WINTER COL

ALSO BY THE SAME AUTHOR

Nothing Personal: The Business of Sex
Dark Trade: Lost in Boxing

MAINSTREAM / SPORT

WINTER COLOURS

CHANGING SEASONS IN WORLD RUGBY

DONALD McRAE

MAINSTREAM
PUBLISHING

EDINBURGH AND LONDON

Copyright © Donald McRae, 1998
All rights reserved
The moral right of the author has been asserted

First published in Great Britain in 1998 by
MAINSTREAM PUBLISHING COMPANY
(EDINBURGH) LTD
7 Albany Street
Edinburgh
EH1 3UG

This edition 1999

ISBN 1 84018 247 4

No part of this book may be reproduced or
transmitted in any way or by any means without
written permission from the publisher, except by a
reviewer who wishes to quote short passages in
connection with a review written for insertion in a
newspaper, magazine or broadcast

A catalogue record for this book is available from the
British Library

Typeset in Van Dijck
Printed and bound in Finland by WSOY

Contents

For my parents, Ian and Jess
– and for Alison

Part One

The Colour of My Shirt

The quiet blue stillness of an early morning in June reminded me of winter on the Highveld. Summer in London was holding. I had my ritual in place, having perfected it over the previous four Saturdays. We woke earlier than we usually did on a weekend, Alison and I, for I needed time to get ready. It calmed me a little to walk slowly up the hill to the tiny parade of shops halfway along the Wimbledon Park Road. I could savour my anticipation and, more seriously, brace myself for the calamity of defeat.

I remembered losing myself more simply in football's last three World Cup extravaganzas. Diego and the Mexican 'Hand of God' in 1986, Gazza and the tears of the *Azzurri* in Italia '90 and Brazil and America in '94 had each dominated a month and more of my life in London. They belonged amongst my greatest memories of the city, filled by heaving nights in open-windowed pubs and bars as London watched and sighed with the rest of the planet. But that was football, the world game.

This is different. This goes beyond sport, this is personal. The 1995 Rugby World Cup, in the new South Africa, in the South Africa of a free Nelson Mandela and a smiling Francois Pienaar, would become history. It felt like the beginning of a new story. It felt like the end of darkness in the last area to surrender – rugby.

All our hurt and shame had begun to recede. South Africa's first democratic election had been held the previous year and, miraculously, the country seemed to be thriving. And, that hazy afternoon, before not only a 65,000 crowd at Ellis Park, but in front of Mandela and the whole nation, the Springboks would face the All Blacks in the World Cup final.

The stroll from our flat to Bruno's baguette shop in SW18 took ten minutes. My journey from South Africa to England, from Johannesburg to London, from Soweto to Southfields, had taken a while longer. I had left almost eleven years before, in August 1984, when the army again came a-knocking. My last two years in the country were spent working as an English teacher in Soweto. I learnt more about South Africa then than in the previous twenty-one years put together. Soweto had been crammed with wit and heat, grime and funk, drinking and soccer – without a single mention of the oval ball or a Springbok. Rugby did not exist in the township. It was the game of apartheid, having nothing to do with eighty per cent of the people.

From the opening match of the tournament in Cape Town, the change from the past was obvious. Although Mandela had allowed the Springboks to keep their name and green-and-gold shirts, everything else felt different. On the same ground three years before, they had lost 26–3 against Australia, the reigning world champions. But, on 25 May 1995, South Africa overwhelmed virtually the same Wallaby team 27–18. They looked as fiery as they had been awkward on their international re-emergence. The blend of bliss-struck black and white faces revelling in the Springboks', the *Amabokbokke's*, victory was an even more stunning sight – a blurring of colours once impossible to imagine in either a South African rugby stadium or on the surrounding streets.

I especially liked the footage of James Small, the team's apparent 'bad boy', being folded up in the arms of a bosomy black mama who must have been at least sixty. As Small stepped off the team bus she engulfed him in a shimmy of a slipper-shuffling dance. He took to it like a young master of the shebeen dancefloor, rocking her gently across the hot tar as the ecstatic ululations rang out in accompaniment.

With his snazzy shades and a walkman tuned to Massive Attack, Small offered white South African sport its first taste of cultural rebellion. Small was different to the other players and he knew it, deliberately cultivating his own brooding interest in boxing and fashion, in writers like Edward Bunker and movies like *Reservoir Dogs*. He had a smart smack of the '90s about him. Small was so far beyond the old country he didn't even have to think about how he looked as he jived around with his big mama. Instead, he just laughed and danced, devoid of the embarrassment which had made so many former Springboks clam up whenever they'd been asked to show a touch of spontaneity.

There was also something more tangible than political PR at work in the informal exchanges between Mandela and the Springboks. While aware how easily he could forge a link with even the most sceptical whites by endorsing Pienaar's team, Mandela was more natural than calculating in the friendly overtures he made to the young rugby men. The Springbok reaction was one of veneration tinged with delight. In a peculiarly South African moment, the country's first black president accepted the ultimate Afrikaans gift of a Springbok cap from the centre Hennie Le Roux with a large grin. Mandela plonked the green-and-gold cap on his silvery head and continued down the line of outstretched rugby-playing hands.

At that stage, in only the first week of the competition, it seemed as if rugby's own answer to Mandela – Chester Williams – had missed his opportunity through injury. Williams was a 'Cape Coloured', the only 'dark face' at the Springbok party. He was handsome and genial with a grin as smooth as his own mix of brown skin and white teeth. Chester Williams was the organising committee's dream-man.

Their nightmare, however, was his torn hamstring. Williams had recovered by the time the first match was played – but, as he had been left out of the original squad, he could not be recalled. The 'Rainbow Nation's' team looked suspiciously bleached; for the Springboks were, yet again, the All Whites.

Chester's face still stared down from every billboard and television screen advertising a World Cup which stretched rugby's usual borders. Beyond Britain, Ireland, France, Australia, New Zealand and South Africa, rugby extended into unfamiliar territory. From Romania to Japan, Canada to Tonga, the Ivory Coast to Italy, emerging rugby countries made their own small impression in quintessential South African cities like Bloemfontein and Port Elizabeth.

But, still, the old dark giants from the bottom of the world, the All Blacks, looked set to make the most massive imprint on the tournament. They realised, more acutely than any other team, that rugby was on the brink of astonishing change. The 1995 World Cup, only the third of its kind, would leave rugby men agog with the prospect of reinventing themselves both on and off the field.

I had always loved a singularly French definition of rugby. Pierre Danos, a three-quarter for the *Tricolores* in the early '70s, had inspired us with his poetic precision. 'There are two kinds of rugby players,' he had once explained, 'those who play pianos and those who shift them.' I was fascinated by both, for rugby's essential appeal centred as much on its grinding forwards as those tinkling backs who jinked and ran.

Yet, in 1995, under Laurie Mains, New Zealand were determined to blur the once rigid certainties of rugby. They would play rugby at a pace that had never been seen before. They would also concentrate on players who could manage both piano tricks. Their captain, after all, was Sean Fitzpatrick, an abrasive hooker who could do the usual front-row thing and carry the weight on his back all day long. But Fitzpatrick was different to his predecessors in the number 2 shirt. It wasn't enough for him just to move huge objects around the field. He also liked to let other teams know that he was fiercely intelligent and competitive enough to suddenly pop up on the wing and run in a little trill of a try. And then, at the next scrum, Fitzy would try to convince his opposite number that he had actually invented the fucking piano.

In the scrum behind him, forwards like Ian Jones and Zinzan Brooke could orchestrate moves in a variety of keys. They were outstanding in tight phases of play but, in the loose, they could run and pass as well as most backs. Zinzan, in particular, with his innovations at number 8, was more like a great conductor.

In an outrageous World Cup cacophony of sound and fury, New Zealand then unleashed Jonah Lomu, a solid slab of six-foot-five-inch, eighteen-stone muscle on the wing. Lomu could run through other teams with three or four pianos strapped to his back – and it would still sound as if his thunderous thighs and flying boots made up a Black version of a Wagnerian symphony.

Lomu became rugby's first genuine international celebrity – with a fame so sudden and so shocking that it spread from South Africa to countries which had never even heard the word 'rugby' before. In the space of a month, the sport had revealed a depth of potential which had only been hinted at previously. The New Zealanders, South Africans and Australians had already stressed their determination to capitalise on that abrupt transformation. Just as they would make the game even quicker by driving through a radical series of law-changes, so they would strive for an even slicker sale of post-World Cup tournaments and stars. The northern-hemisphere countries would have to try and keep abreast of their dramatic modifications – for rugby would have altered forever.

It was not just that professionalism would finally sweep away even the stickiest remnants of amateurism. Rugby, in all but name, had been a professional business in the southern hemisphere for years. The 'Five Nations' had more stubborn amateurs in their ranks – but they could no longer hold back the television and sponsorship money pouring into the highest levels of rugby. The struggle for power, and control of that money, had only just begun.

In a supposedly more routine encounter on the pitch, South Africa's third and final group match was against Canada. But the Canadians, with a couple of meanies in their team, were not about to keel over on cue. In a fractious but otherwise dull clash, which South Africa won 20–0, fighting broke out in the second half. The Springbok hooker James Dalton and two Canadians, the prop Rod Snow and their fly-half and captain Gareth Rees, were sent off. All three were suspended for thirty days – the rest of the tournament in effect – while the Canadian Scott Stewart and the Springbok wing, Pieter Hendriks, were also cited for dirty play. Hendriks' ban lasted ninety days. He had been caught both kicking and punching on camera. The South Africans were distraught – especially at the sight of the bald and wide Dalton bursting into tears after he'd said, in his flat Johannesburg accent, 'It was great . . . while it lasted.'

And then, deliriously, they realised the good news. Chester Williams, the country's dusky darling, could replace Hendricks on the left wing. Williams returned for the quarter-final against Western Samoa at Ellis Park and, with one eye on the impossible dream of starring in Hollywood's first film about rugby, he wrote his own outrageous script. South Africa romped home 42–14 and Chester scored four tries – a Springbok record. The South African headline writers joined the marketing men's rolling, if hackneyed, ecstasy. It was 'Chester . . . Chester . . . Chester . . . Chester!' and 'Cheeky Chester!'

There was another classic South Africanism before the delayed start to their semi-final against France at King's Park. Against all the climatic constants which state that it never rains in Durban in the middle of winter, the downpour continued unabated all day. The pitch looked like a grey river. The Springboks were in danger of drifting out of the tournament. According to our chirpy ITV announcers, an arcane World Cup rule stated that if a semi-final could not be played, for whatever reason, then the team with the better disciplinary record would automatically qualify for the final. The teary Dalton and Hendricks fracas meant that France, without a red card in the tournament, would be through.

Desperate times, our commentator rumbled, demand desperate measures. The South Africans reached deep into their bag of technological tricks and pulled out an absurdly familiar standby from the country's suburban kitchens. Thirty middle-aged black women, all of whom looked like they would have been happier having a jig with James Small instead, waded bare foot through the lapping waves. Each of them wore a typical black South African maid's uniform of white *doek* (scarf), brown jersey and green overall, while carrying that old domestic prop – the mop. They stoically walked up and down the length of the field, mopping away, as a mournful white crowd watched them through the falling rain. It was a more representative picture of South African life than all those dreamy snapshots of Nelson's Springbok cap and Chester's wide smile.

I'd reached for the usual retinue of bitter asides as, on my comfortable London sofa, I also watched the women work. But I began to twitch with increasing anxiety. The cup was floating away. It rained and rained until, an hour and a half after the scheduled kick-off, it eased sufficiently for the teams to finally emerge.

They played on through the returning rain. The two number 10s, Joel Stransky and Thierry Lacroix, swapped penalties before South Africa crawled ahead with a solitary try from Ruben Kruger. With five minutes left, France had set up a billowy blue camp on the steaming green tryline. Scrum followed scrum. The Springboks held on, without pushing France any further back. The great Abdelatif Benazzi came roaring through the wet again. He brushed past Pienaar and Joubert before he stumbled in the slush just as he touched down. Only Small's helplessly pinned body separated the ball in Benazzi's hand from the ground. No try. Another scrum to France. And then another.

At last, amid all the straining and wheeling and collapsing, South Africa were given the put-in. The ball came back quickly towards Stransky and, under immense pressure from Laurent Cabannes and Benazzi, he found touch. The players paddled in exhaustion towards the line-out, with South Africa seeming unable to withstand yet another French barrage. But the whistle saved them. It had been a lottery of a match, a cruel maker of coronaries rather than a fair decider of a World Cup final place. But the four-point difference on the board counted. South Africa 19, France 15.

On the morning of the final, I swung through the opening of my south-west London pâtisserie with a more cautious step than usual. Exactly a week before, in a curious coincidence, I had been one of four men peering at the *pain aux raisins* in an watery-mouth semi-final spirit. Bruno the baker, a self-proclaimed French artist with pastry, knew the three of us standing opposite him on the customers' side of the counter. He was amused while we, unknown to each other, stared back in bemusement. It was his little World Cup tart-breaker. He introduced us according to our respective nationalities. The city boy in his Saturday Hackett wear was England; the gangly grinner in the All Black shirt, naturally enough, was New Zealand; and I, with accent and croissant-shaped figure still intact, was South Africa. Bruno, of course, whom we all knew, was France.

We were all 'pretty confident'; but I thought it significant that the Kiwi and I were the quietest of the quartet. As Bruno and Hackett spoke effusively about likely upsets and a European breakthrough, the tall

Black shirt and I smiled warily at each other. Eventually, after I had done my bit and said a few nice words about New Zealand being the best team in the tournament – at least on paper – he stopped smiling. 'Yeah,' he grunted, 'no worries on that score. But, mate, it's still a big ask. The Springboks at home, in a World Cup final, with bloody Nelson Mandela and God on your bastard side . . .'

He then continued, in minute detail, to explain exactly how the Black shirts would overcome even divine intervention. He didn't even bother to mention Jonah Lomu, because Bruno and the English guy had already indulged in head-shaking debate about hiring a tank as the only possible defence down the left flank. 'We've got fourteen other brilliant players,' the Kiwi murmured as he took a chunk out his baguette and turned towards the door. 'See ya next Saturday, mate,' he said. 'We'll have another yarn before the final . . .'

But on the day itself, I wanted to avoid such rugby chit-chat. I was lucky. 'Your new friend has been in already, looking for you,' Bruno said as soon as he saw me. 'I told him that I've forgiven you for last week and that I'm with the Springboks today…' We managed a relatively sophisticated conversation about my tangled emotions on a day which seemed miraculous merely for happening. South Africa was not the same country I had left. There was hope and a semblance of equality which, when I'd lived there, had always been far from ordinary life. 'Still,' Bruno shrugged, 'to win today as well…'

Even at ten in the morning, we could see four green-and-gold shirts outside the tube. There were South Africans wherever you went in London. But I wanted to watch the match at home, just Alison and me, so that I could measure my jumbled feelings one by one, fold after fold, opening up or closing in on myself in private. It already seemed a day like no other.

I wandered back down the hill again, feeling the sweet drag of memory. I thought of my parents and friends, of Johannesburg and Soweto, of Syd Nomis, my original rugby hero, and Errol Tobias, our first black Springbok. Eventually, I settled on my own past racism, from my boyish acceptance of 'our blacks' to the more naked prejudice I'd shown towards Afrikaners. I had been one of those smug English-speakers who thought the mythical 'we' were superior to everyone else. It was not even as if 'Non-Whites' came into the picture. I turned all my spleen and fear of the unknown onto the Afrikaners. We were the good guys, I'd always say, we were the smart guys. Meanwhile they, an equally mythic 'they', were the bad guys. They were the 'Dutchmen' and the 'rock-spiders' who had invented apartheid; as if we, in comparison, remained untainted.

A more personal truth was that I had really never spoken to an Afrikaner my own age until I reached university. I discovered that 'they' were just the same as 'us' – innocent and clever, fucked-up and guilty. They were also just looking for a way to live. And, again, the same little moment of insular revelation recurred in the schoolrooms and shebeens of Soweto. The black 'they' were also just people. I was a wreck when I left the country but, soon after arriving in London, I put some of the baggage to rest. We were just bloody South Africans, the whole lot of us.

I would forever be one; and yet I was also, in the end, more at home in far-off London. By the time I put my key in the latch, it felt like I had been through the entire maze of my heart. And, after so long, I felt happy. It seemed ridiculously easy, suddenly, to just think of rugby.

Like how the hell was James Small going to stop Jonah Lomu? How could a five-foot-ten-inch man called Small even think about taking on that same huge monster of a wing who had trampled over every team that had crossed his path in South Africa? Six days before, Lomu had ripped England to shreds in the second semi-final in Cape Town. Will Carling called him 'a freak' – but the pictures of Lomu on the move were more illuminating than that strange and stunted word. His extreme power put the squeeze on romantic rugby notions of style and swerve on the wing. Lomu just thundered through, blasting his way clear, shattering his opponents, the whole shebang looking as graceful as a controlled demolition. But there was something compelling about the sight of a building being blown apart, disintegrating stage by stage, floor by floor. I found myself transfixed by Lomu's explosive bang-crash whoosh with the ball. Occasionally, he'd root out a tree-like arm. He'd then snap it into the glassy faces of his smashed tacklers. I'd given up even the thought of yelling 'TIMBER!' whenever another band of frantic foresters from England, Scotland or, God help them, Ireland, had attempted to bring him down. Lomu wouldn't fall. He kept running, seeming to grow ever taller, ever broader with every stride. The effect on his victims was even more startling. Tony Underwood, on the same wing as Lomu, had been traumatised by his encounter. He'd bounced repeatedly off the black shirt like a white-winged fly hitting a wall. Mike Catt, meanwhile, had been laid low like a new strip of blistered tar. Lomu simply ran over him with the heavy roller of his massive legs.

Lomu was terrifying; and yet I was just as disturbed by the veracity of my Kiwi pal's observation that the All Blacks had 'fourteen other brilliant players'. Jeff Wilson was quicker and more inventive than Lomu while Frank Bunce and Walter Little were the world's best centre partnership. Andrew Mehrtens, a jewel of a stand-off, had been the New Zealand back line's revelation of the competition – if, naturally, you put Lomu to one side of the black mountain.

In the forwards, however, the All Blacks were formidable. The Auckland front row of Craig Dowd, Sean Fitzpatrick and Olo Brown were exacting scrummagers; and as canny as they were ruthless. Ian Jones was the finest line-out jumper in rugby while Zinzan Brooke confirmed his ranking as the modern game's smartest and most talented forward. Zinzan even had the audacity to land one of his stupendous drop goals from just over the halfway line during the destruction of England. But my favourite All Black was the withering flanker in the black scrum-cap – Josh Kronfeld, a young and brutally fast number 7 who kept reaching the loose ball first in between searing in like a blackened rocket on Lomu's shoulder to complete another try.

They were that good. They were that frightening – even though the Springboks had Andre Joubert at full-back, Small and Williams on the wing and Stransky and Joost van der Westhuizen at half-back. They had Os du Randt and Kobus Wiese in the tight and Pienaar and Kruger in the loose. Yet, if you had to compare each team man for man, player for player, the All Blacks seemed certain to win every time – except that this was a clash between Springbok and All Black in a World Cup final. We'd also learnt that anything could happen when South Africa faced New Zealand.

The Springboks were coached by Kitch Christie and managed by Morne du Plessis – each of whom, with Pienaar, had inspired South Africa throughout the long build-up to the final. The night before, as the rest of the country wondered and wailed about destiny and Jonah Lomu, du Plessis said softly that, 'a stillness has descended on the camp that is quite eerie. It's not tense. I don't quite know how to describe it. It's the stillness that I haven't felt for a long while in a rugby atmosphere . . .'

It felt suddenly still, too, at the cool centre of our flat in London. The television was already on, but I had turned the sound down. The pictures had yet to cut away to Johannesburg. We read the newspaper previews for a while and then, again, I looked at my watch. Three hours were left. There was more to remember.

5 November 1969

We lived at the bottom of Africa. We were young and we were happy. We also knew, in some vague and dreamy way, that all our luck and sweet moments of bliss were sealed in white. We never spoke about it. There was no need. We were believers. We were special. We were white South Africans.

The sun slid down towards us. The Springboks were far from home that hot Wednesday afternoon. My father said that London was six thousand miles away. Stepping barefoot into our sunlit garden, we shivered. Summer here was not the same as winter there. They said it got worse the further north you went. We were told to just wait and see what would happen when our rugby team trudged across Scottish, Welsh and Irish fields. Our boys' boots would grow heavier the longer they marched. There was trouble ahead.

Even at home, we were often at war with each other. We were the English-speakers. They were the Afrikaners. There were more of them than us, even though they were just Afrikaners while we were Jewish and Greek and Italian and Portuguese and English and Welsh and Irish and Scottish. We were the bright guys. We were the nice guys. We were almost perfect. The Afrikaners, however, were different. Their English was terrible and their accents were thick. They wore safari suits for style and crew-cuts for pleasure. The *Boertjies'* (little farmers') bare feet slapped down against jagged stones and steaming tar. They didn't feel a thing. Their fathers, meanwhile, wore long socks and felt shoes below their short pants. The *ou toppies* (old boys) carried combs inside those brown and green socks. Rows of metal teeth glinted between meaty sandwiches of ribbed sock and hairy leg.

We mocked them at a distance, knowing that they could bash the daylights out of every single one of us. They could turn our white skins black and blue. But that's what made them such good rugby players. Even when they called themselves 'Mannetjies' (Little Man) and 'Tiny', they couldn't fool us. Rugby meant everything to the 'Boers'. We, instead, listened to 7-inch singles and whistled at girls from the top of our garden walls. At school, we played football rather than rugby. While they were ready to die for South Africa on hard *veld*, we were happier kicking a round ball across freshly mown lawns, pretending to play for Arsenal at Wembley.

We knew that they called us *rooi-neks* (red-necks) and *sout-piels* (salt-cocks). They said our necks were red because we were too limey-white to stand the African sun. We just laughed. Most of us were Smartiebrown, having spent so much time eating ice-cream next to the pool. As for being 'salt-cocks', we blushed more shyly. The Afrikaners claimed that we wanted a foot in two countries. With our legs spread so wide, our little dicks dangled in the salty waves.

They were right. All four of my grandparents came from Scotland. My one-armed grandad lived with us and made sure that the *Sunday Post* was delivered by sea to him from Scotland. Every week, with only one hand, he managed to turn the pages and, in his thick Glasgow accent, read the comic strips to me. I loved *Oor Wullie* and *The Broons*. And so families like mine, the McRaes and the Scotts, once of Aberdeen and Glasgow, had links to the past.

The Afrikaners, meanwhile, had cut their own ties with Holland. They had taken hold of an African country and made it their own. We were more ragged. Sometimes, it felt as if we were torn. We wanted the best of both worlds.

We had two faces for the Afrikaners. Behind their backs we turned up our noses, calling them 'hairy-backs' or 'rock-spiders', 'crunchies' or 'Dutchmen'. In front of them, we smiled shamelessly. For eighty minutes against the All Blacks or the Lions, the Wallabies or the *Tricolores*, we loved them with all our hearts. They played out of their skins for our country. We rolled those suddenly gorgeous Afrikaans names round our mouths as if we had been born on the *platteland* (farmland) ourselves. We spoke sugary Afrikaans to each other, saying things like '*Man, daardie Mannetjies!*' (Man, that Little Man!) and '*Ja, net soos Tiny!*' (Yes, just like Tiny!) as if those few words dissolved a delicious trail of pink sherbet on our tongues.

There were different kinds of Springbok – for in South Africa we were not all alike. We were told that the country was like a packet of Smarties, full of many coloured faces: white, pinky-white, light-brown, milky-brown, dark-brown and black. Even if you could find every other colour under the sun in a box, they'd never got round to making any black Smarties. And we would never allow anything but white Springboks.

As English-speakers, our favourite players in 1969 were Tommy Bedford and Syd Nomis. Bedford, my mother said, had an attractive face and a lovely voice. He'd studied at Oxford University and had since become an architect – as well as a great number 8. On the radio they called him 'the flaxen-haired Tommy Bedford'. In the newspapers, they preferred to tag him 'a rebel'. We were more interested in the bushy strips of hair which stretched down the length of Syd Nomis's puffed-up cheeks. Syd's sideburns were full of his fiery acceleration and swerving movement on the wing. We also liked the fact that a good Johannesburg Jewish boy like Sydney Harold Nomis had shortened his name to Syd. He looked exactly like a 'Syd' to us, with a pair of green flares in his wardrobe.

The Afrikaans players were less cool. 'Mannetjies' Roux, in particular, was the mad dog of world rugby. He was a centre the British press called 'The Monster'. They said that when Mannetjies tackled an opponent, he tried to maim him. In 1962, in Pretoria, playing in the light blue of Northern Transvaal against the blood-red shirts of the British Lions, Roux had first hit the big time. Richard Sharp was one of the tourists' stars. A fly-half with blond hair and a big jaw, he'd carved chunks out of other South African provincial back lines. The 'Blue Bulls' were having none of it. And their Mannetjies was no matador; he was the bull. Sharp's flashing jersey made him see red. As the Lion dummied and cut back inside, Mannetjies Roux hit him like a blue train. Sharp fell to the ground. He didn't move. He couldn't move. His cheekbone had been smashed into little pieces.

While the British press called for the face-cracking head of our Mannetjies, Sharp stressed later that the tackle on him had been fair – if brutal. Those two short words summed up the Springbok spirit. We were fair, and the Afrikaners were brutal.

Yet, on international afternoons, we were just South Africans. Together, we were unbeatable. A few months before, the Springboks had demolished Australia by four Tests to nil – winning each match with such violent ease that we began to feel sorry for the poor Wallabies. The British were next; and we grinned at the thought of our big Springboks smacking into their smaller players.

But there were problems. For months we'd been told that the tour might be cancelled. 'Why?' I kept asking my father. The answer made my head hum. Even though they'd never met us, people in Britain attacked our Afrikaans government and the whole country. It made me mad. We knew the Dutchmen better than anyone. We were the only ones who should have been allowed to trash them.

My dad said that the British students and hippies were unhappy because we had no black players in the Springbok side. But the black boys, like us, played football. They didn't even like rugby. How could we select a boy who had never played the game, who actually feared some of the Afrikaners he would have to line up alongside. I knew that Mof Myburgh and Hannes Marais, our steely props, would never have stood for a black hooker dangling between them. No black man would be allowed to put his long arms around their hunched shoulders. In a scrum you had to get so close to the other players. Sweaty cheeks touched sweaty cheeks. Huge hands and heads were put between tree-trunk legs and near salty *piels*. I couldn't imagine a day when an Afrikaans lock like Frik du Preez would put his head between Mof's legs and those of a black boy. It was impossible. You could never talk about black Springboks – it was the same as telling an Afrikaner that Jesus was a black man. They'd become crazed dogs. They'd bite your head off.

But, my dad explained, there was more to it than just rugby. The anti-Springboks said that we didn't live with black people. Yet Maggie, our maid, a black girl my mother's age, had been with us ever since I could remember. We gave Maggie her own tin plate and her own knife and fork which she used to eat our food in her room. We also gave her a tin mug so that she could drink our coffee. We were that close. She was part of our family. Her full name was Maggie Thabang. She had children of her own, about the same age as me and my sister.

Maggie's room was in our backyard, where she would watch us twirl our sparklers on Guy Fawkes night. She cooked and washed and cleaned and even put us to bed whenever my mom and dad went out. Maggie allowed us into her room, showing us how she stacked her bed high on piles of bricks to keep her safe from the *Tokolosh*, an evil dwarf which could be sent to torment her by the neighbouring witchdoctors. My sister and I were terrified of the *Tokolosh*. I asked Maggie if she'd help us put our own beds on bricks so that we would be perched too high for him to reach up and take us away in our sleep. She cackled and told us not to be silly. The *Tokolosh* was not interested in whites. He was only after black people.

They didn't understand our blacks in Britain. They would never have even heard of the *Tokolosh*. Maggie did not mind if the Springboks went overseas or not. She only moaned that her boyfriend, Samson, couldn't live with her in the backroom. Once, the police checked her room late at night, shouting and shining their torches as they climbed over the yard gate. We lived in a 'White By Night' neighbourhood. Only servants could live on our property. No blacks could walk the streets at night. But, in the day, when we played rugby, black people could stroll around as they liked. I wondered if, six thousand miles away, they had a clear picture of our South African lives.

The Springbok manager explained that it was wrong to mix politics and sport. 'We have come to play rugby,' Corrie Bornman said, 'and not engage in politics. We want to mix socially and create a favourable impression among the British people. We have a well-balanced side with no particular stars and we will try to run with the ball at every opportunity. We hope to do a good job and better relationships between South Africa and Great Britain. We have no advance instructions on how to approach the tour and I feel sure all matches will be played.'

The first game had been scheduled to take place that afternoon at the Iffley Road Ground against Oxford University. But the demonstrators had threatened to dig up the pitch. We were surprised to hear on our SABC (South African Broadcasting Corporation) news that the British police were made to back down by 'a few hundred agitators'. We liked the British bobby, especially the helmets they wore, but they were not the same as our flat-capped Afrikaans policeman. Our boys in blue were fearless.

For five days, the venue for the match remained a secret. Then, the mystery ended. The game would be played on 5 November at Twickenham – where we'd show them some real fireworks. With my radio blaring on the warm grass, we sat down to listen to the game.

Television was still banned in South Africa. As Minister of Posts and Telegraphs, Dr Albert Hertzog described television as 'a little *bioscope*' (cinema). He explained that, 'friends of mine recently returned from Britain tell me that one cannot see a programme which does not show black and white living together, where they are not continually propagating a mixture of the two races. We could never allow that in our own country.'

As much as we pined for TV, we loved the radio. The familiar voice of the SABC's Kim Shippey crackled through the wireless. 'Welcome to Twickenham,' he said majestically. We cheered. The Springbok tour was about to start on an autumn afternoon which was 'crisp and beautiful under a cloudless sky'. We roared. Shippey said that conditions were not unlike those found on a typically sunny winter's day at Ellis Park in Johannesburg. We danced. We'd grown used to posh BBC voices telling us on the World Service that rain swept across Highbury or Elland Road. But we knew that the fleeter Springboks needed firmer fields on which to shine. They were magical enough to have carried our sunlight with them to Twickenham.

Meanwhile, student protestors marched to the ground. They were led by a white South African. Peter Hain was nineteen and chairman of the 'Stop the Racist Tour' campaign. It felt even worse that he should be one of our own people. But the police were in control. In cars and on horseback, they surrounded the stadium.

We concentrated on the rugby as Piet Visagie, our brilliant fly-half playing at full-back for the day, kicked the oval ball high into the blue English sky. At the first line-out, a penalty was awarded to the Springboks. From twenty-five yards, Visagie slotted the ball through the white posts. Suddenly, we felt better. It would be all right in the end.

We were wrong. Oxford equalised after seven minutes. We were tentative in the tackle and anxious in the mauls. While the Springboks struggled, Oxford were urged on by their New Zealand scrum-half, Chris Laidlaw. We felt uneasy. We were the best side in the world. But, thirty-two minutes in, we were losing 6–3, after the University full-back, Heal, kicked another penalty.

The second half was no better. Time slipped by. The normally deadly Visagie missed kick after kick. With only seconds left, the Boks remembered how to surge upfield. A savage ruck drove the team further forward. Shippey screamed and Dawie de Villiers snapped a long diving pass into Visagie's hands. He caught the ball and, with joy booming softly in our throats, went for the drop. The ball flew towards the towering posts. But, as we jumped, we heard the cry. 'It's wide! Visagie has missed . . .'

South Africa had lost 6–3 to Oxford University – at rugby. It was the first time the Springboks had ever been defeated by an English club side. I was afraid to think what might happen next.

South Africa lost two out of their next four matches. And we learnt that it was not only the students of Oxford who hated us. Even in Newport, a demonstrator announced that he had begun a hunger strike against South Africa. We stared into the bathroom mirror, pulling at our chubby cheeks, wondering how long it would take to starve to death. But we laughed the next day. The hunger-striker had been spotted at a local café, feeding himself large portions every breakfast, lunch and supper-time. He starved himself the rest of the time.

When the Springboks did win, the victory still tasted bitter. A 12–0 success over Swansea was soured by yet more chanting, marching and swearing at the South Africans. The sight of a young girl leading a charge of fifty hecklers onto the field early in the second half shocked the Springboks. I tried to imagine her face. She might've been pretty, with thick red hair streaming down the back of her open leather jacket. If she was wild enough to run onto a rugby pitch, she probably also smoked.

And if a girl slipped a cigarette between her lips it was a sign that she wanted to be kissed on the mouth. I forgot about the Springboks for a few moments.

But the police finally got her. Five minutes later they'd trapped all the demonstrators at the Mumbles Road end. Punches were thrown and kicks were aimed but the bobbies came down hard. We could feel an ugly hole opening up. We were on one side and the rest of the world was on the other.

It didn't help that the Springboks could not win a single Test – losing 6–3 and 11–8 to England and Scotland and drawing with Ireland and Wales. Off the field, there were mass marches through Edinburgh and London, bomb-scares in Ireland and, everywhere, noisy demonstrations and flying flour bombs, tin-tacks and smoke flares.

In London, a coach carrying the Springboks and Danie Craven, the President of the South African Rugby Board, was stopped by a protestor. He boarded the bus and handcuffed himself to the steering wheel, forcing the driver off the road. Although he was arrested, his actions startled the Springboks. 'The demonstrators made a serious attempt to kidnap some of the players on the coach,' Corrie Bornman complained. 'What is going to happen next? Some of my players could be maimed or killed. The demonstrators seem now to have lost their peaceful intentions.'

I was tired of the tour, of tuning the transistor to yet more bad news. It had been a long three months. South Africa had, slowly, been ground down. We knew that if we were no longer the best rugby team in the world, we were the most despised. Much had changed – even though Corrie Bornman tried to renew his hopes in our rugby future. 'We believe rugby football is a strong brotherhood,' he told his British audience, 'and that the game is above creed, colour and religion. It is only played by law-abiding citizens. We have to stick to the laws of our country as you stick to yours; but we can achieve better relationships through sport – and especially through the game we love, rugby . . .'

Danie Craven, our rugby godfather, sent out a more ambiguous message. 'In South Africa, the blacks, the coloureds and the whites are separate nations,' he argued, 'like Scotland, Wales and England. They are different stock, so they won't ever play in the same side. But maybe, perhaps, like your Lions, one day, we would have such a team, combining the nations. What happens ultimately, that we must leave to the future. Let us see what history will have to say . . .'

Black was the colour of fear. Black was the colour of evil. Black was the colour of death. Every time we went to the movies on a Saturday morning, every time we opened our American comics or read our ninety-nine-cent boy-detective paperbacks, we were reminded. The bad guys wore black hats and carried black guns. They ripped past in black cars and black flying machines. Their hearts, always as black as the ace of spades, were never shuffled. They were in such league with the forces of darkness that we fell for them every time.

But black was also the colour of ordinary life. We spoke about black sheep in the family and black marks on our report cards. We fawned in front of our violent woodwork teacher just so that we could stay off his blacklist. And we thought it would truly be a black day if the *Tokolosh* lived up to Maggie Thabang's premonition and descended on her backroom with his furious black magic.

I remember once looking up and seeing a hundred black faces moving towards me from the bottom of a railway bridge. They climbed the steep 'Non-White' side, a heaving crowd making a low hum of Friday-afternoon noise. My yellow bicycle glided with a breathless hush down the empty 'Whites Only' section. A five-foot-high metal barrier separated them from me. I could see only the bobbing tops of the coloured *doeks* (scarves) worn by the shortest women. But some black men were tall enough to tower over the dented blue wall. A few stared blankly down at me. They winked more often and said, 'Hello, master.'

We were less frightened of the people we called 'our blacks' than we were of a rugby team the world called the All Blacks. We believed that our black maids and gardeners were our pals, that they were forever our wide-smiling natives. We thought there were no hard feelings between us and them – for they beamed when, really, their eyes brimmed with something sadder and angrier.

The All Blacks, however, preferred to tighten their lips. They were 'The Unsmiling Giants'. They were the bleak 'Invincibles'. They were the brutal 'Incomparables'. Even the Afrikaners spoke their name with a smothered awe, for it had been years since a direct comparison could be made between our Springboks and their All Blacks.

There was something about the black shirt, the black shorts and the black socks which made us tremble. We also read the story of the *Haka*, wondering what it might be like to see fifteen All Blacks slapping their huge thighs and screaming 'It is death! It is death!' in a strange language. Other snippets of New Zealand rugby history were equally menacing.

Despite some Kiwi stars having names like 'Tiny' Hill and 'Tiny' White, 'Snow' White and 'Bunny' Tremain, they were sombre giants dressed in black. They preferred to grunt rather than talk, to knock you down when they might have slipped past instead. They were hard men who grew up with a sheep under one arm and a rugby ball under the other. Their countless farms and rugby fields were the only markers of life in the vast emptiness of New Zealand. We'd heard stories of boys our age, in places like Rotorua and Te Kuiti, practising the harsh art of scrummaging on creaking machines in their back gardens. Even the Afrikaners of Pretoria and Bloemfontein did not go that far. But New Zealand was the most fanatical rugby country on earth. They would do anything to beat us, the Springboks being the only team in the world they really respected.

The rivalry between the All Blacks and the Springboks was so fierce that only one side had ever beaten the other in a home series – the triumphant 1937 Springboks. In that year's crucial second Test, a bang to 'Boy' Louw's temple reduced him to a perpetual fit of giggles. The inspirational South African prop ran up and down the length of the Christchurch field, chuckling madly to himself while playing brilliantly. It was one way to unnerve the deadly serious All Blacks.

Their most famous men were always the meanest players, the massive bruisers who locked the flat black pack. Kevin Skinner was the most notorious. To us, his name spelt out the All Black method. His legend had darkened with time.

Skinner had retired from rugby in 1954 but, two years later, the All Black selectors were frantic. After two ferocious matches, the Springboks had squared the series. The foundations of their win were built on a front row propped by Chris Koch and Jaap Bekker. They ground into their opponents with such intensity that the All Black Mark Irwin's ribs cracked under the pressure. Koch and Bekker were also battered and bleeding. Bekker was so badly concussed that, long after the last whistle, he staggered around the dressing-room. Whenever he was approached by a team-mate, Bekker would lash out blindly. He imagined that he was still out on the field, fending off marauding All Blacks. But, being such a tough Bok, he recovered dramatically in hospital and declared himself ready for the third Test.

The Blacks, in turn, reached for Kevin Skinner. He had the tools for the job. Skinner had been New Zealand boxing's heavyweight champion in 1947. His fists earned him an even bigger reputation on the rugby field. He packed down against Koch and, so we were told, hammered the

Springbok. The punches were heavy and deliberate. The South Africans were thrown off balance as Koch wilted. Then, in his most audacious move, to take care of Bekker, Skinner switched from loosehead to tighthead. The result was the same. The Springboks were beaten – in more ways than one. In front of the fittingly named New Zealand referee, Bill Fright, Skinner had terrorised the Springbok front row. The All Blacks went on to win the final Test and the series 3–1.

They returned to South Africa in 1960 – a tour which gave us the most rugged tale yet to wag the immense body of All Black folklore. During the New Zealand trials, one of their lesser-known heroes, Richard Conway, was told that a hand injury would not heal in time for him to be considered for selection. In desperation, the number 8 asked the specialist if there was anything they could do to save his place in the team.

'There's only one thing that will mend that finger in time,' the doctor joked, 'and that's amputation.'

Conway, called 'Red' rather than Richard by the All Blacks, ordered the bewildered doc to get on with it. After an hour of arguing, the chop eventually came and, missing a finger, a bloodied Red made the tour. He played in three losing Tests out of four against the Springboks. Three All Black caps for one finger? Back in New Zealand it seemed a fair exchange. In South Africa, we just shook our heads and whispered the name of Red Conway with the kind of wonder we normally reserved for Kevin Skinner.

They were followed by equally tough successors in the Black scrum. Colin Meads personified the severe face of New Zealand rugby. He was known as Pinetree, while his All Black brother Stan was called 'Snow'. We recognised Pinetree as the hardest of the hard. John Gainsford remembered the day he challenged the huge Kiwi lock. 'Meads grabbed hold of both my wrists,' the Springbok sighed. 'It was like being held in a band of steel. I couldn't move. He looked up and said: "Don't bother, son".'

Throughout the 1960s the All Blacks had played forty-two internationals and only lost four Tests. Under a great coach, Fred 'Needle' Allen, they'd been unbeaten for the previous five years, setting a world record of seventeen consecutive Test victories. The All Blacks' 1967 tour of the Republic had been cancelled after the Nationalist government again put in the black boot. In 1965 Prime Minister Hendrik Verwoerd had promised, on the sunlit banks of the Loskop Dam, that we would never allow Maoris to tour the country. Previously, for the sake of rugby, the New Zealanders had always given in. Even some of the finest players, like George Nepia, had been sacrificed whenever the All Blacks visited South Africa – just because they were Maoris. It was one example of the strangeness of South African life. Whenever we met the All Blacks at home we insisted that they should be all white.

In 1967 the New Zealanders at last resisted. They refused to play against the Springboks unless they could pick whomever they liked. The tour was cancelled. Even after Verwoerd's assassination, life followed the same white track. In 1969 Prime Minister Vorster turned away not only Arthur Ashe but the England cricket team which included Basil d'Oliveira, the South African-born coloured batsman. We were on our way out of international sport.

But, after the disasters of the Springboks' tour only a few months before, our rugby-loving government finally relented in the South African autumn of 1970. If it came to a choice between playing the All Blacks and barring all Maoris, they knew that the Afrikaans *volk* (people) would end up siding with rugby. An oval ball was the only thing which, sometimes, could seem more important than the colour of a man's skin.

In South African terms there were four 'non-whites' in the New Zealand party – three Maoris in Syd Going, Blair Furlong and Buff Milner and, most dramatically of all, a nineteen-year-old Samoan wing called Bryan Williams. Williams had, our newspapers reported, 'darkly flashing good looks' and a 'brilliant white smile'. He also had an irresistible novelty value.

When the All Blacks landed at Jan Smuts Airport in mid-June 1970, three thousand delirious Springbok fans welcomed them. Brian Lochore was the captain and Colin Meads his deputy. We preferred to focus on the obvious pick of the backs – Graham Thorne, Fergie McCormick and Ian MacRae, in whom we took particular delight as he had the same name as my father. But none of them, not even Pinetree, could match Williams. His face shone from our front pages, his name filled the back pages. We could hardly wait to see what kind of rugby player he would make.

They presented him as a saviour in Bethlehem – a cold and small town in the Orange Free State. We whistled admiringly as Williams sliced through the hapless Afrikaners. He scored two dizzying tries in the heady process. Bryan Williams was, already, the star of the tour.

In the following match, an easy win against Mannetjies Roux's Currie Cup champions, Griqualand West, Williams glittered again. At the end, a few coloured spectators ran onto the Kimberly pitch. We knew why coloured and black South Africans delighted in every overseas team's success – and especially in the majesty of the All Blacks. It pleased them to see us face up to hurt. For whenever a South African rugby team lost to an overseas side, even the All Blacks, it took a little chunk out of us. Rugby defined us that clearly.

As Williams was approached by a happy bunch of coloured men, they were intercepted by a group of Afrikaners. A white man hit one of the coloureds and, in a typically South African flash, the fighting began. Each side reached for bricks, bottles and blocks of wood. The rioting lasted for ten minutes before the police finally separated the previously segregated men. A New Zealand spokesman suggested that 'this hard core of white spectators destroyed two weeks of wonderful welcomes in this oh-so-pleasant land.' We wondered anxiously what Bryan Williams made of it all.

The violence spread to the rugby field. The All Blacks suffered casualties. Most seriously, they lost Colin Meads after a brawling match against Eastern Transvaal in Springs. Meads emerged from a ruck with his left arm dangling horribly. He had been kicked by one of the opposing 'Red Devils'. Brian Lochore advised him to leave the field immediately. Meads refused. He played on until the end as New Zealand sealed an emphatic 24–3 victory. Meads had broken his arm; but he comforted himself with the fact that 'at least we won the bloody game'.

Meads was out of the first two Tests – and possibly the entire tour. The fractured state of the Pinetree arm preoccupied white South Africa. We were divided in our response to the break. While his absence left a gaping hole in the black eight, we felt strangely deprived. Meads was indisputably a great player, and we revered rugby greatness even when it came wrapped in a black shirt. Pinetree was also an exceptionally loyal friend to us, standing tall and unbowed against the new anti-South African movement. 'We're just rugby players,' he would say gruffly when asked to justify his presence in a country as reviled as our own.

But, with the first Test careering towards us, the local papers picked up on Boy Louw's suggestion from twenty-one years before. 'When South Africa plays New Zealand,' he had told the 1949 Springboks, 'consider your country at war.' It was the kind of enduring quote which sports-writers loved. They used it relentlessly, evoking all kinds of military metaphors. The Springboks had gone into hiding. They were developing secret and ruthless strategies. Our hard-bitten coach, Johan Claassen, was said to be urging the Boks to die for South Africa.

The All Blacks, meanwhile, were being driven to a frenzy by 'Ivan the

Terrible', a coach with a suspiciously Russian-sounding surname – Vodanovich. Vodanovich demanded a cruel form of discipline from the Blacks. It was intoxicating stuff, as rumour mixed hazily with fact.

The day of the Test was typical of a Highveld winter. Early-morning cold gave way to a clear blue sky and a high sun which, by noon, boomeranged off the hard yellow grass. Quiet settled over the suburbs as, soon after lunch, we retreated to our radios. I sat alone in my room, looking out at the streets below, empty but for a stray black man trudging towards the station at the bottom of the hill. As the commentators gravely tolled the names of thirty players, I saw the lonely walker lift his black hat in greeting. He held it in the air as if offering his own private salute to the All Blacks. Then he strolled towards the shade of a tall tree where Maggie Thabang answered his wave. She was knitting herself a red jersey. With needles and a ball of wool in one hand, she used the other to welcome him over. Even through the closed windows, I could hear their laughter and the odd shouted word of an African language I didn't understand. Our black and white worlds seemed so far apart then as, turning up the radio, I watched them sit down on her checked blanket and share a cigarette under the tree.

Fifty miles away, in Pretoria, the two teams ran out – New Zealand first and then, to a reverberating bellow, South Africa emerged from the tunnel. My heart tightened. Just after 3.30, the green-and-gold shirts crashed into the black. The ball was driven forward before, like a hot breath of dry wind from his native South-West Africa, the Springbok flanker Jan Ellis tore away on a gusting run. He was finally brought down on the 25-yard line. New Zealand had the put-in. They won the ball but were pushed back. Chris Laidlaw fumbled. Ellis's partner, Piet Greyling, hacked the ball ahead. The Springboks hared towards the try-line. There was a jubilant explosion. Dawie de Villiers had reached the dancing leather first. It had taken the Springboks four minutes to score the first try of the series.

Three minutes later, they struck an even more damaging blow. Joggie Jansen, on his international début, partnered Mannetjies Roux in the centre of the South African back line. He was an even more rabid tackler than 'Mad Dog' Mannetjies. Wayne Cottrell, the All Black stand-off, snapped up Laidlaw's pass and, hurtling away from his own backs, attempted to forge an opening on the blind-side of the scrum. It was a clever move on paper. On the rocky surface of Loftus Versveld, it was an awful mistake. Jansen spotted the switch and, dropping his right shoulder, hit Cottrell at chest height with sickening force. The spell of

All Black magic had been broken. South Africa were soon cruising at a giddy 12–0 altitude.

The All Blacks came back. Bryan Williams shook our radios with a devastating jitterbug. He intercepted Syd Nomis's looping pass and side-stepped Ian MacCallum. When he dived over in the corner I looked out of my bedroom window, over the brick wall, and down towards Maggie. Her friend had left to catch his train. She sat alone, oblivious to the breakthrough by a dark-skinned flyer. A cigarette dangled from her lips as her knitting needles clicked in the distance. 12–6 to South Africa.

There were still anxious moments to endure. With less than five minutes left New Zealand were awarded a penalty. Going, on for the injured Laidlaw, took the tap. The All Blacks scissored their way up-field but, then, the snazzily tailored Syd Nomis saved us. He swept between Lochore and MacRae to steal their ball. As he ran, our Afrikaans commentator Gerhard Viviers barked out one word again and again. 'Siddy! Siddy! Siddy! Siddy!'

Siddy crossed the black line with a sparkling plunge. MacCallum converted, lifting the winning score to 17–6. I did my little dance around the radio. On the darkening street below, Maggie had pulled her blanket more closely around her. Late-afternoon cold seeped through the air. She slipped a bottle of gin out of her bag. Maggie took a warming slug, with no hint as to whether it might have been tinged with celebration or sorrow if she'd heard the score from Pretoria.

One Test down and still without Pinetree, the All Blacks approached the second international at Newlands in Cape Town with unbridled fury. In a clash of heads, elbows, fists and boots, twenty-two stitches were sewn through skin while only seventeen points were scored.

'Gee,' Ian MacRae sighed after New Zealand had won 9–8, 'it was hell out there in the foxholes . . .'

The All Blacks' tighthead prop, Brian 'Jazz' Muller, had already won a following in South Africa because of his tendency, at home in Taranaki, to use a lawnmower to trim his garden hedge. He was that kind of guy. After the carnage of Newlands, Jazz reflected silently on the match. For two days he cogitated without comment and then, suddenly, he mumbled to a couple of All Blacks – 'Jeez, that was a beaut game.'

But the third Test in Port Elizabeth was different. The All Blacks had brought back Meads in an attempt to strengthen their pack. Meads had resorted to horse liniment in an attempt for a quick cure, but no amount of rubbing could disguise his own feeling that his broken arm had not yet healed. Hope drained from the New Zealanders as steadily as our tension eased. 14–3 to South Africa.

They reached the same margin in the fourth Test by half-time. But, late on in the second half, Bryan Williams thrilled us with one more party-piece. He popped through the entire Springbok back line to score another spectacular try. By then, the colour of his skin had become less significant than the quality of his play.

South Africa won the match 20–17, and the series 3–1. We were the unofficial champions of the world again. But Bryan Williams had done something more exotic for South Africa. We no longer thought of him as a dark stranger. He was one of us, so much so that he received 1,500 letters from South Africa on his return to New Zealand. We owed him that for, in the winter of 1970, Bryan Williams had become a hero in a white country, a blinding feat for a coloured man in a black shirt.

May 1974

Our yo-yo craze consumed us. For hour after hour, line upon line of us stood with our backs to the sun and spun the coloured halves of plastic along our blurring strands of string. Twenty or thirty yo-yos, turning together, made a low white hum. Afterwards, like magicians in a circle, we shared our repertoire of tricks and taught each other how to loop the loop, make a cradle, build the Eiffel Tower, wash the baby and walk the dog.

In the lazy suburbs, like our yo-yos, we were always more up than down. But it also seemed that for every peak there would be a dip; for every certainty, a doubt. Our problem was that we were as shaky as we were cocky. We believed we were good, we hoped we were fine and, yet, more than anything, we longed to belong – to become a part of the world outside. For we were the Yo-Yo people of Africa. If we were the masters, we were also the lepers. We were rulers and we were outcasts.

As much as we pretended that we didn't care, that we were right and they were wrong, it always did matter. We were only human. We wanted to be liked. We wanted to play rugby and cricket and football against all of you out there. We wanted to be told we were as talented as you, as smart as you, as cultured as you. And when you wouldn't say the words we needed to hear, we hardened. We were thirteen, in 1974, when we first learnt to say 'fuck you', to say 'fuck them'. We said we could cream anyone we liked while, inside, we churned over the same old sour worries.

There was no longer any international cricket in South Africa. Our last Test series had been in 1970 when Bacher, Barlow, Richards, Proctor and the Pollocks swept to a 4–0 win over Australia at home. It had been our last golden year as a sporting country. There was peace and rapture at home, with victory over Australia in cricket and New Zealand in rugby. Since then, our cricketers had begun to waste away. We had lost hope that we would ever follow them to Lords or the Melbourne Cricket Ground. That loss hurt us more than anything.

Yet the Afrikaners kept the oval ball trickling along. We'd begun to wonder if the bloody Dutchmen were smarter than us after all. Since beating the All Blacks, the Springboks had played six Tests in four years. We'd won four, drawn one and, somehow, lost at home to England. But that had been a fluke. The true markers of our continued rugby dominance were planted against France at home and Australia away.

In 1971 we'd played those two series while still basking in the previous winter's All Black win. We felt on top of the world, especially in that place we always called 'Down Under'. At least we understood that Australianism – it was easier to fathom than our commentators' persistent reference to New Zealand as the mysterious 'Land of the Long White Cloud'. We might have been more smitten with America, more intrigued by Europe and more familiar with Britain but, in the end, our white country was most like Australia – except for the trouble, except for apartheid.

Less fanatical than the Springboks or the All Blacks, the Wallabies could surf and swear as well as they could turn their hands to most sports. They were always ready to try more than one thing. Rugby was an obvious example. Our brand of rugby was only one of three variations in Australia. Apart from Union, they played Rugby League and Aussie Rules, games which were not only beyond our comprehension, but beneath our interest. We found it hard to believe that the Australians only played proper rugby in some states. We thought they would've been better off if they had scrapped the other two codes and tried to boost the Wallabies. It was the only way they would live with the Blacks and the Boks.

At the end of 1971, the Springboks ripped through Australia on a thirteen-match tour. Under Hannes Marais they became the first South African team to complete an overseas tour without a single defeat – despite the now familiar demonstrations. But the ageing core of that team – de Villiers, Myburgh, Roux, Bedford, Visagie, du Preez and Nomis – was breaking up.

Our favourite radio-man, Kim Shippey, made us blink back the tears when he wrote of the night that old Frik du Preez finally stepped down in Sydney. In his celebratory book of the tour, *The Unbeatables*, Shippey revealed that, at the last team meeting, the normally garrulous du Preez leant against a wall. His team-mates watched quietly, waiting for him to make one last cracker of a speech while he shifted a beer can from one sober hand to the other. 'In silence,' Shippey wrote, 'they showed their respect for him, and in silence he acknowledged their adulation. It was the most eloquent non-speech I've ever heard . . .'

We were moved by the emotion of our boys in green and gold. They were more than just hard players. They were big men who, when it mattered, also felt sorrow and hurt. Frik du Preez might once have been a 'Dutchman' but, by the end of 1971, he had become our Springbok saint.

His hallowed name had also, in that year, become entwined with that of the first black player to play a Test in South Africa. As a Samoan, Bryan Williams, at least in strictly South African terms, would have been classified as a 'coloured Non-White' rather than a 'black Non-White'. There was a clumsy force about the language of apartheid. Roger Bourgarel, however, was black. But because he was a black Frenchman, rather than a black South African, he was able to play international rugby. Bourgarel was formally welcomed in South Africa, even if he was a rugby curiosity.

In the series' most memorable incident, in Bloemfontein, du Preez crashed through the blue line of French shirts. Only Roger Bourgarel stood between him and a certain try. It seemed a peculiarly South African moment as the bulky Afrikaner closed in on the slim black man. But Bourgarel was as wiry as the proverbial Free State rock-spider. He jumped on du Preez's back and forced him to stumble and fall into touch. A Springbok try had been prevented; and yet the hardcore Bloemfontein crowd rose to acclaim the first black rugby player they had ever seen.

The French team had players of such flair – from Jo Maso, Pierre Villepreux and Claude Dourthe in the back line to the great Benoit Dauga and Walter Spanghero in the forwards. They tended to dash off witty nicknames like 'The Flea' and 'The Butterfly' to their swervy backs while, up front, they dished the dirt. We loved the heady contrast between their artists of the running game and their madmen of the scrum. In 1958, using such a combination, they had become the first team this century to win a series in South Africa.

They were captained then by Lucien Mias whose approach to the decisive Test had always enthralled us. The night before the most important Test in French rugby history, Mias was, in his own words, 'rotten drunk'. He was found weaving around the hotel lobby in Johannesburg by Denis Lalanne from *L'Equipe*.

'But, surely, Lucien, you can't be this drunk!' Lalanne exclaimed.

'Sure, sure, old man!' Mias giggled. 'Nothing could be surer. I've just drunk half a bottle of rum. My sinuses were horribly sore. I had to do something about it. Probably I'll be sick in the night, but tomorrow I'll play like a demon!'

France, having drawn the first Test 3–3, were inspired by Mias to a decisive 9–5 victory. Lalanne wrote the next day that 'Mias did more alone than the eight Springbok forwards put together. He took the ball in the line-outs; he burst through on his own with a series of dummy passes to the backs, tackled, shoved like a madman, yelled, had a hand in all the big movements, and performed such mighty deeds that the South African press, petrified with admiration, wrote that he was "the greatest rugby forward ever seen in South Africa".'

The *Tricolores*, in their blue, white and red, were as brilliant as they were brutal. They played rugby like no one else for, if the mood took them, they could be more skilful and more physical than the rest of us put together. The 1971 second Test showed the French piano-movers at their most unremitting. After Joggie Jansen had done his usual crash-tackle on Maso, forcing the Frenchman to be carried from the field, the *Tricolores* climbed into the Springboks. They held on for an 8–8 draw on the field and a narrow points victory in the bloodied ring of the scrum. But we didn't mind. Rugby was more about violent contact than delicate passing. The French just did everything with a little more passion – and made us love international rugby all the more, especially when Bourgarel again stopped du Preez in full flight just a few feet from the try-line. We learnt our first French phrase through rugby during that tour – *vive la difference*, a curiously fitting saying in the country of 'Separate Development'. On the rugby field, at least, we yearned to taste that difference.

We wanted to play the All Blacks, the Wallabies, the *Tricolores* and, in 1974, most of all, the British Lions. The tour had been postponed, rescheduled, cancelled and saved so many times that we could hardly believe that the full pride had gathered in London. We had not forgotten the humiliation of 1969. Four Tests, two draws, two defeats and a million insults. Our welcome would be different – we would shower them with gratitude for we knew the odds they had overcome in pressing ahead with the tour. They had proved again that they were rugby family. But, still, you always longed to put at least one over a big brother. We wanted a whitewash. We wanted to win all four Tests.

For two long years, politics had prevented any international sport in South Africa. We had many enemies, but we were encouraged to stay strong. We would be all right if we stayed all white. Sometimes it was hard, especially when apartheid seemed to stifle even our favourite sports. The government also upheld their ban on television. Although we read about it voraciously, we never got to see *Top of the Pops* or that month's FA Cup final between Liverpool and Newcastle. We, too, suffered under apartheid. But, as our horizons slowly expanded, we imagined ourselves growing ever cooler, with our posters of Charlie George and Alice Cooper on the wall, and the sounds of Sweet and Grand Funk on the turntable. It became even more difficult to bear the thought that we were cocooned alone with the Afrikaners.

But, with the return of the Lions, we were out of the wilderness. Even more than the All Blacks, whom the Lions had beaten 2–1 in New Zealand in 1971, the British would ensure that our contest would be regarded as a world championship decider. Once we had throttled the Lions, our mastery would be undisputed.

In late May, the grass beneath our feet died and changed colour from shiny yellow to dusty brown. Another sun-filled winter settled across the Transvaal. I had just turned thirteen. Girls, especially those with long brown legs, were becoming even more noticeable to us than squat Afrikaans hookers. But every Saturday afternoon we forgot Nicola and Jennifer, Lucinda and Tracey, and, once more, through rugby, became as one with the Dutchmen. The Springboks were still our boys and, even if the Lions had fielded Ziggy Stardust at number 9, we would have wanted 'Moaner' van Heerden or Klippies Kritzinger to nail him.

The Lions had some great players. We even tried a little Welsh lilt when we chanted their back-line names to each other – J.P.R. Wil-liams, J.J. Wil-liams, Phil Ben-nett, Ga-reth Ed-wards. Unlike Lions from the past, the 1970s generation were no longer merely fancy-dan boys. They had learnt the value of the scrum and the art of intimidation. Under Carwyn James, they had followed a simple rule against the All Black eight in 1971 – they always 'got their retaliation in first'. They clobbered you first and asked questions later. They had become a little more like us.

A month before the tour began, Syd Miller, the Lions' Irish coach, admitted that 'my attitude to the game is the same as the Springboks'.

They have always based their philosophy on the importance of the scrum. Maybe it's because I was a prop, but I also know that you cannot play rugby unless you have a competitive scrum. I remember preaching this at my club back in the mid-'60s. I told them it meant a lot of hard work, but that it would be repaid. It was. We paralysed everybody for three years. The point is that if you have a competitive scrum, all things are possible. Your half-backs can play. Your wingers can run. You can do your miss-moves and your scissors and the rest. All because you are going forward. Equally, if you are going forward, the opposition has to be going backwards. So their half-backs are under pressure. Their loose-forwards can do nothing. Their backs are busy clearing up the mess. All they can do is defend. They are depressed psychologically, too.

'This is where the All Blacks went wrong. All the New Zealand forwards wanted to run with the ball. No one wanted to work. Scrummage technique went out of the window. So when the Lions went there in 1971, with some very good scrummagers indeed, the New Zealand forwards were destroyed in the scrums at both provincial and Test level. The Springboks won't make that mistake. Neither shall we.'

Springbok passion for the scrum had been undying since the historic 1937 tour of New Zealand when a former captain, Paul Roos, sent a telegram which conveyed the holy message in Afrikaans: '*Skrum, skrum, skrum.*' With Boy Louw propping the scrum, the Springboks overpowered the All Blacks – and confirmed South Africa's love for the prop-forward above all other players. If New Zealanders rated fast loose-forwards, Welshmen adored breaking outside-halves and Frenchmen pined for attacking backs, South Africans would have given up everything for a strong prop.

It explained why the Lion we spoke of with most veneration was not Williams, Bennett, Edwards or even Willie John McBride. Rather, we were struck most by Ian 'Mighty Mouse' McLaughlan, the awesome Scottish prop who had wrecked the All Black front row. We were also tickled by the idea that a prop could be named 'Mighty Mouse' – in the same way that we delighted in the fact that our favourite lock-forward was called 'Moaner' van Heerden. We were always a little less subtle than the British. We also assumed that our Moaner would swallow their Mouse.

Syd Miller had also been a Lion in New Zealand in 1959, and he felt that even the All Blacks at home was an easier proposition. 'The point is that the conditions [between Britain and South Africa] are so different. In New Zealand, the conditions are the same. The grounds are the same.

The grass is the same. The mud is the same. The wind is the same. The rain is the same. The matches are all played at sea-level. A New Zealand winter is like a mild winter in Britain. Once you become used to the time change, you might as well be playing in Britain.

'But not in South Africa. The whole set-up is different. The sun shines. The grounds are hard. The grass is different; it's more wiry. The air is thinner and drier. The ball travels further and faster. It behaves differently. It bounces more. It does not sit still for the ruck. And just as the grounds are harder, the games are harder from the point of view of injuries and recovery time. A team tends to have more major injuries in South Africa. Tacklers hit you harder because they can get a more secure foothold and so drive in harder. Line-kicking is different. Place-kicking is different. Tactical-kicking is different. The ball moves in the air differently when one man goes to pass it to another. The hand ruck becomes more important than the ground ruck. And, of course, there is the overriding problem of altitude.'

Like Miller, the Lions' captain, Willie John McBride, had also toured South Africa with the losing 1962 and '68 teams. He had become a similarly uncompromising supporter of scrummaging. Miller and McBride were 'The Ballymena Boys', for they came from the same club in a town near Belfast. Northern Ireland, like South Africa we were told, was a troubled but much misunderstood country. The Protestants of Ballymena were not unlike the Afrikaners of Bloemfontein. Syd and Willie John, like Colin Meads, were part of our culture. They were pure rugby men.

As always, we followed the tour on the wireless. The exuberant commentaries helped concentrate our minds on smaller towns closer to home – from Potchefstroom to Pretoria. At least the Lions were more evocative. As they piled up win after win during their seven-match build-up to the opening Test, we loved the way our commentators called the best British players by their first names, nicknames and mere initials – as if humanising some wild man-eaters. Willie John, Gareth, Mighty Mouse, JPR and JJ were soon as familiar to us as our own 'Moaner', 'Piston' and 'Klippies'.

We also heard some new South African names when the Lions played the hard-tackling 'Coloured' Proteas and 'Bantu' Leopards. These were described as 'Representative' matches – although quite what they represented remained a mystery. But we were surprised when black players like Morgan Cushe and Thompson Magxala were described as potential Springboks.

The South African side picked to slaughter the Lions in the first Test in Cape Town was, naturally, all white. But we were more concerned with our own persecution. Tommy Bedford had become even less popular with the Afrikaans élite by criticising both the structure and the inequality of the game. Unless we changed, he warned, the Springboks would be cast out in darkness. The selectors did not need an English-speaking rebel from Durban to give them advice. We groaned gloomily when Hannes Marais was called out of retirement to resume the captaincy. He was a quiet and seriously uncharismatic Afrikaner – and also a prop. It had never really been a contest, even though we kicked up a fuss about our need for an intelligent number 8 like Bedford to link up with our preferred half-back pairing of Paul Bayvel and Gerald 'The Boot' Bosch. Of course we needed the likes of Moaner and Piston as frighteners, but we didn't want the Lions to think that they were just being mauled by a bunch of Boers. Yet Bosch and Bayvel were excluded, as was the mean-hearted Moaner – which was no way to confront a pack as powerful as the Lions.

Our mood darkened further on the day itself. Newlands was cold and wet. We knew that Mighty Mouse and his sturdy front-row chums, Fran Cotton and Bobby Windsor, would enjoy a cheerful wallow. As on the 1969 British tour, the supposedly fleeter Springboks needed hard and dry fields to shine. Our excuses were safely stored – just in case.

After ten minutes we were up the swampy creek. Despite playing into a gale, the Lions pushed the Bok pack yards and yards, scrum after scrum. Our SABC commentator spoke anxiously of Springboks 'being strangled in the mud'. Although the score was 3–3 at half-time, he made it sound as if the match might already be over. It was – the unyielding Lions suffocated the Springboks. We were so overwhelmed at forward that we hardly saw any ball. The Lions eight – McLauchlan, Windsor, Cotton, McBride, Brown, Slattery, Uttley and Davies – destroyed us. A one-sided 12–3 victory for the Lions had been transformed into a psychological massacre.

At the post-match function, Danie Craven did not try to disguise his disgust. The old rugby president was merciless. 'I have to present a cap and a blazer to Chris Pope,' he moaned as the young wing walked up to accept his colours. 'He created a record by becoming the first Springbok ever to play for his country without touching the ball.' Facing Peter Whipp, another English-speaking débutant, Craven sneered: 'At least he did better than Chris Pope. He did touch the ball once.'

Craven was just as hard on the new Afrikaans Springboks. Looking down on the lock, Kevin de Klerk, a hero of ours from the Transvaal, Craven remarked acidly, 'He looks a big man here, but he wasn't a big man on the field. As for Boland Coetzee, he is the old man of the team – and he played like one.' No one was as cruel as an old Springbok.

The South African selectors panicked. They used thirty-three different players, including twenty-one débutants, in the four Tests. In contrast, the Lions used only seventeen players, with one change forced by an injury to Gordon Brown. Even the emergence of our Transvaal icons, Bayvel and Bosch, meant nothing in the second Test. On the scorched turf of Loftus Versveld, the Lions' scrummaging was relentless. The Lions scored five tries that day, including two from JJ and an absolute heart-stopper from Bennett as he zig-zagged his way through half the Springbok team. South Africa's biggest-ever defeat, 28–9, was mourned by an increasingly hysterical Afrikaans and English press. The entire country seemed on the brink of catastrophe.

Four days later, three friends and I turned up at Ellis Park to see our red-shirted conquerors in the flesh. We were ecstatic to be part of a world record crowd for a midweek game of rugby: 54,996 and the four of us. On a typically crisp Wednesday in early August the Lions faced the South African equivalent of the Barbarians – the Quaggas, named after an extinct species of Zebra. South African rugby felt just as endangered.

In Johannesburg, we'd hoped to show the best of ourselves to the world outside. But the Prime Minister had stepped in the week before. The Quaggas were refused permission to select a couple of coloured players. How could we convince anyone that we were not such old-fashioned baddies when, every step of the way, John Vorster and his cronies were intent on proving that we still lived in the dark ages?

The Lions struggled against the Quaggas. We simmered with excitement, willing the black-and-white shirts to succeed where the Springboks had failed. The match had everything – fierce scrummaging, glistening back-line moves, drama and controversy. The referee, Ian Gourlay, had already allowed a disputed try by Andy Ripley for the Lions and rejected two Quagga tries. Yet, with less than five minutes left, the Lions were only ahead 16–13. We were delirious.

But the Lions were resilient. Mike Gibson broke straight down the middle of the Quagga line and made valuable ground. We were certain that Andy Irvine knocked on but, in the gathering gloom, the ref had eyes less sharp than ours. He missed it and the ball bounced on and into Gordon Brown's arms. He crashed over. Tries, even illegitimate tries, were now worth four points. The Lions, scandalously, were ahead 20–13.

At the end, we wanted to storm the field with most of the other 55,000 – but we were too frightened. The noise was incredible, with boos and yells raining down in an orange shower of *naartjies* (tangerines) and plastic bottles of Fanta. The quickest spectator reached the referee first, bowling him over with a shoulder charge. On the ground, Ian Gourlay covered his head as the crowd swarmed around him. Gordon Brown and a few other Lions dragged him away towards the tunnel. It was one thing to attack a referee, and quite another to take on a Lion as hefty as the Scottish lock.

The Chairman of the South African Referee's Society, Wouter du Toit, was more disappointed with the result than with the reaction of the crowd. Despite Gourlay's black eye and swollen cheek, du Toit declared that the crowd had been 'justifiably incensed' and that the poor ref 'had been looking for trouble with his decisions'.

South African fanaticism knew no bounds when it came to planning a comeback. For the third Test the selectors picked a huge line-up of men mad enough to think they could intimidate the Lions. Moaner van Heerden came in for his first cap – as did Gerrie Sonnekus, the Free State eighth man at, we gasped incredulously, 'fucking scrum-half!' The Springbok management had completely flipped. They were attempting to batter the Lions – and you could not out-slug supreme sluggers like Willie John and Mighty Mouse.

L'Equipe described the Port Elizabeth Test as '*un combat de rue*', literally a street fight. Hunched over our crackling radios, we reeled back in horror at one of the most violent Tests in history. Moaner was in first, viciously raking JPR and hitting Bobby Windsor. Manslaughter followed as the Lions set about the Springboks. Although they never said the number aloud on radio, we whispered it to each other – '*99!*'

In 1962 and '68, Miller and McBride had not won a single Test in South Africa. But they had learnt an Afrikaans lesson. You could never take a backward step against the Springboks, you had to fight them to the bitter end. The Lions did just that, with ruthless efficiency. Whenever the time was right, we read, McBride would bark the '99' command and the Lions would start hitting, and hurting, their opponents. Early in the second half, a broken Moaner limped from the field, his left arm hanging at his side. The Lions were savage – yet they were also spectacular. They crushed South Africa 26–9, clinching the series 3–0, by eight tries to nil.

Although the Springboks salvaged a contentious 13–13 draw at Ellis Park, when Slattery's last-minute try was penalised, the damage had already been done. McBride's magnificent Lions were unbeaten in twenty-two matches, heaping up 729 points against a paltry 207. They had destroyed us. Black South Africans were jubilant. We knew why.

In the end we were less distraught than we were dazed. The long white days of certainty were gone. It seemed as if anything could happen. And it did. None of us was ever the same again.

16 June 1976

On an ordinary Wednesday afternoon, just before five, our shadows meandered up the long hill. Anderson Lane, on our bicycles, was a killer. But we pedalled on steadily. The small gang of us leant back in our saddles and steered our high handlebarred machines towards home. We were the dudes in *Easy Rider*, we were the *peloton* in the Tour de France. We were the cats already announcing which kittens we would try and kiss at Friday night's party in some mom and dad's furry garage.

It no longer felt so bad that we had just played rugby against a Johannesburg school side who were bigger and harder than us. They had thumped us but, what the hell, there was another game on Saturday morning – and one next Wednesday and right through the rest of the winter. After three years of high-school rugby we knew that none of us was ever going to make it onto the Ellis Park pitch. We were preparing for other great things instead, from our first real hangover to our first real girl.

As we climbed that dappled hill we also steeled ourselves. The unyielding tension of an All Blacks tour, our first in six years, was about to begin. In exactly five days, the Blacks were due to touch down at Jan Smuts Airport with a team which promised to be as testing as ever. We reminded each other that Ian Kirkpatrick, Syd Going and Bryan Williams were all returning – with new stars like Doug Robertson and Grant Batty in the back line and Billy Bush, Tane Norton, 'Pole' Whiting and Frank Oliver up front. The Kiwis, captained by Andy Leslie and coached by J.J. Stewart, were unbeaten over the course of three seasons, winning twenty-three matches on the trot while touring Australia, Wales and England.

Since the Lions, we had played only four Tests, all against the French, two at home and two away. The fact that we had won all four helped ease the pain and confusion of '74. But we were still in recovery, and fretting quietly that the All Blacks would do what they had always threatened to do – and win a series in South Africa.

Colin Meads had spoken repeatedly about that Black fantasy. 'If you're ever going to play good rugby,' he stressed, 'you'll play it in South Africa. The atmosphere demands it of you. The contest is hard physically – not perhaps as hard as against the French but consistently competitive in match after match. The sun throws its heat on your shoulders and there is always that feeling inside you, as an All Black, that this is what it has all been about, that this is South Africa and these are the players you most want to beat. What a tragedy if this experience is denied our All Blacks through activities quite divorced from the game of rugby.

'It had been my greatest ambition as a player to go to South Africa and win a series there. For each of the two tours I made there, in 1960 and 1970, my whole training was geared to that end. To beat South Africa in South Africa! What a dream it was. I prepared myself with total determination. South Africa and the defeat of the Springboks was always in my mind. If I didn't run up a hill five seconds faster than when I was preparing for an Australian tour, I was slacking on the job. I got angry with myself. On my runs I'd romance a bit, play imaginary games, go through imaginary tactics. South Africa and Frik du Preez were always there . . .'

We yearned to hear such dreamy words. They soothed our sores. But, as Meads suggested, the All Blacks shared some of our suffering. The tour seemed fated to emulate the cancelled 1973 Springbok trip to New Zealand. The Anti-Apartheid Movements in New Zealand, especially HART (Halt All Racist Tours), were gathering strength. The friendly Kiwis were not used to such internal dissent. They were even more startled to see how their interaction with Springbok rugby had assumed global significance. Twenty-six African countries were about to withdraw from the Olympic Games in Montreal the following month – in protest against the All Blacks.

Bryan Williams tried his best to justify the tour. 'Apartheid gets me down,' he'd told Paul Gifford in the *Auckland Star* the previous week. 'Knowing that I'd probably be in the same situation as South Africa's blacks is not a very nice thought. I do get depressed about it. But if you fight the problem by boycotts, by bullying someone, I think you get resented. If you go there, and discuss it with people, you do get communication.'

We loved Bryan Williams, and could not wait to communicate that ardour to him again. We also tried to convince ourselves that he was right, that if the Afrikaners could swoon once more at his dark and radiant feet we might change the grim way in which the world stared at us. Life in South Africa, still, did not seem so bad to us groovy bikers. How could the world hate us so much when we shouted 'howzit, my china!' to every black walker who gave us a wave? We were even buddies with some of the cooler black *Tsotsis* (delinquents) who hung around on our street corners. We still joked around in our old pal Maggie Thabang's backroom – even if she just clicked her tongue in a toothless grimace when we asked her to call up the *Tokolosh* against the All Blacks. If only they looked a little deeper, we thought, people would see that there was more to us than apartheid.

We'd neared the top of Anderson Lane when I saw the first of the helicopters. I remember pointing just as someone shouted, 'Check the choppers!' The leading helicopter was suddenly followed by another and then another and then two more. There were five of them, flying tightly together, banking away towards the south-west of a darkening sky. They were police helicopters. We could see them clearly silhouetted against the end of the day's streaks of blue, red and yellow. I thought how beautiful they looked as we watched them disappear amid a fading drone of sound.

The surrounding streets were quiet. Our breathless chatter wandered back to the Blacks. We had a shimmering fancy that we might even get to see some of the Tests on TV. After countless Commissions of Inquiry, the government had finally unbanned television. The SABC's transmissions had begun in January. There were two hours of programmes to watch daily, half in English, half in Afrikaans. A bilingual burst of Christmas/*Kersfees* every day. Our parents had all splashed out on a set. In colour, naturally, as we were having none of that monochrome crap. With home-made programmes like *Wilie-Walie* and, more accurately, American imports like *The Brady Bunch*, we had at last hit modern times. 'We've reached the twentieth century!' we'd sigh as we stared adoringly at the Brady babes flashing their white teeth in the most glorious small-screen Technicolor.

There was never really much news on television, just nodding heads telling us how wonderfully the country was doing despite the worst efforts of communist forces. It was so fucking boring. The radio was a little better, although it had already begun to drive me up the wall every morning just before seven. As my dad read the papers with one ear cocked to the news commentary, I fed our stealthy collie a couple more crusts of toast under the breakfast table. It was in such homely moments that I began to absorb how black and white everything sounded. 'Separate

Development' was good, communism was evil. Our boys in the army were courageous, the revolutionary elements in neighbouring Angola and Mozambique were cowardly. John Vorster was God's envoy, Nelson Mandela was the devil. South Africa was right, the rest of the world was wrong. Even then, it seemed to belong more to the numbed pages of our Standard Eight English set-book. We loved *Animal Farm*, but sometimes it seemed as if George Orwell might have lifted his communist pigs' 'four legs good, two legs bad' line straight from a SABC chant.

But there were some interesting programmes on the English service, especially in the late afternoon and early evening. Then, reporters modelled themselves on their BBC counterparts. They spoke in carefully modulated tones, 'the Queen's English' my mom told me, and presented programmes which were about everything from books and films and music to hat stores in London and cheese shops in Paris. Even though they rarely mentioned rugby, I listened to them with my mom and Maggie in the kitchen when I got home from playing sport every afternoon. At five o'clock, there was a magazine programme which took a 'whirl around the world' in sixty minutes. It made me feel casually sophisticated to take a swig of juice from the fridge and listen awhile as we waited for my sister and my dad to return for dinner.

But the news was bleaker, and more localised, that particular Wednesday afternoon. Even my mother's face was clouded as she saw me saunter into the kitchen. As she quietly said hello, Maggie also looked away.

'What's wrong?' I remember asking my mother.

She didn't really know yet – except that there had been trouble all day in the township, in Soweto.

'With the children,' Maggie said softly.

My mother explained the facts she knew. The few we heard were terrifying. The schoolchildren of Soweto were rioting. Some of them were younger than me. The township was burning. The police were trying to stop the fighting, but it was not yet over. They had had to shoot some of the black children. They'd had no choice. They were calling in more men all the time.

I thought of the helicopters. My mouth felt dry. There were more than a million black people in Soweto, and they were only fifteen miles away. There were other townships too, locations like Natalspruit and Katlehong which were even closer. The day had come. I longed for my dad to walk through the kitchen door with his bulging briefcase so that he could tell us that everything was going to be all right.

When he did, it made no difference. We went to bed that night with the news that the townships were 'quiet, but tense'. I no longer believed the radio. I could only imagine the worst. I hunkered down under the winter blankets and said a hushed prayer for my mom and my dad and my sister and Maggie and my friends and my dogs and myself. The night dragged by and, somehow, the sunshine made it easier to bear the next morning. I even listened more closely to the SABC comment. There had been more reported deaths. But we turned to our newspaper for more precise details. There was only one decent morning paper in Johannesburg – the *Rand Daily Mail*, which my parents described as 'liberal'. It was the one Transvaal newspaper which dared to criticise the government consistently, if mildly. Personally, I liked its pop music and rugby coverage. I still turned to the sports pages first, but I also began to read the front and inside sheets of *The Mail*. I began to understand a little more.

Thousands of black schoolchildren, some of them half my age, had gathered early in Soweto on the morning of the sixteenth. They marched in protest against a government decision that they would be taught in Afrikaans. I reckoned that we might have marched ourselves if we'd faced the tedium of studying chemistry and trigonometry in bloody Afrikaans. Trust B.J. Vorster and the fucking Dutchmen. The police decided to cut off the students at the top of a dirt road, just in case they really meant to make good their threat of walking all the way into white Johannesburg. The black kids were singing protest songs and stamping their feet, causing small clouds of dust to rise around them. They waved their banners at the nervous lines of white policemen. And then they started. The children moved towards the police.

They kept singing, making a haunting sound, as the police raised their guns in silent warning. As they walked, some of the older students bent down to pick up stones. As they sang, they began to throw them at the lines of blue. The police fired back. The first bullet killed a thirteen-year-old boy called Hector Peterson, a boy two years younger than me. Another black teenager lifted up the body and, crying, he began to run. The others ran with him, towards the police, their stones and songs soaring through the thin dry air. The riot lasted all day. When black parents returned to Soweto from work on the packed and swaying township trains, they saw the bodies. 'It was like war,' one man told *The Mail*.

And the war continued, with the rioting being intense on some days and sporadic on others. It spread from Soweto, where 179 people were already dead, to adjoining townships and then down through the rest of the country, to isolated parts of the Free State and Natal and right across the Eastern and Western Cape. After a while, we became used to it. But I was shaken by those first days. It became harder to let my eye skip over the 'Whites Only' signs which encircled us. It seemed as if there was nothing I could do which did not involve staying on the strict white side of life. We were on one side of a smudged pane of a glass and 'they' were on the other. We kept going to the movies, eating in steakhouses, driving in cars, following the rugby, while 'they', blurred and smeared, watched and waited.

Even when the All Blacks arrived the following week, the violence continued. John Vorster insisted that there was 'No Crisis'. There were times when the All Blacks must have thought differently. Bryan Williams, Ian Kirkpatrick and two New Zealand journalists, Bob Howitt and Ross Wiggens, were amongst those tear-gassed in the middle of Cape Town when the police tried to disperse yet more rioting students. Tane Norton and Andy Leslie were then asked by a Durban mother, Lynette Phillips, if they would visit her son at Voortrekkerhoogte's military hospital, near Pretoria. He had been on the border, 'fighting the terrorists of South-West Africa and Angola', when he'd stood on a landmine. The boy's chest 'looked like meat waiting for the *braai* [barbecue],' his mother told the startled All Blacks. Leslie declared that 'South Africa is at war'.

In the middle of the tour, we were forced to endure a week-long 'Veld School' trip. The girls were taken to one batch of bush in the middle of nowhere while we were dumped in a military-style camp deeper in the empty Transvaal *veld*. We had grown used to turning up at school in army-style uniforms every Thursday for 'Youth Preparedness', as the education department coyly described our own chaotic marching drills. But it was nothing like the trauma we felt as we were yelled at by hulking Afrikaans army commanders who kept on surprising us all week. Each day's running and crawling through the dust would be followed by bizarre night-time activities. We would either be cajoled into singing old Afrikaans rugby songs around the campfire or made to attend lectures about communism's *Rooi Gevaar* (Red Danger) and rebellious girls who wore T-shirts carrying the number '69'. It was even worse when we taken out in open-backed trucks in the middle of the night. Small groups of us were left in complete darkness, miles from anywhere, and told to use our army compass and the stars to find our way back to camp. We were the kind of soft white suburban kids who could hardly drag ourselves from the next-door neighbour's swimming-pool. How could they think of turning us into teenage soldiers? In the seething blackness of the bush, we were reduced to shivering wrecks, blinking back tears for our mothers and the *Brady Bunch* girls – whom we hoped wore the number '69' on their tight red T-shirts.

We even turned a little against rugby when the Afrikaans leaders resorted to their favourite oval ball metaphors to explain why they were tormenting us. 'We whites,' one of the evening discussion pamphlets read, 'despite the fact that we are in the minority, are in a position of control. This is due to our discipline, unity and advanced technology. Yet few countries have so cosmopolitan a society, with so many ethnic groupings, as we do in the Republic of South Africa. We should never forget that there are so many obvious differences within these various ethnic groups that no signs of mutual harmony exist amongst these peoples. No Zulu would be prepared to live under a Sotho government, any more than Indians or whites would. The position in the Republic is thus, potentially, one of conflict – and a breeding ground for communist insurgency. We must be prepared. But South Africa has found the solution of thwarting the Russian expansionist ideals. That solution lies within her people as bearers of the Christian faith, basic humanity, and the recognition of the principle that separate development offers the only logical solution to the threat of cultural and racial conflict in our country. The struggle to gain the support of the population can, therefore, be compared to a rugby match. He who wins the scrum and controls the ball, scores the try. Gaining this support requires, on the one hand, strong action against the terrorist, and, on the other hand, a passing of maximum friendship and team support to our people as a whole. We need to work hard and stay strong for each other. Just like a rugby team. Just like a winning rugby team.'

Two nights later, there was not even space for a scrummaging allusion. Instead, we were given a serious little tip to polish around the dying embers of our fire. I kept this one, too, for it made me think of Maggie Thabang rather than rugby. 'Today,' that final pamphlet of our week read, 'South Africa is experiencing a total onslaught. They are trying to get YOU! You are the youth of our country. They are not interested in the older generation – you are the leaders of tomorrow. The communist says, "Give me a child between 0 and 6 and I will win the war." They are not in a hurry – they want the whole world and they won't stop anywhere. The insurgents will try to create chaos, as we saw in the Soweto riots. They were part of a communist onslaught. They used the youth, hoping we would panic, but our Prime Minister was too clever and, luckily, handled the riots. The so-called freedom fighters on our borders are not fighting for freedom, but for communism. This can be seen in urban terrorism. In Soweto there are hundreds of terrorists. You must be aware of them. Speak to your servant – she will tell you. If you notice something strange about her, don't be afraid to tell the police. We must be spiritually prepared. We must be militarily prepared.'

We were fifteen years old and, in just over two years, we would begin our stretch of military service. The dreaded army had been on my mind for years, and the more I thought about it the more I realised how closely I associated it with rugby. Every Saturday afternoon, as we waited for the rugby on the radio, we would hear the SABC's *Forces Favourites*, a programme of messages and songs for our boys in the army. Heartbroken soldiers and their sweethearts affirmed their love for each other through rhyming messages and jokes about short hair and long days while choosing Elvis records like *Love Me Tender* and *40 Days*. I would be hanging around for the latest Transvaal match against Griqualand West or, more excitingly and more rarely, a Springbok Test while I listened glumly to *Forces Favourites*, knowing that our compulsory stint in the army had been increased from one year to two.

By the time the All Blacks arrived in June '76, I was so pissed-off with the whole military malarkey that I felt like smashing the radio against the nearest wall every time I heard those fucking favourites of our forsaken forces. I would have given the All Blacks a series victory on South African soil if it meant avoiding that train which would take me away for twenty-four months, perhaps even to the shadowy war on our borders with South-West Africa or Angola.

I'd also become disenchanted with some of my own previous rugby heroes. Jan Ellis, the great Springbok flanker who had survived the 1969 tour and the Lions of '74 to produce scalding performances against the French, the Wallabies and the All Blacks, let us down. He had been chosen to captain a multi-racial side against New Zealand in Cape Town – one of the 'Representative' games which was supposed to convince the world how much we had moved ahead in eradicating the colour bar in sport. Ellis's South African Invitation XV included eleven whites, two blacks and two coloureds.

But old Jan declined the opportunity. At first it was announced by the South African Rugby Board that he had flu, but Ellis himself was more candid in the *Sunday Times*. 'Multi-racial sport anywhere else in the world is okay,' he said. 'I have played against and socialised with Fijians, Maoris and all other kinds – but that was in Europe. When in Rome, you do as the Romans tell you. Here in South Africa, the same thing holds – and I am a white South African.'

Cuthbert Loriston, the president of the Proteas' Rugby Federation, was as damning of those whites who did play in the Invitation side as he was of Ellis. 'For three hundred years, we coloureds have been treated by the whites as sub-human. For the convenience of international rugby relationships, it has now pleased some of them to treat us as equals. But when the need of convenience is no longer there, we shall go back to our life of sub-humanity.'

Of course, despite such head-spinning strife, I still managed to lose myself in the rugby. I thrilled to the sounds and sights of the *Haka*, restored to the New Zealand ritual in South Africa for the first time in decades. Fifteen big men in black roared of war and death and monkeys as they slapped hands and arms and thighs before, with one long scream, they leapt into the air as one. I rocked and reeled as the Springboks and the All Blacks shared the first two Tests – 16–7 to South Africa in Durban and 15–9 to a fanatical New Zealand in Bloemfontein. Hunched over the radio, I was as tense as I'd ever been as Morne du Plessis's Springboks dug out bruising clinchers in Cape Town and Johannesburg – inching and kicking their way through 15–10 and 15–14 nailbiters. The All Blacks were left raging with frustration at the refereeing decisions which went against them – crucial verdicts which even Danie Craven derided as 'mistaken and unfair to New Zealand'. But at least we had won 3–1 again, even if the All Blacks' J.J. Stewart remarked bitterly, 'We outplayed South Africa and South Africa outkicked us. So, okay, it's a kicking game. Goodbye, rugby. Let's all go surf instead.'

We couldn't think too much about surfing, and not just because it was four hundred miles to the nearest whites-only beach. On 21 September, exactly three months since the All Blacks' arrival, the *Rand Daily Mail* reported on the findings of the country's Christian Institute. Since 16 June, the student riots' death toll had passed 300. Some 5,200 people had been arrested in connection with the 'disturbances'. More than 900 people were detained without trial. The police used eighteen different types of torture against the detainees. At least three people were known to have died in their custody. They also had forty-six new security laws to call upon as they cracked down on the townships.

The Afrikaans director of the Institute, the Reverend Beyers Naude, called upon Christians across South Africa to 'exercise their moral responsibility by giving material care to detainees and their families'. But Naude was even more forceful when, in his introduction to the report, he asked, 'Has South Africa now reached the point where it could be called a police state?'

I turned instead to the sports pages. Another rugby season was ending. But, in the spring of '76, a different kind of winter had already begun. The All Blacks were leaving that evening, but my eye lingered over another sentence, a line in which an unnamed black sports leader observed coldly: 'They have the guns, we have the masses . . .'

19 August 1981

'Good Evening. All three members of the banned African National Congress accused in the Sasol Two/Booysens treason trial were sentenced to death in the Pretoria Supreme Court this afternoon. Passing sentence, Mr Justice Charles Theron said that, from their evidence, the accused, Bobby Tsotsobe, Johannes Shabangu and David Moise, had emerged as very intelligent people. They should have known that their actions could have caused the deaths of innocent people. Nevertheless, Mr Justice Theron said that they had committed their deeds with premeditation and with total disregard to the safety of the public. He said he had no alternative but to impose the utmost punishment.

'In New Zealand, the Springbok rugby team have arrived in the town of Nelson. Their manager, Professor Johan Claassen, reported that the players were in good spirits despite their narrow loss in last Saturday's first Test in Christchurch. According to Professor Claassen, the team were welcomed warmly in Nelson and have already begun preparing for this Saturday's match against Nelson Bay. They are also due to attend their first mayoral reception in New Zealand tomorrow evening. There have been no new reports of demonstrations.' [SABC News]

New Zealand was being torn apart. Cities, towns and even families were split in two as the battles between police and protestors became increasingly brutal. A placid country was riven with violent division. New Zealand, because of us, had become a mirror of South Africa.

We, however, were more inured to images of repression and resistance. I was in my third year at university and every week I would attend another mass meeting of black and white students. The songs and the slogans, the marches and the martyrs became part of an everyday backdrop. We were even more accustomed to the sight of P.W. Botha wagging his finger in defiance on television and to the distant rumble of army trucks. It would be wrong to say that we had become blasé, for our feelings were as raw as they were tangled, but we no longer had that slightly glazed look of so many New Zealanders who had taken their first smack in the face.

The time difference meant that pictures from New Zealand were usually beamed back to the SABC in the early hours of match days. At three o'clock on a Saturday morning, I'd usually just rolled in from a long night of drinking in some dingy club where bands like Corporal Punishment, the Safari Suits and the Asylum Kids played songs like *Darkie*, *A South African in Paris* and *Policeman*. I had only a short time left in South Africa. There were only so many university courses I could take before the men in brown uniforms would wait no longer. I'd already decided that when the last call-up came, I would leave the country.

With the drink swirling round my head it sometimes felt as if my heart would crack in those small dark hours. Even then, at the height of my resentment, I knew how much I loved the country. I pinned my forlorn hopes on the sudden breakdown of the South African Defence Force. But we knew it wouldn't happen for years. Sometimes, especially at three in the morning, it felt like it would drag on forever. I would leave and never be able to return.

I'd open another beer and think of everything I would miss when I was gone. It made a change from yelling at my parents about everything I hated in 'the apartheid State'. For starters, I loved quite a few people around me. I was no longer sure how I would ever say goodbye to them. I loved the old white house where I lived. I loved the way the landscape changed as you travelled through the country. I loved the way that even the most harsh and desolate places, like the Transvaal and the Karroo, were beautiful. I loved the sun in winter. And, when I was determined to be sentimental, I'd think of all the Springbok rugby teams I had followed since 1969.

I'd reach for the television. I couldn't help myself. For all my denunciations of the tour, I was still a sucker for the green-and-gold shirts. The Springboks against the All Blacks, as always, was unmissable rugby. I *had* to watch. But, amid the barbed wire and riot police, the baton charges and the flour bombs, it was impossible to forget apartheid.

There had been many moments of shame since the All Blacks' 1976 tour. Under Danie Craven, the rugby authorities claimed that the sport had become 'fully integrated'. There were countless failed attempts to organise both legitimate and 'rebel' rugby tours – and between 1976 and 1980, the Springboks only played one match, against an ageing 'World XV', led by Willie John McBride, in Pretoria in 1977. Yet the desperation of white South Africans to have any form of international rugby did not run as deeply as their refusal to accept political change. Apartheid beat rugby almost every time.

Yet there were some glimmers of difference. A multi-racial tour of Britain by the South African Barbarians in 1979 showcased a shiny blend of fine black and white players – from Errol Tobias, 'Turkey' Shields, 'Pompies' Williams and Soloman Mhlaba to Divan Serfontein, Rob Louw, De Villiers Visser and Gawie Visagie. Guided by the articulate management of the former Scotland international Chick Henderson, the Barbarians opened the way for South Africa's return to world rugby in 1980. Under Nelie Smith, rugby's first professional coach, the Springboks beat an Argentinian-dominated 'South American Combination' called the Jaguars, Bill Beaumont's British Lions and Jean-Pierre Rives's France in rapid succession.

Then, in May 1981, preparing for New Zealand, they made history by selecting Errol Tobias as the first coloured Springbok in two home Tests against Ireland. I remember how the paper fluttered when I read the news. Nelie Smith and his selection panel had stunned us all. After all those years where the idea of a non-white Springbok had been an almost treasonable offence, Errol Tobias would be the first to crack the green-and-gold mould.

We were ridiculously agitated on the afternoon of the Test. Even though, with my dad, we were in place in front of the TV an hour before the game, I had to snap on a snatch of *Forces Favourites* just to make me mad again. I had turned twenty the month before and it seemed easier then to be angry. It was better than being nervous. A few messages to the boys on the border and a burst of the Village People's *In the Navy* put me back in my normal bad mood. There was a ritual exchange about the state of the country between me and my father. But he was the wiser man. He opened a few more beers and we all calmed down. I couldn't believe it. Errol Tobias was about to run onto the Newlands pitch as a Springbok.

'Let's hope he does really well,' my dad murmured. And we all started to panic again. Fuck. Fuck. Fuck it. What if he had an absolute stinker? What if he missed every tackle that came his way? What if every time they passed the ball to him he dropped it? What if everyone refused to pass to him and he failed to get a single touch all afternoon? We could just imagine how the Afrikaans papers would eat him alive as their excuse for Sunday breakfast. He would never get another chance again – and we would be back where we had always been, in a whites-only wilderness.

The poor guy. If we were so worried about him, how was he ever going to find the strength to move one foot in front of the other, and quickly enough so that he could fool the doubters into thinking that he could actually run onto the field in a Springbok shirt? Could he be that brave? Could he be that cool? Even when he was playing out of position, as a centre, alongside the prodigious boot of Naas Botha? Naas hardly passed the ball to anyone, whatever the colour of their hair, preferring to kick it the length of the field instead. So how would Errol even get a sniff all afternoon? We acknowledged the greatness of Botha's kicking. We were less sure how an often dazzling coloured fly-half from Boland would be able to translate his unpredictable jinks and side-steps into the play of an international centre – especially if he was petrified and nobody passed the ball to him anyway. It would be a long afternoon.

But then, suddenly, they were running onto the field. Tobias's legs moved smoothly beneath him, his head held high, if tilted a touch to the left. The cameras zoomed in on him. He was a shy man. Yet he seemed even more reserved, even a little shrunken, as the enormity of the moment pressed down on him. We were quiet too, absorbing our history as it unfolded before us.

It was almost breathtaking in its intensity, at 3.28 on a Saturday afternoon in the autumn of 1981, to see a dark skin inside that Springbok shirt. It seemed eerie, too, that South Africa wore white that day; not in honour of the past, or Tobias's breaking of history, but in deference to the emerald green of Ireland. And then, at last, it came down to a game of rugby. The whistle blew and we all settled quickly – even Tobias. We cheered and clapped his and every other Springbok move. I knew I had been misty-eyed at times. But, remembering my apparently misanthropic role in life, I quickly reverted to being hard and cynical all over again. South Africa, with fourteen white men and one coloured, had won 23–15. So fucking what? It was only a rugby match. Where would Errol Tobias awake next Monday morning, I sneered? He would not wake in a city hotel or a suburban bed. He would be back in his coloured township. What would rugby have changed?

But, then, the post-match replays whirred by again. We jumped once more and punched the air and shouted with the commentator, '*Ja, Errol, Jaaaaaaa!*' as we saw how his rock-solid display had included one especially luminous break which opened up Newlands and sent Rob Louw over for a brilliant try.

Tobias kept his place for the second Test in Durban, which the Springboks won 12–10. And he was selected, too, for the New Zealand tour. On 22 July 1981, we finally saw him wear the green and gold, in a number 10 jersey, when he played in the opening match at Gisborne against Poverty Bay. Tobias shone again that day, catching the eye from the moment he scooped up a horrible pass from Barry Wolmarans and, without breaking stride, sliced through a gap and passed to Edrich Krantz who flew across the touchline. South Africa won 24–6 and Nelie Smith smiled his lopsided smile and asked the crowd of pressmen from New Zealand, Australia, South Africa and England: 'Not bad for tokenism, gentlemen?'

But by mid-August the tour had soured for Tobias. Without any hope of replacing Botha, he was consigned to the dirt-trackers. As the only coloured Springbok he was also forced to bear the most searing public attention in New Zealand, from demonstrators and supporters alike. He became more and more withdrawn, a sad symbol for a bleak tour. But Tobias was not the only miserable South African. The vitriol against the Springboks made the 1969 British version seem more like honeyed acclaim.

The second match of the tour, on Saturday, 25 July, was to be held in Hamilton. Waikato versus South Africa. Instead, cementing the pattern for the rest of the tour, it turned out to be New Zealander against New Zealander. Ten minutes before kick-off, at 3.20 in the morning Johannesburg time, the perplexed SABC studio announcers welcomed us to their screening of the first Saturday match. The reason for their confusion soon became apparent.

At one end of the stadium, to the left of the players' tunnel, a large crowd pressed against the wire fence. Those in front wore crash-helmets. They moved curiously together like a multi-legged helmet-headed insect, searching for an opening. Sometimes they hesitated, as if uncertain which set of legs were taking the right turn. And then, the crowd parted, dividing itself into separate sections, about twenty-five yards apart. The helmet-heads in each group lowered and charged. The fence gave in without even a sigh. They were through. 'Three hundred and more,' our SABC man sighed.

At first they all sat, as if in search of a prize at that weekend's Waikato Musical Chairs. Then, those on the outside of the ring stood up and linked arms. The crowd jeered. After five minutes, a heavy-visored file of riot-police trotted onto the field. The crowd cheered as they took up position along the halfway line. Plaintive 'We Want Rugby!' pleas turned into louder 'Off! Off! Off!' chants. Four more police units jogged across to join their boys in the middle. Together, they approached the

Anti-Apartheid loop. Rugby-mad Kiwis roared – and then groaned as the police stopped a few feet away from the circle.

A man with a loudhailer warned the protestors that they faced arrest. Three stragglers decided they had had enough and walked towards the touchline. Another fifteen minutes passed, taking us a full twenty past the scheduled kick-off. All thoughts of stumbling drunkenly to bed were banished. I sat bolt upright, as if a great big screw had been driven through my hazy head. Orange flares, let off by the demonstrators, curled slowly across the field.

The police hit upon a plan. They would forcibly remove each protestor. After ten minutes they had led away twenty-five people – some of whom departed with a cop on each arm while others fought frantically for their freedom, none more so than a matronly Maori woman whom five strapping policemen struggled to drag away. The Afrikaans commentators noted her 'fierce defiance' with laughter. Five minutes later, a white van drove over the muddied grass and various policemen emerged with boxes of white arrest forms. There were procedures to follow – first of which was to abandon the game and then to take down the name of each demonstrator. 'Unbelievably tragic!' the SABC voice echoed, believing that, like the game, the tour was about to be cancelled.

But it had become a matter of principle, as much for the police and rugby men as the protestors. 'I feel as though I could kill someone,' Colin Meads seethed after the Waikato abandonment. 'Those bastards [the demonstrators] should wear uniforms to identify themselves, so we can recognise them in the street.' We could only imagine what Pinetree would do if given a chance to lay his huge hands on those who had dared put political protest before a game of rugby. After the humiliation of Hamilton, the police were also determined to reassert their authority. They revealed their main reason for calling off the game. They'd received a threat that a terminally ill man was prepared to crash a plane into the main stand. With the buzz of a light aircraft overhead, they had not been willing to take the chance of multiple death. But, from then on, they asserted, they would seize control of the rugby pitches of New Zealand.

At every match, helmeted protestors and baton-hammering riot squads smashed into each other. Helmets were dented, heads were cracked, noses were broken and faces were cut. Suggestions were made that the tour could be counting fatalities rather than just casualties. But, as in South Africa, neither side was prepared to back down. The struggle continued.

Off the field, the first Test in Christchurch was predictably bloody – but the police curbed the time seventy protestors spent on the muddied pitch to minutes rather than hours. Wedged together in a tight phalanx, the 'Red Squad' pushed the activists back. It was the most impressive scrum of a cold but sunny day, accompanied by a willing team of back-line boys who swept up the demonstrators' dropped brass tacks and nails and pieces of glass. The Test which followed was a more tense affair, which the All Blacks won 14–9. But Nelie Smith refused to blame the loss on the fact that, for 'reasons of security' they had been forced to spend the previous night sleeping on local squash courts.

We knew that Smith and Claassen were probably, like most of rugby's top brass, *Broederbonders* (members of 'The Brotherhood', the secret Afrikaans organisation which controlled the country). But they seemed pitiful when skewered and grilled on the New Zealand press conference barbie. They were like two meaty chunks of lamb to the kebab, turning on a spitting spat of questions about apartheid. Again and again, they were asked how they could justify not only the continuation of the tour but the policies of their government. 'We're just here to play rugby,' Claassen would grunt, his face becoming hard and sullen while Smith's half-smile looked queasier by the minute. They wanted to forget about apartheid. Rugby still mattered more than anything to them.

We were disappointed in their reluctance to play South Africa's captain, Wynand Claassen, in the opening Test. Apart from being a tough and bright number 8, he personified the best of New Afrikanerdom. Qualified as an architect, like Tommy Bedford, Wynand Claassen spoke grandly about music and painting and the need for South Africans to open their minds as much as their hearts. He had played rugby in France and forged a friendship with the All Blacks' captain, Murray Mexted. In his absence, the Springboks looked rudderless in Christchurch. There were rumours that Wynand's leanings to the left counted against him.

Another of our favoured picks of the New Zealand tour, Rob Louw, a speedily glamorous flank, had also fallen foul of conservative management. Although Claassen returned to the side for the second Test in Wellington, Louw had been dropped. Despite being easily the best player in Christchurch, Louw was disciplined for drinking away most of Saturday night with some of the All Blacks. The exclusion of Louw, and the inclusion of the twenty-stone prop Flippie van der Merwe, sealed our mournful destiny. Quick-thinking and fast-moving English forwards were out, and ponderous Afrikaans dinosaurs were in.

In the hours before the second Test, I drank long and hard, drowning the misery not only of my imminent leaving but also of the second-last Springbok rugby international. The more we knocked back the beers and the Jack Daniels, the more certain we became that South Africa were about to be deservedly thumped. The Springboks would never again play under apartheid. And in August 1981, apartheid felt like it had a hundred more years to run.

I woke up the whole household when I crashed through the door at 3.15 that morning – but they were growing resigned to my lost ways by then. I tottered towards the TV, feeling as morose as Johan Claassen himself.

And, in wonder, I didn't know how to react when, after half an hour, South Africa led 18–3. I kept jumping up with every score, only to check myself in mid-leap because I was cheering on the *Broeders'* team. But, fuck it, to lead the All Blacks by fifteen points in Wellington was beyond brilliance. It was not quite over yet. New Zealand came back in the second half, but the old Bokke withstood the barrage to win 24–12. The series stood at 1–1 – although there were a thousand more injuries in the battle beyond the barbed wire.

The violence escalated in the last weeks of the tour. Over 1,500 had already been arrested by the morning of 12 September, the day of the third Test in Auckland. Another 400 would follow as the police and the protesters met one last time. It should have been one of rugby's games of the century. The All Blacks and the Springboks, toe-to-toe in the last round, two sides of almost equal talent and commitment, with a win apiece. But we were locked in the dark. As the teams ran out, the orange and yellow flares again climbed towards the winter sky, where a plane circled in slow and angry circles. We thought of Hamilton and the dying Kamikazi pilot who was ready to crash his aircraft into the main stand.

The Blacks and the Boks tore into each other. Eden Park throbbed as the plane flew lower. The teams exchanged early penalties, one each for Hewson and Botha, and the plane dropped its first bombs. Heavy bags of appropriately white flour fell to earth, faster than the drifting reams of leaflets against apartheid. If one of the bombs hit a player, there was no telling what might happen. But these were All Blacks and Springboks, locked in combat in the deciding international. A crazed pilot and a few pesky missiles were not about to deflect them from their ultimate mission.

In the spring air of another early Highveld morning I gave up the pretence. I didn't care if it would also enchant P.W. Botha, Danie Craven and Johan Claassen. I wanted the Springboks to do it – to become the first South African side to win a Test series in New Zealand since the 1937 legends of Boy Louw and Craven himself. The tension cranked ever upwards. More and more bombs hit their target. Our SABC men feared a catastrophe even more devastating than a Springbok defeat – the plane taking a final plunge into the crowd.

By half-time, the pilot had still resisted but the All Blacks led 16–3. But, suddenly, with the wind behind them, the Boks rushed downfield. Ray Mordt scored a try, and then another. With fifteen minutes left, the All Blacks led 19–18. They played on until a flour bomb landed squarely on Gary Knight's squat back, knocking him breathless into the oozing Auckland mud. Clive Norling called Andy Dalton and Wynand Claassen together, and asked them if, considering the danger, they wanted to play on. They looked at each other, All Black and Springbok, steam rising from their heads, and simply nodded – more in respect for each other than in answer to Norling.

They raged on. Shelford tackled Gerber, the ball spun loose and ended up in Rollerson's hands. He looked up and sneaked over a drop-goal in the last minute. 22–18. It was all over, we thought. But the Springboks came back. Dalton knocked on. South Africa won the scrum. Botha scrambled past Mexted and found Mordt who careered over for his third try 22–22, with the conversion to come. Botha, who hardly ever missed a kick, looked up at the tall white posts as the plane turned back for one last attack. He wiped the black mud from his eye and stepped forward. He kicked and, with a cry, I realised that he had sliced it to the right. 1–1, with the last Test drawn 22–22.

Norling refused to blow his whistle. Deeper and deeper into injury time, thirty shattered players hauled themselves up for a line-out and then a scrum. The Springbok hooker, Robert Cockrell, lifted his foot early on his own put-in. The All Blacks took the tap. Rollerson ran at the Springboks. Norling blew his whistle – but not for the last time. South Africa had not retreated quickly enough. Danie Gerber, a genius of a centre, was struck dumb. Norling had pointed the finger at him. Gerber was guilty. South Africa was guilty. Norling confirmed the point with a sweeping gesture. Penalty to New Zealand. Heartache in Johannesburg.

Allen Hewson prepared himself. I hoped he'd miss, but knew he wouldn't. 22–22 was just too neat an end to so fractured a tour. As I slumped in my whisky chair, Eden Park slurred with a-shushing and a-shooshing. The 'Ssssshhhhhhh!' was enough to distract anyone – but not Hewson. His moment had come. The ball climbed and steepled. The fucker had hit it perfectly. It sliced through the middle of the wide open poles. 25–22.

I stared at the barbed wire glinting around the muddied perimeter of the field. In front of it, Hewson's thin arms were held high in a definitive print of triumph. Springboks crumpled, All Blacks frolicked. The tour was over. The game was up – and not only for Springbok rugby but for my life at home. They had already run out of time. I was still running, but I had only a little Highveld breath left.

The television became a blue blur as the pictures from New Zealand cut away into nothing. A whole chunk of my life, my youth if you like, was behind me. I turned off the box and, in the dark, I couldn't see anything.

For the next eleven years, the South African Rugby Board banged its drum of despair. It did not matter to them, even when the country burned or a State of Emergency escalated. They howled on, just like I'd done as a boy, about the injustice of isolation and the hardship of an international sports boycott. Their desperation assumed many forms – the most obvious of which was the relentless lobbying of the International Rugby Board and the tepid 'Tests' they tried to arrange whenever they were knocked back again.

After the cataclysmic trek through New Zealand, the Springboks were forced to award themselves caps for a meagre series of matches against the USA and various South American and 'World' combinations. Only the arrival of the sanction-breaking New Zealand 'Cavaliers' in 1986 constituted a breakthrough for the South Africans. But, playing in black-and-yellow shirts, without the silver fern, the New Zealanders were always Cavaliers rather than All Blacks. For the rest of that violent decade, South African rugby was dumped in a wasteland of its own making. Apartheid and rugby were as indivisible as ever.

And then, the incredible happened. On 2 February 1990, F.W. de Klerk, the last in that scowling line of Nationalist leaders, stretching from Malan to Strijdom to Verwoerd to Vorster to Botha, unbanned the ANC and various other illegal organisations. Even more symbolically, de Klerk announced the release of Nelson Mandela after twenty-six years of imprisonment.

The rugby boys was soon in touch with the ANC, promising to change the old ways of their sport in exchange for a straight route back into the world game. They got their way even sooner than cricket, which had done so much more to open its sport to all South Africans. They also found a path back into the global arena long before the country's most wildly popular game – football. After all the years of connivance and subterfuge, the old rugby men knew how to make the most of the narrowest of openings.

The rugby world was almost as pleased to have them back. On 15 August 1992, the Springboks returned to Test competition. At a seething Ellis Park, they lost 27–24 to Sean Fitzpatrick's New Zealand. But their international salvation almost shattered before the first whistle. The ANC's support of Springbok rugby had been based on an agreement with the new and supposedly 'non-racial' South African Rugby Football Union (Sarfu) that the white national anthem, *Die Stem* (The Call), would not be played before matches. Nelson Mandela also requested a minute's silence in memory of all those who had died during the country's recent unrest.

Both promises were broken. There was no silence. Instead, the majority of the crowd burst into a swaggering rendition of *Die Stem* amid lavish waving of the old orange, white and blue flag of apartheid. And then, as the teams took the field, Louis Luyt, the domineering president of the Transvaal Union, insisted that the anthem should be played again over the loud-speaker system, resulting in a second and even more overblown burst of chorusing. An old white day of rugby all over again. The ANC were so incensed that they immediately withdrew their backing of Sarfu.

Nick Farr-Jones's Wallabies, the world champions, were due to meet the Springboks the following Saturday in Cape Town. But the Australians would not play without the ANC's official clearance. Frantic days of negotiations and furtive apologies saved the Springboks as Mandela relented – with the proviso that South African rugby would be banished again if the events of Ellis Park were repeated. The Newlands crowd took the hint and observed the silence diligently – as they did the annihilation of hapless Springboks by the Wallabies' quick and sustained brilliance. Campese, Horan, Little, Lynagh, Farr-Jones, Ofahengaue, Wilson and Gavin proved how far modern rugby had moved in a decade from the stolid South African past. Australia carved out a twenty-three-point Springbok nightmare – dishing out South Africa's worst-ever defeat. The Wallaby victory was even more clinical than any achieved by the Lions eighteen years earlier. A long road lay ahead – both for the Springboks and the whole of South Africa.

The day was as beautiful in Johannesburg as it was in London. At 3.15 South African time, the two teams walked down the Ellis Park tunnel and out into an almost magical light. Fifteen men were dressed in black, fifteen in green, gold and white. The surrounding clamour circled and climbed to a new pitch as Mandela followed them. Unlike any other politician, Mandela had dressed for the occasion. The colour of his own shirt was also green, with a gold Springbok leaping across his right breast. The number on the back was a six. He wore the shirt that Francois Pienaar had sent to him after the opening victory against Australia. He doffed the now familiar Springbok cap on his head. I looked at Alison to see if, as a non-South African, she found the gesture either absurdly nationalistic or sentimental. She laughed, but her eyes glistened. 'Listen . . .' she said.

They were chanting his name, '*Nelson . . . Nelson . . . Nelson . . .*', that very same name which we had once been told was as evil and threatening to us as the *Tokolosh* had been to Maggie Thabang. Mandela lifted his cap higher and grinned wider. The demons faded beneath the shadow of the main stand. Mandela turned towards the teams.

Sean Fitzpatrick led him down the black rank. When he reached Jonah Lomu, the President stopped. 'You,' he said to Lomu in his distinctive voice, 'you are the one!' Lomu nodded, a little curtly, and Mandela rambled on about how we had heard so much about him. Mandela was enjoying himself enormously and, as he lingered, Lomu almost fidgeted. He was impatient to get his first touch of the ball. He flexed the muscles in his neck. You could tell that big Jonah fancied a run in the sun, across the green length of the Ellis Park grass.

Mandela and Pienaar were in a hand-holding huddle. The old leader had already phoned the Springbok captain, live on SABC TV, to confirm that the Springboks had the backing of all South Africans. But, in the flesh, Mandela had to tell him once more. Pienaar smiled and nodded his appreciation. And the man routinely described in our youth as the world's most dangerous terrorist beamed on. The echoing chant of '*Nelson . . . Nelson*' rose and fell, from every corner of the ground. Mandela held onto James Small's hand, wishing him well, telling him that he had an important job to do for South Africa. Small bowed his head, readying himself for Lomu.

I wanted Mandela to stay on the field for another hour, to prolong that South African moment, to delay the hurtful truth of an All Black assault. But, finally, Nelson drifted away, to watch with the rest of us.

The rugby was rarely scintillating; yet it was impossible to look away. It held us in a grip so tight that there were times that you had to remind yourself to breathe. The All Blacks scored after only four minutes. Mehrtens put over a penalty as coolly as he might have done with his last kick at a leisurely training session. Six minutes later, Stransky answered with an equally steady nerve. 3–3, without a scrum or even the first Lomu touch. It could not last forever. In the eleventh minute, the forwards eventually had the chance to bash into each other, heads just missing as necks and shoulders took the terrible impact. The twin packs lowered and heaved against each other. A minute more and Lomu rose. He was in his own half. He had the ball. Smearing past Le Roux and Mulder in a black blur, he seemed to gather strength as he ran. Lomu had decided to start with a try. But, out of nowhere, the green shirts hit him. Van der Westhuizen was first, with the bulk of the Ox, Os du Randt, crashing down in support with Mark Andrews not far behind.

'Lomu is down!' the commentators screamed, as if an unbeaten fighter had finally fallen, 'Lomu is down!' We were up, out of our seats in a flash of elated relief. Lomu, after all, could be stopped.

All afternoon they blocked and tackled him – Small, Williams, Mulder and van der Westhuizen. The Springbok tackling was hard and brutal, in the style of Mannetjies Roux and Joggie Jansen or plain old South African history, as one body after another was cut down. The All Blacks were as determined. Kruger was denied a certain try, and Small and Williams were closed down as soon as the ball neared them. Stransky and Mehrtens, slightly removed from the surrounding thud and crunch, composed their own private duel. Penalty to Mehrtens, 6–3 to New Zealand. Penalty to Stansky, 6–6. And then, after thirty-two minutes, a drop goal by Stransky. 9–6 to South Africa.

Only three points, amid the unremitting attrition, were added in the second half. They went to Mehrtens, who matched Stransky with a drop of his own. 9–9. The two packs pushed on, with only Ian Jones making a difference in the line-out as he jumped magnificently all afternoon long. But no matter how much ball he won, the Springbok vice clamped tighter.

At the whistle the two teams sought respite on their backs, feeling the grass beneath them and seeing the light die slowly above them. The sound around them swelled and fattened as the entire crowd joined the black choir singing on the edge of the field. *Shosholoza* again. A black workers' song transformed into a South African rugby hymn. Francois Pienaar and the Springboks were back on their feet, the captain in the middle of a circle as he exhorted his players to lift themselves for twenty more minutes. And still, *Shosholoza* rang out, as if one song could change everything.

Ed Morrison lifted his arm to begin the first period of extra time. Mehrtens was given a chance early on, hardly more than a metre inside the Springbok half. And, of course, he took it. 12–9 to New Zealand. Stransky drew level with an easier penalty, if any kick might be deemed easy at such a moment, on the blast of Morrison's ten-minute whistle. 12–12. One last stretch to travel.

The All Blacks wanted to win, but a draw would be enough to give them the cup. No black shirt had taken the long walk, as James Dalton had done. No black shirt had been cited for foul play, as Pieter Hendriks had been. If it stayed at 12–12, the All Blacks would be world champions for the second time. Seven minutes left. The Springboks won a scrum. We all knew what would happen as soon as van der Westhuizen received the ball. He would snap out a pass to his number 10 and Stransky would try for the drop. Graham Bachop knew. Andrew Mehrtens knew, for he would have prepared himself exactly as Stransky did. Zinzan Brooke, Josh Kronfeld and every other All Black also knew. They had to slow the scrum and then stop Stransky. The first put-in led to nothing. Morrison made them go down again. Van der Westhuizen held up his hands, pleading for a fair chance as the black pack wheeled and dropped. Then, the ball was in the tunnel and out at the back. Andrews didn't dally. It was half-back time. Van der Westhuizen made the pass, perfectly. Stransky caught it and Mehrtens was almost on him, barely an arm's length away as the Springbok boot made contact. The ball cleared the outstretched hand and began its spiralling climb. We rose with it as it spun through the air, climbing with every turn. We were in the air ourselves as Stransky's ball dropped just at the moment it passed through the highest points of the Ellis Park poles. 'It's over!' a breaking voice on the box repeated, 'it's over!'

And, finally, it was over. 15–12 to South Africa. Pienaar was on his haunches, fingers squeezing his nose as if they might push back the tears. The others gathered around him. They knelt and said their little prayer as the black shirts fell or walked away in despair. Josh Kronfeld lifted his hands to his head and cradled his black scrum-cap. He rolled his eyes in disbelief. The Springboks couldn't believe it themselves.

But Mandela, the inspirational motivator, the country's great moderator, made them look at the cup and then at the shimmering wash of colour and movement in the crowd. The old flag of South Africa had been lost. The country's new colours swamped the stadium. Mandela, the oldest African on the field, called his Afrikaans hero forward.

'Thank you for what you have done for South Africa,' Mandela said.

'We could never do what you have done for South Africa,' Pienaar answered.

He had one more hand to shake, and then Pienaar was able to turn and lift the cup to his team and the world beyond. His eyes closed for a second as his arms straightened. Behind him, Mandela shook his own green sleeves in a shuddering dance.

The photographers and the TV cameras moved in. Francois Pienaar's face filled the mammoth Ellis Park screen. He was asked what he thought of the 'tremendous support' given to the Springboks by 65,000 supporters across the full expanse of a tear-streaked Ellis Park. Pienaar shook his head and told the interviewer, 'David,' as casually as if he was on his mobile phone to an old pal, 'we had 43,000,000 South Africans today . . .'

And, even six thousand miles away, I was still one of them. I bit down on my lip, hard; and then we laughed rather than cried. We started our jive of a waltz across the room. 'Let's get drunk,' I said.

Part Two

Changing Seasons

Chapter 1
Small Moments

It was cold in Cardiff. Old women bowed their heads, scarves flapping irritably, as they dragged their Tuesday-morning shopping behind them. The men pushed their hands deeper into their coat pockets. They also picked up the pace, hoping to stamp some of the griping rawness from their feet. As we turned left towards the stadium, we did the same. The concrete outline of the main stand could barely be seen through the cloud. It was a sky so low and so grey that, searching for a Celtic streak of brooding romance, I said it might be carrying the whitest snow.

I didn't sound like a velvet-voiced Richard Burton growling a line from a Dylan Thomas story. I sounded like a South African in Cardiff. Two teenage girls skipping school shivered and laughed. But they hadn't even noticed us. They took turns to throw thin and drooping chips at each other outside the nearest burger bar to the Arms Park.

We both thought it might have been different. I guess I had been hoping that we'd be recognised. I would've loved it if some wizened old wing three-quarter had come scuttling across the pavement. 'Welcome to Wales, boyo!' he'd say. He would pump James Small's hand, congratulating him on taming Jonah Lomu in the previous year's World Cup final. Then, he'd cast a mildly bemused eye my way, wondering if I was a prime example of those beefy but deceptively mobile Springbok loose-forwards with a strange Afrikaans name. 'Welcome to rugby country!' he'd chortle. 'I'm off for a pint of Brains with JPR – fancy comin' along?'

James Small's expectations were more realistic. 'Fuck it,' he said, 'I never thought Cardiff would be this freezing! We should be sipping cappuccinos in some cosy café instead . . .'

But we were so close that we pressed ahead. Cardiff Arms Park, only months away from demolition, suddenly looked huge and grand in the surrounding silence. We hesitated at the bottom of the first row of cement stairs leading to the ticket office. They were still advertising seats and standing room for that Sunday's match. *'Wales v South Africa (World Champions), Sunday, 15 December 1996'* ran the message on the blackboard outside the turnstiles and on the damp posters plastered on the adjoining walls. It would be the last major international at the Arms Park. I thought the match would have sold out weeks before. But we had moved twenty years on from the last glittering age of Welsh rugby.

'Oh sure, it's not quite the same anymore,' the smiley gatekeeper told us, 'but it'll still be packed by kick-off. We've only got four or five thousand to shift now – and they'll go. You fellers over for the game?'

Small nodded and looked up at the high curve of the arena as it towered above us. He knew that, in less than three years, a new stadium would host the 1999 World Cup final. James Small would be thirty years old then. In the unforgiving terrain of international rugby, even for a wing, time would be drawing in on him. He'd already said that he could count the seasons he had left on one hand. Small put up a thumb and then a finger. He grinned and added a third digit, which he half-cocked and then straightened. '1997 . . . 1998 . . . 1999 . . .' he counted, reminding me again that the modern rugby player measured his seasons in years rather than just winters.

The sport had changed drastically in the eighteen months since the World Cup. Rugby, having turned fully professional, had become even more draining. It demanded speed, strength and stamina at a new and brutal pitch of intensity. It tested men relentlessly, even if it paid them well. The game's star performers trained and played for eleven consecutive months, criss-crossing the rugby world with dizzying impact. Their rate of burnout had quickened.

'But James,' I argued tentatively as we searched for a way into the ground, 'maybe you'll hit your peak at thirty . . .'

Small laughed throatily. 'Maybe . . .'

'And then what happens?' I asked, tempting him to say that he was already dreaming of scoring the winning World Cup try, against the All Blacks, in Cardiff's Millennium Stadium final.

'Who knows?' Small shrugged. '1999 seems a long way off right now.' He pointed to one of the gates. It was slightly ajar. 'Let's go through here.'

Inside, we crossed the main concourse and wandered past the lines of steel shutters which would be rolled back that Sunday to reveal bar after bar. Although he'd never been to the Arms Park before, Small's rugby instinct took over. He could tell that the dressing-rooms were on the other side of the ground. It was enough for us then to walk though a darkened entrance, over a narrow stretch of paving and onto the field.

We were quiet as we looked around. The sky above seemed lighter and higher than it had been outside. Our gaze moved across the pitch and up the steep banks of seating along both touchlines and behind the right-hand posts. To the left, where people stood, the stand was less imposing but, still, Small whistled gently.

'Quite a place,' he nodded. 'Imagine it full, with all the singing . . .'

We walked across the green and springy surface. Small stretched out a few feet ahead, looking right towards the wing he'd patrol on Sunday. By the time we'd reached the halfway line we stopped again and stared at the old cathedral of rugby. In the Tuesday hush, we seemed far from the drone of the city centre. We looked at each other. It suddenly hit us. We were in Wales, standing in the middle of the Cardiff Arms Park.

'Sometimes,' Small said, 'you get goosebumps in a place like this. I grew up in the '70s when there were all those great Welsh sides. We used to be a little in awe of them. They were better than us then. Y'know, I've never really been a student of the game but, man, some players and some teams just stay with you. For me, the Welsh were always special. I loved JPR and the way he ran with the ball – wherever he caught it.'

We began moving again, reminiscing further with every step. 'JPR, Gareth Edwards, Phil Bennett and all those Welsh guys were always there when we were little,' Small remembered. 'I was five years old when I first stood on my father's shoulders at the old Ellis Park. The Springboks against the Lions in 1974, the year they really fucked us up. It was the last Test and people were screaming all around me. The Lions ripped us – especially the Welsh. That's my first memory of rugby . . .'

Small shook his closely cropped head and lifted his sleeve. 'Look, goosebumps, bru.'

He was right. The tightly chilled flesh on his muscled arm rose up in bumpy little rows of emotion.

'To be here now,' he murmured, 'twenty-two years later, to be on this pitch, knowing that we're playing Wales on Sunday. Jeez, who would've believed it?'

The groundsman for one. 'Oi!' he shouted angrily, waving his arms at us as he thundered across the field. 'What you playing at?'

I explained that we were engaged in a respectful pilgrimage to the home of Welsh rugby – not long before its destruction and even closer to the moment when the Springbok number 14 ran across the sacred Arms Park turf.

'Fuck off!' the venerable keeper snarled. 'I don't care who he is. Nobody walks across this pitch today. Go on! Both of you! Off!'

Sheepishly, we trudged away, wondering if every last rugby sentimentalist in Cardiff had been similarly numbed. Perhaps Cardiff was not even much of a rugby town anymore – an idea which sounded absurd as soon as it left my mouth. If we had taken a similar walk near Ellis Park we'd have cast an eye around for knife-sharpening killers rather than ghostly images of Cliff Morgan or Barry John slicing through the Springboks. No one thought of Johannesburg as some cocooned rugby citadel. Rather, moving with the South African times, it had since become 'The Murder Capital of the World'. Cardiff's own transition from rugby mania to ordinary British city life seemed more sensible, if less startling.

We went for a drink before lunch. I had abandoned my search for the Welsh heartbeat of the game and so, inevitably, they found us. 'You one of the Springboks?' a tough old boy asked Small as we ambled into a pub across the road from the stadium. There was a soft gurgle when Small told them his name.

'You marked that Lomu feller then, didn't you?' one of the others remembered, as I silently took back everything I had said about the loss of Welsh rugby fervour.

'What was that like, then?' another man asked.

'Well,' Small said, thinking of Lomu as he took a sip of his Coke, 'it doesn't feel like you've tackled an ordinary guy when you try to stop him.'

'I'll bet!' the first old boy chuckled. 'But you'll fancy your chances this Sunday.'

'We haven't seen too much of your guys,' Small answered diplomatically, 'but we know you've got some good players . . .'

'That little Robert Howley . . .,' a woman sighed.

'Our best scrum-half since Gareth,' the leading man stressed.

'Scott Gibbs, too,' Small added. 'All those guys who've played rugby league – especially Gibbs. He's got a real physical presence.'

'That's Scott Gibbs all right,' the Welshman agreed. 'But it won't matter on Sunday – you'll have a romp. It'll be one-way traffic.'

It was then that I showed my own crashing variation of the Scott Gibbs crunch. Reaching over to make sure that my recorder was capturing all this sweet off-the-cuff rugby banter, I swept my jug of Brains from the counter. We watched in horror as it smashed on the bar-room floor. Small lifted his brow sympathetically as the Welshmen cracked up.

'I reckon that's what you South Africans are going to do to our boys.'

'The long hard fall of Welsh rugby,' another voice cackled, 'again . . .'

Small looked at me quizzically, wondering if I was drunk already. But, before I knew it, he had bought me another beer. He was very different, I decided, to the player I had read about in countless articles. This was not the man who, some said, personified the title of his favourite book, *No Beast So Fierce*.

A bearded man moved in at Small's elbow. He needed a few photographs.

'Sure,' Small said, with an early crack of a smile for the camera.

'A couple of shots outside?' the man suggested hopefully. 'Y'know, just you actin' casual, gettin' in the mood for the game.'

Small nodded. He turned to me, a vision of flying glass still hurtling through his head 'Have a drink,' he advised, 'and then we'll go somewhere quieter and talk . . .'

'Cheers,' I said.

After a pint of Welsh bitter, my reasons for travelling to Cardiff seemed clearer than ever. James Small was the first Springbok I had ever met. When we shook hands, I'd felt a strange sensation, a sudden and heightened sense of everything the Springboks meant to me. Even when South Africa made me despair, even when I knew what they'd symbolised in 1974, in 1981 and in 1992, I'd always loved them. It was a helpless constant. They were part of me. They belonged to the worst days; but they'd come back for good on the best, on that June Saturday in '95.

In moments of the purest rugby, I could be entranced by the All Blacks or the *Tricolores*. I could forget everything in a fraught World Cup quarter-final between England and Australia. I could thrill to a free-flowing Five Nations exchange between the French and the Welsh in Paris or Cardiff. I could enjoy provincial rugby in the southern hemisphere, and club rugby in the north. But the Springboks transcended rugby.

Small believed that even more than me. He had lived through the conviction longer than anyone else in the Springbok team. And, still, he seemed to feel it more deeply. At the Arms Park, I had sensed the emotion coursing through him, the fervour which made him say, 'I would die for my country on the rugby field.' If someone else had said it, I might have raised a dubious brow or simply covered my mouth to hide the smirk. But not with Small; for, even with professionalism running rife through rugby, it didn't matter. He really meant it.

So I thought of Small whenever I heard older fans, whether they were in Cape Town or Cardiff, grumbling that money eroded the heart of rugby. They feared that the fat salaries, the very turning of rugby into a profession rather than a passion, would destroy the game. They couldn't understand why rugby's young bucks should fly first class from one international hotel to another, or why they should have the choice of any car or home they fancied if they hit the big time. Rugby players were not meant to act like footballers. For the traditionalist, they were supposed to hold down a steady job in the day, practise hard in the evenings and then enjoy a few beers after Saturday's game.

Rugby, however, had become a career – even if the stringent physicality of moneyed rugby made it a short burst of a working life. So there was cynicism in professional rugby. There was disloyalty, too, as players veered towards the dosh, making the most of a honeyed life off the field. They would go for it, as long as it lasted. They would train, rest, play and earn a large pile of cash. Rugby players, finally, had become professional sportsmen.

But, even from the outside, I could see how many disparate types of men made a living through rugby. Some were conceited or complacent, and some were just very dull. I liked another kind of rugby player. I wanted to meet the guys who played as if they lived for rugby and yet, at the end of a game, still had lives which existed beyond sport's narrow borders. With someone like Small, I knew that a lunchtime conversation would quickly wander past the next match in Cardiff and end up somewhere more unexpected.

Yet he was a man who shivered inside when he pulled on a Springbok jersey and caught sight of its colour. I wasn't especially interested in nationalism but, when the Springboks ran out onto a field, fifteen green shirts blurred the present and my past. It did something far more to players like Small, opening up emotions buried too deep to be affected by money. The black jersey, even more so, spread a jolt of feeling across the face of every New Zealander who wore it. Perhaps because it was so hard and visceral, rugby brought such raw softness to the surface.

Some rugby truths would always stay the same. But so much else about the game had changed. Cardiff, so representative of rugby from the 1950s and '60s and '70s, seemed an oddly appropriate place to consider the shock of the new. In the distant southern hemisphere, especially, conventional links had been sharpened to a bright edge by the introduction of two very different competitions. The Super 10 provincial tournament had grown into the glistening Super 12 championship. For the first three months of the season, between March and May, five teams from New Zealand, four from South Africa and three from

Australia produced some rollicking rugby. The pace was cruel, but it created wild levels of entertainment. Rugby had become a serious business.

There had been further expansion. For the first time in one season, the 1996 Tri-Nations saw Australia, New Zealand and South Africa play each other both at home and away in furious back-to-back internationals. The All Blacks and the Springboks then contested three additional Tests in South Africa – a series as gruelling and profound as anything previously seen in world rugby.

In the northern hemisphere, the wheel of revolution spun more slowly. But it was quick enough to have transformed the sport in Britain, Ireland and France. If the administration and marketing of rugby still seemed amateurish in comparison to their brash equivalents down south, the clubs, coaches and players had embraced the concept of professionalism with diligent enthusiasm. It was, inevitably, an idea centred on the hope that there would be enough money to make everyone feel that they were suddenly rich. In England, in particular, there was a naïve belief that rugby could follow football's reinvention of itself as a multi-million-pound enterprise. The crucial difference, however, remained that football was the national game. Even professional rugby would never be able to compete at that level. It would invariably occupy a more specialist enclave, only breaking out during a phenomenon as rare as 'Lomu-fever'.

Yet in New Zealand and white South Africa, rugby was still locked into collective theories of national identity and cultural significance. In those countries, it didn't matter that rugby described itself in newly commercial terms – its true power resided in the enduring passion it elicited from ordinary people. A similar vigour had once energised Welsh rugby but, at least amongst the Cardiff kids we saw that week, there was the odd sight of as many red shirts marked by a Manchester United badge as a green dragon.

Ironically, the spread of professionalism threatened to open that divide between the mid-'70s and the mid-'90s into an end-of-century chasm. The Tri-Nations and the Super 12 had given southern-hemisphere rugby even more impetus. Yet, even in that tight band of three, a gap had emerged. By the end of 1996, South Africa's aura as World Champions had begun to fade. New Zealand, instead, had become the dominant force.

Auckland, captained by Sean Fitzpatrick, won the inaugural Super 12, beating James Small's Natal in the final. Even more historically, South

Africa then suffered the unthinkable. Under yet another new coach, Andre Markgraaff, they lost their unbeaten record in a home series against New Zealand. A magnificent All Black team also beat the Springboks and the Wallabies in all four of their Tri-Nations matches. They played South Africa five times in 1996 – and only lost the last 'dead rubber'.

The Springboks' World Cup image as a unifying social force had also begun to curdle. Having lost an ill Kitch Christie as coach, and inexplicably discarded their inspirational manager, Morne du Plessis, Springbok rugby had been in retreat all year. Markgraaff had dumped Pienaar, replacing him as captain with the quieter and less politically flamboyant Gary Teichmann. While Teichmann was respected and liked within the game, Pienaar's leadership seemed sacrosanct, bolstered as it was by his friendship with Mandela. But Pienaar was out, seemingly forever. It marked the start of another painful period in South African rugby.

Small had never been far from crisis himself in 1996. There were some great achievements, such as the way in which he ended the Super 12 as the tournament's leading try-scorer ahead of Lomu and Wilson. His reputation as South African rugby's most fervent star had been reaffirmed. But, continuing a pattern established years earlier, Small was dropped against the All Blacks for 'disciplinary reasons'. After he'd performed brilliantly out of position at full-back in the first Tri-Nations Test in Cape Town, Small was spotted by a journalist the following Thursday night. He was in a nightclub. Although he argued that he was merely pursuing his growing interest in photography at a fashion show, Small had broken the team's 10.30 p.m. curfew. It was a familiar scenario.

In a curious way, the man and the team seemed the ideal fit. For each, chaos perpetually followed triumph. The Springboks could replace their 'One Country, One Team' World Cup ambition with a gloomy collection of political gaffes. They could lose du Plessis and Pienaar, but it seemed as if they would never shake their infamous president, Louis Luyt. They could win a World Cup against the All Blacks and then, in their next meeting in South Africa, build an 18–6 lead, before collapsing in the crush of twenty-three unanswered points.

But, for both Small and the Springboks, in every forlorn moment there would be a more hopeful undertow. The Springboks always promised to improve, they always intended to escape the shadows of racism. Small, meanwhile, was the lone survivor from the first Springbok team to have emerged in the wake of apartheid, in 1992. Four years later, according to the All Blacks, he was still the best wing in South Africa. Yet in terms of being dropped, fined and suspended, Small was already the most-reprimanded Springbok in rugby history. At the same time he neared two more long-standing records – for the most caps and the most tries scored in a green-and-gold shirt. As he neared those more exalted Springbok marks, I could sense Danie Craven turning slowly beneath our feet. If Small provided a link between the country's variously dramatic recent eras of rugby, he was not reminiscent of any Springbok from the bad old days. He was even unlike some of his newer contemporaries.

While the selectors excluded Small for 'bad behaviour', they chose to play Henry Tromp at hooker against New Zealand. In 1993 Tromp and his father had beaten a sixteen-year-old black employee to death on their farm. They were both convicted and served a short sentence in prison. And then, three years later, Tromp made his Springbok début in a team missing Small, described as 'South African rugby's naughty boy supreme'.

In a radio poll in Johannesburg, 13,000 callers voted that Small should keep his place while a thousand went the other way. A stranger forum of support for Small came from the conservative Zulu Inkahata Freedom Party. Their spokesman, Ed Tillet, said that, if Small so wished, tens of thousands of Zulu Impi warriors could be mobilised to take 'the necessary action on the streets of Durban' to ensure that he was not wrongly persecuted.

The Tromp turmoil, the dispute between Markgraaff and Pienaar, and the news that the country's Minister of Finance, Trevor Manuel, had supported the All Blacks rather than the Springboks, were more serious signals that South African rugby's old wounds of division had reopened.

Rugby had always been an inherently conservative sport. In South Africa, however, there were players and spectators who still assumed that the word 'reactionary' was the highest possible compliment for a tight defence. So when a character like Small sauntered along, brimful of attitude and chock-full of emotion, they trawled through rugby history's books. It was no use. Small was without precedent.

In their attempt to define the way in which Small had changed the once rigid iconography of Springbok rugby, the South African press turned regularly to British football. Without any obvious comparisons in either their own game or their own society, they had tagged Small as 'The Paul Gascoigne of South African Rugby' and 'The Eric Cantona of

South African Rugby'. Beyond the Premiership, and in even more entrenched rebel territory, he was also known as 'The James Dean of South African Rugby'.

Small had always interested reporters working outside of sport. He made news and elicited overblown national reactions irresistibly – whether it was his admission that he had smoked dope or the sight of him crying bitterly after missing a try against the All Blacks and, again, after he became the first Springbok to be sent off in a Test match.

With his magazine looks and TV commercials, his love affairs and break-ups, his reputation both on and off the rugby field turned him into a soap-opera style celebrity. The liberal and un-sporty *Weekly Mail* decided, as far back as 1992, that 'James Small is the closest thing we have in this country to a superstar'.

I knew, too, that Small was troubled by something which made him as compelling as he was confusing. While it caused him no end of unease in his tangled life, it also drove him on in the harsh arena of Test rugby. He did not have the natural brilliance of Jeff Wilson or Christian Cullen, the sheer *élan* of Jeremy Guscott or Thomas Castaignède, but Small had the bravado and resilience to compete at even that exalted level.

By the end of 1996, Markgraaff recalled him for the tour of Argentina, France and Wales. He was immediately back in the Test side, inspiring South Africa to successive victories over the Pumas and the *Tricolores*, scoring two tries against the French.

Markgraaff resorted to that footballing short-cut when he considered Springbok rugby's strange new standard-bearer. 'James Small is the Eric Cantona of South African rugby,' he explained once more to those who had yet to hear it. 'But Cantona has worked hard to improve his discipline and has won much respect for it. We hope that James Small can do the same…'

I preferred the words of Harry Viljoen, an intelligent coach who had worked with Small in both Transvaal and Natal. 'If I've got fifteen James Smalls in my side,' Viljoen said, 'I'll take on anyone else in the world . . .' But, being a rugby man who knew Small as well as anyone, he paused. 'I've just got to teach him not to be so emotional . . .'

Cardiff, Tuesday, 10 December 1996
There was so much feeling in James Small that, facing him across a table, I made a silent decision to write this book. We sat in Cardiff's only Mexican restaurant. It was raining outside but, inside, the Small passion

burned. It scorched through those preconceptions which link all professional rugby players to the conservatism of the game's institutions – from Ellis Park to Twickenham. After Small, it was easy to look beneath just the scores and the competitions, to move beyond the unity of teams and the nationalism of countries. Rugby was also about individual men.

It helped that we had been put together by James's oldest friend and, in the Small vernacular, his 'cultural guru', Josh Georgiou, whom I had just met in Johannesburg. It also meant something that we came from the same place, that we were both still reeling a little from having grown up as white South Africans in such a strange time.

'You know how it was in South Africa then,' Small said as he stirred his third Cardiff cappuccino and I drank my umpteenth Belgian beer. 'We felt so isolated. We felt so insecure about our own culture. Everything was geared to this "overseas dream", to getting the hell out of Johannesburg and seeing how different life could be in London or Paris. I became very bitter. I'd be preparing for a match in Pretoria or wherever when I'd get a postcard from someone in Paris. I'd wonder if I'd ever see what they saw. And fuck, now, the irony is that because of rugby I get to travel the world. So last week it felt like some kind of circle had been completed.'

Three days before, Small had stood in the Parc des Princes in Paris. 'On Saturday, just before the start of the French game,' he said, 'the noise and the colours in the stadium were incredible. I looked up towards the seats where I knew my mom and dad sat. It was unbelievable. I thought then: "This is it! No amount of money anywhere in the world can ever buy a moment as pure as this. I'm in Paris. And, way up there, my mom and dad are watching me play my thirty-fifth rugby football international."

'Moments like that drive me on. It'll be the same this Sunday. I'll think of all the shitty grounds my dad's watched me play at, from school onwards. He'd always sit on his own. He'd get worked up because he supported me like crazy. My old man's got into fights with other spectators because they've always liked to diss me. But on Sunday we'll have made it all the way to Cardiff Arms Park. That moment is just not purchasable.'

Earlier that morning, perhaps an hour after we'd met, James Small had told me about his parents. He did so almost in passing, but there was a tiny echo in his voice. Like so many apparent 'bad boys', the very idea of an unbroken family both inspired and haunted Small. He was exceptionally good-humoured in Cardiff – and mainly because his parents and sister were about to follow him from Paris. They were a family again.

The divorce, which had happened when he was young, hit him hard. Since then, he had hardly ever seen his parents together in the same room; so to have them sitting side by side in Paris, of all cities, had opened him up.

'My mother always provided the stability during my rockiest moments,' he explained, 'but the rugby passion began with my dad. In 1956, Vernon Small played soccer for South Africa. When I was a kid that always meant a huge amount to me. It's always been a passion for me, to follow in my father's footsteps and play for South Africa. Sometimes he even let me wear his Springbok shirt. It was all I wanted.'

'When you were that kid,' I wondered, 'did you ever feel that the Springbok shirt also represented something else?'

'To be honest,' Small said, 'I never really thought about that. It was only later that I began to put everything into context. That first Test of ours, back in '92, against the All Blacks, was very emotional. There had been a lot of pain and isolation. And I'll never forget voting in the first election in 1994. We were on tour in New Zealand and so we were probably the very first South Africans to cast our vote. That was a special moment. But, before that, as a kid, I was just sports-*bevok* [fucked]. Nothing else mattered. Soccer, rugby and athletics ruled my life. Later, when I was around seventeen, I got suspended from soccer for headbutting a referee. That was when I got totally involved with rugby instead. We would have rugby practice on Tuesday and Thursday and games on Wednesday. I was absent from school most Fridays . . .'

While I'd been disdainful of Afrikaners, Small was less judgmental. 'I grew up in awe of a lot of Afrikaners,' he explained. 'And the more I played rugby, the deeper that feeling grew. The higher the level of rugby, the more surrounded I was by Afrikaners. I made it to Craven Week [South Africa's provincial schoolboy tournament] with Transvaal. That was unbelievable. In those days, the main Transvaal school side was supposed to be all-Afrikaans. The A team for Craven Week would be all these hulking guys from Monument *Höer Skool* [High School] and the B team would include a couple of token English guys. And I ended up making the South African Schools side that year – which was almost unheard of. They kept saying, "Who's this fucking *sout-piel* [salt-cock]?" and they've been saying it ever since!

'When I hit provincial level there were guys like Piet Kruger and Andre Skinner – great characters of South African rugby who were also hardcore Afrikaners. In 1992 the only two English guys on the Springbok scene were myself and Evan Speechly, our physio. And when it came to the Saturday night after a game, when the players were put in charge of the team, I would get fucked up. I was fucked up every Saturday night for two straight years. It was my initiation into Afrikaans rugby at the highest level – but, because I was this English *oke* [guy], there was a bit of seriousness in the beatings. I was singled out because they were asking, "Who is this young Englishman? Who the hell does he think he is?" '

'And now?'

'Well, things are different. Our captain, Gary Teichmann, is English-speaking and there're a lot of English guys on this tour. But it's not really an issue. I'm rooming with Jacques Olivier who's Afrikaans and he's a friend of mine – like a lot of the guys. Yet one of the best moments of my rugby career came just after my first Springbok Test in 1992 – at the after-match function this Afrikaans guy in a Northern Transvaal blazer comes up to me. I can see his face right now. And he says to me, in this thick Afrikaans accent, "James Small, I have to say something to you. Listen, we *okes* had all written you off. But we were wrong. As a rugby player you're okay. You deserve to be a Springbok." Then, it was unusual for an Afrikaner like him to even talk to an English-speaker like me. But for him to say that I was as good as the rest of the team – those are the memories that stay with you...'

'As I guess,' I murmured, 'do the tears . . .'

In South Africa's opening post-isolation Test following Mandela's release, against New Zealand, he faced the formidable Inga Tuigamala. Small showed an immediate affinity for international rugby. He made tackles of astonishing bravery and ran with commitment and pace as the Springboks fought back from a disastrous start. In the end, the enduring memory for most was the image of Small knocking on with an open try-line only metres away. If he had held on and scored, South Africa might have completed a shock victory after a decade in the wasteland.

'Oh boy,' Small laughed softly, 'I just bawled my heart out afterwards. I was inconsolable! But, after a while, I was able to look at the whole match and realize that I had done well. They said I couldn't stand up to Tuigamala. He was this hundred-kilo Tongan winger in a black shirt who had been running over everybody. People were calling him the best wing in the world. They said I had no chance.

'I'll never forget the Friday afternoon before the Test. I was with my sister in this pub in Johannesburg, The Moosehead. We were getting something to eat at the bar and these four guys behind us were discussing the team. It was a huge moment in South African rugby – our first Test in years. These guys went through the whole side, player by player. And I was the only guy they didn't want. I went over to the loudest guy and said to him, "Give me your business card and I'll call you after the game!" And he started stumbling, "Oh shit, I'm sorry, I didn't know you were there." I said, "Fuck that! I heard what you said. Give me your card and we'll talk after the game."

'That night I couldn't sleep. My first Test for South Africa and we're playing New Zealand. I was so nervous. I just kept walking round and round the hotel in my Springbok shirt. I eventually went to bed in that jersey. And I thought about what those guys had said about me. The next day, quite early on in the game, there was an opportunity for Tuigamala to steamroller me. He got the ball in their 22. I was hanging deep for a kick but he decided to run. He had a clear thirty yards in front of him to pick up speed. I don't know how I did it but I hit him, knocked him down, got up and ran up the sideline with the ball. And on Monday morning I phoned that guy who had dissed me and I said, "There – fuck you!" and put down the phone. That's how I feel my whole life has been – proving people wrong.'

'But not everyone thinks of you as a martyr,' I pointed out.

'No. You've just got to look at the World Cup.'

'Yeah, you and the rest of South Africa against Lomu . . .'

'Well, with a name like mine,' Small grinned helplessly, 'I was always destined to face a guy as huge as him. And in Johannesburg, my old home town, in the World Cup final. The Springboks against the All Blacks! The whole nation, from Nelson Mandela down, is rocking. You can feel this longing for us to win. But, to be honest, I'm shitting myself.'

A laugh, as sharp and dry as Small himself, slipped out. 'Jonah Lomu's awesome. He's standing tall at six-foot-five and clocking in at 120kg. I'm five-ten and sitting pretty on the same wing at 85kg. And the whole fucking country is saying, "Go on, James, go get him, boy!"'

He shook his head in disbelief. I remembered how, just before the kick-off, Mandela had stopped in front of Small. The President offered the green-and-gold number 14 a curious smile, as sweet as it was grave.

'And then,' Small said, 'Mandela laughed. Very gently. You could see it in his eyes. He was thinking, "Shame! This poor guy is marking Lomu!" Mandela took my hand and said, "You've got a big job to do today, Mr Small!" I'd only seen Lomu once before. It was the Dubai 7s and I didn't know who he was then. He was huge. I thought, "Who's this brute of a lock?" And then I heard he was a wing. I thought, "Oh shit!" He had this walkman on but the headphones were so massive that it looked like he had two orange soccer balls on the side of his head!

'Before the final, it was eerie. On the way to the ground, on the bus, I had my own little walkman on. I was listening to this song, *Hymn of the Big Wheel*, by Massive Attack. It's this beautiful song, with a slow and hypnotic beat, and this high voice sings this one line over and over . . .'

Small and I, respectively full of caffeine and beer, and similarly high on excitement, sang that very line, in the aching falsetto of Massive Attack's Horace Andy, the great Jamaican vocalist: '*and the big wheel, keeps on turning . . .*' I am not a singer, and I don't think James Small is either, but I have the tape to prove it. For a moment we were Horace Andy and Tricky singing for Massive Attack in Cardiff. I was ready to repeat the line again, as it goes on record, but Small was sensibly back on the bus to Ellis Park.

'I'm playing this song over and over again,' he said, as if he'd already forgotten our poignant duet. 'And I could see people walking to the ground, carrying the new flag and these banners which all seemed to have a "Small" name painted on them – telling Jonah Lomu that he had a "Small Problem". Time seemed to slow down. I got those goosebumps again. Like the song, it felt like I had come full circle – after all the heartache I was back on top again. The wheel had turned.

'But, on the day itself, there were other guys who took on Lomu as well. I had a lot of support. Before we went out, Chester Williams said to me, "You just hold him, James, and the rest of us will pull him down." Kobus Wiese also said, "Just cling on to him and I'll fuck him up!" Chester hit him, Kobus hit him, Japie [Mulder] hit him, Joost [van der Westhuizen] hit him, I hit him . . .'

'And how does it feel,' I repeated, 'when you tackle Lomu?'

'When you hit him hard,' Small said after a thoughtful pause, 'it's like hitting a wall. But I got his attention. Jonah's very aware of me on the park. He knows what I bring to the party. I'm this psycho-kid who's not going to stop at anything. He knows I'm capable of going a little ballistic. So we've had some good battles over the last year. And I think I can safely say that there's only one game when he got the better of me – in the Super 12 final, when he scored two tries. Apart from that, I've held my own against him. But I would never class myself as a great player. I'm just a worker. But a very hard and a very committed worker.'

'Are "hard-working" and "committed" also fair descriptions of the Springboks? The All Blacks might have had more flair . . .'

'But we had this incredible desire to win. I don't want to sound philosophical or even religious, but it was down to something deeper. This will sound strange coming out of my mouth but I truly believe that it was South Africa's destiny to win the World Cup. It was almost as if there was divine intervention, that God wanted South Africa to share in some joy, that elation, after so much shit over the years. It was like he was saying, "Okay, South Africa, here's a month of pure enjoyment and togetherness for the whole country – this is yours." And to have Nelson Mandela there, on the day, well, that was just the sweetest moment.

'When we attended the State President's function for winning the World Cup, Mandela comes up and says, "James Small, my son has posters of two white men all over his wall. One of them is Francois Pienaar, which I can understand. But, for some unknown reason, the second man is you!" He laughed but it made me think – jeez, even the President knows I'm supposed to be the bad boy!'

Small often played up to his unhinged persona – for he thrived on the enduring intensity of his role as the country's most controversial rugby player. '*Ja*,' he drawled, 'and the image also pays off sometimes. The media love that "bad boy" thing. And, of course, a lot of the Afrikaner players aren't that media-friendly so I get all this attention because I'm different.'

As early as August 1993, the Small saga had already turned down a bumpier track. As he offered to work alongside Adele Searle, an anti-drug campaigner in Cape Town, the papers revisited his own past. While everyone knew that most South African kids had rolled a couple of joints by the time they were sixteen, Small's indulgences were printed with a breathless puff of shocked revelation.

Charlene Smith's *Sunday Times* feature began with these words: 'Rugby hero James Small used to be the terror of Johannesburg's Northern Suburbs – a *dagga* [dope] smoking drop-out whose future looked bleak.' Smith did her best to write a story of redemption. Although she went into astounded detail about the teenage Small smoking a joint on a golf course, she was relieved to announce that there was a happy ending.

In celebration of the fact that he had not smoked for the previous two years, a local company had pledged to pay the Adele Searle Drug Rehabilitation Centre R300 for every try Small scored. 'Managing Director Angelo Peros', the man coughing up the anti-dope dough, told Smith that he had seen Small 'talking to sixty teenagers. He is the perfect anti-drug symbol for young people. He is incredibly charismatic and great with kids. They gave him a fantastic response. It has taken a lot of courage for James to take the stand he has . . .'

But, the following year, Small was attacked on New Zealand television by Murray Deaker, a glibly provocative TV personality. The theatrical Deaker described Small as 'a danger to all around him'. Freeze-framing moments when the camera zoomed in on Small's typically fierce match face, Deaker declared grandly that 'this absolute nutter' was 'obviously still suffering the effects of his dope-smoking'. After so many decades of abysmal publicity under apartheid, the nervous Springbok management refused Small permission to take legal action against Deaker.

Small's frustration escalated. Later that year he was involved in a 'nightclub spat' with a Springbok water-skier, Ian MacLeod. The 'aggro', as MacLeod characterised it on television, began when a girl 'pinched Small on the bum'. MacLeod's girlfriend, Adele Hattingh, denied that she was the cheeky culprit. On the front page of the *Sunday Times*, as the country tussled with issues of democracy and murder, a cheesy rugby headline appeared: 'I Didn't Pinch James Small's Bum – Adele!'

The *Sunday Times* reported that 'the attractive second-year university student said that, unlike other women, she did not find James Small irresistible'. Meanwhile, another student at the club, twenty-year-old Melany Jackson, claimed that she definitely belonged to the broad church of 'other women'. Speaking in Afrikaans, she was quoted as saying that, when she met Small, she 'was in seventh heaven. He has the softest lips and the hardest body a girl can dream of. It was heaven just to meet him.'

Back in hell, and dropped for the UK tour at the end of '94, Small was less ecstatic. His exclusion from the Springbok team felt like 'someone had reached in and pulled out my heart'.

But Small soon won back his spot in the World Cup squad. Afterwards, in the following weeks of national euphoria, images of Small kicking a ball around the townships seemed the perfect symbol of 'new' Springbok rugby. Photographs of Mandela and Pienaar together at countless functions provided the political seal to bind the entire country to rugby. Yet Small was a little closer to ordinary life. He was still one of the boys on the street.

'I'd say it's been pretty much an even spread of ups and downs over the last nine years,' he reflected. 'At the start of each season I think, "This is gonna be a good year for me, this is gonna be a peaceful year." But then, somehow, I self-destruct or get made an example of. There've been times when I've been in the depths of despair. You know all the incidents. But a lot of those things were blown out of all proportion. The drug thing just got turned inside out and I ended up having to talk like I'd been some sort of junkie. It was ridiculous. Then that Murray Deaker guy in New Zealand rolls these clips of me playing rugby. I'd be about to ruck a ball and Deaker would say, "Look at the maniacal frenzy in James Small."

'Morne du Plessis, our old team manager, would always tell me – "James, you have to be more careful. They're making a big thing of this because it's you . . . they wouldn't care if someone else did it." After a while, you just say to hell with it. I'm happy with my image. It sells and, also, it forces people to give me some space. A lot of them think that I'm going to turn round and deck them!'

But, in Cardiff, Small was intent on discovering a more cultural side to his already complex personality.

'How do you feel about all the Gazza and Cantona comparisons?' I asked.

'When I was compared to Eric Cantona,' Small enthused, 'I took that as my biggest-ever compliment. If I had just an ounce of the skill Eric Cantona has in his left foot, I'd be a happy man. But Cantona also has that immense intelligence.'

Small looked me straight in the eye. He reached for his wallet. He found the neatly folded set of words. 'To achieve happiness,' he read aloud, 'sometimes you have to go through the worst depths of despair. Genius is about digging yourself out of the hole you have fallen, or been pushed, into. Failure makes you succeed.'

The Springbok tyro looked up slowly and confirmed the truth. 'That is a direct quote from Eric Cantona.'

'But James,' I replied, sounding as if I had lived in England too long, 'you support Liverpool!'

'*Ja*, but I love Cantona! You remember what he said about journalists and seagulls . . .'

In true Cantona fashion, Small tore away on a deeper artistic jag, telling me about Iceberg Slim's gritty American novels before skidding down to talk about John Hyatt, Robbie Robertson and the other artists he featured on a compilation album of his favourite songs, *A Small Collection*.

Small also detailed his next venture. 'I've just done this deal with a company called Mr Price. We're gonna do this range of underwear. I've been buying all kinds of samples in London and Paris – I've got a suitcase packed full of everything from boxer shorts to ladies' teddies.'

He chuckled again, as if he could imagine hiring Jonah Lomu for a Calvin Klein-like underwear ad campaign. 'We've got the perfect name.'

'What's that?' I asked.

'Well, it just had to be "Smalls"!'

We were still laughing when I called for one more beer and, adhering to his new discipline as a reformed rugby player and exotic underwear entrepreneur, a sparkling glass of water for Small. 'The thing is,' he suddenly broke off, 'I'm not just that one-dimensional guy they write about. I don't just want to be known as the nut who got kicked out because of a fight in a nightclub. I want to be known as someone who did some interesting things off the field. But, maybe most of all, I want to be known as a great competitor, as a guy who is good to play with and hard to play against. I'm twenty-seven years old now and I've only got a few years left to set the record straight.

'I know that the hardest thing for any sportsman is to give up the game. Who knows how you react when you're no longer "The Business". You not only lose the fame and the money that comes with it – you lose the chance to do something you do best of all. You're just an ex-player. This is my ninth season as a full-time rugby player. So I've had a good run, I've had a long run. And, sure, there are times when you get *gatvol* [fed up] and you don't feel like going away on another tour or to another practice on a Monday morning. But, now, I'm happy. That's a big thing for me to say. Because I'm a very negative person most of the time. Y'know, I don't like flying because I believe I'm destined to die on a plane.'

I could have mentioned that this made him the 'Dennis Bergkamp of South African Rugby' – but his distress was real. 'I always have this feeling of impending doom. If it's not that, it's another thing. I'm always waiting for the bomb to go off. It's as if I can't believe good things can last.

'But, now, life feels good. I'm playing for my country in Buenos Aires and Paris and Cardiff and it feels great. My family are around me. I've got some fantastic friends and a lot of wonderful opportunities outside rugby. It feels like things couldn't be better. I'm going to try hard to live for this moment, to just enjoy it and see if I can put something special on the field next to everything else that has happened off it.'

It was the perfect moment to turn off the tape. I called for the bill. We sat for a few minutes and spoke about our plans for the year ahead. Christmas was only ten days away and it felt like a new beginning awaited both of us. And then the phone rang. As James reached for it in his jacket pocket, I made a slurred crack about how a Welsh Lolita must have tracked down his mobile number. He winked, and then nodded hopefully.

But it was his father. It did not take long for the mood to change. The hurt spread slowly across James Small's face. I looked down, trying to appear fascinated by each and every number printed on our bill. The conversation continued while I worked on my mental arithmetic. Then, I did the right thing. I went for a walk.

Eventually, when I returned to the table, James ran a hand across his cropped head. His eyes glistened. 'That was my dad,' he said. 'He's on his way to the airport. He's not going to wait until Sunday. He won't see me at the Arms Park.'

I hesitated, not quite sure how best to respond. But, as he pushed back his chair and stood up, James Small said the words before I could. 'I'm sorry . . .' He walked towards the door and then turned and shook my hand. He said it again. 'Sorry . . .'

Cardiff Arms Park, Sunday, 15 December 1998
The weather was still miserable. But the green-and-gold shirts shimmered through the gloom. Our eyes were on James Small all afternoon. We were with three older Welshmen who were unfailingly humorous about South Africa's supremacy. It was not the result they wanted, a 37–20 Springbok cruise, with Joost van der Westhuizen scoring three slashing tries. But they took us out to a crammed pub afterwards and told us about the glorious, if dipping, history of Welsh rugby. They lamented the fact that the Cardiff crowd hardly sang anymore – snatches of *Why, Oh Why, Delilah!* and *Bread of Heaven* were all they'd heard that afternoon. We told them about James Small.

In the match itself, Small was injured early on, cracking a rib, but he played on with his usual fire. We cheered every time he touched the ball or brought down a red jersey. The night before, Alison and I, and her brother, Tim, an Englishman living in Cardiff, had gone to visit James and his mother, Vaughn, at the Springboks' hotel. It was an ordinary Saturday night in Cardiff and so the four of us had a few glasses, while James guzzled his water instead.

He was happy again, as I was too, as we stressed to Alison and Tim how sorry we were that the Welsh were about to be thrashed in their last big match at the Arms Park. His mother laughed and told us stories about James as a kid, and how it was not the easiest thing to live in South

Africa when your son kept hitting the headlines as often as Nelson Mandela – if not for the same reasons. 'Ag, Ma!' James would say.

But it was the night before his last game of the season and so, after an hour, we said goodbye. He walked us to the door and put his arm around my shoulders. 'I want you to have the shirt I play in tomorrow . . .' he said.

Twenty-four hours later, even though I still did not believe it, Alison and I swept through those same revolving doors. The foyer of the hotel was packed, but there he stood. James Small had a beer in one hand and a cigarette in the other. It was the end of another year, and his life felt sweet again. He came towards us with his arms opened wide. '*Howzit!*' he shouted.

A minute later he stretched over and gave the jersey to me. It was wrapped in plastic. The mud of Cardiff Arms Park glinted darkly through the shiny surface, already just a memory from a famous ground. I only told him later what it meant to me, that shirt, how the green and the gold had echoed through my life, how it reminded me of everything that was so powerful and unforgettable about South Africa. Then, I just grinned at him, thinking of the moment when I would lift the muddied number 14 shirt out of its glossy wrapping and hold it in front of me, turning only to say to my English girl, 'I love these colours . . .'

Chapter 2
The Black Art

London, Monday, 17 February 1997
Sean Fitzpatrick tapped his thick fingers against the arm of our crushed-velvet sofa. The patter of a piano echoed in the distance. Whispering flunkies and high-heel-clicking air-hostesses drifted across the lobby, flashing their *Come Dancing* smiles in time to the tinkle. Fitzpatrick grinned back but, at the same time, his eyes glazed momentarily. The loop was endless. From Auckland to Brisbane, from Durban to Dublin, Fitzpatrick had been doing the blurring two-step since his first overseas tour in 1984.

He rubbed his ball-throwing hand across his broad face when I asked if he felt he could be anywhere in the world where they played rugby. 'I know what you mean,' he murmured, 'but I took a little walk a few hours ago. It was pretty cold and wet and, y'know, it sorta felt like a Monday in London.' Fitzpatrick smiled easily, suddenly sounding genially sunny on a foul winter night. He told me that he was back in the groove again, that he was in the mood 'for a bit of a yarn'.

It had been different earlier that day. There was no mutual friend or shared background to bind us together. I came cold to Sean Fitzpatrick. He stared at me with steel-capped eyes as I approached him in that same Kensington hotel foyer. It was the look of a man who had lived through the moment again and again. He pulled the shutters down and gazed at me through the narrowed slits. If I'd had a tennis ball in my hand, and been in a more playful mood, I might have tossed it gently towards Fitzpatrick – just to see it bounce off the hard surface of his stare long before it neared his head. But there was something about Sean which concentrated the mind. I got straight down to work, doing my little pitch, trying to sound as unobtrusive as I was pleasant.

'What's that?' Fitzpatrick said quietly after my first smiling mumble had trickled away.

That's the downside of being unobtrusive – it's difficult to make yourself understood. I realised that I needed to speak up, a tad more boldly and clearly. Yet the problem remained that I'd always had more than one picture of Sean Fitzpatrick in my mind. I had seen him talk charmingly on television so many times, just as I had so often seen him bite down hard on his flashing white gumshield, lock arms with his two props and snarl shorter words at the hooker opposite him. Fitzpatrick's canny version of a split personality was fascinating. He was the most urbane TV interviewee in world rugby; yet he was also the game's most ferocious competitor. It seemed like I had hit a day when, off the field and early in a new season, he had decided to drag down the front-row mask.

As I cleared my throat in preparation of a more convincing verbal put-in, it was difficult to forget that Fitzpatrick, for all his media-savvy, did not think especially highly of journalists. In his autobiography he admitted that he and many of his fellow players had considered the inky breed and decided that they 'couldn't see a lot of quality there'. He was even more wary of the UK hack. Writing about previous British tours he remarked: 'You never feel entirely at ease. Perhaps it's the bad weather, the lack of sun, the numbers of people everywhere – but most places seem boxed-in and claustrophobic to New Zealanders used to blue skies and open spaces. It's hard to relax a hundred per cent because there are too many prying eyes, notebooks, tape-recorders, long lenses. At the back of your mind you know a single indiscretion or a mistake will be put under the spotlight and scrutinised like nowhere else.'

I looked at a point slightly over his right shoulder, as if to emphasise my determination not to examine him too closely. I wondered if I should explain to him that, actually, I was from South Africa and I wasn't much of a journalist after all.

The South African angle was a bit of a gamble. Fitzpatrick knew that, to South African rugby fans, he was entrenched as number one on a very long national list of public enemies. South Africans could become almost pathologic about Fitzpatrick, fuming murderously at his ability to psychologically dominate some of their meanest forwards while, also, having an uncanny knack to persuade referees to see decisions his way. The fact that Fitzy himself acknowledged a few of his wily tricks only deepened their antagonism. While he was smoothly diplomatic as soon as the whistle had blown, he had let slip his own view of his detractors.

'I couldn't get over how one-eyed South Africans are,' he revealed in his book. 'Everywhere we went we got the same talk. "Is this the best beach, or what?" "Is this the best meat?" "The best weather?" "The best rugby?" Etcetera, etcetera, etcetera. They've very arrogant about their abilities, too. I spoke to quite a few New Zealand supporters on tour who found them the same. They believe so much in themselves, that only they have the world's great players – everyone else is second best. After about five minutes you get really sick of it.'

The idea, therefore, of confirming that I was a South African who had lived in the brightly lit media-madhouse of London for the previous twelve and a half years did not seem like the massive boost of image I needed. But I knew that Fitzpatrick was too smart to con. So, in the best front-row tradition, I took a deep breath, looked him straight in the still-narrowed eye, stuck my neck out and told him the truth.

'Okay,' he said. 'What can I do for you?'

I told him, still filled to the brim with truth, that I thought the All Blacks were the best team in world rugby. Although I was no expert, it looked to me as if they were on the verge of developing into one of the world's greatest-ever sides. His provincial team, Auckland, who had just renamed themselves the Auckland Blues, were ten days away from beginning their Super 12 defence. And 1996 had been a huge year for Fitzpatrick, the All Blacks and Auckland – they had won everything. It was likely that 1997 would turn out to be even better for all three of them. I told him about the book I intended to write, and my hope that I might trail his teams in New Zealand, Australia, South Africa and Europe.

I had picked up the interview ball. My mouth was running. I could feel its momentum. I was just about to drive deeper into 'The Myth and the Meaning of New Zealand Rugby' when Fitzpatrick broke in with a nod. He'd got the picture. The shutters opened a crack and he looked out at the lounge across the lobby. 'Okay, no worries,' he said. 'What about if we meet over there, round about five?'

My jump through the blackened hoop had lasted less than a minute. Fitzpatrick offered me his hand when I thanked him. It hadn't been so bad after all. If anything, Fitzpatrick's initial caution had been a useful reminder of the old All Black heritage, of those schoolboy days when we'd whispered the legend of 'The Unsmiling Giants'. The black names came back to me, like a schoolyard rhyme: 'Tiny White and Tiny Hill, Kevin Skinner and Colin Meads . . .'

Off the park, those icons were expected to do no more than pull on the black blazer and a pair of grey trousers before they grunted 'Yup' or 'Nah' to a handful of uneasy journalists. Sean Fitzpatrick, as tough as any of those past meanies, had changed everything. He had long been aware of his more sophisticated responsibilities in the modern game. And, more than anyone else in world rugby, he was as slick on the podium as he was fierce in the ruck.

One of the most intriguing aspects of New Zealand under Fitzpatrick, and John Hart, their coach since December 1995, had been the transformation of the All Blacks into a publicity-machine dream. Whether hammering their rivals or commending them dutifully afterwards, Fitzpatrick's beaming boys in black could be trusted to do the right thing. 'Yeah,' he nodded agreeably later that afternoon, 'we've always been very professional in terms of playing rugby – but now we're also paying a lot of attention to our image. We want to ensure that our product becomes the best in the world. The basis will be formidable rugby – but we're striving to improve ourselves off the field, from management strategy down to the look of the brand.'

You might have guessed that, before the advent of full-time professionalism in rugby, Fitzpatrick used to work as a part-time consultant for Coke. Yet, for all the marketing speak, his commercial bonhomie would have meant nothing without the burning inside him. The glowering hooker inside the gleaming man, the squat leader breathing fire through his bellowing pack continued to enthral most. It also explained why some of his opponents described him in cruder language. I'd forgotten how many times I had heard Fitzpatrick described privately by rival Test players as 'the fucking hardest bastard of them all', or some similarly blue-hued compliment.

As just one example, his encounter with the Irish hooker Steve Smith belonged in Colin Meads's big black book of tough tales. Smith hit him with what he described as 'the biggest punch I've ever thrown'. His fist smashed into Fitzpatrick's face, instantly drawing blood. Fitzpatrick took out his mouthguard, spat out three teeth, and then slipped the suddenly crimson shield back between his swollen lips. The stare he shot at Smith, as they prepared to lock heads again, chilled Irish hearts – Smith's most of all.

Fitzpatrick's physical resilience was unsurpassed in world rugby. He had played 118 times for New Zealand, eighty-one of those matches being Tests, the last forty of which he had run out as captain. For ten straight years he had played in every single All Black international, only missing New Zealand's 145–17 massacre of Japan in the 1995 World Cup when he'd stood down voluntarily so that his perpetual understudy, Norm Hewitt, could get a game. Fitzpatrick's ability to withstand pain, and grind through the kind of injuries which sidelined more ordinary men, was bound up in his even more staggering mental strength. It was a psychological hardness of such depth that he did not have to resort to brutality himself. Fitzpatrick would tug at shirts and hold on to arms.

He might even throw the odd sneaky punch if he felt it was required – but he was always more intent on upsetting the equilibrium of his opponents. He would unhinge them gradually, and always mentally rather than physically.

Fitzpatrick talked incessantly on the field, infuriating the men in front of him with his barbed banter which ran a wire around their heads until they could see nothing but the jibing man in the number 2 shirt. And if he wasn't talking or galloping along with the ball, they'd see him lying on the wrong side of a ruck, looking up innocently at the referee as he waited for another penalty for foul play against him. Even the All Black's media-pack that year concurred coyly that 'international opponents have referred to him as the best referee in the game'. But, more importantly for Fitzpatrick, the focus of those same opponents would be smeared by a consuming desire to shut his mouth. They would lash out and be penalised. And their concentration would waver even further as they waited for the penalty against them to be taken. They would get him next time – unless Fitzpatrick or the referee got there first.

Os du Randt, the great South African prop, laughed despairingly when he told me about his various encounters with Fitzpatrick. 'You'll run out into the sunshine on a beautiful day,' sighed the massive Free State man in his most expressive Afrikaans, 'and you'll be muttering under your breath. "*Ja*, today is the day that I'm going to fuck up Fitzpatrick. Today it's going to be his turn. He's done it so many times to me that, this time, I'm going to make him pay." And, naturally, that's what he wants. You're thinking of him rather than playing your own game. It's the same old story. He ends up doing it all over again. We try to sort things out and the referee gives a penalty to them – three points to Auckland or New Zealand. He's helluvu frustrating to play against. But, jeez, at the same time, you have to respect the guy – he's one of the true greats of world rugby.'

Notoriously, the Springboks' Johan le Roux lacked the control of du Randt. He bit Fitzpatrick on the ear, tearing flesh in the 1994 series in New Zealand, and was sent home in disgrace and banned for nineteen months from international rugby. But, before he left, le Roux's wild teeth gave the laconic Kiwi journalists another Fitzpatrick joke. 'Fitzy's fine,' they cracked, 'but le Roux's in hospital with blood poisoning.'

Phil Kearns, one of Fitzpatrick's most ferocious rivals, also maintained a mordant sense of humour. During a Bledisloe Cup match between Australia and New Zealand, the Wallaby hooker and captain shoved two fingers in Fitzpatrick's face after yet another niggling skirmish. 'Well,' Kearns said later, 'I was just inviting him to a barbecue and I wanted to know if he wanted one sausage or two.'

In the plush surroundings of his Kensington hotel, Fitzpatrick chuckled knowingly at such anecdotes. But, later, when pushed a fraction, he did talk convincingly of the need for a hooker to be relentlessly combative. 'I've got little doubt,' he said, 'that hookers are usually the most competitive individuals in a rugby team. All the great hookers I've faced have been the same. They're tough, they're in your face, almost daring you to take them on. That's why I love the position. You're at the very heart of the game, deep in the engine of a team. And I guess that's why the position, as well as those of the props, is misunderstood. From the outside, it's hard to see what's going on. And, sure, you need plenty of strength and aggression – but the best front-rowers also rely on technique and guile. It's not been called the dark art for nothing.'

'With you often depicted as the darkest of the dark . . .'

'Yeah, especially in South Africa!' Fitzpatrick grinned slyly. 'But that can get overplayed a little. The fact remains that rugby amongst the forwards has a crucial psychological element – it's not just a matter of battering into each other. Of course the physical confrontation is at the core of the game but, sometimes, the most important battles are won in the mind. Everyone who knows me in rugby knows that I most respect the players who stand up to the pressure. Of course I'll push it to the very limit, because that's in my nature. I've always been intensely competitive.'

I was intrigued by stories that, as Andrew Harvey, his best friend at school, explained, 'Sean didn't really develop muscles until he was seventeen or eighteen. Before that he was fat, a real porky, a Billy Bunter. He had curly hair – I think it was an afro – and he looked round. But he was tough.'

It sounded to me like the ultimate fat boy's revenge, with Fitzpatrick grafting cunning onto competitiveness with such dedication that he eventually rose to the position which every other kid in his country had dreamed of – captaining the All Blacks. I wondered if his supposedly embarrassing size as a boy had made him even more desperate to succeed?

'The key point was that I hated losing. I couldn't bear it. It's been the same my whole career, whether playing for my school, Auckland or the All Blacks. It didn't matter what size I was – I was just so keen to win!'

'But that issue of size is also so integral to the charm of rugby.'

'Of course! It's great. There's a place for the tallest guys at lock, the smallest guy can wear the number 9 shirt and us fat boys play up front. But, yes, I was sensitive about my size at school. I got a lot of stick about it. It wasn't easy. They also used to pick under-age teams according to weight and there were times when I was just much heavier than guys my age – so I'd be left out of some teams because of my size. You don't easily get over that kind of humiliation when you're young. So, yeah, maybe that instilled an even deeper drive in me . . .'

'Although looking at the All Blacks today,' I said, 'with Ian Jones or yourself popping up on the wing to score tries, it seems as if even the lankiest and the . . .'

'. . . And the roundest,' Fitzpatrick laughed as I hesitated. 'I think Ian Jones is slightly slicker than me when he joins the back line! But you're right – the changes in the game are just incredible. And it's one of the reasons that makes me want to keep on playing. The game is becoming more and more entertaining and I love the style of play we've developed in New Zealand – it's a fifteen-man game and everyone's involved all the time. I couldn't think of anything more boring than trudging from one scrum to another, from one line-out to the next. Playing a dull forward-orientated game. I want to be in there, tackling and running, passing the ball and, yeah, scoring tries too!'

Fitzpatrick bristled with energy and enthusiasm. He looked like he was about to lead a team of Black bucks down the tunnel at Eden Park. He nodded enthusiastically, as if he was saying another silent 'yeah!' to himself. I smiled at his mysterious secret. Somehow, he could kid around with time. I didn't know many other men of our generation who could still pull off that trick. At almost thirty-six, I was two years older than Sean. Then, as I slouched in my chair and he sat bolt upright in his, it felt like a hundred. My head was still recovering from the previous night's high-tackling hangover. I had reached that stage of life where my best side-step was the one I took towards our third bottle of red wine on the occasional wild night in.

I tried to slow the pace a little. 'Is it harder,' I coughed grimly, 'to play the game in the late-'90s than it was in the mid-'80s?'

'It's just so different,' Fitzpatrick marvelled. 'When I started out in representative rugby there was so much scrummaging. And before I even came along, Test packs would be engaging in fifty or more scrums a match. Now we'll do twelve or fifteen. But it is much harder in the sense that it's played at such a pace and everyone is so much fitter. Every team seems better prepared – and so the intensity of the competition is amazing. It's not just Test rugby either. Auckland start this year's Super 12 next weekend with a game in Pretoria against Northern Transvaal and we know it's going to be hugely demanding. The pace will be very quick, the heat will be terrific and the game won't be too far off Test standard.'

'Are you aware of the criticism of the Super 12s in the UK?'

'Yeah, I've heard a little bit,' Fitzpatrick said with a small raise of the brow.

I loved Super 12 rugby's speed and power – and, most of all, the quality of the players who were on display week in, week out for three and a half months. But there was a counter argument that a 42–27 game did not necessarily constitute great rugby. Sometimes, a 16–9 scoreline might disguise the fact that the rugby had been more compelling.

While the theory appeared sound on paper, it was an essentially outdated premise. From a distance, a 42–27 score suggested that the Super 12 was nothing more than a high-stepping splurge of tries through lazy defensive lines. But the points on the board did not explain the startling increase in the levels of pace and skill. Both backs and forwards in the southern hemisphere were able to play modern rugby in a dazzlingly fast and deft style. The revised rules of the game and the increased accent on attack meant that teams tried to retain possession in an attempt to score tries rather than rely on penalties. Some Super 12 sides would even boot a penalty out, to use the ensuing line-out to set up another crack at the try-line, rather than accept three points for a kick. If there was a choice in the Super 12, you had to go for the seven-pointer. Yet, if there were ten tries in a game, there would invariably be twice as many try-saving tackles. Without actually attending a Super 12 match, it was easy to assume that defences were weak. But they were often strong enough to resist four or five successive waves of attack. In the Super 12, tries usually came on the fifth or sixth phase of possession – the tournament, after all, featured the same hit-merchants who wore All Black, Springbok and Wallaby jerseys.

But the whole pro- or anti-Super 12 debate tapped into roots of both nationalism and nostalgia. New Zealanders and South Africans were quick to howl outrage at any British writer who questioned the enduring content of the Super 12. Their response became one of sneering patriotism. 'What would a bloody Brit know about rugby, anyway?' constituted the stock refrain. They would not have seen the markedly improved quality or competitiveness of British club rugby in the late-1990s – so the UK game remained, to them, a faintly amusing anachronism. But even an old-fashioned visit to Gloucester, to see Lawrence Dallaglio's Wasps or Francois Pienaar's Saracens striving for victory at a snarling Kingsholm, would have added some ballast to their airy contempt.

Yet, at the same time, British rugby men were quick to base their own contrasting Super 12 doubts on neatly packaged television highlights. They thought that the faster and looser southern-hemisphere style undermined the traditional gravitas of the game. Few of them would have seen eighty minutes of live Super 12 rugby in searing close-up at Carisbrook or King's Park, at Ballymore or Athletic Park. It was easy to sit back and describe Sky's bundle of Super 12 tries and cheerleaders as a glib variant of basketball. Personally, I was more interested in the opinions of the players. And, whether they had featured in the tournament or, from Lawrence Dallaglio to Gregor Townsend, watched it at a distance in Britain, they seemed united in their passionate admiration for the Super 12.

The key distinction between club rugby in Europe and the Super 12s remained the way in which it was officiated. In the southern hemisphere, the referees were instructed to allow the play to flow as much as possible, to encourage continuity between one phase of play and the next. The team in possession were always at an advantage. Apart from the fact that they were almost certain to win their own line-outs and scrums, they would also escape minor infringements as long as the ball was played quickly and constructively. The officials were most interested in acting within the spirit, rather than sticking to the exact letter, of certain laws. There was little wrong with that decision. There had long been a need for more fluidity, for the game to shed its stop-start mentality.

Referees in the northern hemisphere adhered to the old rule book far more strictly. The game was slower and more pedantic. Yet it was superior to the Super 12 in the opinion of Stephen Jones, the *Sunday Times*'s authoritative rugby writer. Jones was the most vociferous opponent of Super 12 rugby. I did not agree with him – Jones described the tournament as 'rubbish' and declared that 'I absolutely hate it'. However, his writing could not be easily ignored.

'The Super 12,' he argued, 'has substituted a speedy, sanitised, glossy nothing for a physical confrontation. It takes big lungs, but not big hearts. It has lost rugby those delicious moments when two packs thunder at each other, battling grimly for supremacy. Ultimately, it is basketball played with an oval ball, stuff which makes you long for a 3–3 draw in a grim and pitched battle.

'Basketball has always struck me as being a pleasant enough activity but with too much scoring, too few real twists and reversals of the action, to be satisfying. For me it provides one of sport's most anodyne experiences. And now, courtesy of our supposed masters below the equator, we can now derive the same non-experience from rugby. The Super 12 is easy on the eye, but it provides rugby that no longer touches the heart.'

I knew that my own heart would beat faster if I was at a match between Auckland and Natal, rather than Bath against Leicester. But, still, I thought Fitzpatrick would answer Jones' accusations better than anyone. I turned to the black-shirted master of rugby's dark art. Fittingly, he had begun to glower slightly. I asked him if he worried that some of the game's most basic and attritional virtues were being lost as the Super 12 became even quicker and less structured.

'I think differently. I think Super 12 rugby is amazing. Sure, I was pretty sceptical about it at first. But I've been totally won over. I don't agree with those criticisms. It's not the kind of rugby they watch in the UK and so they might think it's all powder-puff, try-scoring stuff. But they're very wrong. Having played in it, I'd be happy to tell anyone that it's an incredibly hard tournament. It's the perfect bridge between provincial and Test rugby. It's also not just a great tournament in terms of the high level of skill or speed or strength of all the teams – there are some bloody awesome hits going in as well. The confrontation is very fierce.

'But, perhaps more importantly, Super 12 rugby is attractive to most people. You might alienate the odd purist but, as far as the rest of the public is concerned, certainly in New Zealand, you can't better it outside Test rugby. The whole atmosphere is great, and the crowds really get into it. That can only be good for the game. Particularly in New Zealand, before the Super 12 concept came along, people were being lost to rugby. Our own provincial tournament was doing nothing for most people. The rugby wasn't always the greatest and the divide between the teams was too wide. No one wants to see Auckland hammer Counties by forty points. There are a lot of other things to do in Auckland beyond watch one-sided and dull rugby matches. But, with Super 12, the teams are much more evenly matched and the international flavour adds real spice. It really captures the New Zealand public's imagination when their teams are up against the South Africans or the Australians. I'm all for the Super 12!'

I didn't need much convincing. I had already booked tickets for the following afternoon's friendly between the Auckland Blues and Harlequins at the Stoop. My London Kiwi friends and I were already in full Super 12 mode, with me outnumbered by the Auckland and Otago brigade. But our southern-hemisphere roots bound us together. Any chance for us to see the tournament's defending champions together was irresistible.

Fitzpatrick himself was less enamoured. Preparing for a Saturday-afternoon Super 12 game in the 40°C heat of Pretoria by trudging through the mud of Twickenham on a wet Tuesday was hardly ideal. 'There's a ruling that you can only turn up in one of the other countries in the same week of your first match. It means that there is no advantage for teams playing away first – because later in the tournament other sides will also have to deal with the travel. So you have to get used to the long flights and playing matches five or six days after you arrive. But the advantage for us coming here is that London is in the same time-zone as South Africa.

'However, it's not easy to prepare in these conditions. On this tour we've noticed how hard it is even to train. We were out Twickenham way today and the pitch was clogged with mud. It wasn't enjoyable. I was also on that BBC footie show [*Rugby Special*] and they were interviewing John Hall at Bath. And the condition of that training pitch was just shocking. The mud was so thick that the guy could hardly lift his boot! It makes you wonder how the players here do it.'

Fitzpatrick, however, quickly turned my question about the gulf between the styles of rugby played in the two hemispheres into an un-muddied exercise in diplomacy. He might have bounded alongside twenty-one-year-olds in the Test arena but, off the pitch, Fitzpatrick considered his words as shrewdly as any election veteran on the night before another big win at the polls.

'Everyone's comparing the two,' he agreed, 'but there are too many variables. The weather for one – how can you play an expansive game on a muddy pitch? Just take a look at Saturday's game at Lansdowne Road [when Ireland lost 46–6 to England in the Five Nations]. Although England eventually scored a lot of points they struggled to play because the pitch was just not conducive to good rugby. Look at that poor Irish winger [Dennis Hickie] – he breaks clear and then trips over a bloody divot! On the same day in Paris, the sun shone and the French and the Welsh played some attractive rugby. England didn't have the same opportunity. So, y'know, if I played here I'd be annoyed by the comparisons being made between me and these blokes down South. I'd be thinking, "Who do they think they are? Let them come play over here for a while!"'

Fitzpatrick chortled at ritual All Black insults from the past – such as Colin Meads's sweeping denunciation of English rugby as comprising 'too many sweatbands, not enough sweat!'. They were no longer pertinent and, anyway, it was part of his psychological strategy to boost his rivals. He smoothly switched his focus to the most positive attributes of the English game. 'I was pretty impressed by the English pack,' he countered. 'The sheer power of their tight five was outstanding but it was more revealing to watch the loosies – Dallaglio and Rodber were excellent but I also liked Richard Hill. He looks like he's got the goods. Johnson at lock is an exciting player. He does a lot with the ball and always puts pressure on the opposition. There's a growing confidence upfront but they're a little unsure about some of the back line. It shows in the way they try to keep it tight for so long. The New Zealand attitude is very different. We have such confidence in all fifteen men. When we look at the firepower we've got out wide we always want to get the ball to them.'

In the blandest All Black lines, you often find the deepest truths. 'We have such confidence in all fifteen men' might read like a bubble of football manager-speak. Yet Fitzpatrick said it with eerie certitude. I looked even more closely at him. He could spin out homilies all night long about the quality of the English pack or the difficulties of running across a sticky training pitch – but, underneath everything, he was a man without doubt. He knew that he was captain of the world's best rugby team. There was no need for him to spell it out, and so he continued on his preferred trip around the vagaries of international rugby culture.

'There is a little bit of difference in the English and the Kiwi attitude,' he confirmed. 'When Auckland played Bristol last week, I saw again that some English players are keen to kill the ball at the earliest opportunity. And when we did a few training sessions with some kids at Harlequins, the young prop was asking us, "How do I spoil the scrum?", and the lock was asking, "How do I spoil their line-out?" I'm not trying to be critical, but that basic attitude – of spoiling rugby – is different to ours. We're convinced that this is our ball, so let's get it out of this phase and move it out to our backs. It's why I'm enjoying my rugby so much.

'Another reason I still play the game is that, unlike this morning, I enjoy the training back home. In New Zealand there are great facilities and good pitches. We'll get up at six o'clock in the morning and more often than not the sun's out. You go down to a firm field and you train and you come back and have a big bowl of fresh fruit, a big orange juice and, y'know, you're on top of the world. Then you might go down to the harbour and water-ski in the afternoon. It's not why we play good rugby, but it obviously helps . . .'

The All Blacks' breathtakingly expressive rugby was dependent on factors more significant than a bit of sunshine, a glistening pile of Kiwi fruit and time to improve their water-skiing technique. Their style of play, coaching and management had taken the game into a different dimension. Under Laurie Mains, they added blistering pace and skill to their traditional bedrock of power and ferocity. In 1996 their back line had become even more explosive with the introduction of the twenty-year-old Christian Cullen. Described as world rugby's 'Discovery of the Decade', Cullen appeared as a deceptively slight, but inherently strong full-back who had the genius to corkscrew his way through five or six tackles while scoring the most head-spinning tries imaginable. His talent was matched by that of Jeff Wilson, otherwise known as 'Goldie' throughout New Zealand. Wilson had become the consummate wing in Test rugby. He could do everything, with lashings of grace and verve. Although Jonah Lomu had been stricken with a terrible kidney illness, the previously unknown Tana Umaga was often as difficult to stop. Alongside these dynamic young back-line stars, those cultured old sweats in the centre, Frank Bunce and Walter Little, had just rolled on in 1996. Justin Marshall was a competent scrum-half while Andrew Mehrtens and the emerging Carlos Spencer provided sublime and contrasting options for the number 10 slot. The All Black back line, with its flat accent on pure attack, was exhilarating.

Yet the previous August, when the team dominated three out of four Tests in South Africa, the success was built on the foundation of a tough, mobile and hugely experienced pack. Their dominance was established upfront where Fitzpatrick and his Auckland allies, Olo Brown and Craig Dowd, presented an unbreakable front row. Ian Jones and Robin Brooke were consistently decisive in the line-outs and almost better in broken play. Their back-row trio provided an even more extraordinary combination – Michael Jones, Josh Kronfeld and Zinzan Brooke. Even the acerbic English rugby writer, John Reason, claimed that the incandescent Jones was the best rugby player he had ever seen. Zinzan also carried out moves which no previous number 8 had ever attempted. Kronfeld, meanwhile, had been the best open-sided flanker in world rugby in 1995 and 1996. His use of the loose ball was breathtaking.

With such a combination, the All Blacks had established themselves as the best and the most glamorous side in world rugby. And, because they were as pragmatic in the tight as they overflowed with flair in the loose, they kept on winning. In footballing terms, they rolled the best of Germany and Brazil into one outrageously successful team.

However, 'off the paddock', as Fitzpatrick put it in plain Kiwi-lingo, the New Zealand hierarchy had been as dextrous. Under Fitzpatrick and the slick John Hart, New Zealand had shed much of the insularity which undermined some of their past sides. It had been no coincidence that France were the All Blacks' bogey team. Whenever the boys in black ran out in Bordeaux or Paris they felt far from home with nothing familiar, from language to tucker, to ease them into their more typical mood of invincibility. But Fitzpatrick and Hart had taken New Zealand to a more worldly level. Whether motivating the team or refining tactical man-oeuvres, reorganising Test schedules or handling the media, the All Black leadership approached perfection.

The business-minded coach and captain taught their players that the power of the modern game sprung from the corporate suites and tele-vision studios. Those brightly lit rooms housed the men who proffered the contracts which had made the All Blacks the most marketable rugby team of all time. But, as Fitzpatrick stressed, alone with me and away from the cameras, his team would not be overworked just to satisfy the ravenous appetites of their paymasters. While the rest of the rugby community were about to flog as many games, and dosh, out of their exhausted players, Fitzpatrick and Hart were insisting on All Black cutbacks.

'This year,' Fitzpatrick said, 'will place an excessive strain on our best players. The Super 12 is extremely demanding and, soon afterwards, we're bang into a series of internationals. We've got Fiji, Argentina twice, the Bledisloe Cup and then it's the Tri-Nations and four matches as tough as anything anywhere in the world. After that we've got the NPC [National Provincial Championship] in New Zealand and then it's back over here in November and December for four Tests. That means twelve Tests, possibly thirteen Super 12 matches and some hard grind in the NPC on top.

'But this programme was put together before John Hart was fully on board. He's said he's not going to allow it to happen next year. In 1998 we'll play far fewer Tests. It might not please some people but we have to put the All Blacks first. It's what we've done for years – and it's the cornerstone of our success. We've got the structure of the game right.

Everything is geared to helping the All Blacks remain at the pinnacle of the world game. We look at some other countries and it seems obvious that there are power struggles within their domestic games. But, in New Zealand, whether you live in Auckland or Wellington, the All Blacks are always the ultimate. Nothing can be allowed to stop them.'

The All Blacks were already preparing for the 1999 World Cup. I wondered if the painful memory of the previous final had eased.

'Well,' he said slowly, 'it helped that we beat South Africa last year but it still hurts to think of the final.'

'And the poisoning story?' I asked, in reference to Laurie Mains' allegation that the majority of the New Zealand team had been poisoned by a fanatical South African chambermaid the night before the final.

Fitzpatrick laughed. 'Oh, that had nothing to do with it. We played very well throughout the tournament but we just didn't clear the final hurdle. South Africa were the better team on the day. It was hard to take. I was lucky because I had already been part of a team which had won the World Cup [in 1987]. But I guess that defines New Zealand rugby. We remember our losses rather than our victories.'

'Well,' I noted, a touch enviously, 'you haven't lost too many . . .'

'No, but I remember every one as clear as a bell. The victories blur but the defeats . . .' Fitzpatrick's face scrunched up in dejection, as if he had just lost a Test that afternoon. 'The defeats are horrible. We just don't like to lose. It's not a feeling we rate much, y'know! It's different somewhere like Wales. The only game they seem to remember against the All Blacks was when they beat us in 1953! But we don't think about the wins so much. We go over the losses again and again. But, then, you can find some positives in defeat. In hindsight, taking into account everything the team achieved in 1996, we might not have developed so quickly if we had won the World Cup. If we had won in '95 then it could have been us, rather than the South Africans, who would have been struggling. There's huge pressure on them as champions. I think our team last year would have been too young to take that pressure. It was better that we could play against the world champions – and beat them in their own backyard. We've gelled as a side, both the old boys and the young kids. We're on the verge of becoming a very special side.'

'Are they the best side you've played in?'

'It's not easy to compare. I was first picked for the All Blacks in 1986 [as part of the 'Baby Blacks', the young team which was selected when most of the established New Zealand players broke the international sports boycott to play for the rebel 'Cavaliers' in South Africa]. We came out of nowhere and we were very inexperienced. But by the time of the 1987 World Cup we had evolved into a very good side – with some truly great players. Michael Jones, Grant Fox, John Kirwan and John Gallagher were all superb. Then, the 1995 team played some outstanding rugby – at a speed no one had attempted before. We were bigger and quicker than the '87 team. Now we've introduced some great young players to the core of the '95 team – and, yes, there are times when I think that this particular side could become one of the greatest ever.'

'Do you feel a little grizzled when you look at guys like Cullen?'

'You bet!' Fitzpatrick replied with matching seriousness. 'But it keeps you young. They're such good kids and it's great to be around them. We have a lot of fun. We encourage them to be competitive with the old boys like me and Zinny and Frank [Bunce]. They love that – and so do we . . .'

Fitzpatrick used to dread training when he himself was twenty and on the fringe of the Auckland team. Andy Haden, the All Black lock, refused to excuse youthful imperfections. 'He was really hard on me,' Fitzpatrick said. 'If I threw in badly at a line-out, he stopped the training session. He'd say, "No, that's wrong!" Sometimes he'd even draw a sketch of what he wanted in front of the whole team. It made me feel pretty small.'

The cruellest humiliation occurred on a European tour when, in the midst of training, Fitzpatrick threw three consecutive bad balls. Haden yelled at him to 'Get out!' and refused to train further until Fitzpatrick had left the field, knowing that he had been dropped. 'It was one hell of a shock to the system. Those established All Blacks wouldn't tolerate sloppiness just because you were a kid,' Fitzpatrick admitted ruefully. 'I can laugh about it now but we treat young players differently today.'

'But has some of the camaraderie you had with guys like Fox and Kirwan been lost with professionalism?'

'Yeah, I think so. Money changes a lot of things, doesn't it? It's really great that we can now just go out there and play, knowing that we've got more than enough money to pay the mortgage each month. But, in other ways, it is now so much more serious. It's a job to a lot of players now. We still have that camaraderie because we're very close in the All Blacks today – but we had a fantastic time in the '80s. A guy like Foxy missed out on the professional era, which is a real shame, but we're still very close friends and I know he wouldn't swap most of his experiences. The professional era is still a bit of a novelty and when that wears off it'll be interesting to see how it pans out. It'll be important to balance the business side with the traditional passion we've always had in rugby, both on and off the field.'

'Is the money a prime incentive in wanting to play on?' I asked.

He answered with winning honesty. 'I would be lying if I said it wasn't. I just love the game but, obviously, the money is also a significant factor. I've been playing for a long time and, for a lot of those years, I didn't make a huge amount out of the game. But, in many ways, that was an advantage for me as a person. I developed my own building business away from rugby – and for most of my career I would be getting up at dawn to go and work on a building site. We'd only train at night. And that was good for me. It opened my eyes to the real world. There are a lot of nineteen-year-olds coming into the game and they only play rugby. That's fine when you're nineteen but, when you get injured, or when you eventually have to retire you're going to be pretty one-dimensional if that's all you've done. So that's why, with Auckland and the All Blacks, we try to get all the young players – no matter how talented they are – working towards some kind of trade or business. But it was easier for us in the '80s. We had no choice. We *had* to earn a living. A lot of the kids in rugby assume that they're already set up for life. It doesn't always work out.'

We spoke about Jonah Lomu, and the bleak way in which the seemingly unstoppable World Cup idol had been cut down at the age of twenty-two. It was impossible to know, then, if he would ever play rugby again. He was not the only Auckland All Black who had failed to start the 1997 season. Michael Jones, as always, was on the list of battle-stricken, while the meteoric Andrew Blowers had also suffered a series of debilitating injuries. Blowers, at the age of twenty-one, was out for months. Rugby was a harsh trade.

Sean Fitzpatrick, however, seemed indestructible. But he paused when I asked him how much longer he thought he could keep playing, having shrugged aside injury for a decade and more. 'At the end of last year,' he eventually said, 'I felt more shattered than I've ever done. This year is going to be even more arduous. But I love playing. My aim is to keep going as long as I can, ideally right the way through to the 1999 World Cup in Cardiff.'

'Do you think you can do it?' I asked my seemingly rhetorical question.

'Yes, I do,' Fitzpatrick answered typically. 'I certainly have the desire . . .'

'How old will you be on the day of the 1999 World Cup final?'

Sean Fitzpatrick stroked his chin, as thoughtful as always. 'I'll be thirty-six,' he said.

'That doesn't sound too bad!' I said with the defiant logic of an old boy.

'No, not to us, I guess,' Fitzpatrick murmured. 'But the game is getting harder. I like to think I've got two years left in me but, y'know, I'll have a better idea the next time I'm in this town . . .'

November seemed years away. I thought about how much rugby Fitzpatrick still had to play, a large chunk of which I hoped to watch in comfort, high above him in various stadiums around the world. He would try to keep beating away at the heart of rugby, game after game, year after year.

'I hope so,' he said. 'But this is the year that will decide things. If I can make it through to the end of 1997, I think I'll be okay.'

I nodded; and he nodded back. 'I hope I do make it,' he repeated. 'Rugby has been my life for so long.'

He rubbed that same ball-throwing hand across his face again; and then he sighed at the truth of his own words. 'I know it's going to be terribly hard to just let go, to have to give up one day . . .'

Chapter 3
Four Countries, One Team

The morning after I met Sean Fitzpatrick, South African rugby reached for the knife again. It felt strange to have witnessed the remarkable survival technique of Fitzpatrick in close-up just as, six thousand miles away, his old adversaries appeared set on self-mutilation. Yet when a country, like a sport, has such a black and white history then red always flows more freely than any other colour.

As the South African murder toll rose steadily, the Springbok rugby authorities slashed away at their 'One Team, One Country' slogan. It was, as always, the same. You could still gauge the mood of white South Africa by examining the state of the national rugby team. And, on 18 February 1997, you did not need to look long to see that the body of rugby was twitching and bleeding again. In the end, and in keeping with so many other guardians of apartheid before them, they had turned the knife on themselves.

Andre Markgraaff, the Springbok coach, was still revelling in his team's success, two months before, in France and Wales. He spoke brave words about restoring Springbok rugby's parity with the All Blacks. As for those blacks closer to home, 'our blacks' as we would have said in our green and rolling suburbs of the '70s, Markgraaff had been more blunt in his delivery. They were 'fucking kaffirs'.

On 17 February, at 8 p.m. Johannesburg time, the exact moment when I said goodbye to Sean Fitzpatrick in his Kensington hotel, a taped conversation between Markgraaff and one of his provincial players, Andre Bester, was broadcast for the first time in South Africa. The recording had been made secretly by Bester the previous October, a few weeks before Markgraaff led Gary Teichmann, James Small and the rest of the Springbok squad on their Argentinian and European tour. The SABC played a snatch of Markgraaff's words on national television.

'It's the kaffirs, man,' he said in Afrikaans. 'It's the fucking NSC [National Sports Council], it's the fucking kaffirs!'

Threatened by Markgraaff's lawyers, the SABC had described the speaker as 'a top South African rugby official'. But the tape had also been made available to the country's national newspapers. Markgraaff's voice was clearly identifiable. The following morning, *The Star* newspaper moved a step closer to nailing him in Johannesburg. 'Markgraaff in Firing Line over Racial Slur Tape' ran the big black headline on the front page. The opening sentence confirmed both the paper's distinct rugby slant and its remaining note of legal caution.

'Andre Markgraaff could be axed as Springbok coach amid allegations last night that he is the official who allegedly made taped racist remarks,' the reporters suggested in a tone as damning as the lawyers would then allow. Markgraaff and Sarfu (the South African Rugby Football Union) tried desperately to find some space in which to retreat. They would have found an old *laager* in 1979 but, in 1997, they had little hope.

Markgraaff flapped around mournfully. 'This is a very sensitive matter,' he blustered, 'and I must listen to the tape before commenting on it – but I defy anyone to call me a racist. I am considered a liberal in my community.'

It made one shudder to think what the rest of white Kimberley was like when, a few hours later, Markgraaff called a press conference in his hometown. He spoke huskily through the tears. 'I'm not making any excuses,' he protested, 'but I was very emotional at the time. I apologise to the black people of this country and to the whites for causing them embarrassment. I've acted in a spirit of reconciliation and I hope you will forgive me. This is not easy for me, and I herewith tender my resignation as coach of the Springbok rugby team.'

South African rugby, once more, was in turmoil – and not just because of its return to the stained language of apartheid. The tape had been given first to Brian van Rooyen, a coloured accountant and rugby administrator. Van Rooyen had been a vice-president of Transvaal Rugby until he challenged Louis Luyt for the presidency of the union in October 1996. Apart from dominating the game in the Transvaal, Luyt was also president of Sarfu and the country's delegate on the International Rugby Board. Luyt had appointed his son-in-law, Rian Oberholzer, as Sarfu's chief executive and his son, Louis Jnr., as manager of Ellis Park. He had no difficulty in outvoting van Rooyen – especially after Luyt had insisted that the selection procedure should be conducted as a show of hands. Like Don King, his closest equivalent when it came to using intimidation and manipulation to entrench his sporting power, Luyt would never step back gracefully. King Louis would have to be hacked down instead.

Brian van Rooyen decided that he should have first swing of the axe. During his years with the Transvaal Union, and in the typical fashion of the dedicated accountant, van Rooyen had gathered together reams of financial statements. He had all the information, he said, to bring Luyt and Sarfu to their knees. He was not bluffing. Four days before that definitive blackening of Markgraaff's name, on 14 February, van Rooyen sent a Valentine Day's greeting to Louis – in the form of an announcement by Steve Tshwete, the South African Minister of Sport, that Sarfu would be subject to a state investigation into their running of rugby. On the basis of van Rooyen's 500-page document, the government's taskforce would probe issues of racism and financial irregularity within Sarfu.

Luyt was indignant. Apart from immediately threatening to sue Tshwete, he declared that Sarfu would not accept the three-man investigation. While they would meet reluctantly with the taskforce member from the Department of Sport, they were not willing to talk to the two representatives from the National Olympic Committee and the National Sport Council – or, as Markgraaff had described them, 'the fucking NSC, the fucking kaffirs!' The rugby war had begun; and a bizarre alliance had been formed against Sarfu, Luyt and Markgraaff.

In the wake of Luyt's sneering response, van Rooyen made public the contents of 'the Markgraaff tape'. He confirmed that the recording had been given to him by Andre Bester, an alleged far-right sympathiser who'd also captained Griqualand West, the province which had elected Markgraaff as its president of rugby. Bester and his brother, Piet, a member of the AWB (the neo-Nazi Afrikaner Resistance Movement), had both failed to convince Markgraaff that he should renew their contracts with Griquas. Filled with resentment, Andre Bester telephoned Markgraaff soon after he had also axed Francois Pienaar from the Springbok squad. In decrying the English media's attacks on him for dropping Pienaar, Bester tricked Markgraaff into his blue tirade against black South Africans.

'The whole fucking Pienaar thing is politics,' Markgraaff fumed to Bester, 'the whole fucking country is behind him – in terms of the press. [The SABC's] *Top Sport* is the media. TV is the government. *Top Sport* is the government. It is a kaffir station . . . it is for the kaffirs . . . it's the government, the whole fucking lot, it's the government. That guy [Pienaar] can be walking on fucking crutches, but they still fucking want him . . . it's the kaffirs, man . . . it's the fucking kaffirs.'

I had met Francois Pienaar three days after Christmas, in Windlesham, in deepest Surrey. Pienaar had been in England a week; and he was about to begin an unexpected new career as a player with the previously unfashionable North London club, Saracens. It had just started to snow then, the first of that winter's heavy fall, and I'd felt for Pienaar and his wife, Nerine. While he said all the right words about his newfound commitment to Saracens and their millionaire owner, Nigel Wray, he admitted that he was still recovering from his fall-out with Markgraaff. The previous year, in 1995, he had been at the pinnacle of international rugby. Everything had since dipped and smudged.

Alison and I spent a couple of hours with the Pienaars that freezing white English morning, while Francois spoke movingly about South African rugby and how Markgraaff had 'soured the sweet taste' of his rainbow team. Pienaar did not want to be left open to accusations 'of bitterness now that I've been dropped'. When I did write about him, we concentrated instead on his enthusiasm for the different challenge of British club rugby and his first game in the black shirt of Saracens – a hard and icy encounter in Bath.

I called him again on the night that Markgraaff resigned. He was typically friendly but, still, I could hear the weariness in his voice. 'It's not been a good day,' he sighed. Apart from Markgraaff's racism and van Rooyen's accusations against Sarfu, a Springbok player, Johann Ackermann, had been named that same afternoon for his illegal use of anabolic steroids. It had not been the best Wednesday afternoon in the turbulent history of Springbok rugby.

While neither of us was surprised to hear of Markgraaff's lapse from liberalism, the ramifications swirled through Pienaar's head. Much of what he and the 1995 team had achieved, in conjunction with Mandela, lay all around him – in tatters.

It was ironic that Andre Bester, of all people, should have exposed Markgraaff. Apart from their links with the AWB, an organisation which threatened to 'drive blacks from the face of the earth', the Bester brothers had apparently alienated even their own white team-mates. The Griqua captain, Kobus van der Merwe, said that whenever the Besters played against teams which included a black player, 'they were openly and embarrassingly racist'. Van der Merwe stressed that, in contrast, Markgraaff had 'never made racist remarks against any other racial group in public'.

I laughed at that 'in public', but Pienaar just sighed again. 'Man, it's terrible. We've gone back to those dark old days . . .'

'In South Africa, the blacks, coloureds and the whites are separate nations – like Scotland, Wales and England. They are different stock, so they won't ever play in

the same side. But, maybe, perhaps like your Lions, one day, we would have such a team, combining the nations. What happens ultimately, that we must leave to the future. Let us see what history will have to say . . .' (Danie Craven, London, February 1968)

History had had its say and, apart from the odd year of promised change, South African rugby was found to be rotten to its very core. Almost thirty years on, old Doctor Danie's invocation of 'Separate Development' in rugby appeared as pertinent as ever. It was with relief that I turned away from those rigid lines of colour and considered his secondary theme of nationalism. I had lived in Britain long enough to agree that Scotland, Wales and England each saw itself as a distinct country. Only the Protestants of Belfast, Ballymena, Portadown and the rest of Northern Ireland appeared especially passionate about the idea of a 'United Kingdom'. The rest of Britain, unless you believed Norman Tebbit and the Young Conservatives, had finally dropped the 'Great' prefix along with the rest of its uncomfortable colonial past.

The almost as embarrassing 'Cool Britannia', which tried to convince us that Oasis were the hippest group in the world and that the Union Jack had a swinging future if it was wrapped ironically around a super-model from Croydon, had already begun to fizzle and fade. It was time, as one of many such songs said, to go back to your roots. Welsh music was suddenly jumping, Scottish writing was still pumping and the Irish continued to do a little bit of everything, much to everyone's delight. It was also fantastic to live in London – every nation in the world seemed to be represented on most trips to the pub or through the Underground and, as always, the majority of English people I knew suggested that, actually, their roots were Welsh, Scottish or, most probably, Irish.

I sometimes wondered if my own Celtic lineage was more pronounced with my four Scottish grandparents and my own parents' decision to go for the unfortunate 'Donald George' name-tag. But I was still awaiting the emergence of the first great stream-of-consciousness novelist from Aberdeen or Glasgow who was also a 'Donald' or even a 'George' – until then, as my friends said, I was sticking to my 'South African thing'.

But I liked the idea that an often nebulous concept of 'Britain' was fed by four such strong and distinct cultures. I knew that whenever emphasis was placed on the 'strong and distinct cultures' of the Zulus, the Cape Coloureds, the Xhosas or the Afrikaners I would act differently. I would moan long and loud about Hendrik Verwoerd and Danie Craven and, finally, churn out slightly fresher platitudes about 'the new South Africa' being 'one country' in pursuit of a 'non-racial society'. But that was one of the consequences of having grown up under apartheid. You ended up searching perpetually for colourless clichés to describe the country of your birth.

In London, it seemed natural and healthy to tap into even *Oom* (Uncle) Danie's 'four countries' riff. In rugby, especially, the idea was fixed in past battle and glory. Whether it was in the east carpark at Twickenham or the headier bar-rooms and pubs of Edinburgh, Cardiff and Dublin, British and Irish rugby thrived on its inherent division. The French might have called it *Le Tournoi* but to the English, the Scots, the Welsh and the Irish it was always the Five Nations.

It was a tournament of tradition and truism. Everyone wanted to beat the English, who were supposed to always bring a huge pack of forwards, a kicking fly-half and an ability to wear down their smaller neighbours so that they could score a few tries late in the second half. The Scots wanted to thump the English most of all, and they would call up the spirit of Culloden to do so, but they were less predictable against the rest. The Welsh would have some flair and passion, or *hwyl*, as rugby fans had learned to say, but they would always hark back, like the rest of us, to JPR, Gareth and the '70s boys in red. The Irish were, inevitably, 'terriers' and 'whirling dervishes' for the first hour and then, in the last twenty minutes, they were usually outgunned by the bigger British and the quicker and more elegant French. I was as guilty as the next guy in the pub when resorting each January to those Five Nation proverbs.

The 1997 version had been a typical example. England beat Scotland, Ireland and Wales – but lost a 20–6 lead against the French at Twickenham when Lamaison, Carbonneau, Califano, Merle, Benazzi and Magne came roaring back to sweep the *Tricolores* to a surprise 23–20 win and the Grand Slam. The other matches were typical of recent Five Nations encounters – some great players, some fine moments, lashings of tension but, otherwise, beyond a lovely game of running and passing between the French and the Welsh in Paris, mostly predictable fare. I still watched every match with gathering interest, however; for, ten weeks later, the Lions were on their way to South Africa for the first time in seventeen years.

In deference to the Irish contingent, the touring party were known simply as the Lions – rather than the British Lions of past generations. But a vague fear remained that the squad would be so swamped by English players that the previous British and Irish tag would be rendered virtually obsolete. The strength of rugby in the four countries was undoubtedly centred in England. A natural over-population of local rugby players, reflecting the crowded streets of any English high street, was supplemented further by a widening stream of imports from the other four nations as well as the southern hemisphere. As a result, the English First Division or, in yet another aping of football, 'The Premiership' as it had since been renamed, had become intensely cosmopolitan.

Saracens, once that sweet and trembling little club in Enfield, exemplified the change with seemingly reckless panache. They had been bought by Nigel Wray who, following the examples of fellow millionaires like John Hall of Newcastle and Chris Wright of Wasps, thought that club rugby had potential as some kind of sporting futures market. There were times when it was tempting to jeer softly in the direction of these money moguls, but the sheer scale of their task made me feel more sympathetic. I was still the sort of sap who tended not to bother opening all those depressing white envelopes containing dully computerised sheets of paper that even Nigel Wray no doubt insisted on calling 'bank statements'. It was true. I would not have been able to bring down either Louis Luyt or Sarfu – because I would never have quite got round to reading or even opening those statements detailing their alleged financial misdemeanours.

With such a deep-seated economic affliction, it was indeed odd that I should be one of the many who wondered just how the hell those financial wizards were going to balance their rugby club books. The sums were basic enough for me to understand. A crumbling old ground in Enfield could hold no more, on an exceptionally good day, than 7,500 paying customers. With the bizarre structure of the English game meaning that there were some months when Saracens would be lucky to host one match in four weeks, the numbers on the credit side of the account were hardly of the booming variety – especially when they averaged under 4,000 a match. While any financial cutie worth the shekels in his offshore bank account knew all the sporting buzz-words of 'merchandising' and 'spin-off', it was safe to claim that the streets of north London were hardly seething with replica Saracens shirts. So where was the money coming from – apart from inconsistent gate receipts and a slice of Sky television money?

Wray and the Saracens management soon became aware of the problem – which probably explained why, on one raw and sodden Sunday in January, I'd had to shell out £36 for two tickets to see Saracens play Wasps in a cup match. I had done my years of hard yakka on the terraces of the Arsenal North Bank in the 1980s and early-'90s and so I liked to think I knew all about spectating hardship. But we had grown soft in the subsequent years. When we were not sniffing out the *goujons* of fish or smoked salmon bagels now on offer at Highbury, Alison and I would sigh blissfully at the quality of the seated view and the pristine shine of the Gunner toilets. And, rather than paying a rugby price of £18 each in 1997, we were only asked to cough up a more reasonable £12 to welcome Arsène Wenger and his illuminating recipes about the correct intake of broccoli and mineral water.

Saracens was a more startling culture shock. Francois Pienaar, used to Ellis Park, was bewildered by the poverty of the dilapidated Enfield ground. '*Ja*,' he agreed politely, 'it is a bit old-fashioned . . .'

It was also hard to see how his paymasters could recoup much from the tiny bars and greasy burger vans which constituted match-day facilities. So, I took out my calculator. 7,500 x £18? Well, I was trying to be generous and so I imagined that we had actually bought a tatty programme, a thin burger and a plastic container of warm lager. I tapped the revised figures into the machine. 7,500 x £24 = £180,000. It wasn't too bad, and it would go some way to paying at least one member of a large squad. Unfortunately for them, Saracens could not charge eighteen quid for more mundane league matches. They also only pulled in 7,500 fans for one other game. If they were playing, say, Bristol or Sale on a wet Tuesday night, they would be lucky to get 3,000 – which was ten times less than Arsenal were guaranteed every home gate.

Yet Saracens' star imports – Pienaar, Michael Lynagh and Phillipe Sella – were all on impressive football-style contracts. They deserved their money, too, for they each occupied an iconic place in world rugby. Pienaar had captained the current World Champions to glory; Lynagh had scored more points than any other player in Test rugby; Sella was the most capped international of all time, beating even Sean Fitzpatrick with his staggering 115 caps for France. More significantly, the South African, the Australian and the Frenchman had proved that they'd come to Enfield to play as hard and as well as they possibly could. They were not there just to pick up a fat cheque at the end of each month; but, still, if I had been Nigel Wray, I would have followed my own financial strategy and put those unopened bank statements to one side. The alternative was for him to pore over the bad news and sink into endless worry about what he had actually been thinking when he decided to move into the 'business' of English rugby.

The benefits on the actual churned-up pitch of Enfield, and on rugby fields across the Premiership, were more heartening. The English game had changed radically since the 1980s. Bath were no longer assured of winning everything. In fact, in 1997, Bath were sinking as deep into mud on the park as shit in the boardroom. In true football fashion, they lost a couple of coaches along the way and many more matches. They ended up gasping in pursuit of a top-four place which would assure them of the European Cup money they needed desperately in the 1997–98 season. Leicester were also less imperious than they had been in recent years. Although Bob Dwyer, as coach, and Joel Stransky at fly-half, World Cup-winners both, guided them to the Cup in a dreary final against Sale, they lost the championship to a resolute Wasps side led by Lawrence Dallaglio.

It had been a tight finish and Wasps only won the title on the final Saturday of the season. My own enthusiasm for the British game had increased markedly. Although I was not about to switch my primary allegiance from either the Super 12 or the Currie Cup, I now went to English club games, watched the highlights of every month's grudge match in Wales, followed the Scottish and Irish results in the small print of the paper and recorded Stuart Barnes and the rest of the admirably professional Sky boys every Thursday and Saturday. It was either a sign of madness, or more positive proof that my passion for the international scope of rugby had begun to burn.

Alongside my enthusiasm for Pienaar, Lynagh, Sella, Stransky, Dwyer, Cabannes, Lacroix, Tuigamala, Lam, Mitchell and the rest of the foreign legion of players and coaches, I had my own list of local favourites – all of whom were contenders for Lions stardom. And, as the selection date neared, it became pleasingly apparent that there was a spread of nationalities amongst my preferred Lions. While England were likely to supply almost half of the thirty-five-man squad, players from each of the three remaining countries had the class to match any of their world rivals.

From Wales, Rob Howley was a little gem of a number 9. With Joost van der Westhuizen and Australia's George Gregan, he had a claim to strike as the world's best scrum-half. In the centre, Scott Gibbs and Allan Bateman offered a red-shirted partnership which combined the lethal with the exquisite. If he was a less exciting stand-off than the mercurial Arwel Thomas, then Neil Jenkins at either fly-half or a more shaky full-back was still the equal of any place-kicker in Test rugby.

If the Irish pack had had the Welsh back line behind them, then they might have been even more motivated. The heart of their green eight had missed the Five Nations. But Keith Wood, an inspirational captain and hooker, had fought his way back from a terrible shoulder injury.

After sixteen months away from the game he had shown, in the last weeks of the English season for Harlequins, that he was destined to be one of the Lions' main men. Jeremy Davidson was an emerging force in the line-out and Eric Miller, on his international début in the Five Nations, looked to have exceptional ability. Both young forwards had also been toughened considerably by a season with, respectively, London Irish and Leicester.

The Scots supplied the speed and power of Alan Tait, the instinctive and often audacious running and jinking of Gregor Townsend, as well as the leadership of Rob Wainwright. But, more significantly, they provided the acumen of Ian McGeechan and the ardour of Jim Telfer. McGeechan, who would coach the Lions for the third successive tour, and Telfer, who'd teach the forwards a thing or two about commitment on the hard fields of South Africa, were the Lions' most crucial selections.

But with Fran Cotton as manager, Martin Johnson as captain, and seventeen of their countrymen alongside them, England ensured that predictions about their dominance of the final squad were accurate. Both Cotton and McGeechan had been members of the Lions team which had so blighted the lives of white South Africans in 1974. They knew how essential it was to take a pack of forwards and a captain whose very presence would spell out to the Springboks that they would not be intimidated. The basis of the scrum, it seemed certain, would be English – with Martin Johnson ready to set a formidable example.

Personally, I was less intrigued by big Martin than I was by Lawrence Dallaglio. But it was impossible to quibble with Johnson's captaincy, for he had the kind of brick-wall stare which many hardcore American boxers would have loved to steal every time they appeared at a weigh-in or listened to a referee's pre-fight instructions. You knew that Johnson, like Scott Gibbs in the back line, would not shrink from the physical challenge of facing Os du Randt and Mark Andrews.

Jeremy Guscott was the most naturally gifted player in the Lions party but, to me, it looked like his head was as big as his talent. The Englishman I followed most closely, instead, was half-Italian. Lawrence Dallaglio had the granite jaw and the rugged mental edge to back up Johnson and Wood in the Lions' most telling forward exchanges. He also had pace and a good pair of hands in the loose – which had meant that, for a while, England had played him out of position as an open-side flanker. Jack Rowell had also made a mistake earlier that year in choosing Phil de Glanville ahead of Dallaglio as England captain. I had little doubt that Dallaglio was the best number 6, and captain, in Britain. But he also had the kind of expansive life outside rugby which revealed his intelligence and complexity. With Keith Wood, Gregor Townsend and Rob Howley, he formed a quartet which encapsulated the Lions' quality and diversity.

They were the kind of players – an Englishman, an Irishman, a Scot and a Welshman – who had the ability to blur my otherwise one-eyed support of those Springbok boys. As the South African rugby public banged the whitewashed drum, already bragging about the certainty of a 3–0 Springbok sweep to compensate for the same embarrassing scoreline in favour of the 1974 Lions, a part of me in London wanted Dallaglio, Wood, Townsend, Howley and the Lions to do better than anyone expected. I was also hoping for a 3–0 South African win but, in terms of a less nationalistic outlook on life, I would have been content for the Lions to remain unbeaten throughout the rest of the tour. Perhaps, finally, I was becoming a little more worldly.

Before the Lions left for South Africa at the end of May, I called James Small. It was cold and wet in Cape Town, he said, but he loved the way the winter rain swept in from the south-west and across the face of Table Mountain. He told me that he was 'starting to settle again' after his sudden move from Durban. But, inevitably, we were pulled back to the rugby.

'This is going to be a huge season for South Africa and, hopefully, for me too,' he said as we switched into interview mode. 'To play against the Lions would be one of the highlights of my career. I'd put it on a par with playing the All Blacks. It's that momentous. The Lions are the northern hemisphere's representative side. Maybe British rugby has fallen behind the southern hemisphere but the Lions are as big a name as they've ever been.'

In the first few months of 1997, Small had shone more during his off-the-field activities. Media coverage of his private life was as exhaustive as ever. He had met his new girlfriend, Christina Storm, during a modelling shoot for *Femina* magazine. They were looking for a 'sexy fashion shoot' with a top model and an 'independent and spunky' rugby player. Small played his role with the usual brand of 'one hundred per cent commitment'.

'We were hoping for some chemistry,' Kundra Bowley, *Femina*'s fashion editor, told the *Sunday Times*, 'but we got combustion.' James Small was, once again, 'The Don Juan of South African Rugby'.

After his success the previous year, Small had not been eligible for the 1997 Super 12. Clearly, he was not a New Zealander. The New Zealand provincial teams supplemented their own squads by using a draft system. John Hart and the All Black selectors helped Auckland and the four other New Zealand Super 12 sides select the best players whose own teams had not qualified. In contrast, and to the detriment of Springbok rugby, the South African provinces remained divided. It meant that internationals like Small, whose new team Western Province had finished outside the top four in the Currie Cup in 1996, were excluded from the southern hemisphere's premier tournament.

Amid much controversy, Small had bought himself out of his lucrative contract with Natal, then the Currie Cup champions, to play for the notably weaker Province. He was tired of small-town Durban life, he said, and in need of a change. He was also keen to play for his mentor, Harry Viljoen, the new Western Province coach.

I wondered if the latest batch of publicity, and his lack of Super 12 rugby, had affected him.

'I just don't read any newspapers,' he laughed. 'As for the rugby, I know there are some disadvantages for me in not playing Super 12 this year. But both my body and mind feel really fresh. This is going to be a long season for us – the Lions, then the Tri-Nations and then another European tour at the end. To start with the Super 12s in March and go right through to December at such an intense level is hard. I'm only looking to peak from the first Test against the Lions in June. That can't harm me in the long run . . .'

In the short-term, as he closed in on the record of Springbok caps, I worried about the selectors.

'Don't, bru!' James joshed. 'The selectors know what to expect from me. I've been around forever and my game is not going to change over-night. Sure, I'm not being exposed to the selectors at the moment, but I've been around and I reckon they know what I'm capable of. We're blooding a new coach again and the Springbok team is going to need as much know-how as they can find. I reckon I've picked up a bit over the years.'

We were both bored with the Andre Markgraaff saga, and Small breathed grimly when he said, 'Shit, we've had five coaches in the past four years. On the tour back in December we'd started to sort things out again. Everybody found their place in the squad. Now with a new coach, Carel du Plessis, who hasn't done much coaching at all, there's a whole new ball game. Players don't like this kind of uncertainty because it kills your confidence. So, right now, it's very unsettled in South African rugby. We've got all this shit off the field and, on it, no one knows what the new coach is thinking or which players he might want to use. We're starting from a clean slate – again!'

The Lions' own slate, meanwhile, was clouded by history. In rugby terms they were shadowed by the imposing legend of 1974. Whether their arduous thirteen-match itinerary was considered in South Africa or Britain and Ireland, they were trailed by allusions to that great team. It felt like their more immediate predecessors had been expunged from the sporting lexicon. Bill Beaumont's 1980 Lions had lost 3–1 to the Springboks but, still, previews of the 1997 tour reached inexorably beyond them and back to Willie John McBride's side.

Political and cultural pressures within the Lions camp had to be addressed. If division remained central to the allure of the Five Nations, McGeechan and Telfer could not allow it to grow inside the Lions. They had to break the national cliques and different styles of play and create a team from the best of four countries. They had five weeks in which to banish those old themes of prejudice and mistrust.

The tour started slowly, with a stuttering 39–11 win over the mediocre Eastern Province and a horrible 18–14 escape in the mud of East London. The South Africans sat back in contemptuous expectation – if the Lions struggled so badly against Border, how would they cope with the Super 12 provinces, let alone the Springboks?

The third match of the tour was in Cape Town, against James Small's new team, Western Province. As we would learn later, the Lions paid significant attention to their first meeting with a Springbok. Andy Keast, the Lions' coaching adviser who had worked extensively with Small in Natal, played tapes of his old pal to the watching British and Irish players. They had all heard of Small; and Keast seemed determined to hammer home his image as a wayward wing.

'You see here,' Keast said during a team meeting filmed on the *Living with Lions* video-diary of the tour, '[Small's] actually waiting and he's trying to pull the inside defenders across.' Keast gestured to the frozen sight of Small on the TV screen. 'When he plays for the Boks, especially early on, and in big games, he does the opposite early. He wants to fly in because he's very . . . [Keast paused] . . . messed-up in the head, basically. And he likes to prove a point.'

Ian McGeechan supported the Keast tack. 'As far as James Small is concerned,' he said, 'he will want to make it "The James Small Show" tomorrow. He'll want to prove to South Africa that he's their best winger. He'll want to run it and get involved and, in that respect, his rugby will be very undisciplined, because he'll be trying to get involved in everything.'

With John Bentley, the rumbustious former rugby league left-wing, Small made most of the headlines following the Lions' surprisingly comprehensive 38–21 victory over Province. Bentley played well and scored a couple of tries – and yet two distinct Small moments underlined the sharpened tension of the tour. In the first, Small smoothly moved up a gear and rounded Bentley with a speed and power which explained why he had played thirty-four more Tests than the Yorkshireman. But on his way back to the halfway line, he ran towards Bentley and, by moving his hand and mouth, spelt out that old English word of 'wanker'. After the match he also claimed that Bentley had gouged his eye in an earlier maul – an accusation which Bentley denied.

Fran Cotton's response, again captured on *Living with Lions*, tried to downgrade the traditional legend of All Black and Springbok supremacy. 'I guess most people have just read this crap in the paper from James Small,' he said. 'I'll tell you now, I've seen it so many times from New Zealand and South Africa – really, what you've succeeded in doing on Saturday is putting the seeds of doubt in and now they're looking for just anything to wind it up.'

Jim Telfer was more concerned by the way in which Garry Pagel and Keith Andrews, the ageing Western Province props, had so buckled their English counterparts, Jason Leonard and Graham Rowntree, that every Lions scrum had squeaked. Bentley and, in particular, Robert Howley and Gregor Townsend at half-back might have caught the eye, but Telfer honed in on the glazed look of his front row.

Before the second midweek game, against the Mpumalanga Pumas, who used to be more prosaically known as South-Eastern Transvaal, Telfer was exacting in his preparation. Tom Smith, Keith Wood and Paul Wallace were forced to scrum down forty-two times in one forty-six-minute block. The endurance test began with Telfer screaming and the hydraulic scrum machine hissing but, by the end, the coach and his apparatus had swapped sounds. Telfer pummelled his Celtic trio so effectively that, when the match finally rolled round, they flattened the hapless Pumas. They provided such a solid platform that Davidson, Back, Wainwright, Bateman and Evans could be as scintillating as they were deadly in a 64–14 cull. Only a career-threatening injury to Doddie

Weir, whose knee was savaged by a kick-happy Marius Bosman, ruined Telfer's improved mood. Weir was out of the tour; but the Lions were just starting to rumble.

The Mpumalanga captain, the previously taciturn Tobie Oosthuizen, admitted, 'We were beaten by a supreme team.' And with the Irish, Scots, Welsh and English all playing a significant role, it looked as if the poor Pumas had also been hammered by a united team.

But against Northern Transvaal, the Lions first Super 12 opponents, the selectors went back to their blueprint. The first six pack numbers were given to Englishmen – Rowntree, Regan, Leonard, Johnson, Shaw and Dallaglio, with Ireland's Eric Miller at open-side and Wales's Scott Quinnell at eighth-man. The opening Test was exactly a fortnight away and it appeared time to bed in the English. But the 'Blue Bulls' of Northern Transvaal plucked a few roses on a beautiful Highveld day when the sky matched the colour of the home side's shirts – if not their hearts. The Lions looked slower and weaker at forward as Northern's pack drove them back with quick and hard hits. If Howley, Townsend and Guscott could outwit the locals with gleaming footwork, they lacked a consistent flow of good ball to dominate the match. And, while he both created and scored tries, Townsend also showed his fallibility when he gifted a try – which turned out to be the difference between the two sides. Northern Transvaal 35, Lions 30.

It looked even worse at half-time on the following Wednesday, when the Gauteng Lions, formerly Transvaal, led their namesakes 9–3. But a fine try by Austin Healey was followed by a seventy-metre wonder from Bentley who wove his way across the lush length of grass. Under the Ellis Park lights, even the old Transvaalers stood up drunkenly to acclaim the tour's most intoxicating try. After that crucial bounce-back – a 20–14 win – Bentley made the headlines and Guscott was voted Man of the Match. More significantly, Smith and Wallace had stood up to the Gauteng pile-drivers in the scrum. Even the strong and technical Argentinian prop Roberto Grau had not been able to budge Wallace. Ever since the late withdrawal of Peter Clohessy, the cheery Wallace had bloomed in tandem with the eerily quiet Smith. Telfer, at last, had the right men for his essential front-row seats.

The Lions cantered through their last two pre-match Tests – a startlingly easy 42–12 romp against Natal who, on Carel du Plessis' instructions, did not select their internationals, and an equally convincing 54–22 dismantling of Nick Mallett's Emerging Springboks. Even the devastating loss of Howley with a dislocated collarbone at

King's Park was shrugged off – as soon as Howley's tears had dried and he'd flown home to Cardiff. The absence of the Welsh captain worried the British press. The Lions management, however, wore a more impassive mask. Matt Dawson, they pointed out, was McGeechan's playmaker, alongside Townsend, at Northampton. They also had their pack in place and, behind them, the snipers and bombers, Guscott and Gibbs, Evans and Tait, were ready to fire. In the last few sun-filled days before the first Test they began to sense that, if they could hold the Springboks for the opening thirty minutes, they might yet cause an upset on a scale even greater than the blitz of '74.

Newlands, Cape Town, Saturday, 21 June 1997
Table Mountain had disappeared the night before, lost at first to a black sky and then to the smoky layers of early-morning mist which seeped in from the sea. As if to deepen the looming drama of the day, storm clouds moved in just before noon. They hung over the mountain and the city below. A persistent and gusting wind dragged the smell of rain and salt across Sea Point and up towards the leafier suburbs, like Newlands, where the Springboks and the Lions had gathered for the coming struggle. Beyond the briny damp, you could feel tension snagging in the Newlands air. The grim afternoon dragged past. Each team seemed to personify an anxious fighter waiting for the bell.

It was a longer Test day than usual. The kick-off had been pushed back to 5.15 p.m. so the match could be seen on M-Net's *Open Time* between five and seven – which meant that even non-subscribers to the cable channel could watch the Test. When they burbled on M-Net about South Africa being lost to the rugby for those two hours, they spoke only of the white country. Rugby was, even after Mandela and Pienaar, and post-Markgraaff, still only a white game, a white metaphor, a white hope. The mass of flag-waving South Africans and singing British and Irish fans were almost exclusively white. Alongside us, on pavements and street corners, coloured children and black men sold our beers and Cokes, our *boerewors* rolls and packets of *biltong*. The doleful face of a coloured boy had been painted in the country's new colours – but it looked less like his own wish than a marketing ploy by his mother to sell a few more fishcakes from the wire grate of her tiny *braai*.

The noise of a 50,000 crowd lifted high above the swirling wind. Like a giant wave, it boomed over the curled lip of the main stand and crashed down again on the pitch below. In the tightly packed stadium, it sounded strangely intimate. I wondered how many of the Lions might be intimidated by the intensity of our emotion. Eight of the Springboks – Joubert, Small, Mulder, van der Westhuizen, du Randt, Andrews, Strydom and Kruger – had won a World Cup final. Their captain, Gary Teichmann, like Henry Honiball, Naka Drotske, Adrian Garvey, Andre Venter and Andre Skinner, had played Super 12 and Tri-Nations matches against the harshest All Blacks and Wallabies. Only Edrich Lubbe, at inside-centre, was still an international novice – with one Test cap, against Tonga.

The Lions' back line had a considerable mix of class and professional know-how, but there was more uncertainty upfront. Only Martin Johnson had been tested at such a ferocious pitch. But he had never played before with Jeremy Davidson, the young Irish lock who had forced his way past England's Simon Shaw. And while Leonard, Regan and Rowntree seemed to have lost their usual Five Nations cohesion, it was still a massive risk to ask Keith Wood to hang his scarred arms on the young shoulders of Smith and Wallace. As well as they'd done against the Pumas of Mpumalanga and the Lions of Gauteng, the weight of the Ox – Os du Randt – and the gravity of Garvey would prove a more demanding burden.

Yet there was a radical positivism in Telfer's decision to go with his stocky Celts. Smith and Wallace were notably shorter than du Randt and Garvey. The Springbok bruisers would have to dig far lower than usual to uproot their opposing front row. The British props were also more mobile than their typical counterparts in the northern hemisphere. The onus was on them to not only match du Randt and Garvey in the scrum but to gallop alongside them in the loose. But at least they would have Woody screeching beside them, as he had done all week while the Lions eight assaulted the scrum machine. Their vehemence was echoed in the Springbok training camp. The only difference between the twin sets of screams and phlegm-mangled roars were the few words each side occasionally used. For the Springboks it was a bilingual concoction of '*Jaaaaaa!*' and 'Yes! Yes! Yes!' while, with Wood and the Lions, the elation of the hit was marked by a counting mantra – 'Let's fuckin' hit these fuckin' cunts . . . one, two . . . fuck it, again, one, two . . . let's fuckin' hit this fucker!'

Wood was one of the most impressive swearers I had ever heard. As he told me later with a shamefaced grin, he hit a dressing-room peak just before the first Test. He was caught on camera as he tinkled seventeen variations on 'fuck' in F major during a plangent twenty-second stretch. Yet Telfer and McGeechan had more than the lash of the Limerick tongue in mind when they settled on four Irish players for their original Test selection. Apart from Wood, Wallace and Davidson, they also chose Miller to partner the English flankers, Dallaglio and Hill, in a bold but skilful back row.

It was one of the most dynamic examples of the Lions' ability to weld together such a disparate group of players – for the idea, pre-tour, that the eventual pack would be half-Irish would have seemed ludicrous. But, even when Miller was forced to drop out on the Thursday with flu, the Lions had managed to utilise their best individuals in an even spread of national talent. With the replacement of Miller by Tim Rodber, the Test side consisted of six players from England and three each from Wales, Scotland and Ireland.

But, for the Lions, four countries meant no anthem. The jersey-clutching Springboks, meanwhile, sang their twin-anthems for South Africa – and, as always at the rugby, a tentative *Nkosi Skelel'i Afrika* melted into the white-hot reverberation of *Die Stem*. But James Small, equalling Frik du Preez's and Jan Ellis's record of Springbok caps, sang each with equal passion, his eyes closed and his fist clamped tightly against his shirt. I remembered Ellis's refusal to captain a multi-racial South African side against the All Blacks in 1976 at that same ground. 'I am a white South African,' Ellis had thundered with the clapped-out logic of apartheid. Twenty-one years later, I hoped he was watching Small – his opposite in every way, except for the fact that they had both run out thirty-eight times in the old green and gold.

As the noise deepened, Colin Hawke from New Zealand lifted his arm. Neil Jenkins took a couple of steps forward and drew back his foot in a jerky arc. The ball climbed and climbed until, with a delighted bellow from the South Africans, it crossed the left touchline.

The Lions had made their first mistake. The front rows turned back to face each other on the halfway line. Fifteen seconds had passed when they locked arms and prepared for the impact. They crouched and bent their backs. Lifting their heads, they stared at each other. Twenty seconds into the game, the hit came. The Lions skidded back almost instantly. Du Randt, Drotske and Garvey quickly tightened the clamp. They squeezed and pushed again and back went the Lions once more – two steps, then three. Joost van der Westhuizen, at the back of his own advancing scrum, had seen enough. He spun the ball out to Honiball whose own kick was as stunning as Jenkins' had been nervous. The ball rolled and rolled, end over end, until it finally found touch a few metres from the try-line.

Newlands resounded as much in homage to the forwards. 'Welcome to the southern hemisphere, boys!' someone cracked behind me as Smith, Wood and Wallace trudged thoughtfully to the line-out. After the shock of the scrum, Wood needed to compose himself and find Johnson with an accurate throw. The ball flew from his arm but Johnson couldn't hold it. The scramble was on, and Wood was in quickly, as if to make amends. The ball went dead. Another South African put-in, deep in Lions territory.

'A pushover!' the same mocking voice broke through the bedlam.

Smith, Wood and Wallace, a small firm in a dark court, awaited judgement. Joost bent down, the ball switching casually from hand to hand, as he looked over his shoulder at Honiball. The packs ground into each other. We held our breath as their necks took the terrible strain. The ball was already at Teichmann's feet. The Boks pushed again at the red wall. But, this time, it held. Teichmann picked up the ball and roared in. He was tackled. Honiball followed him. He was tackled. The pattern was set.

The scrum went down again. Du Randt leaned in hard on Wallace who was packing as low as possible. Wallace pulled the Ox down with him, collapsing the scrum. Penalty to South Africa. Edrich Lubbe stepped forward, carefully wiping his brow and the ball. The sky above him was black and the white ball sailed prettily when he struck it. 3–0 to South Africa, four minutes in.

Davidson rose majestically a minute later to win his first of many line-outs. Dawson passed to Townsend who fed Gibbs on the charge. But Honiball timed a scything knee-high hit to perfection, enhancing his reputation as world rugby's best tackler in a number 10 jersey. Gibbs was up quickly, mindful of his own renown as a tank. His shirt was torn but he looked happy, Scott Gibbs, for that was the kind of rugby he loved. The Lions had started to play; and the Springboks were soon penalised. Jenkins stepped up from full-back and made sure. 3–3, after seven minutes. The series was on.

Fifteen minutes later, Small booted out a penalty close to his right touchline. The Springboks were less than five metres from the red line. Teichmann was looking for a seven-pointer. At the line-out, Drotske aimed for Andrews. The big Springbok caught it cleanly and fed du Randt. Os peeled and drove away as if he were casually tossing an orange skin out of his speeding car. There was no stopping him. He crashed through the barrier. Try to South Africa.

But, between the thirty-third and the thirty-fifth minutes, Jenkins threaded two sweet pearls through the blue-and-white poles. 8–3 to the Springboks had become an 8–9 half-time deficit.

The Lions went further ahead early in the second half. After Gibbs had chopped Snyman down, as if he understood that the Afrikaner's name meant 'Cutman', du Randt came in over the top at the resultant ruck. Bang in front, and forty metres out, Jenkins was never going to miss. But back came the Springboks. Teichmann ran hard, gaining five metres with every tackle he brushed past. He had made fifteen in total when, with a delicate one-handed pass over his shoulder, he found Russell Bennett, on as a substitute for the injured Lubbe. Bennett caught the ball and, within a few strides, he was over. The Springboks were a point ahead, at 13–12. One became four when Honiball kicked an easier penalty than his missed conversion.

Jenkins clawed three back with another penalty. Eight minutes were left and a solitary point still separated the two teams. And then it happened. Honiball, like Joubert, had made more mistakes than he usually did. He kicked out on the full. Wood was ready; as was Davidson, his leaping target. Wood picked up the return pass and put his head down. Dallaglio followed him in. Ground was gained and they still retained the ball at the next scrum. The Lions pack, by then, worked like a vice. Open, shut, hold, squeeze. Dawson waited, looking for an offside decision and another Jenkins penalty. But the Springboks stayed bound. Dawson hesitated a second longer and then he picked up the ball. He began a mazy little run, dragging Kruger and Teichmann with him. As if he were copying the South African captain's earlier moves he lifted his right arm and prepared to pass over his shoulder. Teichmann took the hint and held back, preparing for the interception. He had been sold a dummy instead. Kruger bought it too and, in a flash, Dawson was clear. He looked as if he couldn't believe it – but he kept running, outstripping Joubert, and crossed the green line with a smack of joy on his shocked face. Teichmann's hands were on his hips and his head ducked down just as Dawson's arms pumped the cold Cape Town air. 20–16 to the Lions. Guscott tried to seal victory with a sneaky little drop goal, but the ball drifted past. At the drop-out, the Lions reached for their now obligatory big tackles. One more scrum – to the Lions.

Jason Leonard trundled over to replace the limping Smith. Leonard held Garvey and Dawson set Gibbs loose. He hammered past two men and, via Davidson, fed Rodber who had played magnificently all evening.

Rodber reached Tait with a long floater. There was enough space for the Scot to glide over. His right fist milked the British acclaim.

25–16. It was unbelievable. The Lions had won. The red shirts were dancing and gleaming. It was 1974 all over again. They had found us out. I looked down and saw Gibbs, Townsend, Dawson, Smith, Wood, Davidson and Dallaglio. I had to nod my head in deference. The Lions came from four countries but, on a winter night in Cape Town, they had become one team.

Chapter 4

Hard Hit

The entire front page of Sunday morning's *Rapport*, the most powerful Afrikaans newspaper in South Africa, was shrouded by tragedy. In huge green letters, tinged with gold, the headline captured the anguish of Afrikanerdom: *BOKKE, O BOKKE!*

A full-page colour photograph of Matt Dawson, surrounded by Venter, Strydom and van der Westhuizen, with Tom Smith lying on the ground behind them, was subtitled, in funereal black: 'Hungry Lions Beat Tame Boks in Tough Newlands Test'. The rest of the world and domestic news meant nothing on such a morning. Even the yellow flash in the top corner, alongside the date and the price, carried an all-encompassing threat of rugby overload: 'Everything About the Tough Test Inside'.

The *Sunday Times* editors were as concerned by the catastrophe. Their own lead story was capped by a similarly desolate headline: 'BOKS: WHAT WENT WRONG?' Various reasons for the Springboks' defeat were listed – ranging from complacency and arrogance to selection blunders and provincial rivalries. Each mistake was shadowed by a large black dot.

There were repetitions and variations on such themes in all the country's white-run newspapers. The Springboks' inexperienced coach Carel du Plessis, after only his second Test, was said to be feeling the pressure, while Louis Luyt had stayed away from Newlands because of his enduring unpopularity. We knew what white South Africa thought about the state of Springbok rugby. But there were other voices too, rugby voices raised against issues more bleak than the result of one game.

'I'm just an ordinary guy,' Brian van Rooyen said, 'a normal man with a family, a coloured guy of average means. But I can feel the full weight of white rugby bearing down on me. These guys are furious with me. They're out to hammer me.'

Exactly four months had passed since van Rooyen's allegations against Sarfu had led to a government probe into racism in rugby. The same amount of time had elapsed since Andre Markgraaff's 'Kaffir' tirade had been made public. Fifteen months had also slid by since van Rooyen had first become embroiled in his increasingly bitter struggle with Luyt. It was difficult not to shudder whenever Luyt warned, 'I have one more fight to fight – Brian van Rooyen.' The next murky round looked certain to end painfully for the coloured accountant. At the beginning of July he was due to appear before a Sarfu disciplinary committee.

'One of the charges against me,' he murmured, 'is that I've brought rugby into disrepute by implying that Sarfu are racist. But let's start with the Markgraaff tape. If that's not racism, then what is? Sarfu knew about this tape months before. They deny it, but I've got the evidence to show otherwise. Markgraaff himself admitted that he knew about the tape before they played the first Test against France. He knew, Sarfu knew – but they tried to hide it. They hoped it would just disappear. In the same way, they hope that the government investigation into rugby will disappear. It will not. I promise you – this story still has a long road to travel . . .'

Rian Oberholzer, Sarfu's chief executive, claimed that 'we've proved over the years that we're not a racist organisation'. Van Rooyen remained insistent. 'Racism is alive in South African rugby,' he stressed. 'R7,000,000 [just under a million pounds] was supposedly used to develop black rugby. When I first challenged them in March 1996, I asked two simple questions. "How was this money spent? Where are the benefits?" I'm still waiting for answers. There are none.'

I asked van Rooyen how he had been drawn to rugby.

'It's ironic, really, but I was born in Kimberley, in Markgraaff's home town,' he explained. 'Of course, being coloured, we lived in one of the poorer areas, a slum called Colville. My father was a general labourer, as was my mother. We had little money – and I knew all about apartheid from an early age. We saw rugby as coming directly out of the system. But my father pointed out that there were coloured and black people who also played the game. And so, with his encouragement, I decided to try rugby when I was about fifteen. It was a game I came to love. But, also, I played it because black rugby, SARU (South African Rugby Union) rugby, could be an instrument to help you vent your anger at the system. There were only two disciplines in which you could express these feelings – the Church and black rugby. The rest were banned.'

Even as white kids in the '70s, we knew the difference between the coloured players of the Federation, like Errol Tobias, and the more militant members of SARU.

Van Rooyen agreed. 'Those who affiliated themselves with the whites played for the Federation. We were different. We knew that the problems went deep. It was not enough that someone like Errol Tobias could be picked for the Springboks. The discrimination did not disappear just because they allowed one exceptional coloured man to finally wear a green jersey. There were so many other players who were just thrown away by rugby – as if they were rubbish. The same trouble continues today.'

'How did you feel in 1995,' I asked, 'during the World Cup?'

'Well, I was sceptical. To be honest, I think we, at SARU, sold our souls when we united with the white board to form Sarfu. I was studying in England at the time of the unification talks. I came back on a Sunday and I was told that the final meeting was being held on the Monday – when my name would be put forward for an executive position in the Transvaal. But, as we now know, it wasn't a unification – it was a takeover. We were used so that the Springboks could play Test rugby again. Frankly, Sarfu have been a disaster. They seem interested only in preserving the status quo. I yearn instead for a truly representative team – a team drawn from each and every corner of this country, whatever its colour. I would like to see a team my own sons might dream of playing for . . .'

Sarfu pointed to its 'Development' squads of 'UPA' (Under-Privileged Area) players – 'UPA' being, it seemed, the correct post-apartheid rugby term to use when describing black and coloured players. Sarfu had also tried to introduce a quota system in which each provincial union's 'B' side, or 'President's Team', would have no less than an 8–7 ratio of 'UPA' and white players. The plan had yet to be successfully implemented. Brian van Rooyen was contemptuous of all Sarfu's initiatives.

'I would go as far as saying that the situation today, in 1997, is worse than it was at the start of the 1980s, when apartheid was at its most entrenched. In 1980 Errol Tobias actually played for the Springboks. Where is his successor today? Why should our kids want to play rugby when they see how corrupt and racist it really is? The situation is grave – personally, the way things are going in South African rugby, I think we only have two more years before the game is completely dead in the black community.'

'So what's the solution?'

'The solution is simple,' van Rooyen said with the conviction of the polemicist he had recently become. 'We need to renegotiate the terms and split rugby into two separate camps. This should not be done along racial lines, but in terms of professionalism and amateurism. Let Sarfu continue its money-spinning deals with M-Net and [Rupert] Murdoch. Let them belong to the professional circus of rugby – but let us carry on with the development of the game at the grass-roots.'

I could not agree. As long as all the money pumped into South African rugby by M-Net and Sky was only made available to those on the white peaks of 'professionalism', then black and coloured schoolboys would remain bound to the martyrdom of grass-roots rugby. If the New Zealand Union could use a sizeable chunk of the All Black millions to develop opportunities for the future likes of Lomu and Umaga, it seemed bizarre that South Africa should revert to such antiquated division. The chasm between Sarfu and all those 'lost' players needed to be crossed rather than widened.

I only had to think of the black students I'd once taught in Soweto. Some looked as if they had been born to play rugby. With the intelligence and strength, the pace and skill they had shown as teenagers in 1984, passing a football across the township's dirt streets, they might have hit their very peak on a Saturday night in Cape Town, in 1997, against the Lions. It was pure fantasy, of course, because they had loved football and hated rugby. But some of those boys had grown up to be as big as Johnson and Dallaglio. I knew how much Dallaglio loved football. But, because of his size, he was always going to be a rugby player rather than a footballer. Some of my Soweto stars might have done the same – if they had been given the chance to see that rugby could carve out a different future for them. I wondered what kind of team the Springboks might make one day – if, as in van Rooyen's softer dream, they could draw on players from the whole country.

Meanwhile the British press pack, following the bigger news story of the Lions, grew in number every day. Another slice of Lions history was being carved out of the granite of a hard and absorbing South African series. I was due to rejoin the tour in another few days; but, first, I decided to take a little trip and travel through some of the traditional rugby-playing areas of the Cape. I would drive out to the Boland, a beautiful area of mountains and valleys, of rivers and farms, where the coloured communities loved rugby.

I had arranged to meet Jeffrey Stevens, a twenty-year-old winger from the Western Cape town of Worcester, whom Sarfu were touting as the face of 'new' South African rugby. I would then retrace my steps to the winelands of Paarl and the home of a more famous coloured winger, Chester Williams. From there, I would climb the mountains before dipping down towards Caledon, about an hour and a half from Cape Town, where Errol Tobias still lived. The three of them ran like a coloured chain through Springbok rugby. Stevens represented the apparent brightness of the future, Williams the 'rainbow-hued' present and Tobias the darker past.

As my car left Cape Town I turned on the battered old tape-deck and listened to the words of one of the country's rare black rugby prospects. In Johannesburg the previous week, I had interviewed Macdonald Masina, an articulate and talented twenty-two-year-old from Soweto. But, in a familiar tale, Mac Masina had not even held a rugby ball until he was sixteen.

'Ag,' his voice came nonchalantly through the tiny speakers, 'you know how it was. We thought rugby symbolised apartheid. I was at school in Soweto, playing soccer when this Afrikaans headmaster came along. He said we had to play rugby instead. We were definitely not interested.'

Mac's rasping chuckle sounded even more wiry as the car picked up speed. I turned up the volume. 'But when we heard that trips to Cape Town would be involved,' he said, 'it became more appealing. We were the only rugby-playing school in Soweto so we always had to play against white sides. One of the schools in Johannesburg was St Johns, a pretty posh place out in the Northern Suburbs. They liked my style and so they offered me a scholarship. At first I was very dubious. Why leave my Soweto buddies for some white school? But my dad said it was an opportunity to get a better education as well. And, sure, it's worked out fine for me so far.'

Masina had since played centre for the Gauteng Lions 'B' side, made Sarfu's 'Elite Development Squad' and been chosen for the South African Barbarians sevens side in Paris. 'It's going okay,' his voice echoed, 'but I would like to establish myself in this province and then, one day, it would be great to play for my country.'

Gauteng had yet to field a black player in their provincial side. Masina had much to learn on the rugby field but, even as one of Sarfu's chosen 'Elite', did he still worry about discrimination?

It was suddenly silent in the car. The morning sun shone against a blue mountain, reminding me of the way that, when I spoke to Mac, it had streamed through the window of his small room in Johannesburg.

'Well, the thing is,' he eventually said, 'as a black player you never really know what they think of you. There is racism in rugby. It's just that you can never be certain when it's being used against you . . .'

Even in a place as gorgeous as the purple valley through which my car wound, you could not escape. This country had hurt so many people. Mac Masina, I hoped, might be one of the lucky ones. But I did not think it would be easy for him to change his life through rugby. I had seen him play in a town called Brakpan for the Gauteng Falcons, formerly Eastern Transvaal, against Scotland 'A'. He had done well but, clearly, he was still a long way from being good enough to fulfil his fantasy of becoming the first ever Springbok from Soweto. His struggle to become a better rugby player was essentially a lonely experience. He told me that none of his old friends played the game. While he had met 'many cool white guys' both on his rugby scholarship and during his various representative appearances, it was difficult to move beyond the colour of his skin.

'Some notice you just because of your colour,' he shrugged, 'others dislike you because of it. What can you do?'

As I took the exit for Worcester, I heard myself ask Mac about Jeffrey Stevens. 'Ja,' he said, 'I know Jeffrey. We've played together a few times. He's a very quiet guy. But he's a very cool guy. He's also a very good player. But those guys from the Cape, coloured guys like Jeffrey, they've been playing rugby since they were small boys. Their culture, you know, is different to ours here in Johannesburg. Their language is Afrikaans and, y'know, in South African rugby, that helps.'

Two years younger than Masina, Jeffrey Stevens was further down the track. Although he lacked the bulk and muscle of established Super 12 wings – and was dwarfed by New Zealanders like Lomu and Vidiri – Stevens had a shimmering talent. Sarfu had big plans for him. In 1995 he had been picked for the first South African Schools side to include black players. He had also represented the national Under-19s and played for the Springbok sevens side in Hong Kong early in 1997. Sarfu's slickest PR minds, mindful of their tarnished reputation, pumped out slogans like 'Reach Out Through Rugby' and promos endorsing 'various new development initiatives for the under-privileged'.

Jeffrey Stevens's image was invariably used to colour the Sarfu rhetoric. It was more than opportunism. I had seen footage of the graceful figure Stevens cut as he sliced through an opposing back line. In one move he looked like the Jeremy Guscott of Boland as, gliding past outstretched arms, he aimed for the try-line.

At his home in Worcester, he seemed curiously untouched by the surrounding political machinations. When I asked him how he felt about Sarfu using his face to present a different slant on South African rugby, he looked blank. He had not seen all the press packs Sarfu had dished out to the visiting contingent. I pulled out their latest media guide. He laughed delightedly as he stared at himself on the cover – wearing a Junior Springbok shirt as he sidestepped a rival wing.

'Do you think it looks good?' he asked shyly in English.

'It looks great!'

'There was a time,' Stevens said as he tapped the booklet and switched back into Afrikaans, 'when I never thought I'd wear this shirt. My uncle, Pieter Claassen, was an outstanding centre. He could jink past ten men. He also had great vision. He was like Danie Gerber. He could see a gap before anyone else. He should have been a Springbok. But he was the wrong colour.'

While he was too reserved to say so in public, Stevens opened up at home and reflected on the troubles in South African rugby. 'There are disappointments. The Markgraaff tape is one example. Before South Africa played New Zealand last year, Markgraaff invited me to train with the Springboks for the whole week before the Test. It was great. I was made to feel part of the team. James Small would step aside so that I could take his place in the back line. We would practise moves and the ball was going down from Joost [van der Westhuizen] to Honiball and Mulder and out to me. Whew, it was amazing. Markgraaff treated me well. He was like the rest of the team. He didn't see me as a "coloured", he saw me just as a player. So, this year, when I heard what he said on that tape . . .'

Stevens trailed away, and then looked up at me again. 'Y'know, it reminded me that I supported the All Blacks in 1992 when South Africa came back into world rugby. I couldn't give my heart to the Springboks then. My real hero was John Kirwan, the All Black wing. I wanted New Zealand to win because I was angry about things in this country.

'But things change. Our house was packed for the World Cup final in '95. Fifty people were here, in this room. All coloureds, born into rugby. But me and my dad were the only Springbok supporters. We were supporting James Small against Jonah Lomu! We wanted South Africa to win! Everyone else was cheering the All Blacks – they said the Springboks excluded us. But we had Chester Williams on the left wing. That was something. I was so happy when the Springboks won. It made me want to play for them – one day.'

He was still years away from that day. But Nick Mallett, Stevens's provincial coach at Boland who would, late in 1997, become the new Springbok coach, had already thought of such a day. Jeffrey's eyes glistened in his parents' front room as I read him some of Mallett's words, words which had appeared a few months before in the *Cape Times*: 'Jeffrey Stevens must be nurtured,' Mallett said. 'When he plays for the Springboks, it will be because he is the best in his position. His background, heritage and skin colour will have nothing to do with it. They will pick him because of his brilliance.'

I knew that they had picked Chester Williams for the same reason. After Lomu, Williams had been the most photographed player in world rugby in 1995. Like Lomu, too, Williams had been out of the game for the last year and a half. In 1996 he tore the cruciate ligaments, broke a bone and snapped a cartilage, all in his right knee, during one freakish moment on the field. A year later, almost to the day, in his comeback game for Western Province, the other knee buckled. It was also bad – 'but not so bad,' Chester insisted as he rubbed the injured knee, 'this time it was just the ligaments which were torn.' But he ended up in hospital again with another year of rugby wiped out. 'Maybe this time next year, in 1998,' he said, 'I'll be playing at full tilt again. Until then, it's just a case of waiting . . . and thinking.'

Williams had a long mental battle ahead of him. Beyond the boredom and the pain, he had to deal with doubt. He told me about the nights where, unable to find sleep, looking up at a darkened ceiling, his wife breathing quietly beside him, he wondered if he would ever play rugby again.

'There are bad moments,' he said, 'but ninety per cent of the time, I can put the doubts to one side. Then, like now, I believe that I will wear my Springbok jersey again.'

But, in South Africa, Chester Williams could never be just a rugby player in convalescence. He was a star – but he was also an icon and a symbol and all the rest of those words which he believed belonged 'on computer screens and in newspapers. I want nothing more than to be seen as a rugby player. It's impossible. I'm always the "Coloured Springbok" or the "Black Pearl". It's the same every year. I always wish I could just be another player. I want to go out there and try my best without having all this pressure that I am playing on behalf of every single person in the "New South Africa". But I understand. People want to see coloureds and blacks in the Springbok team. They want to use them to make a statement about the country. But, like every white guy in the side, I'm just an ordinary player who wants to do well for himself and his team and his family and, *ja*, in the end for the country. That's it. It's hard to deal with the other stuff – and it's not going to be any easier for guys like Jeffrey Stevens. I told him this when he came to my house last week. I told him to try and block out everything people are saying. Some say he could become the next coloured Springbok – others say he is far too small to make international rugby. How many other twenty-year-olds have that kind of pressure? But it's always been the way – just think how much harder Errol had it, when he became the first of us ...'

Late that same afternoon, when I reached Caledon, Errol Tobias spoke bitterly at first, but then beautifully. We moved beyond his initial suspicion when he heard about my father and me cheering his Test début in the strangely white shirt of the Springboks against the green of the Irish in 1980. We spoke about the hurt he had endured on the fated 1981 tour to New Zealand, and of his feelings of rejection. He then tore into the way 'the *Broederbond* ruined rugby in this country' and lambasted 'Louis Luyt and his Sarfu cronies for trying to keep apartheid alive in rugby'. He told me, 'I am with Brian van Rooyen. I phoned him and we agreed to work together. He needs the support and I am going to help him. We're going to fight these *Broederbonders* in Sarfu. We're going to drive Louis Luyt out! Because when I look at Luyt or I hear those words, "kaffirs . . . fucking kaffirs!", on the Markgraaff tape, I have to ask – has everything we've been through in this country changed nothing? Has it all been a waste of time?'

But, as the light faded and we turned to his love, to rugby, Errol's face crinkled and softened. The anecdotes rolled from him, as amusing as they were poignant. He remembered how he was part of the first coloured team to beat a white side when the Federation whipped a wailing Northern Free State, or the 'Purple People-Eaters' as they called themselves. He laughed at the way heavily bearded Afrikaans Springboks like Louis Moolman had stared at him 'like policemen' when he first went on an overseas rugby tour – only dropping their baleful glares when he cut through the opposition and set up a try for 'big Louis' under the posts. He spoke about Nelie Smith, his Springbok coach, 'a *Broederbonder* – but a man who so loved rugby. An Afrikaner who gave me a chance in the end.'

He explained what it had meant for him to become a Springbok: 'The night when I came home to this same house, the moment when I pulled on my South African shirt and cap . . . as I stood in the lounge here, before my family, tears in our eyes, waiting for the flash of my wife's camera. That was a moment when I thought, "*Ja*, Errol, all the pain was worth it . . ." '

And then, as darkness closed in, we moved down to the bottom of his small garden, to the room where he kept his six Springbok jerseys, an All Black Maori shirt and all the rugby colours he had received from players around the world. Errol Tobias said then that, despite everything, he had only one regret. 'Man, I wish I could have had a chance to play for South Africa when I was at my best. I got my first Test at thirty. At twenty-four – I'm telling you, Don, I was a different kind of player to the guy you know!'

Errol rolled up his sleeves. Surrounded by his glass-framed shirts, he gave me a scintillating demonstration of his youthful expertise. He picked up an old leather rugby ball and, with a few metres on either side of him, and a few more in front, he skipped and sold me a dummy. I stood like a white statue. He danced around me, showing me his favourite moves, the breath catching at the back of his forty-seven-year-old throat.

'Look, Don,' he said as the movements began, 'this is how I played twenty-three years ago. I loved Phil Bennett, Gareth Edwards, JPR – that kind of classy guy! Before them I was mad about Mike Gibson. I was mad about Cliff Morgan, a great Welsh number 10, a master of the subtle play, a man who taught me one of my favourite moves when I met him in London. He showed me this pretty little number . . . look, watch . . . did you like that? That was only the start of my tricks. I would also stand stock still and then move quick off the mark, take a big sidestep and roll a little grubber into the box . . . like that . . . you see . . . it was great to play that way. It's why I like this Lions fly-half so much, this Scottish boy, this Gregor Townsend. Man, he is schooled in the old-fashioned way! He is a runner! A jinker! A side-stepper! A little marvel! I tell my son – watch this young Lion play! He plays with inspiration! This is the way I always tried to play.'

Durban, Friday, 27 June 1997
At lunchtime, the day before a momentous second Test, I met Gregor Townsend. He was the kind of Lion whom Telfer and McGeechan had always wanted. A talented player who took risks, a player who relied more on instinct than caution. He made mistakes but he was not afraid

to try different ideas. The coaches were emphatic that they needed men, like Townsend, who were fresh and intelligent and open.

Townsend told me about the inspirational quality of Telfer's words as they entered the strange new world of South Africa. Those same words were captured on *Living with Lions*. 'I've coached Lions teams before,' Telfer said, 'and we've complained and carped about this, that and the next thing. And I've likened it to the British and the Irish going abroad on holiday. The first thing they look for is a fucking English pub, the second thing they look for is a pint of Guinness and the third thing they look for is a fish-and-chip shop. They don't take on anything that is good or decent or different abroad. If we do that we're sunk. [So] we don't go back bitching, we don't go back carping, "Oh, we did this at Twickenham or the Arms Park or Murrayfield." No, no, no! Those days are past. What's accepted over there is not accepted over here. From now on, the page is turned. It's a new book, with different attitudes . . .'

Townsend was as happy talking about Iain Banks's novels as Henry Honiball's crash-tackling. He had played in Australia and he longed to play in France – as much for the change in culture as the switch in rugby. He eventually wanted to play in the Super 12s, because he loved the kind of rugby he had seen – but he was also intrigued to know what it would be like to live for a while in New Zealand, South Africa or Australia again. His girlfriend, Claire, was on her way for the last week of the tour. Once the final match had been played, and the rest of the Lions had left, they would stay on in South Africa so that he could see the country in close-up, for himself, as Gregor, rather than as a professional rugby player. They would then move on to Zimbabwe and 'taste another slice of Africa'.

I knew he would understand the touching significance of Tobias's words about him. 'I've always wanted to learn about South Africa from first-hand experience,' he said. 'I studied politics at university and so I guess my feelings about apartheid were always there – but I wanted to see the country with my own eyes. Now that I'm here I've just been struck by the different kinds of people and cultures, the way in which Cape Town is so different to Durban which is the opposite of Johannesburg. I love those contrasts. I'll see much more once the tour's over – but there've been moments which have gone beyond the usual routine. About six of us went to Soweto and then in the Boland we met a whole lot of coloured kids who were just crazy about rugby. I like the skills those little kids have too . . .'

'And when someone like Tobias calls you an "old-fashioned" stand-off, do you take that as a compliment?'

'Yeah, I do. I am a professional and I have to show discipline. Last week, I showed that I can kick when there's a lot of pressure and absolutely no space. But, most of all, I love to run with the ball and look for the break. I love moving the ball out wide. If I didn't enjoy my rugby I'd retire. You've only got about ten years in the game so you have to enjoy it.

'At Newlands last week there was no space. It was the hardest match I've ever played. The South Africans are just so quick and so hard you can hardly draw breath. So we couldn't play the kind of attacking rugby we've done against the provincial sides – but the challenge was tremendous. And, near the end, the emotion was so high, especially when Matt Dawson went over for his try. I can still see us now, jumping up and down – and that's why you play rugby, for those intense pleasures.'

I wandered over to talk to another one of those special Lions, Keith Wood, who had perhaps the most vocal roar on tour. He personified all that was best about the Lions. Wood was outrageously passionate and committed. But he also listened, as well as he talked. And whether the Lions were in Vanderbylpark or in Durban, I had my most stimulating conversations with him. He was as ready to entertain me with stories about rugby fervour in Limerick as he was keen to hear about the wild streets of Johannesburg. He would tell me about some of his witty encounters with South African girls and then teach me a thing or two about the ancient art of falconry. That was Keith Wood, a bald but brilliant twenty-five-year-old – an all-round sort of guy. But, above all else, he was a son of Limerick.

'It's very satisfying,' he admitted in Durban, 'that four Irish lads were picked for last week's pack. But we've also fought hard against that kind of nationalism. This is the Lions. And Jason Leonard defines that spirit. At the start of the tour he was a certainty – but Paul Wallace, who didn't even make the original squad, took his place. Yet Jason has been superb. At every training session he's been brilliantly constructive. There's been huge back-biting on previous Lions tours. The difference this time is that we're all moving together into the professional swing. So it's very strange – I'm leaving the tour with friends from all four countries.'

Rob Wainwright, the Scotland captain, had made a similar point when he said to me, 'We've come from these different countries with our own pre-conceptions. For a lot of Lions, their only previous contact with players from the other three countries has been on the field – where they may play like snarling baboons. I had only met Graham Rowntree, for instance, on the pitch. In the Five Nations, he's an uncompromising and very aggressive prop. And yet I've shared a room with him on this tour and found that he's quiet and kind – he's a really nice chap.'

Woodie was a little earthier than Wainwright, a clipped and well-spoken army doctor: 'Yeah, Rob's right. But, at the same time, I've told these new pals of mine that when we next play against each other, I'm going to kick them in the nuts if I get the chance! I expect them to do the same to me and have a pint with me afterwards.

'But the intensity of this tour has been incredible. I've loved it – the buzz, the huge crowds, these magnificent stadiums. The first Test was awesome. We went through the whole range of emotions. Trepidation and anticipation at the start, desire and anxiety in the middle and sheer exhaustion and elation at the end. When Taitey [Alan Tait] scored the decisive try, I felt such a rush of emotion. I was all over the place at the end of that match. I felt physically, emotionally and psychologically at sea.

'It had been a very hard and physical encounter – especially up front. Y'know, as a hooker you're totally involved for eighty minutes. It's great. But during a Test against South Africa it's very difficult to go from the huge impact at those scrums to throwing the ball in at a line-out. The two disciplines are such opposites. The scrum is so much about aggression whereas the throw at the line-out requires a deft hand. It's an art all on its own – an art which, I have to admit, sometimes goes a little wayward in my hands! But tomorrow, I'll have to perform better than ever – in the scrums, at the line-outs and in the loose. It's going to be a big one.'

'And how do you prepare for such a big match – in the last hour?'

'Sometimes,' he said, 'I put on my Walkman and listen to Leonard Cohen.'

'Wow,' I whistled. 'I bet Fitzy doesn't listen to *Bird on a Wire* when he's changing next to Olo Brown and Craig Dowd.'

'Probably not,' Wood agreed in his soft brogue. 'But I just love Leonard Cohen. His voice, the words. It is melancholic, but I like that.'

'Did you listen to him last week?'

'No, last Saturday, facing the Springboks for the first time, I was in a different mood. I was buzzin', I was bouncin' off the four walls. Then it hit me – pure nervous energy. I was physically sick ten minutes before kick-off.'

'You mean . . .?' I hesitated. The image of Woody opening his mouth to do something apart from crooning *I'm Your Man*, seemed startling.

'Yeah, I was doin' the business all right. Retching, vomiting – the works. And then, bang, we're on the field and I'm runnin' around like a man possessed! Waiting for that first whistle . . .'

'And Neil Jenkins kicks out on the full,' I remembered.

'So he does,' Wood agreed.

'Your first scrum as a Lion, fifteen seconds into the match . . .'

'It was terrible! The hit came so quick. They pushed us back a couple of yards and I thought, "Shit, this is gonna be even harder than we thought!" It was pretty unnerving. But as I ran across to the line-out I analysed it. We hadn't concentrated as hard as them. We hadn't matched their intensity. From then on we did. That's why we won the Test. That's why to win tomorrow, to win the series, we've not only got to do it again – we've got to be even more intense, we've got to be even more fierce because those boys of yours are gonna be on fire . . .'

James Small told me later that it rained again in Cape Town on the afternoon of the second Test. Instead of running out at King's Park for his record-breaking thirty-ninth cap, Small nursed his torn hamstring at his flat in Clifton. He watched the first half of the Test and then he could stand it no longer. He went outside and stood in the rain until it was all over – as if the drizzle could douse the blazing.

There were times in Durban, on the evening of 28 June 1997, when I did not know what to do with my own sense of burning. The atmosphere at King's Park was even more electrifying than it had been at Newlands. It began with two hundred Zulu dancers taking to the field just before five o'clock. I had seen my share of tribal dancing over the years, having had a father who was invited to a compound every other month to watch the ritual. I thought I had grown immune to the steps and the chants – but, perhaps because you don't usually get to see a couple of hundred Zulu warriors toyi-toying in Wimbledon Village on a Saturday evening, I was impressed by the King's Park spectacle. The towering stands swapped their 'Ole, Ole-Ole-Ole!' chants for rhythmic clapping as the dancers lifted their feet in time and stamped down hard on the green turf below.

'It's a little like Rorke's Drift, isn't it?' an old English gent suggested as, from our chairs on the very touchline, we felt the reverberation.

A few minutes earlier, I could have reached out and tapped Gregor

Townsend on the shoulder as he practised his kicking. I could have sung the first few lines of *Tower of Song* to Keith Wood as he honed his throwing arm by aiming for Jeremy Davidson on the near touchline. But I was more anxious that Woodie might end up vomiting over me with his familiar nerves.

He looked okay, though, when the Lions followed the disappearing Zulus and ran onto the field. They had perhaps 10,000 supporters in the ground so their welcome was resounding. However, it was a whisper compared to the bedlam which greeted Gary Teichmann's Springboks. On his home ground, and facing a second consecutive home series loss, Teichmann ran hard. He looked very tall and very determined as he swept past me, his head cocked slightly to the right in concentration.

As much as I liked Townsend, Wood, Dallaglio and the absent Howley, I stood up for Gary. I clapped harder than I had done for years. I am not sure how many more times I must have leapt from my chair that long and sapping night. I did so in despair each time the Springboks missed another easy kick at goal – and they missed every single one that Test, six in all. With their slobbery kicking they kissed away fifteen points in the steamy Durban air. They scored as many through three tries – van der Westhuizen, Montgomery and Joubert – and each time I was up, with an arm above me. After that last try, with twenty minutes to go, it was 15–9 to South Africa.

But I slumped a little every time Didier Mene gave another penalty to the Lions. There was little point even hoping, because we all knew Neil Jenkins would not miss a kick all night. His first three penalties were followed by another and then another. 15–15 with seven minutes left. If Jenkins had kicked for South Africa and Honiball, Joubert and Montgomery for the Lions, the score might have been 30–0 to the Springboks. Their amount of possession suggested as much – but the Lions made thirty or more hard hits in a sustained stretch of heroic defence.

They just kept tackling and tackling and tackling. And, then, with four minutes left, they neared the green line. Davidson won a line-out and Townsend went for the try. He was blocked but the ball trickled back to Dawson. He turned and looked. And he saw Guscott, the bloody Jeremy. Dawson passed. Guscott caught it. He looked up. And then kicked.

18–15 to the Lions and who else but Guscott wheeling away, taking the series with him. I did not jump from my seat. I could move nothing but my head. I was the proverbial nodding dog in the back seat of a crashing car – except for the fact that my head did not move up and down. It moved from left to right, from right to left, saying a grim and silent 'no, no . . .'

Less than an hour later, in the press suite, Guscott did not know whether to beam or smirk. But I could not quite get over the sight of Gary Teichmann walking alone into that heaving room.

'Could I have a Coke, please,' he asked at the counter. The woman behind the bar did not hear him. And there he stood, the captain of a distressed Springbok side, a team which transcended sport in a divided and violent country. I thought of Andre Markgraaff and Errol Tobias and all the men who had worn that same green blazer. Gary Teichmann, I knew, was a better man than most – and he just wanted a drink. His team had lost again and, in a fortnight, they would face the All Blacks. He was tired and thirsty. Yet no one else had heard or seen him. He waited. At last, she saw him.

When he had his drink in hand, he took a quick sip. Then, with a little chew of his lower lip, he walked through the noisy ranks of press and TV men to the table at the front. I felt for him. A hush settled gradually over the hot room. Gary Teichmann sat down. And then he looked up at the hundred-odd faces staring at him. He knew. They were about to ask him again – about the troubles of South African rugby.

Chapter 5
Black and Blue

An ordinary winter week in Johannesburg. A clear blue sky stretched across one dry July day after another. Black workers walking to and from work carried balaclavas rather than umbrellas, fearing the chill rather than any rain. The cold early mornings and the low afternoon sun were the plainest reminders that the season had settled. Even though the Lions had departed, having lost the last Test at Ellis Park, rugby was everywhere. The Currie Cup had resumed with matches from every Friday to Sunday, while newspaper editors dispatched their writers to Kimberley, not in hunt of either Markgraaff or van Rooyen but in pursuit of the country's future black and white stars at the schoolboys' national Craven Week. More importantly, the All Blacks had arrived the Thursday before to prepare for their opening Tri-Nations match, that coming Saturday at Ellis Park.

There was another kind of season in Johannesburg, an endless season where violence was the hardiest perennial. The bloodied loop ran from January to December. By mid-July, I had been back in South Africa for six weeks. The high walls were as familiar as the slanting sunshine, the hum of electronic gates as quiet as the still Highveld days, the glint of a gun as hard and shiny as the dead grass. We spoke about Johannesburg murder in between deciding whether to see *Fargo* again or opt instead for a caffe latte in Rosebank, at Ninos, the hip little joint in which James Small owned shares. While stories of torture drifted from the kitchen radio, we watched slow-motion replays of Josh Kronfeld's two searing tries for New Zealand against Australia the previous Saturday in the Bledisloe Cup.

That week, radio reports from the Truth and Reconciliation Commission into apartheid made for grisly listening. It was not easy to absorb the exultant Kiwi voice of Murray Mexted whooping on television, 'It's Carlos Spencer, with a peach of a reverse pass to Kronfeld . . . and over goes Josh for another blistering try!' The flatter accent of Captain Jeffrey Benzien, a South African security policeman, kept cutting through to explain how he had rarely needed more than thirty minutes to 'break a detainee'.

Benzien had been the most notorious interrogator of anti-apartheid activists in the Western Cape in the 1980s. At the hearing, and as part of the search for both 'truth' and 'reconciliation', Benzien was confronted by some of his past coloured victims – like Ashley Forbes and Peter Jacobs, former ANC guerrillas who were amongst the few who had held on beyond his usual half-hour mark.

'When I was arrested,' Forbes said to Benzien, 'do you remember saying to me that you were able to treat me like an animal or a human being?'

'I concede I may have said it,' Benzien agreed.

The policeman then admitted to Jacobs, 'The normal interview with you was robust and very long. It was obvious you were playing for time. I resorted to using the wet bag on you.'

Benzien was renowned for his use of the technique. He forced a wet bag over a victim's head and pulled it tight until suffocation neared.

'How did we react physically to your torture?' another of Benzien's detainees asked.

'There would be movement, distress,' Benzien recalled. 'All the time there would be questions being asked. Do you want to speak? As soon as an indication was given that the person wanted to speak, the air would be allowed back.'

But Peter Jacobs would not give in to the bag. Benzien had had to shock him instead.

'You'd undress me,' Jacobs reminded him, 'tie my blue belt around my feet, put on handcuffs with cloth over my arms to prevent marks. You used it [electric shocks] on me quite a few times. When I thought I was dying, you said, "Peter, I can take you to the verge of death many times, but you will talk."'

'I concede,' Benzien said, 'that might be so . . .'

When Jacobs asked why he had not made such an admission in his application for amnesty from his past crimes, Benzien said, 'I could not bring myself to put it on paper..'

I had strewn papers all over the floor of my parents' lounge. It was like being fifteen again, making a mess at home – except that there were metal grilles across every window and an armed security patrol on the street corner outside. The newspaper reports, also, did not make for teenage reading. Apart from printing old tales of torture from that week's TRC, *The Star* and *The Weekly Mail* covered stories of violence from present-day Johannesburg. Rob Kaplan was a wealthy thirty-six-year-old businessman who lived in the Northern Suburbs. He had made most of his money from owning three IBM computer-training schools. But, as *The Weekly Mail* stressed, 'Rob Kaplan should be dead.'

While his two-year-old son slept in an adjoining room, Kaplan had been attacked by a group of men who had broken into his home. In the end, Kaplan somehow survived 'five gunshot wounds, sixteen stab wounds, torture with a hot electric iron and a vicious pistol-whipping to the head'. The worst moments came when Kaplan could not find the key to his safe.

'You don't give us the key, we're going to give you the special treatment,' one black robber threatened. They reached for the iron.

'The most remarkable thing happened after the first burn to my arm,' Kaplan explained. 'My body switched off. It was a miracle. I felt no pain, yet I could smell my flesh burning and I saw the smoke . . .'

The Star's front page featured a lighter tale of survival. A large colour photograph of Tony Liversage, South Africa's cruiserweight champion in 1950, was accompanied by a 'Muggers' Target (70) Routs All Five of Them' headline. A beaming Liversage stood in a classic boxing pose while, below, he explained how he had beaten up the gang in Rissik Street.

'I had been told it [downtown Johannesburg] was dangerous,' the septuagenarian bruiser was quoted, 'but I wasn't expecting trouble. It was shocking the way they coolly strolled over, one grabbing hold of my arm and another my other arm. I let one have it with my knee as he was frisking me for cash. Another then drew a knife and said: "Now we're going to kill you." But I'm still quite fit and so I managed to immobilise them.'

Liversage's effective form of immobilisation entailed plunging his fingers into one of his attacker's eyes, punching another in the mouth and elbowing a third in the face. 'I guess my reflexes haven't changed all that much since the old days, although I wouldn't advise anyone else to try it,' he remarked as he showed the reporter the toothmarks gouged into his fist.

Life in Johannesburg was a scream. The All Blacks preferred a quieter and safer life. They knew Johannesburg – so they'd set up camp in the smaller Afrikaans city of Pretoria, an hour away from the worst trouble.

Pretoria, Tuesday, 15 July 1997
A new scrum-machine glistened in the sunlight. The huge contraption, so silently monstrous only thirty minutes earlier, had been reduced to a

quivering chorus of squeaks and hisses. It had been subjected to a terrible grinding. Feathery slivers of foam floated above it, separated from their casing by the battering. You could not miss the deep and wide indentations the three-headed front row had formed in the sighing leather cushions.

At almost noon, four days before the All Blacks faced the Springboks, Sean Fitzpatrick and John Hart called for yet more bodies. Twenty beefy Afrikaans teenagers were already peering uncertainly from the top tiers of the wheezing apparatus. Another ten boys clambered on, leaving space for two eighteen-stone front-row forwards from the once notorious Pretoria police to squeeze their way onto the wooden support beams at the back. The machine creaked sadly.

A few feet away, their tops ringed with dark circles of sweat, seven forwards waited for their captain to return. Fitzpatrick walked back slowly, seemingly lost in a reverie of fatigue. Hart waved to Justin Marshall, who had left his yelping backs at the opposite end of the field. As the ball spun down the line in the shimmering distance, moving from Spencer to Ieremia to Bunce to Wilson to Cullen speeding on the outside, the backs sounded even younger than the boys piled on the machine. Kiwi voices rang out breezily in the sapping heat – 'Go, Goldie, go!' to Wilson as he showed another electric turn of pace, and 'Yesssss! It's Cullie, Cullie, Cullie!' whenever Cullen sliced through four or five tackles. They were having fun.

It was different amongst the forwards. Relief only rose from the copious spitting of phlegm from the back of their dry throats, or in the occasional bellowing burp as yet more water was taken on board. The pack made its corner sound like an abattoir rather than a playground. Zinzan Brooke, who had welcomed me with his brilliant grin and a 'Good ta see ya, mate!' catchphrase, took charge of the slaughter. Although they had been bending metal for twenty minutes, Brooke was not yet happy. His language turned the thin Highveld air a shade of butcher blue.

'Saturday,' he snarled, 'we fuck them from the first scrum. But we've gotta go lower. We can drop down a few more inches. In lower, in harder! Let's fucking work!'

Fitzpatrick, hanging loosely on his props, Olo Brown and Craig Dowd, finally tightened his grip. They had linked arms in more than thirty-five Tests – and a hundred-odd games for Auckland. Their ritual was unchanging. They eyeballed the metal monster calmly before digging in their heels, preparing for the strain. The heads of two locks sprouted suddenly between the trio's trunk-like legs. Ian Jones and Robin Brooke had already broken the world record of Tests together as a partnership. By the end of 1997 they would have locked the New Zealand scrum for the fortieth time. The loose-forwards – Josh Kronfeld, Taine Randell and Zinzan – settled down on the sides and at the back.

At Marshall's feint with the ball the eight men smashed into the machine. From his crouch, Hart could see that the sweat on each nose only needed to fall a few inches before hitting the dirt. But Zinzan barked, 'Lower! Lower!' The black octopus flattened and squeezed itself into a gravity-defying horizontal plane. The machine skidded backwards, helpless against such a well-oiled concertina of pressure. Their black boots marched in time to Zinny's 'Little feet, little feet!' yodel. They howled in unison, a sound wild enough to lift the hair on even the most cropped Afrikaans head.

Marshall allowed respite after thirty seconds. There was an almost hysterical laugh from one of the big Pretoria props when he craned his head round and saw how far they had been shoved. 'Good scrum!' Hart shouted. 'Twenty-nine to go!' And back and forth they pushed, this way and that, bulldozing the machine from one wing to the other.

The dark rumble was broken only by Hart's words of praise and Marshall's urgent plea to 'Keep it on, keep it on, keep it on!' He extended the moment further and further. The screams sounded unbearable. Something, it seemed, would have to snap. Eventually, Marshall called 'Break!' The rest of us winced in sympathy. One day, these men's bodies will remind them of such mornings. Fitzpatrick and his exhausted pack slipped to the ground.

Hart was delighted but, when I walked over to him, he told me that the hard yellow grass was too dry, making it easier than usual to propel a machine pinned down by thirty-two bodies. 'The Springboks will be a bigger ask in the scrum,' he grinned cheerfully. I nodded politely but the massive policeman shook his head. 'No way,' he said gravely.

Hart, however, was insistent: 'This is the biggest challenge the All Blacks have ever faced. I don't think any side has ever been asked to overcome the odds we now face. On Saturday we play the Springboks at Ellis Park. The pressure will be tremendous. And then, just seven days later, we fly to Melbourne and face Australia before rugby's first-ever 100,000 crowd. We're playing our two arch-rivals on successive Saturdays. And yet we've got to fly across God knows how many time zones and thousands of miles! It's ridiculous! It's too much to ask . . .'

He paused, stroking his chin, before adding the inevitable All Black rider – 'But, with this team, you never know. We're trying for the impossible . . .'

The extent of Hart's grip on New Zealand rugby made it strange to remember that it once seemed as if he would never coach the national team. He was derided as being 'too clever for his own good' and 'a jumped-up publicity merchant' by a large section of the country. Some of that derision stemmed from the natural divide existing between Auckland and the rest of New Zealand. Hart had helped create Auckland's long-standing domination of the NPC and the city, already moving towards its current provision of a third of the national population, was not shy in proclaiming the power and sophistication of its rugby team. Wellington, Canterbury and Otago were less impressed by the 'Auckland mafia'.

Hart's business background also evoked suspicion. In the more down-to-earth sectors of New Zealand, motivational and marketing skills were considered less important than plain honesty. Hart would manipulate people and situations for the benefit of either himself or his teams. He was also happiest when he was in complete control. He had not worked well as an assistant coach to Alex Wylie in 1991.

Hart, like Auckland, could never be just another hound in the pack. It was top dog status, or the kennel. But when Wylie departed, the New Zealand Board turned to Laurie Mains – who also did not get on with Hart. Out in New Zealand rugby's cold backyard in 1993, Hart barked that he was on the verge of abandoning coaching.

Wayne Shelford, the great 'Buck' of the 1980s, was scathing in his criticism. 'The overriding thing [about] John Hart is his ego,' he said. 'He wants to be number one, to put his successes on his CV. It's his corporate culture mentality – the survival of the fittest. It's why he says one thing to one, a different thing to another. He does it to keep producing the best. But it's his ego too. He always wanted to promote "his" guys.'

Even those who had benefited from Hart's tenure were not always complementary. In his autobiography, written after Mains had beaten Hart to the All Blacks, Fitzpatrick voiced his own reservations. While he had only played thirteen games during the last season and a half of Hart's Auckland rule, Fitzpatrick showed a striking insight into the man behind the coach.

'I think Harty's a great motivator and a great coach,' Fitzpatrick wrote, 'but his weakness is that he plays too many people off against each other. Through sheer strength of personality he manipulates players. At times this approach creates insecurity and disharmony among the team. No doubt Hart rationalises his methods by saying that the end justifies the means, but they certainly create friction. Having said that, he probably brings out the best in most players and certainly achieves results.

'Harty is political. He manipulates people very cleverly. He'll admit this – it's his way of ensuring no one gets complacent. It's effective, but not a comfortable experience. When I was playing for Auckland I know Abo felt the same way. Harty would say something to Abo and then he'd say something else to me. We'd find out that there were different versions by comparing stories. But he was the best Auckland coach I've known. He knew how to get the most out of each player, what to say and what not to. He is a complex man – there isn't just one John Hart – but for me, like most of the team, Harty seemed to press the right buttons.'

After the '95 World Cup loss, Hart took over that December, with the promise that he could do things his way – as long as the team kept winning. Even though he inherited a great side, Hart soon established himself as an international coach. If, off the field, he paid copious attention to image, on the rugby pitch he stressed that simplicity was a strength rather than a limitation. His teams concentrated on the rudiments of rugby, both in training and during matches.

Hart warned his players repeatedly not to 'get bogged down with technicalities'. In his 1993 book, *Straight from the Hart*, he wrote that, for example, 'I don't believe in power scrummaging for the sake of it; I believe in the forwards delivering good ball to the backs. The only way backs can operate effectively in the modern game is to receive the ball on the front foot with the opposition backs retreating. You don't have to drive the other pack back yards at a scrum: if the ball is delivered quickly, a nudge forward of a foot will achieve the objective of preventing their backs from coming up flat and pressurising your back line. The nudge backwards also restrains the opposition loose-forwards since, if they detach, their scrum is in danger of being shunted back yards. The reverse applies on the opposition put-in: I wanted their scrum put under pressure so their backs were on the back foot and our loosies were coming off an advancing scrum to nullify their attack.'

Hart's strength was his clarity. He did have neat corporate sayings, but they were shaped by logic rather than blather. His code at Auckland had been 'SAPS' which translated as support, accuracy, pressure and simplicity. 'Some teams are awfully complicated in their back play – instead of focusing on doing the simple things to create space on the outside or support up the middle. If you are manipulating the opposition one on one and have your lines of attack right, you can open up the best defence . . . accuracy encompasses everything a team does, from kicking to touch to delivering the ball from a scum. Every lapse in accuracy, every unforced error, has a repercussion . . . pressure means taking it to the opposition when you have the ball and depriving them of time and space when they have it through aggressive defence . . . I wanted my players to be offensive tacklers who smashed ball-carriers backwards, halting the momentum of the attack and causing them to spill possession . . . Auckland took support play to a new level but the word has a wider meaning: the test of a good team is how it responds when an individual is under pressure or the team is struggling in a particular phase of play.'

He surprised some by asking Fitzpatrick to stay on – but Hart was too astute to discard a player of such magnitude just because he had been at the centre of the last régime. He needed Fitzpatrick's adroit toughness to weld the core of the Mains team to his own style of management. Fitzpatrick gave Hart the bridge he needed to lead his modernised version of the All Blacks into a different stratosphere. But Hart also appeared able to select the right new player at just the right time.

A month before, in June, Hart picked the twenty-two-year-old Taine Randell to replace the seemingly irreplaceable Michael Jones. After only a couple of Tests, Randell had proved himself an exceptional addition to the back row. He was already assured of his role as Fitzpatrick's successor.

While the South African, Australian, British and Irish administrations tore themselves apart in the rush to dump their next coach or latest batch of players, the All Blacks offered a model of decisive planning. After victory, continuity was their favourite word. Apart from Randell, Hart had introduced a stunning array of talent – Cullen, Umaga, Spencer – without skipping even a momentary beat.

As they began their last hour of toil for the day, Hart mixed the most grizzled All Blacks with the greenest members of the squad, dividing them into small groups which blurred the differences between age and experience. In the hot Pretoria sun, he gave the ball to different trios of players who had to try and pass a defending duo carrying their padded tackling gear with mean intent. So Brown, Spencer and Ieremia would run at Fitzpatrick and Kronfeld and, once that move was over, be followed in by Allen, Bunce and Cullen as contrasting positions and styles dissolved into one whooping Black band. As Fitzpatrick tried to chase down Spencer and then Cullen, with laughter following his initial seriousness, it was odd to remember his own stories of humiliation at training sessions with Auckland in the mid-'80s. Andy Haden and the grim-faced Blacks of the past might have disapproved of such equitable frivolity – but Hart's words, as he clapped his hands, were resounding: 'Good work! Good work! Good work!'

An hour after training, looking as fresh as if they'd just woken from an indulgently long lie-in, two of the new brigade drifted over for another 'bit of a yarn'. For Josh Kronfeld, as sharp as Christian Cullen was affable, the old days were hard to believe. 'It's very different being an All Black today,' Kronfeld said after he and Cullen had stretched out in the hotel garden. 'It helps the younger guys when they see legends like Zinny and Fitzy walking alongside them, encouraging them, thinking about the game constantly. They're there to help us, rather than to trip us up. They're incredibly supportive – but they won't let us get complacent. You saw how competitive we were this morning. It was ferocious stuff.'

'With Zinny shouting most of the time!' Cullen recalled cheerfully.

'Yeah,' Kronfeld nodded, 'but a guy like Zinny is also pretty thoughtful, he doesn't ever stop analysing the game.'

Kronfeld nodded at Cullen. 'Y'know, Cullie looks laid-back but if he ever gets round to having a bad game, he'll be the first one to say it. And out on the training pitch he knows I'm going to nail him every chance I get, just to prove it's possible to stop him. Another reason we're getting a lot of praise is that the network of New Zealand rugby has been beautifully set up. It's easy for us to perform because everything is taken care of for us. Not too many teams have our structure and unity.'

'Yeah,' Cullen murmured lazily, 'all we've got to worry about is going out there, training and then playing. It's great. Sure, there's a little bit of pressure when you pull on the black jersey because everybody expects you to win. But we're not going to mess up if we can help it.'

The astonishing way in which Cullen stepped through an opposing team was as far from 'messing up' as rugby could get. 'If you start with Christian at full-back,' Kronfeld agreed, 'you're starting with a rare talent. Jeez, I don't think even he knows what's he's going to do half the time! He sees things the rest of us never see. He takes gaps that hardly exist. I just wish he'd pass the ball to me a bit more . . .'

'Hey,' Cullen exclaimed on cue, 'you take a guy like Josh, a loosie, and whenever I look over my shoulder he's the first one I always see! When you get tackled he's the first to win the ball back. He's a bit of a leech, really.'

Kronfeld grinned. 'Maybe the backs take it for granted that our pack is going to be moving forward all the time. But, being a little closer to the action, I marvel at our tight five. At the sharp end, our front row, those tough old Auckland boys, are just not going to take a step back for anyone. They make everything easier for the rest of us. If you look at the locks too, individually they have wonderful skills. Robin Brooke has the ability to snaffle line-out ball at crucial times. Ian Jones is amazingly consistent – he can win you ball all day. And they're both liable to pop up alongside you in the loose.'

'Jesus!' the appropriately named Christian interrupted. 'Josh! Are you going to go through the whole team, one by one!'

'I easily could – we've got players I could talk about all day . . .'

'Did you both want to be All Blacks more than anything?' I asked.

'No, not really,' the unconventional Kronfeld said. 'I didn't follow rugby a whole lot until Michael Jones came onto the scene. I never really thought about being an All Black. I just wanted to be like Michael Jones. Yeah, I wanted to be like Mike! He just played with such imagination. He brought new qualities to the game. At that time they were getting really hung up on having huge loose-forwards in New Zealand and Michael just blew them away. He played with such daring, such subtlety. So my dream was a Michael Jones dream, rather than an All Black one.'

'Whereas for me,' Cullen countered, 'it was just such a massive thing to become an All Black!'

'Perhaps it was something I never thought I would attain,' Kronfeld said. 'You know the All Blacks are so awesome that it seems a long way away when you're young. But when you lock into an individual like Michael Jones, who is an All Black, then you start to put the two strands together. So when I was eighteen or nineteen I'd caught onto the Black fantasy . . .'

'And now that it's a reality?'

'It's great,' he murmured.

'And the downside?' I asked.

'Well,' Kronfeld said, 'the only downside I can think of is when you can't go to the pub with a mate to have a beer and a yarn.'

'Yeah, I miss that, too,' Cullen agreed.

'We know it's part of the job,' Kronfeld said, 'and we don't get pissed off but, yeah, sometimes, it's difficult if you've got some guy who just won't leave you alone. You know, you're happy to smile and shake his hand but, eventually, you're with someone else too. But in a place like Dunedin, where I live, it's cool. Dunedin's not really big and so all the locals have access to the All Blacks. They see me driving around every day so it becomes old hat. I can come and go as I please.'

'Yeah,' Cullen agreed, 'they're pretty used to me in Palmerston North, too. People just wave or say hi to you there.'

'But for the Auckland guys,' Josh suggested, 'it's more difficult. Especially the likes of Fitzy and Zinny and Michael and a superstar like Jonah Lomu. They walk around Auckland and people who've never seen them before start hassling them because they're really excited to see them in the flesh.'

Although they were very different from each other – with Kronfeld as layered as Cullen was uncomplicated – there was an instinctive affinity between them.

'We both wear the black shirt, I guess,' Cullen said in his quiet drawl. 'We might come from different parts of New Zealand and we might do different things both on and off the park, but we're All Blacks.'

It was a definition as simple as one of John Hart's direct coaching drills – and no less effective for its straightforward tone. I liked the way they had both cast aside their professional rugby personas, their big Black cloaks if you like, and had sat together with me, to talk rather than just be interviewed.

Kronfeld, like Small, was not just one of the boys in a rugby team. While Hart praised 'imaginative thinkers', I suspected he would be more content with the corporate team-ethic Fitzpatrick had picked up at Coke. I knew more clearly that the questions I wanted to ask the two All Blacks were not the same. For Christian, it was better to be lighter and more relaxed. But, for Josh, anything went.

'No worries,' said Christian. 'No dramas,' said Josh, when we decided together that, for the sake of work, I would talk to each of them in turn. In the end, I spoke most of all to Josh.

Josh Kronfeld loved art, surfing and the blues. Unlike previous All Black forwards, he painted and drew, rode the waves and played harmonica in a band. He had been to university and had worked as a teacher. He also wore a distinctive black scrum-cap which, in 1995, he'd covered in white anti-nuclear messages while playing for Otago. The New Zealand

Union's fear of a diplomatic incident in France that year was, luckily for them, averted when Kronfeld was injured.

'I'd thought carefully about what I could do about protesting against nuclear testing,' Josh said. 'I'd figured putting something on my head-gear was one way of doing it. I like to show there's more to rugby players than just playing the game. I'd been told I couldn't have any message on my headgear while I was playing for the All Blacks in France. It's a shame I didn't play because, if I had, I'm sure I would have sneaked on the field once with a message on my headgear.'

I might have been tempted to call him 'The James Small of New Zealand Rugby', if he not been so obviously sure of himself.

'If you begin with my name, I guess,' Josh explained, 'it's obvious that my roots are a little different.'

'Joshua Kronfeld' I agreed, 'does not sound quite the same as Colin Meads or Tiny White . . .'

'Yeah, I'm German-Samoan.'

'It's quite a mix . . .'

'I suppose it's been mostly a European kind of life in New Zealand. But when I was younger I didn't think much about my roots. I've since been to Western Samoa and, as time passes, I become more and more interested in the culture. It's part of who I am. I've never been to Germany and I'm not sure if the name still exists over there. All I know is that my great-great-grandfather came to New Zealand. He married into a Samoan family and they had seven sons. One of those was my father's grandfather.'

In the 1930s, Josh's great uncles, Frank and Dave Solomon, were the first players of Samoan descent to play for New Zealand. Frank had also been the last player to play wing-forward in a black shirt. After the 1931 Test against Australia, the position was banned – which ended the old 2–3–2 scrum formation where the wing-forward stood to one side to provide either defensive cover or act as an extra attacker. It was a slot which would have suited Kronfeld perfectly. But I was more interested in his response to South Africa.

'Well, it's an interesting country. We're aware of all the troubles and of the role rugby plays in white South African life. And, sure, I really look forward to the day when the Springboks have a wider range of players to select from. Chester Williams really proved his ability in the World Cup – for us it's a scary thought to think that there're potentially a million more South African rugby players out there. It took a while to happen in New Zealand but now we've got a great mix of guys from all communities. That blend certainly adds to the All Blacks – you know, we've got a strong balance between the North Island and the South Island and we've got the dynamic input of the Polynesian rugby cultures into our game.'

Kronfeld himself came from Hawkes Bay but had ended up as a South Island god to the students, the 'Scarfies', and rugby zealots in Dunedin where he played his heart out for Otago. 'I just love Dunedin,' he confirmed, 'and it's very much my home now. But, yeah, originally I'm a Hastings boy, from Hawkes Bay, on the east coast of Napier Island.'

Hawkes Bay had once been a powerhouse of New Zealand rugby. And while it continued to supply the likes of Kronfeld and Randell to university towns like Dunedin, it no longer maintained a serious presence in senior rugby. 'Years ago,' Kronfeld explained, 'the All Blacks were drawn mainly from the country's farming communities. Most of your great names amongst the old forwards were of farming stock. Even in more recent times, from the '60s to the '80s, from Colin Meads to Richard Loe, the farming boys were very dominant. The townies didn't get much of a look-in against those big strong guys whose work on the farms had given them a lasting strength and fitness. Hawkes Bay was a big farming community and so its links with the All Blacks were vital. But there's less money in farming and so the region holds fewer opportunities for young people. There's a lot of unemployment – and most kids move on out. They go overseas for a while or they go to university – somewhere like Dunedin.'

'Has the loss of that farming base weakened the All Blacks?'

'Not really – perhaps natural fitness has been replaced by the kind of fitness you build up in the gym or in a professional training setting. It's just different – as I guess it must be elsewhere too . . .'

Welsh rugby had lost its mining communities and South Africa, also, relied less on its own farmers from the *platteland*. Kronfeld nodded. 'So each country finds alternatives to their old cultural traditions. But, in New Zealand, a region like Hawkes Bay still has a very high standard of schoolboy rugby. They're still producing players.'

'What were you like as a schoolboy player?'

Kronfeld shook his shaved head. 'You won't believe this,' laughed the man who had been tagged 'Chrome-Head' when he took a razor to his hair just before the '95 World Cup, 'but I had a very different look then. I had really long hair. I would also get it beaded.'

'Which must have gone down a treat in rugby circles!'

'Tell me about it,' Josh sighed wryly. 'Selectors take a look at all that hair and they begin to wonder. I made most of the representative sides – except at national level.'

'Because of the hair?' I wondered.

'The hair didn't help – but I'm not saying that was the reason. I guess unlike some of the rugby guys then, I was my own individual. I didn't have anything to do with rugby – other than the fact that I loved playing it. Now, it's different, with professionalism. You have to be intensely committed. I really love playing for the All Blacks and I like the Super 12 scene but, dare I say it, there are other things I like to do beyond play rugby.'

Josh Kronfeld would always be my favourite All Black. I loved the way he played the game – with a furious and fearless intent, putting his body in places where he knew he'd be trampled and kicked. I also liked the fact that I could talk to him about the blues and boxing, and about the way he felt when a huge breaker curled over him or when he drew one of his 'little pictures'.

We made plans to meet in England and Ireland, in Auckland and his beloved Dunedin. I looked forward to all those illuminating moments when he would explain the yearning both inside and out that black shirt marked with a 7.

'To play open-side,' he said, 'you need to be a bit of a loner. A number 7 is not a back and he is not really a forward. He's lumped together with the forwards – but when the forwards are training and working on their line-outs, he stands at the back looking stupid and perhaps a little lost. As an open-side you don't do much in the pack. You push in the scrum but you have to break away as quickly as possible to make the tackle. You have to tackle both forwards and backs. And you're the guy out front, the man racing ahead, the one who has to turn over the ball for everyone else. You feed the ball back to your forwards. You secure the ball for your backs. You create play for the forwards, you create play for the backs. You pack down with the forwards but you run with the backs. You work for both but you're not really part of either. You have to be a little different.

'If you look at most teams, their open-side will carry his badge of difference. They'll be a little more individual, a little more isolated by their character. It's that difference, that sense of being apart from the others – some might even see it as a slight strangeness – which makes the open-side flanker more unusual than most rugby players. Look at Michael Jones. He was unique. He was a committed Christian. He wouldn't play on Sundays – even if it was a World Cup Final day. That's different. Look at Jean-Pierre Rives, slightly on the margins with that shock of hair, playing beautifully. Now, he's working as a sculptor. I'm not trying to put myself in the class of those guys – but I have some of their spirit. I'm always going to be me. On Saturday I'll be hidden behind my black cap but I'll be looking at those colours in the huge stands and, then, I'll start running . . .'

Ellis Park, Johannesburg, Saturday, 19 July 1997
New Zealand and South Africa had played each other forty-eight times before. Three matches had been drawn. The remainder had been split exactly down the middle. Twenty-two wins for the All Blacks. Twenty-two wins for the Springboks.

In terms of the immediate past, the All Blacks had a clear advantage. While the South Africans had torn themselves apart as they kicked away the series to the Lions, New Zealand had casually destroyed Fiji, Argentina and Australia. But the rugby history of the two countries exerted such a powerful hold over both the green and the black shirts that I had reason to hope that Gary Teichmann's battered boys might match Fitzpatrick's seemingly superior team. There was also the 'Ellis Park hoodoo' – a superstition that both Fitzpatrick and Hart were keen to dispel.

But the fact remained. South Africa almost always beat New Zealand in Johannesburg, in the seething atmosphere of a fanatical stadium. The stands had soared imposingly a fortnight before, overflowing with those colours which Josh Kronfeld always noticed. The Springboks had ripped through the weary Lions. They had also picked a fly-half, Jannie de Beer from the Free State, who could kick his penalties.

Carel du Plessis, the beleaguered South African coach, had also stuck with some of his novice internationals in the absence of more seasoned World Cup stars. Russell Bennett, Percy Montgomery, Pieter Rossouw, Andre Snyman and Krynauw Otto were in. Andre Joubert, Japie Mulder, Hennie le Roux, Joel Stransky and Kobus Wiese were still out in the wilderness – either through injury or, more bluntly, because they did not fit du Plessis's 'new vision' for Springbok rugby. Henry Honiball and James Small clung on – to the bench at least.

John Hart was surprised. 'I don't know what you feel as a South African,' he had said in Pretoria, 'but if I was in charge over here, Honiball would be one of the first names I'd put down. He has such a great physical presence, both in attack and in defence. And you know what I think about James Small. It suits us that he's not playing because I think he brings so much to the Springboks.'

'He should be leading the team out on Saturday,' I moaned, 'on the day he breaks the record for the most Springbok caps.'

'I know,' Hart agreed sympathetically. 'I'm sure they'll bring him on some time during the course of the game but, knowing James, that's not how he'd want to break the record. It's not what he really deserves. He's the kind of player who should get an ovation from the Ellis Park crowd.'

For a long while on that cool and overcast Saturday evening, it looked as if the bench would be their final resting place. The Springboks did not need either Small or Honiball as they slashed at the All Blacks with shocking ferocity. But it was exhilarating, too, as Teichmann inspired them to heights they had not come close to reaching against the Lions.

After a de Beer penalty in the third minute, Teichmann brushed past Zinzan Brooke. The line was shining in front of him. He plunged forward and slipped his characteristic little link ball to Drotske. It was perfect. The green number 2 was over even as Marshall clattered into him. De Beer's success with a difficult conversion from the left touchline was almost as impressive. South Africa 10, New Zealand 0. Six minutes on the clock.

It took another seven before the opening scrum – which I assumed was an omen. The green and black packs had only locked for the first time in the '95 final after eleven minutes. Those were the kind of hopeful scraps I had begun to devour. But they meant less when you were watching the singular brilliance of, in the words of the ecstatic Kiwi journalist sitting next to me, 'Buncey – the oldest bull on the paddock!' The thirty-five-year-old Frank Bunce reached deep inside his black-rimmed box of sorcery to find two spectacular side-steps which seemed to electrocute three shock-haired Springboks. The Lions had complained about the lack of space given to their backs. Bunce seemed able to invent a gap or a hole whenever the dark fancy took him. He cruised in under the red-and-white poles. 10–7.

The All Blacks' scrum began to work its own more brutal magic. Stripped and glossed earlier that week in the Pretoria sunshine, the black wall not only stood firm but began to push back. There was one especially unforgettable moment when, after twenty minutes, we heard Zinzan's bellow from deep within the battle. The locks in front of him responded perfectly and, with Dowd, Fitzpatrick and Brown, they flattened and tightened their shove. The Springboks moved back a precious step.

But de Beer hit a drop-goal from forty metres to extend the lead to 13–7. The Springboks had also managed two more turnovers and, in the loose, the All Blacks were looking increasingly haggard. They were not used to being harried and cornered with such relentless determination. The South Africans kept coming at them until, after twenty-seven minutes, they found themselves a few metres from the black line. They had the put-in.

Van der Westhuizen broke and then fired a flat Johannesburg bullet of a pass. Bennett was only a few metres away when the ball hit him. But he held on and was through. De Beer kicked the tiddler of a conversion and then another penalty. 23–7.

John Hart's basics, his 'SAPS', had been blown apart. New Zealand looked a little smaller, a little more ordinary. The All Blacks were slipping away, into the dark of Doornfontein where, in the streets outside Ellis Park, you could smell the danger and the defeat. They were lost in a wild place.

The night before, at the Johannesburg Zoo, a gorilla called Max had been shot by an intruder. A burglar, fleeing the police, had climbed the wall of the zoo and jumped into poor old Max's enclosure. No one in Johannesburg was safe in their bed. The startled gorilla was gunned down by the gangster who, in turn, was shot by the police.

Like the gun-slinger, Max was in intensive care after he had been rushed to the Milpark Hospital – with that old Jo'burg standby of 'severe gunshot wounds'. We were pulling for him, the whole country, but the All Blacks would have been happier even in that bastion of apartheid, at Loftus Versveld in Pretoria – anywhere but downtown Johannesburg.

But then, as if in homage to Max, they came back from their mugging. They came back, mouths open wide, screaming.

Van der Westhuizen attempted to set up another attack with one of his distinctive chips. But his kick was knocked down by Wilson, by the electric Goldie, who charged after the madly spinning ball. It eventually sat up in pert expectation before bouncing delightedly into his open arms. Wilson gave his try-scoring throttle the merest of turns. Spencer converted. 23–14. The gap still seemed wide.

But, from de Beer's kick-off, Zinzan careered forward, using his hefty shoulder to open another dark-green door. Marshall, Spencer, Stensness, Bunce and Wilson swept through, using the ball to revolve forward. Wilson decided to show van der Westhuizen how to chip a ball. Being Goldie, it bounced again perfectly. Spencer only had to close his hands around the oval shape and dive over. 23–19. In two minutes, without a Springbok hand touching the ball, the lethal Blacks had scored two tries and twelve points.

Small came on for Bennett at the start of the second half, showing scant emotion as he became the most experienced Springbok of all time. He swept down the left touchline as if he might yet make it an even more historic night. But an old warrior pulled him back – Zinzan, in his last Ellis Park Test.

I could not believe it when, after forty-eight minutes, Norm Hewitt took off his jacket. He jiggled his beefy legs and his throwing arm. He did not make a graceful sight – but it was an original image. Fitzpatrick had never previously left an All Black match. He did not look like he was going to break the habit either. On the far touchline, Fitzy aimed for Jones – and hit him. The ball swept down to Marshall and Spencer and on to Bunce. The third of the serious old-timers – a centre older even than Zinzan and Sean – began to move. He picked up speed with a staccato little run. Then, Bunce reached for the stiletto and, with noise all around him, he did the damage, slicing soundlessly down the middle of the Springboks. The gap burst open. He swept through with the insides of the Springbok defence, van Schalkwyk and Montgomery, trailing behind him. Bunce's regal run had begun on the halfway line. His try was as beautiful as it was deadly. With Spencer's conversion from close to the corner of the 22, the scores were level.

However, the impossible had happened. Sean Fitzpatrick limped away towards the bench. He shrugged as he picked up his training top. Hewitt was on; and it looked like he was on for the rest of the match. For 'Stormin' Norm', waiting on the sideline since Old Testament days, it seemed as if rugby miracles could still happen.

26–26 became 29–29 as another de Beer conversion was matched by a Spencer penalty. And then it was 32–32 as the two fly-halves swapped their order of penalties. Spencer again took the lead when he made it 35–32. With three minutes left, the Springboks were close. They scrummed and scrummed but, still, the All Blacks held. But there was one more twist.

Josh Kronfeld, bless him, I said, was caught offside. Penalty to South Africa. De Beer was close to the right touchline, but he had already scored twenty-two points. He needed three more, to maintain that sweet symmetry of twenty-two Test victories each. As de Beer bent down to place the ball I suddenly thought of Naas Botha's kick in New Zealand in 1981. The score, then, had also been 22–22. Botha missed; but

Hewson didn't. 25–22 to New Zealand in 1981. But that had been in the dark days. In 1995, Stransky had turned a 15–15 stalemate into an 18–15 victory with his famous World Cup drop-kick. But that had been in the good days.

After the last six months in South Africa, it felt as if we had slid down towards the bad side again. I feared divine punishment – or the kind of bleak Gauteng karma which had almost done for Max the gorilla.

De Beer kicked. The ball curled in towards the high poles. It shone in the night air and then, in a smudge, it hit the right pole and bounced away. New Zealand 35, South Africa 32. Three points' difference in the end, each point like a lash across the back. A lash for Andre Markgraaff. A lash for Sarfu. A lash for Louis Luyt.

Chapter 6
On the Black Road

Windsor, England, Monday, 3 November 1997
They arrived early that morning, wearing black. Black jackets, black crew-neck tops, black pleated trousers, shiny black shoes, long black suitcases. There were forty of them, moving in a black phalanx of muscles and quiet smiles. They breathed the air of exaggerated politeness which screenwriters have always associated with the most dangerous men. The impact was immediate.

The All Blacks were described as a natty bunch of undertakers, a silent Mafia hit-squad, a menacing Blues Brothers posse and, inevitably, as The Men In Black. John Hart, however, spoke of them in more evocative terms at their opening British press conference.

'We have a vastly experienced side now,' he said, 'but it's not an old side. I look at our pack and, after three days together in an All Black environment, even after a gruelling year, they're like spring lambs again.' Hart grinned wolfishly as our eyes scanned the room. We, feeling sheep-like, were surrounded. The All Blacks lined the walls behind, alongside and in front of us. I saw Josh Kronfeld in the far corner, his chair at the end of a long black row. He caught my eye and, a cool surfer even in Windsor, he gave me a little wave and a grin. I waved back and then stared at Hart's other tasty lambs as he introduced them one by one. Sean Fitzpatrick sat next to him at the main table. But the others were closer to us – Olo Brown, Craig Dowd, Ian Jones, Robin and Zinzan Brooke.

Zinny in Windsor was exactly the same as Zinny in Pretoria. 'Good ta see ya, mate!' he'd said when I first walked into the hotel. I was pleased that he had remembered me. But, a moment later, as the laundry-man walked past, Zinny said the same thing to him: 'Good ta see ya, mate!'

Zinzan's eyes glinted at Hart's allusion. Once, sheep-shearing had meant even more to him than rugby. When Zinny was fourteen he could take the clippers to three hundred sheep a day. 'I think in those days I wanted to be a Golden Shears champion,' he told Bob Howitt in *Rugby Greats*. 'The All Blacks weren't a serious consideration. I loved the oily smell and feel of the wool and the battle with the rams and those cranky ewes.'

Zinny, on his last All Black tour, looked happy in Windsor. Craig Dowd looked bored. Olo Brown resembled a mildly cranky ram rather than Hart's spring lamb. But we took the coach's point. Olo would have preferred to lock his black horns with a scrum machine rather than endure the gaze of the British rugby media. The big boys in black were ready for the last five weeks of a season which had begun ten months earlier.

Olo and Fitzy had begun touring in February when Auckland arrived in England for their Super 12 preparation. And 1997 had been much the same as 1996. Auckland's Super 12 championship had been followed by the All Blacks' Tri-Nations triumph. After their 35–32 comeback at Ellis Park, they destroyed Australia a week later in Melbourne with a magnificent first-half display before easing home 33–18. They did the same trick against the Wallabies in Dunedin and then dished out a record 55–35 thumping of South Africa in Auckland. The Springboks' worst-ever defeat removed Carel du Plessis from his position as coach.

Hart was more impressed by the Johannesburg-Melbourne sequence of Black wins. 'I think those back-to-back victories are the greatest ever achievement in New Zealand rugby,' he said to me later as we sipped our coffees and ate our curling triangles of sandwich. 'But this tour presents a new opportunity. Whatever I said up there earlier, on the podium, I do know that there's physical tiredness and mental frailty after eleven months of ceaseless rugby. I reckon if we come through these next few weeks, we'll be a pretty good side . . .'

We looked round at the boys stretching and yawning, not knowing if the thirty-hour flight or another press conference had been more taxing. Hart told me that there were at least six other young players he had left at home who would 'definitely come into the 1999 World Cup picture'. With Zinzan heading for retirement, Xavier Rush, in particular, was a name for the Black future. But, still, Hart's current party cut a mighty picture. Beyond the forwards, the backs mingled freely in hunt of something more substantial than another cucumber sarnie. Together, they made a peerless collection.

But the pressmen and television cameras had eyes only for one man.

Josh Kronfeld grinned again and nodded at the media scrum. 'Oh boy,' he said, 'you can tell that Jonah's back . . .'

The memory was as vivid as the day had been hazy. On 18 June 1995, on a beautiful winter's afternoon in Cape Town, Jonah Lomu had found world fame as 'a monster of a man'. After Lomu had scored his fourth try to complete New Zealand's World Cup semi-final destruction of England, the South African radio phone-ins had echoed ceaselessly.

'How the hell do you stop Jonah Lomu?'

The most common answer, with a logic which dredged the murderous soul of Johannesburg, was to 'reach for the bazooka'.

I could still hear the scream of the commentators when the green shirts hit him. 'Lomu is down!' I could still feel the little leap we made, spilling beer on the carpet, whenever the words came. 'Lomu is down!' In the end he was just a man. Like the rest of us, Jonah Lomu could be dragged down at any time.

Two and a half years later, in the lush garden of that country hotel near Windsor, as forty-odd British journalists tracked Jonah Lomu relentlessly, I remembered that some things are always the same. Despite everything that had changed, despite every terrible thing that had since happened to him, Jonah Lomu was still a 'freak'. I was no better than the rest and, not wanting to miss one moment of the grotesque press-show, I shoved my way through the breathless ruck. My tiny recorder found its spot beneath the vast shadow of Jonah's head.

'My darkest moment,' Lomu said shyly, 'was when I was eating two chickens a day. I jumped on the scales and saw I was 148 kilos [almost 24 stone]. I thought, "Gee, boy, what's going on here?"'

We chuckled in sympathy as, all the while, we spooled the reel through our heads, imagining surreal pictures of huge Jonah devouring the chickens. His appetite had always been as legendary as his power on the wing. Before he made his All Black début, much was made of the fact that Lomu used to eat fourteen boiled eggs for breakfast while a McDonald's lunch would consist of 'six Big Macs, two hamburgers, a twenty-piece box of chicken nuggets, two large milkshakes and a Coke'. Dinner, a more serious affair, 'would last for hours'. But that was then – and everything a mammoth eighteen-year-old ate turned into hard packs of furrowed brawn.

The clocks in England had just moved back into wintertime. I shivered a little in the Windsor chill. But I also pictured the Lomu photographs I'd since seen. Over the previous eighteen months, rugby's very own 'force of nature' had been stripped of all his bite and might. His increasingly sallow face became bloated and puffy, his suddenly lumbering body slack with lethargy. The barest glance was enough to tell you that he was sick. Chemotherapy burned a hole through his blackened eyes – and yet even then none of us really knew the hollow extent of his illness. It was no longer a case of whether he'd play rugby again. It had become a grim matter of whether a twenty-one-year-old man might ever feel well again.

'I wish I knew half the names of the things they gave me to take,' he sighed as we pressed in closer. 'I don't even know the name of the disease, mate. It starts with, um, something like "g" and ends with something "syndrome".'

Nephrotic Syndrome was a rare disease of the kidneys which consumed all protein before it could be absorbed by the body. 'The side-effects,' Hart explained, 'are horrendous. Jonah's a remarkable man just to be here. When people understand the illness he had and the horrific treatment he received, it's a great testament that he's even up and on the rugby field again. But he's only played a couple of warm-up games after being out for so long. I'm not expecting great things of him on this tour. He's here for the future . . .'

But the press were still locked into the past. I moved away when I heard, for at least the tenth time that morning, the same question from a different voice of questing excitement. 'Jonah, how did you feel after that World Cup game against England?'

I sat on a low wall with Fitzpatrick. 'You forget what poor old Jonah has to go through every time he's with the All Blacks,' he sighed as we watched the media maul roll chaotically on. The reporters and cameramen jostled and tussled for the best position to record Lomu's mildly bewildered words. It was as if they knew that there were only a few minutes left to score their last Lomu quote for the day.

'Well, it must make a nice change for you,' I said to Fitzy, 'not having everyone crowding you instead . . .'

'That's true,' Fitzpatrick laughed. 'Good on ya, Jonah!'

'So how are you?' I asked him, trying not to look down at his injured knee.

'Yeah, I'm good,' Fitzpatrick nodded positively. 'It's not been easy these last few months – but I'm here. It feels good to be back.'

After limping off at Ellis Park, Fitzpatrick had, once more, made a miraculous recovery. He led the All Blacks in Melbourne and, also, in the two remaining Tri-Nations matches in New Zealand. But, since then, he'd gone under the knife. Officially, the cartilage operation had been a success. And yet I had also heard that there was nothing any doctor could do to improve that painful right knee. After so many years of hard rugby, it was just about worn through. Bone ground against bone – with most of the sinews and ligaments in between lost somewhere amid those floating memories of his previous ninety-one Tests. It would be hard to keep the knee intact after the past ravages. Rest could only do so much – for, even after a few months away, his knee would still be old and battered.

'Yeah, it's definitely made me think,' Fitzpatrick said. 'I've realised how fortunate I've been to get through eleven years of international rugby without an injury. I guess it's incredible that this is the first time I've had to really cope with injury. Two or three weeks ago it still wasn't feeling good and I had severe doubts that I'd even make this tour . . . but we've both made it, me and Jonah. He's had to deal with a serious disease – I've just had this old knee of mine turn a wee bit dodgy . . .'

The first match of the tour was five days away. I knew the indestructible Fitzy would make it but, still, I went through the reporting motions.

'Will you play on Saturday?' I asked.

Fitzpatrick smiled broadly. 'I'm available for selection . . .'

'And then, a week later, it's Ireland in Dublin . . .'

'Yeah, that'll be interesting. The Irish boys will give it a rip.'

'Have you ever played against Keith Wood?'

'No, but I know Keith. He's a good guy – and a very competitive hooker. I'm really looking forward to playing against him. But I'd better not get carried away. I've still got to survive those Welsh boys up in Llanelli this Saturday. I hear that they're playing really well . . .'

It seemed inconceivable that there might be any doubt about the line-up of that Saturday's shadow Test team. I knew that all the usual boys would be selected. Fitzy would be back with the Auckland front row, Jones and Brooke would lock the line-out, Zinny would be at the back with Kronfeld and Randell on the flank. With Lomu and Walter Little still easing gently back into the All Black scene, the back line picked itself – except that there were persistent rumours that Christian Cullen was being pushed hard for his place by Todd Miller, a nephew of the famous Going brothers and an almost perfect Cullen clone. Miller, after two years away from rugby while 'attending to Mormon missionary duties', had burst into the full-back reckoning with a series of sensational performances for Waikato in the NPC. He was only twenty-two, a year older than Cullen.

The rumours were probably John Hart's way of giving Cullen a motivational nudge. A couple of days after their arrival in Windsor, the side was announced – and Cullen, like Fitzpatrick, was in. The only surprise was that Andrew Blowers, the young Auckland tyro, had been given a game in place of Zinzan. Although there had never been any real danger that he would be left out, Cullen insisted that 'I was nervous when we got together to hear the team. Todd Miller's been playing really well – so there was a small worry nagging away at the back of my mind. It was a relief when I heard my name being read out first.'

While we shared a juice, Cullen reflected on yet another startlingly successful year. 'Mate!' he laughed softly, 'the wins are starting to blur. We've played so much rugby this season that it's hard to pick out one game from the other.'

'Does that make it less enjoyable?' I asked.

'Aw, no, not at all. I love playing. There's nothing better. And the idea of pulling on that black shirt over here thrills me as much as it ever did. I guess that's why I was fretting just before they called out the names for Saturday's team.'

Cullen had played eighteen Tests and scored eighteen tries. Seven of those had come in his first two matches. He scored a hat-trick on his début against Western Samoa and followed it up with four more against Scotland. Yet his try in the All Blacks' last Test – a sixty-metre slasher against Australia in Dunedin – had been even more impressive. Midway through the first half, the Wallabies' Stephen Larkham hoisted a huge up-and-under into the winter sunlight. Deep in his own half, Zinzan Brooke shouted, 'My ball!' so loudly that his call rang out high above the noise of a packed Carisbrook. As soon as he'd caught it, Zinny spun the ball out in a long white arc. It sailed through the air for at least twenty metres until it landed perfectly into the arms of an already running Cullen. He was just outside his own 22 as he looked up. He had room to move. As he ran you could see his mind ticking over coolly, rolling one word out in front of him as if he liked the flat momentum of its repetition – 'space . . . space . . . space . . .'

By the time he had reached halfway he was moving too quickly for most of the lagging cover defence to reach him. Whenever someone seemed to be nearing, Cullen altered the angle of his run and turned up the velocity. His speed and vision burned a widening hole through the gold shirts as he crossed their 10-metre line. Cullen looked around as he ran, his radar zooming him through the open spaces. He was in the Wallabies' 22 before he had to reach for his best side-step. George Gregan didn't know which way to turn as Cullen whooshed towards him. While the Black feet shimmied and crossed, an Ali shuffle for

Carisbrook, Gregan swivelled towards his own line. His head twisted over his shoulder as he tried to decide which way Cullen might swerve next. But Gregan was left holding nothing but the hyphen in zig-zag as Cullen dazzled past him with another sudden shift in step. Jason Little managed to touch Cullen as he swept in under the posts – but it might as well have been a congratulatory slap on the back.

Frank Bunce had still scored more Test tries than any other current All Black. He had managed twenty in forty-six internationals. Cullen, having played twenty-eight Tests fewer, was only two tries behind. I tried hard to coax some of that on-field eloquence and insight from Cullen – even though one of the things I liked most about him was his lack of pretence. He knew that he did not have the words. I imagine he also thought it was vaguely stupid to even resort to language in an attempt to recapture such blurring rugby moments. Why use words when, if you had to see it again, you could watch it on video? But he was a polite and patient young Kiwi – and so he tried to give me what I wanted.

'I just love running with the ball,' Cullen said. 'I love to counter-attack and to score tries. It's great when things go well. You start a move from inside your own half and, suddenly, the hole opens up in front of you. I'm always looking for space and, if I see it, I go for it. If there's only one or two defenders then I'll have a little run at them. If there's more then I'll look to pass to one of our guys.'

Cullen had a genius for running through other teams and scoring sensational tries. But, otherwise, he was just an ordinary guy. We spoke for another thirty minutes, but only used ten to talk about rugby. Cullen had heard that 'the Welsh are pretty tough and passionate about rugby'. He liked the idea that there would be singing in Llanelli. He had seen the Irish Development squad in action in New Zealand. 'They were thrashed pretty much every game – but, on their home turf, I'm sure the full Irish side will be fired-up.' Cullen had enjoyed playing at Twickenham the previous year with the New Zealand Barbarians. 'We won in the end but it was quite hard at first. It's an awesome stadium and the crowd made quite a bit of noise. And those forwards of theirs are big. I reckon England will again go for a pretty huge pack. It'll be interesting to see if they try to run it a bit more, though. It might give me a few more chances.'

And then we put the tape away and spoke instead about golf, his new girlfriend and the holiday they were planning to take in Western Samoa. I asked him about his nickname – 'The Paekakariki Express' – and he told me about his small home town and of all the fun he had as a kid playing with his older brother, Shane, in their Paekakariki backyard. He also confirmed with a blush that it was true that he could bench-press more weight than anyone else in his Super 12 side – 'except for the two props!'. But, more than anything, we talked about how much he was looking forward to getting home in time for a hot and sun-filled Christmas, 'with not a rugby ball in sight . . .' The twenty-one-year-old wonder leaned forward with a sigh of a smile. 'It's been a long year, mate, a really long year . . .'

Stradey Park, Llanelli, Saturday, 8 November 1997
It was also a long drive to Llanelli. Saturday morning in London was cold and rainy; and it became even colder and rainier the further west Alison and I drove. We stopped in Bristol for lunch. It was great to forget about rugby and pretend that we were to about to bump into Roni Size or Beth from Portishead or one of the Massive Attack boys. Bristol had become less a rugby town than an innovative movement in British music. Josh Kronfeld would have loved to be in Bristol – but the All Blacks were already wending their way from Swansea to Stradey Park in Llanelli, a town which Christian Cullen argued was harder to spell than Paekakariki.

In 1972, on a dark Tuesday in October, the All Blacks had lost 9–3 to Llanelli. The Welsh town, as Fitzpatrick had predicted when we'd met at the start of 1997, had not forgotten the victory. The passing twenty-five years had only deepened Welsh pride in that historic win. Such was the fervour, in both the town and the club, to play New Zealand again, that Llanelli had announced a few weeks before that they would withdraw from the European Cup rather than miss the opportunity. But, the week before, in a European play-off for the quarter-finals of the Heineken Cup, Llanelli had lost 24–20 to Rob Howley's Cardiff. They insisted that even if they had won, they would have given Bath a walk-over into the semi-final so that they could keep their All Black date. I understood the reasoning for I still preferred the idea of watching a massacre in Llanelli than a tight and fascinating contest between Bath and Cardiff. Like the Welsh, I could not get enough of that Black magic.

But Llanelli were in crisis. Apart from the fact that they no longer had players of the calibre of J.J. Williams, Phil Bennett and Derek Quinnell, or a coach as great as Carwyn James, Llanelli had been on the verge of bankruptcy. 'Within six months of the first professional season,' Llanelli's

Ron Jones told the *Sunday Times*, 'we had wiped out the accumulated assets built up over the previous 125 years.' They had not been able to keep pace with the changes in the game – and particularly with the spiralling wages of their playing staff, who knew how much money they might make if they crossed the Severn Bridge and headed for the English Premiership. Amateur and part-time administrators were suddenly expected to compete in professional sport's brutal marketplace. They were soon lost.

At the start of the year they had been £1,400,000 in debt, after losing £800,000 the previous season. Llanelli had staved off financial closure by selling their ground at Stradey Park for £1,250,000. They, in turn, would have to lease the small stadium back over thirty years for an annual fee of £125,000. Their loyal supporters had subscribed a further £500,000 in a share offer. But the contrast between Llanelli, the Scarlets, and the All Blacks could not have been greater. The New Zealand RFU had just signed the biggest-ever contract in world rugby – a $68,000,000 deal with Adidas.

In Wales, Llanelli were not alone. Neath, Swansea, Pontypridd and the national team all struggled – while popular support for rugby had ebbed once more. I wondered doubtfully if the rise of Welsh pop music, the cinema multiplex or even the computer had eaten into rugby's traditional constituency. Instead of Welsh boys spending late afternoons and all weekend either playing or watching rugby, they could pick up a guitar or tap away on the Internet.

But, as Josh Kronfeld pointed out, even at the bottom of the globe, modern New Zealand offered as many diversions as any other Western country. He did stress, however, the significance of New Zealand's relatively meagre population – 3,500,000 compared to, say, a city like London's 8,000,000. 'Like Wales, we're only a small country – but I guess we're also perceived to live at the bottom of the world. That makes us pretty determined to make a mark in rugby. New Zealanders are a pretty hardy breed. They like to be outside. They like a physical confrontation which is hard but fair. And they also tend to be very committed when they put their minds to something. And, when it comes to rugby, it's not only our number-one sport. It's something far deeper than that. It's a huge part of our culture and it's bound up in shaping our national identity. It means a lot to people when we're described as the best rugby-playing country in the world. And so the All Blacks are a very magnetic force. People are drawn to them. They want to be part of the All Blacks in some way whether they're there as supporters or whether they're young boys dreaming of playing for them one day. The black jersey represents something very powerful. And as long as the team continues to do well, and the organisation of the game remains effective, we should uncover more great players.'

That crucial sense of rugby being used to shore up national identity seemed as good a reason as any to explain the dominance of All Black rugby. The passion for rugby in New Zealand burned brighter than it did in Wales, or even South Africa. It was also built on a coherent structure which evolved constantly in an effort to improve the All Blacks. Every week I read another story about dissent and turmoil in Welsh rugby. And every weekend there were so many Welshmen turning out for Richmond or Bath that the once endemic power of the club game in Wales had crumbled. There were a dozen fine French club sides and perhaps ten in England. In Wales, only Cardiff had the potential corporate muscle to match Toulouse or Brive, Bath or Newcastle. At least Swansea – with the differing likes of Scott Gibbs and Arwel Thomas – had a side to match and even outstrip the current Cardiff line-up. But the rest, including Pontypridd and Llanelli who had both qualified for the European Cup, were struggling.

It was dark and wet in Llanelli when we finally found a muddy field in which to park. The small houses huddled down into the damp. Llanelli did not look to be a town on the rise. And yet the club were attempting to redefine their culture. After the share offer, there had been dabblings with corporate identity, rebranding, merchandising and a few other big-city ploys. Apart from the garish design of the Scarlets' new logo and shirt, it was difficult to spot the other changes when we finally reached the club bar. The room was awash with beer, sweat, tattoos, big bellies, even more ample bar-women and yet more beer. Brains wherever you looked, and Welsh wherever you listened. We drank our own warm pints in their plastic cups and tried to work out the correct pronunciation for the £3 *Rhaglen Swyddogol y Gem* (official souvenir match programme) for the match between *Clwb Rygbi Llanelli v Seland Newydd*.

We were soon in the Llanelli swing – especially as we kept being mistaken for New Zealanders, both by the locals and by the visiting groups of London-based Kiwis. Outside, the weather had improved slightly. The black sky was spitting rather than raining and the wind had dropped to a chill breeze. A red-jacketed Welsh Royal Regiment marched and played with gusto on the pitch and we enthusiastically cheered the arrival of Jenkins – not ginger Neil from Pontypridd, but Jenkins a haughty but impressively good-tempered Welsh goat. We were so close to the pitch that we reached out and patted his smelly white head.

Llanelli suddenly felt a good place to be on an early-Saturday evening in November – especially when the steaming Stradey choir of 14,000 began to sing *Sospan Fach* and *Land of My Fathers* with a breathtaking beauty. We loved the singing – and especially the irony that, twenty minutes earlier, it had sounded as if all 14,000 crooners had been burping less melodically in the bar. The All Blacks, no doubt as part of John Hart's marketing strategy, ran out to the sound of Will Smith and *Men in Black*.

Yet it was more strange not to see either Zinny or Fitzy. Fitzpatrick's knee was still hurting and, for the first time ever, he had stood down from an All Black team. It was hard to believe. An era was closing in world rugby.

But the *Haka* remained. It was easy for Alison to understand all the preceding fuss about the All Blacks. As the Scarlet shirts of Llanelli flapped in the wind, foolishly waving red rags at fifteen black bulls, the New Zealanders launched into the eye-rolling, face-splitting, tongue-wagging ritual. In the absence of both Fitzpatrick and Brooke, Norm Hewitt made the leader's opening *Talite! Talite!* call. The men behind him answered with a shuddering stamp and a *Kamate! Kamate!* roar. Fitzpatrick and Brooke watched in silence.

In the background, Alison had her eyes trained on my favourites – Christian Cullen was all seriousness and soft shouting while, a little apart and a second in front of the others, Josh Kronfeld seemed lost in his scrum-cap-covered world of the open-side. He was preparing himself for the slight isolation of the number 7 position – that lonely slot where he ran with both the backs and the forwards but never felt wholly a part of either.

The New Zealand leadership, however, were joined at the hip in their dismissal of All Black complacency. 'I think you will find,' John Hart predicted generously, 'that we have never beaten Llanelli by much more than twelve points. There has been nothing [in past encounters] you could call decisive. So we are expecting a challenging game at Stradey Park. Llanelli will be a really motivated team who will have the benefit of tremendous home support. If they do manage to get into the match and take a hold, watch out!'

'A good result for us will be to win,' Hart went on to suggest. 'If we succeed with style, so much the better. I am not a person to talk about winning by so many points. People who do that show arrogance and a total lack of respect for their opponents.'

Sean Fitzpatrick, no doubt rubbing his wounded knee in consolation, supported his coach. 'Welsh crowds are the most passionate in the world,' he stressed, 'and that includes South Africa. The supporters are only a couple of yards away from the players on the touchlines and really get behind their side. I have told our people they have not experienced anything like it. When we came over in 1989, it was the club sides that really tested us. The only time we pulled clear was in the international match. We are going to need to play well tonight.'

They did – despite the icy surface. The treacherous conditions did not bother the likes of Randell and Kronfeld, Wilson and Cullen, for they just put their skates on. Cullen was in first, of course, after only five minutes, slicing across Llanelli as if he was a ghost of the ice rink. They hardly laid a finger on the pale number 15 all night as Cullen drifted by for three more tries of his own – the best of which came from a rare Llanelli attack when their outside-half, Warlow, managed a break. He was quickly dumped for his impertinence and Cullen scooped up the bobbing ball. He chipped ahead, caught it and, from inside Black territory, ran the Scarlets ragged and red. He left them gasping as he raced fifty metres and touched down with an easy grace. 'Wow!' we shouted to each other. I couldn't believe it – Christian Cullen, despite his protestations of weariness, looked even better than he had done three months before.

Wilson followed him in with two matching gems – as did Hewitt with a more robust brace of tries. Fitzpatrick seemed pleased for his old understudy. 'Well, Norm's had ninety-one Tests to see how it's done,' he joked. The rest of the thirteen tries came from Kronfeld, Jones, Marshall, Ieremia and Zinzan, who came on for Josh after the first fifty minutes of slaughter. Mehrtens battled with the gust and swirl of the wind, and eight conversions were, thankfully for the Scarlet faces, missed. Llanelli only managed a Warlow penalty – but we stayed to the last whistle, so exhilarating were those Black destroyers. At the end, through the misty rain, the scoreboard carried the startling score in matching black and white, making it a night to remember in West Wales: LLANELLI 3, SELAND NEWYDD, 81.

Gareth Jenkins, the Llanelli coach, who had been one of that legendary 1972 XV, was as shocked as his players. 'For a while,' he admitted, 'I felt frustrated and puzzled. What were we doing wrong? I couldn't work it out. Eventually, I realised that the two teams were simply a class apart – and we were seeing things from the All Blacks which we've never seen in rugby before. Let's face it, we didn't know what the hell was happening to us out there. There are things that we are trying to build into our rugby that they do automatically. They always had five players against three, not by accident but through method. We applaud ball retention and think we are developing along the proper lines when we get it right. They just expect it every time, and do it every time. They have a panoramic view of the rugby field and make decisions that don't even occur to us. We're not a bad side but they produce such organisation and continuity that we couldn't compete. When the boys walked into the dressing-room afterwards they were shaking their heads. The first thing I did was laugh. It lightened the moment. And then I asked them, "Well, what did you make of that then?"'

'The main point about the All Blacks,' Josh Kronfeld reiterated, 'is that we are intensely competitive amongst each other. That comes out on the field – we're disappointed if we win without style. Losing is not even part of the equation. We don't even consider it.'

It was one thing to wallop Llanelli – but, as Kronfeld stressed, there was a difference when it came to internationals. Against Australia in particular, in the Tri-Nations, New Zealand had been devastating in the first half of both matches. The Wallabies, however, had come back after each break. 'I get disappointed,' Kronfeld said, 'when people say you were brilliant for forty minutes but you didn't turn it on as much in the second half. John [Hart] mentioned it in passing a couple of times and the media really jumped on it and made a big thing as if we're a one-half side. We always try to play hard for the whole eighty minutes. But people forget that, in Tests, we're playing some good teams. We built up a big lead against the Australians in Dunedin but they aren't a scabby side. They were very determined and they also have some excellent players – so things eventually settled down into a more typical Test. We had also had some great moments against South Africa – but they are the World Champions, after all, and they were very tough at Ellis Park.

'But the press and the public often think we're going to post fifty points on the board without even blinking. But at the top level the opposition really raise their game. I think it's getting harder. If a player like myself, or more usually Jonah Lomu, comes out and does something extraordinary then, next time, he's going to be watched more closely. Teams will double up on him. There's less room to move but more pressure to repeat the magic.'

Josh, as always, spoke honestly. 'In some ways,' he admitted, 'it's a shame that we're over here at the end of such a huge season back in the southern hemisphere. It would be lovely if we could come over when we're feeling fresh and revitalised. Don't get me wrong: the guys want to keep playing good rugby but for some of them the whole rigmarole of travel and training is starting to get to them after almost eleven months on the road. It's easier for guys like me and Mehrts [Mehrtens] because our girlfriends are coming over for the last week of the tour.

'I'm also lucky that I've been going out with Holly for ages. It would've been harder if we'd just met at the start of professionalism last year, because the demands on the players are huge. We're away so often that it has to impinge on our private lives. When you come home after a long trip it's hard to settle back into the old routine immediately. You want to be with your partner but you also need some time to recover.'

Kronfeld had been less fortunate with injuries in 1997. Although he had played in all New Zealand's Tests, he had missed most of the Super 12s and the NPC with various shoulder and elbow injuries. 'As per usual,' he said, 'in my position with the way I play, injuries keep cropping up. I know I'm still young at twenty-six – even for a rugby player – but it is getting tougher each year. The injuries begin to gather up and the body is slightly less supple than it was a few years ago. I guess I've also thought about it a little more, what with Michael Jones being out all season and Fitzy having to miss out. It's very hard. But the time will come for all of us.

'However, at the moment I suppose I still run round thinking I'm eighteen years old. But there are also times when I'm sitting at home and my ankle's aching and my shoulder's hurting. And I'll think, "Shit, I never used to have this problem! Am I just getting old or are the injuries catching up with me?"'

Josh laughed. 'I think we all play with pain most of the time. And it's easy to forget when you've got another Test coming up fast. I've never been to Dublin before and I've heard it's a fantastic city. I can't wait . . .'

Dublin, Friday, 14 November 1997
At five o'clock that afternoon, in the foyer of the Burlington Hotel, Josh Kronfeld was surrounded as usual. There were friendly boys with shining faces and older men bearing darker rugby scars more shyly. They kept coming, offering him books and posters, shirts and jerseys, even their hands and arms – and rugby ball after rugby ball. He signed everything, answering every question with a little crack.

At last, Kronfeld looked up and saw me. He could tell that I had already heard the bad news. Two days before, on the Wednesday, John Hart told him that his number 7 jersey had been handed to Andrew Blowers. For the first Test of the tour, against Ireland that Saturday, Blowers would play while Kronfeld would watch, from the bench.

Kronfeld was only three years older than Blowers and, if he had suffered from injury throughout 1997, his replacement had battled even more. At the peak of his career, it seemed unthinkable that Kronfeld should be dropped – especially when Blowers, as fine a player as he was, was more a blind-side flanker.

Josh's hurt at losing the black shirt was almost unbearable. 'I'm still in shock,' he said softly to us. 'I couldn't believe it when I heard.'

I asked him if Hart or any of the other All Black management had explained why he had been dropped.

He shook his head. 'I just don't know . . .'

His pain was different to the normal scenario of disappointment in sport. There were no sudden tactical changes or disciplinary measures. It was more complex than that. I did not say it to Josh, but I wondered if Hart was sending out another of his mixed corporate strategy messages. I wondered if he was using some of the hard-edged man-management ploys which Sean Fitzpatrick had described as 'effective but uncomfortable' during their Auckland days together. I knew that Hart was willing to cause individual insecurity if he thought it would be for the team's overall benefit. He had decided to press the button against Josh Kronfeld – seemingly just to shake things up a little.

'What's been the reaction amongst other people?' I asked.

'I spoke to my parents,' Josh said, 'and apparently it's big news back home. There's a bit of uproar . . .'

'I bet there is,' I said, knowing how much Kronfeld was revered in New Zealand – particularly on the South Island.

'Yeah,' he sighed, 'but it's not going to change anything. I'm still going to be on that bench tomorrow . . .'

'I'm really sorry, Josh,' I offered, not knowing what else to say to him.

And then, in a moment more moving than any other in my All Black year, he suddenly smiled. 'I'll be okay,' he promised. 'I've just got to get that jersey back. I can't think of anything else – this team means too much to me.'

But he was big-hearted enough to immediately think of us. He made us laugh as he squared-up playfully. He knew that I was married to a woman who did the best Chris Eubank impersonation this side of

Brighton. 'C'mon, Alison,' the big All Black said as he took a step forward with his bunched fists and curling grin, 'show me your Eubank!'

At Lansdowne Road the following afternoon, the All Black fans carried their own black-and-white posters of protest: 'No Hart – Bring Back Josh!' And, after an hour, Kronfeld finally did return in place of Blowers. By then, the All Blacks were cruising again after they'd sailed over the initial rough waves of Irish ardour. For the first thirty minutes, inspired by a magnificent Keith Wood, Ireland had not only held New Zealand but, miracle of miracles, actually taken the lead. Their 15–14 margin was built on two opportunist tries by Woodie – the second of which had us on our feet as he did the supposedly impossible and out-sprinted Jeff Wilson to touch down Eric Miller's hack ahead.

But, as against South Africa three and a half months before, the All Blacks turned up the burner just before half-time. Even without Fitzpatrick who, in the days before the Test, had at last admitted that he was 'pessimistic' about playing on tour, the Black machine was on track. Mehrtens coolly slotted two penalties and then Marshall jinked through for a try under the posts. A 14–15 deficit had abruptly become a 27–15 jaunt. In the second half, with Wood having to be replaced after he could no longer ignore the effects of a crunching Blowers tackle on his gammy ankle, New Zealand kept possession by driving the ball down the middle rather than trying to spread it wide. In one awesome fifteen-minute stretch, Ireland only managed twice to lay hand to ball. 63–15 was, in the end, the terrible thumping everyone had predicted.

Keith Wood was certain that he had just played against the world's best team. 'New Zealand are a much better side than the Springboks,' he said. 'They're much craftier. You saw how they changed their game after half-time. South Africa, to their detriment, did not change at all in the first two Tests against the Lions. One of the things you have to do is to stop them continually recycling the ball until your own defence cannot hold out any longer. But, at the same time, they can also play the game so well in other areas. The All Blacks can attack you from anywhere . . .'

The Irish coach, the former Bath stalwart Brian Ashton, was more sombre in his assessment. 'The All Blacks are now so good,' he said gravely, 'they're running out of teams to play . . .'

Chapter 7
A Green Light in Paris

Bistros, bridge, English cricket and European languages were not usually listed on the CV of a new Springbok rugby coach. But Nick Mallett was different. Two months before, in September, when Mallett was announced as Carel du Plessis's successor, attention focused on his cosmopolitan personality rather than on a more pedestrian detail – he was the seventh Springbok coach in the five years they had been back in world rugby.

John Williams had been a dinosaur from the old régime; Ian McIntosh an outstanding coach who fell foul of the maddening Louis Luyt; Kitch Christie a World Cup winner who became seriously ill; Gerrie Sonnekus a mistake who did not last long enough to oversee a single training session; Andre Markgraaff a political disaster; and Carel du Plessis a novice who failed to win the trust of his own players. Yet, as wide and varied as that list read, none of those men, either individually or together, could match Mallett's eclectic range beyond the rugby field.

It was strange to learn that, while studying politics and philosophy at Oxford, Mallett had gained his Blue in bridge and had also hit three straight sixes off Ian Botham. His Blue in cricket, following another in rugby, came soon after he had scored a half-century and taken five wickets in an innings of a first-class match against Glamorgan. I already knew that Mallett had enjoyed an expansive rugby career in France and Italy, but it was more unusual to hear that, while in St Claude, north of Lyon and not far from the Swiss border, he had run his own bistro. Unlike any previous Springbok coach he was also fluent in French and competent in Italian.

As impressed as he was by those culinary and linguistic skills, a friend of mine saw the definitive break with past Springbok culture in Mallett's confession that he actually read books by Stephen Fry. Ironically, a different Stephen Fry had captained the Springboks against the Lions in 1955. But we knew that Mallett meant the modern English dandy and aspiring renaissance man, who had even played Oscar in *Wilde*, rather than his less erudite rugby namesake.

Mallett himself had been born in England and had once made the final trial for the English Test team – pushing the then existing back row of Uttley, Neary and Scott close with his ability to play at both eighth-man and on the flank. But he was, in Afrikaans, *'n ware Suid-Afrikaan* (a true South African). He had been brought up in Cape Town, and had gone to school in Grahamstown. More significantly, in rugby terms, he had been schooled in the rigorous local scene – moving from junior and university rugby to helping Western Province win the Currie Cup four times before he was capped for the Springboks in 1984.

At Oxford, he had been known as 'The Incredible Hulk'. I suspected that Mallett's nickname was more a consequence of his competitive physicality than his refined prowess at the crease or the bridge table. Like many South African forwards, Mallett could be as blunt as he was rugged. He did not have any traditional English characteristics – he was not reserved or overly modest. He did not deal much in irony or ambivalence. Mallett was as straightforward as most of his Afrikaans predecessors. Yet the growing myth suggested that his time in Italy and France had grafted on a fierce emotion and a willingness to protest angrily if the need arose. There were times when Nick Mallett's press made him sound like he was a cross between Danie Craven and Jacques Fouroux – except that Mallett always had his bridge and cricketing background to set him apart from such crass comparisons.

More strikingly, Mallett had the coaching credentials and strength of personality to give the blundering bulk of South African rugby a hard shake. He had spent two years with Rovigo in Italy, five years with St Claude and four with Boulogne-Billancourt in France. There, he had first revealed his ability to blend disparate rugby cultures. 'French rugby tends to be loose and unstructured,' he explained to the *Sunday Times*'s Dan Retief, 'with everyone running with the ball. So I coached ordered pattern play. It helped that in those days you could maul the ball forward and keep it. We took a lot of teams by surprise.'

On his return to South Africa he transformed a struggling False Bay club side and then went on to work with Jeffrey Stevens and an emerging Boland. As before, at Boland he took charge of a team with limited resources. Yet Mallett was able to implement a radical improvement through basic tactical changes and management skills. Like Hart and McGeechan, Mallett was adept at conveying his game-plan clearly and effectively. Although he stressed the need for imaginative and attacking rugby, he was more emphatic that, when played well, it was an essentially simple game.

Unlike Carel du Plessis, Mallett actually led his teams. He simultaneously made players feel that they were involved in many of his decisions – from matters of discipline to ways of training. But, like Hart, he never ceded control.

While he thought that the Springboks' World Cup win had been 'fantastic for the country', he suggested that a 'more honest position would have been a top-four place – as opposed to being the best team in the world'. Mallett claimed that the subsequent law changes suited New Zealand most and helped stretch the gap they'd opened up on the rest of the rugby world. 'They became far better than us,' he admitted. 'We were more a kicking side and had very good line-out forwards – because we used to cheat a bit and lift – but now they allow lifting, so their line-outs, which weren't a strong aspect of their game, have become equal [to ours]. Their skill levels are also that much higher.'

Mallett also named two All Blacks as modern rugby's most impressive players: Zinzan Brooke, 'the consummate footballer', and 'bloody Fitzy – you have to admire his durability, the way he plays, his sheer presence . . .'

Yet in Paris, in the days following the All Blacks' Dublin blitz, it was not patriotism which made me think that Mallett might be able to provide a sustained challenge to New Zealand. It was also not the new coach's startling ability to switch between French, English, Afrikaans and Italian as European and South African journalists pressed in on him. It was not even his political credibility, which allowed him to say, 'Springbok rugby has long been regarded as the preserve of the white man, especially the white Afrikaner man. I would like to change that and return to the exhilarating feelings of 1995 when the whole country felt positive about the game and everyone was behind the Springbok team.' It was not the fact that, in his first Test as coach, South Africa had hammered Italy in Bologna, scoring nine tries and winning by more than thirty points. It was not just the potential they had shown in outscoring France by five tries to three during their victory in Lyon. There were other factors.

Apart from rebuilding their shattered confidence, Mallett encouraged the Springboks to play an effervescent fifteen-man game. He'd restored Adrian Garvey and James Dalton at tighthead and hooker because, like Os du Randt, they were the kind of abrasive but extremely mobile front-rowers who loved to run and pass the ball. At inside-centre he had selected a thirty-two-year-old veteran, Dick Muir, who had never previously played international rugby. Muir's direct and generous play opened up space for the entire back line. Mallett had also moved Andre

Snyman from the wing to his more natural position at outside-centre. Suddenly, set up by Muir, Snyman's hard running and strength on the break were being utilised. Even more dramatically, Mallett switched Percy Montgomery, who had been so shaky in the centre of du Plessis's flawed plan, to full-back. It was the perfect launch-pad for a player of his explosive pace and attacking instincts. Montgomery was given licence by Mallett to run and take on players in a style which suggested that Christian Cullen's lessons in the offensive art of wearing a number 15 shirt had not been lost in Cape Town.

James Small and Henry Honiball were both given increased influence on the wing and at stand-off – and Small's individuality off the field was handled deftly by Mallett who, with an imaginative stroke of irony, appointed him head of the players' disciplinary committee. Small responded to the new responsibility. He doled out discipline with all the rigour of a man who had been so often on the other side of the fence that he knew every little excuse and duck-out clause before the latest culprit could even give voice to them.

Mallett also made previously doubtful players believe that he had enduring faith in them. Krynauw Otto, a big lock from Pretoria, had been accused of lacking the heart for real battle. But Mallett told Otto he could forge a partnership with Mark Andrews which would take the Springbok line-out at least as far as Wales in 1999. He reacted instantly by standing up to French bruisers like Olivier Merle.

But, most importantly, Mallett had established a cohesive partnership with Gary Teichmann. They were determined to lead South Africa into the next World Cup on a platform of continuity which, until then, had appeared to be the sole preserve of New Zealand.

Mallett and Teichmann also favoured a dynamic brand of rugby – where the emphasis was placed squarely on ball-retention and try-scoring. To match the All Blacks, it was a change in attitude the Spring-boks needed to embrace. If they were given a penalty they would punt the ball out for a line-out and attempt to score seven points from the resultant throw, rather than settling for a more conservative kick at the posts. Their bold approach was beginning to work.

It was easy to pick up on Mallett's growing optimism. 'I really believe,' he said, 'that we lost against the Lions and in the Tri-Nations because of bad man-management and planning. It was not the fault of the players. That's why 1997 has been such a frustrating year for Springbok rugby. But, now, I am handling the players in a non-South African way. I am not being dictatorial. I am being consultative and constructive. I am looking for players who play intelligently but who, above all, play for the benefit of the whole team. We want to change the perception that South African rugby is just played by brawny guys from the Highveld who can only grunt. I want people around the world to stop thinking of us as being brutal and parochial. Our results will always be the most important criteria but I also want people to see that we can play with imagination and verve.'

Mallett might have sounded like an All Black coach – except for his increasing desire to look at the potential dilemma facing New Zealand rugby. 'Their greatest strength, their experience,' Mallett said of the All Blacks, 'could soon turn into their biggest weakness. I believe we now have the team to exploit that weakness. They can't get away from it. Their leading players are ageing fast . . .'

Brooke had only three more Tests to play. Fitzpatrick was limping like never before. Bunce was only months away from his thirty-sixth birthday. Although the Black conveyor belt rolled on, even New Zealand could not just shrug aside the loss of such a trio. In contrast, the international player whom Mallett admired most after Zinny and Fitzy was only approaching his peak. For Mallett, Gary Teichmann was the first name he wrote down on every Test sheet. His assessment of his captain's contribution was characteristically to the point: 'Gary has been bloody good, Test after Test. It's been an extremely difficult year but, to me, Gary has shone brighter than ever . . .'

Gary Teichmann had come through difficult times. There had been enough dark moments to suggest that 'Heart-Ache' might have been a more appropriate middle name than the grander 'Hamilton' he'd been given at birth. In 1995 Teichmann had been one of the unfortunate quartet who'd been axed when the Springbok squad was cut from thirty to twenty-six players only days before the World Cup. Although he returned later that year to play against Wales, in a match where he scored a try, Teichmann was again described as being 'desperately unlucky' when he was excluded from the party to play in Italy and England in November '95.

When Francois Pienaar was injured early on in the series against the All Blacks in 1996, the twenty-nine-year-old Teichmann had the unenviable role of taking over the captaincy – even though he'd just come into the team. At a time when Pienaar's popularity was near its zenith, Andre Markgraaff decided to make Teichmann's appointment permanent. Beyond having to endure the national demand for Pienaar's reinstatement – with the call coming from Mandela downwards – Teichmann had to confront his own black place in history. He had just become the first Springbok captain to lose a home series to New Zealand. It did not matter that the All Blacks were then at their peak – Teichmann had, in South African rugby terms, literally sinned in failing to inspire his country to an historic fightback.

The mood lightened briefly at the end of '96. Pienaar had left South Africa for Saracens and Teichmann led a rejuvenated Springbok squad through Argentina, France and Wales. And then, just as Teichmann was returning to a new Super 12 season with Natal, the Markgraaff bomb dropped. The man who had placed so much faith in him, at the expense of Pienaar, was exposed as a fraud.

While du Plessis retained Teichmann, the shadow of Pienaar still lingered during the Lions tour. Teichmann was compared constantly with his predecessor. But the image I had of him after the second Test at King's Park, as he waited alone for a drink before he turned to face the media, had moved me more than any picture of Pienaar holding the World Cup. Teichmann, in defeat, cut a deeply sympathetic figure – mostly because we sensed how much he yearned to win.

The two Springbok captains were distinct personalities. Pienaar was a charismatic politician who had a flair for finding snappy soundbites as quickly as he could assess a situation whether on the fringe of a scrum or in the heart of a boardroom. Teichmann was far quieter and much happier in the company of his own team. While he was unfailingly polite, he did not relish the attention which accompanied the position.

I asked James Small about the differences between the two men. While he respected Pienaar, and said that 'Francois has an unbelievable ability to read a game – he is better than any other player I know in being able to judge when a team should change its tactics', Small suggested that the players felt closer to Teichmann. 'Gary is a player's captain. You always feel that his heart lies with the team. Francois was different. He could move easily between the political and playing sides. He was as comfortable dealing with the media or the administration as he was playing rugby. Francois was a very skilful leader both on and off the field. But I don't think I'm being disloyal to him if I say that the players feel a little closer to Gary. If he had a choice, Gary would prefer to stick with us rather than have to do all the other stuff. Francois is a national icon. Gary is our captain . . .'

I knew what he meant. I also liked Pienaar but I was always conscious, as with Fitzpatrick, that he was a master of the interview. Pienaar and Fitzpatrick had both handled so many media assignments that you could not ignore the smoothness of their answers. They both spoke beautifully, and sometimes from the heart as well as the head, but I found it easier to strike a more instant rapport with Teichmann. With Gary, it did not matter that he was not as scintillating as Pienaar in carving out quotes. I didn't mind that he spoke plainly and rarely deviated from the point of the question. He did not philosophise or reflect on the past in evocative detail. He merely answered each question as honestly and as diplomatically as possible. It was enough for me.

Teichmann exuded such sincerity and warmth that it felt to me, from that first morning in Paris, that we were more likely to become friends than stick formally to our official roles of professional player and persistent questioner. I guess that Small had something to do with it for, thanks to the man in the number 14 shirt, Teichmann knew a little about me when we met. It changed the tenor of our interview – and so we spoke, without the tape, as much as we went through the question-answer routine.

I learnt that Teichmann, even though he loved Durban, was happiest when he could leave the city and head out to his father's farm where people were less bothered about the latest rugby palaver. There, in the Natal farmlands, they worried about more important things – like the weather. He had grown up on a farm in Zimbabwe, where he'd been born in 1967 and lived for the first twelve years of his life. But after a long and terrible war and, fearing more trouble, the Teichmanns moved to Natal. Both his parents' families were originally South African and, having visited Natal during most school holidays, the adjustment had been relatively easy for him. The main change was switching from cricket and football to a sport of which he had known nothing in Zimbabwe – rugby. It had been more difficult for his father, a livestock auctioneer. They had had to start all over, having left most of what they owned in Zimbabwe. But his dad began farming again and Gary thought that one day, after his life in rugby, he might return to a simpler farm life himself. For the moment, outside rugby, he had developed a small earth-moving business.

In Durban, his wife had just given birth to a little girl, Danielle. As hard as it had been for him to leave them to go on tour again, Teichmann almost glowed in Paris when he spoke about his baby. It helped explain why he was never in trouble with the press. Even as Springbok captain, Teichmann was not hounded by either the public or the media – it was difficult for them to pursue him when he was so obviously content to spend most of his free time at home, with his two girls. He joked that he was happy for James Small to churn up the newsprint while he settled for the quiet life.

But, within that quietness, there was a clink of steel. Sitting next to Teichmann, drinking our Parisian coffee, I was acutely aware of the resolve he always showed on the rugby field. It was not just his height and lean build of sixteen-stone strength which told of his power at the back of the scrum. It was more the look in his eye when he talked about the All Blacks or playing at the Parc des Princes. He was a well-balanced and calm man – but there was something beyond the tranquillity. Teichmann had become an outstanding international but, more than anything else in rugby, he needed his team to match him. It was two years away, but I could feel it. He wanted the World Cup.

Before even meeting Teichmann, my admiration for his resilience had sharpened considerably. As Mallett had said, Teichmann was the only Springbok to enhance his reputation during that chaotic South African winter. It was difficult to imagine any previous Springbok captain surviving a shock series loss to the Lions and two catastrophic away defeats to Australia and New Zealand. But, as a number 8, Teichmann's soft hands and little link passes were as sumptuous as his driving play was seamless. He set a huge-hearted example on the pitch, while his composure in the face of various Sarfu political scandals offered rare restraint. Teichmann had provided the only themes of consistency throughout that turbulent year. He'd even managed to instil a measure of cool insight into the hysterical criticism of his players, insisting that the 'crisis' had never centred on a lack of talent or desire.

The real problem, rather, was embedded in the archaic structure of the 'Old South Africa' where rugby continued to be ruled by Louis Luyt's iron rod. 'Have you heard?' Teichmann asked in Paris. 'Luyt got in again,' he said with a wry smile in reference to the latest Sarfu power struggle in which big Louis had won a surprisingly easy vote against Mluleki George and Keith Parkinson to retain the presidency of Sarfu. We did not need to say anything else. The accusations of racism and financial impropriety, and a seemingly endless government investigation, provided a doleful echo to the clatter of defeats and sacked coaches.

'For sure,' Teichmann sighed, 'it's not been an easy eighteen months. We've lost some important matches and, when you go down at home to the All Blacks or the Lions, it hurts all the more. On top of that, as we all know, there've been problems off the field. All the negativity starts to affect you and, sometimes, it's hard not to let it bring you down. Even if you just focus on the coaching situation it's difficult not to be affected. It seems like we manage to find a new coach every six months . . .'

His laugh was muffled. We both shrugged, two weary South Africans worn down by the old saga. But there was a reason to be cheerful in France. A bistro-running, bridge-playing coaching maestro could at last support Teichmann.

'Nick's done really well,' Teichmann enthused, 'and it makes all the difference if your coaching and management is up to scratch. It takes so much off the captain's shoulders and, as a player, you start enjoying the game again. To be honest, just before this tour, I was shattered, as much mentally as physically. When we had our first training sessions under Nick my heart wasn't really in it . . .'

'I guess you were counting the days until the end of this season . . .'

'I'd be bullshitting you, Donald, if I said otherwise. You know I'm never going to turn down the opportunity to play for the Springboks but, *ja*, a little of the shine was taken away this year. In the first week, I reckon Nick could quickly see that I wasn't quite giving it a hundred per cent. You go along with things and you don't complain but, deep down, you're not going to give anything extra in training. That's not the kind of player I normally am but I was just so fed up that I was doing the minimum. But Nick and the guys quickly turned the thing round. Suddenly the whole atmosphere lifted and we were back feeling positive again. It was a great feeling because it hadn't been easy playing the Lions under a new coach. And then to have to start all over again seemed even more difficult. But Nick's very charismatic – it's easy to feel full of hope when he's around.'

Teichmann remembered his contrasting dejection in the King's Park press room five months before. '*Ja*,' he nodded, 'that was one of the very lowest moments. It was a lousy feeling. I really didn't want to have to go up there and explain away another defeat – especially one at home. But, at the same time, I knew I had to do it. And I also felt it was right to point out that the Lions were a very professional outfit. They took on a really tough tour where they had no easy games – and yet they came through in the end. I was happy to give credit to them, even if we should have beaten them. The first Test was a tight affair and in the end they beat us fair and square. But, really, at King's Park we were all over them. But there were some strange decisions and – whew – their defence was outstanding.'

'Did you underestimate them?'

'I think our newspapers just assumed that they were going to roll over

– but, as players, we really respected them. If anything I'd say we over-trained before the first Test. But that was the coach's decision. I think we should have been a bit more relaxed going into that Test. And we certainly didn't underestimate them in Durban. There was just so much pressure on us . . .'

I wondered how much he and the other players had suffered from all the emotional 'Bokke! O Bokke!' and 'Boks – What Went Wrong?' headlines as well as the ensuing public chagrin.

'We've been hurt by some of the criticism,' he admitted. 'I sometimes get letters from guys who haven't considered the whole scenario. They don't assess our performance in light of all the changes in coaching or the injuries we've had. They just hammer us over a specific defeat. I remember how one of the first letters I got really hit home. I just thought, "How can a guy sit down and write something like this?" Look, we accept that we haven't done well in terms of what South Africa expects from the Springboks but the reasons often lie far beyond the players themselves.'

Were there still provincial and linguistic divisions?

'I don't think that applies anymore at Springbok level. But, *ja*, it was different a few years ago. I remember when I was in the army. They asked all the guys who had played Craven Week to step forward. Whenever a guy was from Northern Transvaal or the Free State the army coach was very happy. But when they asked me who I'd played for they just laughed. In those days Natal had won nothing. We were this English province that no one took seriously. So I wasn't considered a big deal in army rugby. But things have changed a lot. Natal have done well and most of that provincial division has disappeared when you get to Springbok level. But it's a very different story among the administrators. Unfortunately, all those problems of disunity have affected the running of our game. I think this is why the All Blacks are a little ahead of the rest of us now. Their whole structure works for the players' benefit. Until we do that, the All Blacks are always going to have the edge.'

I asked Teichmann the obvious question: 'What's it like to face the All Blacks?'

'They're very good,' he agreed. 'They've got great players and it's not easy to knock them out of their stride. But we did it at Ellis Park and we were also ahead for a while at Eden Park – but they always come back at you. So, *ja*, they are the best side at the moment. But, at the same time, I have to say that until this trip they've been lucky with injuries. I know Fitzpatrick's battling at the moment but they've had an incredible run.

A lot of that, I guess, is down to their training and preparation – but they've also had some good fortune.'

'How would you compare the Springbok team which lost to the Lions to this team in France?'

'We're now so much better. There's no question about it. Nick has introduced a new dimension to our game. We didn't play that well in Lyon but we still posted thirty-six points pretty quickly. In the first two Tests against the Lions we only made a handful of opportunities. Now we're creating an enormous amount of chances. Nick's whole philosophy is built around a simple aim – to create as many opportunities to score tries as possible. Sure, this means that we take a few risks but we're always looking to score tries rather than penalties.'

It was the morning before he led the Springboks out at the Parc des Princes for that famous old stadium's last rugby international. Even in the plush and mammoth luxury of the Hotel Concorde Lafayette, a small tug of anxiety could be sensed within the South African camp. The mood was good; but there was an undertow of trepidation.

'*Ja*,' Teichmann said, 'I can also feel it. But this time tomorrow the tension will be far worse. It's going to be a very big game. If we win tomorrow, we'll have started to build real momentum. But if we lose . . .'

His voice trailed away – but the grim thought remained. 'The French, as we all know,' he continued, 'can be very unpredictable. Last week we were way ahead before they started to cut loose. We'd scored five tries before they got their first. They had nothing to lose so they started to take chances. They scored three tries pretty quickly. [Olivier] Merle came on and he fired them up a bit. But the main thing is that we gave away possession. We've got to learn not to do that. It's important to keep the ball, as a team, when you're on top. You can't let a team like the French come back at you – because I think the new style of professional rugby, which is all about speed, could really suit them. They have fantastic ball skills and if they can pick up the pace they'll be very hard tomorrow.

'They're never easy to beat at home – just ask the All Blacks. They really battle over here. The French have beaten them quite a few times over the last ten years. We've done better. We've tended to win in France. Last year we also beat them twice and so they're going to be even more determined tomorrow, what with it being the last game at the Parc . . .'

Aware of the looming history of the day, Teichmann still felt that the Springboks were on the verge of something groundbreaking. 'I do feel that we have the players and the game-plan to transform our rugby.

There are signs that we can play in a style which is much more exciting than past Springbok teams. If we play to the best of our ability tomorrow we should win. It's not going to be easy, but a second straight win against the French would be fantastic. It would be a huge boost after such a bad year.'

Gary Teichmann looked down at his big hands. He spread them wide and then closed them again. His last words were said quietly. 'We really need this win . . .'

That afternoon, James Small took me down the road for my tiny glass of beer. His season in South Africa had ended well. He was on the wing for du Plessis's last match – a belated 61–22 thrashing of the Wallabies. He had also helped Western Province win the Currie Cup – an outcome few would have predicted when Small had left Natal eight months before.

Under Mallett, he had dazzled in the first two Tests of their European tour. He had scored twice against Italy and also against France in Lyon. Those tries meant that he was only one away from yet another Springbok record – Danie Gerber's nineteen Test tries. Whatever else they said about Small, he was on the verge of turning the record books into his best answer.

But, as always with James, there were other subjects to talk about besides rugby – Paris most of all. It represented everything we'd once yearned to discover in those years when it seemed as if we'd be stuck forever in the Transvaal.

When he first reached Paris, in 1992, he'd look up 'at all these mysterious Parisian houses and dream of a day when I might see inside them for myself.' Earlier that week, Small had had one of his 'best-ever nights – just an evening at home with a friend, his wife and two kids. A family dinner in Paris. I just sat there, listening to the music, drinking some Bordeaux, thinking, "This is even better than the dream . . ."'

That friend, Richard Escot, a French rugby writer, had known Small for years. He understood him better than any other journalist and, once more, he had written beautifully in *L'Equipe* of 'the difference' in Small, a difference which always appealed to followers of French rugby.

Small shook his head, but in pleasure. 'Hey, I love France! I love Paris! But, tomorrow, at the Parc, my bru, we're still gonna kick some butt!'

A cold greeny-grey fog slid across Paris late that afternoon. The symbolism seemed too obvious even for a French melodrama. But *Les Tricolores* looked as befuddled as they were lost. Even their great icons – Philippe Saint-André, Abdelatif Benazzi, Jean-Luc Sardourney, Philippe Benetton and Christian Califano – had a smack of dismay about them.

France had just played their final Test at the Parc des Princes, their cherished and imposing citadel of rugby. Yet, even in a soft mist of nostalgia, they could not find relief. They were too bewildered by the shock of the moment; by the fact that, for the first time in their history, they had conceded fifty points.

As they disappeared into the dark maze of tunnels running beneath the old stadium, their words drifted by in a blur of awe. Jean-Claude Skrela, their coach, wailed gently that 'it was like running into a green wall'. The verdict of his captain, the magisterial Saint-André, sounded equally stunned. 'I have played against the Springboks perhaps seven times. But nothing from the past prepared me for this. The same players have put on so much muscle and yet they run even faster than before. It's incredible. The South Africans have moved to a level where we cannot compete. They are stronger and quicker than us and now they also play with an intensity which is like nothing we have ever experienced. It's new rugby.'

Pieter Rossouw equalled Chester Williams's World Cup record by scoring four of the Springboks' seven tries – the best being his second and third. For number two, Andre Venter opened up the French with a bullocking charge. The back line were right behind him. Montgomery and Small then exchanged lightning passes to let Rossouw loose. His long legs tore across the damp grass. The touchdown looked easy. Five minutes into the second half he turned his opposite number, David Venditti, inside out as if he were a designer coat on its way to the cleaners. At the end of his run he did the same sartorial trick to the elegantly muddied Saint-André. The two Frenchmen dropped to the floor, more like old blue socks to be brutal, while Rossouw crossed the line for his hat-trick.

Snyman, Teichmann and Honiball scored tries of their own – and the fly-half added all seven conversions and the one penalty which the South Africans did not attempt to turn into another try. Raphael Ibanez, replacing del Maso at hooker, managed France's solitary try. Lamaison converted to add to his earlier penalty. France had at least made double figures; but South Africa, recognising the cricketing pedigree of their new coach, had their half-century.

And 52–10 was just one measurement of the Springboks' superiority. The earlier sight of Garvey, Venter, Andrews and Teichmann flattening *Les Bleus* was a more lasting quantifier. The South African pack had been formidable – just as their back line had been clinical.

Small, in his beloved Paris, trotted round the park in a French jersey. It was Benetton's number 6. Teichmann, also in blue, did not jog even a step ahead for, as Small had said, the Springbok captain was happiest to be at the heart of his side. Their wide smiles burnished the gloom. Rapturous acclaim rolled down the steep banks of concrete seating. The venerable Parc, for all its sadness, rose as one in a sweeping gesture of acclaim. The best rugby it had ever seen had been saved for the very last.

Chapter 8

An Autumn Break

The season in England was only three months old but the cracks ran deep. On one side, the twelve newly professional Premiership clubs glowered. Their league was more appealing and competitive than it had ever been and yet, at the end of November, it appeared to have been put on perpetual hold. Across an ever-widening gap from them, the Rugby Football Union had apparently forgotten to contract any of England's leading players. While they had neglected that little issue, they had managed to cook up a taxing itinerary for their national team. Over the absurdly crammed space of four successive Saturday afternoons, England had been assigned dates with Australia, New Zealand, South Africa and, once more for luck, the All Blacks. It was scant consolation for the new England coaching team – Clive Woodward, once of Bath, and John Mitchell, from Waikato and Sale – that their southern-hemisphere rivals were equally weary after ten straight months of demanding rugby.

If the opportunity to see the Wallabies, All Blacks and Springboks thrilled fans in England, another international disruption infuriated club rugby's affluent owners. Newcastle's John Hall, Saracens' Nigel Wray, Wasps' Chris Wright, Gloucester's Tom Walkinshaw and Richmond's Ashley Levett comprised the most high-profile quintet. They looked unlikely to burst into any barber-shop routine about the joys of autumn.

English rugby was in a mess, with stray remnants of the unlucky first thirteen weeks of the season spread over a sprawling variety of surfaces. Ironically, each separate sector was interesting. The international month was a mostly stimulating, if still unbalanced, contest between rugby's contrasting hemispheres. The fiery Heineken Cup had reached the semi-final stages in Europe with the harder-edged French clubs supplying three of the four teams which would meet again on the weekend before Christmas. Brive would play Toulouse while Pau travelled to Bath. The English Premiership, meanwhile, had opened intriguingly on 23 August 1997 and, in that weekend's most significant match, the newly promoted Newcastle won a tight match at Bath, 20–13. It was a tasty harbinger of a change in the old English order with Newcastle and Saracens ready to take on the more traditional powerhouses of Bath and Leicester, as well as the reigning champions, Wasps.

Saracens, with Francois Pienaar established as player-coach, also began with a win – beating Sale away on Sunday, 24 August. However, their next league match, at their new home in Watford, at the football ground, had to wait six weeks. On a miserable Wednesday evening, on 8 October, they only counted 5,000 to see Pienaar, Sella, Lynagh and the rest beat Richmond 15–9. Saracens had signed Peter Deakin as their marketing guru. While he'd achieved marvels in rugby league with the Bradford Bulls, he had a more imposing task in Watford. He began that night with dancing girls, a giant walking Jaffa Cake and a remote controlled toy truck which brought the kicking tees onto the ground every time there was a penalty. It was hard to imagine, then, that it was enough to attract the additional 17,000 needed to fill the stadium.

Apart from the weather, Saracens had not been helped by a break in the league programme. As they had not finished in the Premiership's top four the season before, they failed to qualify for the Heineken Cup. So while Wasps, Leicester, Bath and Harlequins faced the best of the French and the Welsh, as well as Scottish and Irish combinations, throughout September and October, Saracens and Newcastle were consigned to the second-tier European Conference. Saracens were grouped with Neath, Narbonne and Castres – tough sides of considerable tradition and yet, at the same time, hardly the charismatic names to light up a non-rugby town like Watford. As long as Saracens were compelled to play Neath at home one weekend before travelling to Narbonne the next, it was virtually impossible for Wray, Deakin and Pienaar to build a consistent support base. They wanted a football-type structure where their fans were guaranteed an accessible league match every weekend – with a home tie at least once a fortnight.

It was a uniform view amongst the Premiership clubs. Owing to England's onerous commitments in November and December, the league champions had been badly affected. Wasps' chairman, Chris Wright, was indignant that even though Wasps had hosted the European Cup-holders, Brive, in a money-spinning quarter-final tie in early November, they did not have another home match until 30 December – an end-of-year Tuesday-evening downer at that. No home game for almost two months meant no gate receipts and no growing supporter base. And then, at the end of January, the Five Nations would begin – removing a full league programme every other week until early April. For the clubs, it was disastrous.

Wray and Wright underlined the sport's financial plight. Rugby's professional business was being run into the ground by amateurish administrators. Although all the Premiership clubs, with the exception of Bristol, had negotiated sponsorship deals which secured their immediate future, their long-term prospects were decidedly cloudy. Bristol's fate – £2,500,000 in debt without a sugar-daddy in sight – was a stark warning to the rest. Even Harlequins, derided as London fat-cats, had lost one of their financial saviours in early October when John Beckwith ended his involvement with the club. Without a fundamental restructuring, the remaining proprietors were adamant that they would follow Beckwith's lead.

The *Sunday Times*'s Stephen Jones and Nick Cain explained the further reasons for chaos. 'Until 1995,' they wrote, 'even clubs in the top divisions in England and Wales employed only a handful of people. Then, the leap from the high board. Instead of an intermediate stage, where the game went semi-professional, every English club and most Welsh clubs went fully professional.

'The going rate for salaries was artificially inflated, by sheer panic that a club's players were going to be enticed away overnight and, more specifically, because the riches of Sir John Hall, who bought the ailing Newcastle club, allowed Newcastle to pay massive salaries; hardly Newcastle's fault, but an inflationary precedent. Every club realises that salaries are way too high. Even Mike Burton, the sports impresario who handles the affairs of nearly three hundred players, agrees. Harlequins' wage bill is thought to be in excess of £2,000,000 a year and they have two players on £100,000.

'Ironically, the image of rugby as an impoverished sport is spectacularly inaccurate. The Rugby Football Union could bail out the insolvent British Athletic Federation from its petty-cash box. Could England's football team sell out Wembley every Saturday for four consecutive weeks, with tickets only available to club members, not the general public? All four of England's autumn rugby internationals, three at Twickenham and another at Old Trafford, are sold out. The gate receipts alone from those four matches will bring in well over £8,000,000. Television money is pouring in from BBC, ITV and BSkyB to the four home rugby unions and to France. But these funds flow mainly into central coffers.

'The RFU is a massively expensive bureaucracy, and also sucks up funds for its huge development programmes. Whereas central cricket funds are largely distributed to the nineteen first-class counties, the

RFU assists thousands of smaller clubs as well as its own infrastructure. This means that the RFU's lifeboat for the major clubs is small. This season, the Allied Dunbar Premiership clubs receive only £500,000 each from the RFU, despite the fact that they provide England's international players. The club owners are still incensed by the low level of central funding.'

But the clubs themselves kept on spending. Harlequins still had money left over from their aborted Beckwith deal – and they promptly went out and signed up Zinzan Brooke for a reputed £400,000. Brooke was due to join the club early in 1998, soon after he had played his last game for the All Blacks. As wonderful a player as Zinny had been for years, it seemed a huge amount to pay for a retired international. There were also a few doubts. Would Brooke adjust easily to London life? And, more notably, how would he settle amid the tangle of politics which still dragged Quins down to a level some way from the All Blacks' exalted heights of organisation?

The Premiership's own wider injection of professionalism, however, had hardened the edge which the Lions needed to win in South Africa. Of the thirty-eight Lions, only six appeared outside the English league. The clubs had also made domestic rugby a far more colourful place – with the 1997–98 season becoming even more exotic with the arrival of the Fijian wonder Waisale Serevi at Leicester and the French captain, Philippe Saint-André, at Gloucester. Premiership weekends were not just about English, Welsh, Scottish and Irish voices – the array of accents stretched around the world, with French, Italian, American, Canadian, Argentinian, South African, Zimbabwean, Australian, New Zealand, Fijian, Tongan and Samoan inflections making themselves heard above the cultural whirlpool.

The benefits, at least for Woodward and Mitchell, were mixed. The good news was that emerging English internationals like Tony Diprose and Will Greenwood learned much under Pienaar and Dwyer, and by playing alongside Sella and Stransky. There were also gains to be made when promising props like Gloucester's Phil Vickery were put through the blender by wizened campaigners like Northampton's terminator from the Cape – Garry Pagel. The downside, however, was equally obvious.

A large portion of Premiership talent, by virtue of nationality, was simply not available for England selection. In November 1997, Richmond had a virtual team of fourteen 'non-English qualified' players. The trend was the same wherever you looked – as far as England was concerned, Harlequins had thirteen 'foreigners', Bristol twelve, Bath and Saracens eleven each, Newcastle ten and on and on. In defence of the spending spree, some argued that the best fifty or sixty English rugby players would emerge alongside the international galaxy. While local journeymen on the fringes of the Premiership would suffer, it would not be to the detriment of the England team. A strong Premiership meant a strong England.

The flaw in an otherwise plausible theory remained that club coaches, fearing the axe if results went against them, preferred to buy in experience and class for the key decision-making positions. The number 10 shirt was rarely one to be filled by callow English youth. On a Premiership weekend it was quite likely that the following fly-halves would star: Australia's Michael Lynagh (Saracens), South Africa's Joel Stransky (Leicester), France's Thierry Lacroix (Harlequins), New Zealand's Simon Mannix (Sale), Western Samoa's Earl Va'a (Richmond), Scotland's Gregor Townsend (Northampton) and Ireland's David Humphreys (London Irish). In contrast, with Newcastle's Rob Andrew already retired from international rugby, there were only four credible fly-halves who were eligible for England: Paul Grayson (Northampton), Mike Catt (Bath), Alex King (Wasps) and Mark Mapletoft (Gloucester).

If Catt was more properly considered for a place in the centre, where he always looked more incisive, the list was reduced to three. King and Mapletoft were untested at international level while Grayson was still weighed down by his reputation as a pedestrian and kicking stand-off. Moreover, recovering from injury, he still had to finally nail down his slot at Northampton ahead of Townsend – who had been Ian McGeechan's preferred choice for the Lions when both players were selected for the trip to South Africa. Townsend could play inside-centre and Grayson had turned out at full-back – but you could hardly expect McGeechan to base his eventual club selection around England's need for Grayson to play consistently at fly-half.

It was just one indicator that the clubs' agenda was not sufficiently broad to benefit English rugby in its entirety. The idea that, in New Zealand, John Hart might have to pick his first-fives from only a quarter of the teams in the NPC was too ludicrous even to contemplate. Although ACT's David Knox had spent three months in Durban, as a replacement for Natal when Henry Honiball was away on Springbok duty, the same principle applied in South Africa. In the southern hemisphere, the acme of rugby would always be found in those shirts belonging to the All Blacks, the Springboks and the Wallabies. Each of those country's best players were contracted to their national squad which, inevitably, had first call on their services. In contrast, the club owners in the Premiership implied that they owned England's best performers – on the basis that they were the only ones paying the players every month.

They knew that they could not block the autumn series against the southern hemisphere or the 1998 Five Nations. But there were brooding hints that the clubs would adopt a tougher stance at the end of the season when their exhausted players were due to go abroad again on international tours. The lines of battle were carved into a block of intransigence – with the RFU's Cliff Brittle and Fran Cotton scraping away at one end and the clubs at the other. It would be a war about power, money and ego.

The RFU's appointment of Clive Woodward as England coach had also been a protracted and embarrassing affair. His predecessor, the often curmudgeonly Jack Rowell, had every right to feel spiky about the way he was treated in his last months. By mid-'97, Rowell had not translated his success with Bath into international plaudits. But he still did not deserve that rugby-committee speciality – blustering prevarication – as the RFU decided whether he should continue while they touted the job to Auckland's Graham Henry and Northampton's Ian McGeechan. They failed to appoint either. Rowell resigned, while England wondered whom they might turn to next.

In the end they went for Woodward – and I wondered if they would also suffer from the Springboks' 'Carel du Plessis Syndrome'. Like du Plessis, Woodward had been a dashing three-quarter in his own playing days. His coaching experience, while not quite as limited as that of du Plessis, was less impressive. It certainly did not have the copious clout of Hart or even Mallett. Woodward was assisting Bath's own fledgling, Andy Robinson, when the offer finally rolled round. While he was clearly bright and enthusiastic, Woodward still had some way to go before he could claim real coaching gravitas. He spoke with panache and excitement about England's future but the suspicion remained that he would not readily receive the help he needed from either the RFU or the clubs. While he had a huge white mountain to climb, his next step always looked in danger of being swept away by an administrative and political avalanche.

But he made some astute decisions. It was an inspired move to co-opt Sale's Kiwi, John Mitchell, as his hardbitten mentor to the forwards. He also rectified Rowell's error, and named Lawrence Dallaglio as his captain – although he refused to confirm the permanence of that appointment. Gary Teichmann knew that he would take the Springboks through to the World Cup, as John Eales would for the Wallabies – and even the twenty-two-year-old Taine Randell knew that the All Black job would be his as soon as Sean Fitzpatrick finally stepped aside. Dallaglio was clearly in that class of player and, on the outside, it seemed odd that Woodward should refrain from making a similar endorsement of his own captain.

But his admiration had been vocal on 29 October when he met the media to announce his choice of Dallaglio. 'He is right up there in world terms,' Woodward confirmed. 'He would be in many people's World XV after being outstanding for England and for the Lions.'

Woodward was as bullish when asked to assess England's autumn schedule – which also marked his début as an international coach. 'The aim is to defeat the three visitors now and win the World Cup. By the time we finish this series of four Tests, we will have a very clear idea of who can and who cannot operate at this level . . .'

Woodward, in keeping with his own inexperience, had opted for youth when he made his first selection for England's clash with Australia on 15 November. Alex King and Will Green, Dallaglio's young team-mates at Wasps, were given crucial berths at fly-half and tighthead – while two twenty-year-old greenhorns from Bath, Matt Perry and Andy Long, came in at full-back and hooker. The fact that Perry played centre for Bath and that Long had only made six first-class appearances did not deter Woodward. It seemed an exceedingly brave decision to take on Australia with a front row whose hooker, only the season before, had been playing South-West Division II rugby for Bournemouth.

King had to withdraw through injury – and so Catt was switched from centre to fly-half. The more boyish forwards also did not last. Long was replaced after forty minutes, making way for the more strident Richard Cockerill. The young hooker became an abject figure as he was banished to the backwoods for the rest of the season. It had been the selectors' fault, rather than his own, that the English scrum had caved in so quickly. Green was also dropped for the next Test.

Although Catt did well before he was injured, and Perry looked to be a genuine discovery, England were woeful. The Australians were little better, failing to gel under an excellent new coach, Rod Macqueen, who had taken ACT to the Super 12 final earlier that year and subsequently replaced the maligned Greg Smith. On the evidence of the video-recorder and the damning press reports, it was hard to believe that these were the world's third and fourth best sides as they ground out a dreary 15–15 draw. Woodward and Dallaglio admitted to being 'shattered' and 'very disappointed'.

England improved the following week at a far noisier Old Trafford but still lost 25–8 to New Zealand – who restored both Josh Kronfeld and Jonah Lomu to the Test team after their convincing midweek performances against an 'Emerging England XV'. It had taken Josh exactly a week to make good that promise to regain his jersey. Andrew Blowers was back on the bench. The All Blacks were not overly stretched by England in Manchester, but neither did they sparkle as usual. Attention focused more on peripheral details – such as Cockerill's laddish reaction to the *Haka*. As Norm Hewitt led the All Black chant, Cockerill stood nose-to-nose with him before pushing him back slightly. Hart said later that Cockerill had insulted New Zealand's indigenous culture. He also deplored the punch Martin Johnson threw at Justin Marshall and was disdainful of the fact that England had indulged in a lap of honour despite losing by seventeen points. The English players defended their post-match jog-and-wave as being more a 'thank you' to the supportive Old Trafford crowd.

Johnson was banned for England's next match, against South Africa – which Hart expected to follow the trend of whippings for the boys from the North. 'Over the weekend,' he said on the Monday after the Manchester needling, 'South Africa made a major statement for southern-hemisphere rugby by scoring fifty points in France. Australia beat Scotland comfortably and we outscored England by three tries to one. The gap comes about because European rugby doesn't have the intensity of games in its competitions' structure. There is nothing that matches our Super 12, and players here are not being consistently exposed to top-class rugby. England have additional problems because I think the clubs have far too much power over players' contracts – and where will England's stars of the future come from when there are so many overseas internationals playing domestic rugby?'

Mallett, also in London, touched his cap in the Kiwi direction. 'I can't say to the guys, "Don't go and play in England",' he said in reference to the likes of Pienaar, Stransky, Pagel and, more worryingly for Springbok rugby, the lock Fritz van Heerden who had just interrupted his international career in preference for a large contract with Leicester. 'But rugby must not lose the feeling of what an honour it is to play for your country. That can't be quantified in terms of money. I could not imagine any New Zealander going to England rather than playing for the All Blacks. My job is to get that sort pride back in our rugby.'

While he had made more than a start in Paris, Mallett was determined to play down the significance of a record result. 'I don't think for a moment,' he stressed, 'that we're really forty-odd points better than the French. They caught us on a good day. We caught them on a bad day. I was a little surprised by the score but I always believed we had the potential to play the way we did.'

Mallett was also emphatic that, despite the eulogising of his bold approach, he was not willing to play the same way every week. 'You have to win! You advance so much quicker if you win, even if you've played badly. I'm not going to commit myself to just one style. Rugby is too practical a game for that. You have to consider your opponents, the game, the pitch, the weather – all those variables.'

The Springboks had scored twenty-one tries in three Tests under Mallett; but he went for the most basic truth rather than settling on that glistening statistic. 'I'll take penalties to win a Test if that's what it takes. The guys in this team are very bright and they have great leadership qualities. You can utilise this instead of trying to stifle it. I've always tried to handle players the way I would have liked to be handled myself. I was an English player in an Afrikaans environment where fear was almost more important than respect. We've changed that . . .'

Mallett's favourite leader, Gary Teichmann, echoed his coach when we spoke again in London. 'It was just fantastic,' he murmured when remembering Paris, 'an occasion which we'll never forget. Just the fact that we played the last Test at the Parc was special, but the way we performed made it even more memorable. It was the best performance from any Springbok side I've ever been involved in because, even in terms of taking all the opportunities that came our way, we never let up. It felt great to play so well . . .'

His thoughts had already switched to Twickenham. 'Hopefully, against England, we'll perform the way we should. I think we're in for a very competitive match because South Africa and England are in the same boat. We're both under new coaches. We're both desperate to win, and with some style too. Having faced the Lions, we know that England will ask us some hard questions. Like the Lions, they're extremely tough to break down . . .'

It did take a long time. After quarter of an hour, England led 11–0, and they held that lead until the fortieth minute. Two Catt penalties, which were surpassed by his general kicking for the corners and his fluid running, had been followed by a Nick Greenstock interception and try. The Springboks were ragged for the rest of the half, until just before the whistle when they pulled out a Black trick and scored a critical try.

After Catt had crashed into Honiball's knee – which left him concussed and out of the match – Adrian Garvey crashed through the hapless embrace of a trio of English huggers to score a converted try. At 11–7, without Catt, England were helpless, and pointless, under the Springbok crush. Garvey, Dalton and du Randt rumbled across Twickenham like twenty-first-century tanks while the back row of Teichmann, Venter and Andrew Aitken scorched across the turf in an epic encounter with Dallaglio, Back and Hill. Andrews and Otto were dominant in the line-out and the Springboks were as daring as they were exquisite at the back.

Honiball excited me with huge looping passes across the face of his own try-line while Small and Rossouw shifted powerfully down the flanks. Snyman and Andrews also scored startlingly brilliant tries. Snyman's solo burst of genius came first, after fifty-six minutes. On the halfway line he hesitated before he went with his instinct and broke through the diving English midfield. He was away from the flagging flankers in a fluttery blink of a lash. With the space to dance he dazzled past Perry. It was a try as sweetly lethal as Frank Bunce's Ellis Park slasher had been five months before.

Four minutes later he started a breathtaking eight-man move, described by Stephen Jones as 'an absolute masterpiece of continuity', which ended with Andrews crashing over in the corner. 29–11 was the second record-breaking score on the smash for the green mallet – with England conceding more points than ever before in a home Test.

Afterwards, Woodward insisted, 'I still believe we can win the World Cup in 1999.' But he also admitted his own doubts about English rugby: 'Catt's injury dealt us a heavy blow, not least because he had been playing brilliantly. The question now is where do we go from here? Tell me where the English-qualified stand-offs are. Mike is out for three weeks, Alex King is still unfit, Grayson was earmarked for the midweek England A game at Leicester, but we're going to have to rethink the whole issue now. I've been talking about empty cupboards for weeks but now we're looking at the empty shelves.'

For Woodward, it was 'a nightmare scenario. The young English guys haven't come through because they can't get a game [in the Premiership]. We're going to have to front this one somehow or other because, if not, I'll be sitting here in two years' time still whingeing. I'm determined to put it right but there's going to be pain along the way. It's not rocket science to work it out. We need more top-class competition for English players. The European Cup is brilliant but the English teams in it are not English. We wouldn't need another tier of competition if they were. As it is, we do.

'We need to field four teams of fifteen English guys against the best in France, Ireland and the like and then play off against the best of the southern hemisphere. I don't care what you call the teams – regions, divisions, whatever – as long as English guys get exposure. We have a pool of as many talented players as South Africa. They're just not being allowed to come through.

'I was quoted as saying the other day that English rugby was laughable. It's not. The system is. And I used the term to describe the way people like John Hart see it. You explain it to him and he just shakes his head and laughs. I'm not whingeing. I'm just trying to state the facts. It's a really bad situation.'

The whole vexed question of regionalising English competition in the European Cup was at the heart of the RFU's bitter dissent with the clubs. At rugby headquarters, Fran Cotton was pushing the concept hard while, elsewhere, the owners were emphatically resistant. If Wasps, Saracens and Richmond were forced to combine into an exclusively English London XV, all the plans and signed cheques of Wright, Wray and Levett would bounce into oblivion. Both sides were pitching for change. The chairmen wanted their clubs to grow ever stronger and the Premiership more concentrated. In contrast, Woodward and particularly Cotton and Brittle wanted a structure which pooled the best players – irrespective of their club affiliations – into regional teams along the model of New Zealand rugby in the Super 12.

Nick Mallett was more conscious that the English, whether turning out for a club, a region or their country, had to change the way they played. 'They need pace, power and dynamic thrust. You only need to compare the two sets of props. If you look at Adrian Garvey and Os du Randt, ask yourself how many times the pair of them laid their hands on the ball and then compare their contribution with that made by the English props. I think that the English were forced to give so much of themselves just to hold Os and Adrian in the scrums that, when it came to other areas of the game, they were twenty metres off the pace. It was a key advantage for us. The same thing applies through much of the English team. After they've won third- or fourth-phase possession, they want to put the ball in the air rather than try and break down their opponents through any other means. To create opportunities you have got to take risks. The tries we scored were all created from risks.'

Mallett also warned the British press against excessive Kiwi-fever. 'We have been unquestionably motivated,' he said, 'by you scarcely mentioning our existence these past couple of weeks, realising your love affair with the All Blacks, calling them the "dream team" and the "best-ever team" and all that. But examine closely the respective form in each of our last two matches. It's not the All Blacks who have broken records in Paris and London, is it? It's about time you guys started looking in our direction again.'

That afternoon, across town, at Wembley, the All Blacks had squashed the homeless Welsh 42–7 – with Christian Cullen scoring three tries to raise his own record to twenty-one in the same number of Tests. Sean Fitzpatrick also made a cameo appearance near the end, to rack up his ninety-second cap. But the British media were understandably agog at the prospect of an All Black-Springbok clash. Frank Keating, in *The Guardian*, wished it could take place in London the following Saturday: 'What a resounding final could have been played had someone had the wit to arrange it. Nor would any wise man, on the evidence of the past ten days, have presumed a confident bet on the souped-up and written-up All Blacks beating these renascent and sparklingly athletic South Africans.' Mick Cleary, in *The Daily Telegraph*, agreed: 'What a pity the two countries are not playing off next weekend. Now that would be a contest.'

Alison and I went out partying that night in London with James Small, his girlfriend, Christina, and another friend from Johannesburg. The day before, James had also noted wryly that I spent a lot of time writing about the majesty of the All Blacks. He just laughed when I mentioned it again a few hours after we had swapped old Twickers for Soho. 'Hey, let's forget the rugby for a while,' he said.

It was one of those nights. At one point, in the middle of a stream of head-opening jugs of drink in a heaving Riki Tiks, we had already decided, as one does in such blissfully blurring moments, that the five of us, and all our other friends, were really going to open up our cultural empire which would allow us to live and work simultaneously in London, Paris, Amsterdam, New York, Las Vegas, Sydney, Tokyo, Cape

Town and even old gun-toting Johannesburg. We felt that wild. We had another drink. We felt that cool. My hiccups started about then. In the end, James even took us dancing, swanning us through the line of clubbers who parted at the first sight of the Hanover Grand's massive bouncer's nod of recognition: 'James Small!' He'd remembered him from the year before. But we didn't last too much longer. My hangover, however, did.

A week later, on the last Saturday of the Springbok season, 6 December, in Edinburgh, a spring-heeled and remarkably fresh Small entered the individual record books again. He responded to his green-shirted friends' desire for him to get his name down in history with two of South Africa's ten tries in a whopping 68–10 demolition of Scotland. In his forty-sixth international, Small scored his nineteenth and twentieth tries – which took him one clear of Danie Gerber.

The Springboks had dazzled with thirty-five tries in five European internationals – and also dished out their third consecutive record drubbing. Scotland's defeat was their worst ever – far worse even than the famous 44–0 loss to South Africa at Murrayfield in 1951. 'We were absolutely outstanding in the second half,' Mallett enthused after the Springboks had added fifty-four points to their half-time lead of 14–3. Percy Montgomery was the undoubted star, matching Small's duo with two of his own, eight conversions and as many scything runs. For Rob Wainwright it was 'the finest display I've ever seen by a full-back. He's a devastating attacking force . . .'

The Scotland coach, Rob Dixon, concurred sadly. 'South Africa gave a tremendous example of modern rugby. We know we have a problem. We have a small playing base and these are the best players we have. It's obvious we are falling further behind the southern-hemisphere teams.'

While Mallett admitted that 'to break three records in five Tests has exceeded all our expectations, we've yet to play the other top teams, New Zealand and Australia. We'll not know where we really stand until we play them in next year's Tri-Nations.'

But that was another merciful seven months away. That was next season; and after another strange and tumultuous year, James Small was smiling again. He kept on coming back, more than any other Springbok before him. But, with Christmas less than three weeks away and a celebratory ski trip in Austria for him and his Western Province team-mates, it was at last time for a small break from rugby.

If it was also the end of the year for the All Blacks, Lawrence Dallaglio knew that his own season was not even halfway through. And, for the fourth consecutive Saturday, he had to drive his huge frame through another southern storm. The oval omens were not twinkling for either an inspirational twenty-five-year-old or his flattened team.

New Zealand were still firing. While recovering from our Small night out, I had watched a video of the All Blacks at Wembley. There were some gorgeous passages of play. Cullen was blistering, Randell majestic, Kronfeld ravenous and Zinzan Brooke as inventive as ever – but not even they could steal the plaudits from Ian Jones and Robin Brooke who swooped in the line-out and across the lush turf with lofty grace and dash. Fitzy's twenty-five minutes, meanwhile, illuminated the fact that Taine Randell had been the player of the tour. A change of the Black guard was ready – as soon as Fitzpatrick made the painful decision.

It had also been Zinzan's second-last match. He did everything which made us love him. He cut and clipped beautifully across the grassy paddock, a champion shearer to the end, in between flipping the ball backwards through his legs to set up Marshall's try and then, in the last movement of the game, dropping a trademark thirty-five-metre goal. Afterwards, sticking to vintage Kiwi, Zinny reacted in bemusement to the media's acclaim for his younger brother's delightful dummy and white bow of a pass which allowed Cullen to score his second try. Zinzan said, 'He caught the ball and then passed it – that's what rugby players do. What are you getting excited about?'

It was the kind of stuff which John Hart loved. He had also not forgotten Martin Johnson's Manchester punch, Cockerill and the *Haka* or that strange lap of English celebration after defeat. 'It's going to be a big game against England A on Tuesday,' he said grimly, 'and a huge match against England at Twickenham on Saturday. I can already feel us getting up for it now. We really want to win – and win well.'

Twickenham, Saturday, 6 December 1997
It was less than ten months since I had first met him in London and, then, it would have seemed unbelievable to hear Sean Fitzpatrick say, half an hour before kick-off, 'I'm trying to be philosophical, but I'd love to be out there.' After his brief excursion at Wembley, Fitzpatrick was back in the stands. His season was over. He was gearing himself up to try again in 1998; but he knew that his career might already be over. There

was also sadness that, whatever happened, he would never again play with Zinny.

Zinzan Brooke, playing his hundredth game for the All Blacks, and his fifty-eighth Test, walked out slowly in front of the rest of his team. Frank Bunce in his fiftieth and last-ever international as well, followed him. The two black shirts soaked up the adulation stoically, waiting for the younger thirteen to run out and join them. They came out at a trot – Marshall, Wilson, Cullen and Kronfeld with his typical black-capped, hunch-shouldered amble onto the field. Randell was just ahead of him, moving with quiet assurance. There were many more Black days ahead, for all of them, even without Fitzpatrick, Brooke and Bunce.

'Those journos keep asking me about it,' Zinny had said, 'wanting to get me to cry on television or something. But I'm not going to do it. The All Blacks are far bigger than any man.'

The anthems were sung. And then another, 'Swing Low, Sweet Chariot', was reached for yet again as the two teams stood twenty metres apart during the *Haka*. I wanted to hear the cries of the All Blacks instead. But Cockerill smirked – still a chubby Jack-the-Lad – as if he had decided to let them get away with it. I thought of Fitzpatrick's earlier words: 'They played very well at Old Trafford – we played pretty badly but still won by seventeen points. We'll be trying to eradicate those mistakes we made.' Richard Cockerill, I suspected, would have cause to regret his smarmy fighter's smile.

But England came out fast. Within less than a minute, Bracken ran a penalty a second after it had been awarded. The Black tackles finally arrived and, in the mêlée, England were awarded another penalty. As if in homage to Nick Mallett, they aimed for the touchline near the corner.

It was all white. They kept it flowing. Grayson, amazingly, was standing as flat as a plain, catching Bracken's speedy passes and firing them out fast and wide. Meanwhile, they were still running a chain. Healey to Bracken to Hill and back to Bracken and then out to Grayson and onto Greenwood. Zinzan hit him hard with a black clatter. But Back and Healey carried it forward until, at last, after two minutes, the move ended. Penalty to New Zealand, and a chance for a Black hand on the ball. Marshall, matching Bracken for pace, tapped and passed to Mehrtens whose kick only reached Rees on the right of the English half. The winger from Sale showed the ball to Lomu, as if it were on offer, while he ran at him. And then, *à la* Goldie, he chipped and collected a perfect bounce. Rees was away, at a tempo which not even Zinzan could stop. Bunce and Kronfeld veered across in cover but they were too late.

After four minutes of English pressure, a try for Rees in the corner.

5–0 to England became 10–0 after eleven minutes when Healey and Greenwood, showing the understanding of Leicester flatmates, combined down the left flank. Greenwood weaved through the Black maze until Marshall finally pulled him down, only for Hill to follow up and dive over. Mehrtens' penalty in the fourteenth minute mattered even less when, two minutes later, de Glanville tackled Bunce, and Dallaglio hacked it ahead. With another Zola-like tap of the boot, the ball was over the line with the England captain falling on top of it. I couldn't believe it. Dallaglio threw a roundhouse punch into the hazy air as he ran away from the try-line. Grayson converted. England 17, New Zealand 3.

They kept up their point-a-minute rate with another Grayson penalty after twenty minutes. At 20–3 the All Blacks were reeling. They were making mistake after mistake as if they had lost themselves in the weary depths of one match too many. But they had been down three times before that arduous season – at Ellis Park, Eden Park and Lansdowne Road. Each time they had come back convincingly. But, in London, they were shattered. Mehrtens started the slow climb back with two penalties. But, even at 20–9, the All Blacks looked fitful.

The New Zealanders came out on the back of a rollicking. Four minutes in and Wilson and Zinzan swarmed at the line. Brooke slid it back to Mehrtens who scored under the white sticks. 23–16 became 23–19 after another easy penalty. New Zealand were at last spreading the ball wide, out to Wilson and Lomu on the wing. But they were also more predictable than usual. Cullen kept trying those buttery and rolling runs when a pass would have made a more slippery change.

But, after an hour, they finally jangled a lead from a Lomu run. When Jonah was yanked back, Bunce passed to Mehrtens who ran in behind his own up-and-under. The ball boomeranged out of the leaping arms of Mehrtens and Perry and into the path of 'The Bull' – Mark Allen. The bald prop put his skull down and charged at the line. The ball came back to Marshall who, fifteen metres out, gave it to Little who accelerated past four white shirts for a simple score. England 23, New Zealand 26.

We sat back, imagining it was all over. But England, if a little more ragged, were still courageous. Hill, Greenwood, Dallaglio and Perry all aimed for the line. The Black wall held until, with ten minutes left on the clock, they were penalised. Dallaglio went for the points. Grayson kicked the penalty. It was a draw. 26–26.

The black shirts darkened a shade at the whistle. They looked dejected. They had had enough rugby for the year. The white shirts were muddied – but the English were also restrained after an extraordinary Twickenham tie. Most of the men seemed bedraggled and a little unsteady. It was enough for both teams to reach for each other's hands.

Lawrence Dallaglio, his head wrapped in a bandage, walked slowly towards a blank-faced Zinzan Brooke with an outstretched arm. He knew what the moment meant, not only to New Zealand but to world rugby. Zinzan took Dallaglio's hand. The English captain reached round to embrace him. Zinzan, the great Zinny, answered him with a silent wrap round of his own brawny arms. They held each other for a second and then, with a few words from Dallaglio and a nod from Brooke, they broke.

For the last time, Zinzan Brooke turned and headed for the black tunnel.

Chapter 9
From Sudbury to Ballymena

On a late Friday afternoon in crumbling old Sudbury, in the first month of a new year, as the winter sun faded across a muddied training field, it seemed the right time to ask Lawrence Dallaglio the question. Mike Tyson provided the link. I was not surprised. I knew why Dallaglio was interested in fighters. They occupied terrain even more physically brutal and politically tangled than his own.

In his oval domain he was depicted more simply as a lantern-jawed super-hero who had, the month before, miraculously inspired his country to brief parity with the All Blacks. Beyond rugby, Dallaglio was also courted by a snaking queue of marketing moguls tantalised by the commercial appeal of his chiselled face and gregarious personality. Yet all that was less stimulating than a man who wanted to think first about boxing and boxers.

So we moved, inevitably, onto the rusted life of 'Iron Mike' and reflected a little on Tyson's sour comment, in 1991, that he felt like the oldest twenty-five-year-old on the planet.

'But how old do *you* feel?' I wondered, thinking that Lawrence Dallaglio was the most mature twenty-five-year-old I had met anywhere, stretching way beyond Sudbury. I remembered all that had happened to him; and the massive responsibilities bearing down on him, both professionally and privately. He was a father and a captain, England's best rugby player and a national icon in waiting, a calm but relentless man.

I was twelve years older than Dallaglio, but it seemed as if I was closer to a lost and shiftless youth. Yet he was not staid or pedantic – and his liking for a good drink and a long night-out was firmly established. Rather, it was his clarity of purpose, framed by an unflinching gaze, which made him appear remarkable.

Dallaglio burst into laughter, suddenly proving that he really was born in 1972. 'Hey,' he exclaimed, 'I feel twenty-five!'

'Like an ordinary twenty-five-year-old?' I persisted.

'Yeah, course I do!', he said, before giving due consideration to his role as the English game's most credible saviour and complex personality. 'But maybe I had some kind of premonition when I was younger. I

remember always looking towards the kids who were two or three y
older than me. I veered naturally towards them. And, ultimately,
build a bank of experience from everyone and everything that you are
exposed to – whether that involves pain or joy. You draw on the past to
help make decisions in the present . . .'

Dallaglio sometimes spoke in great big chunks of meditative speech.
It became obvious again that he was different to the usual star who
scorched across the tabloids' back pages. His effect on other rugby men
had been equally evident an hour earlier when he ran the Wasps' training
session with cool authority. Then, he had settled on more blunt words as
he drilled his squad. Even the older players were content for Dallaglio to
work them with a mix of instruction and banter. He seemed as
comfortable showing the backs the angles they should run as he was
slapping the hefty rump of Simon Shaw with a 'C'mon, mate!' gee-up.

If his name sounded Italian, his voice echoed with London. He was
born in Shepherd's Bush to an Italian father and a mother who was half-
Irish but almost definitively English. 'I've always loved London,' he
stressed. 'There are so many colours around you, so many cultures. You
develop differently if you grow up in London. You're maybe a little
sharper, a little tougher – just because you have to be. It takes time to
adjust to if you come in from the outside, because it's so vast. But it's a
fantastic city.'

After almost fourteen years, I shared that love of London. There was
even a soiled kind of beauty in Sudbury as its wan sunlight dipped over
the bumpy field and bounced off the smeary glass of the clubhouse
window. Wasps only trained in Sudbury now. From the start of the
season they had shifted back to Dallaglio's original patch, or 'manor' in
my best Mockney, for home matches. When Chris Wright bought the
club in 1997 he decided that they should share the Loftus Road football
ground in Shepherd's Bush with his other sporting acquisition, Queen's
Park Rangers.

'I always had this very strong London identity,' Dallaglio continued.
'West London if you want to be even more specific. Born in Shepherd's
Bush, always a Chelsea supporter, now living in Ladbroke Grove, playing
again in W12 . . .'

'But with an Italian name and an Italian father,' I said.

'Yeah! Y'know, I've always sounded and looked like I'm from London.
But I'm proud that we've also got this other side to our family – our
Italian side. It made life as a kid a bit more special. Me and my sister
were given a typically Italian start in that way – with a very loving and

family-orientated background. I can remember junior matches when my mum and dad would be the only ones watching on the touchline. But I always had loads of friends who knew nothing about rugby. I've always liked that – 'cos at home we were relaxed and amiable, in that very Italian way. All my friends would come round and eat about fifteen plates of food each while we sat around the table together.'

'What did your dad do?' I wondered, imagining ritual pictures of Papa Vincenzo Dallaglio smiling benignly at the head of a long Italian family table covered by a spaghetti-sauce-splattered gingham tablecloth, with photographs of Inter Milan and the Pope hanging on the wall behind him.

As if he could spot the red, white and green clichés spooling through my head, Dallaglio chuckled throatily. 'Surprisingly enough, being an Italian,' he paused dramatically, 'my dad was in the catering business. But as we grew older he expanded into lecturing about the food and beverage business instead, so that he could spend more time with us. My parents could see where we were going. For my sister it was dancing while for me, at first, it was football. I used to have this dream of becoming a professional footballer. I started out at left-wing and then, as I got bigger, they moved me to centre-half.'

'Shepherd's Bush's answer to Tony Adams?'

'Yeah, something like that. But when I was thirteen, because I'm Catholic, I went to Ampleforth College which is a Catholic boarding-school near York. It's one of the great English rugby schools. It was very strange for me at first because I had spent all my life in London – and suddenly I'm at this school in a beautiful but almost desolate part of Yorkshire. And wherever I looked I saw rugby field after rugby field. At first I was a wing. But, y'know, this being English rugby, I didn't get much sight of the ball! So I moved to centre and then to forward. To be honest, because of the style of rugby, I didn't rate the game much until I got to number 8. And then I really took to it.'

By the time he was playing first-team rugby, Dallaglio showed signs of the physical power and footballing skills which would eventually allow him to dominate opponents in a way few other English players could match. But his rise with Wasps and England was still years away when, in 1989, while he was still sixteen, tragedy came to the Dallaglio family – and many others.

His older sister, Francesca, was killed in the *Marchioness* disaster. The boat had been hired for a summertime evening party along the river. It was packed with a large group of young Londoners who were emerging dancers, actors and models. They were not just drifting down the

Thames. They all felt as if their lives were headed for somewhere meaningful. But they went into death instead. The *Marchioness* was hit by another boat. It sank before Francesca and the others could be saved from drowning. The sense of loss and of waste was overwhelming.

A few years later, Lawrence Dallaglio took to living on a house-boat on the same river where the *Marchioness* had sailed on the night Francesca died. He found a home on the water, near Twickenham, which made him feel closer to his sister than he did to rugby. Dallaglio was able to talk about that time to me, but he had no need to spell out how it had marked him forever.

I also felt the emptiness of the questions I might have kept on asking. Even if I had known him better I don't think I would have wanted to say, especially in a rugby clubhouse, 'How did you feel then?' or 'How do you feel now?' I could guess the answers. But there was a sentimental danger in reducing Francesca's death to being just a motivational adjunct to his success as a rugby player. If it had made him a deeper and more serious man, the impact it had on him at the back of a scrum seemed obscure. In the coarse terms of rugby, the only tangible link to his sister's dying was Dallaglio's suggestion that his disappointments on the field remained within their smaller sporting context.

That night, as we drank an appropriate bottle of Italian red at our own table, I told Alison how much Dallaglio had impressed me. I talked and talked, for it had been almost a year since I had been similarly struck by Sean Fitzpatrick. Even though he was nine years younger than Fitzy, Dallaglio had that rare presence which allowed him to match his All Black counterpart. Dallaglio could also stamp his personality on anything he did – whether it was playing rugby with an abrasive edge or holding court in interviews. Dallaglio, again like Fitzpatrick, liked to be in charge. And he did not need to use force to get his way. I had already watched a few English press conferences where Dallaglio waxed politely, without giving away any snippet of consequence. It was another Fitzpatrick art.

While it probably gnawed at some that he had tangled his Catholic roots by merely living with his baby's mother, all that mattered to Dallaglio was that he loved his girlfriend, Alice, and their ten-month-old daughter, Ella Francesca. Dallaglio's sole concern, that Alice would be subjected to tabloid scrutiny because of his shock-horror status as an 'unmarried father' and England rugby captain, had already disappeared. He was not about to be dictated to by anyone – whether around a ruck or the cot.

After Will Carling and his brand of surly men, Dallaglio provided the most refreshing possible change at the head of English rugby. It was impossible, especially that week, to avoid comparisons with Carling – England's first professional captain. Carling was about to sever his £125,000-a-year contract with Harlequins. His retirement would soon follow. I had never met Carling; and so my preference for Dallaglio had more than a touch of partiality. But Carling seemed to personify many of the negative facets which his southern-hemisphere rivals still used to castigate English rugby. To the outsider, Carling could appear cold and arrogant with a tedious bias towards a kicking game. He was also big on vacuous bubbles of corporate double-talk. It seemed as if Carling became more interested in selling his 'inspirational winning strategies' to businessmen than in improving the turgid quality of English rugby. Carling, however, had done much to break the mould of amateurism. His 'fifty-seven old farts' jibe at the blazered RFU officials still resounded through the chaos of the English game.

Much of the media and most city boys thrived on the idea that Carling represented a late-'80s boom in English rugby. But I had never believed in Carling's England. I was more excited by the fact that England were captained instead by a big Shepherd's Bush geezer of a charmer whose full name was Lawrence Bruno Nero Dallaglio.

But rugby, too, had hurt Dallaglio. He'd been excluded from the 1995 World Cup squad and, two years later, he had also been wounded by Phil de Glanville's appointment as Carling's successor. Dallaglio had virtually been assured that he had the job. But, if anything, those small moments of failure had intensified his determination.

'I've always known, from an early age, that this is what I would do,' he stressed. 'Nothing would stop me. So "doubt" has never been a word to cross my mind. I've always had this really strong self-belief. And, now, rugby is increasingly about mental strength. I think this England team can find it too. Against New Zealand we took a huge step forward. We matched the All Blacks and, for large parts of the game, we simply outplayed them. They came to Twickenham with this massive aura around them. You could almost feel it – it was as if they believed they were unbeatable. It's something they've built up over the years and it's quite hard to shake. But, after fifteen minutes, I remember thinking, "God, they really are feeling vulnerable now!" You could see it in their faces. We'd rocked them . . .'

I could still picture that startling opening quarter when England carved open their 20–3 lead. It had made me understand anew that

Dallaglio was as ferocious as he was gifted, a roaring leader who had the ability to lift England – not only in the gushy old Five Nations but in the more harsh black, green and gold realms of southern-hemisphere rugby.

'I think it's no coincidence,' Dallaglio suggested, 'that the Australians improved so much in the late-'80s when they popped across the Tasman and played the All Blacks two or three times a season. I really believe that, if we get the chance to meet that quality of opposition on a regular basis, we can eventually conquer the world. But we've got a hellavu lot to do to get there, because there's a quantum leap from being there or thereabouts to actually being the very best . . .'

Consistency of performance was still the main difference between New Zealand and England. If the All Blacks had slumped a little at the very end of their season, they had played magnificently throughout the last two years. England, in contrast, had been execrable, ordinary and then briefly exhilarating in the space of a month.

'Well, we were together for four weeks and, in a sense, it was like a tour. It took us time to get over the message to all the players that we had to change our way of playing. We had to learn that, as John Mitchell told us, to beat the All Blacks you have to go out there and score thirty-five points. You have to score tries. We were still stuck in the old mind-set when we started out and that's why the Australian match was such a disappointment. But by the end of that round of internationals, we'd finally started to gel and the reason we did so well against New Zealand is that we didn't play the way they expected. They thought we'd kick the ball all over the field in the typical English way – but we ran the ball, we used our heads, we found space, we scored tries. You have to be direct in rugby and you need that grinding physicality which English packs relied on throughout the '80s. But, most of all, you need to be clever and flexible when you play the All Blacks or the Springboks. You have to find variety and you have to be able to retain possession and use the ball with both guile and pace. In that 26–26 draw I think we showed both for long stretches of the game. We should have won but we couldn't sustain the quality. Perhaps it was a good thing in the end – if we'd won, an awful lot of English people would have been walking around under a cloud of illusion.'

Dallaglio also distanced himself from the Carling years. 'For me, the negative rugby which England used for so long was never inextricably linked to long-term success. I always thought we'd be found out at the highest level. It happened in 1995 when, in the World Cup, the All Blacks came out against England and thought, "Right, we're going to do some things they'll never expect . . ." They blew us away in the first fifteen minutes. We've got to be able to do that – and more than once.

'I'm not saying the All Black way or the Springbok way should be the English way. We haven't got the wonderful ball-handling skills of the New Zealand front five because the build of their players tends to be different to ours. With guys like Ian Jones they have these lanky, athletic players. You can't expect a Martin Johnson to suddenly emulate Ian Jones. They're too different. The same thing applies to the Springbok forwards. They tend to be bigger, heavier and stronger than the All Blacks. I think that in England we have a mixture of the two styles. We have some very physical and aggressive forwards and, personally, I think they have the ideal frame for modern forward play. We just need to be more ruthless. We have to believe we can become the best rugby team in the world. It's not going to happen this year – but we've got to believe that it will happen in 1999.'

'But,' I countered, 'will the structure of the game in England allow that? The All Blacks this season will play seven Tests and their stars will run out in only twenty-five or thirty matches . . .'

'Yeah, you're right,' Dallaglio sighed. 'Last season Martin Johnson played fifty-five matches. We can't go on like this much longer. Something's got to give . . .'

The strain was already starting to show. It seemed obvious that Dallaglio thrilled more to playing for England against the All Blacks before 75,000 people rather than turning out, as he would that Sunday, against Gloucester before a measly 4,000.

'It's a bit of a roller-coaster,' he agreed. 'Mentally, it's very hard to keep up for every single match. It takes its toll. But that's our fault. The New Zealanders and the Springboks think we're completely crazy. Our players have to give their all game after game, whether they're playing for their country or their club.'

Until the last few days of the old year, Dallaglio had been banging away without a single win for nine straight matches. In five club games and four internationals, his record between October and December 1997 was 'downright embarrassing. It was played nine, lost seven and drawn two. When you consider that Wasps are the English league champions, it's very hard to take. It was horrible. I hate losing. Whenever it happens it's like I'm being tormented. The feeling will only go away when the next win comes. But, whew, it was a long time coming.'

Alison and I, more out of duty than pure rugby fever, had seen the end of that Wasps' drought. On the second-last night of the year, we trudged to Loftus Road where not even the sponsors' free glasses of Drambuie could raise the temperature of a mundane club encounter. Wasps beat Richmond 22–18 with a very late Paul Sampson try which Dallaglio had set up with another crunching tackle. It was only Wasps' second home match of the Premiership; and yet it was often more tempting for us to follow the progress of a small but brave caterpillar as it crawled through the white hair of an oblivious old boy huddled in front of us. I guess we should have told him but the caterpillar was doing no harm and its curvy manoeuvres sometimes seemed more riveting than the flat rugby. It was one of those games. You had to look hard for anything to justify our freezing in a barren open-side stand when we could have been in a warm little pub up the road in Notting Hill.

Dallaglio growled. 'Yeah, it wasn't a whole lot of fun to play in either – but we were ready to take any win! Now we've got to keep it going and beat Gloucester this Sunday. Otherwise, we'll be back under that terrible pressure again. But you learn more from life, and about yourself, when things are difficult. I can take some positives from all that's happened over the past eight or nine weeks. I've stored it in the experience bank. I'll be even stronger for coming through this . . .'

'It seems a very English characteristic to turn adversity into a positive,' I said, 'and yet you seem so much more cosmopolitan in your personal life.'

'I don't think there's such a difference between me as a rugby player and as a private person. You can tell a lot about me just by the way I play. I've never really bought into that idea that the "bulldog" spirit is enough. But the English – whether it's in rugby or football or cricket – tend to do their best when they've been totally written off. I want us to be motivated by other reasons. I want us to be more sophisticated and smarter in the way we prepare ourselves for matches. And it goes back to what we were saying earlier about London and my own background. I think it's an advantage that I can draw on the best of two cultures. I think it's an advantage that my dad's the sort of guy who can speak five languages. I think it's great that we were never brought up in a hundred per cent roast beef way . . .'

Unlike the rest of the Twickers hierarchy and spectating set, Dallaglio lived in a ceaselessly modern and culturally varied world. He embraced change rather than convention. It was one of the primary reasons which instilled real hope into the otherwise hollow state of English rugby.

'But Lawrence, apart from being a new dad and being the best rugby player in supposedly the world's next best rugby team, what else do you like to do?'

'Well, I love football and Chelsea and a whole lot else but, y'know,' Captain Marvel spread his huge mitts helplessly, 'it's not like I've got a lot of spare time on my hands . . .'

Inevitably for a man so focused on his profession, Dallaglio admitted that he'd found *Living with Lions* in his own Xmas stocking from Santa.

'Have you watched it yet?' I asked.

'Yeah, a bit of it . . .' he mumbled evasively, 'but, luckily, I'm not on it much!'

'Yeah,' I agreed, 'it's mostly Keith Wood . . .'

'Right,' Dallaglio laughed, 'Woodie saying "fuck!" in a hundred different ways!'

'Sounds like you might've preferred a video on Chelsea,' I suggested.

'Absolutely!'

At twenty-five, Dallaglio had already sorted out his priorities and his responsibilities. He might moan every time Wasps or Chelsea lost, but then he'd move on. He'd get back on track, saying, as he did when we parted in a darkening Sudbury, 'I just need to win another match this weekend . . . and then another next week and then another . . .'

Soon after I'd met Lawrence Dallaglio, I travelled again to Ballymena – a small Protestant town in Northern Ireland which clung staunchly to its religious and political conservatism. While Dallaglio spoke of 'conquering the world', Ballymena's vision was more parochial. If Dallaglio personified a newly professional sporting business in England, so Ballymena's rugby club represented the old amateur game in Ulster.

Ballymena had never been easily stirred by the lure of change. Thirty miles north of Belfast, with every mile marking another year of trouble in Ulster, the town was bound tightly to tradition. Rigid loyalties had begun to shift elsewhere in Northern Ireland, with uncertainty looming at every turn, but life in Ballymena continued slowly and steadily. The suburban streets were clean and pretty, lined by rows of rolling green gardens and large white houses. It was a comfortable and friendly town – even though I could not forget that its Loyalist leader and honourable member of parliament, the Reverend Ian Paisley, preferred to depict himself as a furious model of intransigence.

Paisley wagged his stubby finger, shook his massive head and barked out the word 'No!' as often as possible. He was a big man who also liked to wear a bowler hat and an orange sash while shouting out quotes of biblical retribution. He and his followers were similarly taken with marching and waving the flag and promising that they would never surrender to the enemy. It was all so reminiscent of those past Afrikaans leaders that I reeled whenever I saw Paisley and the Orangemen. I was almost sick with the dizzy sense of recognition.

Whenever I was in Ulster, I saw the analogies with apartheid deepen. You could smell the prejudice and the fear, you could see the barbed wire and balaclavas, you could feel the eyes of the soldiers and of blank-faced violent men shifting up and down empty roads. When I went to east Belfast one night, to the Protestant area, the first taxi-driver said he couldn't take me all the way. He was from the other side. And when I visited a friend on that side of the city, to the west, he, a Catholic and a Republican, couldn't believe that I had based myself in Ballymena for a week.

'Ballymena,' he sneered, 'thinks it's the middle-class, moneyed intelligentsia of the Unionist movement. It's even worse than east Belfast. Ballymena is full of shite . . .'

But I stayed on in Ballymena and, even if I mocked Ian Paisley, I did care about a number of people who lived in the town. Perhaps because I was such an outsider – and maybe more because I had lived in whitest South Africa – I could suspend judgement. And I found that, just as in Pretoria and Bloemfontein, there were good and decent and interesting people in Ballymena. I was welcomed at their rugby club in a way that moved me, such was the attention I found at every turn. Ballymena soon became the only club side I really supported anywhere in the world.

Initially, I had chosen Ballymena as a route back into my South African past – for Willie John McBride was their president and Nelie Smith their 'Director of Rugby'. Smith had been a Springbok selector during McBride's 1974 Lions tour and had also coached South Africa in successive series against Argentina, France, Ireland and, in 1981, during the fateful tour of New Zealand. He'd been brought to Ballymena by McBride and the Lions' 1974 coach, Syd Miller, whose own links with the club remained as strong as ever after forty-three years.

The opportunity to spend time with those rugby icons, McBride and Miller, and to meet Smith, was irresistible. Many of the strategies used to inspire the '74 Lions had been tried out first in Ballymena club games. But Ballymena also provided a break from the hard-core echelons of pro rugby. There were times when I needed to feel that rugby was still a game played for the simple love of it. As much as I cherished my time with the All Blacks and the Springboks, I wanted to remind myself what rugby meant to more ordinary men.

I remember spending a miserable Monday afternoon on the soggy rugby fields of the Ballymena Academy on the Galgorm Road. The rain was persistent but I stood and watched the young schoolboys train. They practised a fast maul which one of the boys tagged a 'Kronfeld', after All Black Josh. When I told Josh about his fame in Ballymena he just rocked with delight and said, 'Wow!' While the 'Kronfeld' rolled on, the school's coach, Barry Coen, kept popping over to entertain me. He was a witty and gentle man.

A few weeks from then I was due to arrive in France. Any anxiety I'd felt about coping without even the most basic French was swept away with the Ballymena rain. As little rivulets ran down our faces, Barry Coen marvelled at the kind of rugby he had watched in towns like Agen and Dax. Every August he and his family drove across France and down to the south-west and, in between all the eating and the drinking, they went to as many early-season club games as possible. My own enthusiasm for the skill and physicality of French rugby began to quicken again that dank day in Ballymena. We must have made a strange sight – a Protestant Irishman and a white South African standing in the rain becoming more and more French-like in our hand-waving excitement as we discussed the rugby I would see when Brive played Dax.

Our little circle was completed by Nelie Smith. The mud stuck to our feet as we walked across the adjoining pitches – 'just like in Wellington', Smith recalled wryly in reference to New Zealand in 1981. But we soon returned to our mutual celebration of the French. Smith was a close friend of Pierre Villepreux, who coached the national French side with Jacques Skrela, and he predicted sagely that *Les Bleus* would be devastating in the imminent Five Nations. By the time we had reached the school's tiny cloakroom, and Barry had cracked open a packet of chocolate biscuits for Nelie and me, our attention had wandered back to Ballymena.

I knew that Ballymena was not the first place in Ireland, let alone the world, you would visit in search of revolution. Yet, and I said this softly to Nelie and Barry, in a whisper compared to the foghorn used by Ballymena's own 'Mr Angry', something radical was stirring on the edge of town. It would not have tickled the Reverend Paisley's fancy, but the fantasy of winning an All-Ireland title excited rugby people all over Ulster.

'*Ja*,' Nelie chuckled, 'that's what we all want to do. We want to change things here. We want to make a little bit of history in Ballymena . . .'

Later that night, Willie John McBride helped explain the charm of that Ballymena dream. 'I joined this club forty years ago,' he chortled. 'I first played for them in 1958, just a year out of school. I had never played before. My father died when I was four and we never had much time. Rugby was after school and we had to get home to work on the farm. But, four years after starting the game with Ballymena, I played my first two Tests for the 1962 Lions in South Africa. That's when Syd and I first met Nelie – he captained the Free State side that held us to a draw.

'But, despite all my games with the Lions down the years, I stayed with Ballymena throughout my career. Sometimes it was strange. One week you'd be playing against France before 50,000 in Paris and the next Saturday you'd turn out in the Towns Cup in front of a few hundred in Ballymena. But, in those days, loyalty was everything. I could never see myself playing in any other club colours but the black of Ballymena. My last game was in 1980 – meaning that I'd played for the club in four separate decades.'

McBride, like Miller, went on to coach Ballymena and then become their President. 'At the beginning of last season, just as the game turned professional, and all the mad business of inflated fees and wages began,' McBride explained, 'we sat down and considered our position. Rugby was changing crazily. We could see that there would be many English clubs who would pump silly money into people's pockets. But it can't last. There's no way that the game can be sustained at the level it's reached. It's nonsense!'

McBride had the winning habit of interspersing the seriously intense stare of the marauding lock-forward with abandoned laughter. 'It's absolute nonsense!' he hooted. 'So we sat down and asked ourselves a simple question – "When the madness settles down, do we still want to be a premier club in Ireland?" The answer was an emphatic yes. I never thought the solution would be for us to turn completely professional. We just don't have enough money. We have a handful of players who are already earning a full-time living after signing contracts with Ireland and Ulster – but the rest of the team have to hold down jobs and train in the evening. Can you imagine them doing that at bloody Wasps these days! So we have one foot in past values, in having a tightly knit team who play for the sheer love of Ballymena – and then we have another foot in a bolder future. We've done something that no other club in Ireland has dared do. We've poured all our resources into coaching. We've gone for an international coach who will transform our whole rugby culture. We've gone for Nelie Smith – who I think is the best coach in the world.

'Y'see, we refused to follow the trend of other clubs in both Ulster and Munster. They decided to pay their players and they brought in these "hired guns" to play on short-term contracts. We took our more radical step in consultation with our own players. We asked them what would keep them at the club. After all, Jimmy Topping could've signed a huge contract with a London club. But the boys were unanimous: money was not the issue. They wanted to stay with Ballymena, but they also wanted better coaching. And Nelie Smith is working wonders – not only for Ballymena but for the whole of Irish rugby. And, boy, we all need a lift!'

Irish rugby had had a bleak year in 1997. Ireland lost to Italy in both January and December, home and away. The 37–29 and 37–22 defeats were depressingly familiar, with the Italians even showing more fire in the once sacrosanct Irish bellows of commitment and spirit. Apart from sneaking home 26–25 against Wales in Cardiff, not much had gone right for them. At least the sixty-one-point All Black tornado had been expected. But they had also been outplayed by France, England and Scotland.

In Ireland itself, the domestic game struggled as never before. With professionalism spreading ever wider, yet more Irish players had been enticed across the water. The four star forwards picked for the Lions' first Test pack in South Africa – Wood, Wallace, Davidson and Miller – featured in a huge billboard advert which could be seen all over Ballymena. But they were actually far away, being paid by their Allied Dunbar Premiership teams. Even the lesser-known likes of David Humphreys, a talented international stand-off whom Barry Coen had coached at Ballymena Academy, were now based in England. For those who remained in Ireland, the chances of finding glamour or even a living through rugby were notably meagre. Instead of being a flagship competition, the supposedly élite All-Ireland League had been a poorly supported procession – easily secured the previous season by Shannon. The trend appeared irreversible, for Shannon's victory merely continued the Munster clubs' domination of Irish club rugby. Cork had won the inaugural championship, but throughout the rest of the '90s the title had stayed in Munster where Shannon, Garryowen and Young Munster ruled. Willie John McBride dreamed that Ballymena would become the first club from Ulster to break that southern monopoly.

I was fascinated by the cultural contradictions running though Ballymena and Irish rugby. While the town's political representative, and the vast majority of local people, refused even to consider breaking away from the UK to form a united Ireland, their rugby club's overwhelming focus was resolutely Irish. They looked forward to those crucial weekends when they would travel south to play the 'Masters of Munster'. Their respect for the rugby heritage of Limerick bolstered their belief that the All-Ireland League presented Ballymena's most enticing challenge.

Similarly, the national team was selected from both the Republic and Northern Ireland. The most famous Irish rugby men of all time – McBride and Miller – were from Ballymena. Like their only current international, James Topping, McBride and Miller had always played for a united Ireland in the Five Nations and against the southern-hemisphere teams. Whenever I was in the North it seemed to me as if Irish rugby had pulled off a breathtaking breakthrough across the political divide.

There were still divisions beneath the surface of Ulster's supposed rugby unity with Dublin and Limerick. But it remained an intriguing sporting and cultural combination. It also had the appeal of rarity – for, in football, the two Irelands played under separate flags. Northern Ireland, a footballing country which had given George Best to the world, had done little since they beat Spain in the 1982 World Cup. The Republic of Ireland, under Jack Charlton, had achieved wonders in the 1990 and '94 finals – but they'd also since wavered. Yet there were few suggestions that the two teams should unite, as they did in the more conservative world of rugby.

After seeing all that rugby had done to disunite the old South Africa, how could I resist the Ballymena dream of a first All-Ireland championship?

By October 1997, Nelie Smith and I spoke on the phone almost every week, having struck up an unexpected rapport from the moment we met. Our friendship, rich in paradox, said much for the way in which rugby could bind together different men.

Reliving so much of what rugby had meant during apartheid I kept stumbling across Nelie Smith's name. My own memories of him were troubled. When Smith was at his zenith, coaching the Orange Free State as well as the demo-ridden Boks, I was at my own intransigent worst. In my later teenage years, and especially during my early twenties when I was driving every day into Soweto, I just raged – as if I suffered rather than benefited from the country's white bias. I blamed the Afrikaners for apartheid – especially the men in power, whether they were the prime minister or the Springbok coach.

Smith's own place at the centre of apartheid-era rugby would always be pinned down by his coaching of the 1981 Springboks. Yet, at the same time, he was also the national coach when Errol Tobias became the country's first 'non-white' Springbok. Amid all his bitterness towards the *Broederbonders*, Tobias had stressed that Nelie Smith was driven more by rugby than apartheid.

Yet I went to Ballymena in search of a confrontation with that past. I imagined that I would eventually quiz Smith hard about his role in rugby and apartheid. There were even times when I could see myself writing about the 'confessions' I would prise from the old Bok. It's hard for me to admit that now. But, facing him, I lost any desire to put him in some interview dock. I liked him too much. I liked him from that first autumn day in Ballymena when, as the usual rain fell, he told me about his life.

He even made me laugh when we talked about Bloemfontein. He told me about his own suburb's unending supply of Free State sporting heroes – a litany of talent which included one Fritzie Kleynhans, the 'World Tongue-Twisting Champion'. Nelie swung with the sweetest nostalgia when he said, 'Y'know, it's very difficult to roll the tongue and twist it as many times as possible in a minute. But, oh, Fritzie, he was tremendous . . . Don, you would have loved to have seen the fast roll of his tongue!'

But our mood grew more sombre. Nelie Smith was still suffering. He had known his wife since he was twelve and she was eleven. Forty years later, Nelie spoke of their childhood in tender detail. They had started going out seriously towards the end of high school – and were together until she finally died of cancer in September 1995. She was named Anna; but everyone called her 'Orna', Nelie said, 'because she was just so pretty – just like an ornament. So the name stuck. She was Orna to us. As far as I was concerned she was very beautiful. She was always so neat and tidy. She liked to dress well – very neatly, you know – and she liked to keep herself very trim and very fit. But then, all of a sudden, her strength was gone.

'In the last year, things were very hard. My oldest daughter was in America then and we had to tell her that her mother was dying. So she came back to South Africa to see her one last time. At the end of her holiday, there were tears because she had to go back to America. We took her to the airport. It was a very painful moment for all of us. As we sat on a bench at the airport, I reached out and took Orna's hand. We were waiting for our daughter's plane to take off. I remember how unusually cloudy it was that day. And, as the plane climbed and disappeared into those clouds, my wife turned to me, with tears in her eyes, and she said, "Nelie, it's so final . . ."

'As it turned out, my daughter gave up everything in America to come back to Bloemfontein so that she could help me care for Orna. She was with her mother twenty-four hours a day – and I was with them too. It was the first time in my life I put rugby second. In the build-up to the 1995 World Cup, Louis Luyt had asked if I would be interested in coaching the Springboks again. This was before they appointed Kitch Christie. It was a Sunday evening and my wife was sitting only five metres away from the phone. She had been expecting the call and she had said, "Please, Nelie, don't use me as an excuse. I know how much it would mean to you to coach the Springboks again – especially in a World Cup . . ."

'But, Don, how could I? She had given up everything for me and my rugby. It was time for me to be there for her. I said, "Listen, Louis, I'm afraid it's impossible. My wife needs me . . ." I put down the phone and she started to cry. She said, very quietly, "Thank you . . ." I have never regretted that decision. In the very last months we were allowed to keep Orna at home. There were three times, always late at night, when I had to call the doctor out. The little pump we had to push the morphine into her was not strong enough. Her pain would be unbearable. Sometimes, it was like watching an animal being tortured. It was awful. But at least we were there for her. She died at home. But I think of her often, here, in Ballymena . . .'

After hearing such words, said as they were in a soft Afrikaans voice which was as steady as it was sad, I had no heart to hound Nelie Smith. We did speak about rugby in the 'old days' and he enthused that he 'had never met a more polite man than Errol Tobias – he was such a gentleman and one of the hardest workers I have ever encountered on the training field. And Errol, you know, I wanted him in my Springbok team, not because he was a coloured, but because he was a tremendous rugby player.' He recalled the 1970 All Blacks, the 1974 Lions and the 1981 New Zealand tour so vividly that it felt as if we were back in South Africa and he was with the Springboks and I was at home again, listening to the earliest matches on the radio and watching the later Tests on SABC TV. We had both made strange journeys to end up in Ballymena –

and I did not care that my twenty-year-old self would have sneered at my sympathy for Nelie Smith. I had learnt a little since 1981. I could see all that was good and touching in a fifty-three-year-old Afrikaner from Bloemfontein, a man struggling with pain and memory in rainy Ballymena.

At Eaton Park, where we sat, and where Ballymena played their rugby, the bright yellow banners of corporate sponsorship still shone beneath the grey winter clouds. Cable & Wireless, in the midst of a £50,000,000 advertising campaign, had injected £100,000 into Ballymena rugby. It was their first venture into the British sports market. Their previous team sponsorship had a more sensational international ring, linking the company with the West Indies and the mighty likes of Viv Richards, Curtly Ambrose and Brian Lara. But Ballymena had their own legends – Willie John McBride and Syd Miller – and the corporate money enabled them to bring over their old Afrikaans chum.

As Smith said, 'Whenever Syd and Willie John came over to South Africa we got together. I've always been close to them – but Willie John took me by surprise when he asked me to coach Ballymena. It was a real bolt from the blue. I was coaching Griqualand West in 1996 when that great All Black side come over. It was a real battle but I decided that we should take the New Zealanders on at forward. My Griqua team really surprised them and, in the end, the All Blacks were relieved to get away with a draw.'

While I picked up on the political link with Andre Markgraaff and Andre Bester, Nelie explained how a provincial team could match the All Blacks. When Markgraaff became Springbok coach in 1996, Smith stepped in to assist Griquas. His captain against New Zealand was Bester – who would soon trick Markgraaff into making the infamous 'Kaffir' tape which caused such turmoil in South African rugby early in 1997. But Nelie had already moved on to explain McBride's offer.

'That night, Willie John, who was at the All Black-Griqua match, asked me if I would consider joining Ballymena. I had never been to Ireland before and I was very interested in helping them do well. I had better offers elsewhere but, in rugby terms, this was by far the best challenge. And with Willie John and Syd's involvement, I knew that Ballymena would be a very special club. They're rugby people.'

If the mix of Afrikaans and Ulster accents was vaguely bizarre, the similarities between the Orange Free State and the Orange heartland of

Ballymena were obvious. '*Ja*, Don,' Nelie chuckled, 'you're dead right. But I stay out of politics. We're only really interested in rugby at this club. I've tried to create a winning culture in Ballymena. Even though most of the boys are not professionals, they've worked extremely hard. Last season, from being bottom of the league when I joined, they finished fifth. They also won the Ulster League and Cup. This year we have already won the local Ulster championship. In fact, counting last season, we're unbeaten in twenty-seven out of my twenty-eight matches. We're top of the All-Ireland League at the moment as well – so the dream continues . . .'

As in England, the structure of the game in Ireland had its complications. The first three months of the season were given over to local competitions – the Ulster League in Ballymena's case. The majority of their fifty- and sixty-point victories had been achieved without thirteen of their players who'd spent September and October playing for the Ulster provincial side against Wasps, Swansea and Glasgow in the European Cup.

They were destroyed by 'that bloody awesome Dallaglio' and the English club champions; but the witty and passionate Ballymena boys were quick to point out that the primary difference centred around professionalism. As their captain, a fiery hooker called Steven Ritchie, remarked dryly, 'It's difficult to compete against someone like Dallaglio when some of your team have spent the day counting money in a bank or working on a building-site . . .'

'Yeah,' his international wing, James Topping, agreed, 'the difference was obvious in the second half of our evening game. We kept the score down to 14–13 at half-time but ten of our boys had worked all that day. They just overpowered us in the second half. They were fitter, faster and stronger – a guy like Lawrence Dallaglio is about two stone heavier and five yards faster than most of our forwards. You could tell that he was captain of England and that he had fourteen other full-time professionals alongside him. But things are a little more even in the All-Ireland – especially when we've got legends like Nelie and Willie John to inspire us.'

Like Topping, I found it hard to resist McBride's enthusiasm, particularly when the big man's face opened up in unrestrained delight. 'We're unbeaten and ahead of Shannon and Garryowen and Young Munster and St Marys!' he laughed. 'And now we're rightly telling ourselves that this year we've got the best chance we'll ever have to win the thing. If we get a fair wind, I really think we could make history and become the first club from Ulster to do it. What a story that would make . . .'

I followed that story with increasing ardour. Whether in France or Australia or New Zealand, I found myself scouring the small print for Ballymena's latest score, to see if the fantasy could be fulfilled. Perhaps it was because I had washed away some of my old teenage angst by actually meeting Nelie Smith. Perhaps it was the memorable Saturday night we had at the McBrides' home in Ballyclare as Nelie, Willie John and I watched a recording of Free State reaching the 1997 Currie Cup final by beating Gary Teichmann's Natal – a result which left Smith almost breathless with delight. Perhaps it was because I had felt so oddly special when, at the launch of Cable & Wireless's sponsorship of Ballymena, Willie John called me out to the front so that I could pose for the local paper's photographer alongside McBride, Miller and Smith – as if I really was the right fourth man to feature in such a celebrity square. As the camera flashed I thought how much I would have loved that photograph in the South African winter of 1974. Perhaps the merging of that then and now explained why, as I packed my bags for Paris and Brive, I was already working out how I might make it back to Ireland to see Ballymena take on Shannon at the end of the month in Limerick. Their top-of-the-table All-Ireland encounter would clash with the European Cup final between Brive and Bath in Bordeaux on 31 January. I compared the significance of each for a long moment. And then I picked up the telephone.

'Nelie,' I said, 'we'll see you in Limerick, hey . . .'

Chapter 10
Allez Racing, Allez Brive

I began my journey through French rugby in an open-plan Parisian office which doubled as a fashion warehouse. In an elegant old building, found halfway down a cobbled alleyway just off the Arc de Triomphe end of the Champs-Elysées, I realised again that what may look *très chic* in Ballymena or Sudbury does not necessarily cut the Dijon in Paris. I had actually dressed for the occasion, wearing my full Christmas-present finery. It was still a bit of a novelty but, married to a woman who wanted to improve me, I suddenly had a wardrobe which included a shirt by Hugo Boss, a Paul Smith jacket and jeans by Katherine Hamnett. I wore the whole shebang for my first French interview, feeling mildly sorry for Lawrence Dallaglio that *Papa Noël* had brought him a video of *Living with Lions* instead.

The only problem was that old body of mine. It obviously still considered itself too cerebral, its own euphemism for 'bulky', for another designer-clad image. I was, after all, the only man in the world whose Armani coat had been described as a 'comfortable-looking anorak' by one ignorant dolt after another. I could put up with such misconception in South London for, even if English fashion had produced Vivienne Westwood, John Galliano and Alexander McQueen, there were still plenty of cool dudes in SW18 who thought that slipping on a Chelsea shirt was pretty damn exquisite. Paris, naturally, was different.

As I waited for Franck Mesnel to arrive, his office overflowed with a beautiful stream of young Frenchwomen who drifted up and down the stairs. Contrary to that weary cliché that Parisians are always surly and haughty, they could not have been sweeter as they offered me coffee and smiled sympathetically. It was as if they could see past my outer labels and right into the heart of that old Anglo-Saxon struggle with all things *à la mode*. We hardly spoke a word of each other's language, but there was an instant and mutual understanding. They were in fashion. I was not. I was way out of their clothing line. Once that had been established, I began to enjoy myself.

Franck Mesnel's company, Eden Park, was named after the ground in Auckland where, in rugby's first World Cup final in 1987, he had played for France against New Zealand. Although the French lost to an All Black team including Sean Fitzpatrick, Mesnel still thrilled to the sound of Eden Park. With four fellow French rugby players from the Paris team, Racing Club de France, Mesnel had set up a sportswear business which had since grown into a multi-million-pound empire. In ten years they had opened more than two hundred Eden Park shops across France and were about to unveil their first London store in Mayfair.

Their logo was famous throughout France. It consisted of a pink bow-tie which was also a symbol for the romantic brand of French rugby we had always loved. France, spins yet another truism, traditionally play rugby like Brazil play football. If the Brazilians are always expected to bend and caress a round ball as if they're frolicking across a sandy beach, so the rugby maxim decrees that the French are supposed to run and pass the oval ball with enchanting flair. And of course they do – even if, unlike Brazil and France's own football team, they're yet to win a World Cup.

But the All Blacks, Springboks and Wallabies all confessed to some real fear of the French. They were more than just a team of piano-players – for in Toulouse and Brive they could call upon some of the most formidable piano-movers in world rugby.

Since I had first arrived in Europe, in the mid-1980s, *les Bleus* had briefly tried to cut back on the aesthetic tinkling of their running game in favour of a forward-led plan which relied on big and aggressive men whipped up to a pitch of almost pathological intensity. Under the small but fiery Jacques Fouroux, a great scrum-half turned national coach, France's own love affair with the All Blacks was taken to an extreme obsession. For a couple of years they had followed Fouroux's battering diktat that only immense and totally wired forwards could hammer France to rugby greatness. It could not last. Essentially, the French could not abandon the sense of freedom and unpredictability which distinguished their rugby.

Despite the catastrophic 52–10 loss to South Africa eight weeks before, they still wielded outrageous potential. They could blend the genius of Thomas Castaignède and a blue flash of back-line runners with forwards like their prop Christian Califano, an alarmingly strong tank in both the tight and the loose. Castaignède and Califano ran with the rich patter of French rugby history in their every step – for theirs was a legacy of creativity and imagination like nothing else in world rugby.

If the All Blacks wore a silver fern on their breasts, and the South Africans a Springbok, it seemed strangely appropriate that Franck

Mesnel and his 'Show-Bizz' rugby troupe at Racing, the same quintet of men who had formed Eden Park, should have preferred a pink bow-tie. But it was only one example of their fantastic celebration of *Tricolores* rugby. Their cheeky homage had begun, in fact, with a beret. Exactly eleven years before, in January 1987, Racing faced yet another harsh rugby test against Bayonne, close to the Spanish border. But they decided to have some fun along the way. Mesnel, Eric Blanc, Jean-Baptiste Lafond, Yvon Rousset and Philippe Guillard had all been part of the Racing team which, the previous year, had finished as runners-up in the notoriously tough French championship. The first three were established in the national team. Yet, because they were from Paris, they were still regarded with suspicion in the southern heartland of French rugby. They decided to live up to their image as jokers. All five of them played the entire match against Bayonne with a Basque beret plonked jauntily on their heads.

Three months later, in the quarter-finals of the French cup, they ran onto the field with club blazers buttoned over their hooped rugby shirts – which they described as 'elegant dress for the occasion'. They still won the match. In the semi-final, against a feverish Toulouse, in that rugby bastion of Bordeaux, they wore golden boots and the longest possible shorts in a natty early-twentieth-century-style. Again, they won – either despite, or because of, their sartorial gamble. In the final at the Parc des Princes they were less lucky against Toulon, but were even more memorable for playing in their now illustrious pink bow-ties.

Their shenanigans continued for the next four years. Racing and the 'Show-Bizz' boys transfixed the whole of France as they played breath-taking rugby with even more breathless jollity. In April 1988 they painted their faces black before a match to 'pay tribute' to their black friend and fellow player, Vincent Lelano. The following April, the famous five played in skull-caps in a cheery nod to their menacingly bald rival, Didier Camberaberro. They made it to the final of that championship a few months later. During the pre-match introductions they presented President Mitterrand with a pink bow-tie of his own. At half-time, the retired Yvon Rousset ambled across the Parc in a black suit. He carried a silver tray and a bottle of the best French champagne with which to replenish his Racing team. They kept the fizz in their second-half play against Agen and secured 1990's *Championnat de France*.

They were the kind of stories you were meant to tell with a shrug, for in France one shrug led to another and then another. As connoisseurs of the shrug, the 'Show-Bizz' party at Racing knew that French rugby itself had an infinite variety of shrugging techniques – from the side-step to the hand-off, the shoulder-charge to the shoulder-drop. More significantly, the French shrug could spell out various rugby emotions, whether fuelled by audacity or despair, defiance or boredom.

I remembered Franck Mesnel from countless Five Nations' afternoons and all three World Cups, in New Zealand, England and South Africa. Up close, across a small desk in a tiny office in the basement of his building, he looked even younger than he had done on television. He had also qualified as an architect while playing international rugby. Yet he wore his erudition lightly. At the same time, his humour did not belie his thoughtfulness as he reflected, in perfect if Gallic-accented English, on the myth and the meaning of French rugby and those bizarre Racing days.

'We were,' Mesnel explained, 'always looking for a way to express our idea that the best French rugby combines rigour and fantasy. You know, just because you play well you don't have to be serious all the time. Yes, French people have always played with excitement but, sometimes, before or after a match, there is too much gravity. This is because rugby in France has always been very institutional. It can be very rigid when they plan their leagues and their cups. "You must do this!" they say. "You can't do that!" But we were students and we were from Paris so, when you compared us to rugby men in the south, what could they expect? But we wanted to tell them that even in Paris, where you have theatre and cinema and jazz and literature, rugby also exists. The journalists gave us this name, "Show-Bizz!" Maybe they thought we were just trendy, good-looking students who liked to joke all the time. But, for us, it was just a release of spontaneity.'

'What was the reaction when you wore pink bow-ties and drank champagne at half-time?'

'I think we surprised many people – especially in the south where rugby is taken very seriously. They could not believe what they were seeing! We were not typical French internationals. We were Parisian rugby players. I think we maybe started our jokes because, as rugby players, we were lost in Paris. You know Paris – it feels it is too important to give up its cultural identity to a game like rugby. It's okay to do that in Toulouse or Brive but here, in Paris, rugby means very little. At Racing we did not have the support they have in the south. Sometimes it seemed as if the players were also the spectators. You know, it felt like there were more of us [players] than them [spectators]. So we thought, well, let us entertain ourselves while saying something about our rugby culture.

'Everyone else in French rugby hated Racing. They hated us because we were from Paris. That's rugby, that's people! What can you do? Ours is a conservative sport. In rugby, because we are Parisians, we are all dogs! We are all homosexuals! Even outside the little world of rugby, in France itself, everyone thinks that every Parisian man is a homosexual. This is very amusing to us. We enjoy the idea. As students we have many cultural and artistic interests so we decide to play with this joke. If we are called the homosexuals of French rugby we will be happy! We will laugh! We will wear our pink bow-ties!'

'Did people in a rugby town like Toulouse ever regard your little jokes as offensive to their rugby tradition of seriousness and masculinity?'

'Of course!' Mesnel shrugged. 'Some people always misunderstand. Our Rugby Federation and its president took the most offence. They tried to stop us. But, in rugby, as in life, when you have a strong idea you almost have to be excessive. You have to push it to the limits. The press and the public understood this. They admired our spirit. I think it was only dangerous when we started with the berets in Bayonne. The beret belongs to the Basque people. That is its origin. So there was some *hazard*. They could have thought we were disrespectful. But, you know, the way we wore those berets and the way we played, the crowd could tell that we had no aggression towards them or the beret. In fact we wore the beret in honour of the great Basque tradition. At the end we threw our berets to the home crowd in acknowledgement that, as a symbol, the beret belonged to them. Their response? Magnificent . . .'

'Where else,' I wondered, 'but in French club rugby?'

'Nowhere. Exactly. In the French joke there is French seriousness. There is appreciation of a people's culture. There is appreciation of our people's rugby. It is so unique it must make one laugh.'

We both chuckled on cue, with my own shoulders suddenly shrugging in emulation of Mesnel's. But he broke off to resume a more scholarly tack.

'Could I make an analogy for you?' he asked softly.

'Certainly,' I replied, sounding more Parisian by the moment, as if Franck had just asked if he could crack the first egg in the making of my lunch-time omelette.

'It is like a lawyer who wears a red clown's nose while defending his case in a court before 2,000 people. Everyone is just staring at his red nose – thinking, "What a clown!" To win his case, his defence must be better than good. If he is not exceptional he is just ridiculous. It was the same with us at Racing. We took big chances. If we did not perform exceptionally we would also have been just ridiculous. It was a very fine motivation. You see, it goes back to the heart of our understanding of what defines great French rugby. Without rigour – the rigour of hard training and exceptional play – the fantasy means nothing.'

I loved the way that the best French teams had always thrown the ball around the field as if they were tossing a little lemon back and forth to each other at a picnic on a hot summer's day. But, I also understood why Jacques Fouroux and his disciples had turned away from 'fantasy' in favour of 'rigour'. Without the forwards to win that oval lemon there could be no summery joy or pleasure. Threatened by a huge England pack in the 1980s, and by the then dour masters in Black shirts, the French believed that they would be dominated if they did not react accordingly.

'Yes, you are right,' Mesnel agreed, remembering a time when he won many of his fifty-six caps at fly-half, 'but it was another of those big paradoxes we love in French rugby. At the time we had backs like Serge Blanco and Philippe Sella – the most extraordinary players. And Jacques Fouroux knew that he couldn't change his back line – he took us as we were. He would go away with the forwards ten minutes before a match – but, first, he would wave at us and say, "You boys go away – I don't need you. I am with the forwards now."'

'So were all those stories true? Did Fouroux make the forwards bash their heads against the wall and against each other before kick-off?'

'Yes, of course. Jacques Fouroux is very original. If I had to go on holiday with someone I would chose Jacques Fouroux because he is a very funny man. But when it came to rugby it was very serious. As you know, he is a little man but he had to find very big and strong players. It became an obsession with him. It went too far, I think. But there was also logic in what he did. I think Fouroux understood better than anyone that the French rugby player has a very Latin temperament. We are, after all, Latin people. And we need to find the right motivation. We lack what the Anglo-Saxon countries have. They will always be sensible. They will convince themselves that a rugby match is important. Sometimes, and we don't know why, we find it hard to see what is so special about another rugby match. We cannot motivate ourselves unless we do something unusual. At Racing we did our tricks and dressed up in funny clothes. With Fouroux he would scream and shout and hit his forwards so that they would be motivated. Our techniques were not the same – but we were both searching for inspiration.'

Despite its renown for flair, French rugby had a reputation for savagery. Even Sean Fitzpatrick had said that the French were the hardest and most physical rugby players he had ever faced – with 'hard' and 'physical' sounding like polite descriptions for dirty play. I asked Mesnel if the parable still applied. Did French rugby consist only of 'artists and butchers'?

Mesnel laughed again. 'Yes, probably! But, no, seriously, I can say that it is different now. The majority of French rugby players are more Anglo-Saxon in their psychology now. At least they try to be. They try to keep hold of their emotions. They no longer do things the Fouroux way. They try to be professional. The game even at club level is not so violent. The players are calmer. But for some of the older guys, like [Olivier] Merle, it is still difficult. He has the cameras on him but he will still do something wild and violent. He cannot stop himself. The Anglo-Saxon countries can control themselves better so, often, they will beat us because of that.

'But we must be careful not to say one nation is like this all the time, and another like that. The cultures are not so opposite sometimes. Here is another paradox. The French people often make this mistake – they say that the British are very conservative. They say they are too reserved and too serious. But there are crazy people in England! In Scotland, Wales, Ireland! Look especially at London – it is full of crazy people and so it is a fantastic city. I have always said this. The British are very controlled in their emotions but, every day, for five minutes, they will go completely crazy. They will do something even more wild than anyone else. It might only last for five minutes but, in that time, they show such capacity for craziness. I love it! Some say it is the eccentric in the British. I say it is the artist in them. In the fashion world this is recognised. Today the most eccentric designers, the craziest designers, the best designers are the British . . .'

'But they went into fashion rather than rugby . . .'

'It's a shame. But I think British rugby is trying to change. They need to show more imagination, even though they must keep what is best about their own game. It is the same here. We need to become faster and stronger – but we need to keep our essence. We find pleasure in risk-taking. There is always danger but, when the risk works, it is beautiful.'

'Has French rugby lost some of that fantasy in the professional era?'

'No, I don't want to say that,' Mesnel grinned. 'When I was a player I always heard old players saying, "Oh, it was better in my day . . ." So I must be very careful. It is different. When we were at Racing, Bob

Dwyer, the coach of Australia, worked with us for a year. I like Bob, he is a very nice man and a great coach. But it didn't work out with us at Racing. It was a very interesting clash of cultures. Bob found it difficult to work with French players. We were not open to his culture of rugby. When we were training he would say, "We must do this practice routine ten times!" The French players would do it five times and then they would stop. "That's enough!" they would say. And Bob would say, "No, you've got to do five more! I said ten times!" The players wouldn't listen. They would just shrug. It nearly drove Bob Dwyer mad. Now, maybe they would react differently. In the professional game, the teams from around the world have taken the best of each other's culture. France will be more disciplined this year – but it worries me that the players with the most flair are now from New Zealand and South Africa and Australia. In Paris a few months ago the Springboks played "French" rugby – except much faster and better than ever before. We have to find that higher level of fantasy ourselves . . .'

I told Eden Park's arch-fantasist that I was about to leave Paris for Brive.

'Ah, Brive!' Mesnel smiled. 'You will find it very interesting. It is the opposite to Paris. Here, no one thinks about rugby. There, it is everything! And, in the week before the European final, it will be even more crazy! It will be rugby, rugby, rugby! At Brive, they want nothing more than to be champions of Europe again . . .'

'And what if you were playing in the European Cup final next week-end,' I asked the hypothetical teaser, 'with your old Racing team . . .?'

'Wouldn't that be beautiful!' Mesnel said softly. 'Because for all the success we have in business, for all the money we make, nothing has ever come close to giving us the same feeling we had when we used to run out for the big match! It was incredible. I would love to do it again next Saturday! I would love to see what we would wear for a European Cup final!'

Franck Mesnel considered the point for a long while and then, he sighed, with pleasure I thought. 'I am sure we would look very different to Brive…'

Brive-la-Gaillarde, Saturday, 24 January 1998
On a cold and late afternoon, just before five, the stadium in Brive was lit from above by brightly arcing floodlights and, from the west, by a gaunt winter sunset. It did not take us long to walk from the main town

to the Parc Municipal ground, guided as we were by the glare and the shuffling crowd of Brive men chatting earnestly about rugby. We could tell it was rugby because, after a day in a small town where it seemed as if every single one of its 50,000 inhabitants was rugby-mad, my ear had become attuned to an accent which verbally stroked Brive's favourite names – Arbizu, Carbonneau, Lamaison, Magne, Penaud, Van Der Linden and Venditti.

If McDonald's numerous 'Fast Chicken' outlets and a flat line of tin-shed warehouses fringed the edges of Brive, the old town centre was as pretty as we had been promised. Lying in a valley surrounded by the green hills and fields of the Corrèze farming region, Brive's ochre-coloured stone buildings and black-tiled rooftops made us feel as if we had, at last, arrived in deepest France. The rugby-fever was also as pronounced as Franck Mesnel had suggested. In every shop and bar-room window there were pictures of the men in white and black, or sometimes blue, shirts. The same message was pinned across each photograph and poster – *Allez Brive . . . Allez Brive . . . Allez Brive*. In the specialist Brive rugby club shop in Rue de Paris, and in the many 'exclusive' Brive rugby bars, the main images were taken from the 1997 Heineken Cup final in Cardiff. There, Brive had put on an astonishing display of running and driving rugby which had crushed Leicester 21–8. It was the culmination of a competition which, as *The Independent*'s Chris Hewett stressed, overshadowed its international counterpart. 'Cast your mind back to the bleak midwinter,' he wrote in a preview of the 1998 club competition, 'and wallow awhile in the great, spine-tingling moments of the 1997 Five Nations Championship. You will not need the day off work – a few seconds will suffice – for apart from the brass-necked cheek of Arwel Thomas at Murrayfield, Lawrence Dallaglio's elephant-lunged Twickenham try against the French, the subtle perfection of Christophe Lamaison's performance in the same match, Jeremy Guscott's part-time brilliance in Cardiff and the majesty of Olivier Magne's Grand Slam score against the Scots at the Parc des Princes, last season's international showpiece was anything but.

'Now compare and contrast the pure theatre generated by the Heineken Cup, which began as a half-cocked, Johnny-come-lately affair without rhyme or reason or, crucially, the modern-day oxygen of tele-vision coverage, but somehow evolved into an absolute show-stopper to place alongside the Super 12 extravaganza south of the equator and, if you prefer blood-and-guts drama to try-laden soufflé, even put to shame. Club or country? Only one winner, it seems.'

Apart from the British journalist's ritual description of the Super 12 as akin to something light and fluffy – an analysis based once more on try-scoring TV highlights from a 12,000-mile distance – Hewett's breathless assessment was spot-on. In the 1997–98 Heineken Cup, the intensity of rugby played by Brive, Toulouse, Pau, Bath, Leicester, Wasps and, more occasionally, Harlequins, Cardiff and Pontypridd, was consistently more absorbing than a mundane domestic international. With blanket coverage on Sky, the profile of the European clubs had also risen sharply. Only the unbalanced structure of the championship – that northern-hemisphere rugby perennial – shadowed the competition's future.

The problem was caused by the widening gap between the French and English clubs at the top and the Welsh, Scottish, Irish and Italian combinations at the bottom. Of the twenty teams in a five-pool Heineken Cup, there were four each from England, Wales and France, three from Scotland and Ireland and two from Italy. On paper, the cultural mix was great – with, for example, Pool A offering disparate visits to Leicester, Leinster, Milan and Toulouse and Pool E skipping between Caledonia, Llanelli, Pau and Treviso. On the pitch, the balance of power was badly askew.

By December 1997, only Bath threatened the imposing trio of Brive, Pau and Toulouse. The French had already won the first two Heineken competitions, with Toulouse preceding Brive in 1996. Even in that year's second-tier European Conference Championship, for those clubs which had not qualified for the Heineken, France supplied seven quarter-finalists. It was ludicrous that they should have the same number of representatives in 1998 as Wales and only one more than Scotland or Ireland. The English Premiership were even more indignant. As Dallaglio asked, 'I'm not knocking the competition but is it right that we should have to play twenty-two tough league matches to get in while the Irish provinces have only to beat Connacht to secure a place?'

Having watched players from Ballymena wear their hearts out for Ulster against Wasps, it was hard to argue with the English captain. There was no doubt that Saracens, Newcastle, Northampton and the rest of the Premiership – and, even more particularly, Colomiers, Agen, Castres, Stade-Français and Perpignan in France – had infinitely superior players to the amateurs of Ballymena. There was something awry when Sella, Diprose, Weir, Archer, Rodber, Townsend, Sadourny, Benazzi, Castaignède and the Lievremont brothers were isolated from Europe's main club competition.

While the RFU's Cliff Brittle and Fran Cotton argued for regionalism, it was obvious that the clubs held sway in both England and France. And as long as the present European Cup structure remained in place, the competition's very existence would be endangered. Yet, as the Celtic nations counter-claimed, if Ulster and Munster, the Scottish Borders and Glasgow were simply wiped away, the difference in playing standards would widen more drastically. The Five Nations would become even weaker as the club game within Ireland and Scotland withered yet further.

The only even-handed solution – to expand the European competition so that the French and English contingent could be doubled without completely excluding the Celts and the emerging Italians – was already unlikely. The exhausted players could not be expected to tot up any more matches, and yet the Allied-Dunbar sponsors would hardly allow the loss of any Premiership games in favour of more European encounters for the competition at Heineken.

Consequently, the English clubs announced that week that they would withdraw from the 1998–99 Heineken Cup for 'both commercial and competitive reasons'. Commercially, they wanted the share of Sky and Heineken money which was paid instead to the Irish and Scottish regions and the weaker Welsh and Italian clubs. They also wanted an unbroken league programme every weekend, from the start of the season until the first Five Nations break in the New Year. While fewer games would mean fresher players, the loss of European competition would be catastrophic for northern-hemisphere rugby. The only hope was that Bath would become the first English club to win the cup and persuade the others to rejoin them for the following season's defence. The clubs' obstinacy, however, hardened.

Brive had already threatened to withdraw from their beloved European defence for more controversial reasons. The otherwise engaging cultural concoction of the Heineken Cup had fermented into a more poisonous brew. On 14 September 1997, a day after Pau and Llanelli had sunk into trench warfare, the champions of Wales, Pontypridd, came to Brive. In an appallingly filthy match, the violence reached its nadir early on. After punches and kicks had peppered the opening quarter, a mass brawl, involving twenty-seven of the thirty players, exploded in the twenty-fifth minute when Pontypridd's strident New Zealand number 8, Dale McIntosh, crashed into the Brive scrum-half Philippe Carbonneau, long after the ball had been released. Carbonneau, in the sardonic words of a couple of French journalists, was 'no angel', and he was caught later on camera head-butting Stuart Roy in the face – but McIntosh's attack infuriated the Brive flanker, Lionel Mailler. He dished out some damage of his own. The mayhem spread across the field as the two teams set about their task of deciding which could be the more brutal.

Eddie Murray, the outgunned Scottish referee, eventually sent off both McIntosh and Mailler. The acrimony soured when McIntosh gestured mockingly at the packed banks of Brive supporters as he walked around the field. The fighting resumed. Although there were occasional outbreaks of rugby, as Brive squeezed home with a last-minute pushover try, the 32–31 result was a more appropriate boxing scorecard for three bloody rounds – each of which seemed to last twenty minutes.

The main twenty-minute bout of bare-knuckle violence, however, was saved for darkness. That Sunday night, in Bar Le Toulzac, just around the corner from the club shop, a number of Brive back-line stars were drinking when a contingent from Pontypridd arrived just after 10.30 p.m. It did not take long for bottles, chairs and tables to join the flying fists. Like Carbonneau, Lamaison's nose was broken, while Venditti's face was cut and his right hand was badly bitten. All three had to be taken to hospital while, the next morning, a trio of Ponty players – McIntosh, the hooker Phil John and their new South African centre, Andre Barnard – were arrested just before the Welsh flew home. They appeared in court on the Monday afternoon on a charge of 'violence and degradation'. Although they returned to Wales later that night, they were threatened with a possible two-year prison term and a heavy fine for the 'wilful damage' to Le Toulzac once police investigations had been concluded.

'I have never seen anything so violent in all my life,' Lamaison told Ian Borthwick in *The Guardian*, 'and I have never been so frightened. It was like being in a Western. People were throwing doors, chairs, glasses; they were completely hysterical. I even saw bottles smashed on the bar to be used as weapons. If the cops hadn't arrived and thrown in the tear-gas bomb it could have been even more serious. I sincerely believe some players would have been killed.'

Even a hard nut like Carbonneau admitted on French radio that 'before the police came, we were really afraid'. For the more sensitive Lamaison, it would take weeks for the psychological trauma to dissipate. Yet there was little respite for Brive. Six days later, they had to travel to Bath and then, the following Saturday, return to 'the hell of Pontypridd'.

Lamaison insisted that they would not play at Sardis Road. 'It would be impossible for us,' he stressed. Brive also demanded the immediate expulsion of Pontypridd, with a life-ban from Europe for McIntosh, John and Barnard. They also requested a fortnight's break in order to recover from their injuries. All three demands were politely refused by the European administrators. Instead, both clubs were fined £15,000, with an additional £15,000 suspended pending 'good behaviour'. The Toulzac bar massacre was declared 'beyond rugby's jurisdiction'. Brive were instructed to play in both Bath and Pontypridd.

On a summery September afternoon in Bath, Carbonneau was missing. He had been left behind in Brive while Lamaison, looking like Hannibal Lecter in a blue-and-white mask of bandages, stayed on the bench. Venditti, still sporting his Toulzac bruising, played at centre. Despite their melancholic air both before and after the match, Brive played with superb spirit and only lost 27–25 when, with the last kick of the match, their Argentinian marvel, Lisandro Arbizu, missed a forty-metre penalty.

'For us,' the brooding Brive coach Laurent Seigne said, 'the real dream is to play matches like today. Last week we played a semi-civilised team. It's quite impossible to play a match in Pontypridd against those kind of players. I would prefer not to play them. The main problem is the security of our players both on and off the pitch.' Seigne's words were translated by an interpreter but, then, as if he knew that the harshness of his meaning had been softened, the coach grunted an English word of his own in a closing reference to the Pontypridd players: 'Animals . . .'

But the European Cup mattered enormously to Brive and so, amid much gnashing and wailing, they made the Welsh journey. Incredibly, a drawn match passed off without further incident – except for the fact that it set up another return match in Brive to decide which of the two teams would qualify behind Bath from their particular 'Group of Death'.

The British rugby media analysed, in copious detail, what Stephen Jones in the *Sunday Times* described as the 'psyche behind French rugby which has earned a reputation in the rest of the world as the dirtiest environment in the sport. And is that reputation deserved? Consider the views of people who have played there. We spoke to eleven well-known non-Frenchmen who have extensive experience in the country. All, to a man, found it a violent experience.'

Jones quoted two Cardiff players who had been part of the Brive squad which had won the 1997 Heineken Cup. Gregory Kacala, the Polish flanker, recalled his time at Brive in pithy terms. 'One minute it is quiet on the field. Then, boom. It all goes crazy, completely crazy.' For

Tony Rees, 'the French and the Japanese are similar in one respect. They must never, ever lose face. Consequently, things boil over and some teams have frightening reputations.'

Jones suggested further that 'Laurent Seigne's winding-up procedures in the dressing-room are infamous, and include punching his own players . . . it is surely instructive that all last week the French media were blaming Pontypridd, not Seigne's Brive, for causing the trouble.'

I found it equally instructive to see such a focus on French guilt. 'At the very least,' Jones argued, 'the French are either beastly themselves, or they bring out the beast in others. The litany of incidents, historical and recent, with eye-gouging and head-butting apparently almost a Gallic custom, is far, far too long to tell a lie.' Jones did attempt to balance his view by quoting Jean-Pierre Rives's and Serge Blanco's defence of their countrymen. He also admitted that 'it is certainly true that the British and Irish tend to regard their own sins as high-jinks and the French as murky foreigners. There has been little comment, the French say, on the brutal punch by Mick Galwey of Munster on Keith Wood of Harlequins.'

But, in conclusion, Jones wrote: 'France must admit their own violence, and that it is endemic. Even Sale, returning from a Conference match against Montpellier last week, came back with facial injuries caused by punching and gouging. France are beyond doubt the most talented northern-hemisphere rugby nation. But indiscipline is marring that promise. They must change. This is not a biased Anglo-Saxon view. It springs from the ache of longing for the true French.'

Yet, it was essentially a simplistic concept to speak of the 'true French'. As Franck Mesnel explained, *Tricolores* rugby was 'based on paradox'. 'Rigour' and 'fantasy' were his chosen words and, if their poetry stripped some of the menace from French rugby, they provided an intriguing insight into the complexities of the game played by *Les Blues* and the powerful clubs below them. I was less interested in the views of 'non-Frenchmen'. I wanted to hear most from those close to the heart of the game in their own country.

But, first, there was pure spectacle. Brive, as usual, had been unhappy in the build-up to yet another match. Seven days before they faced Bath again in the Heineken final, they'd tried to persuade Dax to postpone that evening's league encounter. It was not surprising, considering all the stories of internecine bitterness in French club rugby, that Dax refused. When Raphael Ibanez, only two days away from being named as the new captain of France, led Dax out on the dot of six, the vehement booing and sinister whistling made it seem as if the entire town of Brive, rather than a mere quarter of 12,000, had turned out to vent their spleen.

I cocked a brow at Alison, but she was already aglow with the sudden change in mood. The Brive band hit full stride as the voices around us burst into riotous song. Carbonneau and the blue shirts skipped across the sparkling green grass. They might as well have been running across golden sand, for the musicians in the crowd had slipped into a cheeky rendition of *She Wore an Itsy-Bitsy Teeny-Weeny Yellow Polka-Dot Bikini*. It was surreal – the brass band were electric. But we loved it. For its size, the ground rocked with more colour and noise than any other rugby stadium I had ever experienced. Brive against Dax, on an ordinary league day, had an atmosphere almost as profound as that which filled King's Park and Ellis Park when the Springboks played the Lions and the All Blacks. It was *that* hot in Brive – especially with *les Brivistes* burning furiously.

Carbonneau went over in the first minute, with Penaud in the fourth and Venditti in the twelfth also scoring tries – all converted by Lamaison. Brive had scorched into a 21–0 lead. Their passing was crisp, their running like lightning, with the try-scoring backs supported by thunderous forwards like Magne, Van Der Linden and the hooker Travers, a startling Bruce Willis lookalike. Lamaison, playing at inside-centre alongside the elusive Arbizu, kicked immaculately – landing four penalties in the first half. At the break we were breathless. 33–5 to Brive, and thirty-three gorgeous ditties from the band too.

If it slowed a little for Brive in the second period, as they allowed Dax to put some points on the board, a 55–29 thumping made it seem as if they were saving themselves for Bath in Bordeaux. It was again possible to see why, even if Toulouse were consistently the best team in France, Brive had yet to lose in Europe. In the Heineken Cup quarter-finals, Brive had beaten Wasps in London. Toulouse, meanwhile, had destroyed Harlequins 51–10. In his last European match, Will Carling admitted: 'I haven't been on the receiving end of anything like that since the All Blacks game in the semi-finals of the World Cup. That was one of the great performances by a club team. They were hugely impressive. I can't see anyone beating them . . .'

But, if the mood took Brive, they could match anyone. Their December semi-final in Toulouse, against the home giants, turned out to be a sublime advert for French rugby. It ended 22–22 after extra-time, but Brive went through to the final after scoring a try more than Toulouse. Lamaison had been spared the most terrible agony after slicing a conversion wide in the last minute of ordinary time.

Against Dax there were no such traumas. There was also no violence and no dissent. Dax knew they were lost but, for Brive, there was rigour and fantasy and music. When we looked up at the packed stand above, *les Brivistes* were singing, *les Brivistes* were dancing. Franck Mesnel, I knew, would have approved.

Richard Escot, the premier rugby writer in France and a friend of a Francophile called James Small, knew what he liked most about the oval game. 'It is the chance,' he confirmed as we sat in the sunshine alongside a glistening lake at the end of a winding road in Brive, 'to meet some perfect gentlemen, great players and good comrades. This is the beautiful thing about rugby – that you meet men of the calibre of Lisandro Arbizu, Lawrence Dallaglio, James Small, Gavin Hastings, John Rutherford, Serge Blanco, Jean-Pierre Rives, Philippe Saint-André, Jo Maso. There are so many extraordinary people in rugby. For me it's like meeting an impressionist painter or a classical musician. These men are incredible. They have something special inside. We're lucky, in rugby, to have such men.'

Although he watched a couple of games every week, and spent day after day, month after month, year after year, writing about players, rugby still energised him. Richard Escot was the least jaded rugby journalist I had ever met. It was partly because he was interested in so many things beyond rugby but, also, it stemmed from the way in which he worked for *L'Equipe*. As a specialist daily sports newspaper, *L'Equipe* gave Escot far more space than his English-speaking counterparts had in their own publications. The culture of rugby journalism in France was also different. *L'Equipe* tended to assign individual journalists to specific teams. Rather than jeopardising a reporter's impartiality, the technique actually deepened that writer's understanding of the players in a particular side. If it entailed compromise in the sense that the journalist did not report on everything he saw or was privately told, it did provide a more compelling and intimate insight into the workings of French rugby. The relationship of trust between Escot and the Brive men, for example, was very different to that which existed between the press and the players I had seen in Britain, South Africa and New Zealand.

Before choosing Brive in 1996, Escot had followed Toulouse between 1985 and 1990 and then Toulon in the early-'90s. 'They were both very interesting clubs,' he said. 'For example, Toulouse was built around a new idea of how rugby could be played. The idea that a prop could act like a centre was introduced by Toulouse in 1985. They were ahead of everyone. They worked together like a family and I became very close to the players and the two coaches – Villepreux and Skrela who are now in charge of France. But Brive is very special. The interesting thing about Brive is that three years ago, until Laurent Seigne came in, they had not won anything. They were thought of as a good club – but not a top club. Seigne changed that. We have our differences sometimes, of course, but I like the way Laurent Seigne brings his team together. He chooses quality players who have a big heart and a strong mentality. People who are warm. He sticks to a simple way of playing. Before Seigne, Brive lacked aggression and toughness. Not now. I never imagined they would be European champions but I thought there was an adventure in Brive.'

Escot had read Tony Rees's and Stephen Jones's comments in the *Sunday Times*. He laughed quietly. 'Oh yes. A week after Tony Rees said those funny things he was sent off and banned for three months for kicking someone's head. In Brive he never kicked anyone. Seigne does not abuse his players. You have to understand this particularity of French rugby. We need a tough warm-up – for we are like children sometimes. Perhaps, after all, French rugby is most reminiscent of childhood. There is a lot of joy in the play. And I would say that most rugby players in France want to entertain themselves, their friends and their family. They love to play with their hands. I think it's our Latin blood, our Italian blood. As in life, in rugby we talk best with our hands. But we also need to psychologically motivate ourselves. Again like a child, we sometimes need to be frightened to understand the seriousness of something. Jacques Fouroux used to stand his players in a circle around him. He would head-butt each player – just to be sure the players were ready. And the players liked that. They were waiting for that!'

It made for a grisly, if captivating, image – the big French forwards leaning down to take the full force of little Jacques's crashing head in the face. But I could not imagine Josh Kronfeld or Gary Teichmann accepting such 'motivation'.

'No, of course not,' Escot agreed. 'The All Blacks, especially, don't need to do this. They have their own history and their own quieter way of preparing. But for us, under Fouroux and now sometimes Seigne, it is part of French rugby's psychological drama and atmosphere. But don't make the mistake of confusing it with violence. It has nothing to do with violence. It has to do with collective drama.'

It was a beautiful phrase, but did that 'collective drama' induce violence on the field?

'The game in France is less violent now. The players are more controlled. With France, under Villepreux, it is different. But, maybe, against South Africa in Paris, it would have been better if he had taken the Fouroux way! That would have at least frightened those players into playing better – because we are temperamental. I always say we, the French, are lost somewhere between dignity and vice. So, yes, violence has always been part of our game. Violence is what happens when uneducated people act when they're in danger. And, in France, rugby is not an upper-class or even a middle-class sport. It is not taught in high schools. It is not an institution at universities. We have usually relied on players who have come from families of farmers and manual workers. We don't have that philosophy of education in rugby. We only see it as a sport and a pleasure. So the onus is on the club. The club is the key to French rugby. Provincialism and regionalism can work in the southern hemisphere – but not here where the club is everything. There is one club in every town. That is why French rugby is so strong at club level – but it also explains why we sometimes struggle at national level. There is a lot of division.'

'Would a player from this town, for example,' I asked, 'think of himself more as a Brive man than a Frenchman?'

'It would be Brive first, France second. They have such a strong feeling for their club. You see, in France, rugby is often seen as the best way to start a war with your neighbour. The French like that. The country was divided a long time ago. For example, Brive and Toulon have a very bad feeling between them. It's an extremely strong animosity. They will always fight each other. When Brive play a European Cup match on a Sunday, Toulon will arrange to play their league match at the same time, just to make people choose. You're either for Toulon or you're for Brive. In the European Cup final this weekend, Bath's best supporters will be in Toulon. And yet Toulon is only twenty-five miles east of Brive. And that's why French club rugby is so strong – because it is very passionate. The emotions are rich because these rivalries go back hundreds of years. The feelings run deep not just because of what happened last season but because of what your town did to my town so many centuries ago!'

Escot laughed again. 'This is French rugby for you! It's very hard!'

'Would you say it's harder to become champions of France than it is to win the European Cup?'

'Oh, it's much harder, much, much harder! When I told my friend Stuart Barnes last year that Brive were not the best French team he laughed at me – but my argument was that they never surprised another French side with the way they played. Their game is more suited to the Anglo-Saxon way. Brive are more like an English side sometimes. They are very organised. They play the same direct pattern. In French rugby this is not enough. A side like Toulouse are better because they have a wide range of options and solutions. Brive's play is so direct it's almost square. If your defence can stop Venditti and Van Der Linden they're in trouble. They only have Plan A! When they're very motivated they will beat Toulouse. They held them in the semi-final. At home these last few weeks we have seen them play two beautiful games in the league to again beat Toulouse and Dax. But those two sides were not at the top of their motivation. Also, if Brive can beat Toulouse in the quarter-finals, I do not know if they can beat, say, Colomiers in the semi or Montferrand in the final. The league starts on 1 August and the final is on 1 June – you have to be consistent for a long time. Brive are not as consistent as maybe four or five other French teams.

'I also think it will be better for European rugby if we can have an English champion on Saturday – and Bath can win – but Brive are doing good things too. They are part of the move away from the problems we had in the Jacques Fouroux era. I like Fouroux but there was too much emphasis on the pack. We had that square idea of playing rugby based only on strength and forward power. England also did this – but in France it went against our natural inclination to use the ball to talk with our hands. It is one of Brive's main qualities to have both the rigour and the pattern of a solid forward platform and the French ability to pass through the defence. There are plenty of players in Brive who have those talking hands . . .'

Thormond Park, Limerick, Saturday, 31 January 1998
After more than two weeks of French eloquence, whether delivered by hand or mouth, I supported Brive from afar, on an afternoon when the sun shone in both Bordeaux and Limerick. In Brive I had been charmed by Christophe Lamaison, until our lack of a shared language defeated us, and especially by Lisandro Arbizu. The young back from Buenos Aires was thrilled to have a chance to speak English again and to gasp at the 'rugby fanatics of Brive' – a phenomenon to which he was still growing accustomed after only six months in French club rugby. With Richard Escot translating, Olivier Magne also remembered his most significant match against English opposition in evocative detail. 'At Twickenham

last year, in the Five Nations, it felt like we were at war with the English. They hammered us in the first half. I lay down on the pitch at half-time. I was exhausted. But, as I stared up at the sky, I suddenly thought of my grandfather fighting in the First World War. He was in the trenches. And I thought how much he suffered for France. So how could I feel tired after a little rugby? I stood up and said, "Okay, we have to fight. We can't surrender. I will die for my jersey first." And so we did. We fought back and we won – and I could then run around Twickenham carrying a French flag. On Saturday, I will fight even harder for Brive . . .'

The more solemn Laurent Seigne and Philippe Carbonneau concentrated only on beating Bath. They said that the team needed to escape from the pressure of their town.

The day I left, I heard that 30,000 of Brive's 50,000 population were planning to travel to Bordeaux – half with tickets and the other in the dreamier hope of finding some way into a sold-out ground. Ballymena, in contrast, brought only a coach-load for their crucial match against Shannon. With Willie John and Penny McBride, their daughter, son-in-law and granddaughters, we were part of that small throng in a packed Thormond Park. The gates closed on 12,000 – with 11,900 supporting Shannon and a hundred shouting for Ballymena.

Nelie Smith waved at us from the touchline. He then started to chew the skin on top of his right thumb. Ballymena were top of the All-Ireland League, having won every single match up until then. Their dream of finally toppling the 'Masters of Munster' had edged closer to reality. But Shannon, the champions, were the only other unbeaten side in Ireland.

At first, the sun kept glinting across the play of both my adopted teams for the day. Ballymena rocked Shannon and quickly built an impressive lead. Brive, similarly, were 15–6 ahead at half-time. Early in the second period the French packed down seven times, in close succession, only metres from the Bath line. Seven times they drove for the try, and seven times the Bath defence held. If they had scored, it might have ended then. Across the sea, if Ballymena had not knocked-on three times with space all around them, it could also have been all over in Limerick.

But back came Shannon in Munster. And back came Bath in Bordeaux. The fate of two such different matches seemed oddly entwined. The European Cup final and an Irish league game were both decided in the very last minute. Shannon scored a desperate try in the far corner to finally gain the lead. Ballymena's All-Ireland fantasy began to curl and die in that moment. And, in the eightieth minute too, Jon Callard coolly landed a penalty in south-west France. It was his fourth, and accompanied his own try and conversion. The old man of Bath had scored all their points. For the first time in the match they were in front, 19–18.

As the Ballymena boys cried a little at their final whistle, there was just time in Bordeaux for Arbizu to miss a drop goal from a perfect set-up. For the first time, Bath were champions of Europe. Shannon, meanwhile, once again led the All-Ireland.

A few hours later the young men from Ballymena, rejuvenated by their healing black draughts of Guinness, started to sing the night away. They had only lost a rugby match; and it was still a Saturday night in Ireland. More than half of the team had to be back at work in Ulster by Monday morning, in their banks and on their building sites. They did not want to cry in Limerick any longer. They wanted to sing and get drunk.

Nelie Smith looked benignly on, a soft drink in his hand and a softer expression on his face. 'They tried hard,' he smiled at Alison and me. 'And it was nearly enough. It was only in the very last minute that Shannon scored that try . . .'

'Oh, come over here, will ya, Nelie,' one of the front-row men shouted, 'and let's have another sing-song . . .'

We decided to slip away into Limerick, leaving Nelie and his Ballymena boys, knowing that there would be far less happiness on a Saturday night for the professionals from Brive.

'*Allez Brive!*' we said ten minutes later, clinking our bottles of beer, '*Allez Ballymena!*'

Chapter 11

Les Bleus

The Five Nations Championship had never appeared more vulnerable. Time had finally caught up with a tournament which had traded in nostalgia for so long. The malaise had been creeping closer for years but, befitting the pace of modern rugby, it plummeted in abrupt tandem with the advent of professionalism. Another split opened in an already fragmented tournament. As much as the last romantics insisted that anything could happen on a wet day in Dublin or Edinburgh or Cardiff, the chasm seemed deep and dry when the 1998 fixture list was printed.

Even the reams of Five Nations handbooks and colour supplements, containing bright previews and mistier reflections, struggled to curb the doubt. There were a few ritual declarations that 'The World's Greatest Rugby Tournament' was about to begin, but you could sense the straining. It was impossible to sustain the veracity of such a claim when, all around the antique edifice, the crumbling continued. For many, it was easier to concentrate on surface oddities rather than structural flaws.

Much inky newsprint was expended on the fact that the 1998 championship would only begin in February and end in April, thus breaking aeons of tradition where January and March acted as cosy midwinter bookends for international rugby in the northern hemisphere. There was mild uproar that there would be two Sunday matches – a television-driven decision which cut to the heart of the fact that the Five Nations was as much a riotous social escapade as a serious rugby contest. The England prop and all-round Bath and Chelsea party-man Victor Ubogu lamented the Sunday shift in *The Observer*. '[Dublin] has always been one of those hazy places where you stay up all night and somehow find your hotel in the morning, and that is why the decision to play some games on a Sunday is such a shocker. Imagine not being able to sample Dublin's delights because you've got to be back at work the next day.'

There was further confusion and consternation – confusion because the levelling effects of a wet day in Cardiff were redundant while Wales played their 'home' matches in London, and consternation that a large portion of the BBC's television coverage of the tournament had been consumed by Sky and ITV. It was also confirmed that, from the year

2000, Italy would be allowed their overdue entry into the Six Nations. There was significance in each of those alterations – yet none compared to the cataclysmic shift in playing standards which had changed the tenor of the tournament forever. The overall history of the Five Nations contained a remarkably even spread of championships for each country – Wales (33), England (29), Scotland (21), France (18) and Ireland (17). Yet it was hard to predict another outright Celtic victory.

It even took some effort to recall that, up until the last World Cup, the 1990s Five Nations had still coughed up the occasional surprise. At the very start of the decade, Scotland had completed a memorable Grand Slam by defeating England in Edinburgh. Ireland had also beaten England in successive years, winning 17–3 at Lansdowne Road in 1993 and, even more startlingly, 13–12 at Twickenham in 1994. France had also suffered, losing badly to Wales in 1994 and, even in Paris, to Scotland the following year.

There seemed to be no chance of any repeat in 1998. The tournament would run the same course that it had done the previous year. To the cynic, and the realist, England and France would each beat the Celtic countries while their own encounter would decide the Grand Slam. The remaining matches would be of a more dubious quality, with Wales just a step ahead of the Scots and the Irish. There were even mutterings amongst some of the English and French players that they aspired to a different kind of 'five nations' – one in which they could join the tougher triumvirate of New Zealand, South Africa and Australia.

It was possible to imagine that, by the time poor old Italy made it through the millennium door, the northern-hemisphere showcase would have been downgraded further by post-World Cup English and French ambitions to compete more regularly at the peak of international rugby. The existing Five Nations divide was exacerbated by the certainty that the 1998 championship would be decided on the opening Saturday when England travelled to Paris. Once that finale was out of the way, so the jibes ran, the real jokey stuff could begin.

I found it more depressing than laughable. Apart from the fact that I lived in Britain, I could not find any pleasure in another narrowing of rugby's horizon. Whereas football had became increasingly egalitarian, and accustomed to results where Tunisia beat Germany and Norway thumped Brazil, rugby had become less democratic. There had once been eight rugby powers – the 'Five Nations' and the southern-hemisphere trio – with the ability to beat anyone in the world on a given day of rugby. There were now, at a stretch, only five. The 52–10 thrashing of

France by South Africa, and England's failure to beat any of the southern-hemisphere teams at home in the autumn had even raised doubts about that revised figure.

Nick Mallett and Rod Macqueen had revamped their South African and Australian teams. Together they would test the All Blacks with renewed severity. At the start of the Five Nations there was less certainty that either of the European giants could consistently cross over into such an exclusive club. Unless they did, and unless Wales, Scotland and Ireland raised their game, the hope that rugby might develop a more global perspective would be redundant. Argentina, Italy, Western Samoa, Canada and Fiji had closed in on the Celts' third tier of play, but that was not enough. Rugby needed a strong European dimension at the very top to provide it with contrast and colour. Instead, at the start of a new year, and a new Five Nations, discord and dejection prevailed.

Wales, the standard-bearers for so long, agonised over their decline and the accompanying dispute between the Union and Cardiff. The WRU, anxious about the loss of so many of their players to England, had managed to secure a ten-year 'loyalty agreement' with seven of their eight senior clubs. But their kingpin, Cardiff, refused to sign the nebulous contract, arguing that they could not commit themselves to the Welsh League while the future of rugby was so murky. Cardiff regarded their prosperity as being more closely tied to England and France. As long as there was a chance of an expanded Heineken Cup or European Super-League, they would refuse to limit themselves to domestic rugby. The schism highlighted Welsh problems in coming to terms with professionalism. Their hope that the pain of adjustment would be eased by the 1999 World Cup had also begun to splinter. There were persistent rumours that the new Millennium Stadium in Cardiff, like Wales itself, would not be ready in time.

The Scottish rugby psyche was even more ravaged. While they could attribute their record loss to South Africa in December to a 'freakish' Springbok display, the Scots could not describe the Italians in similar terms after they had been beaten 25–21 in Treviso. It was their tenth defeat in twelve matches. The inevitable departure of Richie Dixon as coach appeared less newsworthy than a despairing attack by Gavin Hastings. The former captain fumed to *The Scotsman* that 'Scotland looked frightened and played with less flair and feel for the game as I think I have ever witnessed before. Where has the heart gone? It has been ripped out of everyone connected with the game in this country.'

It did not help that Scotland were engaged in their perennial debate about whether their leading home-based players should be gathered along club or regional lines. But Hastings focused scathingly on a lack of individual commitment. 'No More Excuses: It Is Time For The Guilty To Go!' ran *The Scotsman*'s indignant headline. It would be a bonny old time in the Five Nations for the hapless Scottish boys.

The atmosphere in Ireland was more mournful than vehement. As we left Limerick, we could not avoid the feelings of Irish trepidation. 'Irish and Scots Lost In A Mist' declared *The Sunday Tribune* in their lead article on the Five Nations. I turned the page. The 'Lion To Roar Ireland On' headline was more upbeat, but the feature on Keith Wood could not fail to point out in its opening sentence that the bald man in the green number 2 shirt led 'an international side that is now expected to lose. Of eleven caps to date, he has been involved in just two victories – over the USA and Japan – and had to retire nine minutes into the latter of those games. It's the sort of statistic to induce depression or at least undermine self-belief.'

While Ballymena's recent challenge had offered Northern variety to the All-Ireland League, their impact in international terms was non-existent. Ireland would still rely on a perilously tiny band of men from the English Premiership and Munster to represent them in Paris, London and Dublin. Under a cerebral Englishman, Brian Ashton, they were also attempting to cast off their old Five Nations heritage of 'giving it a lash' to play a more expansive fifteen-man game. It was not a style to suit a team of such meagre resources. As one bleak Munster man croaked to me in Limerick, 'Even "damage limitation" now looks an impossible ambition for us . . .'

France, meanwhile, were buried beneath their own crisis. The extent of the Springbok-induced trauma in Paris became more obvious the longer I stayed in France. In Castres, an hour from Toulouse, even the usually high-jinking Thomas Castaignède stopped smiling when I asked him about the South African defeat. He spread his hands wide and shook his head grimly. Even his new shock of peroxide-blond hair seemed to stand on end as his eyes opened wide.

'Oh!' he literally gasped. 'It was a bad day! Our worst day in rugby! We cannot recover so easily from that match. It was like a nightmare! I was injured that day. And, later, to be truthful to you, I was glad I could not play. But I was also unhappy because that was my country losing so badly. I was in Manchester, commentating for French TV on the All Blacks' match against England. Everybody was saying the score from

Paris to me. I can't believe it's happening so quickly. Seven-love! Fourteen-love! Fifty-love! I want to shout, "It's impossible! This cannot happen to France!" But it did happen. And now we have to suffer.'

In Agen, I heard a more sober assessment from a man who had played that day. Abdelatif Benazzi, France's Grand Slam-winning captain in the 1997 Five Nations, spoke initially about that stunning French triumph at Twickenham. 'Last time we started the Five Nations,' Benazzi said in his thoughtful if halting English, 'we had young players. They were not experienced. Sadourny, Califano, Merle and me – we were the only very experienced players. So when we arrive in Twickenham we find the English to be very big favourites. It meant we arrive in a relaxed way. But we had a big inspiration – no one expected us to win. The England start was very good. It was very English. I lost for five years against England. I know how they play. They apply so much pressure, pressure, pressure. In France we say this is how England have played for a hundred years. It was the same at Twickenham. But I am the captain and I know the game is eighty minutes, not forty. At half-time I have the opportunity to change things. I did and we won. We won the Five Nations. But, now, I cannot think of that. Now, all the time, in my head, is a different match. South Africa 52, France 10.

'It was a big tragedy for us. It was terrible. For one week I could not sleep much. Only one hour here, one hour there. All the time I see this score in my head. I see South Africa scoring tries. It was very painful. I knew that French rugby would have to change. The shame was too much. We knew many of the players would not play for France again. We expect the same for the coaches. We expect trouble for them.'

Pierre Villepreux and Jean-Claude Skrela, however, were given one last chance. But a quietly hysterical edge surrounded their Five Nations approach. Apart from having to endure the psychological fall-out from the Parc des Princes, and then opening *Le Tournoi* against England, the French had the added burden of playing at the new Stade de France.

Jo Maso, the French team manager, attempted to lighten the cargo of doubt when a radically different side was named in late-January. 'We saw the way England played in their draw against New Zealand. That's why we have formed a team based on strong defence, on speed and sheer enthusiasm. We have been deeply hurt by the humiliating result against South Africa, but this is a chance for us to bounce back. Playing England in the first official game in our new stadium is a great event. It should also be an uplifting experience for this young side.'

Rafael Ibanez, their new twenty-four-year-old captain, had yet to start an international. Unsurprisingly, his guard slipped a little more quickly in the week preceding the match. 'If we lose on Saturday,' Ibanez said with a trace of nervousness in his voice, 'with a new team in a new stadium, the French public will really be up in arms . . .'

It proved at least that the Dax hooker grasped the national mood. The local press, in contrast, seemed to think that the selectors had lost their own hold on reality. Ibanez had only made six appearances as a Test substitute and he was widely considered to be some way behind Agen's Marc Dal Maso as second-choice hooker. Villepreux and Skrela claimed that Ibanez was attuned to their 'rugby vision' but his sudden elevation to the captaincy seemed to carry a mild tag of panic. Less controversially, the coaching duo had dispensed with the services of Cabannes, Lacroix, Leflammand and Merle. It appeared that the injured Saint-André and Ntamack would also not be needed for future French engagements.

A question-mark hung over the similarly wounded Benazzi, although the big man from Morocco tried to convince both himself and me that his international career was not yet over. 'This is my big hope,' he said in Agen. 'I do not want my international career to end with that game against South Africa. That would not be good for me. So I believe I will be back – even when I hear so many people all over France saying, "Benazzi, Cabannes, Merle – they are all finished!" All I know is that the coaches phoned me after the South African match. They say that the older players must go, but that they still want two of the experienced men. They still want Sadourny and they still want Benazzi. That was very big news for me. Even if I cannot play in the Five Nations I will come back and join these younger men. They have a very big job . . .'

The task which England themselves faced was diverted both by their transitory success against the All Blacks and their more enduring political bedlam. That twenty-minute blast against New Zealand was still sufficiently fresh to encourage the notion that, in contrast to France and the Celts, England might drive through the Five Nations on a fifteen-man surge. But their internal circus was a more telling diversion.

Bath's success in beating Brive was largely negated by confirmation that the English clubs intended to press ahead with their decision to boycott the next Heineken Cup. The organisers of the tournament, the European Rugby Cup (ERC) committee, had emphasised that they were willing to concede substantial ground on all the issues which had proved to be contentious to English First Division Rugby (EFDR) – the clubs' representative body. The ERC were willing to increase the number of

English teams in the competition and to add significantly to their slice of Heineken Cup revenue. The EFDR simply ignored the gesture, indicating that nothing would persuade them to change their tack. They had a bloodier war to fight first, against Cliff Brittle and Fran Cotton, who had enraged them with another call for England's leading players to be contracted to the Union and for representative regions to replace the clubs in Europe.

Meanwhile, down the bruised flank of a different skirmish, but still the same war, Northampton had made a further call to EFDR arms. They had resolved to deny permission for their internationals – Matt Dawson, Paul Grayson and Tim Rodber – to tour the southern hemisphere with England in the summer. Most of their colleagues in the league were expected to support their stand. They were expected to be only the first in a dictatorial line of judgments which would reassert the clubs' power over the RFU.

As long as the swaggering chief executives did battle with Brittle and Cotton, a pair determined to prove that they were infinitely harder than their names suggested, Dallaglio's pursuit of a new England supremacy would be perpetually undermined. He, naturally, resisted the gloom. When we'd shut the lid on the tedious politicians and considered the schedule of Five Nations matches, I offered sympathy that England should have to travel first to Paris. Dallaglio, instead, insisted that, 'No, mate, you're wrong! It's the best possible game to start the Five Nations.'

'Why?' I asked. 'Surely you would prefer to play Ireland at home first and then take on Scotland and Wales, before facing your hardest match?'

'Not at all. I think it's fantastic we're playing the French first. I have a tremendous amount of respect for them. And Skrela and Villepreux will get things right – they're highly intelligent and they've got a hellavu lot of talent to call upon. So have we! Let's face it, the old Five Nations has come in for a bit of a hammering and if we can kick off the tournament with a brilliant match in an amazing stadium, so much the better.'

'But I know you're more concerned about England than the Five Nations.'

'Yeah, course I am. But from England's point of view it's a great game to start the tournament. Everyone should be really up for it – because if you're not going to be motivated for the French in Paris you might as well pack it in. So we've said, "After the high of the All Blacks, why not pick up where we left off by starting this tournament against the French?" As we all know, on their day, France are capable of destroying anyone – but they also know that they never have it easy against England.'

Considering all that the French could produce between their twin tenets of 'fantasy' and the more ominous 'rigour', I asked Dallaglio towards which pole *Les Bleus* might lean in the Stade de France.

'I think they've got some immensely talented players,' he said with the careful smile of a debonair diplomat. 'I tend to think of them more as flair players. The press often overplay the angle that they're capable of producing dirty sides. Rugby is an intensely physical game. Sometimes it's brutal. The French know how to impose themselves. They're not shy about making their mark – but the best sides are always physical. I know that they're going to be doing everything they can to erase the memory of their loss to South Africa but, at the same time, we can't worry too much about them. At this level you have to have confidence in yourself. And I really do. We all do. It'll be another chance to forget about all the politics and show the world what we can do on the field . . .'

By the time England had settled at their Versailles base, four days before the Five Nations began, Clive Woodward sounded more tentative. 'I'm feeling more nervous,' he admitted, 'than I was over the four games we played against the southern-hemisphere sides before Christmas. The Five Nations brings its own kind of pressure because we're expected to win the championship – there are no prizes for coming second.'

The usually professorial Pierre Villepreux echoed the French apprehension. 'We have to be more rigorous in defence,' he sighed, as if he'd already banished its blue colleague of 'fantasy' to the bin of academia. 'That much is certain. We need players to put themselves on the line.'

Skrela added his own statistical measure by suggesting that 'for matches at this level you have to make a minimum of 120 tackles. In the South African match we managed only seventy. Players have to recognise that defence is the basis for everything. If we want to be able to attack, then first we have to perform on a defensive level. The modern game demands that.'

L'Equipe described the revised *Tricolores*' philosophy in a banner headline: '*Operation Defense*'. Mick Cleary responded quickly to such unusual French stringency. 'Something strange is afoot in Paris,' he claimed in *The Daily Telegraph*. 'For it is England, those dull, pragmatic souls by tradition, who are setting pulses racing with their bright, adventurous inclinations, and it is the French who are obsessed with tightening it up, closing it down and erecting a wall of resistance.

England the epitome of flair, France the ally of method and organisation. Cross-dressing comes to rugby.'

The 06.19 train from Waterloo could have been heaving with every last dancing transvestite from Eurostar's version of the Tunnel Club. We still would not have noticed. The first couple of hours of our journey made for a grumpy drag. A day-trip to Paris, then, seemed the most unpleasant idea I had dredged up in a long time. This book was killing me. I vowed to never, ever, get out of bed again with the futile purpose of travelling hundreds of miles to watch another rugby match. I was tired. I was fed up. Fuck the rugby. Fuck, especially, Five Nations rugby. I just wanted to go home.

As we neared Paris, however, we had a coffee and a croissant. We started to cheer up. Yet we were hardly as bubbly as the quietly braying group of Barbours who had just cracked open another bottle of Veuve Clicquot at the end of our carriage. They had begun drinking soon after we had gone under water. But even they needed to see daylight again to really let rip. Their rugby talk was still relatively lucid. The tallest gent confessed the concern he had felt while reading Lawrence Dallaglio's column in *The Times* that morning. Dallaglio claimed that he was, the man read, 'particularly interested in France's selection of what amounts to five number 8s in the pack . . .'

'Five?' one of the others snorted.

'Number 8s?' asked another.

'Bloody hell!' someone else said.

'Exactly!' the first man exclaimed. 'Just what are the bloody French up to this time?'

'What does Lawrence think?' the roundest chap asked more sensibly.

It turned out that Dallaglio believed that France had finally 'moved away from the days of Olivier Merle towards a very athletic pack. Maybe our playing philosophies have moved closer together.'

'Never!' someone countered, as if a dawn start at Waterloo had stirred the old fighting blood.

I looked out of the window. The train raced past the outer suburbs of Paris. It was fantastic to be back in France.

'Y'know,' I said to Alison, uttering my first long sentence of the day, 'I'm really glad we've come. I can't wait to see the stadium. I can't wait for the match . . .'

The journey from the Gare du Nord to the Stade de France took less than five minutes. Yet we could only see the grey base of the stadium as we peered across the wasteland which then separated it from the station at St Denis. The clouds were heavy, enveloping the upper reaches of a ghostly apparition built on the site of a former gasworks. It was late morning and, before the crowds, the quiet was eerie. We began the walk, soon veering right towards the white tents which at least promised that the match had not, seemingly like the stadium, been abandoned.

Earlier in the week, the threat of a cancellation had been serious. A bitter couple of winter weeks had frozen the pitch on the Stade de France – whose designers had dispensed with undersoil heating to, so ran the official line, 'avoid artificial growth of the grass in winter'. With France's hosting of the football World Cup just over four months away, it even seemed possible that the rugby would have to give way to save the newly laid stretch of grass. But, with an English heating company's mildly ironic help, the pitch had been 'microwaved and defrosted under a double rubber blanket and twelve hot-air blowers'. It might have sounded like a latex-queen's dream of a snug night-in, but it did the trick. The match, off the icy track at last, was back on again by Friday lunchtime.

Twenty-four hours later, with the drink starting to work its own magical thaw, we felt our first Five Nations flush. It made for a curious moment, as we surveyed the cultural divide in our tent, wondering whether we were on the side of 'rigour' or of 'fantasy'. What we did know, however, was that we clearly stood on the side of the tent hosting all the English fans. We were with the drinkers. On the other side of the rope, the French sat at long tables eating a two-course meal. A ramshackle but oddly endearing Parisian brass band played what sounded like a Gallic version of the Pogues' songbook – raising more applause from the drinking set than the more silent diners.

Yet there was no football-fan-style animosity, just a cheery acknowledgement of the strange difference between those of, as Franck Mesnel would say, 'Anglo-Saxon stock and those of a Latin temperament'. A small carafe of red wine was shared by three or four Frenchmen, while three or four pints of beer were each swallowed by every Englishman, Alison and me. At least we were happy as we exchanged politely disguised burps – ours induced by beery froth and theirs by an excellent-looking onion soup and *coq-au-vin*. 'Cheers,' we said, as we decided to have another quick beer instead of crossing over for a wolf-down of Stade de France cuisine.

By the time we had reeled out of our white tent the clouds had disappeared and the sun was out – which I took to be yet more evidence that a few beers always sort out a mildly unsettled start to the day. The stadium glinted futuristically, its open top cantilevered high above us in an oval welcome. It might have been the beer but the Stade de France seemed to float hugely in front of us, a stadium of such graciously imposing beauty that we felt like finding a bottle to toast the architect.

Once inside, with sunshine streaming through the sliding roof's curving glass and steel perimeter, it seemed as if £270,000,000 was a snip for such a stadium. It made Twickenham seem even more cold and dreary.

By the time most of the 80,000 crowd had found their seats, the two teams had gambolled at length across the green field. Even from a giddy height, Dallaglio looked big-jawed with determination in the warm-up. But my eye also kept skipping across to Castaignède's flash of dyed blond hair.

'When I did this in the beginning of January,' he'd told me in Castres, 'I phoned my mother. I say, "Mama, mum!" and she say, "Yes, Thomas?" And I say, "Mama, mummy, do you love me?" She said, "Yes, yes, I love you!" I ask her, "Even when I do something bad?" She shouts, "What did you do, Thomas?" I tell her I change the colour of my hair. She just says, "Oh, is that all? I'm glad it's not something so bad." But that's my mother. Everyone else thinks I'm crazy. But, after a few more weeks, I'm not the only one in French rugby with blond hair. Some of the other players follow me . . .'

That afternoon, Castaignède also led the English players on a dizzy dance through a roaring Stade. Castaignède's little feet blurred as his silvery hands fed the similarly quick and inventive Stephane Glas, Christophe Lamaison, Philippe Bernat-Salles, Jean-Luc Sadourny and Christophe Dominici behind him. But Castaignède proved again that he was a brave man as well as an ethereal magician. He tackled relentlessly, making a tenth of the 120 team-tackles Skrela had demanded. In front of him, Carbonneau, Magne, Ibanez and, especially, Califano were as glittering as they were robust. The whole French team, in fact, played as if the very sanctity of *Tricolores* rugby depended on both the effort and the wit they could summon in Paris.

There was a pure simplicity to France's rugby as Carbonneau worked in seamless conjunction with his bold pack. The Brive bruiser stuck close to them, ensuring that they applied the basics with devastating concentration. They destroyed England upfront, reducing their front five to rubble in the scrums and, despite Archer's efforts, in most line-outs. Without any platform, the English back row of Dallaglio, Back and Hill were forced to retreat. And then, with Carbonneau at their heels, the blue pack drove on, opening up the Stade with one magnificent forward phase after another. Califano was a bullocking presence, whether his cropped head dropped low to almost lift Darren Garforth off his sliding feet or, instead, when he aimed for the try-line during a typical charge through the white shirts.

The Toulouse prop's own fantasy, of one day playing at centre next to Castaignède, appeared ready to bloom into reality. But Glas proved to him that, as great as he was at running and handling the ball, even Califano did not quite possess the range of subtle passes and sublime angles of running. Glas played through the centre with geometric precision, a blue-shirted architect for the day. He designed the second French try with a perfect little bridge of a pass to Sadourny which drew Rees in, as if he were a stick figure on a drawing board, and created a curvy little overlap for the spare wing, Dominici, to race past a bemused Catt and Hill.

Clive Woodward admitted: 'All our Englishness came out and we became quite conservative, which is something I don't want to have in a team I'm coaching.' Instead, Woodward was forced to endure the sight of his side kicking the ball repeatedly, and usually down a Gallic gullet, missing a dozen tackles while conceding an almost matching number of turnovers. Dallaglio, incredibly, had the ball ripped from him as often as anyone else. Even worse for England, their pack was shunted around the Stade and their line-out creaked.

In the most elementary terms, England were bad. In the more exalted realms of both authority and finesse, France were inspired. And yet, somehow, after an hour, France were only 18–14 ahead after Back had scored a messy try for a falling English pack. A drop-goal by Sadourny and a penalty from Lamaison, in answer to another three points from Grayson, lifted the score to 24–17 when, in the last minute, Glas sliced though the English defence. He followed up his delicate chip to the right-hand corner only to knock-on just before he touched down. In combination with disallowed tries for Castaignède and Dominici, it made up the missing fifteen or twenty French points which would have more accurately summarised English disappointment and French delight.

'Of course the score flattered us,' Woodward admitted. 'It would have been a travesty had we got out of there with a win or even a draw. Our biggest problem was spilling the ball in contact. We kicked far too much ball away and, even in the second half, we did not fire out of the blocks. We did not have enough pace, while France ran almost everything and did not kick anything back at us. I've no explanation for it – we were just terrible.'

After the elation of Twickenham, the daze of the Stade. The rugby press, which had tried to support Woodward's talk of 'vision' and winning the World Cup, were becoming increasingly frustrated. While normal service had been resumed with Catt putting boot to ball as often as possible, the rest of the team appeared uncertain whether they were meant to be running and passing or kicking and simply grinding out a result. Robert Armstrong, in *The Guardian*, argued that 'Woodward's insistence that England can play a fast, all-purpose game flies in the face of the evidence. However, if he intends to persist with a high-risk strategy, the England coach should take advice from a world-class coach such as John Hart, Kitch Christie or Bob Dwyer. Woodward, likeable and honest, sounds at times like a bright undergraduate who has wandered into the senior common-room and finds himself a little out of his depth. His flimsy record as a club coach is beginning to count against him; at this critical time the England manager Roger Uttley needs to remind him that England are neglecting the basics in the set-pieces and in defence.'

The French press, meanwhile, were thrilled at the maturity of their new captain and his young side. Raphael Ibanez did not gloat at his earlier doubters. 'We had excellent motivation,' he said enigmatically before reverting to the basics upon which France had added their customary verve. 'I was pleased that we got our tactics right. Our defence was good and that is always a key factor at international level. But we won't be complacent after this win because I'm disappointed that we didn't take at least two or three other try-scoring chances.'

Jean-Claude Skrela, especially for a man who had just seen his team 'salvage the soul of French rugby', also tried hard to be a little more Anglo-Saxon than Latin in his ensuing reflections. 'This job is done,' he said quietly, 'but we have to be prudent . . .'

Scotland, Skrela murmured, were next. He sounded like a man who had come through the Five Nations' most glorious ranks and still believed in its competitive spirit. 'The Scots always make it tough for us in this tournament. Remember, the last time we beat England in the first game we then went and lost to Scotland . . .'

Chapter 12
Five Nations Blues

After it was all over, and France had won their second successive Grand Slam, and England had beaten Wales, Scotland and Ireland in the descending order in which they eventually finished the championship, Lawrence Dallaglio and I sat in his flat's living-room and compared notes. I had seen three-fifths of the tournament before heading for the contrasting Super 12 whirl in New Zealand and Australia. Dallaglio had been through the whole ten weeks. The experience left him more certain than ever.

'Not too many people are willing to tell the truth about the Five Nations,' he said, 'because the truth hurts.'

He took in the lightest of breaths, not out of hesitation but, rather, as if he had already set himself for another hard tilt at trouble. Then, calmly, he began. 'The Five Nations is not conducive to producing the kind of rugby which will lead to you becoming the best team in the world. I'm sure the French will tell you the same thing. If we want to compete at the highest level we have to play far more in the southern hemisphere. You just cannot compare playing there to playing in the Five Nations. When we came together as Lions, the British and Irish players showed that we can respond to that intensity. As the tour progressed so we grew as players. But, to be blunt, when we're back in the old Five Nations there is this terrible temptation to fall back into a comfort zone of mediocrity.

'We tried to resist it but I was quite disappointed by England. I felt we slipped back. But whenever I say anything along these lines I get heavily criticised. Not too long ago some guy wrote to me and called me a "shit-head" because I'd said that I would be lying if I claimed that the pace of the games we played pre-Christmas was not totally different to the pace of the Five Nations. I could also have added that, against the southern-hemisphere teams in November, first- and second-phase possession was nowhere near good enough. You need to be so much more positive. You need to retain the ball and use it – over and over again. Against those guys, because they defend so well, you need six, seven, even eight phases to score. It's a big step up. But people don't want to hear that – they still want to believe that the Five Nations presents the ultimate in world rugby. Clearly, it doesn't.

'The French, of course, were the best team we faced in the competition. They were very good. They play with such flair and passion. But, in many ways, even that game highlighted the frustrations of the Five Nations. When we play France, it's not like in the Tri-Nations where South Africa meet New Zealand or Australia. They play each other home and away. We only get one crack at the French every year. It seems wrong. They're far and away our strongest rival in the northern hemisphere and yet we only meet them once a year.'

The blue-hued memory of Paris still hung over Dallaglio. 'The disappointment still runs deep,' he said, as if he could see the match unfolding on the blank TV screen.

'What went wrong?' I eventually asked, remembering how he had stressed his delight that England were playing first in Paris.

'Yeah, I did believe that. We'd trained fantastically before the match and we were a little too confident – maybe we'd been up our own arses after the New Zealand game and just expected that things were going to happen for us. We went into the game as clear favourites and we have to learn how to cope with that, like the All Blacks have to do year after year. With a new captain, eight new players and a new stadium, it was a big day for France. So they hit us with a very aggressive game. They were much more committed in the scrummage and they were hitting harder in the tackle. Yet, as well as they played, we let ourselves down. We were missing tackles while they were tackling in twos and threes. You could see their motivation in every tackle. They were hungrier than we were.'

Dallaglio spoke fiercely, almost as if he and I were about to run out of his flat, down the stairs and through the front door to take on the French pack on a stretch of Ladbroke Grove tar. 'We can't allow that ever to happen again! We've got to have even more fire than them! We've got to go in harder than them – every time!'

I felt ready to take on anyone, to say, 'C'mon, captain, let's go get 'em!', but Dallaglio had returned to reality. He sifted through the rubble and found some hope from even that dreadful day.

'It felt like we played particularly badly and they played very well – and yet we still stayed in touch. That was the main positive.'

'It must have been hard, though, to keep that in mind at the official dinner . . .'

'Yeah, that Saturday night wasn't the greatest. I sat at the main table with their captain, Ibanez, the French rugby president and the English president. It was a long and lonely night . . .'

'What was Ibanez like?'

'He was okay. Pretty impressive in fact – and typically European. He spoke French, Spanish and English! So it was fine being with him – it's just that those Five Nations dinners can be a bit of a chore if you're stuck up at the top table and you've lost the game a few hours before . . .'

Dallaglio was thoughtful. 'Every great side has to have mental scars. The current All Black side lost to England in '93 at Twickenham, and they went away and revolutionised the way they played under Laurie Mains. They played brilliant rugby for the next couple of years. Then, in 1995, they lost the World Cup – but they've come back even better than before. In a way, you need that ammunition to really start firing. You need some pain to build the mental strength. I'd rather lose now, and learn something from that loss, than sail through and then see England lose in a World Cup semi-final . . .'

'What effect did that game have on the rest of the Five Nations?'

'Clearly, that result galvanised the French. They really caught fire and they played some great rugby against Scotland and Wales. They were outstanding. For us, the French game was a classic case of losing some of the confidence we'd built up against the All Blacks. I also felt we regressed a little when we played Scotland and Ireland. But there were some better moments against the Welsh.'

When they faced Wales, England had not won one of their preceding seven internationals. Midway through the first half at Twickenham, after the unfailingly classy Bateman had scored two tries, Wales led 12–7. It was yet another serious English wobble. But, then, the rarely seen 'other side' of English rugby burst open. England scored four tries in the last fifteen minutes of the first half to canter in 34–12 at the interval. They added four more in the second period with a stunning spell of running rugby.

'We stayed positive and stuck to our expansive style,' Dallaglio recalled. 'When we were down a few alarm bells were clanging. We could have just kicked and tried to win on penalties. But we had a real crack at them. It paid dividends. Yet, for me, the most heartening thing was that we scored sixty points and, afterwards, we still saw huge room for improvement. Especially on defence. We gave away four tries – and that's just not good enough. In our next two matches, against Scotland and Ireland, we allowed two tries each time. You could see that there were problems with our fitness against Scotland because we flagged and they went over twice in injury-time. If we're going to compete in the World

Cup we've got to become fitter and more technically proficient. The team which wins the World Cup won't give away eight tries in three games. The All Blacks, the Springboks and the Wallabies all build from an outstanding defence. The French are now also prepared to defend for eighty minutes and more. It's the only way . . .'

Dallaglio's Five Nations assessment, like all the French, British and Irish players I spoke to, kept reverting to that southern-hemisphere loop. He even felt that one of the few redeeming features of the tournament had been the introduction of referees from New Zealand and Australia. 'It was no surprise,' he insisted, 'that, with a New Zealand ref, we scored sixty points against Wales. When France played Wales and Scotland they scored fifty points both times and, again, it was no surprise that the officials were Australian and New Zealand.

'Of course we had Welsh journalists moaning that it was a disgrace because the game was allowed to move continuously. But then I really disagree with Stephen Jones that Super 12 rugby is powder-puff stuff where no one contests the ball. At least the southern-hemisphere referees have an empathy with the game. They want to keep it flowing and that makes for entertaining rugby. Some would argue that it's not to the letter of the law. Personally, I'm more in favour of their style. At least they're consistent. You know where you stand with the southern-hemisphere guys. Here, there are so many shades of grey that there's little consistency. The rugby is variable and, too often, it's slowed down by too much whistle.

'Beyond a handful of reporters, almost everyone else will tell you, whether they're players or spectators, that the best rugby in the tournament came on those days – England against Wales and the French against Scotland and Wales again. The gap between the teams was wide but the best players could shine. At least we had that . . .'

On the second championship Saturday, 21 February, exactly a fortnight after our visit to the Stade de France, *Les Blues* had travelled to Murrayfield while England hosted Wales. It was a day of record scores. Most significantly, it marked the first and the second time a team had conceded fifty points in a Five Nations match. After the Scots had been destroyed 51–16 and the Welsh had been decimated 60–26, Finlay Calder, the former Scotland international and British Lion, declared: 'Our players are now playing not only for their survival but the survival of the Five Nations. I have to say that if it carries on like this it won't survive for very long. Scotland, Wales and Ireland are going to be cast aside. People watch sport in the hope that the underdog can win. But when the underdog has no chance of winning it becomes very difficult to remain enthusiastic.'

France had won only once at Murrayfield in the last twenty years – in 1994 when, with a 20–12 scoreline, they at last broke that strange Scotch egg. The fact that, four years later, they could obliterate Scotland, winning by seven tries to one, hurt many of the old tartan stars. Apart from Calder, both David Sole and Gavin Hastings, again, castigated their successors for a lack of passion. Gregor Townsend told me how hurt he and the other players had been by accusations that it looked as if they hardly cared about the size of their defeat.

'It just wasn't true,' he said when I visited him in Northampton. 'So much was made of the fact that, at the end of the game, we smiled when we shook hands with the French players. Fingers were pointed at me because I put my arm round Castaignède and had a few words with him. There were photographs of us together, having a wee laugh on the pitch – as if it would've changed anything if we had refused to shake hands. I have enormous respect for guys like Castaignède and Carbonneau and Lamaison and Sadourny and Magne – they're great, great players.

'There had been a little incident on the field earlier when I'd stopped Castaignède and, as we fell, I accidentally hit him in the balls. It was completely unintentional and I just wanted to let him know that afterwards. So I told him and we had a laugh about it. Y'know, one of my favourite images in sport is that photo of Bobby Moore and Pelé together, exchanging shirts in the 1970 World Cup. England had lost but it didn't make any difference to Moore's attitude. And just because he smiled at the end didn't mean he had tried less hard in the game itself . . .'

I knew what Townsend meant; but I also knew how such a quote could be misconstrued. In 1970, Moore's England had played astonishingly well against the great Brazilians. Their subsequent 1–0 loss was a noble defeat. I suspected that Hastings and Sole would be quick to point out that a 51–16 thrashing at Murrayfield, following so soon after a record loss to South Africa, was devoid of similar honour. But it was churlish to criticise the young Scots for applauding their opponents off the field. The difference between the two sides was so vast that no manner of snarling would have brought about a Scottish victory. They lost the match not in the eighty minutes it lasted but, rather, in the preceding eighteen months when the gap between the Celtic nations and England and France had opened even more drastically. Townsend and the others suffered for the last few years' laxity in the structure of Scottish rugby.

'The game in Scotland has now moved away from the clubs,' he explained. 'The top players based in Scotland are contracted solely to their districts. Last season there were four districts and you played about six games for your club – the rest was District and European rugby. But now they won't play at all for their clubs. Some of the clubs think it's better because at least they'll now know who they can select on a consistent basis. But I think the club game will suffer even more because there'll be no international players on show and so the sponsors will drift away. I can't see how it will encourage young players to join the clubs – and so I sometimes worry that the gap between us and the French and the English might widen rather than narrow in the next few years.'

Like many of his international contemporaries, Townsend played in the Allied Dunbar, for Northampton. But I knew he was in the midst of deciding whether he should move away from the turbulent English club scene. In keeping with his love of French rugby and his constant yen to explore different cultures, Townsend was enticed by Brive rather than his beloved Scottish Borders. It was the right move for a player as intelligent and as inquisitive as Townsend. In the meantime, he yearned for Scotland to play with a touch more French 'fantasy'.

'We've been playing the wrong kind of rugby for the last few years,' he argued. 'Scotland will never have a pack which will dominate the top teams. At best we'll just about hold on in the forward exchanges. So we have to try and run the ball. We should have done this years ago. In the old days, when Sole and Hastings and those boys won the Grand Slam in 1990, the rules of the game were very different. Then, you could get away with a kicking game – especially when you had, like Scotland, such a great back row. It was kick and chase. But, since the mid-'90s, rugby has become a very different game – it's now all about running with the ball in hand. Against us, the French did that to perfection . . .'

For the first ten minutes Scotland had been able to ruck impressively but, then, the French took over. They controlled the ball at forward and, mixing with the backs, spun it wide and long. Three tries exemplified France's superiority. They all carried a Brive stamp. For the first, Olivier Magne, playing a towering match at open-side flank, ran fast and hard, burning off the first few straggling Scots. Magne looked strong enough to carry the ball another twenty metres but, instead, looking up, he decided on another option. As if he was Townsend or Castaignède, he used a delicate grubber to thread the ball through the defence. It bounced and bounced until, with Bernat-Salles swooping in, it seemed to freeze in mid-air. The French wing caught it and took a short jog over the line for a try which should have been named after Magne.

In injury-time, the Brive number 7 concluded a French move of svelte handling at high pace. He forged through another opening to slip a gift of a pass to an eager Castaignède. Their quickness of thought, the speed of their running off the ball and the alacrity of that final exchange was bright enough to illuminate even the stranded Scots. They simply stood in the blue glare. Castaignède dotted down under the posts. A minute earlier, Magne's club captain, Carbonneau, had burst round the side of a scrum to intercept a clearing kick with such deft zeal that, again, the Scottish defence had been helpless. Carbonneau completed a try which would have been ridiculously simple – if it had not needed brilliance at its very source.

As Townsend noted, 'The French no longer necessarily pick the biggest players – but now they consistently pick their best ball-players. Their wingers are not huge guys but they're fantastic rugby players. Their centres always use their heads to play rugby. And you've got forwards like Magne and Califano coming inside to link with Carbonneau and keep the ball moving, playing it from hand to hand. It's terrific rugby.

'But it's not only the French way. Look what the South Africans did to them. That Springbok result was phenomenal. They were just so clinical. I think three of their tries that day were length-of-the-field efforts. It certainly shook the French – and, in the Five Nations, they were a much better side for that defeat.'

For the sake of the European tournament itself, the key question remained whether Scotland, Ireland and Wales could follow France and turn their own humiliation into even a more modest form of rugby triumph. I think we both knew the answer. Gregor Townsend smiled, a little sadly, before he said, 'I guess we have to be realistic. We know we're some way behind the top five countries. We can't just ignore the fact that Scotland and Ireland lost to Italy this year. Wales only just beat them. So the four of us are probably grouped together – although I heard Nick Mallett say that Italy are better than Ireland and Scotland. He also said that we'd finish bottom of the Super 12!'

Gregor laughed, mainly because he was probably the most ardent supporter of the Super 12 in British rugby. 'I just love it!' he confirmed. 'I'm amazed when I hear people in England slag it off and say they'd prefer a dull 12–9 game. They miss the whole point about the levels of skill and pace and fitness and commitment in the Super 12. There is some bad defence sometimes, but, boy, there're also some massive hits going in. A lot of those teams would blow anyone away. I really want to go over and have a crack at it myself – once the World Cup's over and, hopefully, we've had a better time of it with Scotland!'

Townsend and the Scots had at least won their opening match – a mournful affair in Dublin which marked the end of Brian Ashton's uneasy tenure as Ireland coach. He was replaced by Warren Gatland, a former New Zealand hooker and Sean Fitzpatrick understudy, who had established himself as a coach at Connacht. 'I'm fortunate,' Gatland said, 'that, having played and coached in Ireland since 1989, I understand the Irish psyche. Each of the Five Nations has its distinct playing style. Ireland's game has traditionally been fast and furious, and I do not want the players to lose sight of that . . .'

Gatland seemed far less lucky to begin his international coaching career with a match in Paris. After they had cut through England and Scotland, the French were expected to chase their highest-ever score in Five Nations rugby at home to the Irish. We smiled politely the day before the match, on 7 March, when Gatland said, 'Of course we're rank outsiders. Ireland's record in Paris is depressing – but I'm trying to eliminate all negative thoughts from the squad. Words like futile have been used about our visit, but if we can be disciplined, creative and get a work ethic going, we can come away with something far higher than the public expects.'

The public were expecting a sixty-point thrashing so Gatland's choice of the word 'higher' seemed ominous. Would Ireland come away with the seventy-point mark breached at the Stade de France?

Willie John McBride, in Ballymena, had told me that playing in Paris was the hardest of all Five Nations experiences. He also stressed that 'of course we've got limited resources compared to France, but that's nothing new. I think the problem runs far deeper. With this professionalism lark I honestly feel our rugby culture is being eroded. Personally, I would only pick players who were based in Ireland. I think the cultural identity of each country has been sapped by all the money which has lured the Irish, Scots and Welsh over to England. I don't think it does anything for the international game. I certainly don't think playing in the English league is doing our players much good. They look burnt-out and they lack the fire and passion which Irish sides have always had. If they don't find it in a hurry against France, we're in for a terrible thrashing . . .'

Ironically, in the solitary but most amazing surprise of the 1998 Five Nations, France only just beat Ireland 18–16 – after trailing 13–3 and 16–6 for much of the match. Ibanez scored the winning try seven minutes from the end and, still, Ireland came back to almost gain a victory which, as Castaignède said later in Castres, 'they really deserved. They were better than us that day. We thought we would win easily. It was a big shock. They should have won – you know, that day, the Irish were very . . .'

Castaignède's cheeks ballooned and he puffed his chest out in extravagant pride. 'That was Ireland,' he said as he reverted to his normal shape, 'they were so proud it made them giant men . . .'

Keith Wood shook his head when he relived his own Paris memory. 'Y'know, there were some really weird feelings in the build-up to that game. We had been diabolical against Scotland and the French had been fucking brilliant in their first two matches. The Scotland match had been one of the lowest points of my rugby career. So, before France, it was a little eerie. At a team meeting the evening before, I asked everyone to say something – I was looking for just a sentence from each player. And one of the boys came up with this line – he said we were shit-scared of being shitless. And we were. We were terrified that we were going to be humiliated. We were terrified that it was going to be the worst-ever Five Nations defeat. Everyone presumed that we were going to be slaughtered – and that was the feeling in our camp.

'But we used that fear. Every single one of us was scared and we were willing to do whatever was necessary to avoid humiliation. The fright was so deep that it dragged us to a great height for that match. I always say that when you're underdogs you have to stay in the match for twenty minutes and then work in blocks of ten minutes at a time. We did that and we hunted down every ball. We swarmed all over them. Our defence was manic. I could see it after the first ten minutes – the French were totally shocked by our intensity.'

Wood, as usual, made the biggest of all hits. In desperation, Ibanez, his opposite number, hit him early in the second half, 'with a beautiful punch to the back of the head. I'd run myself into the ground and Ibanez saw me stand, legitimately, on one of their players. I'll give credit to him. He came after me, in defence of his struggling team. I got into a bit of trouble for calling it a "beautiful punch" and for not citing him – but, in my heart, I couldn't criticise him, even if he could've broken my jaw. He did what he thought was necessary. And it worked. I was woozy and I had to go off . . .

'Afterwards we were devastated that we'd lost. But, eventually, it did sink in – we'd achieved something special. By ten o'clock I was out of my tree. I even abused the French team in my post-match speech but, Jesus, I was drunk and it had been so long since we'd been good enough to almost beat them. It also proved that there was still a real heart to the Five Nations – that was very important to everyone. We lost a little of that spark against Wales – and we panicked whenever we got in their 22 while they seemed to score every time they got a chance. But, in the last game, against England, I really enjoyed myself. It was one of my best matches this season. It was 15–0 at one point but we dug it out and, in the end, I thought we played okay. 37–15 to them. They didn't bury us as everyone had predicted . . .'

France, however, buried Wales at Wembley the following afternoon, on Sunday, 5 April. Their 51–0 victory secured the biggest-ever win in Five Nations history and their most decisive Grand Slam. Gareth Edwards, writing in *The Daily Telegraph* the day after French mastery and Welsh mortification, admitted: 'The Grand Slam I was involved in exactly twenty years ago seems a long way away from the modern game. The disappointment felt in Wales this morning is born of the standards expected of players from a country which has had so much tradition and pride. It is still difficult for Wales to come to terms with their inadequacies, and compete at the highest level. It was abundantly clear on the lush Wembley pitch that the type of game that Kevin Bowring is preaching – the ball-in-hand game played at pace – is not possible at the moment with this Welsh team. Players who are outstanding week in, week out for their clubs have found it difficult to come to terms with the pace, tenacity and pressure applied at international level, especially against sides like France and England.'

A fortnight later, the passion of Edwards's most impressive descendant at scrum-half sounded even starker. When I met Robert Howley in Cardiff he was still in recovery from such a devastating loss, but his admiration for *Les Bleus* remained undimmed. 'The French were simply awesome,' he said softly. 'Last year, at the Parc des Princes, we were still able to compete against them. But, at Wembley, they were incredible. The most basic difference between the two sides was pace: the French were electric. Also, they have fantastic ball-handling skills and they now tackle like demons. On top of that, they have fifteen decision-makers. Castaignède was out of this world. Looking back on it, you almost have to laugh at some of the options he took. But he has that spark of unpredictable genius to make it work. And then you have a guy like Califano making the sort of decisions a number 9 is supposed to take. That's not fair! A prop is just meant to put his head down and scrum – but not these days. It was just a complete performance from the French. It was even better than the one the All Blacks gave against us at Wembley. For the French, our game was like a summer's afternoon of touch rugby.'

Howley, however, was bleakly aware of the consequences for Welsh rugby. He began by explaining that, as captain of Wales, he had fulfilled his 'childhood fantasy'. He looked across the Cardiff club ground and stressed that 'every kid had an ambition to play for Wales. I was born in 1970 and, so, by the time I was aware of rugby, we had all these stars for us to emulate. Gareth Edwards and Phil Bennett and JPR – their names go before them, to be honest. To have followed them is a privilege.'

I told Howley how, the month before, Richard Escot had faxed me some even more evocative French quotes on the grandeur of Welsh rugby. While preparing an article for the Wembley programme of the Wales v France match, Escot had spoken to the current French back line about their own red-tinged recollections.

'When I was a boy,' Philippe Carbonneau told him, 'on every Five Nations Saturday my mother would put a big bottle of Coca-Cola on the little table in front of the TV. My brother and I would watch every game which involved Welsh players. We were never fed up with rugby when Wales were playing. My older brother had bought an extra video showing the best try of the Five Nations and so, every day, we sat in front of the screen, completely astonished by the great Welsh team. I mean, those red jerseys in the '70s!'

His Brive team-mate, Christophe Lamaison, agreed that *Le Tournoi* was a ritual: 'Watching the Welsh enlarged my life when I was a kid . . . Gerald Davies was my favourite! What a flash!'

France's most experienced back, Jean-Luc Sadourny, said, 'When Colomiers, my club, came to Bridgend to play in the [European] Conference, I suddenly found myself in front of J.P.R. Williams. I was unable to say anything to such a hero. I just stood there – mute. He was so kind to everybody, easy and fine. A champion! And I found myself such a kid compared to him. Sixty caps or whatever don't make [me] a legend. JPR is – naturally!'

The red message had been similarly drummed home during Thomas Castaignède's earliest days. His father, Pierre, had also been an outside-half. 'Over and over again,' Thomas said, 'my father would play all the games that Barry John illuminated with his sheer class. And perhaps because I'm not a bodybuilder of a fly-half myself, his ability to avoid defences and then turn them into pedestrians pleased me so much . . .'

It was lovely stuff, and Howley agreed that it was echoed all over the rugby world. But, in 1998, Wales's leader on the field could only see turmoil both before and beyond every touchline. 'In Wales we're very parochial,' he said bluntly, 'and the effect of that can be seen very clearly in our rugby. When I was with Bridgend, as long as we beat Cardiff everything was okay. It made our season to win just that one game. Lately, it feels a bit like that in the Five Nations. As long as we beat England, everything will be okay. But it won't. Even if we'd come close to beating England this year, our problems would remain in Wales. They're very serious – and England did score sixty points against us as well!

'It's not just a case that they have better players than us. In fact, before the match we looked at the two teams and, especially in the back line, we thought that we had the edge in a number of positions. But, after a pretty bright opening, we played badly. Twenty-six minutes into the game we were leading by six points but, then, there was a hellish bombing. In the next fourteen minutes we touched the ball six times. In that time, England had eight scrums, six line-outs and scored four tries. I still maintain that any international side of quality would have done the same with that amount of possession. England just cranked things up and we were lost. Our pack got a lot of criticism but our troubles go much deeper than that. They start, as always, a long way off the field . . .'

It felt appropriate that we should be sitting in one of the Cardiff executive boxes at an empty ground on an ordinary Tuesday afternoon as Howley dissected the problems of his country's domestic game. 'As it currently stands, the Union are trying to get all the Welsh clubs to sign a ten-year loyalty agreement. All the other clubs signed, but Cardiff were not prepared to do the same because they felt the future of Welsh rugby was unstable. We don't know what will happen in the game next season – let alone in five or ten years' time. Will there even be a Heineken Cup next season? And, if not, what quality opposition can Wales expect to face? So it started that way, and there've been a lot of squabbles since.

'As players it's very difficult because we're caught in the middle.

We're signed to Cardiff and we're signed to the Union. I know that the fact that the English boys are not signed to their Union is causing them a lot of problems but, here, it's very difficult to work for two pay-masters. But, rugby being rugby, we don't expect things will change for a long while. It's now a professional game being governed behind the scenes by amateurs. And in Welsh rugby there are too many egos – and when the struggle is about power and money, the egos run rife.

'I sometimes think that people in Wales are very envious of success. They don't like to see people getting on in life. I think Cardiff is a massive club. We're the best club in Wales and one of the best in Europe. Everyone wants to beat us in Wales. It's a problem in the sense that we want to play a brand of rugby that you see in the Super 12 – and that can only help Wales internationally because England and France are already a long way down that track. They know that's the way they have to play to compete with the southern hemisphere. But it's very difficult to play that kind of game in Wales because everyone just wants to stop us playing. They want to shut us down on the field because we're the big-city club, the glamour club. It doesn't make for very attractive or enjoyable rugby. I think it goes to the root of our dilemma.

'I don't believe that Wales can fund a fully professional game. I think that it's more realistic to admit that we can only sustain two wholly professional outfits. Cardiff is financially self-sufficient. The others all have doubts hanging over them. Perhaps Swansea can join Cardiff and take on the best of the English and French teams both on the field and in the boardroom. I know it goes against the grain of Welsh rugby sentiment to say that, but it's the truth.'

Eight clubs played in the Welsh League's top division – and yet you could often see almost as many Welshmen playing in the Allied-Dunbar for Richmond as there were in the black shirts of Neath. Would the lure of the English cheque-book, I wondered, hasten the decline of the Welsh League?

'It has already. Personally, I want to stay here. It's a massive honour for me to captain my country and so I want to be based in Wales – especially when we're hosting the World Cup. But I'd be lying if I said my rugby was improving by playing solely against other Welshmen. We're such a small league that we know each other's play inside out. And, yeah, without wanting to sound disrespectful, it's sometimes hard to motivate yourself for the domestic club games. I have personal pride in my play. But rugby is all about peaks and troughs and, let's face it, there are a lot of Welsh club games where you can just cruise through.

'We get accused of being anti-Welsh at Cardiff because we want more than that. We want to regularly play the best French and English club sides. The Welsh guys at Richmond also get accused of being anti-Welsh because they're earning a living in England. But they're playing a higher standard of rugby week in, week out. That can only benefit Wales when playing France, England and the big boys from the south . . .'

'So, Rob,' I asked, 'what's the solution?'

'At the highest level of the game,' he said with serene certainty, 'I would like to see a fully fledged European competition. I think that there should be sixteen teams. Two Welsh clubs and between six and eight clubs each from France and England. If you went for six from the French and the English, you could have a representative side from both Scotland and Ireland. I don't think either of those countries could sustain more than one professional squad because so many of their best players are playing in England anyway. If you had sixteen teams, it would mean your top players would be playing thirty matches a year with the international games on top. That would be more than enough – and it would actually help the best Welsh, Scots and Irish players.

'Instead, we've got this vicious circle. The clubs want to keep the top players but there is a disparity between demand and supply. Yes, the demand is high but we just don't have the depth in Wales. There might be a massive pool in England and France but we simply don't have that many top-class players. So we end up with mediocre players demanding high-class salaries – and the whole thing spirals downwards . . .'

'But would the chairman of even a struggling Welsh club like, say, Neath agree that the national league in Wales should be restructured so that it plays second-fiddle to a European championship?'

Howley shrugged. 'Of course he wouldn't. That's exactly our problem! And it doesn't only apply to Wales. The chairman of Northampton has to ask himself the same question. "Are we for Northampton rugby or English rugby?" Whether you're in Neath or Northampton, surely the ultimate goal for any player would be to play for his country. Surely the needs of the country must come first. But how many chief executives of struggling rugby clubs will agree? They'll try to keep the existing structure as long as possible. That's the parochialism that exists in rugby – not only in Wales but in all the home countries. It's meant that, apart from the French, this has not been a great Five Nations for any of us . . .'

The huge scores against the Celtic nations could, at a stretch, be explained by the presence of southern-hemisphere referees and by the fact that, as the former Welsh international Steve Fenwick suggested in *The Guardian*, 'the ball-in-play time is far higher now than it ever has been. So more tries are going to be scored. It was significant that, against Wales, England kicked for touch when awarded penalties rather than going for goal. Because the game is played at a faster pace now it is easier to rattle up a large score.'

A coherent argument could also be made that each country had suffered previous slumps. As Jim Renwick cracked, 'If you think Scotland are struggling now, what about the '50s when we lost seventeen matches in a row, including a 44–0 home defeat to South Africa when a try was only worth three points? We have been here before. England and France are monopolising the tournament, but when I was playing it was Wales who invariably contested the championship.'

But the 1998 Five Nations did not appear to be a mere example of a cyclical dip. It looked more like a crisis. The problems of Welsh, Scottish and Irish rugby ran too deep, and the nature of modern rugby was too quick and brutal to provide any form of cover over the widening cracks. The tournament would not die, but it was hard to believe that it would regain its former lustre. Yet, like so many, I longed for a return to the flair and the fire of the best Welsh, Scottish and Irish teams of the past. World rugby needed a strong and vibrant Five Nations. Instead, we had trouble and woe – without end.

I asked Rob Howley the same rhetorical question I had put to his friend from the 1997 Lions, Gregor Townsend: could Wales or Scotland or Ireland follow France's lead and turn a catastrophic defeat into a dynamic new era of Celtic rugby?

His answer was equally honest. 'No, I don't think any of us can. We don't have the strength or the depth of players. Compared to France and England, we're still very small nations . . .'

'But so is New Zealand,' I said.

Rob Howley's smile was rueful as he murmured, 'I haven't got an answer for that one . . .'

Chapter 13

Summer's Over ... and We're All Happy

'Wakey-wakey!' the Kiwi voice bubbled and crackled as the plane banked to the left, 'this is your captain speaking . . . and, folks, as you all know, having flown with me so many times before, I, Captain Speaking, am the world's most famous pilot . . .'

The blue information screen flickered through the red-eyed gloom. Local time: 4.26 a.m.

Just what I needed – twenty-eight hours in and a stand-up comedian had taken over the graveyard shift. I'd left London early on Sunday afternoon, flown through a missing Monday, and, at last, made it into a bleary Tuesday morning over Auckland. It was not the right time for Captain Speaking to make his showbiz entry at the Mile-High economy club. I yearned instead for one of those Kiwi pilots who modelled himself on the bluntly efficient 'Unsmiling Giants' from All Black history. Then, it would've only required a flick of the mic and a curt 'Yup' to let us know that we'd reached New Zealand.

Two minutes of airy witter later my inner scream, for a Colin Meads grunt-a-like to throttle aviation's answer to Noel Edmonds, was finally answered. The silence was blissfully sombre, broken only by the lowering screech of the engine and a heavy clank of wheels opening up beneath us. And, at 4.40 precisely, as the plane taxied across the runway, a different voice, a deeper and more mysterious voice, said the only six words we needed to hear. 'Welcome to the city of darkness . . .'

It could not have been more appropriate. On my first visit to the dark heart of rugby, New Zealand's largest city had turned all black. For ten days, downtown Auckland had been without light. The longest power-cut in history might have been a warning to the world's most electric team but, even at five in the morning, I saw it as a more poetic symbol. For thirty years, for three long decades of rugby, I had wondered what New Zealand might look like. And, strangely, my dream had been right – it was black, black, black.

But, on the southern edge of the city, the airport still had electricity. So the drowsy face of the man at passport control had lit up when I slipped my little blue book across his high white desk.

'South African? Mmm – good on ya, mate! You enjoyin' the Super 12?'

I knew, then, that I had truly arrived in New Zealand. It was 5.25 a.m. and we were already into it. I did my best and, when asked, gave my opinion of the new 'tackled-ball' law and its impact on the Super 12.

'You're dead right, matey,' my passport-pal enthused, 'but I reckon it'll suit you South Africans more than us. Unlike us and the bloody Aussies, you fellers don't go to ground so much. You prefer to stand in the tackle, don'tcher?'

The snaking queue of British backpackers behind me listened dolefully, too weary even to contemplate a gang-tackle which would not only bring me down but open up their exit from airport hell.

Finally, after an exchange of our picks for the Super 12 semi-final spots in May, I was through – and into the baggage lounge where, as an empty conveyor belt trundled round, I joined the others and stared at a television. We were deep into injury-time of a game played at Ellis Park the previous Saturday. I already knew the score, as did everyone else, but that did not stop the murmuring approval of 'here it comes, here it comes' from the surrounding rugby buffs as the Blues and the Cats scrummed and wheeled near the South African try-line. When the Australian referee, Wayne Erickson, lifted his arm to signal a penalty try and a disputed 38–37 Auckland win, another soft roar swept through the terminal.

'Good for that Aussie!' an admiring baggage-handler sighed.

'Good for those Blues!' his friend enthused more loudly. 'To win at Ellis Park is a big ask!'

'Yeah, specially when we were bloody 32–11 down . . .'

'Pure ticker!' the second man in overalls nodded as he banged his left breast.

It was pure madness, too, but I loved it – even jetlagged and wasted in the dawn of a summery and already humid Tuesday. By the time I'd eventually picked up my bag and left the building, an orange sun had peeled away the last remaining sliver of dark-blue sky.

'Oh yes, it's lovely all right,' George the taxi-driver agreed, 'but the blackout continues, even in daylight! You won't be able to get a milk-shake or a cold beer anywhere in the centre of town – the power's still down . . .'

Big George looked more concerned about the loss of his milkshake run, for ice-cream had been the 'only thing which stopped me goin' mad in the weather we just had . . .' It had been one of the hottest New Zealand summers on record, and even a Fijian like George had struggled to cope with the blistering heat. 'And now,' he sympathised, 'these poor rugby buggers gotta run round the paddock pretendin' it's winter already . . .'

As we drove through Auckland, with each suburb looking a little brighter and prettier than the last, George murmured proudly: 'Biggest Polynesian city in the world. I been here twenty-five years and you won't believe the changes I seen. It's a nice big melting-pot these days . . .'

We had turned into Remuera, where I was due to stay. I had already told George I was South African and so he winked at me when he chuckled, 'But round here it's now pretty much a place for white folks. It'll seem like you've come home.'

If anything, a lush and hilly Remuera reminded me more of suburban Durban than the old Transvaal town where I had lived – especially up the steep climb of Seaview Road, which lived up to its name when we reached the top and saw the ocean below. 'It's very nice round here,' George grinned, 'very nice!'

I'd chosen my bed-and-breakfast from a guidebook, and had settled quickly on Remuera. It was described as 'one of Auckland's most attractive locations, adjoining the funky bars and restaurants of Parnell' – which sounded more than fine to me. But there was a romantic rugby reason for my homing in on one of the few Auckland names I recognised. It had taken me only a few moments to remember why I knew the name 'Remuera'.

I'd dug out Bob Howitt's *New Zealand Rugby Greats* – volumes 1, 2 and 3 – and read again that 'those inside-backs who have been terrorised over the years by Michael Jones, flanker, can blame a rogue barbed-wire fence in Remuera for what they've had to endure. Until he attended intermediate school, he was a highly promising second-five with all the necessary skills to carve a future for himself in midfield. But when he and his brother Derek went to their Uncle Niko's house to play tennis, Michael snagged his leg on barbed wire while searching for a ball. The leg was ripped wide open and took some time to mend. His coach at the time, Al Kay, concluded that because the injury would impair Michael's speed, he should move into the forwards and suggested the new position of flanker.'

Many rugby connoisseurs around the world described Jones as the most complete player of the last dozen years – if not of all time. I suppose the vague hope lurked that my B&B would be the exact house where Michael Jones had slashed his leg. It was not that the barbed wire would have made me nostalgic for Johannesburg but, rather, that it would have been a wonderful story to tell the two flankers I had interviewed most for this book. Lawrence Dallaglio and Josh Kronfeld, an English 6 and a Kiwi 7, had both spoken of Jones in awestruck terms. I could still hear Josh's voice, almost breaking with delight, when he'd told me in Pretoria, 'I just wanted to be like Michael Jones! Yeah, I wanted to be like Mike!' I thought how great it would be to take a small piece of barbed Remuera wire to Dunedin, for Josh; but, of course, it didn't happen.

Jones was back from one more catastrophic injury and, in the absence of Fitzy and Zinzan, had returned to captain the Auckland Blues. Everywhere I went in New Zealand over the next month, the name of Michael Jones elicited words like 'legend' and even 'god'. Yet, in my Remuera house, they'd not even heard of him. I had so suckered myself into believing in rugby myth that I half-expected every living-room in New Zealand to be covered in photographs of All Black greats stretching from Tiny Hill to Goldie Wilson. But Margaret, who used her home as an occasional B&B, admitted the more balanced truth. She and her nineteen-year-old son, Charles, she said with a dismissive wave, 'are not very rugby-orientated in this house. We're far more into the arts.'

Sean Fitzpatrick, I might have argued, had described the best front-row shenanigans as a 'dark art' – but I was too caught up in enjoying the irony that I had ended up in a New Zealand house so untouched by rugby.

In Auckland I met Jonah Lomu and Michael Jones, Andrew Blowers and Josh Kronfeld, Graham Henry and Carlos Spencer, Fred Allen and Kevin Skinner. It was a line-up great enough to send a shiver down not only me, but almost every New Zealander I knew. But, in Remuera, with Margaret and Charles, it meant nothing.

'Oh, they're on the television all the time, those rugby chaps,' Margaret sighed. 'I just try to ignore them – which, admittedly, can be a little challenging in New Zealand . . .'

I asked Margaret if she could name one current All Black.

'Well, there's that Fitzpatrick fellow,' she said thoughtfully. 'I suppose I've heard him say a few impressive words.'

Margaret was surprised, if not quite doubled over in distress, to hear that Fitzpatrick was still struggling with his damaged knee and had postponed his return to rugby until at least the end of April.

'Oh well,' she shrugged.

So, over breakfast, we did not analyse the rival claims of Stormin' Norm Hewitt and Anton Oliver for Fitzpatrick's All Black jersey.

Instead, at the start of each new rugby day in Auckland, I usually listened to Charles practise his cello beautifully while Margaret told me of her latest plans for a trip to Italy in the European summer. It was all very civilised and charming, and I learnt more than I had known before about both Tuscany and London's Royal Academy of Music – the different destinations towards which mother and son were moving. And, then, lowering the tone, whenever Margaret went to answer the phone, I'd sneak in a quick gander at the paper's sports pages to catch up on the latest Super 12 developments.

Remuera was a cultured reminder for me to flatten my more warped ideas about All Black mania. I already knew that not every South African, and not even every white South African man, lived for rugby – it just took some adjusting to reach the same understanding about New Zealand in Auckland.

On my first afternoon, the coffee-shops stretched invitingly down the sunny stretch of Parnell Road. There was also a great-looking bookstore; and I decided to pick up something to read with my opening drop-kick of Kiwi caffeine. Sweeping past the impressive displays for Rupert Thompson's *Soft* and Peter Carey's *Jack Maggs*, I aimed straight for the rugby section. I found my magazines. A bare-chested Christian Cullen stared out from the cover of *NZ Rugby Monthly*. The weekly *Rugby News*, meanwhile, featured a glossy photograph of Mark Robinson, the young All Black scrum-half, running out of the sea in a tight costume and red life-saver's cap.

'You must like rugby,' the demure girl at the bookshop counter observed sagely. She was reading Don De Lillo's mammoth *Underworld*. My rugby mags looked ridiculously flimsy in comparison to the huge weight of her book. I grinned at her gormlessly, wanting to tell her that I actually knew that *Underworld* was not about scrummaging technique on the South Island.

'I said you must like rugby,' she repeated softly, with the kindly smile one turns on the perennially disadvantaged.

'I'm South African,' I eventually muttered, as a form of excuse.

'Ah,' she said, 'that would explain it then. You'll feel at home here – everybody likes rugby . . .'

'Even you?' I asked eagerly.

'Well, that's everyone but me – and my friends . . .'

We laughed, awkwardly, before her eye was dragged down to the level of the *Rugby News* cover again. 'But I like that!' she enthused. 'That's almost witty for a rugby magazine . . .'

Against a backdrop of blue sky and even bluer sea, the words were separated into two by Mark Robinson's red cap and glistening torso. It was another definitive *New Zealand Rugby News* headline: 'Summer's over . . . and we're all happy!'

But it was still scaldingly hot outside. The coffee could wait. I headed for the nearest bar instead. Inside, it was cool and, even better, they were showing a repeat of the previous Friday's Super 12 match between the Canterbury Crusaders and the New South Wales Waratahs. I drank my beer and watched the rugby, feeling that I had found New Zealand's true soul.

The 1998 Super 12 had begun a fortnight before, on 27 February, with Friday-night matches in Dunedin and Cape Town. Josh Kronfeld's Otago Highlanders had upset the more touted Queensland Reds, led by John Eales and including backs like Herbert, Little and Horan. At Newlands, a Cullen-inspired Wellington Hurricanes had overrun a dazzled Western Stormers side whose own back line starred Small, Montgomery, Muir and Rossouw. 26–19 to Otago and 45–31 to Wellington – and yet two more victories for New Zealand rugby.

But if Kiwi power remained a constant, much else had changed in the Super 12. There were the Americanised names, for a start. In South Africa the four newly regionalised teams ran out under the bizarre banners of the Coastal Sharks, the Golden Cats, the Northern Bulls and the Western Stormers. There was a more gradual move in New Zealand to avoid associating their Super 12 sides with specific cities or provinces. Auckland, Waikato, Canterbury, Otago and Wellington were often referred to by their descriptive tags – the Blues, Chiefs, Crusaders, Highlanders and Hurricanes. The Chiefs had even picked up the toma-hawk and slashed the Waikato prefix into oblivion. Including North Harbour players like Ian Jones, Mark Robinson, Frank Bunce and Walter Little, and playing matches in Albany and Rotorua, rather than just Hamilton, it no longer made commercial sense to limit the team's appeal. It was also far easier for North Harbour and Bay of Plenty fans to support a team called 'The Chiefs' – especially when, three months later, their provincial teams would run out against Waikato in New Zealand's domestic NPC.

The (Wellington) Hurricanes tried to achieve a more ambivalent reconciliation – a difficult task when they were drawn from nine dif-ferent unions. In the capital, they were billed relentlessly as the Wellington Hurricanes. However, when they played in towns like Palmerston North and New Plymouth, they were called 'The Hurricanes'. In the same way, the Otago Highlanders in Dunedin became 'The Highlanders' when the team played at the bottom of Southland, in Invercargill.

Australia was spared such trauma and nicety. Without the depth of players from the wide expanse of a country still dominated by Rugby League and Aussie Rules, the three Australian Super 12 teams could concentrate their efforts in Brisbane, Canberra and Sydney. But, as keen on Super 12 hype as the New Zealanders and South Africans, they also traded under suitably wacky and 're-branded' Super 12 names – the ACT Brumbies, the New South Wales Waratahs and the Queensland Reds.

In the more important terms of rugby, it made for a fascinating contest as the dozen teams criss-crossed three countries. Over twelve weeks, in a programme to decide which four teams would qualify for the semi-final play-offs, each side met the other – with either five or six games at home, and the rest away, depending on the draw. For the watching public, the ideal schedule entailed a couple of Friday-night matches, two on a Saturday afternoon and one that night, with a humdinger on the Sunday. The time difference meant that TV coverage of an average Super 12 weekend could span an impressive sixty hours – leaving ample time between live games and recorded transmissions to stock up on essentials and get some sleep. But some weeks only featured five matches, allowing two teams the opportunity of a bye to recuperate from the travel and the competition's searing pace.

The game had been remorselessly quick during the first two years of Super 12 rivalry. Yet, in 1998, the teams' representatives decided to crank it up another notch. They wanted outrageously fast and free-flowing rugby which appealed less to the purist than a new kind of supporter who, primarily, was looking to be entertained by running, passing and try-scoring rather than absorbed by a more attritional or tactical struggle.

The Super 12 had become rugby's brutal equivalent of one-day cricket – held, preferably, under floodlights and with the full razzmatazz of an open-air pop concert. And just as world cricket had finally accepted the one-day variant as an entertaining and often compelling sideline to the real five-day Test, so the Super 12 had become compulsive viewing in the southern hemisphere. It also provided a vital bridge between provincial and international rugby. The Queensland Reds against the Wellington Hurricanes was not a Bledisloe Cup match between Australia and New

Zealand – but it demanded far more skill and strength than an ordinary provincial encounter.

Yet, just as limited-overs cricket diluted the concentration of an opening batsman who might normally strive to occupy the crease all day, and also shortened the run-up of his opposing fast-bowlers, so the Super 12 attempted to tinker with the grinding set-pieces of traditional rugby. The scrum had never been a central component of Super 12 rugby. Unless a knock-on was blatantly forward, or a throw at a line-out badly askew, teams were allowed to retain possession. Rather than having to turn back and pack down at the point of a mild infringement, they were allowed to move forward more positively. Line-outs and scrums, therefore, were not contested at length in the Super 12 – which, especially for British critics, diminished rugby's previously central struggle between two sets of forwards.

The 1998 series of law-changes were initially problematic. In a concerted effort to avoid the disruption of movement, a tackled player was instructed to release the ball. The more experienced referee allowed a second or two's delay, which gave other players enough time to pick up the released ball and drive forward. But, even after two weeks, the law was subject to wildly varying readings, with the result that some players looked bewildered whenever an approaching tackler closed in on them. Fearing a penalty against them for slow release of the ball, they tried to avoid the tackle by passing it to the nearest man.

Super 12 rugby, therefore, had become even more frenetic – and a little more like Rugby League. Extravagant passes along extended 'back lines' often replaced the essential ruck and maul amongst the forwards. There were more interceptions and turnovers. Ironically, it also led to more mistakes. Desperate passes went clearly forward or were knocked-on so awkwardly that the breathless ref had no option but to reach for the whistle he was supposedly meant to have swallowed.

Both Michael Jones and Graham Henry, respectively captain and coach of the Auckland Blues, the only team ever to have won the Super 12, admitted their concern when I met them just after their return from the opening couple of away matches in South Africa. 'It's certainly changed from last year,' Jones agreed. 'It's pretty helter-skelter now. I think they want to make the Super 12 even quicker and more sensational, but I don't know if they're actually achieving that goal. Perhaps it'll settle down after a couple of weeks, when we've all adjusted to the new law. But, right now, I'd have to say it's a little chaotic . . .'

'Just before the tournament began there was a meeting between the coaches and the referees in Australia,' Graham Henry explained. 'I was in England – but some of the coaches were not happy with the amount of time it was taking for the player going into the tackle to place the ball. Continuity was being lost. So, in theory, the change is a good one because it aims to keep the ball alive. But, in practice, people are turning before the tackle and so the ruck and the maul are being taken out of the game. Without those structures, it's hard to play and it's even harder to coach. But, for most of the fans, it's great to watch. Right now, in the Super 12s, we're playing a fifteen-man game of sevens . . .'

Henry, then only four months away from becoming the new coach of Wales, was sharply aware of British scepticism. When I asked him about the apparent 'commercialisation' of rugby in the Super 12 – stretching from the pompom-wielding cheerleaders to the frantic law-changes – he reacted with his usual brand of laconic acerbity. 'Look, this is not England where 80,000 bods will turn up at Twickenham to watch any kind of rugby just because it's a Five Nations match. In the UK, that kind of rugby is as much a social event as anything else. It's a chance for some old boys to turn up, take in whatever rugby's on offer, and then go off for a gin-and-tonic after the match with someone they knew at public school. That's fine. But, when they're looking at the Super 12, the UK critic should really get his head out of the sand.

'New Zealand's population is tiny – three and a half million. Rugby is our national sport, but we also have to work very hard to entice enough people into the grounds. Our core audience is full of middle-aged men. That's not wide enough. To make the game pay, we need to pull in teenagers and "twenty-something couples" and women – who are all looking for an all-round afternoon's or evening's entertainment.'

It was another sober reassessment of my mythic understanding of Kiwi rugby culture. The All Blacks, and rugby in general, dominated New Zealand sport, to the extent where the state of the national team could still shape the country's collective mood. But that 'obsession' did not stretch to a point where tens of thousands of people would just turn up automatically with fifteen or twenty dollars in hand to pay for an ordinary game of rugby. It helped explain why the Super 12 had been such a huge success in New Zealand. After so many years of humdrum pro-vincial rugby, overwhelmed during the last decade by Auckland's mono-tonous success, the brighter, faster and more testing encounters with South African and Australian opposition had brought back the crowds.

The success of the Super 12 had also helped quell the last vestiges of a threat from Rugby League. While Rugby Union had always been certain of its central place in New Zealand culture, there had been a surge of interest in League during the mid-'90s. The subsequent emergence of the Auckland Warriors, a professional team which competed in Australian Rugby League, had been noted with trepidation by the Union administrators. Soon after their inception, the Warriors were drawing home crowds of 25,000 – which was often far in excess of the number who would turn out for another Auckland union romp in the NPC. But, since the Super 12, the Blues were back on top as Auckland's most popular rugby team – in any code.

'It's inevitable,' Graham Henry said, 'that we're going to have some teething trouble with these changes to the game. But, on the whole, we're moving in the right direction. Ultimately, the Super 12 is a very tough and a very cut-throat competition. The teams are very even and they're all very intense about winning. You could argue that a lot of mistakes are being made out on the field, but we have to be realistic. The season's just a few weeks old. After a couple more games everyone will find their feet and you'll see a fantastically tight and abrasive tournament. It's going to be hell for the players, and especially the coaches, but it'll be great for the spectators and the TV people. Every team is capable of beating the others. It's going to be a real old dogfight . . .'

In their first match of the tournament, in a rainy but unbearably humid Durban, the Blues had been comprehensively outplayed by the Coastal Sharks. 25–8 was a bad defeat and, although they had escaped with that last-minute penalty try win at Ellis Park, they had been adrift by twenty-one points until the poor old Golden Cats ran out of puff. I was especially interested in the Super 12 fortunes of the Auckland Blues – and not just because of their determination to win the tournament for the third year running. I felt that the fate of the Blues and the Blacks might be inextricably intertwined. Both Auckland and New Zealand looked as if they would have to, somehow, survive the loss not only of the great Zinzan Brooke but, also, their most resilient talisman – Sean Fitzpatrick.

In December, when I had last seen Fitzy, I had always felt that he would make it back in time for the Blues. He thought so, too. We were both wrong. Instead of answering painful questions about his future, he was going to make one last-ditch attempt to overcome his hurtful knee. He told himself, and us, that he could still do it – but the unspoken prognosis was bleak.

Graham Henry tugged at his chin doubtfully, if diplomatically. 'He thinks he'll be back. I'd love him to be back. But he's got to prove it to me and then to the All Black management. Whatever they might say about the Super 12 in the British papers, it's a very harsh tournament. He won't be able to come straight in at this level – he'll have to try and play some club rugby at the end of April. But his knee's pretty bad. It could be a sad end to a great era . . .'

In the absence of one great New Zealand captain and front-row specialist, I decided to seek out two older icons – Kevin Skinner, the ultimate All Black prop, and Fred Allen, New Zealand's rugby's definitive former coach and captain. They were an especially robust pair of septuagenarians, Skinner at seventy-one and Allen at seventy-eight, who would take me a step back from the hectic whirl of modern rugby. I was particularly curious, too, to hear what they made of Super 12 rugby.

I turned to Skinner first because, with Colin Meads, his Black name had resonated through the Springbok history of my childhood. In 1976, twenty years after the famous South African tour of New Zealand when Skinner had returned from early retirement to 'sort out' the massive Afrikaner props, Chris Koch and Jaap Bekker, his legend still echoed through newspaper reports and our games in the back garden. Billy Bush and 'Jazz' Muller, the new breed of All Black in '76, were the 'toughest New Zealand props since Kevin Skinner'. Yet, even then, we read that they weren't quite as hard as Skinner. Even his very name – Skinner – conjured up images of a butcher of a prop.

But Kevin Skinner, of course, could not have been more generous when I called him in New Zealand. 'No problem, Don,' he boomed down the phone, 'I'm more than happy to have a yarn . . .'

I drove out to Henderson, on the outskirts of Auckland, where he and his wife lived. It was another special rugby moment for me – to meet Kevin Skinner, of all the All Blacks, at home in New Zealand. Strangely, he even reminded me of my father when he opened the door with a grin and a big handshake. He had a wide and open face, and he was balding badly on top – not that he minded having lost so much hair at his age. He also had the inevitable old belly; but he still looked strong and fit, with powerful forearms and a broad chest. He was barefoot, and dressed in blue shorts and a striped shirt.

'Still pretty fine weather, hey, Don?' he said as we padded over to his den.

'It's great, Kevin,' I said casually, as if I had been popping over to the Skinners' ever since my earliest days in short pants.

There was a photograph of Skinner, in an All Black jersey, on the mantelpiece. He looked unbelievably young and handsome. 'I was twenty years old then,' Skinner laughed, rubbing his wrinkled face. 'Incredible to look at it now, isn't it? We were on our way to South Africa – for a bloody tough tour. You boys won all four Tests! And every provincial match we played was a real battle too. I weighed about fourteen stone five then and I was packing down against these big South Africans who were all sixteen stone and more. Hell, at the end of it, I had a neck like a bloody ox. It was nineteen and a half inches thick – just from packing down in the scrum. I had to move up to a size nine shirt just to close the collar round my flaming neck!'

He chuckled at the memory. But it also defined one of the most obvious distinctions between old and new rugby. 'Oh boy!' Skinner exclaimed. 'They hardly know what a scrum is these days! In the 1949 and '56 series against the Springboks we'd pack down for forty scrums a game. Every time there was the slightest knock-on we had to go back for the scrum – even if we had already retrieved the ball. The ball was put in again and again – it was like the babbling brook!'

I laughed, but Skinner had already pushed on. 'The game's very different now. I like Super 12 rugby and some of these fellers are magnificent specimens. I also think the park has a lot of atmosphere these days. I think too many mistakes are made but, still, I enjoy it. Hell, I'm on my feet with the next guy when Ian Jones, a lanky lock like him, is suddenly haring down the wing, ball in hand, before he throws out a long beaut of a pass. It's marvellous.

'But, if they're not careful, they'll lose some of rugby's charm. The forwards are just not competitive in the tight-phases anymore. No one fights for the heel against the head in the scrum – not when the ball's being put under the bloody feet of one hooker! I can remember way back in 1937 and then again in '49 how our Has Catley and your Jan Lotz used to go at it hammer and tongs at every scrum, trying to win every ball. It was terrific – people would just go to the rugby to see which pack of forwards came out on top. They didn't mind that the score was 6–3 or 8–5. I miss that kind of intense forward battle. Also, if someone got hurt on the paddock, they had to stick it out. There was none of this swapping your players round and bringing in fresh legs from the bench.'

All morning we went back and forth, babbling up our own little brook of constant chat, moving from the then to the now with an easy sort of pleasure. But, always, Kevin Skinner made me realise how rugby had changed beyond recognition. As demanding as the modern game had become, he said, 'The players today are spared a few chores. When we went out to South Africa in '49, we left New Zealand at Easter and we got back in October. It took us nearly six weeks to sail to Africa on a cargo boat and then, once we were there, we had nine nights on the trains. It's no wonder that most of us gave up playing before we were thirty. We weren't being paid to play rugby – we had to bloody well work. I moved into the grocery game soon after I got married – and, well, eventually rugby had to go. I had a living to earn.

'But, now, we've got people like old Fitzy hanging on, trying to keep going when he's got a buggered knee and he's thirty-five years old. Don't get me wrong – I think Fitzpatrick's one of the greats. So are Zinzan Brooke, Michael Jones and Frank Bunce. But they're all old boys. Zinny's off to England and Buncey's battling with injury and old Michael Jones is also trying to hang on in there. But I think Michael Jones is very fragile now. Fitzy's fragile. I'm not saying the boys are greedy because they've put a lot into the game – but they can see the gold. I think Sean would have pulled out a year or two ago if there hadn't been the chance to earn some gold in the Super 12 and with the All Blacks. But I'm not blaming him for trying to come back – it's just that the game's changed and, quite rightly, they want to make the most of it.'

I asked Skinner if it was possible to compare players from different eras, now that rugby had literally reinvented itself.

'There's a big gap between the rugby of my generation and the rugby of today. But, y'know, I see John Hart quite a lot these days. I like the bugger, even though he's a dictatorial little so-and-so, a real little schemer, but sometimes I have to take issue with him. He's saying these All Blacks today are the best ever. Well, maybe they are – but there's a lot of slack in these lax rules. If we played under their rules, sure, they would have hammered us. But if they'd had to take us on under the old laws – well, you would have had a different story to write about then. I think we'd have held them in the old game . . .'

There was just time for us, in the end, to revisit the myth of '56. 'Don,' Kevin Skinner told me, 'there's been more rubbish written about that series than anything else in the whole bloody history of rugby. We had a few buggers as reporters then and they coughed up this bullshit about me punching the Springboks into submission – and everyone believed them! There were a lot of lies told about those matches. I'll tell you the truth, instead. The All Black selectors had made a mistake. They picked Mark Irwin and Frank McAtamney when they should have called in Snow White from Auckland. Snow was a prop – full-stop. You couldn't buckle bloody Snow! But poor old Irwin and McAtamney were put under terrible strain by Bekker and Koch.

'So they called me back after the All Blacks had lost the second Test. I felt ready to have another crack. I asked the boys what had been going on and they said that they were feeling intimidated by the Springboks. I turned to Tiny Hill and Bob Duff and I said, "Blokes like you? Being intimidated! Come on!" So I decided to stand up to these Boks. Chris [Koch] liked to barge in the line-out. So I said, "Chris, if you come over the line again, I'll knock your bloody block off!" He didn't do it again. At half-time I asked Ian Clarke if he wanted a bit of a breather against Bekker. So I took over on that side. And Bekker and I took a couple of swishes at each other – but we both missed. The rest of it was bloody rubbish!'

It seemed ironic that we had once thought that his name spelt out rugby in its most brutal form.

'I used to get fed up being this bogeyman to every bloody South African rugby fan,' Skinner admitted. 'But, now, it doesn't bother me. And, y'know, it has its good points. I get to meet young fellers like you who still want to have a yarn with an old bugger like me . . .'

Fred Allen had no doubts. 'That old bugger, Kevin Skinner, was the best prop we ever had. Skinner is a New Zealand legend – but, unless you played with him, I don't think you can quite understand how good he was in the scrum. He was a great prop. Strong as anything, but what technique!'

I took Fred Allen at his word. He had been the most successful All Black coach of all time. From 1966 to 1969, his New Zealand team were undefeated in thirty-seven matches – sweeping series against the Lions, Wallabies and *Tricolores* as well as roaring through Europe in 1967 with an All Black side still regarded by most who saw it as the best-ever team to tour the UK. As Auckland's coach he also achieved a record twenty-five consecutive defences of the Ranfurly Shield. Fred 'Needle' Allen was a coach without peer in New Zealand rugby.

As a twinkling first-five, he had also captained the All Blacks twenty-one times – leading them out in every Test in which he played. His only mistake had been his decision, as the touring captain, to drop himself during the Springbok whitewash of the All Blacks in 1949.

Fred had not been known as 'Needle' for nothing – he was a fierce and demanding coach. Bob Howitt, in his *Rugby Greats* opus, stressed that 'Allen possessed the special capacity to get inside and motivate the men who wore the All Black jersey. When Colin Meads yawned once, Allen glowered at him, "I'm not boring you, am I, Colin?" On another occasion he criticised Tony Steel for diving across spectacularly in the corner for a try. "You could have run in at least fifteen yards closer to the posts," he told him. Steel never again dived over. And when, following one particularly torrid session, Kel Tremain shouted, "You're a bastard, Allen," the coach promptly ordered everyone out for a further five minutes' training. "You're here," said Allen, "because Tremain called me a bastard." And he wouldn't let them finish until they'd completed three sweeping passing rushes without dropping a ball.'

But, as he opened his own door to me in Tindall's Bay, near Whanga-paraoa, about an hour outside Auckland, it seemed as if the needle had long left Fred Allen's hand. His grip was firm and friendly, even though it was partly covered in shaving cream. Fred's face, meanwhile, was a white mask of foam.

'Bloody hell, Don,' he chortled, 'I'm like a blinking slow coach today. You're bang on time but you've caught me a bit short! I'm still in the middle of this shaving lark!'

Fred was in his shorts, bare-chested and barefoot. I liked the casual style of these All Black legends. Before he left to finish his shave and have a shower, he showed me down to his storeroom at the bottom of the stairs. Then, still wearing his foamy beard, he'd hauled out box after box of yellowing clippings which charted his career both as a player and as a coach.

'At least you'll have something to read for the next ten minutes,' he cracked.

I could have spent all day in Fred Allen's house, reading his story in All Black history. There would've been a dozen more boxes, too, if Allen had not lost five of his best years as a player during the Second World War. Apart from a few friendly games in the desert against the South African and Australian soldiers, he did not play at all from 1940 to 1945. I had only got as far as the first few clippings about the great 'Kiwi Army' side, which he led through Britain in the immediate wake of the war, when Fred called me up to his balcony.

It was another gorgeous day, and we sat in the sunshine looking down at his peach trees and at the blue bay of sea which curled round the edge of his garden. 'Have a squizz at this,' Fred said, as he produced another newspaper clipping.

It was black and white, rather than yellow, having been printed only a few weeks before. In the photograph, Fred stood on a bowling green with Bob Scott, the great All Black full-back from the 1940s and '50s. Under a familiar headline of 'All Black Legends Fred Allen and Bob Scott', Needle's opinion on the state of modern rugby was quoted. I was struck by its immense generosity. Allen spoke of the 'magnificent athletes' and the 'stunning rugby' being played 'by such an exciting new generation of great young players'.

'Well, it's true,' he said. 'You take a young feller like Cullen. I think that boy's a genius. He has such beautiful balance – it's absolutely incredible. And he's not the only one with individual brilliance. If you look at our back three with the All Blacks, we're laughing. Cullen, Wilson, Lomu. I only worry that Cullen's going to get injured because, with the way he ducks and weaves, he's going to cop a knee or something. But I also think Cullen can improve as a player. John Hart came over to say hello to me at the Auckland Cup race day and I congratulated him on the year he had in '97. But I said, "Harty, you've got to get Cullen releasing the ball. He's fantastic when he beats three or four but then he should work it wide." And Hart said he's been telling him the same thing. So we'll see.

'As for old Jonah, I know he's still struggling a bit, but he's slowly coming back. And what a player he can be! Awesome! I remember Gavin Hastings coming over to me at breakfast during the World Cup in '95 and he said, "Fred, how the hell do we stop this bugger?" And I really like Gavin, he's a lovely bloke – but what could I say but, "Goodness, Gavin, I don't think a tank could stop this Lomu feller!" And when the All Blacks hammered the Scots I really felt for Gavin – Jonah just ran right over him.

'We've also had some great ability amongst the forwards over the last ten years. Fitzpatrick's up there with anyone I've ever seen. So is Zinzan. And Michael Jones. I had to pick a world team last year – y'know, one of those "Best of all Time" jokers. And, on the open-side flank, I had Michael Jones. So, with those sort of players, I think New Zealand rugby's been in great shape these last few years.

'The only disappointing thing is that, at the top, it hasn't been as competitive. Without being too disrespectful, this Louis Luyt bloke has stuffed up Springbok rugby in big lumps! The poor old Springboks have been a bit of a disaster since the World Cup – but now, with Nick Mallett, they're coming back. I said, "Harty, you'd better watch these Springboks in 1998! They're closing the gap on ya! They're looking really good now!" And he said, "Fred, I'm aware of the threat! It's a serious one!"

'You South African buggers are going to really run us close this year – and that can only be good for rugby. The Aussies are back too. In Horan and Herbert and Eales they've got exceptional talent. And then there's Burke and this Stephen Larkham – he really is something extra. So it's boiling up nicely in the Super 12, with the Tri-Nations to come!'

Allen had hit full stride when, with a sudden and polite 'Excuse me a moment, Don,' murmur, he stood up. He wheeled out of the room and, a second later, came back with an airgun in his gnarled hands. The old All Black stepped to the edge of the balcony and, with his back to me, raised the gun without a word. He fired a single shot.

By then, I had jumped out of my chair, almost as high as the smoke twirling from his rifle.

'Don't worry,' Fred said, 'it's just one of those bloody blackbirds eating my peaches . . .'

He put the gun away and then, calmly, continued with his assessment of the increased rivalry in southern-hemisphere rugby.

I had to steady myself; and so I asked him what he thought of James Small. 'He can be a bloody lunatic, sometimes,' Fred said, 'but he's a very good footballer. And such a competitor – so fiery!'

I wondered what Allen disliked most about contemporary rugby. 'I don't like this draft system. I know why they're doing it but it means that players are just being shunted around. They just play for any old team. They have no allegiance to the shirt. But, otherwise, the only rule that they've really got to look at is this tackled-ball hoo-ha. It's plain stupid at the moment. You can't release it in a second if some guy's holding on to you. Most of the penalties being awarded in the Super 12 are all because of this silly law. It's also taking away the ruck. Now I've never been a lover of the maul but the ruck is at the heart of our game. In the old days, your forwards would simply ruck and drive over the ball and set up a platform for you. Now there's less structure. They jiggle this way and they jiggle that way. I guess it's what the public want. But I would never decry the Super 12. Y'know, I still get given two tickets for every game and, Don, you can always find me there – at the Park . . .'

Rugby Park, Hamilton, Friday, 13 March 1998
On a grey and sullen morning, with rain sweeping across the end of summer, I drove to Hamilton. The seventy miles passed slowly, and I had time to see the New Zealand of my imagination. The cold and the wet, the rolling green hills and the heavy banks of cloud had always been in

my head when I had thought of New Zealand as a kid. And, in 1981, when I was twenty, and Nelie Smith led the Springboks across a warring country, the rain and the mud seemed as enduring as the police and the demonstrators.

The day before, when the sun still shone, I had driven over to Eden Park in Auckland. It was not a stadium to compare to Ellis Park or, especially, the spanking new Stade de France. My memories of Eden Park, unlike Franck Mesnel and the pink bow-tie contingent, were bound up in the Springboks' 1981 tour – for at Eden Park the flour bombs had dropped from the hovering plane during that final Test.

Fred Allen was a friend of Nelie Smith and so, inexorably, we had returned to that tour. I was astonished how, finally in New Zealand, my recollections of 1981 were so sharp and even pungent. I reached the ground through a slip road at the back. A white corrugated fence ran around the perimeter of Eden Park. As I slowed to look at the blue and white stands and the high rugby poles in the distance, I saw the scrawled words: *No Tour.*

They were written in huge capitals and covered one whole section of ribbed metal. I never did find out if they were part of the original protest, and had been left there as a salutary reminder of the way a rugby tour had so divided a country, or if they were a simply a middle-aged rebel's more recent attempt at nostalgia. I took a photograph anyway, at least to prove that it had not been a dream.

Rugby Park held as powerful a link to 1981. For it had been in Hamilton, at the same old decrepit ground, that the Springboks' second match against Waikato had been abandoned. I could still see our old television beaming back the pictures to Johannesburg – images of protesters and riot-squads, of a mass sit-in on the Rugby Park field and of a plane circling above, supposedly manned by a pilot ready to crash into the grandstand.

I sat in that exact stand, amongst the 24,000, for that evening's top-of-the-table clash between two of the tournament's unbeaten sides, the Chiefs and the Hurricanes. Both had begun the Super 12 with remarkable gusto. The Hurricanes had won in Cape Town and Pretoria, while the Chiefs beat Canterbury and then Queensland, in Brisbane.

The hype was enormous – and the noise at Rugby Park was out-rageous, mainly because the Chiefs used a PA system to blast out music throughout the match. It was tense and exciting, but also scrappy rugby, with our attention being diverted as much by the DJ's choice of song to illustrate each new emotion in the home crowd. When Christian Cullen set up Tana Umaga for an early Hurricanes try, and later followed it up with a gorgeous chip for Alex Telea to race over for another, the mixmaster reached for his Alanis Morrisette collection and hammered out *Ironic*. But when Mark Robinson scored an absolute cracker, bursting round the side of the scrum and through a huge hole, he played Blur's *Song 2* with its celebratory whoops. From then on, whenever the Chiefs neared the try-line, a roll of Indian wardrums reverberated. And, at the end, as the travel-weary Hurricanes came back with another Telea try to secure a narrow 22–19 victory, Rugby Park echoed with The Verve's *Bitter Sweet Symphony*. It was not Twickenham; but neither was it an example of the best Super 12 rugby which Fred Allen, Kevin Skinner and I still loved.

The post-match press conference was a small affair, with a dozen New Zealand journalists and me. But it did provide a lovely bridge between the past and the present. Earlier, it had been all Super 12 noise and colour but, inside a small room in Rugby Park, we could have gone back ten years or more.

Errol Brain, the Chiefs skipper, and Frank Oliver, the former All Black lock and famously grumpy Hurricanes coach, lived up to everything I yearned for from New Zealand rugby. With sweat and mud streaked across his serious face, the great Brain, or 'EB' as you called him in Kiwi rugby lingo, nodded approvingly when he was asked to consider the merits of the Hurricane pack.

'Shew,' EB sighed, as fair as he was blunt, 'those boys of theirs were well drilled, hey! Guys like Norm [Hewitt] and Bull [Allen] love that pick-and-go style. I said to our boys, "Let's just get the ball and hold onto the damn thing!" But they were pretty well drilled!'

I also liked Frank Oliver. 'Our boys need a rest,' he grunted. 'We've been on the road thirty days. So you can see why I get grouchy. In the second half, our wheels came off. The boys had the thousand-yard stare on. The heads were lolling. They looked like they were goners.'

'But the boys pulled through in the end, Frank . . .' someone ventured.

'Yeah, they're a pretty game bunch. They could've folded, but we've got some strong little critters in this side.'

'There was some good defence tonight, Frank,' a local man suggested.

'Yep, our defence was huge,' Frank nodded. 'Although we don't call it defence – we call it attacking the player with the ball.'

'You must be happy, Frank,' another voice suggested wryly.

'Well, this is pretty big. Three wins on the road. Fifteen points in the bag. So, yeah, if you wanna push me, I guess you could say I'm happy.'

Frank Oliver scowled and, on tap, the furrows poured from his head. There was an awkward silence – and then someone else asked if there had been a particular highlight, 'apart from the way you attacked players with the ball'.

Frank thought for a moment – an old All Black again. 'Yeah,' he said with half a smile. 'There was one scrum. We buckled them. And then we shunted them backwards. That was good . . .'

The reporters made their notes, and a more comfortable hush filled the room.

'That's us, boys,' Frank Oliver said, suddenly as quick as a Christian Cullen side-step, 'we gotta go . . .'

Chapter 14
The Big Man from Pukekohe

I drove in and out of Hamilton twice that Friday the thirteenth; and neither for luck nor pleasure. Hamilton just happened to be halfway between Auckland and Rotorua. It was a flat and plain town, named after an obscure British army officer. If a huge poster for the 'Mad Butcher of Hamilton – Best Meat in Town' had the virtue of conviction, there was less certainty elsewhere. The local hot-spot, Celebz nightclub, looked a shrunken building. Situated across the rainy street from Pet City and Burger King, its pink neon sign almost blushed at its own star-struck pretence. Even the use of inverted commas on the city's welcoming billboard suggested a tentative irony: Hamilton – 'Where It's Happening!'

Beneath a 'Cow Town Aims to Be a Now Town' headline, the lead story in that morning's *New Zealand Herald* reported that 'Hamilton, the country's fifth-biggest city, wants to shrug off its reputation as Dullsville and stamp itself on the map with a dynamic new image. In an effort to lose the cow town tag, the city's marketing gurus are banking on a new lease of life from a new name. Promoting Hamilton is mission impossible, they say. It is viewed as a city with no pride and no soul and residents who cringe when they tell people where they live. The new marketing department found the task such a nightmare it decided to change the product altogether – to Waikato City.'

The appropriately named Mrs Mavora Hamilton, an executive officer of the Waikato Chamber of Commerce, was against the 'reprehensible' loss of her urban namesake. But 'the acting-chief executive of the Tainui Maori Trust Board, Tom Moke, said the Maori tribe Waikato-Tainui, after whom the region was named, was very supportive of the city also bearing its name'.

The city council had still to decide whether they would hold a referendum on the subject, but the *Herald* remarked that, 'the identity crisis may for once put Hamilton at the head of the queue. In tackling a case of colonial cringe it may pave the way for other towns around the country to move on. Already Palmerston North is eyeing a name-change.'

As a South African, it was all strikingly familiar. For every old Dutch root in Afrikaner towns like Pretoria, Swellendam and Stellenbosch, there would be a British hand in the naming of Durban, Harrismith and Newcastle. The end of apartheid, we'd always assumed, would lead to a dramatic renaming process of places once entwined with delusions of white supremacy. South Africa would become 'Azania' and Johannesburg, Bloemfontein and the rest would soon follow – with the old-style Springbok tag for the national rugby team one of the first to be dropped. Yet, in one of Mandela's many gestures of reconciliation, most were allowed to stay; while the disappearance of others was more gradual. It took time for a province like Transvaal to become Gauteng, and for the South-Eastern Transvaal to re-emerge as Mpumalanga. Even old Jan Smuts Airport melted slowly into the 'new' Johannesburg International.

There was another South African parallel in New Zealand's bilingualism. Hamilton, like most towns, offered both an English 'Welcome' and a Maori *'Haere Mai'* greeting. It was a more lyrical equivalent of all those 'Welcome/Welkom' signs from my youth. The translations crossed over into most official instructions and directions along New Zealand's sole motorway. If the country only needed that one linking highway, the different languages provided a more accurate guide to its cultural diversity.

The 150-mile journey from Auckland to Rotorua swept through a large swathe of both colonial and Maori heritage. On the Auckland side of Hamilton, a café on the Hampton Downs advertised its 'Devonshire Teas' while, over the Waikato River, I drove through a town called Cambridge. But then came Putaruru and Tirau, Rotorua and Te Kuiti. While there were also symbols of newer cultures in the 'Hot & Spicy is Back!' promise from the KFC in Cambridge, and in the presence of 'New Zealand's Only McDonald's-Themed Gift Shop' on the edge of Rotorua, I was more taken by the blend near Tirau.

At a Maori rugby club ground, at either end of the field, lines of woolly sheep grazed the green tufts of grass sprouting from the base of the unpainted wooden poles. Oblivious to the importance of their work, the bleating flock were preparing an old pitch for another new season of a sport which, more than ever, spanned the different colours of New Zealand.

Even in the darkest South African days, we had been deeply aware of the role Maori rugby played in the New Zealand legend. If anything, the Maori and Polynesian Island players were most often at the centre of our All Black interest. I had so many memories of Bryan Williams, a Samoan flyer on the wing, and the mind-opening impact he'd had on our white lives during the 1970 tour. New Zealand, then, included three other Maori players in their thirty-man squad – just over a thirteen per cent Polynesian and Maori influence in an otherwise 'white' All Black party. Yet, in the last Test I had seen New Zealand play, at Twickenham in December 1997, nearly half the team could claim mixed descent. There were men like Josh Kronfeld – with his unusual blend of Samoan and German ancestry – and others such as Jonah Lomu, a Tongan by birth.

From the outside, the blend seemed to have unfolded seamlessly. A few positions had yet to be settled in the 1998 All Blacks' team. With Zinzan Brooke's retirement, a loose-forward slot alongside Taine Randell and Josh Kronfeld needed to be filled. The leading quintet of potential replacements consisted of Michael Jones, Andrew Blowers, Isitolo Maka, Filo Tiatia and Todd Blackadder – the first four of whom were Samoan or Tongan. It was a similar situation on the left wing where Lomu, Vidiri and Umaga were the prime contenders. The only 'race' issue centred around the varying pace each brought to the position in combination with their respective levels of power and skill. It seemed that what the Springboks usually lacked – some colour – ran right through the All Blacks.

New Zealand rugby, however, was not a completely spotless amalgam. A few stubborn stains remained. That pesky cousin, Rugby League, had just sliced open a supposedly healed wound when the Auckland Warriors captain, Mathew Ridge, suggested that Polynesian players, owing to 'genetic differences', did not seem as durable as most white players. It was soiled old ground – and reminiscent of that covered in late-'80s English football when Ron Noades, then the crass chairman of Crystal Palace, suggested that black players were invariably 'found out' by the 'hard white men' in the arduous winter months. It was a laughable theory which had been treated with suitable derision in England.

Yet Sean Fitzpatrick, on business in Sydney, was quoted by the New Zealand Press Association as saying, of Ridge, that 'he's right to an extent. Polynesian players do need to be handled carefully. Look at Inga Tuigamala – he didn't really reach his potential at union, but once he was in a professional [league] environment, where his fitness was monitored, he was sensational.'

The NZPA reported that 'while many critics of Ridge's comments have held up All Black and Auckland flanker Michael Jones – a Samoan – as an example of a Polynesian whose fitness is unquestioned, Fitzpatrick implied Jones was an exception rather than the rule. "There are Polynesian players who need someone like Michael Jones to guide them and maybe in a team like the Auckland Warriors, where the majority of the players are Polynesians, the guidance is missing."'

I knew that Fitzpatrick was far from being racist. But he sounded as if he was trying to blunder across an uneasy stretch of Kiwi territory. Essentially, the Ridge rubbish filled the small racial divide which still, despite all the changes, existed in New Zealand rugby and life.

I thought, for a moment, that Rotorua was burning. But the thick misty clouds in the distance were not made by smoke. You could smell it, the reason why they had given Rotorua its 'Sulphur City' nickname. The steam and the gas from the natural geysers, hot springs and mud pools hung over the town, with an aroma as mildly stinky as the billowing haze was surprisingly pretty. Against a stormy sky, the white steam curled from drains and cracks in the road and around the green banks of bushes and trees. It was at its most dense when drifting from large open holes in the ground, around which little stone walls had been built in the adjoining stretches of parkland.

Rotorua had been inhabited by the Maoris since the fourteenth century. Its name, with *roto* meaning 'lake' and *rua* being 'two', derived from the fact that it was the second lake the tribe had discovered in the Bay of Plenty. The town remained at the heart of Maori culture, which also explained why there was such a collection of *haka* photographs all over Rotorua.

I found my way to Rotorua Boys' High, knowing that some of my first questions would be best answered by a man called Chris Grinter. Apart from being the deputy-chairman of New Zealand Schools Rugby, a head-master and a first XV coach for the last nineteen years, Grinter had also been the middle-aged white man who had first persuaded Jonah Lomu to play rugby.

Grinter was tall and his grey hair was cropped short, but there was no severity in his manner. We got off to a great start. It turned out that there were three South Africans on the Rotorua staff, and one of them had been to the same school as me. It was a long way from a Transvaal town, and a South African state school, to Rotorua High. But Grinter beamed with delighted interest. 'Gee,' he said enthusiastically, 'isn't that a super coincidence! But I guess, as South Africans and New Zealanders, we've always tended to get on famously . . .'

'Is that just because of rugby?' I asked.

'I think the rugby link is enormously strong between the two countries. But so is the cultural diversity. At a school like this, for example, the mix is almost a fifty-fifty blend. Half our boys are of Maori or Polynesian Island descent. And in schools rugby, as in the senior game, that's very significant. The Polynesian boys add so much to the traditional brand of New Zealand rugby. It's why the schools on the North Island are always the hardest to beat. On the South Island, the Otago schools will only have two or three players from a Maori or Pacific Island background. But at a school like Wesley, in South Auckland, where Jonah and I first met, there's rarely more than one white boy in the side. And Wesley, like Rotorua, have been very successful in recent years.'

Grinter had also coached three immensely talented national schools sides – the most illustrious of whom was his 1987 team which included future All Blacks like Va'aiga Tuigamala, Walter Little, Pat Lam, Jamie Joseph, John Timu, Craig Innes, Jasin Goldsmith and Jason Hewett.

'The impact of the Pacific Islanders and Maoris on New Zealand rugby has been tremendous,' he stressed. 'In many areas of New Zealand, League is the game of the Maori and Pacific Island people. Rugby League is very confrontational and that appeals to many of the young men. It's interesting because, off the field, most of these boys are very shy and will avoid any form of dissent – for it's the way they've been brought up, with this great respect for older people. But, on the rugby field, they're very keen to be involved in a fast and hard game.

'Since more and more players have come over to rugby, many of our antiquated ideas have changed. Years ago there were many negative attitudes in New Zealand rugby – it was said that the Polynesian boys were quick-tempered and aggressive on the field. Some even said that they lacked focus off the pitch and couldn't easily discipline themselves. It's a lot of nonsense because these boys are very discipline-orientated and that's what makes them such wonderful sportsmen. It's significant that, because of their religious beliefs, most of the boys I've worked with don't smoke or drink. They've been very close to their families and they've worked quietly but very determinedly. That's why, these days, our schools sides are very strong in terms of a Pacific Island input. For the white boys who've come through the ranks lately and made it to All Black level – players like Christian Cullen and Anton Oliver – it's been a very tough and rigorous schooling. They've had to show a lot of resilience in standing up to these strong, tough and very dedicated Pacific Islanders.'

I wondered if a player of recent Tongan or Samoan extraction would consider himself primarily as a New Zealander once he had made the national schools side.

'I think, first and foremost, he would see himself as a Tongan or a Samoan. That's where their roots are found. That's where they feel they most belong. The Pacific Island culture, after all, is very strong. But New Zealand is where they live and so there is also a strong bond to this country. And, in terms of their aspirations, there is no doubt that they see themselves as New Zealand rugby players. The lure of the All Black jersey is powerful – and the game has also turned professional. So, many have turned away from League. That's wonderful for us . . .'

I asked Grinter if he had seen the latest round of doubt about 'Polynesian durability'.

'It makes me quite angry,' he said, 'when I see some of the old myths being perpetuated every now and then. But, fortunately, I don't think anyone takes serious note of it. I just point to Bryan Williams. He was a tremendous player and a great ambassador who also went on to qualify as a lawyer. Everything changed in New Zealand rugby once Williams came along in 1970. He started the All Blacks' great wave of Polynesian talent. And, now, his good work just grows. We all know how much Michael Jones is loved by the rugby public and yet he's also built a life for himself beyond rugby. Michael has a couple of degrees in geography and town-planning. Olo Brown, meanwhile, is an accountant as well as an icon to young front-row forwards across New Zealand. And then, of course, we have Jonah who is bigger than anyone, in every sense, in New Zealand rugby . . .'

Grinter was the principal of Wesley when Lomu's parents contacted him in 1991. They were desperate to 'get Jonah off the road to ruin'. From the tiny Tongan island of Ha'apai, where 'little Jonah' had been born as a thirteen-pound baby, Lomu's family had moved to South Auckland when he was seven years old. Compared to a Polynesian island, South Auckland seemed harsh terrain. Jonah was a massive boy and, in a troubled environment, he resorted to violence.

By the time Grinter accepted him at Wesley's Methodist College, Jonah had lost his best friend, Danny Sekona, and his uncle, Dave Fukoa. Both were stabbed to death, just two more fatalities amidst gang strife. The Lomu family hoped that a religious school and an inspirational headmaster might save their son from an identical fate. They could not have guessed then, by moving to Wesley College in Pukekohe, that Jonah Lomu would eventually find a fame which transcended anything else New Zealand had ever known.

Rugby, however, was not the first route to Jonah's salvation. 'No, it's a little ironic now,' Grinter explained, 'but with Jonah we turned first to boxing. You see, he came to us at Wesley as a . . .' Grinter hesitated for a moment as, with headmasterly precision, he considered the most diplomatic euphemism. 'Yes, I think it's safe to say that he came to us as a reasonably wild third-form boy. He was a little difficult to handle at first but I wouldn't say he was a problem. He displayed a lot of those South Auckland . . . [another pause] . . . tendencies – which make education quite a challenge in an area like Pukekohe. He was a big boy, even at fourteen, around six foot three and weighing ninety-six kilos [fifteen stone]. He had a lot of pent-up emotion. I understood what he was going through. So, in his difficult moments, I'd give him the key to the gym. I had hung a couple of boxing bags from the ceiling and I'd say, "Jonah, go down there for a wee while and see if it'll help you to hit the bag." And it did – he soon learnt to go down there on his own whenever he felt the need.

'Things went well. Jonah found a measure of calm and he came more out of himself. He was less angry. He was more positive. I remember that he wanted to play League and I said, "Okay, Jonah, you can go and play League – but on one condition." "What's that?" he asked. And I said, "That you come and play rugby for the school next season." So we had a deal – and that's how I was able to coax Jonah Lomu into rugby.'

'How did he do, at first?' I asked.

'With his size, and a wonderful athletic ability, he was a rugby sensation from early on,' Grinter affirmed. 'I played him at lock. And that year Wesley beat Gisborne High in Invercargill in the National Schools final. We had a huge pack – our front row was as heavy as the All Black front row. But Jonah was the man of the match – and no one would believe me when I said he was only a fourteen-year-old fourth former.'

I'd heard stories of the immense power Lomu wielded even then – his punches being heavy enough to sometimes knock the boxing bag clean off its chain. Chris Grinter nodded quietly. 'Yes, he had incredible strength and punching power. But I think it's much more interesting to note that, since those days, I have never seen Jonah throw a punch on the rugby field. You never see him show any violence and in many ways, knowing the difficulties he overcame, I'm more proud of him for that than anything else.'

Grinter looked thoughtfully out of his office window in Rotorua. The late-afternoon weather had begun to clear. 'You know, I've thought about this a lot over the last few months. There is so much to admire in Jonah

Lomu. Soon after he had come back from his illness last year and made the All Black team again, I asked him to visit this school of mine. And he came down to Rotorua and he spoke before a thousand people at our assembly for twenty minutes without notes – and I remembered the very shy boy I had first met at Wesley, a boy who had absolutely no eloquence about him at all. And I felt moved as I thought, "Yes, Jonah, you have come a long way . . ."'

A mere twenty-two miles separated the swish and hilly Auckland suburbs of Parnell and Ponsonby from the flatlands on the southern edge of town. The gulf, in all other ways, was much greater. South Auckland occupied a darker world than the sleek 'City of Sails' where huge yachts and expensive jet-skis dazzled in the harbour and along the packed marina of bars and restaurants. In Papatoetoe and Pukekohe, places less evocative than they sound, the surroundings were bare.

When I arrived in Pukekohe I searched for some trace of glamour. There was none – not even in the Bluegum Motel or the Pukekohe Hot Rod Club, and clearly nowhere near Bernie Thickpenny's Panelbeaters, adjoining the low grey building hosting County Manukau's Funeral Services. I thought of the friends and family that Jonah Lomu had lost, stabbed to death not far away.

Later that week, Lomu told me about the 'jungle attitude' which had then blighted South Auckland. 'There was a lot of violence in the neighbourhood,' he said, 'and that impacted on me. It was very basic. If you didn't know how to fight, you got beaten up – or even worse. So I became very aggressive. I used my size to intimidate guys. I would hit first and ask questions later. I became pretty hard-nosed. Because, y'know, life could be cruel . . .'

But, on a sunny autumn day in March 1998, waiting for Jonah, life seemed less threatening. A soft breeze lifted a waft of manure as if in reminder that Pukekohe was as close to Manukau County's rural communities as the southern sprawl of Auckland. A white banner strung across the main street of the town advertised that Saturday's annual 'Onion, Potato & Grape Festival at Pukekohe Park'. The two teenage Lomu clones who stood beneath the fluttering pennant looked as if they couldn't give a fuck. One had eyes only for his Gameboy while the second, the larger kid, gazed at the gigantic poster of Lomu which covered the local sports-shop window. Like Jonah, both he and Gameboy had coloured the front tuft of their black hair with a blond shock of dye.

He caught me staring; but instead of glaring he simply grinned. He pointed to Lomu in the window and put up his thumb.

I wandered over and discovered that both boys were from Wesley College, which I'd visited on my way into Pukekohe. My new Wesley pals were the dead-spit of mean young extras from either a Wu-Tang Clan video or the cult New Zealand film, *Once Were Warriors*, a harrowing dissection of modern Maori life where gangs and drink mattered more than rugby. But, as it turned out, my homeboys were also very sweet and very funny, describing themselves as good Catholics and emerging All Black rugby heroes. 'Just like Jonah,' the taller Maori chuckled throatily. 'It's just that we're not as good as Jonah, we're not as cool as Jonah.' Gameboy chipped in with an admiring shrug – 'But who is, brother, who is? Lomu rules!'

Watching them, I could imagine Lomu six years before. At Wesley, and replacing the pull of the gang for the crunch of the pitch, Lomu's own rugby hero had been the then incandescent Michael Jones. 'Oh, I was just the same as all these Wesley boys today,' Lomu laughed when I told him later that week about his latest pair of Pukekohe fans. 'Michael Jones was my idol. In those days, because of my size, Chris Grinter always played me as a forward. And, y'know, to be honest, I wanted to be Michael Jones. I had Michael's haircut. I'd stand at the back of the line-out exactly like Michael did. I had the exact same pose – y'know, hands in the air! Then, after his first big injury, he came back with his knee strapped. So I used to strap up my own knee. There was nothing wrong with it – but I just wanted to do everything he did. That's how I really got into rugby, that's how I developed my love of it. And I got where I am today because of rugby – it's taken me so far . . .'

Phil Kingsley Jones, Lomu's ebullient manager, knew exactly how far he had flown. Lomu had rocketed so deep into stardom that he was out of our reach. 'Listen,' Kingsley Jones said when I'd first called him to request a meeting with Lomu, 'fellers like you don't know the half of it. You think you can just call up out of the blue and me and Jonah are gonna jump for ya! Well, there's no way we're gonna jump. I've got half the bloody world phoning me up asking for a piece of this boy's time.'

It had been easy to set up my interviews with Skinner, Allen and Grinter. I had just picked up the phone and asked if I could pop over for a casual chat. But it was not the way Phil Kingsley Jones worked.

'So,' he queried down the line, 'what's in it for Jonah?'

I admitted that old Phil had rolled a tough one my way. I could not pay Lomu a fee for his time. I had no 'Big Fat Don' burger for him to endorse. There was no new hospital ward I needed him to open. I just wanted to have a yarn. And, even though he had lived in Auckland for almost fourteen years, I knew that Phil would not be seduced by the 'yarn' word.

While I hesitated, Phil spoke sharply. 'Look, I'm just a working-class bloke from South Wales. My family are from a mining community. We're used to bloody hard labour. We're used to working underground. And once you've done that you'll understand that you get nothing for nothing in life.'

'I understand totally, Phil!' I said with the hard-working simper of a sycophant who knew how to fawn above ground.

'So,' Phil repeated, 'what's in it for my boy?'

I told Phil that I would write a flattering piece about Jonah in *Esquire*.

'Yeah?' he said bluntly. 'Well, I've got every fucking magazine in the world clamouring for a feature on Jonah. You know what?'

'No,' I admitted.

'There's this Italian magazine – called *Colours* or something – and they've just voted Jonah one of the world's most beautiful people!'

My cloying prattle was not working. I tried a less sticky approach. I was interested in 'Lomu – The Man!', rather than 'Lomu – The Myth!'. I let the italics in my voice echo into the mouthpiece.

'Oh yeah?' Phil said. He had heard it before.

Even worse, it was time for me to put another coin in the phone-box. It was difficult. One hand covered my left ear, so that I could block out the steady roar of the mid-morning traffic. The other hand, clutching my tape recorder and the phone, was even more essential. I unblocked my ear and popped in a few more coins. Phil's voice was lost in the noise.

'Pardon?' I shouted.

Phil sighed. 'I said that's all well and good but someone's still making money out of Jonah at the end of it . . .'

'Not me,' I assured him.

'Well, someone along the line is exploiting his name to sell some-thing . . .'

I was being worn down. 'I know Mike Tyson,' I said rashly. It sounded like a threat. I blustered on quickly and explained: 'Well, I interviewed Tyson. And I didn't mess Mike around. I never got in his way. I never took up much of his time. I'll be the same with Jonah . . .'

Phil snapped out another fast jab. 'My boy has it far worse than even Mike Tyson! I think Jonah Lomu is the biggest sports star in the world. The demands on the boy are incredible. So that's why I'll use an iron fist and put it in the face of most people who come our way. I have to protect Jonah!'

Curiously, for all my efforts to persuade him otherwise, I agreed. I thought Tyson was still more notorious than Lomu was famous – but, as for the rest of it, he was right. There was no benefit for Lomu in meeting me. He was the most sought-after celebrity rugby had ever known, a superstar who symbolised his newly professional sport as obviously as Tiger Woods represented golf, Michael Jordan illuminated basketball and Tyson himself darkened the gloomier world of boxing. Lomu needed a manager like Phil Kingsley Jones – a guy who would happily burn off all the leeches.

'I understand,' I said truthfully.

Phil paused, perhaps surprised at our sudden agreement. 'Put something in writing,' he suggested, 'and I'll think about it . . .'

I was in like a shark. I asked him if I could glide over with a letter in an hour.

'No promises, mind . . .' Kingsley Jones warned.

We got on well, from the moment he poked his head through the open garage door of his home in Manukau City. He was dressed in a vest and shorts, a small barrel of a man who was as affable in person as he had been curt on the phone. We were instantly 'Don & Phil' together, a bit like a chubby version of the crooning Everly Brothers. He showed me round the garage he was in the midst of turning into a home gymnasium. Then, he took me over to meet Jonah's dad – 'He works for me,' Phil explained, 'which is just another sign of how close I am to the whole family.'

We went up to Phil's office and I marvelled at the huge Lomu jerseys which covered the walls. Each had been given to Kingsley Jones, as a thank-you from Jonah at various stages of their rollicking ride through rugby. For the next hour we chit-chatted away. We understood each other; and so I was able to relax. I did not push too hard for the elusive interview. It was enough to hear some of Phil's stories, especially those retracing the days when he'd been in showbusiness. As a stand-up comedian, Phil had even won a Butlin's 'Search for a Star' competition in the late-'70s. I was impressed.

He also liked boxing, which helped. We bantered back and forth, supposedly sealing our bond when I mentioned the 'On Being Welsh' banner and Celtic manifesto we had passed on the way up the stairs.

'My brother-in-law's wife is Welsh,' I said meaningfully.

'Really?' Phil said politely.

'Wales, South Africa, New Zealand . . .' I murmured passionately, 'the three great rugby countries . . .'

Phil nodded. 'As you know, Jonah's wife's a South African girl.'

'Tanya,' I confirmed in a flash. I wanted to shout, 'Phil, we're practically family!' – but, remembering our telephone conversation, I opted for caution.

'She's a great girl,' Phil smiled at the thought of Tanya. 'She's even tougher than me! Together, we make sure that Jonah's okay.'

Kingsley Jones looked seriously at me. We weren't kidding around anymore.

'That's why I wasn't so friendly before,' he explained. 'Jonah's not my client. He's my pal. And so many people want to take a chunk out of my pal. I'm not going to let that happen. He's had too hard a time of it already . . .'

Phil rocked back in his chair, and tapped the envelope I had given him. 'But I tell you what,' he said. 'I've got your letter now . . . let me have a chat with the boy and see if he wants to meet you . . .'

Eden Park, Auckland, Saturday, 14 March 1998

In the blunt terms of his once-rocketing rugby career, Jonah Lomu had taken a few steps back. The devastation of Nephrotic Syndrome cost him more than a season or two of his prime rugby-playing years. In New Zealand, it had also rubbed away a little of his lustre as a contemporary legend. As Lomu struggled to regain full fitness at the start of another Super 12 campaign, the two most potent attacking players in world rugby were widely considered to be Christian Cullen and Jeff Wilson. If Cullen and Wilson were certainties for the 1998 All Blacks, Lomu was in the unusual position of having to fight for his Test spot.

In Britain, still reeling from the 1995 World Cup and all those Pizza Hut commercials with Lomu and the Underwood brothers, the threat of Joeli Vidiri and Tana Umaga seemed incredible – as it would have done less than two years before in New Zealand. But the depth of All Black rugby, and the severe nature of Lomu's kidney ailment, meant that an intense pressure was bearing down on him.

After his opening two appearances in 1998, in Durban and Johannesburg, Lomu's form, like the rest of the Auckland Blues, seemed decidedly patchy. In contrast, Umaga and his Hurricanes were flying. For his first home game of the season, at Eden Park in Auckland, under the narrow-eyed scrutiny of John Hart and the All Black selectors, Lomu knew that he had to shine.

The Blues faced the Otago Highlanders, a tough and rapidly improving team including Josh Kronfeld, Anton Oliver and Isitolo Maka, who'd replaced the injured Taine Randell. Jeff Wilson, who would have been patrolling the same wing as Lomu, was also out. At least that gave Lomu some respite. After a fitful opening fifteen minutes on a hot and humid afternoon, following a showery morning, Lomu dropped a high pass as he slipped across the slick turf. The Auckland crowd groaned – as they did even more mournfully when the Otago full-back, Brendan Laney, slipped past Lomu's despairing tackle.

But then, a minute later, as if reaching within some fiery Pukekohe memory, Lomu tracked Laney and hit him with a tackle of such force that he lifted the number 15 off his feet and cartwheeled him over his shoulder. Eden Park erupted, for that was the freakishly awesome Lomu they remembered. Jonah had just begun. Twenty yards from the Otago line he barged through three tackles and, with three more hapless Highlanders hanging onto him, he crashed over – only for the referee to call them back for a five-metre scrum despite the television replay's confirmation of a legitimate Lomu try. It didn't matter. Lomu came again, banging his way clear, opening up a big bright path for his fly-half Carlos Spencer to set up another try with a gorgeous little reverse flick to Robin Brooke.

Early in the second half, Lomu fielded a difficult high kick steepling over his left shoulder. He caught the ball and called 'Mark!' – giving himself time to find touch with a relieving kick. 'Well done, Jonah!', the previously taciturn Graham Henry enthused from the seat in front of mine. 'That's great play!'

After seventy-two minutes, Lomu's beefy stock rose even further – a snappy break sending him hurtling down the touchline, his speed clearing him of everyone but a lone Otago straggler. But Lomu needed only half a hand-off to send the tackler to ground. 'Go, Jonah, go!' the rest of the Auckland coaching staff chorused as their arms pumped in unison with Lomu's hurtling legs. A rapturous Eden Park throng, which had emitted a low growl of anticipation whenever the ball neared Lomu, were on their feet. They bellowed as he scored his first Super 12 try of the year. John Hart's toothy smile filled the television monitors. Lomu, it seemed, had pleased everyone – apart from the dejected Otago team. Kronfeld left the field with an ankle injury, and the Highlanders slipped away to a 41–22 thumping. Jonah and the Blues were back on track.

In the dressing-room ten minutes later, there was no surprise when the television crews called for Lomu. As he walked through the sweltering doorway, and into the white light, he looked my way and grinned – it had been a fine day and there was just one more job to do. 'Hello, mate,' he said as he stretched out his broad hand to the blazered TV head who was rushing towards him with his silver microphone. 'Good game?'

Manukau City, South Auckland, Sunday, 16 March 1998
In person, Jonah Lomu was impossible to resist. And it had nothing to do with size, for the things I liked most about Jonah were found in the little moments. I liked the way he insisted on leaping up to fetch me yet another of 'those great creamy biscuits', and how he winked slyly when Phil Kingsley Jones convinced me that 'Jonah has a beautiful singing voice – the boy would make a great record'. And I liked the fact that Jonah then broke in with a little tap on my knee. He cocked a brow, looked me in the eye and almost giggled. 'Aw, Don, I wouldn't listen to Phil. Nah, I don't think I've got a singing voice at all.'

His grin just widened when I pointed out Phil's own showbiz pedigree.

'Exactly! You tell him boy!' Kingsley Jones said. '1977 Butlin's finals at the London Palladium and I pipped Stan Boardman, the Scouse comedian. I was in the business for years. I know a few things and, Jonah, you can really sing! We've also had people from Las Vegas telling us that Jonah could fight for the heavyweight championship of the world. I believe he can act, too, if he wants. I said it at the World Cup in South Africa. And my mate, Terry Godwin, a rugby writer, called and said, "You shouldn't have said that. Jonah's just a rugby player." And I said, "Fuck ya! This boy can do anything he likes."'

There was something beguiling about the Phil & Jonah Show as they ripped through their Little and Large routine – 'That's Phil in a nutshell,' Lomu cracked as he patted his manager on the belly, 'little and large!' They had known each other long before the World Cup, stretching back to Jonah's Wesley College days, when Chris Grinter called up Kingsley Jones.

'Chris phoned me,' Phil recalled, 'and said, "This boy should be in the Counties development squad." But when I heard he was fourteen, I just laughed. "Fourteen! The boys in my squad are at least eighteen." But Chris persisted and I went down and took one look at Jonah and he was in my team. We've been pals ever since.'

Rather than finding a slick media guru or marketing man to act as his manager, Lomu had turned to a former Welsh miner and comedian. 'Well,' Lomu explained, 'I'd seen how sports people often end up with managers they don't really know. And they just get jerked. I wasn't looking for some agent. I was looking for someone I could work with as a mate. Phil was the only guy who fell into that category. When he said to me, "Listen, boy, I don't know the first thing about management," I said, "It doesn't matter – you're good enough for me."'

And they were good enough together that, once the double-act had been reeled in, Kingsley Jones retreated and allowed Lomu to speak for himself. He did so with a lucidity that was almost surprising, considering his tentative early years when a voracious media hounded him.

'I was very shy then,' Lomu admitted. 'It came out of my childhood. The Polynesian way is to keep your head down. You only talk when you're spoken to and you never look anyone in the eye. It's the way we were brought up; it's our way of showing respect. But I have to act differently now – and it's getting a little easier all the time.'

I wondered if it was harder on the field, knowing that there were two or three men marking his every move, knowing that Vidiri and Umaga were being mentioned as All Black rivals.

'The hardest thing,' he admitted, 'has been getting the confidence back. Going out and doing it like it's natural, to play without being afraid to try something. I guess that's been missing. But yesterday [against Otago] was a step forward. Now it's just a matter of always feeling that you've got that licence to play with freedom. You can't worry about how the other guys chasing your spot are doing. I'm enjoying the challenge.'

As Kingsley Jones had complained, expectations around Lomu were such that he was never allowed a quiet game. He sometimes looked as if he was trying to score a couple of tries every game, with half the opposition hanging on him. But it was no longer so easy for him. It was no longer 1995.

'Yeah,' he sighed for the first time, 'but the illness has given me another perspective. I'm just thankful to play again. That's why I play – not for money or fame but because I love it.'

'And when your illness was at its worst?' I asked.

'Whew,' Lomu whistled through his teeth. 'It was tough. The doctors thought it would be a long time before the medication helped. But I was different to other patients. It started to work almost immediately. I'm still not really right but I know what I'm dealing with. I know I'm probably going to be on medication for the rest of my life.'

'Did you think it was the end?'

Lomu hesitated, looking oddly hurt. 'There was one time. I was on the couch at home, watching rugby on TV. And it just hit me. But Tanya clipped me round the head and said, "That's enough, boy!" I was fine after that.'

He was without bitterness, even though he had once felt so unstoppable. 'I had to accept that life can't always be good,' he said evenly. 'There have to be bad times . . .'

'It's not easy being philosophical . . .' I suggested.

'No, it's not. But I'm different since I was that kid at Wesley. That's why Chris Grinter was so significant. He knew I needed to get some anger out. He knew I needed the boxing bag. It worked. The week after I first hit the bag, I got clobbered on the rugby field. I knew I could hammer this guy who hit me, and I was tempted to whack him back as usual. But, instead, I just smiled and walked away. I was in control. That's how I escaped the violence and focused on rugby.'

'And if it hadn't been for rugby?'

'Boy, I don't like to think about it!'

I knew about the deaths and I knew, too, that some of his old friends were still in prison. But, that Sunday, I thought that he was different. Even with all the ravaging strangeness of his huge fame he was not, like Tyson, a victim. He was not the 'freak' of popular myth. As he grinned again, there was a light calm about him. It might have taken a tiny organism in his kidney rather than a bazooka to bring him down, but he was on his way up again. The dark days were fading.

'Do you always feel,' I asked, 'as if you're in control?'

'Not before the All Black games,' Jonah said softly. 'That's when you get so nervous you want to spew with the tension – the black shirt means so much. The World Cup was the worst. I remember, just before the first game, against Ireland, I was so wound up. I was actually vomiting with nerves and shock . . .'

'And after destroying England in that semi-final?'

'Numb. I'd put myself in this little box to block everything out – it took a while to realise what had happened . . . but then I was happy. And that's how I still try to play. I feel the passion before the game, then I try to stay calm on the field. I don't need to hurt anyone. I just want to play with all my heart. That's why I reckon that whatever happens, I'm going to be okay, I'm really going to be okay . . .'

I believed him. As Phil Kingsley Jones meandered back, Lomu's humour resurfaced. 'Hey,' he asked, 'do you want to hear about my best day ever?'

'Sure,' I said, hoping for a little scoop from the big man.

'It was the day I told Phil I'd organised him a permanent parking spot at the airport. He was so happy. He was like a little kid. But, once we got to the airport, he found out it wasn't free parking. It was a $145 slot. Phil was going crazy. But I kept quiet, looking out the window, acting all innocent. And then, the moment came . . . oh, I loved it! Phil had to take out his cobweb wallet!'

'He's done some terrible things,' the Welsh Spiderman said darkly. 'I once went on this diet where I could only eat one piece of bread a week –'

'Oh yeah,' Lomu jumped up excitedly. 'The fruit diet!'

'And then he'd take me into McDonald's –'

'And I'd order four double cheeseburgers,' a deadpan Lomu sizzled, 'and then I'd turn to him and say, "What about you, Phil? Would you like anything?" And he'd be glaring at me and I'd come in with my killer-line: "Aw, yeah, you're on that fruit diet, aren't you, Phil?"'

I saw Jonah Lomu the following day too, on a sun-filled Monday. We met first at a gym in Newmarket, just down the road from Remuera, where he and the rest of the laughing Blues worked the heavy weights. As Olo Brown and Craig Dowd pumped metal stoically, Lomu skipped over to say hello. 'Oh, mate,' he said. 'I've been struggling. You shoulda seen the circuits we just done. It was so tough. I was waitin' for my second wind. I just kept saying, "Where are you, second wind, where are you?" And you know when it finally came? On the very last circuit of fifty!'

But, during a dappled late-afternoon's training session at Eden Park that day, he ran and passed the ball to his Auckland pals with such vigour and determination that jubilant cries of 'Jonah! Jonah! Jonah!' echoed around the empty ground. And at the end of it all, drenched in sweat, walking beside his captain, the gently composed Michael Jones, Jonah Lomu said, as if to the world as much as me: 'It's still good, mate . . .'

Chapter 15

Swimming with Sharks

After ten days in Auckland, my one-man version of a Super 12 tour began to roll. But seven towns, six hangovers, two islands, a couple of countries and no exercise in the next five weeks was a more gentle schedule than most itineraries in the southern-hemisphere draw. In that same period, Gary Teichmann and his Coastal Sharks faced a more typical routine, playing five matches while travelling through ten towns, those same two islands and three countries. But, hey, what were a few towns and another country between a Super 12 team and their new mascot?

Older and fatter than almost every single Shark, I was a soft mini-man compared to the great whites and hard hammerheads of Super 12 rugby. Considering the difference in size and age it seemed natural that I should run a few steps behind one of the giants – and the Sharks, South Africa's best team, were my most obvious pick.

I had chosen well. The Sharks were on a ravenous roll, having bitten through both the Blues and the Western Stormers before they left Durban for Australia. It had taken them thirty-one hours to reach Canberra, having flown via Johannesburg, Harare and Perth. Four days later, in their third match of the tournament, they met the ACT Brumbies, the 1997 finalists. Despite the jetlag and a half-time deficit, they eventually tore through the Brumbies, scoring six tries in a 41–23 kill.

I'd arranged to meet Teichmann and his black-and-white fins in the chillier waters of New Zealand rugby. We knew that the most dangerous Super 12 teams still trawled across Black seas. The way in which the Wellington Hurricanes had swept through South Africa, and then held on the following week in Hamilton, left yet more brightly bobbing markers of Kiwi power.

Nick Mallett and Rod Macqueen, the Springbok and Wallaby coaches, had already expressed misgivings about the sustained commitment of the New Zealand sides in each country. The Blues' and Chiefs' victories in Johannesburg and Brisbane had been almost as impressive as the Hurricane blowing through Cape Town and Pretoria.

As a precursor to the Tri-Nations, Test rugby's most significant annual event, it seemed as if a successful regional tournament would once more be at the root of an imposing All Black year. To give fresh hope to the Springboks and the Wallabies, a South African or an Australian Super 12 side had to somehow outstrip five teams from New Zealand.

South African provincial rivalries had supposedly been set aside in an attempt to follow the Kiwi model and incorporate all the country's best players in four local Super 12 teams. Beneath their glitzy names a serious rugby point remained. The South Africans had originally put forward their previous year's Currie Cup semi-finalists. In 1997 the entire Western Province team had missed out even though, a few months later, they became the best team in the country by winning the Currie Cup. If the old model had been adopted in 1998, South Africa's three other Super 12 representatives would have been Free State, Natal and Gauteng (formerly Transvaal). Pretoria-based Springboks like Joost van der Westhuizen, Andre Snyman and Krynauw Otto would have been excluded from the Super 12. Emerging stars like Franco Smith, Stefan Terblanche, McNeil Hendricks and Marius Goosen, who played for the unfashionable Griqualand West and Boland, would have been similarly isolated.

As far back as the Lions tour nine months before, Sarfu and provinces like Natal and Free State had exchanged Super 12 vitriol. In a clash which echoed the chaos of the RFU's call for regionalisation and the English clubs' refusal to compromise their own identities, Natal led the fight against provincial mergers. They had worked hard to establish themselves as the country's premier rugby power both on the field and in terms of merchandising. Sarfu's insistence that they should dissolve into a new franchise for the southern-hemisphere showcase infuriated them.

On the pitch, the Coastal Sharks were essentially the Natal team, including an array of Durban-based Springboks like Teichmann, Andrews, Garvey, Honiball and Joubert. The key points of dispute, as always in professional rugby, were economic. The provincial union were horrified by the prospect of losing two home gates as well as dropping the sponsorship plug of the 'Natal' name.

Yet, for the sake of South African rugby, the provinces conceded – even if Natal had to be coerced by a High Court ruling. They accepted the new regional arrangement; a tough compromise which should have encouraged the English clubs and the RFU to attempt a similar resolution of their own conflict. At least Natal managed to negotiate the move of only one home game from Durban – with their encounter against the

Chiefs rescheduled for Port Elizabeth. In exchange, however painfully, they became the Coastal Sharks and called up a few Eastern Province and Border players. More notably, they also took advantage of a new draft system. With Mallett's encouragement, they picked Terblanche on the wing from Boland, Chris Rossouw, the 1995 World Cup-winning hooker from Gauteng, and Boeta Wessels, a young utility back from Griqualand West.

Western Province, similarly, became the Western Stormers – with only a few players added to their squad from Boland and South-Western Districts. With four wings already in the Stormers squad – Small, Rossouw, Williams and Paulse – Mallett's inspired hand could be seen guiding Terblanche towards Durban and Hendricks to Pretoria. South African rugby, at last, seemed to be using its collective head.

The transition was more complicated elsewhere. Gauteng, Northern Transvaal and Free State each wanted to be the dominant union in a Super 12 enterprise, thus ensuring themselves the bulk of home fixtures for their own stadium. Free State argued bitterly against their enforced link with Luyt's swaggering Gauteng – knowing that plum ties against the likes of Auckland would always slide across to the Ellis Park plate. Their official rationale was equally convincing. It made logistical sense to combine Gauteng with Northerns, as a mere fifty miles separated Johannesburg from Pretoria.

Instead, Sarfu insisted on establishing a tenuous chain between the 'Cheetahs' of the Free State and the 'Lions' of Gauteng. The hapless Golden Cats were born – an impressive team on paper, but a cattish disaster in reality. Apart from a gaping divide in outlook, the two cities were separated by a four-hour drive. The resulting training sessions were not noticeably harmonious. In terms of playing personnel, Free State and Gauteng were also unsuited. They boasted the country's two leading hookers – James Dalton and Naka Drotske – and initially opted to alternate the pair every week. Apart from undermining any hope of a settled front row, it also left either Dalton or Drotske on the bench every other week. The Northern Bulls and Western Stormers, meanwhile, did not field a hooker of similar Test standard in their own teams. South Africa, still, could not match New Zealand's overwhelming unity in using the Super 12 for the benefit of their national team.

The startling European gains made three months before by Mallett's Springboks shrank quickly. Stars from that tour – Small, Montgomery and Rossouw in the back line, and Dalton, Erasmus and Venter amongst the forwards – struggled in the Super 12. After three weeks, the Bulls,

Cats and Stormers could not claim a win between them against Australian and New Zealand opposition. Already, it was down to the Sharks. They were one of only two unbeaten Super 12 teams. But it seemed ominous that, in second place, they should be sandwiched between two meaty New Zealand sides. They were a bonus point behind the Hurricanes and four ahead of the re-emerging Blues.

By the time we reached the South Island, a wintry evening rain had begun to fall. Big men, and bleak questions, circled the Sharks. We were alone in New Zealand; and set for a long swim through the cold and the dark.

Another town, another taxi. My driver from Dunedin airport was a Maori man in his mid-fifties. Rangi Anderson, unsurprisingly, loved rugby. He had played one game for Waikato, as a centre, at a time when Kevin Skinner was the youth-team's coach. Skinner had replaced Fred Allen. 'Ah, the irony!' Rangi sighed when he heard that I had just met both men. 'But that's rugby. You'll always find a link with someone who likes rugby . . .'

We struck another, seamlessly, when Rangi nodded, without any prompting from me: 'When we think of South African players we think of your James Small. We love him in Dunedin – he's such a passionate footballer.'

Yet Small had not started the tournament with his usual dynamism. After a widely publicised and relatively drunken pre-season scrap with his team-mate, the truculent prop Toks van der Linde, Small had lost the momentum which had seen him end 1997 with the Springbok record for both caps and tries. In his last Super 12, in 1996, Small had also established himself as the tournament's top try-scorer. He was not set for a repeat performance.

With growing concern, I read in the *New Zealand Rugby News* that 'James Small won't easily forget the working-over he received from Alex Telea' – the Hurricanes wing who scored two tries against him in the opening match. In his next game, against his old team, the Sharks from Natal, Small was concussed as the Western Stormers were crushed 32–17 in Durban. He was out for at least a fortnight. I expected that he would eventually find his way back into form – but, until I next saw him, I thought it best to concentrate on Teichmann and the Sharks.

'Oh yes,' Rangi agreed of the Sharks' Australian prelude, 'to beat ACT away is a very big win.'

Canberra, before the Shark attack, had seemed impenetrable. ACT had won every single home match since the Super 12 began two years before. The Otago Highlanders, the Sharks' next opponents, had lost the week before against those same Australians – a succession of results which, as Rangi confirmed, meant that 'your boys are now second in the league. We're second from bottom. Friday night, I'm afraid, will be do-or-die for us. Look, you can see Carisbrook in the distance . . .'

The stadium's floodlights illuminated the valley below as we wound down towards Dunedin. 'So that's the famous "House of Pain" . . .' I said.

'Well, sir, to be completely accurate,' Rangi corrected me, 'we call it the "House of Taine" these days.'

Taine Randell, on the verge of the All Black captaincy, was still injured. But the Highlanders were rejuvenated by the prospect of Jeff Wilson's return against the Sharks. 'Goldie, Goldie,' Rangi hummed, 'how we love him here . . .'

'And Josh Kronfeld?'

'Of course,' Rangi exclaimed as he thumped the steering wheel, 'Josh is the god of Dunedin!'

I had seen Kronfeld briefly in the bowels of Eden Park, in a dejected Highlanders dressing-room after they'd been worn down by the Blues. Kronfeld limped towards me and shook his shaved head. He wore only a white towel; and beyond his muscled bulk I could see the hurt that spread from his damaged ligaments to his open face. He had battled with injury for years and, against ACT, had taken another bad knock on the leg. Without the back-up of Randell, he had forced himself to stay on the field in Canberra for the entire match. It had made the game in Auckland eight days later even more painful.

'It's the Super 12, mate,' Kronfeld had said softly, 'so there's no respite.' As he bent down to rub his throbbing ankle, with the steam still rising from him, he looked up at me with a strange expression. 'I can deal with the pain . . . it's losing like that which really hurts.'

His sore body spelt out the brutal impact of Super 12 rugby; but his grin was a more forceful reminder of the tournament's enduring appeal.

'We've got your Sharks at home next week . . .' he murmured.

'Yeah,' I said with the enthusiasm of a sadistic voyeur, 'it'll be my first visit to the House of Pain . . .'

Josh smiled curiously again, as he tugged at the bandages wrapped around his feet. They finally came free and he leant back wearily against a white wall. 'You'll like Carisbrook,' he said. 'There's quite an atmosphere.'

'Will you be okay by Friday?' I asked with a touch more sensitivity.

He nodded as he rolled the bandages together into a tight ball. 'I'm sure.'

'You won't risk more permanent injury by playing on?'

'The only way I'm going to fix this for good,' he said as he looked down, 'is if I have an operation. But that'll put me out for a season. That can't happen for the next few years. It's not too bad. I just live with it. As long as we start to play well again, I can play through anything . . .'

As we neared Dunedin, Rangi Anderson said, as if he had seen my memory, 'Oh, there's no doubt about it . . . Josh Kronfeld is as tough as any great All Black from the past. I think he's probably as tough as old Kevin Skinner used to be. Teichmann's boys will fear him most on Friday night...'

The Sharks were staying at the upper end of Dunedin while, paying for myself, I had booked in downtown at The Statesman. It had sounded vaguely grand when selected from the 'Small Hotels' section in my mildly erratic guidebook. I hoped that it might represent Dunedin's moderate equivalent of those 'intimate' but impossibly expensive London establishments like The Basil or The Halcyon. My optimistic economic slant was encouraged by the book's one-word description of The Statesman – 'Cheap'.

If I was taken aback by the brevity of detail, I consoled myself with the thought that I had arrived at the heart of the South Island. In those crucial New Zealand terms of rugby, Dunedin had once been home to famously hulking packs of Otago forwards who preferred to ruck rather than talk. Kevin Skinner, perhaps the most legendary of all southern front-row men, had promised me that 'they don't waste too many words down there – they're good and solid rugby people'. I imagined that a decent master of the South Island ruck had written my hotel report. Why squander breath and ink on flowery words like 'discreet', 'exclusive', 'gracious' and 'secluded' when you could settle on one as frugal as 'cheap'?

The usually loquacious Rangi had been curiously sphinx-like when I asked him to drop me off at The Statesman. After we had engaged in our Super 12 repartee, I decided to press him a little more closely about my home for the next week.

'So what's The Statesman like?' I asked.

The charmingly polite Rangi pointed out the beauty of the Otago countryside.

I agreed and then tried again. 'Rangi, tell me about my hotel . . .'

The kindly Maori man coughed in embarrassment. He rolled down his window and allowed the rain to spit on his face, as if he was accepting punishment for what he was about to confess. 'The Statesman . . .' he began, before stopping to once again wind-up his window.

'The Statesman?' I insisted.

'Ah,' Rangi squirmed in his seat, 'I would say it is a . . . uh . . . a very central hotel . . .'

'Central' worried me. 'Quiet' would have been acceptable. 'Clean' would have been better. 'Intimate', even in estate-agent speak, would have been great. But 'central' was worryingly neutral.

'Cheap & Cheerful' would have been clichéd. But, together, 'Cheap & Central' sounded sinister. I began to understand both Rangi and the guidebook's precise use of language when we at last reached The Statesman. It was bang in the middle of Dunedin – which, as Rangi implied, was the best thing you could say about a building whose peeling paint seemed to change colour from dingy green to dirty brown depending on the time of day or the way you tilted your head to read its twin-promise of 'Affordable Accommodation' and 'Victuallers Since 1874'.

Rangi left me with a bolstering hand-shake and a 'very good luck!' wish. I needed it. The Statesman, let's say, was neither The Basil nor The Halcyon. When I saw my cupboard-less box of a room, with an ancient bed which sank so low it at least swept a small stretch of dusty floor, I groaned. The dark walls were so close that the echo bounced back in a damp snap – which explained why I could already hear the heavy snoring of the man next door. I would not feel lonely, not with the shuddering snorer and the whispering mould on the bed-head for company. I felt like the shock-haired guy from *Eraserhead* as I stood alone, listening blankly to the incessant hum of noise. A red sign flickered through the collapsing curtain, casting an eerie light across the tiny room. I looked through the grimy and rain-spattered window. Across the street, the flash of neon was steady, switching back and forth between the same two red words: OPEN. Blink. MASSAGE. Blink. OPEN. Blink. MASSAGE.

'You settled in okay, pal?' my host asked a moment later as he poked his head around the creaking door.

His name was Ian, a deaf old boy in his early-sixties, who was as ready to scratch his head at my complaints about the snoring and having nowhere to keep my clothes as he was willing to offer a grinning compromise.

Ian's hearing-aid had 'gone up the bloody Swanee – I can hardly hear a thing, pal, even when I turn the volume up all the way.' So, squashed together, mouth to ear, I yelled out my list of objections.

'Yeah,' Ian nodded, 'I get your drift . . . it is a little rough, I guess. But the owners just up and left me to take care of the place. And, mate, I'm not even getting paid anymore . . .'

We were already on our way to becoming genuine pals, Ian and I, when he suggested a settlement of sorts. I was booked in at The Statesman for seven nights. 'Mate,' Ian said, 'if you stay here all seven nights, I'll charge you for one . . .'

I hesitated, even though it meant that I would be paying about twelve pounds for the week. It still entailed spending seven nights on the set of *Eraserhead*.

'C'mon, pal, I'll look after you real well,' Ian promised after he had waited in vain to read my motionless lips. 'Tell you what – you give me your doo-dahs and I'll wash 'em for you at no extra charge . . .'

I wasn't quite sure what he meant by 'doo-dahs' until he hollered again: 'You know, pal, all your smellies . . . your little socks and your little doo-dahs. I'll do 'em all. We've got a washing-machine in The Statesman – and, believe it or not, it's still working. How's that for service?'

As I told Gary Teichmann the following afternoon, Ian and I made our doo-dah of a Statesman deal. I wouldn't get much sleep – not with the lumpy bed, the snoring and the massage parlour's blinking neon. But at least I would be able to wear another clean set of doo-dahs to the House of Pain that evening.

Teichmann just raised a brow and laughed. He was getting to know me, and so he put up with the bizarre behaviour. 'Ag,' he said, 'it's just great to see another South African. I think you're going to be our only supporter tonight . . .'

All the more reason, as Ian might have hooted, for a sparkling set of doo-dahs. But, with kick-off only three hours away, it felt like time to get serious. Dunedin was not Paris, and The Statesman was certainly not the Concorde de Lafayette, but Gary Teichmann and I became a little closer in New Zealand. With some players, it might have helped that I had travelled so far for an interview and a match, but there was no need to flatter Teichmann. He was, as usual, open and kind. We spent as much time sorting out my invitation to the post-match function as we did assessing his remarkable form in the opening weeks of the Super 12.

Even the New Zealand rugby press had Teichmann streaking ahead of 240 other southern-hemisphere players. After three rounds of matches he led both the 'Best' and 'Fairest' tables charting individual achievements. He had already scored three tries and showed such composed leadership and driving creativity that the New Zealanders hailed him as Zinzan Brooke's natural successor as the world's finest number 8.

'*Ja*,' he agreed a tad reluctantly, 'I reckon I'm playing pretty well. I started off not too badly against Auckland. It was the first time we'd beaten them in the Super 12. We put them under a lot of pressure and, as New Zealanders, they weren't used to that. It wasn't the greatest match – a lot of mistakes were made. But there was no stage in the game when I felt we were in any danger of losing. I think it helped that we had been written off by almost everyone. No one gave us a chance. They were the champions and we're supposed to be also-rans this season – so we had a point to prove.'

Teichmann had another statement to underline against the Western Stormers. There were wild press rumours that the twenty-one-year-old Bobby Skinstad threatened the Springbok captain's place in the team. It was rubbish; but, still, Teichmann had been inspired while dominating both Skinstad and the Stormers. 'I was determined to have a really good game,' Teichmann said, 'and I did. We then followed it up with a win in Canberra which meant that we had made a real breakthrough in each of our three matches. We've beaten the Super 12-holders, the Currie Cup champions and we've also taken away ACT's unbeaten home record. So, hopefully, we're on a roll now . . .'

Teichmann did not deal in snappy soundbites, but my respect for him flourished in tandem with his plain delivery. I also felt the startling intensity of his rugby passion when he moved in and listened closely to my stories about the snatches of time I had spent with various All Blacks in Auckland. I did not tell him anything that he did not already know; but there was a vigilance in his listening which spoke of the searing determination he brought to his captaincy of both the Sharks and the Springboks. He was looking for a way, any way, to find a chink in the All Black wall.

I liked Teichmann most because he had the strength of personality not to hide himself behind any tricky quirk or showy flash of persona. He was just himself, an ordinary guy who happened to be a remarkable rugby player. I thought that the combination, and his ensuing calm both on and off the field, made him extraordinary. Sean Fitzpatrick, his closest contemporary, did not particularly like the media, but he invariably reached for his most charming quotes. He knew some of us better than we knew ourselves and so Fitzy could always give us what we wanted. In the end, he knew that it would help him. But Teichmann was different. In Dunedin it seemed to me, as a guy who was not always confident enough to be so straight, that Teichmann possessed a powerful gift – especially for an inherently shy man. It was the talent of self-belief; a readiness to accept himself for who he was, without recourse to ambiguity.

It did not prevent me looking for metaphors. With another physical Super 12 match looming, I asked Teichmann about tension, comparing him to a fighter awaiting his walk to the ring. But he was too sensible for another haymaker of an analogy. 'At the moment, I'm not nervous,' he explained instead. 'When we get on the bus and drive to the ground, I'll start to feel a little tense. But it's no use getting uptight before then, because the nerves will just burn you up. If you worry about the game all day it'll do you no good. It's best just to keep your mind off it . . .'

'How do you manage that?' I asked.

'Well,' he said, 'with this team it's really easy. The guys are very relaxed. Most of them have played at this level so many times before. So it's easy to pass the time.'

'How did you do that today?' I persisted.

Teichmann, Andrews, Garvey, Honiball, Joubert and the rest had spent the morning at the movies. They'd loved *Good Will Hunting*, which I could understand because, in their different ways, they all had abilities and feelings you would not usually discuss in a world as relentlessly masculine as Super 12 rugby.

'Shew,' Gary said, 'this tournament is so hard – there's hardly room to catch breath. So to get away to a film like that is a real break. Otherwise it just grinds on. It seems as if the Super 12 gets harder ever year. The other teams are better prepared than before, the hits are bigger and the travelling gets more difficult . . .'

Teichmann told me how his baby, Danielle, had been ill in the days before the Sharks played ACT in Canberra. Whenever his wife, Nicky, put her hand behind the little girl's head, it caused pain – a sign that she might have picked up meningitis. But, 9,000 miles away, Nicky decided not to tell him until after the match. There was nothing he could do to help at such a distance.

'Luckily,' he said, 'it turned out that the baby was fine – but when I heard, after it was all over, it made me realise again how hard it is for me to leave home every time. I'm thirty-one, and I want to be with my family. But it's not easy to do that when you also want to win the Super 12 . . .'

Teichmann always told me that, as an international, he was aiming for a World Cup peak in 1999. After that tournament, he suggested, it would only be provincial rugby and fatherhood for him. But, before then, I knew he wanted three things in rugby – the World Cup, a Tri-Nations championship and the Super 12.

'I'm just thinking Super 12 at the moment,' he countered. 'It's hard enough to win that. After beating Auckland and the Stormers, to travel to Canberra and then Dunedin is really difficult. Otago are very hard to beat at home. We've always struggled here. Two years ago, we thrashed them in the first half and, before we knew it, they came back and beat us. The Carisbrook crowd are very passionate. They're mostly students and they really inspire guys like Kronfeld and Wilson. They never know when they're beaten . . .'

'You've already whipped Auckland and if you win here tonight,' I speculated, 'and then go on to beat Wellington next Sunday, do you think you'll have started to break New Zealand's psychological edge? Could the Springboks then beat the All Blacks?'

'Let's just win tonight,' Teichmann said, 'and then we can think about the rest of the year. Let's win away in New Zealand and then, Donald, I promise you, I'll buy you a beer tonight . . .'

Carisbrook, Dunedin, Friday, March 20 1998
Thursday's rain had drifted away. It had been a beautiful day in Dunedin. The temperature might have been cooler than in Auckland, but Friday night at Carisbrook was still crackling. Despite its nickname, the re-developed House of Pain was neither a dingy nor a furtive abode. It was full of blazing light and swollen noise. Gary Teichmann had also been accurate about the crowd: 19,999 New Zealanders and one large Shark mascot electrified Carisbrook. I quickly abandoned the idea of trying to compete with the painted faces and blue-and-yellow costumes and banners of the 'Scarfies', the students from Otago University. Their favourite ditty, the insistently nagging, 'Otago . . . Highlanders . . . Otago . . . Highlanders . . . Welcome to the House of Pain!' blared out over the PA. It might not have been the greatest song I had ever heard, but it featured a bluesy harmonica solo by that cool dude in the number 7 shirt – Josh Kronfeld.

But, like the musical surfer in the blue scrum-cap, my concentration soon homed in on the rugby. The Highlanders and the Sharks defined Super 12 rugby at its most vibrant. In more traditional terms, it featured a recharged Otago against an expanded Natal. For all the law-changes and blasting snatches of old Bonnie Tyler's *It's a Heart-Ache* whenever the Sharks scored, you could not escape the compelling reality that a New Zealand team were embroiled in battle with their most tenacious rivals, rugby men from South Africa. There were ten tries, five to each side; but there was also more astringent front-row clattering, terrific tackling and an imperious back-row display from both Teichmann and Kronfeld.

The Highlanders were schooled rigorously in the basics of forward play. If the All Blacks had built their iron machine of the last five years on the unshakeable foundation of an Auckland trio, Dowd, Fitzpatrick and Brown, it suddenly appeared as if their successors had arrived at Carisbrook. Anton Oliver, at hooker, and his two massively impressive young props, Carl Hoeft at loosehead and Kees Meeuws at tighthead, dented the more experienced Springbok front row of Garvey, Chris Rossouw and Ollie le Roux. They shoved and shunted with a taut adhesion which suggested that time had finally unpeeled for the Auckland veterans in the Black shirts. Otago, those rugged bastions of so many great New Zealand packs, were marching forward again.

At number 8, they had also introduced Isitolo Maka – a powerhouse at the base of the scrum. Maka was a twenty-two-year-old giant, running fast at six foot seven with an eighteen-stone bulk. He was also from Tonga; and Jonah Lomu had told me the week before how even he had been a little smaller than Maka at schoolboy level. Lomu just pipped the bigger Maka to the number 8 slot in the New Zealand schools side but, five years later, Isitolo did a passable impression of big Jonah at eighth-man. He lacked the lush hands and tactical nous of Teichmann but, for sheer impact, Maka was astonishing. Like Teichmann, he also scored two tries that night – and he made it possible to imagine an All Black World Cup pack in 1999 consisting of six men from Otago. Three in the front row and, with Randell and Kronfeld on either side of Maka, three at the back.

Otago, of course, also had Jeff Wilson. And, against the Sharks, he returned to play full-back. His sheer presence lifted the fresh-faced boys around him. The Highlanders dug their hooks deep into the Sharks. They were 14–0 up after eleven minutes. The South Africans briefly narrowed the gash to 21–17 but, in the second half, they bled almost as many points. But the size of the Otago lead fluctuated continually, with a fling of Highland scoring being followed by a chunk of Shark tries. After eighty minutes of pounding there were six points between the teams – three conversions from the mop-haired blue-and-yellow number 10, Tony Brown. Otago Highlanders 41, Coastal Sharks 35. On the sliding scale of Super 12 league points it also meant that the Highlanders picked up five for a win and for scoring at least four tries. The Sharks picked up two bonus points – one for their own fourth try and another for keeping the winning margin to less than seven. For at least a brief while, they returned to the head of the table.

Gary Teichmann still bought me my beer, and a few more besides, that long Dunedin night. We began at the typically tedious cocktail party – where Teichmann and Wilson made their obligatory speeches and swapped yet another set of ties while Mark Andrews entertained me with stories of his turbulent love-life. 'I get to meet girls because I'm a Springbok rugby player,' the big lock grinned down at me, 'and then, hell, I lose all my girlfriends because I'm a rugby player . . .' It was a Super 12 night in New Zealand and, as Andrews sighed, that meant he was away from home again. 'How am I going to keep the future mother of my children happy,' he cracked mournfully, 'when I'm never at home?'

Andrews was hugely amiable – even when he itemised the 'basic personality clash' between him and 'our good friend, James Small'. But he was at his most interesting when we spoke about the All Blacks. Kronfeld told me that Andrews had the most notorious reputation amongst the New Zealanders – 'He's always doing chirpy and niggly things, holding on to you, shoving you in the back,' Josh said. If Andrews was happy to hear of my own liking for Kronfeld and Cullen and Lomu, he pointed out the stark divide between the Highlanders and the Sharks at the post-match party. The Otago boys took up one side of the room while the Natal guys stuck together in an opposite corner.

'Look, I've got nothing against them,' Andrews explained, 'and when I've finished playing rugby I'd really like to sit down and have a few beers with some of the All Blacks. But, until then, we can't have any real personal contact. Rugby is about causing hurt. In the Super 12 you're really smashing into guys – and it's not easy to do that if they're your friends. That's why it's so tough to play against other Springboks in this tournament. We've lost to the buggers so many times that I don't have any problems crashing into a Kiwi . . .'

For Kronfeld, however, Teichmann was regarded in the Black pack as the hardest but fairest of all Springboks. 'Aw, mate,' Josh said admiringly, 'Teichmann is just such a hard bastard. But he's also really clean. He just gets on with the game, y'know, and that's what I love most . . .'

On the Sharks' bus back from Carisbrook, Andrews just laughed as Teichmann modestly ducked his head. 'You're right to have him as the hero of your book,' Andrews said. 'There's no dirt on Gary. I've known him a long time and I've looked hard for a little dirt – but the guy's as clean as a whistle. Now, shit, even the All Blacks accept it . . .'

We all went out later for a few more beers. Most of the Sharks knew, from their previous Springbok and Super 12 visits, that the best spot in Dunedin on a Friday night was a rocking little place called Bowlers. It was not too surprising to briefly bump into Josh, Goldie and the other Highlanders just after midnight at the back of Bowlers.

'Yeah,' Josh said, 'but it's actually only one of the hot spots in town. There're a few other interesting places too . . .'

But we were happy enough at Bowlers; and Teichmann made sure that I was never left out of the Shark tank. He kept my beers coming, occasionally allowing me to buy him one. It had been a bruising game, and a disappointing first loss in the Super 12. But Teichmann had again played a towering match, even getting up from 'a bad bang in the balls' to score the second of his tries. As the crammed bar whirled around us, he was relaxed and calm.

'We'll beat them, eventually . . .' he promised as Wilson and Kronfeld were surrounded by eager locals. Even at one in the morning, they were still All Blacks – as much to Teichmann and the watching Henry Honiball as the more enthusiastic Scarfies.

'Every time I pick a side,' Teichmann murmured, 'I write down his name first. Henry's the kind of player who can beat these New Zealanders . . .'

Honiball smiled softly and clinked his bottle of beer against mine – before nodding at a new line of Otago fans who wanted to pay homage to the Springboks. The Sharks shook hands patiently with the shiny-faced, beer-fuelled Kiwi kids. 'Bad luck,' they shouted over the music, 'but you're still great players . . .' A few of them, not quite sure if I was a chubby prop like Ollie le Roux or the Sharks' new secret weapon, slapped me on the back and said, 'Well played . . .' We laughed but, standing with Teichmann, Honiball and Joubert in Dunedin, I was as close to Springbok fame as I would ever be.

Even Jeff Wilson seemed caught up in the mystery of my elevation to the Sharks squad. He sauntered over and put his arm around Teichmann and me. 'C'mon, guys,' he said, 'look at those babes. It's Friday night . . .'

As married men, Gary and I just smiled politely. As soon as old Goldie had left, no doubt to have a dance as if he was shimmying down the All Black wing, Teichmann and I stepped deeper into the shadows of a corner. The Springbok captain nodded thoughtfully, as if he could imagine bringing down Wilson and the rest of the black shirts later that year, in the Tri-Nations, in Wellington and then in his home town of Durban. He turned to me again and said, 'They talk a lot when they win . . .'

We both had another sip of beer. It was late and we were tired; and still yearning for that black silence.

Chapter 16
South Island Surfing

A hungover Saturday; and not even a dark slurp of coffee could help. The *Otago Daily Times* was still dancing. It felt like I'd taken another nail in my already banging head, but I hammered on. I squinted hard, focusing on the purple-thumbed prose. Brent Edwards, the affable local rugby man in Dunedin, was a proud and happy Highlander, as his opening paragraph revealed: 'Heroes all. That was the unanimous verdict of the Carisbrook crowd after the Otago Highlanders upset the Coastal Sharks in a Super 12 rugby thriller last night. The Highlanders vanquished the previously unbeaten Sharks with a captivating mix of gutsy, technically sound forward play and imaginative running by the backs. It was the perfect start to Otago's 150th anniversary weekend as the young Highlanders dug in with the same fortitude as their forebears who founded the province.'

It all contributed to a disturbing start to the day. Ian, my distraught doo-dah man at The Statesman, had woken me early. He had lost a 'little feller' in the dawn wash. I looked at him blankly, fearing that a helpless young urchin had been drowned while washing my latest batch of underwear. But it turned out that the 'little feller' was one of my socks. I commiserated briefly with Ian and then ran screaming from The Statesman and slap-bang into a smiling contingent from supposedly the first boat to have reached Otago from Scotland on 23 March 1848.

I began to think that I had taken a tab of acid the night before because, wherever I turned, it felt like my head was being opened up as easily as a small tin of Otago tuna. The hallucinations were strong and consistent. Downtown Dunedin swarmed with hundreds of people dressed in traditional nineteenth-century garb. There were bonnets and beards, long black dresses and top hats. As I reeled towards the Octagon in the centre of town it seemed, as sure as Ballymena had turned orange so many years before, that the Presbyterian pioneers had come back to life in Dunedin. One big win in the Super 12 on Friday night and, suddenly, the whole town had turned completely crazy.

Eventually, it sank in. The ghostly apparitions were actually participating in the 150th anniversary costume competition. By then, a couple of hundred men on horseback and a motorcade of Victorian jalopies had joined the parade. I went searching instead for my head-clearing shot of late-twentieth-century caffeine. At the resolutely modern Ra Bar, they appeared oblivious to the quaint colonial celebrations drifting past. The waitresses, with their nose and tongue studs glinting in the morning sun, swayed leisurely to a soundtrack which, set in the 1990s rather than the 1890s, offered a cooler blend of British and New Zealand culture. Cornershop and Finley Quaye merged into a local drum-and-bass collection – reminding me that, apart from grinding forward play, Dunedin had once been mildly famous in obscure London music circles as New Zealand's answer to American towns like Athens, Georgia. If The Clean and The Chills had not quite reached the heights of REM and the B52s, they were responsible for creating the almost mythic 'Dunedin Sound' on the equally legendary Flying Nun label.

As a disgruntled South African teenager, I used to swap compilation tapes with a New Zealander who lived in London. He introduced me to the Dunedin 'groove' – while reminding me that Otago was home to the world's fiercest rucking technique. The nostalgia felt so soothing that I knew the coffee was working. But I also remembered that, as Nelie Smith had said, the battered 1981 Springboks had preferred the South Island to the North. The anti-apartheid demonstrations were at their most intense in northern cities like Auckland, Wellington and Hamilton. The far South, especially all the way down in Invercargill, had been less fraught. Seventeen years later it was still noticeable that, in comparison to the Polynesian themes which ran through Auckland, the South Island presented a more obviously European version of New Zealand life.

In Dunedin, especially on an anniversary weekend, it was impossible to miss the Scottish slant – running from Carisbrook to St Andrews street, home of The Statesman. My morning paper confirmed that 'as Otago celebrates 150 years of European settlement, no one can deny the important role Scottish Presbyterians have played in shaping the province. However, Scottish Presbyterianism has never been a spectacular or flamboyant religion. Its influence in Otago has been both enormous and subtle – in fact, thoroughly Scottish and understated.'

Dunedin was known as the 'Edinburgh of the South' – and, like its inspiration, it was both a pretty and an often rainy city. Yet if its ancestors had been Scottish church-members, which presumably meant that they had not been outstanding rugby players, Dunedin had since turned oval. It was a great rugby town. My slow recovery continued as the clock ticked towards that afternoon's first Super 12 match.

I ambled over to the Champions of Otago sports-bar, where the 'Hall of Fame' featured ornate images of local icons from Kevin Skinner to Josh Kronfeld. I saluted both All Blacks as I found a stool in front of one of the many television screens. The place was heaving and I accepted the barmaid's suggestion of a calming pint of Speights – Otago's addictive bitter.

'Hard lines,' she smiled, 'for last night . . .'

My South African accent had obviously been flattened by my late-night session with the crash-tackling duo of Honiball and Teichmann.

'I thought the Sharks played really well,' she said.

'They can play better,' I grunted before I told her, truthfully, how impressed I had been by the Highlanders.

'Yeah, we turned it on, didn't we?' she grinned blissfully. 'Now all we need is for the Chiefs to beat the Blues . . .'

I raised my pint to the South Island girl. Like Gary Teichmann, I longed for the day when South Africa would again beat New Zealand at rugby – but, despite our pain, I loved being in Dunedin on another Super 12 Saturday.

Like the rest of the bar, I decided to support Errol Brain's Chiefs against the Auckland Blues. The Otago sway against Auckland was predictable. The South Islanders would always be stacked against big-city Auckland. My own preference for the Chiefs was more Shark-like – having lost twice before to the Blues in the knock-out stages of the Super 12, I hoped that, without Fitzy and Zinny, Auckland might slip out of the top four and open the way for Teichmann's team.

In the fourth week of the competition, the Super 12 had begun to settle and harden. The Blues against the Chiefs, at Eden Park, was uncompromising rugby, with only three tries being scored. The defenders were ruthless, and the bodies fell in time with the constant crashing.

'Gang-tackling!' the Speights-girl marvelled as she poured me another beer and the Blues captain, Michael Jones, absorbed yet more punishment.

Jones got up and took his place at the back of the scrum. Although no longer as formidable as the marauding likes of Isitolo Maka, he was, as an approving barman said, 'still the great Michael . . .'

I thought of Sean Fitzpatrick and the vivid way in which he had described the young Jones when we'd met in London. 'Michael Jones,' Fitzy explained, 'was lithe and quick and clever and deadly. He was very alert. He could anticipate how a move might shift across a field, like a stalking panther. And then he'd pounce and he would be away, with the ball under his arm and his mind moving as fast as his feet. He was so imaginative. And when I hear the name "Michael Jones", that's the figure I see, even now . . .'

On the Super 12 screen, Jones picked up the white ball and went on the drive. He crashed into another colourful wall of tacklers. Rugby was harder than ever. Ten years before, it had been far easier for Jones.

I still owned the video-tapes of Jones at his glorious zenith in the 1987 World Cup. And I had since heard so much about him from all the players in this book that I could hardly believe it when, six days earlier, he walked over to me in that Auckland gymnasium. 'I'm Michael Jones,' he said as he stretched out his hand.

'I know,' I admitted.

Jones was a month away from his thirty-third birthday. The lines had begun to crease around his eyes when he smiled. But he breathed freely as he gathered himself from yet another training stint. He looked strong. But I could not shake Kevin Skinner's voice from my head. 'Michael Jones is very fragile,' the old All Black had declared.

Nine months earlier, in a one-sided Test against Fiji, Jones had suffered a terrible injury. His career was over – again. Just like it had supposedly ended in 1989.

'That injury was far worse,' Jones affirmed in his high but quiet voice. 'In 1989 it was very serious. I ran for a ball and stuck my leg out to boot it on. But this Argentinian flanker dived at the same time. He landed on my leg. It just twisted and cracked. It was the worst pain. I tried to move my leg, and I couldn't. The knee was shattered. The joint had been utterly dislocated and all the nerves around it were dead. I shouldn't have been able to come back from that injury – because there was only one ligament left to work the knee.'

'How many ligaments do you normally have?' I wondered.

'Four . . .'

Jones tapped that same knee, his left. 'That was nine years ago. It should have been the end of my career. But I had faith . . .'

Jones, 'The Ice-Man', had been a matchless number 7; and all the great open-sides, as Kronfeld said, carried 'their badge of difference'. In 1995, Kronfeld had been picked for the All Blacks because Jones would not compromise his Christianity and play rugby on a Sunday. And television, the god of professional rugby, wanted at least one World Cup semi-final to be played on the Sabbath. The All Blacks played in Cape Town on a Sunday afternoon, against England, on the day when Lomu and Kronfeld tore up the white shirts. Jones's career on the open-side was over. He switched to the blind-side and the black number 6.

'But when you were injured last year, at the age of thirty-two,' I asked him, 'did you not think, then, that it was at last over?'

'If I did,' Jones mused, 'it was for a very short time.'

'How long? I said, recalling how world rugby had again lamented the passing of a genius.

'Maybe a couple of seconds. I felt it was God's will that I should play again. I'd work hard – and the rest would be in the Lord's hands . . .'

I didn't feel awkward, hearing such fervour. And neither did Michael Jones. 'You see,' he said, 'after what happened in 1989, each day I have since spent on the rugby field has been a bonus. Since my first injury, I've understood how much I truly love rugby. So when I play, now, I just find pleasure.'

For the aching Jones, it must have been a strangely painful pleasure to return to 1998's intense Super 12. At half-time, the Blues were 16-6 down and the Chiefs' tackling looked increasingly vicious. Jones tucked his hands behind his scrum-cap as he trudged away.

'Poor Michael Jones – he looks shattered,' the Otago girl noted.

'I'd still take a shattered Michael Jones before most players,' another barman suggested.

The legend had not lost all its lustre. But Jones was too bright not to accept the slow rusting.

'But is it odd,' I'd asked him, 'when, as kids, players like Josh and Jonah thought of you as a god . . .'

As soon as the blasphemous word left my mouth, I tried to catch it. It was too late. It was out. I was mortified.

Jones laughed and patted me on the arm. 'No, no,' he said, 'it's okay. I just feel very privileged that these guys acknowledge me. I get a lot of satisfaction from playing with them now – even though I'm a bit of an old man compared to them. But Josh and Jonah have become my friends – it's like with Zinny and Fitzy. We've been so close, for so long . . .'

'How is Fitzy?'

Jones hesitated. 'It's too early to tell. But he's really good with me. He rings up before every Super 12 game. I also try to encourage him. The thing is, with guys like Fitzy and Zinny, you can never count them out. Fitzy is the most mentally tough guy I've ever known. If anyone can come back from his injury, it'll be him. It's his attitude, his professionalism. A normal person might crumble – but not Fitzy.'

Lomu and Cullen, the latest All Black icons, represented New

Zealand's cultural diversity with relaxed certainty. Yet, before them, Fitzpatrick and Jones had smoothed the path. They might have been of contrasting Irish and Samoan descent, but Fitzy and 'Ice' were united – both as All Blacks and as urbane New Zealanders.

I asked Jones what he thought of Matthew Ridge's recent comments on the 'Polynesian factor' in rugby.

'I don't believe in archetypes,' Jones said politely.

Yet Lomu had spoken of a 'Polynesian way, of a shyness which had to be confronted'. Was there any truth in that?

Jones was emphatic. 'Definitely! You're brought up to be seen and not heard. It can actually stifle your development – not just on the rugby field but as a person. I'm a New Zealand Samoan. I was born here, but I've always been closer to my Samoan side. My dad was a Kiwi but he passed away when I was very young. The rest of my family is Samoan – so it's a strange mix. It's almost like you're a schizophrenic. It can be confusing. In the white environment, in a rugby environment, you act in a certain way. In your own environment you act differently, perhaps more naturally. I was probably more comfortable in a sheltered Polynesian setting. But, through rugby, I came out of my shell. I developed my social skills and so I was able to move between the two worlds . . .'

'Does that schizophrenic existence continue today, for younger players?'

'I think so. But I think the important thing is not to lose our Polynesian culture. The New Zealand I love most takes the best from both cultures. You cannot turn your back on other people. We have to co-exist. And that's why, sometimes, I worry about the younger players. They're twenty-one or twenty-two and rugby's all they know. They're not developing themselves in any other way. While professional rugby can be great, it also has a lot of traps. It can stunt your growth as a person. But, fortunately, that's not always the case. Look over there, at Andrew Blowers . . .'

Playing alongside Jones and Mark Carter in the back row against the Chiefs, Blowers was also recovering from injury. But, slowly, the three All Blacks had begun to claw back possession from the Chiefs. A try by the Fijian toughie, Joeli Vidiri, had levelled the scores at 16–16.

In Auckland, hearing Jones's reference to Blowers, I had thought immediately of Dublin and the day of Kronfeld's exclusion from the All Black Test XV. John Hart chose Blowers to play open-side flank against Ireland ahead of Kronfeld. It was madness. Blowers wasn't as quick as Kronfeld or as good on the ground. Although I was not a South Islander, or even a New Zealander, I knew how much the All Blacks needed Kronfeld's speed to the breakdown as well as his relentless foraging. But, more importantly, Josh was my pal. Like the whole of Otago, I was indignant. In a private announcement, I declared that John Hart was on my black-list. Andrew Blowers, through guilt by association, was similarly black-balled.

But, in Auckland, I wanted to meet Blowers. I hoped that he would be cold and arrogant, so that I could confirm my antagonism in print. They were so insidiously likeable, those All Black Kiwis, that I yearned for a prat to come along. It was time for some mutual antipathy.

'I was always very shy,' Blowers admitted when, probing the source of his malevolence, I asked him to describe his background. We both paused. He was a week away from his twenty-third birthday. 'I still am pretty shy . . .'

Bloody hell, I thought, another tender moment. 'Why?' I demanded.

'I just am, I guess,' Blowers said. 'But it's interesting, I think . . .'

'In what way?' I asked in my most disinterested voice.

'I think it says a lot about New Zealand – and the different ways in which we're brought up. My dad was Scottish. And his mother lived in Scotland. But I was mostly brought up by my mum and she's Samoan. And there's this kind of shyness in Samoan people . . .'

'Yeah,' I conceded. 'Michael Jones just said something quite similar. He called it an almost schizophrenic existence . . .'

'That's pretty accurate. As young Samoans, we wouldn't contradict anyone. We'd tell people what they'd want to hear. But then, when we got home, we'd be as loud as anyone. You know, we'd be joking and tackling each other.'

'So was it a disadvantage, growing up as a Samoan?'

'Not at all. I didn't encounter prejudice. And that's why rugby's been so great. It's given us a chance to shine. I started out playing League, as most of my friends did. But I always preferred rugby. It was just a dream of mine to get that black shirt. And I did it in your country, in South Africa – this amazing country where there's such passion for rugby.'

Blowers had made his début in the All Blacks' groundbreaking 1996 series win over the Springboks. Despite that, and my early determination to dislike him, I already rated Andrew Blowers. Shit, I liked the guy. Blowers was also intriguing because he'd made his international début for Western Samoa, before the All Blacks whisked him away. As Chris Grinter had suggested, if a New Zealand-based Samoan still revered his island culture, his rugby ambitions were invariably Black.

'Absolutely,' Blowers agreed. 'In the Pretoria Test in '96, when we clinched the series, I came on for Josh near the end. I was really young but, still, the enormity was there for me too. In the back row with Michael Jones and Zinzan Brooke, we were just New Zealanders – and we'd done something which meant so much to the country back home.'

Kronfeld had explained previously that there was a stark, if humorous, difference between New Zealand and Samoan rugby culture. Blowers picked up the black and blue threads and ran with the story. 'In New Zealand, rugby's very serious,' he affirmed. 'Winning is everything. And when you make a mistake you sometimes just want to be swallowed up. It all feels so important.

'It's different in Samoa. They love it if you make a mistake – even if you're playing for their team. The Samoan people just roar with laughter. They clap and scream. It'll be the highlight of their afternoon just because you dropped a high ball. I like that attitude. It's based on laughter.'

I noticed how little laughter there was in the Champions sports-bar. Anguished howls subsided into silence. With only a few minutes left, the Chiefs had lost the lead. All afternoon, a wordless couple had sat across the bar from me. With their stares fixed on the screen, they had not spoken for almost two hours. Every twenty minutes, the man gestured silently for another round of drinks. A tonic water for his girlfriend and a beer for him.

At the final whistle, he at last moved his lips. 'No!' he said. Jones, Blowers and the Blues had won again – 25–23. The woman squeezed his arm. They finished their drinks and, in the hush, he slipped his hand into hers and walked towards the door. Rugby could be a painful affair in New Zealand.

But, through the hurt, sometimes there was compassion. 'It's funny you should mention Dublin,' Andrew Blowers had said. 'See, Josh and me – we were room-mates. So when we got the news I was obviously happy for myself but I had a lot of thoughts for Josh. You know, when you're the incumbent and you lose your Test spot . . . it's hard.'

'How was Josh – with you?'

'Aw, Josh was great. I knew he was really disappointed – but, with me, he was so positive.'

Andrew Blowers, after all, was as interesting as he was sympathetic – and some of his words still echoed through my head months later. I had asked him one of my usual questions – 'If it hadn't been for rugby, what would you have done with your life?' Most rugby men I knew just shook their heads and uttered a whistling or gurgling sound – as if it was a thought they did not dare contemplate. But Blowers had considered it many times before, in detail.

'It's not just a case of "what if?",' he said. 'I've decided that, after rugby, I want to work in a real job. I'm going to apply to the police – to see if there's some kind of positive work I can do with kids. I look around and I see people who haven't had a fraction of the opportunities I've been given. I see how many kids are just lost. You know, we have one of the highest suicide rates in the world. I can't believe it. Whether you're on the North Island or the South Island, New Zealand is such a beautiful country – but, all around us, so many people are taking their own lives…'

'Why?'

'We don't really know. Why should more people commit suicide in New Zealand than most other countries? It's a scary thought. And that's why I just want to get out there, to see if there's even a few people I might help one day . . .'

If rugby was usually a consolation in New Zealand, there was a growing fear that South Africa and Australia might soon overtake the All Blacks. The Springboks and the Wallabies were, once more, respectable and even threatening international opposition. Nick Mallett's arrival in New Zealand, to follow the differing fortunes of his Super 12 teams, marked a strange outpouring of admiration for a Springbok coach. If the Kiwis had never quite got the hang of the old Bok leaders, from Nelie Smith to Naas Botha, they could immediately identify with Mallett and Teichmann. 'They're pretty similar to us,' I heard again and again – which was the highest possible compliment in New Zealand rugby.

If the All Blacks were breaking up – with Brooke gone and Fitzpatrick, Bunce, Jones, Little and Dowd clinging on – a new set of Super 12 heroes were needed. That national desire helped explain why, the following afternoon, a different bar in North Dunedin shook with roars of 'Hurricanes . . . Hurricanes . . .' and cries of 'Do those Aussies!'. At the bottom of the North Island, the Hurricanes faced John Eales's Queensland Reds. With the Coastal Sharks basking in Queenstown on a four-day retreat before they faced the Hurricanes themselves the following Sunday, it was left to me to support the lonely Reds. After three straight victories, and with that afternoon's game in hand, the Hurricanes were only a point behind the Sharks. The poor old Reds, meanwhile, had lost their opening brace – against the Highlanders and the Chiefs – before they posted their first win against the Canterbury Crusaders, a surprise 35–9 thumping of the New Zealand provincial champions.

In Wellington they showed their renewed resilience. They were buffeted by one Hurricane assault after another. The Australians had sublime attacking players in Ben Tune, Tim Horan and Daniel Herbert – with Jason Little left on the bench for the first time in a ten-year career – but they had no option but to hurl their bodies at the massive Hurricane waves. It was heroic stuff, and definitive proof that the tenor of the Super 12 had shifted back towards ferocious defence. The gruff New Zealand commentators gasped in admiration.

'Really,' Brent Anderson said on the touchline, as yet another Hurricane forward bled from the head after a crunching Red tackle, 'those northern-hemisphere journalists saying that this is powder-puff rugby had better take a look at this – the hits that have been going in from this Queensland defence are very, very tough indeed . . .'

Murray Mexted snorted in agreement: 'Certainly the defence here is a bit better than what I saw this morning . . . Wales against Ireland in the Five Nations was what we call powder-puff tackling.'

That Red weathering of the Hurricanes was another engrossing and dramatic example of Super 12 rugby. The tackling never let up and, after more than thirty minutes, Queensland led through two long-range penalties from the Australian captain and lock, John Eales. But neither side could hold back the likes of Cullen, Umaga, Tune and Herbert for an entire eighty-minute period. The Hurricanes scored four tries, but the even more stunning Reds replied with five – two of their best coming from their substitute number 10, Shane Drahm, a young Aborigine who silkily side-stepped and dummied his way across the line. The second half was as exhilarating as the first had been brutal. Queensland, shimmering with Australian promise, had scored thirty-five points into the gusting Wellington wind for a breathtaking 41–33 win. They had also picked up five points to the Hurricanes' solitary bonus.

The Super 12 had caught fire again. After the first month of matches, the Sharks and the Hurricanes each had sixteen points. The Blues were a mere two behind, with the Reds closing in on twelve. The Sharks, however, still held the top slot, having scored one try more than the Hurricanes. As the numbed Dunedin bar absorbed the revised log position, I muttered a quiet 'Yes!'. It was another light promise that a change in the old Black order might be approaching. In ascending order, the nationality of the leading Super 12 teams read Australia, New Zealand, New Zealand, South Africa.

'I don't care if tomorrow's a public holiday,' a bearded man yelled from the back of the bar. He pointed at the list of teams. 'That ain't good news. Those bloody South African and Australian critters are comin' back at us...'

On Otago's 150th birthday, the streets of Dunedin still flowed with Victorian fancy-dress, but Josh Kronfeld looked more casual. He'd been for a surf that morning, at the beach near his home in St Claire, and his mood was typically balmy. Although his cross-cultural plan of taking me to a Japanese restaurant for lunch had been spoiled by the continuing Scottish celebrations, he came up with a tasty alternative. Even if there weren't too many places open on a public holiday in Dunedin, Josh knew of a little hideaway where he could buy me a burger and a Speights Distinction.

'Best beer on the South Island, mate,' he said as he eyed his own mineral water and pasta salad with resignation. There was still a cut over his left brow – a remnant from another bash he had collected a few weeks before in Canberra. But he glossed over the deeper hurt I'd seen in Auckland, when he had been hunched over his damaged ligaments.

'Amazing how a win wipes all that stuff away, isn't it?' he grinned. Three days had passed since the Sharks match – and another five were left before the Highlanders' next Super 12 scrap against the Golden Cats. Kronfeld was eager for another Highlander climb up the Super 12 ladder.

We would travel to Invercargill for that next South African encounter, as part of the Highlanders' deal to take Super 12 rugby out of Otago and down to New Zealand's least glamorous province – Southland. The Super 12 had begun to blur the country's traditional rugby and cultural borders. Rural unions like Southland, Taranaki and Hawkes Bay had lost much of their power as the southern-hemisphere's regional tournament dwarfed the National Provincial Championship. If the Super 12 came a close second behind the Tri-Nations, the NPC had been reduced to an obligatory chore for the leading All Blacks. A similar situation had developed in South Africa, with many of the Springboks hoping to be spared from all but the most important Currie Cup matches.

But Kronfeld loved to play for his adopted province. It had become his permanent home – ever since he'd fallen in love with Dunedin after leaving Hawkes Bay for university. Jeff Wilson and Taine Randell had also swapped Southland and Hawkes Bay for Otago. The 1998 Super 12 draft had further expanded the drift of rugby players across the country. Jeremy Stanley, son of the great All Black centre Joe Stanley, had been picked up from Auckland – as had Isitola Maka. Their arrival in Otago had made the Highlanders a more varied team. Tongan families like the Lomus and the Makas tended to move to Auckland, rather than the South Island – and so the Super 12, even if it had weakened the NPC, helped spread an even healthier mix of different cultures around New Zealand.

Kronfeld, with his original German and Samoan blend, nodded approvingly when I updated him on my interviews with Jones and Blowers. While their Samoan roots were more recent than his, he still felt a bond with both players. 'And it's not just because we're all loosies either. Andrew's a really good bloke and so, yeah, I could handle losing my All Black place to him for a week. I wouldn't have wanted it to be longer than that but, shit, I wouldn't wish anyone to fail. That would be the worst thing I could do. So, in Dublin, I gave him a few ideas to use against the Irish and I said, "Play well, Andrew." And I meant it . . .'

Kronfeld's form in the latest Super 12 had been scalding enough to burn off any doubt about him retaining the Black number 7. He was, back to normal, way out in front of anyone on the open-side. Blowers had moved to his rightful position as a blind-side flank and Jones was trying to either regain that jersey or the number 8 slot in the All Blacks. Kronfeld preferred to recall his own heady passion for Jones on the open-side. 'In Hastings, as a kid, I thought I was doing some pretty cool things on the rugby field. But then I'd see Michael Jones on TV and he was doing really freaky stuff. He just blew me away. The way he could dominate a game and create magic out of nothing has never left me.'

We both understood that, a decade on, Jones' career was receding – despite his stoic courage. Kronfeld, too, believed that Fitzpatrick would not return.

'It's not going to be easy for the All Blacks,' he suggested. 'This year we could lose four of the best players the game's ever seen. Sean Fitzpatrick. Zinzan Brooke. Michael Jones. Frank Bunce. That's a staggering amount of talent and experience from one team . . .'

Kronfeld provided a link between that quartet and the younger brigade of All Black dazzlers. At twenty-six he filled the gap between young stars like Cullen and the older sweats in the pack – Dowd, Brown, Ian Jones and Robin Brooke. He was perfectly equipped, too, to compare the various great All Black teams over the last three seasons – the Lomu-charged 1995 World Cup outfit, the 1996 side which beat the Springboks three times out of four in South Africa and the unbeaten '97 collection. 'To my mind,' he said, 'last year's team was not as good. For talent, enthusiasm and dedication I'd take the '95 and '96 sides for sure. If our World Cup side had to play our '96 team I think it would be a draw every time. There's nothing between those two teams. They were both outstanding. In 1997, I think we started to see ourselves as being larger than life. The Aussies and the Springboks were in disarray and we took advantage of that. But it didn't mean that we were quite the same team we'd been the two previous years. I think it's fair to say that some of the guys were fringing a little and didn't do as much work on the field . . .'

'You certainly looked tired against England at Twickenham . . .'

'Yeah, but we have to be bigger than that. I think a lot of the guys didn't really want to be over there on another tour. We wanted to play the rugby all right, but the rest of it was a grind to some of the team. I remember we had a barbecue before the tour and we were all getting excited that our season this year would end two months early, in October. I think that's a good indication of our state of mind when we reached Twickenham . . .'

'Do you think there's a danger of an All Black burn-out this season?'

'Not for me, personally. I reckon my game was just coming right in the UK. I had been put under a bit of pressure both physically and mentally. I was fighting to nail down my place again – so I had plenty of motivation. Some of the other guys were a little more on the cruise. But, for me, the whole of last season had been a bit of battle because I had so many injuries . . . but I'm having a pretty good Super 12 so far.'

Although the early weeks of tackled-ball chaos had cleared a little, there were still problems with the differing interpretations of the new law. 'Yeah,' Josh moaned, 'I get called the most penalised player in New Zealand rugby! And it really pisses me off because it comes down to some weird interpretations. But that's my only gripe about the Super 12. It's a great tournament, and I'm feeling really keyed in. I'm getting back to my very best . . .'

We reminisced again about his exceptional World Cup, a series of matches which had lit up my path from Johannesburg to Dunedin. 'I wanted to play so well. And I was really fit – I wasn't trying to shake off so many niggly injuries . . .'

'Was that the best rugby you ever played?' I wondered.

'I think the series win in '96 was more intense – but, for pure rugby, I played some of my best stuff way back in '93. I think my body was leaner then and I just had so much energy. I was all over the field like a bloody rabbit! I guess I was just younger then . . .'

'Although not with the same knowledge . . .'

'Definitely not – I was just establishing myself in Otago then. I was so quick, though, I'd get to the ball every time. I think the big difference is that then I didn't really know what to do with the ball. I'd get there and maybe thirty per cent of the time I wasn't doing too much with it. Whereas now, I still get to the ball and I do something positive with it every time. I'm much calmer and more thoughtful. I don't always talk a lot but, as a senior player now, one thing I do tell the younger guys in the Otago side is that they've got to get in a position to receive the ball and then do something creative with it. They've got to use their heads a little more.

'It obviously takes time to translate that energy of a twenty-two-year-old into the experience of an old hand. And in the beginning you can get overwhelmed and just try to play on pure adrenaline. When I came into the All Blacks I was kinda intimidated by the likes of Zinny and Fitzy. They were pretty huge figures and they spoke a lot. I'd played against them at Auckland and they were really difficult opponents. They'd stand on your ankles in rucks and they'd be talking to you all the time. Zinny and Fitzy and Robin Brooke would gauge what they could get away with – and Fitzy would talk to the ref and then give you a little whack or a kick behind his back. It wouldn't hurt, that wasn't his intention. But sometimes you'd retaliate and they'd get another penalty. It's not the way I play the game but, whew, those boys were so good at what they did. Two or three of them alone could unsettle opposing Test teams. They were just so canny and psychologically imposing.

'So when, suddenly, I was called into the All Black squad before the World Cup it took a mental adjustment to step out alongside those guys. I used to think they were real cocky bastards but, when you're on the same side as them, they're great. They go out of their way to help you. And, slowly, as we trained together and went through mock-scenarios, I saw that I could match them and sometimes, especially on the aerobic stuff, outdo them. You start to accept that they're just human and so it becomes easier to gain that confidence. It was then that I started to think, "Yeah, maybe I can be an All Black . . ." And when it happened it was just so important to have those old boys alongside me.'

'How badly will the All Blacks miss them this year?'

Josh Kronfeld paused. Only three months were left before the next round of southern-hemisphere Tests. He tugged at his ear thoughtfully.

'I think we'll only realise how much we miss them when we run out as All Blacks again – and we see how many of those faces are missing. It's gonna be tough – what with the Springboks and the Wallabies sharpening up. I think the Tri-Nations, like the Super 12, is gonna be hugely competitive this year. A lot could change over the next few months. I think we're in for some really interesting times . . .'

Chapter 17

Rain and Hurricanes

'When you reach Invercargill,' I had been promised by more than one cynical New Zealander, 'it'll feel like the end of the world . . .'

There was some geographical truth to the jibe for, after Ushuaia in Patagonia, at the bottom of Argentina, Invercargill was the world's most southerly city. Yet it occupied more central territory in New Zealand life. If British and South African rugby fans loved their exhausted quips about the slow sheep-shagging existence of the average Kiwi, then the rest of New Zealand turned up its collective and disjointed nose at the woolly saps who actually came from the bleating hell-hole of Invercargill.

I liked the place. It helped that I had moved up a notch from The Statesman to self-catering and self-doo-dah-washing accommodation on the edge of town – and across the road from the 'best Chinese take-away in Invercargill'. After an afternoon of washing my smellies to a radiant backdrop of satellite television, there seemed few finer places to spend a Super 12 Friday evening. Like half of Invercargill, I nipped over to pick up a 'Beautiful Weekend Combo' of garlic prawns, nutty chicken and fluffy rice and got back just in time to snap open a can of Speights as the rugby beamed in from Canterbury on Sky.

I was missing Alison like crazy but at least I had a cold beer, my piping Chinese and the thought that cursory highlights of that night's match would only make the British Sky screens in nine days' time, on the following Sunday. I had been away from home a long while but, in Invercargill, it suddenly all seemed worth it. A live screening of a vital clash between the NPC champions, the Canterbury Crusaders, and the Super 12-holders, the Auckland Blues, made Invercargill my Paris for the night.

I was not the only romantic on the South Island that autumnal evening. Twenty minutes before kick-off, a Canterbury couple were married on the Christchurch pitch. I was only surprised that the bride wore a white meringue rather than a black-and-red Crusader dress. But, even at the Super 12, some traditions remained. After the wedding, the jousting horses appeared, with their riders' metal helmets and wooden lances harking back to, we were told, 'ye olde Canterbury'. The eventual rugby was also pretty Chaucerian – furious entertainment at a fast and bawdy lick with Jonah Lomu at full charge and the Blues on a knightly roll. 31–24 to Auckland – and the Blues back on top of the Super 12 for at least a day.

It was still Friday morning in London, and time for me to phone home with all my news.

'How's Invercargill?' Alison asked.

'It's great,' I enthused. 'It's only Friday night and I've already seen a wedding and a cracking game of rugby . . .'

Invercargill, Saturday, 28 March 1998
As flat as a tack, and as quiet on a Saturday as Bloemfontein on a Sunday, Invercargill was the perfect place to meet Os du Randt. There were no distractions, either for the immense Springbok prop or me. We just sat back and talked about rugby and New Zealand, du Randt in Afrikaans and me in English. Occasionally, as our confidence and intimacy grew, we would switch an occasional sentence into each other's language, with the Ox's English being stronger than the creaky yoke of my Afrikaans.

'*Ja*,' he agreed, 'Invercargill feels just like home. We've just flown in from Australia and I have to say I'm more comfortable in New Zealand. They're not really interested in rugby in Australia – but, here, it's just the same as South Africa. Rugby is the thing! So they treat us like kings – just like we treat them back home. In Australia, they're not so bothered. I guess it proves the closeness of New Zealand and South African culture. And we have a hellavu rugby history between us. We're the two countries everyone wants to beat – while our own eyes are always on each other. It's a very special, and respectful, relationship.

'For example, there's no doubt that my toughest opponent in world rugby is Olo Brown. He's short, enormously strong and good in the loose. He's the best – and it's a real grind to match him. But we have a lot in common. He's a quiet guy but we had a *lekker* [great] conversation after the Auckland game in Bloemfontein last year. He came over to my place and we had a fantastic time. He's very tough in the scrum – but so bright off the field. It's terrific to have such a rival.'

'But it must have been hard to stay so upbeat about the All Blacks these last few years . . .'

'*Ja*,' Os brooded. 'There've been a few times when they gave us a really good *klap* [slap]. It made my heart sore. Since the World Cup it sometimes felt as if God was walking with the All Blacks. They seemed untouchable. And it bothered me. I would think, "Why have we been forsaken?" And it rolled around in my head until I reached a point where I thought, "But this is so self-centred! God is obviously with all of us. He's not on anyone's side..."'

The idea that rugby was a religion in both white South Africa and New Zealand had long been a cliché – but in Afrikaner circles it was a sacrilegious distortion to claim that rugby was more important than God. Rather, God's guidance was often regarded as the most significant component in rugby success. Yet, during the multi-racial South Africa's longing for the World Cup, 'God' and 'will' became rugby and cultural buzzwords amongst even non-Afrikaners. I told du Randt how I remembered 'James Small talking of "divine intervention" – he said that, during the World Cup, it felt as if God had decided that, after all the trouble and division, South Africa should come together in a moment of elation.'

'Hell,' Os breathed mistily, 'did James really say that? Jeez, I'm impressed! It's strange – because I felt the same thing. I believed God was leading us to victory. But then, after the World Cup, it felt as if he left us. But the truth was that, once more, we had begun to tear ourselves apart.'

Our best moments together were always our most honest; as when I confessed to Os how, years ago, I had blamed Afrikanerdom for everything that went wrong not only in South Africa but in my own fucked-up life. He understood, as I did too when he described his own early years in Eliot as a 'typical life for an Afrikaner on a *platteland dorp* [small farmland town]. We lived on a farm. And it was the farm that my father's father had farmed. My dad, naturally, was also a farmer and we lived a completely Afrikaans life. It was very sheltered. We had no television – and I didn't even bother with the radio. So there was no need for me ever to speak or even understand English. I have to laugh now but, whenever I was in class and we were meant to learn English, I would slip an Afrikaans rugby book into my English set-work. I had no interest in learning English. You guys lived in another world to us. And isn't it ironic that, now, as a professional rugby player, I travel to Britain, Australia and New Zealand and I yearn to speak better English – and I think, fuck, I should've studied English! It would've made my life so much easier . . .'

Yet it was another of the enduring ironies of South African life that a *platteland* Afrikaner like Os du Randt was fluent in Xhosa; while I, an English-speaking liberal and township teacher who had left the country in moral indignation, could muster only a handful of words in any black African language. Meeting Os du Randt in Invercargill, like talking to Nelie Smith in Ballymena, helped rip up my most outdated theories about Afrikanerdom and South Africa. Os, even if it was just for his role in the World Cup-winning *Amabokbokke*, had done far more for the country than I would ever do. There was catharsis in my admiration of du Randt, a sense that, as different as we were, he could teach me more about the country than I might once have dreamed.

'But, Os,' I asked later, 'what did you really think of us *sout-piels*?'

'*Ja*,' Os laughed, 'I'm a little ashamed to say it now, but we could never believe it whenever an English *oke* made it into the Springbok team. We never thought you guys could play rugby – not really. We always thought that we had a huge advantage over the English *sout-piels*. You guys were soft. If we played an English school we said that these guys are going to come at us like maniacs for fifteen or twenty minutes. And then they'll blow-up. They couldn't last the pace. We were just too physical. After twenty minutes our superiority would start to show. And of course it's rubbish. In fact we lost to many English schools but I guess we would never admit it to ourselves. Just like you guys thought we were stupid, we thought you were weak. And, shit, now I'm playing for a great Springbok team which is coached by an Englishman and captained by an Englishman. And look at our pack and at all the English guys – Teichmann, Garvey, Dalton, Andrews . . .'

Mark Andrews had also grown up in Eliot, but on the English side of town. Later, he went to boarding-school in the coastal city of East London. 'Ag, it was just typically South African,' du Randt confirmed. 'I always heard that there was this English rugby player from Eliot but we never had contact with anyone beyond our Afrikaans community. It was only when we reached provincial level that I met Mark – and, now, we're putting Eliot on the map, hey!'

Even as an Eliot schoolboy, du Randt played front-row rugby 'in a style that was all my own. Without TV and the radio to influence me, I didn't have any rugby heroes to follow. I preferred to play with flair, to be very mobile. In the scrum, at primary school, it was too easy for me just to rely on my strength. Like some of these old New Zealand guys, from the age of two or three my dad would encourage us to work on the land. By the time I was five or six I was doing men's work. We'd be up at five in the morning and we would plough the fields until late in the evening. I became very strong, at a very young age. On the rugby field it felt like I could crush anyone.

'It was only when I started playing first-team rugby at high school that I had to develop some scrummaging skills. I was packing down against boys who were two or three years older than me and they were at least as strong as me. But I was never really interested in the scrum. I used to get into a lot of trouble because, even then, I just wanted to be a really fast prop. I wanted to run around the field with the ball under my arm. I wanted to score tries and make tackles and be totally involved in the game. But, then in South Africa, as in New Zealand, they had this idea that the prop should only do the "donkey-work". But the donkey-work was so boring. If I just had to go from scrum to scrum and lift guys at the line-outs I'd have given up rugby years ago. I used to just tell my coaches, "Listen, I don't care what a prop is supposed to do. I'll scrum, but I'll also handle the ball and tackle in the loose. If you don't like it, don't pick me."

'Of course I had to change my attitude a little because if you're going to prop for the Springboks then you had better learn how to scrum properly. So I started paying more attention at scrummaging practice. In the last two or three years my technique has improved and I'd say I'm just above average in the scrums now. I add much more in the loose. And I'm really lucky that modern rugby has become an "entertainment sport". Before, especially in South African and New Zealand rugby, you had these helluva huge and slow props. They were colossal and they dominated upfront – but that's all they did. It was a grim business. But, now, the scrum does not dictate the game like it once did – it's become as important for a prop to run and pass and tackle and, sometimes, even to kick. It suits my style of play perfectly.'

'And Nick Mallett's . . .' I noted.

'Exactly! On our European tour, Nick kept saying that if the five tighties make four tackles each a game then that's twenty tackles less for the loosies and our backs to make. And we did it. We each averaged four hits a Test, which is pretty good going. But Nick's been such an inspiration to Springbok rugby. He's totally in tune with the demands of the new game and he picks the right players in the right positions. Against the Lions it was the complete opposite and we were in chaos. But Nick has an extremely hard character. He's tough and he's brutally honest. He doesn't bullshit you. If he's going to drop a player he'll tell him exactly why he's being dropped. And there's no point arguing with Nick because he knows his own mind. As players, that's so great for us because we know where we stand. Nick Mallett is not a *twee-gat jakkels*.'

Afrikaans is rarely a lyrical language. Yet it has some singular phrases

– and '*twee-gat jakkels*' is up there with the best of them. It literally means a 'two arse-holed jackal', which is a more graphic variation on the old 'two-faced' chestnut. The jackals, clearly, had left the Springbok side and were instead devouring du Randt's Golden Cats.

The Cats had limped into Invercargill on the broken back of two Australian hidings – losing 25–10 to New South Wales and 37–3 to ACT. Even worse, the team was riven with disunity. Du Randt himself had been badly injured and was due to fly back to South Africa the following afternoon, once he'd watched the Cats play the resurgent Highlanders.

'I think I'm going to be out for the next few months,' he sighed, 'and while I'm not going to miss the provincial arguments and squabbles we've had in the Super 12, I hope I can get back in time for the Tri-Nations. Nick Mallett has turned the Springboks into a special force. He knows that once a side is divided into little cliques then it's sure to hit trouble. And that's what happened to us in the Super 12. Basically, the Cats have been a real mess. Some of the guys feel that Sarfu have had a say in the selection of the team and there's not too much harmony around at the moment. But, look, it's only our first year of playing regional rugby. There were bound to be problems. The New Zealanders have been doing it so much better and so much longer than us...'

The Free State Ox considered his words and then, with all the hopeful gravity of a farmer from either Eliot or Invercargill, he nodded defiantly. 'But we can do it. With Nick Mallett, we can beat the All Blacks this year – as long as we work hard together as a united team and a united country. Wouldn't that be sweet?'

A few hours later, at the rickety Homestead Stadium, that sweetness seemed as elusive as ever. At half-time, the woeful Cats were losing 40–3. The Otago Highlanders had run in five tries without even stretching, scoring the first after sixty-one seconds and another three minutes later. I was pleased for Josh Kronfeld, as the Highlanders were on their way to a top-four spot in the Super 12 – but, as even he had said, the Cats were a team not only without claws, but also lacking a heart.

They needed Os du Randt. Earlier that morning he had explained how he prepared himself for a Super 12 match. 'I play the whole game in my mind before kick-off. I go through each scenario of play. I call it "The Hero Game" – because in my mind I become the hero. I'm the guy who fucks everyone up.'

If he'd been fit, du Randt would have required a dreamy 'Super-Hero

Game' to compensate for his hapless team. But, dressed in an immaculate blue shirt and beige suit, he shook his head and shrugged – it was embarrassing to be a South African in Invercargill. I hid my own head when the huge Southland farmer next to me murmured in bemusement to his even larger pal: 'Hey, Snowy, are you really sure that eight of these bloody hopeless blighters are Springboks?'

After the second half had mercifully wound down, with the Cats restricting their loss to a mere thirty points, 57–27, Snowy and I ignored the South Africans trudging from the field. We concentrated instead on the line of awestruck men and young boys queuing up for Taine Randell's signature in the grandstand. We still awaited Sean Fitzpatrick's official retirement, but Randell seemed to be only weeks away from the All Black captaincy.

Snowy and his friend watched the smitten, hazy-eyed faces gazing at Randell as he patiently signed his name, again and again.

'Some of those old boys must be fifty if they're a day,' Snowy said, 'and even a naked Elle McPherson couldn't bloody shift them. You'd think they were looking up at the face of Christ . . .'

'You never know, Snow, they might be doin' just that . . .'

As if it spelt out some dark omen for that afternoon's match between the Hurricanes and the Sharks, cold wind and lashing rain swept across the Invercargill blackness. I left town at 5.30 a.m. on Sunday morning to make my flight back to the North Island. Five hours later, the day had turned even nastier in Palmerston North. The rain was torrential, the wind a veritable hurricane. Waiting for the worst to pass, I sat for an hour in the tiny airport concourse with a bowed crowd of Wellington fans.

The storm pounded against the thickly glazed window, sounding like a threat of biblical retribution for yet more Super 12 blasphemy on a Sunday.

'It's pretty bad today,' someone eventually said, more optimistically, 'and that has to help the Hurricanes . . .'

'Yeah,' someone agreed, 'but the wind will be fiercer than this at home. The Sharks wouldn't have had a prayer at Athletic Park . . .'

Wellington's provincial stadium held 40,000 compared to a more modest 18,500 at Palmerston North's Showgrounds. The additional revenue would have neared the $200,000 mark and provided an arena for a game between, until at least that afternoon, the Super 12's two leading teams. But, drawing on players from nine different unions, the Hurricane management's plan to switch the venue had to be abandoned. Regionalism, at the core of New Zealand's previous success in the Super 12, had to be respected – as did partisan small-town fever. In the weeks preceding the game, a third of Palmerston North's 63,000 population had signed a petition demanding that the Sharks clash be played at the Showgrounds rather than in Wellington.

The New Zealand capital, however, would host South Africa in the Tri-Nations in early-August. I stared at the bleak March wind and rain in Palmerston North, fearing the midwinter weather the Springboks might endure in Wellington. My spiritual discourse with Os du Randt had left its mark. I was ready to make a pact with the devil – even if he always wore black. If the Sharks, somehow, beat the Hurricanes, could that please ensure a Springbok victory later that year? But, crossing my fingers, I warned the bad man. If the Sharks went down that Sunday then all Springbok bets were off.

Palmerston North Showgrounds, Sunday, 29 March 1998
If the wind had not dropped, at least the rain held off for an hour. There was even a snatch of sunshine as Pieter Muller lay flat on the ground and stretched out his arm. He held the ball with one finger, and Henry Honiball kicked into the gale. The Sharks had won the toss and, with me winking at Old Nick, elected to play into the wind.

The South Africans were ready; and both Muller and Honiball landed early with distinctive crash-tackles. But, with the sun, out came Christian Cullen with his definitive ray-gun of a run. He left two men for dead and then fired a flat bullet to Bachop, who looked for Umaga. But Stefan Terblanche, that flying wing on the draft from Boland, swept like an icy wind through the gap that separated Bachop from Umaga. He took the ball with him as well and, after six minutes, streaked away for the first Sharks try. 5–0.

Cullen, kicking in the absence of the injured Jon Preston, landed a penalty soon afterwards – and encouraged the rampaging Filo Tiatia. The big flanker, moving like a fast-falling coat-stand under the combined weight of Joubert, Muller and Terblanche, crashed over in a corner. Suddenly, it was 8–5 to the Hurricanes. As if in celebration, the breeze breathed a little harder.

But Honiball and Teichmann knew how to blow back. The Springboks calmly followed a mazy run from Terblanche with an effortless link.

They opened up a long corridor of space for Muller. He ran hard and, as Monty Python began to whistle over the PA, it was 10–8 to the Sharks. We were looking on the bright side of another Palmerston North storm – as at half-time when, after a penalty each from Honiball and Cullen, the Sharks held on to a narrow 13–11 lead.

With the wind, as well as forty minutes of outstanding ball-retention and ferocious tackling behind them, the Sharks went for a quick kill in the returning rain. They started with a duff penalty. Twenty metres out and bang in front, Honiball hit the post. The ball bounced back into play and Doug Howlett, the new Hurricane wing, opted to run. He was tackled by Jeremy Thomson and, in his anxiety, popped the ball up in the hope of hitting another Hurricane. But Terblanche was too quick. Another interception and, instead of three points from an easy penalty, the Sharks had taken seven. 20–11.

Three minutes later the Hurricanes' best hope, Cullen, was cut down again by Muller. At the resulting scrum, Kevin Putt, the mouthy Kiwi ex-pat in a number 9 Shark shirt, whispered up the blind-side. He must have made thirty metres before he slid a pass to his full-back. Joubert then fed Terblanche who, with Howlett closing in on him, returned the smooth compliment. Joubert caught it again but, almost instantly, as Howlett and Cullen veered in to block him, he made a Michael Jordan-like pass back to Terblanche. It was basketball, for a moment, but with such skill that Terblanche had time to side-step Cullen again and hit his hat-trick. 25–11 after fifty minutes.

The game was over in another seven. Cullen skidded past Honiball, and was hit with terrible force by Wickus van Heerden, the younger brother of mean Moaner. Cullen slumped to the ground. He didn't move – either when Shaun Payne went over for the resulting try or when Honiball landed another conversion. Cullen, as rugged as any other All Black, had to be helped from the field.

And 32–11 became 39–11 when Muller scored his second try in driving rain. With cheery arrogance, before anyone could stop him, the soggy Springbok prop Ollie le Roux stepped up and kicked a touchline conversion. The Australians had a lanky lock who could boot the ball a bit – but we had fat props who, with the merest glances and the daintiest steps, could do the same trick. As the ball soared through the posts, le Roux reeled away in delight and, as a lone Shark in the press box, I hit the roof.

A Sharks victory in the cold and the wet seemed, then, to mark a symbolic end to New Zealand's glistening rugby dominance. Even when the Hurricanes reduced the final deficit to 39–23 with two late tries, the wind and the rain no longer mattered. The long Black cloud over the Super 12 had at last, I thought, begun to break.

The following morning, Christian Cullen walked over to my table with a bad limp and a shy grin which curled up towards his black eye.

'Shit, Christian,' I murmured in consolation, 'what a shiner . . .'

'I thought you might like it, mate,' he said. He took a quick slug of juice and the sliding orange in his glass made the underside of his eye look purple.

'When did it happen?'

'Gee,' Cullen pondered, 'I'm not really sure. The tackles were flying in thick and fast. Your boys nailed me a few times yesterday . . .'

I shuddered at the memory of Wickus van Heerden pasting Cullen against the muddy grass with that huge roller of a hit.

'Yeah,' Cullen said with strange relish, 'that was a pretty good one – but I think I picked up the shiner a bit earlier. Anyway, the eye doesn't hurt at all . . .'

'That's good . . .'

'Nah,' he continued with a grimace, 'it's the knee that's killing me. It's really sore – the ligaments again . . .'

I knew that Cullen and the Hurricanes were due to play again that Friday night in New Plymouth. It was against the wayward Golden Cats but, still, if Andre Venter found some form and came roaring round the scrum with his intent stare pinned on Cullen, it could spell yet more danger.

'Aw, mate, no worries, I'll be okay by Friday . . .'

'But will the Hurricanes?' I asked, slipping away from *Casualty* and back into the locker-room.

'I hope so! It's been really strange. We win our first three on the road and then lose the next two at home. We can make all the excuses in the book but the truth is that we're no longer the team we were three weeks ago. We talked about it a lot last night but we couldn't figure it out. I suppose that when you're away on tour in South Africa you feel you're in for a really tough ride and so you play a little tighter. We had a real spark in Cape Town and Pretoria. But, back in New Zealand, I've noticed the dressing-room's been quieter. I think maybe the guys were absorbing the fact that we were on top of the Super 12. That's a pretty big high. And we didn't handle it so well. Not like Natal – gee, they played so well yesterday. They were much better than us . . .'

'All the marketing men in Durban will be glad you're still calling them "Natal" . . .'

'I just get confused with all the new Super 12 names. Y'know, Bulls and Cats and Sharks start to blur. When I see Honiball and Teichmann and those guys, I just think, oh yeah, they're those hard Natal boys. It's the easiest way.'

Cullen had been a literal and proverbial Hurricane for two Super 12 years – but he had also shown unusual loyalty to his home union of Manawatu and played for them in the second division of the NPC rather than for Wellington. For a player who could devastate opposing Test teams, the minor league was an embarrassingly easy runaround. While I'd always been impressed by Cullen's provincial constancy, it was inevitable that he would have to move permanently to Wellington in 1998.

'Yeah, it's time to make the change,' he agreed. 'I think both me and the [Manawatu] Union have been good for each other but obviously Super 12 has just exploded in New Zealand – and there's just too big a gap between playing against teams like we did yesterday and then stepping down a division a few months later. So I'm leaving Palmerston North once the Super 12's over. It'll take a little adjusting, perhaps, but a lot of the Hurricanes are based in Wellington so that'll help. Anyway, it's not like I'm moving to London or anything. Wellington's even closer to my old home town . . .'

Paekakariki was less than thirty miles from Wellington and yet, although he was still close to his family, Cullen admitted that 'I haven't seen my old buddies for ages. Y'know, the guys from school. It's difficult. It's pretty hard to get the time to go back and see everyone while we're away most of the year. And when I do get some time I just want to be on my own, at home, or with my girlfriend . . .'

Christian and I had a giggle; for the first time in all the interviews we had done over the last year he did not have a new girlfriend to tell me about. 'Yeah,' he laughed, 'it's the same girl this time. But, shit, we don't get to see much of each other. Y'know, even when we went away on holiday at the end of the season, it was crazy. We went to Western Samoa and, yeah, maybe I hadn't thought that one through. We got there and it suddenly hit me – oh shit, they're even crazier about rugby in Samoa than they are in New Zealand! The people were great but I was an All Black again and wherever I went it was rugby, rugby, rugby . . .'

It was one of modern rugby's many quirks that its most marketable and exceptional player was one of the quietest of men. Like Lomu, Cullen would have preferred an anonymous life to stardom. Yet, naturally, he had had to appoint an agent to deal with all the offers. So whenever I went to the movies in New Zealand I chuckled; for there would be Christian, grinning through yet another wide-screen commercial. He did them relatively well, and yet I knew how much more content he would have been on the couch at home rather than on some glaring film set.

'Yeah,' he admitted, 'there're three of four of them around at the moment. But I guess if they pop up you have to take them – well, so they tell me, mate . . .'

'Are you happier now than before?' I wondered.

'Well, life was simpler. You know, before rugby took hold of me, I was cruising around, doing much as I pleased. But, now, sometimes it can seem a bit of an ordeal. But I guess the old days and a more normal life will come back soon enough. I hope it doesn't happen for a long time but I'll have to retire one day. So I just try to live from game to game and switch off – when I get the chance. Y'know, I'm only twenty-two but my rugby career could end tomorrow. I could get wiped out on the field and it would be all over. I thought about it this morning. I woke up and I felt really sore. And I was just so glad that it was nothing serious because, mate, at the end of it all, even when we have to lose, I still really love the rugby . . .'

Frank Oliver had no doubt. 'He's a strong little critter,' the Hurricanes coach said of Cullen, 'and as long as his body holds out, he should be around for fucking years. Nah, I've got no worries about Christian. He can handle it – everything from the hard hits to the huge fame. He's got it sussed. He'll go and have a game of golf later today and he won't churn over the fact that we lost. He's different to a lot of these kids. He'll keep a lid on the bullshit – he knows it's not the end of the fucking world. We lost yesterday but nobody's dead. Nobody lost an arm or a leg. The sun came up on schedule this morning. Life goes on . . .'

At the end of a long scowl, Oliver's face lit up with a huge smile. I knew him as a mean All Black lock from the late-1970s and, even more since then, as New Zealand rugby's bluntest coach. But, while there was both gravitas and blunt common sense in almost everything he said, I'd begun to suspect that Oliver's notoriously glowering persona was little more than a wily front to obscure his inherent good cheer. Oliver, after all, belonged more to the Colin Meads generation of curt All Black forwards rather than Sean Fitzpatrick's shinier brand.

As a teaser, I wondered how much he had enjoyed listening to *Bitter Sweet Symphony* and *Ironic* whenever the Sharks ran in another try. 'Bloody hell,' Frank brooded for a moment before he barked out a laugh, 'they're not in my fucking record collection. But, oh shit, what can you do but go with the times? It's all part of the bloody circus! I was more concerned about my boys out on the field. They didn't like the pressure. Not like Auckland or the bloody Sharks! Those boys soak up bloody pressure. Teichmann? Honiball? Joubert? The bigger the occasion the more they love it. My boys just bagged it. We've got a great player in Cullen and a very good player in Umaga. But the rest of the team are bloody workers. We seem to cope better if we're not expected to do well – and that's because my team's drawn from nine unions. Wellington haven't set the world on fire and the other eight unions are strictly small-time. So the boys have had trouble coming to terms with being the top dogs. It's a hellavu fucking tournament and they were looking down thinking, "Shit, we might win this thing if we keep going. But are we good enough?" Yesterday we found out.'

As another temper-stirrer, I wondered what Oliver made of the perpetual British criticism of the Super 12.

'Yeah,' he admitted on cue, 'I want to shoot the fucking bastards sometimes. But, actually, if you take the southern-hemisphere bias out of it for a wee while, then they do have a valid point in some instances. Some of this stuff we see is a bit bloody frothy. I'm sure in England they think, "Fucking hell, this is rubbish!" Look, I know my team has always wanted to ruck the ball quickly, run with it and then whizz the bloody thing wide. We haven't had guys who've ever thought about kicking the ball so they might turn a back line. Maybe we should start to do a few things which tweak the game a little rather than go at it pell-mell all the time. I guess that's why a few Pommy journos are up in arms. They see the stuff in the middle – the wild passes and the sloppy tackles – and think it's all frothy and rubbishy. So they miss the more obvious point that, in this competition, some of the scrummaging and tackling and finishing is as good as anything you'll find in Test rugby.

'But the important thing to realise is that, ultimately, this is not international rugby – it's still a regional or a provincial tournament which provides a bridge into the high-level rugby you'll see in the Tri-Nations. The All Blacks play a much tighter and more disciplined game – as do the Springboks. The Sharks against the Hurricanes will not be the same as South Africa against New Zealand. But, shit, seeing some of the Shark tackling yesterday you'll understand why the Springbok defence is going to be hard to crack this year. So, yesterday, my boys had to learn a big lesson. And this is the beauty of the Super 12. It teaches our southern-hemisphere players how to operate under less space and less time. And that's why, down south, we're still better than the bloody Brits and even the French . . . we've got boys coming up through the ranks who're playing against awesome rugby men from Australia, South Africa and New Zealand week after week in a fucking hard competition.'

One of those players was Josh Kronfeld's Otago friend and Frank Oliver's twenty-two-year-old son, Anton. After five more weeks of Super 12 rugby, the young Oliver had been earmarked for Sean Fitzpatrick's All Black shirt at hooker. 'Yeah,' Frank conceded with gruff tenderness, 'the kid's done well. Fitzy looks like he might be really crook this time. The word is that he's not coming back – much as he'd love to. So Anton's in with a shout. Y'know, last year, when he made the All Black tour to the UK it was pretty lump-in-the-throat stuff. And I'll have to somehow contain my pleasure if he breaks into the Test team this year . . .'

I asked the old dad if the All Black shirt mattered as much to New Zealanders his son's age, and younger, as it had done when he had been a Test player.

'Aw, yeah,' Frank almost smiled again, 'definitely. It's still every New Zealand kid's dream to wear that black shirt. We've been bloody good at rugby for so long – and we're still right up there. Everyone wants a touch of the magic. The Black shirt still retains a little bit of mystery. But, shit, you know this already. You're a bloody South African!'

Breakfast with Frank Oliver, on one of my last days in New Zealand, was less a humorously profane encounter than something more moving. As a forward from the All Black team which toured South Africa during 1976, he was part of my youth. 'Shit,' Frank sighed, 'those were tormented times. Remember all that shit about the Olympic Games boycott in Montreal 'cos we were on tour in a rioting South Africa? Maybe, in the end, they were right. But, then, we didn't worry too much. We just wanted to play footie against your bloody Boks . . .'

Frank Oliver came from the old days, from a time when New Zealand forwards were gruff bastards in black. But he was a far more interesting and sympathetic man than the rugby myth suggested. After a meaningful pause, he leant over and said, in a naturally dark growl, 'Don, I hate to admit it, but there's also some real mystery in your boys' bloody green-and-gold shirt . . .'

In Wellington, on the very last day of March, the day before I left New Zealand, the circle tightened yet further. The troubles of 1976 and 1981 were meant to have passed forever. But South Africa was still a divided and violent country. Rugby, meanwhile, remained an enduring symbol of that weary struggle.

I spent a sunny but blustery morning drinking coffee and writing postcards to my family and friends, both in South Africa and England. I sat across the street from the Flesh Wounds piercing and tattoo parlour and watched a funky stream of babes and slackers drift by in search of their latest metal stud or inky stain. Christian Cullen, I guessed, would give Flesh Wounds a miss once he moved into town. He'd picked up enough gory cuts and scrapes, as well as his colourful bruises and more serious bangs, for the novelty of pain to have faded.

Springbok rugby was subject to a different wounding, to a more familiar psychological scarring. In South Africa, words like 'racism' and 'rugby', 'boycott' and 'Springbok' were still bolted and branded together. I'd read in the morning paper how the National Sports Council (NSC) threatened 'drastic measures' against Louis Luyt, Sarfu and Springbok rugby. Unless Luyt and the Sarfu executive resigned within fourteen days, the NSC would call for the immediate international isolation of South African rugby – as well as the removal of the Springbok name and emblem from any future national team.

The NSC were furious. They had pointed out months before that South African rugby did not 'reflect the national demographics'. The NSC also underlined the 'almost exclusively white composition' of both the Springbok rugby team and the four Super 12 squads. Of the 120 players selected for the southern-hemisphere tournament, only four were coloured – Chester Williams, McNeil Hendricks, Breyton Paulse and Deon Kayser.

Dan Retief, the rugby writer for the South African *Sunday Times*, explained that 'first to call foul was Mluleki George, a powerful figure in sports circles as president of the NSC. An ANC parliamentarian, who was a key figure in the sports-based anti-apartheid movement, George mooted the possibility of South African rugby again becoming the target of boycott action. He also sent shivers of apprehension through the rugby establishment by saying that he would be looking to Sarfu to honour a "promise" that at least six members of the Springbok World Cup squad in 1999 would be black.'

But, as Retief suggested, 'With the best will in the world, no black rugby player is currently good enough to win a place in the Springbok side. Judged purely from a rugby perspective, Chester Williams has spent two years out of the game recovering from injuries. In the interim, an outstanding player such as Pieter Rossouw has been found to add an extra dimension to the Boks' number 11 jersey. The other players in the running are also wingers: Breyton Paulse and McNeil Hendricks. The former does not possess the physique to contain the likes of Jonah Lomu, Joeli Vidiri, Joe Roff or Tana Umaga, while the latter, although tough, physical and brave, is not yet up to the standard of the players he would need to displace. [The coloured hooker] Dale Santon played nineteen minutes in his only Springbok game against France "A" in Toulon last year before Nick Mallett – a coach fully committed to the principle of affirmative action – had to pull him off so that South Africa could start to win some line-out ball. Mallett, who coached Santon at Boland, afterwards described it as "the hardest decision I've ever had to make", but felt it would not only have been damaging to the team's chances but to Santon's confidence if he had allowed him to struggle on.'

Retief also stressed that 'however prejudiced the selection may have seemed, there are simply no other black players available who are up to the standard of the Super 12. Perhaps all that is needed is a little patience. At school level there are a number of black kids who can really play – kids who were introduced to rugby because it was their school's sport and for whom it is a first-choice game. They are on their way and I, for one, remain convinced that the influence of the coloured players in South African rugby is going to become as great as that wielded by the Maoris and Pacific Islanders in New Zealand. Whether this can happen quickly enough to pacify the politicians is another matter altogether.'

It could not. The NSC were incensed that Sarfu had forced Nelson Mandela to appear in court. For hours, Mandela stood in the dock and defended his sanctioning of a state investigation into racism in South African rugby. 'Adding to the conflict,' *The Dominion* newspaper reported, 'yesterday [March 30] saw the expulsion from rugby of Brian van Rooyen, the man whose dossier of allegations triggered the appointment of the judicial commission of inquiry. Sarfu said on Sunday that the former Transvaal Rugby Union vice-president was guilty of "launching a very violent attack involving claims of financial mismanagement, corruption and racism against the leadership of Sarfu, the back-up for which was demonstrably absent".'

It seemed a long time since, only nine months before, I had met van Rooyen in Johannesburg. Since then, so much had happened; but so little had changed.

Threatened by the cancellation of the 1998 Tri-Nations and the loss of all rugby ties with South Africa, the New Zealand Union, as in 1976 and 1981, promised to plough on regardless. Their chairman, Rob Fisher, stressed that 'essentially it's an internal matter between the South African Rugby Union and its government. It obviously has some implications for us. But Dr Luyt is a very clever person and I have every confidence that he'll do what is best for rugby and come to a solution . . .'

'Yet,' *The Dominion* concluded, 'John Dobson, editor of *SA Rugby* magazine, described the stand-off between Sarfu and the NSC as the most serious issue facing South African rugby since its international re-admission in 1992. "It is much more than just a domestic issue," Dobson said. "The situation is very grave . . ."'

Chapter 18
An Australian Spiderman

April in Sydney; and, with blue skies over the long rolling beaches and gleaming white Opera House, Alison seemed brighter than ever. Three months before, in early-January, while planning my Super 12 tour, I'd had my one and only momentary doubt. Our bank balance had taken more than a single huge hit. It cowered like a mewling Golden Cat after being crunched in quick succession by Isitolo Maka and Jonah Lomu. This book had left it limping and bleeding. We were that deep into the red stuff. But, together, we had been to Enfield and Llanelli for the sake of rugby. We hoped for a last exotic twist before the end of this journey.

I sat down and did the sums. They didn't thrill me but, still, I came up with a suggestion. We could just about afford to be together down under for ten days – if I cheated and wrote off Alison as my tax-deductible and utterly essential Super 12 body-masseuse. I left the choice to her. New Zealand or Australia? It was, of course, a trick question. The answer was obvious. New Zealand, definitely, every single time.

I could not believe it. It was fucking crazy. Somehow, she considered Sydney a more attractive option than Hamilton, Dunedin, Invercargill and Palmerston North. I suspected it was less a gender issue than one of nationality. Alison had been born in Surrey. She was English. So, naturally, when she thought about the Antipodes she pictured Bondi Beach rather than the Wellington Hurricanes. She fancied a tan and our dining out on 'Surf 'n' Turf' and drinking chilled bottles of Australian Chardonnay while looking over the splendour of Darling Harbour. No wonder Lawrence Dallaglio despaired of Five Nations rugby. The English, even my informed wife, had still to grasp the significance of watching the Super 12 in New Zealand. Rather than being absorbed by the Highlanders' future All Black front row of Hoeft, Oliver and Meeuws in a damp South Island setting, Alison was seduced more by the lure of our needing to buy high-factor suntan oil in Sydney.

I could understand her desire for us to act out all our favourite scenes from *Neighbours* and *Home and Away* on sandy Australian soil – but, beyond the soapy art, where was her rugby soul?

Yet a serious midwinter query became a summery irrelevance when we at last hit Australia together. The weather was stunning, the sea was warm and the city was gorgeous. We were in Sydney. It was fantastic. We were Jason and Kylie, bronzed and carefree, having a surf and a smoothie in between stumbling into the transvestites' bar around the corner in King's Cross. It was, in a way, freedom from rugby. Freedom to see the hookers stepping out for work at one in the morning, and not to automatically think of either Sean Fitzpatrick or Keith Wood. Freedom, too, in the hotel we stayed, where the word 'red' had a light and a zone around it, not to ponder the Saturday-night fortunes of the Reds against the Blues, as Auckland visited Queensland. Sydney was terrific, an even better bet than the House of Pain and Eden Park. I bowed again to my wife's wisdom.

However, on our fourth night in town, I felt the first bad tug of withdrawal. The craving began, slowly at first and then more deeply and urgently. I needed a shot. Like any habitual user, I'd already staked out the area and found a place – just in case. And, on Saturday evening, I needed to get straight. I couldn't help it. Under the hot lights, with tumultuous noise and spinning colour amid that sweet rush and crush, the Reds and Blues were irresistible.

I began to list the usual excuses. It was work. It would provide an interesting cultural contrast from my New Zealand experience to watch a live Super 12 match in a Sydney bar. Halfway through the tournament it was, almost, important for us to see the game.

'It sounds great,' Alison said, more simply.

It was a pretty great game – especially for John Eales, the Australian captain. I'd explained Eales's unusual qualities to Alison. Some of his team-mates called him 'Nobody', as in 'nobody's perfect', but I quickly ticked off his line-out prowess and running in the loose, his exceptional place-kicking and unruffled leadership. 'And,' I concluded in another effort to convince Alison of these rugby boys' winning versatility, 'it says here that "not only is Eales an outstandingly consistent and competent footballer, he is, quite simply, a great bloke".' I looked up meaningfully from my copy of *Australian Rugby Review*, a publication I carried everywhere in Sydney – even when we went for our midnight drink at Club Iguana. I found it essential reading; and so I continued my extended quote about the Wallabies lock.

'In spite of his 200cm frame, he is not an imposing fellow off the field. His friendly disposition and genuine interest in talking to the average punter is refreshing. It often appears that Eales will do anything for anyone. But Eales is a natural-born leader, both on and off the field . . .

some say there is no finer example of an international football captain than John Eales.'

We'd got the gist of it by then and I only needed to skim through a quick survey of Ten Things You Didn't Know About John Eales. And so now we know that John Eales always puts his left boot on first when dressing for a match and that he couldn't live without his watch. Even more in keeping with his undoubted appeal, Eales confessed that his favourite food was still 'Grandma's Pasta'.

All lovely stuff, of course; but, as Frank Oliver might have said, 'a bit bloody frothy' when set against Eales's play that night. After twenty-four minutes, he stepped out of a red phone-booth disguised as a Queensland line-out, and raced across his half of the field. He reached the far corner just in time and, flying through the humid Brisbane air, brought off a miraculous crash-tackle on the Blues' Adrian Cashmore. A certain Auckland try had been averted by Captain Fantastic. In the thirty-second minute, close to the right touchline at the opposite end of the pitch, he kicked a curling wonder of a penalty – to follow an earlier penalty and conversion to extend Queensland's lead to 13–5.

Two minutes later, his comic-book fame was assured. Penalty to the Blues and, from forty metres, Cashmore prepared himself for the kick. He struck it beautifully. The camera followed the white ball as it looped towards the Red poles. The Fox commentators were already announcing another three points in the Blue bank when Spiderman took off. He jumped soundlessly into the black sky, as if hoisting himself up an invisible thread, and waited for the ball to drop. It would have cleared the crossbar by a foot had Eales not stretched out his long arm and tapped it down as casually as if he were dropping another live fly into his springy web. Instead of just applauding, the South African referee, Andre Watson, blew for a knock-on – which was like accusing Spiderman of a slip when he abseiled down the side of a building while pursuing the forces of darkness.

But the Blues were suitably stunned; and it was mostly Red from then on. Eales landed all six of his kicks, dominated the line-outs and even turned up at scrum-half during a phase of possession which set up Shane Drahm's gem of a try. The game ended with Eales, forty-four metres out, stepping up to score his final penalty as the Australian commentator, Chris 'Buddha' Handy yelled, 'That is a mighty victory! Queensland Reds, 33. Auckland Blues, the reigning champions, 18. And that's eighteen points in the game, too, to Mr John Eales! He's a marvel!'

*

The Australian Rugby Union had just announced their intention to spend $1,200,000 on marketing the game across the country. It was their most lavish promotion to date. Brian Thorburn, the ARU's marketing guru, suggested, in pithy electoral-speak, that they aimed 'to appeal to the broader market and drive our dollar further with a campaign that will capture the swinging voter, the sports fan who hasn't made up his mind whether to watch AFL, League or Union.'

It was Australian rugby's perennial fate to compete against the more popular and wealthier oval codes. Aussie Football and League, with cricket, dominated Australian sport. While there was always passing interest in rugby, it belonged amongst the middle tier of more individual sports like tennis, golf, athletics and swimming which enjoyed periodic outbursts of national enthusiasm – especially during winning Aussie performances in events of international relevance.

'But then,' one of our Australian friends said, 'if you got 100,000 Aussie blokes together and gave them a beer each and asked them to watch two flies climb a wall, they'd be into it for the whole race – as long as they could place a bet and the local fly came in first . . .'

The ARU were more optimistic that they could take a tilt at Rugby League – in much the same way that League had attempted to take on the traditional strength of Union in New Zealand a few years before. They had been encouraged by the split of the thirteen-man game into two warring camps in 1997 – the Australian Rugby League and the Super League. Although a new and supposedly united twenty-team League competition had begun the previous weekend, the rugby men were hoping to pick up some stray supporters still disenchanted with the squabbling.

But, if anything, the temporary demise of League had bolstered the position of Australian Football across the county. The *Australian Rugby Review* confirmed that the 'AFL is clearly the number-one code nationally and it took full advantage of the League war to strengthen its foothold in the Brisbane and Sydney sports market' – cities which, traditionally, were League and rugby territory.

Although nearly 100,000 people had been attracted to the MCG to see the All Blacks hammer the Wallabies in the 1997 Tri-Nations, a state like Victoria was still engulfed by Australian Football fever. In Melbourne, Perth and Adelaide, the Super 12 was of scant consequence. But at least the Australian Rugby Union had a potentially outstanding national team to sell to the uncertain masses. They were hopeful that the Wallabies would rekindle the fleeting euphoria of their World Cup win in England in 1991. Centred around Eales in the pack and featuring Test rugby's most sparkling back line, they were led by a coach, the discerning Rod Macqueen, who looked as if he might rival the All Black's Hart and the Springbok's Mallett.

Yet, without a national base, the limitations of Australian rugby remained. In an attempt to open up Victoria and Western Australia, the ARU had scheduled the Wallabies' two home Tests in the Tri-Nations for Melbourne and Perth. But, first, as Super 12 fervour spread through New Zealand and South Africa, the rugby Aussies displayed their latest promotional gimmick.

According to Glen Campbell, a director of the advertising agency which had won the contract to publicise rugby, 'two and a half million Australians per year go to or watch rugby from time to time. They have a positive disposition to rugby and they are the "floaters" the ARU wants to convert. If we can appeal to these people we could see a dramatic increase in rugby's following. They may not be conversant with all the laws, but they will form allegiances to teams. Our campaign will educate people on the rules, characters and heroes of the sport – as well as demonstrate the attributes of the game and show sports fans what rugby can offer them over other codes. For example, it is far less predictable than League and has unique attributes.'

The ARU and its advertisers had settled on a 'thought-provoking and insightful message' with which to sell rugby. I had yet to hear what John Eales made of it all, but the ad man suggested that his creative team of copy-writers had 'cleverly taken the instinctive behaviour and unpredictability of animals and directly correlated them to the game. Animals are very skilled at what they do and live in a very competitive environment. Thus they need superb skills to survive. It is amazing how these and other aspects correlate between the animal kingdom and rugby. Animals come in all shapes and sizes, just like players; in nature, animals have different jobs to do, just as players on the field have different roles.'

In South Africa and New Zealand we had already been down the dusty road of the Ox, Os du Randt, and the Bull, Mark Allen, but the Aussies were aiming 'wilder and higher'. The marketing boffins had persuaded the Wallaby scrum-half, George Gregan, to spend ten hours with body-painters so that they could transform him into a 'snarling cheetah'. The result was splashed all over the press and on billboards, with a naked but appropriately spotted Gregan bounding across the page in a dazzling impersonation of a cheetah. Meanwhile, Matthew Burke, the Wallaby full-back, was depicted as a 'menacing bird of prey', with huge wings sprouting from his back as he perched on top of a rugby cross-bar.

The posters were accompanied by slogans like, for Gregan, 'Rugby, Go With Your Instincts' and, for Burke, 'So you've cracked the defensive line . . . now meet the full-back!' They were not quite punchy enough to turn Melbourne and Perth into metropolitan versions of rugby-mad Dunedin or Invercargill – and even the innovative cross-breeding of John Eales and a spider seemed unlikely to impress the more brusque Aussie Rules and League crowds.

The *Sydney Morning Herald*'s rugby columnist, Spiro Zavos, found more significance in the emergence of a new Catholic schoolboy rugby tournament in Sydney – primarily because it would feature seven schools which had previously been Rugby League enclaves. 'It is a matter of sociological fact,' he explained, 'that Australian rugby is a class game; a middle- and upper-class game. In New Zealand, rugby is a national game. The aim of every New Zealand boy is to play for the All Blacks. The aim of Australian boys is to play for the NSW Blues, the Swans, or the Rabbitohs, or the Kings, or – perhaps – even for the Wallabies.'

Zavos stressed that, up until the First World War, 'Rugby Union rather than Rugby League was played in most Catholic schools. But men's rugby closed down for the duration of the war. Rugby League, however, continued to be played at all levels. Boys playing rugby in the schools, therefore, tended to favour League over Union as there was no future in Union when they left school. At the Catholic schools there was another incentive to turn to League. Rugby was identified as the Empire's game and the official winter game of the Australian Army. There was a strong element inside the Catholic community, especially bishops, priests and brothers with Irish backgrounds, who were bitterly opposed to Australian intervention on the side of Britain, the enemy of a united Ireland. Rugby Union is still suffering from the events of 1914–18. The western suburbs of Sydney, the creator of hundreds of fine Rugby League players, has virtually been a dead area to Australian rugby. This is the equivalent of, say, the tough suburbs of Auckland being a dead area for New Zealand rugby . . .'

From the outside, no matter how many glitzy ad campaigns were run or Catholic school competitions were inaugurated, it still looked an ultimately futile sporting war. Rugby lagged far behind. And, for that small Aussie mercy, the rest of world rugby gulped in relief. The brilliant Wallabies, a poor third in their own land, were closing in fast on both the Springboks and the All Blacks.

Sydney Football Stadium, Sunday, 5 April 1998

If Os du Randt still preferred New Zealand to Australia, Gary Teichmann was far happier in Sydney. Dunedin and Palmerston North, after five days in Canberra, had been another arduous grind through New Zealand. The rugby had been typically hard and sapping, with cold and sopping weather a regular backdrop. Yet the surrounding Kiwi obsession with rugby was even more draining. Wherever he went in New Zealand, Teichmann was recognised as the captain of the old enemy – and, even if the attention was devoid of animosity, the demand for a word, a prediction or a statement was constant. Sean Fitzpatrick had found South Africa to be a similarly taxing experience, especially when the locals would collar him and demand a confession of either his own insidious evil or South Africa's comparative superiority.

The Sharks had set up camp in Manly for the week. As Sydney virgins, our pleasures were simple. Even the boat-trip from the harbour to Manly was enough to induce a pant of delight on our part. For Teichmann, there was more sustained relief in the fact that he and the Sharks could waft around Manly and raise barely a glance. 'They really don't care about rugby round here.'

Christian Cullen had been as thrilled by the relative insignificance of rugby in Australia. While reliving his extended Western Samoan hand-shake and back-slap of a holiday, he had mused more wistfully that 'we should've gone some place where they're not at all interested in rugby – somewhere like Oz would have been good . . .'

Yet there was still rugby ardour in Sydney. We were entertained by the local newspapers' demand for the New South Wales Waratahs to show 'much more mongrel' in their clash with the Sharks. While the stray dogs were let loose on the Waratahs for losing against the Northern Bulls and the Western Stormers in South Africa, they were also said to have had cruel luck, poor refereeing decisions and shoddy flight-schedules set against them. The week before, their 33–30 lead against the Stormers was lost when James Small slipped in with a last-minute try. Unless they could salvage a win against either the Sharks or the Blues the following week in Auckland, another Super 12 season in Sydney would end in obscurity.

It was not totally parochial analysis either. As Peter Fitzsimons, in the *Sydney Morning Herald*, asked, 'Lest we forget, the Coastal Sharks – is that a crook name, or what?' But the Sharks' exploits in New Zealand were also noted. With a game in hand they were a point ahead of the Hurricanes and two ahead of the Blues and the Highlanders. A third

Shark victory in four matches in Australia and New Zealand would almost certainly ensure the South Africans home-ground advantage in the play-off stages. It would be yet another 'dog-fight', the preview writers predicted.

As far as the Australians were concerned, they were right. 'Mongrel' and 'crook' did turn out to be the key words on a gloriously sunny Sunday. Initially, everyone in the crowd seemed to be engrossed in smearing ice-cream over their own faces, as if a stickier lotion would block the hot early-afternoon rays. But the locals were soon jumping up repeatedly as the Waratahs licked in with one try after another. Out on the boiling field, the 'crook' Sharks turned 'mongrel'. Richard Harry, the NSW Wallaby prop, said afterwards, 'You name it, it happened today. It was like the Crimes Act – biting, gouging, stomping . . .'

After he had been sin-binned for a 'violent shoulder-charge', Mark Andrews was sent off for trampling a Waratah. The New Zealand ref, Paddy O'Brien, waved him on his way with a droll 'See ya later . . .' quip. Although we didn't realise it at the time, as Harry said, 'more serious X-certificate stuff' had already reeled past. After thirty-three minutes, we saw the Waratahs captain, Michael Brial, and O'Brien call Teichmann over. On the evening news later that night, it was possible to hear O'Brien say to Teichmann, 'That's a bite', as he and Brial pointed down to Richard Harry's arm.

Harry told the press that 'the scrum screwed and the next thing I knew I was bitten. I've never been bitten before. I wonder what I taste like?'

The question was eventually put to Wickus van Heerden, the guilty Shark. Big Wickus couldn't come up with a decent answer – beyond admitting his guilt and shame.

Although the Waratahs were easy 51–18 winners, all the headlines fed off the same theme. We had 'Shark Bite!', 'Shark Attack' and even 'Shark Bites Man!'

We circled the strained after-match party, only really enjoying our beer with Gary Teichmann and Jeremy Thomson – who explained that Andrews, Rossouw and van Heerden were about to be cited by the Waratahs management for foul play. Teichmann and Brial still had to endure the polite ritual. They made their complimentary captains' speeches and exchanged ties, while avoiding any formal mention of the bite.

But the Waratahs coach Matt Williams was a little more emphatic. 'Let's just say Richard Harry has the forensic evidence,' he informed the media. 'He's been bitten on the pig's trotter.'

The Australian phrasing tickled us – but, ultimately, it was a far more damaging nip on the trotter for van Heerden than Harry. The Shark flanker was speared the following evening. SANZAR's southern-hemisphere judiciary banned van Heerden from rugby for eighteen months. Andrews' own citing was quashed – with his dismissal being considered sufficient punishment – while Rossouw received a three-week ban for excessive stomping.

The Sharks were appalled by the severity of the van Heerden judgement. They pointed to the light sentence handed out to Kevin Yates of Bath. Although Yates denied his guilt, a huge chunk had been bitten out of Simon Fenn's ear in a cup match in England. Fenn, also an Australian, making his début for London Scottish, had his head swathed in bandages for almost a week after the Bath chomp. Close-up photographs of the bite on Richard Harry's arm suggested that an elastoplast bandage had left a more significant impression than van Heerden's teeth. Although the ban was reduced to a year on appeal, van Heerden's career, at the age of thirty-three, was effectively over. Biting was inexcusable and van Heerden deserved some form of ban – but his teeth were not nearly as sharp or venomous as those wild gnashers in the Bath scrum or in Mike Tyson's bloodier ring.

Ballymore, Brisbane, Thursday, 9 April 1998
On a gentle and sultry Queensland evening, rugby again seemed to be a game of both innocence and virtue. Alison and I sat at the bottom of an empty grandstand and watched the sun dip down across the banks of pastel-shaded seats and the darker shade of grass which looked so lush that Shane Drahm soon slipped off his boots. We listened to the abandoned yelling and laughing of men who were ten or fifteen years younger than us. It was just an ordinary session of training for the Queensland Reds; but, for me, it unfolded as something more lyrical.

Whether it was the sight of the tiny Drahm skipping across the turf in his bare feet, or the way in which the light faded over Brisbane as Eales climbed high to deflect another drop-kick before it crossed the bar, images from that Thursday evening will linger longer than most of the more dramatic rugby moments I've seen over the past few years. The match-day stadiums and seething games have their place but, now, they have also begun to blur, with a flash from one match tinting and curling into another from a different game. But an otherwise mundane Queensland day has become almost crystalline with memory. I later met and interviewed Drahm, Ben Tune and John Eales and yet, even though each was interesting and accommodating, when I think of Australia now, and even of this book, I remember Ballymore. I can still imagine fifteen shadowy figures running together, shouting again and again, the noise rising and falling as the ball moves from hand to hand in a looping criss-cross of an impossibly green field. Perhaps it has lasted so clearly because, then, I was nearing the end of my own stretch of travel. Also, in comparison to Lomu and the Auckland Blues in a similar setting at Eden Park, the Reds appeared as more ordinary men in Brisbane. They looked and sounded like any young team, almost harking back to a simpler time when rugby practice would always be on a Thursday evening – wherever you played in the world.

Such a romantic view had been shaped by the fact that, even though I was thrilled to see John Eales, Tim Horan, Jason Little, Daniel Herbert and Ben Tune in such close-up, even their names did not quite match those of the best Brisbane Broncos or North Queensland Cowboys. Our friends in Brisbane had all been brought up on League. They were mildly interested in rugby but, plainly, they regarded a comparison between the two codes as ludicrous. Rugby, for them, would never match League. If, in their worst nightmare, they were forced at gun-point to turn away from League, they would look next to Australian Football for their best oval bet. They were sports-mad – and so golf, tennis, cricket, boxing, swimming, canoeing and even British soccer were always on the Brisbane agenda, with rugby only sliding in next on the list.

I would rave about Ben Tune, the fantastic twenty-two-year-old Wallaby wing, and our League pals would nod appreciatively – before pointing out that there were literally dozens of similarly talented backs in League. Gary Teichmann believed Tune was the one Australian with a Cullen and Lomu-like ability to destroy an opposition back line; and the Queensland Red flyer had been hunted diligently by League buyers ever since he'd exploded into Super 12 and Tri-Nations rugby in 1996.

'Funnily enough,' Tune said when he joined me in the stand, 'I started playing League at first. I was born and raised in Queensland – and most kids round here love League most of all. It's a really great game and I played it until I was about fifteen. At the start of high school, I'd also really got into rugby. I managed to keep both going for a while because I played Union on Saturdays for my school and League for a club on Sundays. I loved mixing the two – but, I guess because it was my school's sport, rugby slowly took over.

'There's no doubt that if rugby had not gone professional I would've moved over to League. It's been a huge boost for rugby that guys can now earn a decent living in Union. Before that, so many guys were lost to League. It still happens – but perhaps more because League is so ingrained in the sporting culture of Australia. In the more basic terms of contracts, rugby's starting to compete. After my first deal with Queensland ended at the end of '96 I had a couple of tempting offers from League teams. The best was from the [North Queensland] Cowboys and so, because I've always been taught to keep my options open, I went up to Townsville for a few meetings with them. They were pretty interested in my switching codes and I liked the look of their set-up. But I came back down here to Brisbane and weighed it up and, because I'm doing okay with the rugby, I decided to stick to Union. I'm not saying I would never consider another offer from League but, at least for the time being, I've got no doubts. I love the rugby. And especially the Super 12 . . .'

Tune stroked his jaw, which he had broken three months before in a Super 12 warm-up, and grinned. 'What a tournament, hey! Are you enjoying it, mate?'

I gave my inevitable answer. The Super 12's positive impact on the Wallaby players was equally obvious; but I wondered how much of an impression the tournament had made on Australian sport.

'It's basically been confined to Brisbane, Canberra and Sydney,' Tune admitted, 'but in those cities the impact has been huge. Last Saturday night, when we played Auckland, this place was rocking. It was pretty wild. A capacity crowd – and people were really getting into the rugby. Some of them would have been lured across from League. The Super 12 is narrowing the gap on League. Rugby is now so much more appealing to most Australians because it's become such a spectacle. The Super 12's also done wonders because we're taking on the Kiwis and the South Africans on a weekly basis. That little international flavour really appeals to a lot of Footie and League fans.

'Also, rugby players, since professionalism, have become fitter and stronger and more skilful than ever before. I've got to mark a guy like Jeff Wilson and he's become the complete footballer. He can run, he can step, he can kick, he can tackle. He's the kind of bloke that, if you're not one hundred per cent on top of your game, is going to make you look silly. And he's far from being the only one. The teams are also a little different this year. A side like the Wellington Hurricanes try to keep it pretty loose and very pacy. They win the ball quickly and then spin it wide. We're a much more structured team – but the contrast is really healthy. It's also why, even as the defensive lines have tightened so much in this year's tournament, you're still almost guaranteed six or seven tries every Super 12 match – and, shit, that's just so great. Y'know, mate, I don't want to offend anyone, but when I sat down last month and tried to watch a few Five Nations games I didn't get very far. It wasn't exactly thrilling rugby . . .'

John Eales was even more politely insistent. 'I would back any one of the top Super 12 sides against every single Five Nations team. They might beat a Super 12 side on some one-off occasions but, on a regular basis, we'd usually win. You're never going to test such a theory but I feel that playing week in, week out for three months, considering all the travel and the strength of this competition, the European countries would find it very hard to reach even a mid-table slot. This year, the intensity has risen even more and, most significantly, defences in the Super 12 have been outstanding. Teams are having to reach deep into their most creative moments to create enough magic to get past the wall. This is an exceptional competition.'

There was an almost evangelical fervour amongst the southern hemisphere's best players for the Super 12 – which was, yet again, enough to convince me. But I was more intent on investigating the end of Eales's long limbs as he undid his laces and pulled off his boots. They looked like feet in his red socks. But, with a blackening sky over Brisbane, I would not have been surprised to see a more original set – with perhaps two spring-heels and eight hairy suckers on each foot to help him shoot into the night sky and settle on top of the Ballymore stand. But, as the socks peeled away, I saw that they were merely long and broad feet, with a few little tufts of hair here and there, ending in two neat rows of five toes.

'But John Eales,' I wanted to protest, 'these are just dull and ordinary feet!'

'I hope they don't smell,' Eales murmured as I stared down at them.

I wondered briefly if this was where the 'Nobody' nickname came in – if nobody was perfect, then perhaps the other Reds had uncovered their captain's sniffy flaw.

I breathed in deeply. Just fresh air. 'No, they're pretty good . . .'

'Great!' Eales smiled genially.

'I guess all these stories of the Australian Rugby Union turning you into a spider to sell the game have been getting to me . . .'

Eales folded his socks neatly and laughed. 'Yeah, it's kinda strange . . .'

'Is it a compliment,' I wondered, 'being compared to a spider?'

'I'm not really sure. But it'll be interesting. I think they've been saving the transformation of me into a spider for last . . .'

'Meanwhile Spiderman was out at work again this evening. I saw you practising a few more penalty knock-downs out on the field . . .'

'Aw, we were just mucking around, really . . .'

'Had you attempted it before Auckland? I asked.

'I think I did it in a club game once – but it's not something I'll make a habit of in matches. The overwhelming majority of penalties are just too high to reach anyway.'

Five days had passed since Eales's knock-down of Cashmere's kick – but the pictures kept rolling on television while the stills of his jump and block were studied in intricate detail in the Australian newspapers. AFL coaches were called in to confirm that Eales's innovation had given them the idea of possibly using players to lift defenders to block shots in their own game. The *Sunday Mail* in Brisbane even wondered if 'the ploy could be taken a step further, with Eales being lifted higher by team-mates or even forming a ladder or pyramid by standing on shoulders. If the human pyramid was ruled legal, it would virtually end penalty-kicks at goal. The pyramid could be formed not only under the posts, but also ten metres in front of the kicker.'

One astonishing moment of athleticism had given rugby more free, if mildly absurd, publicity than the entire million-dollar 'Laws of Nature' promotional campaign. Eales had, yet again, proved himself to be Australian rugby's most priceless asset. And the 'good bloke' shtick was not a PR ruse either. Eales did not have much of a clue about what I was doing but, in the midst of training, he'd sent over a message to apologise for the delay. And then, an hour later, just before he had to begin kicking practice, he came over to check that I could put up with another fifteen-minute wait. 'I'm really sorry,' he said, 'that all this is taking so long . . .'

But he had the talent to match the charm. In *The Guardian*, in November 1996, the Australian writer Greg Growden had explained the source of the Eales legend to a British readership. It was a story not dissimilar to Spiderman's exploits against Auckland in the Super 12. 'One day in 1990 this young, lanky kid who struggled to fit into a Brothers' club jumper emerged from nowhere to become an absolute menace of a lock forward during a Brisbane first-grade match,' Growden wrote. 'John Eales was winning all the line-outs, running all over the place as if he were the second full-back, making try-saving tackles, chip-and-chasing, and showing ball skills that would do even an Ella or a

Campese proud. Then came the ultimate. The opposition had kicked from their own goal-line towards Eales, who was standing about forty-five metres away, virtually on the side-line. According to those who saw it, and that number multiplies by the year, this six-foot-seven-inch gangly monster leapt to grab the ball with his outstretched fingers and then, in the next stride, put ball to boot to slot it between the posts for the most breathtaking of drop-goals.'

In South Africa we had revered the legend of 'Okey' Geffen and 'Tiny' Naude – tight-forwards who could also kick goals. But, in the modern and more demanding era of Super 12 and Tri-Nations rugby, Eales's versatility was unmatched. If Zinzan Brooke could also land a long drop-kick, he did not kick penalties and pack down in the middle of a scrum.

'That's the most difficult part,' Eales stressed. 'As a lock it's all very intense and abrasive – whether you're jumping in the line-out or shoving in the scrum. A full-back or five-eight might get involved in the odd ruck but it's not really such high-impact stuff. So when I have to kick a penalty or conversion it's quite hard to switch off that hyped-up physicality and settle into a more composed state of mind. You obviously can't kick well if your heart's beating fast and you're grinding your teeth – you need to settle into a more serene kind of rhythm which, as a lock-forward, is not the easiest thing sometimes . . .'

'You did pretty well against the Blues . . .'

'Yeah, I was lucky enough to land every one. It was one of those nights, I guess. As long as I'm getting time to practise in the week I'm generally okay with the boot. I try to have a session at least three times a week. Sometimes it might be for only twenty minutes – but then there are times when I'll kick for a good hour. But, ideally, if we've got a decent kicker in the side, I'd be far happier for them to do the job. Especially when we're playing teams like the All Blacks and the Springboks. The week before those Tests is always quite fraught. It's not like a Super 12 match for Queensland where we know our line-out drills and combinations backwards. With the Wallabies we come together from basically three Super 12 sides and we have to work hard on gelling together. And then, as Australian captain, there's also quite a lot of media pressure in the build-up to those games. So if I can do without having to kick, it's one less thing to worry about . . .'

Eales had also passed the Super 12 captaincy to David Wilson – such were the demands he already faced. Perhaps most onerous of all, despite the smoothness with which he played the role, was his position as the face and voice of Australian rugby. 'Well,' he agreed, 'this season we're working hard to try to make some inroads into League turf. It's not easy because, as amazing as the Super 12 has been again, it's not available on free public television in Australia. It's on Foxtel which is one of our sports cable stations. It'll be the same with the Tri-Nations. The average person doesn't have Foxtel – which means that some great quality games between Queensland and Auckland and, say, Wellington and Natal are not being seen on live television.'

'But Foxtel are coughing up the money . . .'

'Exactly. That's the problem. We need that money coming in with the new professional game – but, for the sake of long-term rugby, I wish all sports were on public television or, otherwise, they were all on pay TV. But, at the moment, they're paying our bills. And they're allowing us to be competitive with Rugby League salaries. This year, there're twenty League clubs – and so they need a lot of players to fill all those squads. They're inevitably going to try and pick up some of our best rugby players. But now we're in a position to hold them off . . .'

'So no chance of Spiderman popping up in League?'

'Oh no,' Eales shuddered. 'I just haven't got the build for League! And I've never really been that interested in League. It's always been rugby for me. And I think we're in for a few fascinating years in the game. Beyond the next two Super 12s and Tri-Nations, we've got the World Cup coming . . .'

'Do you think you'll have beaten the All Blacks a few times by then?'

'Potentially, we can beat them. I know they've dominated both ourselves and the Springboks but, this year, we could come back at them. It's up to us. They're going to be as professional and as motivated as ever – and we've got to rid ourselves of the confusion of last year . . .'

'Beyond the off-field turmoil, what's been the main difference between you and the All Blacks?'

'It's a matter of consistency of performance. The All Blacks play a calm and composed game and they can sustain real pressure for a period of twenty or even thirty minutes if they need to do that. The Wallabies and the Springboks have played well in short bursts – for five or ten minutes. We haven't been able to sustain it over the course of an entire Test. And the All Blacks can do that – and they've done it Test after Test, year after year. It almost seems effortless to them . . .'

Eales shook his head. All around us, darkness had settled across Ballymore. It again looked black. But there was no need for fear – we were with Spiderman.

Like Batman, he was a man of good thinking. 'But the Super 12 is really helping. We're getting used to playing them so often. You know, beating Auckland last week was a start. And Natal beat Wellington away – so maybe we're closing in a little each week. So, yeah, we're going to have a real crack at them this year. They're not supermen. They're only human. They also have frailties . . .'

A couple of nights later, on a humid Saturday in Brisbane, there were fewer heroics from Spiderman and the Reds. Instead, it was attritional rugby from the old days of rugby realism. Queensland and the Western Stormers ground into each other with grim tenacity, banging heads up-front and smashing into each other at the back. The Stormers managed a couple of tries through Robbie Fleck and the more dazzling Bobby Skinstad, but they also conceded thirteen penalties. Colin Hawke, the New Zealand referee, did not penalise the Reds once – an anomaly which stemmed primarily from the Reds' extreme discipline.

It was tight and jarring rugby and, after he had succeeded with two out of his first three penalties, Eales took a terrible knock to the head. Naturally, he played on, but he called up Shane Drahm to kick the remaining three scores – a conversion and two long-range penalties. Reds 19, Stormers 14. As if in deference to our imminent departure from the southern hemisphere, it had been a game and a scoreline more reminiscent of a scrap at Leicester or Gloucester.

London, for us, was only days away. Ordinary life, and reality beyond the Super 12, was about to return. But, still, there was time for one last rip in Brisbane. As we disappeared into the night, we thought of James Small. We missed him. We had planned to meet in Brisbane. But Small, continuing his disastrous Super 12, had been injured again. While Stefan Terblanche was flying for the Sharks, Small was limping for the Stormers. He'd pulled out of their Australian and New Zealand tour even before the team left Cape Town. Both Ballymore and Brisbane, without him, were not the same.

I knew, too, that Nick Mallett would have turned his hard stare on the space which Small was meant to fill, both in Super 12 and Springbok rugby.

'James will be back,' Alison promised.

But, even then, I worried about him. And I worried, too, about South African rugby. The Sharks had won in Durban that afternoon. They were still on top of the Super 12 – leading Auckland by a point and Queensland and Wellington by four. But, off the field, the doubts escalated. The troubles were rolling again. The Australian Rugby Union awaited urgent assurance that the safety of the Queensland Reds would be guaranteed when they travelled to Johannesburg and Durban to play the Sharks and the Cats in early May.

Even the marketing and television men had begun to brood that the Super 12 would mark the end of South Africa's involvement in world rugby. Nike, the Springbok sponsors, had written to Sarfu to express their concern about the returning notoriety of rugby in South Africa. Russell Macmillan, the chief executive of Supersport, the Johannesburg company which owned all the local broadcast rights to Super 12 and Test rugby, and effectively sustained the country's professional game, was particularly disturbed by the intransigence of Louis Luyt.

'No one person is bigger than the sport,' Macmillan insisted. 'It is clear that the issue is no longer just rugby. The tragedy is that the fight within rugby has degenerated into black against white. The cancellation of any incoming international tour because of a boycott will also mean the cancellation of all existing [television and playing] contracts. Financially, rugby in South Africa will be destroyed – I believe forever.

'Louis Luyt must be honest with himself. He must ask himself if staying on as president is in the interest of the game. The only answer is an emphatic "no". Luyt must go.'

While the Afrikaans newspaper *Rapport* hailed Luyt as the 'only leader who is willing to fight for the rights of the Afrikaner', Mluleki George repeated the NSC's message. 'If Luyt and the Sarfu executive do not meet our ultimatum and quit, they must face the consequence of an international boycott. Luyt must know that his position is non-negotiable. He has to go.'

We needed Spiderman, Batman or any man to knock down big Louis. But Luyt remained immovable.

'No man is my master,' Louis Luyt warned. 'I bow to no man. I bow only to God.'

Chapter 19
Pantomime, Again

Chaos and darkness, everywhere. From Brisbane, the Western Stormers flew to Christchurch. On the day we returned to London, the Stormers' huge prop, Toks van der Linde, sat slumped in his hotel room. Mark Keohane, a South African rugby writer, described the scene in New Zealand's *Rugby News*.

'His hulking 125-kilogram frame,' Keohane wrote of van der Linde, 'had the presence of someone with an eating disorder and all of his 1.96 metres in length appeared sandwiched between two hands that doubled as elbows of support. Van der Linde, head bowed in disgrace, had just been told that he would be going home. It was not unexpected. Earlier, when the management committee had convened for the disciplinary hearing, van der Linde had been forewarned. "Expect the worst . . ."'

For the troubled Toks, it was a familiar scenario. Five months before, on the Springboks' European tour, Nick Mallett had also sent him packing on the next flight back to South Africa. Van der Linde had kicked a French opponent in the head. Then, in pre-season training, Toks and James Small had indulged in their snappy round of sparring. But, as Keohane stressed, in Christchurch, van der Linde had committed a far greater sin, 'a blasphemous act in the new South Africa'.

Approached by a black South African woman in Christchurch, Toks turned truculent. When she asked him to acknowledge that she was also a South African, van der Linde called her a 'kaffir girl'. He did not speak in anger, as Andre Markgraaff had done a year before when Andre Bester provoked his 'kaffirs' rant against the SABC and the NSC. Van der Linde reached more casually for the old language.

'The words, said without thinking, did not shock,' Mark Keohane wrote. 'It's the instinctiveness which shocks. Van der Linde, tutored in the ways of the new South Africa and educated for the past three years on the global stage when touring with South African rugby teams, reverted to what came naturally when challenged. The country boy from Senekal surfaced, admittedly at the most inopportune time of his career. There can be no opportune moment for racism, but van der Linde's three-word outburst, on the eve of the judgement of Sarfu's court battle against the government, is the equivalent of rugby suicide. The press releases were sent in every form: telephonic, e-mail, fax and pigeon post. The national governing body deplores racism. The national governing body will not tolerate it . . . rugby, in its troubled times, is desperate for a scapegoat.'

Sarfu had also uncovered a rare ally in Mr Justice William de Villiers. A judge from the days of apartheid, de Villiers upheld Louis Luyt's allegation that Mandela's appointment of a judicial commission to investigate racism in rugby had been 'illegal'. But if Luyt felt he could celebrate victory, it was not for long. Sarfu had made an appalling mistake in taking Mandela to court. In a country where the majority of people ignored the sport, the image of Mandela being forced to answer circuitous questions for five hours was far more provocative than the loss of the Springbok emblem and the end of international rugby.

Mluleki George's own reputation was not unsullied. Apart from his political career and presidency of the NSC, George also led the Border rugby union – and it appeared as if the sport had begun to erode rather than develop further in the traditionally strong rugby-playing black areas of his own constituency. Yet the sweeping contempt for Luyt meant that George had support across the country. He pledged to escalate the fight against Sarfu – despite the court ruling.

Bill Jardine, the veteran rugby administrator and Gauteng president of the NSC, warned that 'Sarfu must not think they can go against the core of the people and get away with it. Organisation of protest action will start and countries will be contacted and told not to play rugby here, and why.'

The following month, at the end of May, Ireland were due to begin their South African tour – to be followed in June and July by Wales and England. As the first to face the crossfire, the Irish expressed their 'deep concern' about visiting a country of such strife and division.

Rugby, once more, had become a despised metaphor for white intransigence and black anger. It might almost have made me nostalgic for my youth, if I had not felt the need to hang my head in familiar and weary despair.

For Francois Pienaar, the pain was more acute. 'The sport should have grown after our win in the World Cup. It should have gone from strength to strength, but it's heartbreaking that it is at this point now. I can only hope that there is an amicable agreement. If there are boycotts, then who loses? Rugby loses in the end. To me, it would also mean a great deal to lose the Springbok emblem. It would be very disappointing, especially after what we achieved in 1995. Everyone supported the Springbok symbol then. It stood for unity, rather than segregation . . .'

I thought it curious, but also strangely hopeful, that I turned again towards Nelie Smith, a Springbok coach when the green shirt had stood only for segregation. We had once been so far apart. In 1981, when a fractured tour marked the end of Springbok rugby for almost a dozen years, Nelie had been stunned by the ferocity of feeling against him and white South African rugby. I was twenty, then, and already veering away, in disdain, in a different direction.

Seventeen years later, within a few hours of landing in London from Brisbane, I called Nelie. Every Monday morning for the last six weeks, whether in New Zealand or Australia, I had hunted down the previous Saturday's Ballymena score. It was rarely good news. In my absence, and I knew it was a coincidence, Ballymena had suffered in the All-Ireland League. They had never recovered from losing their first match, in Limerick, against Shannon. A reel of successive losses had ruined their early-season success. They were out of the top four and the play-off places to decide the champions of a united Irish league.

The dream was over. And, again in a doleful coincidence, the nightmare had returned. South African rugby, just as a homesick Nelie Smith prepared to leave Ulster for Port Elizabeth, had reverted to type.

But Nelie had more faith. After he had graciously accepted my Ballymena lament, and enthused about my 'really tremendous' Super 12 tour, we turned to the troubles of home.

'But listen,' Nelie said, 'it's going to be okay. I know Louis Luyt very well. He's a hard character. But this time . . . uh-uh . . . he's gone too far. He's on his way out, Don, I'm telling you . . .'

There was chaos and darkness, too, in British rugby. If the problems were less starkly emotive than in South Africa, they were even more tangled. While I'd wafted round New Zealand and Australia, snippets of UK rugby politics filtered down through the astounded press agencies and newspapers.

'They're gone absolutely bloody crazy over there,' more than one Kiwi or Aussie sneered when they heard that I lived in London.

As I surveyed the carnage, especially in England and Wales, I just had to shrug in stunned agreement – as I did with Chris Hewett's summary of English rugby's demented 'civil war' in *The Independent*. 'Start by taking all the available hypocrisy, chicanery, secrecy and misinformation and mix in some power politics, a pinch of paranoia and a dash of playground petulance. Now add a monster helping of self-importance, season with a few outright lies – great big whoppers of the barefaced variety are very much in season – and hey presto, there you have it: English rugby union, 1998-style. Half Watergate, half Alan Partridge.'

While the Super 12 sharpened the best players in the south, the Guilty Two hacked away at British rugby with the blunt instrument of pointless argument. The RFU and the clubs were a real pair of jokers, a right old English comedy duo who could churn out the pie-in-the-face and head-in-a-bucket routine all year long. They were *that* professional. Even if, in British rugby, the pantomime season never ended, the RFU bruisers and the millionaire clubbers were always ready for another slapstick performance. The only difference was that the players and the spectators had given up shouting, 'Look out, he's behind you,' whenever Dame Fran Cotton or the costumed horse hiding Sir John Hall and 'Twinkie' Barwell stalked each other. Instead, exhausted cries of 'Stab him, stab him!' and 'Kill him, kill him!' echoed around the game, in the vain hope that one last bloody jape would bring the fucking curtain down on a tedious farce.

When I'd left England for New Zealand in early-March, Keith Barwell had just forbidden his Northampton internationals from making themselves available for England's summer tour of the southern hemisphere. The chairman instructed his players that they needed rest in June and July to prepare for Northampton's 1998–99 season. Barwell's colleagues in the Premiership prepared to follow his dictatorial lead and win another round for club rugby.

'Everyone is getting completely fed up with England,' Dick McGruther of the Australian Rugby Union moaned, 'and I don't mean just one or two unions. England have to stick by IRB [International Rugby Board] regulations, just like everyone else, and make sure that their best players are available to tour. If they don't, the IRB can sanction punishment against England.'

A week later, Clive Woodward announced that Northampton's Paul Grayson, Matt Dawson and Tim Rodber would be excluded from England's squad for the remaining Five Nations games against Scotland and Ireland. 'If they don't want to play for England they can just go away and play for their clubs and I'll find someone else,' Woodward said. 'I can't be held to ransom. I'd like to think the England players will do what they said they'd do when they signed their international agreements earlier this season. Our objective is to win the World Cup in 1999. I've told the players this is potentially putting a knife through our dreams. I can't possibly run an English team if a third party suddenly decides at his whim that his players aren't available. It's akin to someone ringing up and saying, "I want you to play in pink shirts with blue dots on and if you don't I'm not releasing the players . . ." '

Despite the boyish analogy, Woodward had made his point. Within hours, while Barwell was away on a skiing holiday in the Alps, Northampton's coach, Ian McGeechan, undermined the clubs' parochial strategy by announcing that 'Rodber, Dawson and Grayson are set to tour. My role is to groom more players for international rugby, not fewer. I will not allow our players to be denied the chance to play for their country.'

Assuming that one more battle had been won, Cliff Brittle stressed that 'the total financial success of the RFU depends on one thing – the success of England. People are not interested in the clubs. What people are interested in is the national team.'

Yet again, Brittle sounded as out of touch with the new appeal and hardened competitive edge of English club rugby as the stupid fat guy at the end of a bar in Invercargill who wheezed, 'Our local third team would probably beat any of those Pommy club sides.' I wondered if Brittle had already picked up his pre-booked ticket for that Sunday's 20,000 sell-out of a table-topper between Saracens and Newcastle. It was obvious that English rugby would never be able to rival football's massive club followings, but the strides Saracens had made in the space of one breathless year were startling: 20,000 would be the biggest ever crowd to watch a game of club rugby in England. While King's Park in Durban could pull in 50,000 for the Coastal Sharks, the Saracens' turn-out in Watford at least matched some Super 12 attendances. There were clear signs, too, that the best English clubs could maintain crowds of that size as long as they expanded their own grounds or, more often, shared stadiums with football clubs who were accustomed to catering for such numbers.

English club rugby, whatever Brittle suggested, was on the rise – both in terms of growing popularity off the pitch and in a compelling rivalry on the field. But, as hard as it had become to win the Allied-Dunbar Premiership, it would never be an ambition to rival the headier English dream, however fanciful, of winning the World Cup. And that fantasy would remain unchanged, no matter how long the players' chairmen rambled on about their obligations to fat club contracts. There was no need to ask Dallaglio or Dawson, Johnson or Perry, if they would prefer to beat New Zealand or Newcastle, or if they imagined one day holding the World Cup before the Tetley's Bitter Cup.

Yet both Brittle and the club owners seemed unable to fathom that, as much as they tore at each other, their futures were inextricably entwined. England's potential depended on improved competition at club level – both in Britain and Europe. Brittle and Cotton, in their brave declarations of creating a 'Club England' through regionalised competition, ignored the fact that the heart of the English game, as in France, centred around the clubs themselves. England's international prospects would be diminished rather than enhanced by substituting a bristling club tournament for a more anodyne regional version. The RFU did not need to blindly emulate the Super 12's merging of provincialism with regionalism. Rather, they needed to somehow graft on to their own domestic rugby the unity of purpose and willingness to compromise which distinguished the leading southern-hemisphere teams. The strength, beyond sheer playing talent, of the Auckland Blues and Canterbury Crusaders in New Zealand, and the Sharks of Natal, depended on two interlocking themes. They had built from a foundation of history and passion for their existing provincial identities and then added, in conjunction with their national coach, a more flexible ability to draft in individual players to bolster weaker areas of their team.

I thought it significant that Christian Cullen and John Eales constantly referred to the Coastal Sharks as 'Natal'. They recognised the basic difference which separated the Sharks from the more pitiful Golden Cats. The Sharks, essentially, were Natal; while the Cats were a hopeless amalgam of Free State and Gauteng, a regional mish-mash of a team who managed to lose the best attributes of both their constituent parts. And yet the South African discovery of the Super 12, the Sharks' Stefan Terblanche, was not a Natal player – he was a draft pick from Boland, a small province which would never have the muscle to compete against the likes of Auckland or Queensland.

In their own different ways, Auckland, Canterbury and Natal operated as 'club' outfits – at least in the sense that they were closely knit teams who played with immense conviction. When established English clubs like Bath, Leicester and Gloucester – and their newer contemporaries like Saracens and Newcastle – already had such pride, it seemed nonsensical for the RFU to obliterate that existing vitality. They needed to work with the clubs to create a structure which could one day rival, rather than merely attempt to parody, the Super 12.

Yet, to achieve that seemingly unattainable goal, they needed the clubs, in turn, to show some form of co-operation. In their own rush to imitate football's Premiership, the clubs seemed to have forgotten that the national game also needed a successful international team to stimulate more widespread interest in the sport. It was no coincidence that league attendances in English football always rose sharply in the immediate wake of a World Cup. As parochial as football fans inevitably were, whether they supported Bury or Fulham, the thrill of Michael Owen scoring a goal against Argentina lasted way beyond the summer. It encouraged otherwise sensible men to believe that they might see something similar in a more mundane league encounter. Similarly, in rugby, if England somehow held or even beat the All Blacks or the Springboks, it would inevitably entice a few more souls to the English club game in the ensuing weeks or months.

The RFU and the clubs, as deep as their hatred ran, needed each other. But, from March onwards, you would not have believed it. Soon after the 'Club *v* Country' impasse at Northampton had been diverted, the clubs put forward their blueprint for an expanded Premiership, increasing the First Division from twelve to fourteen teams. Considering their promise to protect their exhausted players from overwork, it seemed bizarre that the club owners should wish to add another four matches to the 1998–99 tally of league fixtures – until you realised that two more home games each would mean just a little bit more lolly. Yet a brace of matches against both London Scottish and West Hartlepool would not produce a more finely honed Martin Johnson or Lawrence Dallaglio in a World Cup year.

Cotton and Brittle rejected the proposal and, instead, presented the clubs with another revised European Cup package. Brittle hailed a considerable breakthrough, claiming that European rugby had been guaranteed by an offer which allowed more English clubs to compete in the competition at a far better rate of financial return. Before Brittle could finish applauding his RFU management team, the clubs had turned away with a flat 'No!' printed on their departing backs. In response, Brittle wrote to each Premiership club, warning that he had the power to withdraw their Tetley's Bitter Cup gate receipts unless they reconsidered his European plan.

Keith Barwell described Brittle as the 'Boris Yeltsin of English rugby' – which was certainly true in the sense that he presided over a desperately crumbling economy. The top clubs had made a combined loss of £13,000,000 in the preceding season. In one typical example, Chris Wright's Loftus Road plc, which owned Wasps, had seen their original stock market valuation of £1 a share in January 1997 plummet to a mere

20p fifteen months later. The game's multi-national backers were looking equally fretful and fidgety.

Paul Charles, in *The Guardian*, explained how the prospect of widespread television coverage had encouraged an early rush of sponsors in the first dizzy year of full-time club rugby. 'The electronics giant, NEC, became one of the first multi-nationals to inject money into the professional era. It agreed a three-year contract, with Harlequins, at the start of the 1996 season. "Many of our products are business-orientated and the rugby crowd is primarily in business," said Taka Furuhashi, NEC's senior UK promotions executive. Now, because of Quins' poor performance on the pitch, the Japanese are getting restless. "If they are losing, you feel as if you are losing too. We will monitor the relationship and re-evaluate if Quins continue to do badly."'

Without NEC, or a suitable equivalent, Harlequins would not be able to make their monthly payments on Zinzan Brooke's two-year £400,000 contract. Yet as great a figure as Zinny remained in world rugby, NEC received scant kudos from their association with him. Without any exposure for club rugby on public television, the majority of Britons in the high street would probably suggest an Australian river if you asked what 'Zinzan Brooke' meant to them. Sky still failed to hit the million-viewer mark for their otherwise astute and live Saturday-afternoon coverage. The figures for their Thursday-night *Rugby Club* were far worse – as mournfully pedestrian as the magazine programme was jet-propelled by shrewd enthusiasm.

'Clubs just assumed that rugby union could become fashionable,' Justin Urquhart-Stewart, a director of Barclays Stockbrokers, told *The Guardian*. 'They thought that a bunch of Jeremys in their Rover Discoveries could suddenly be replaced by the masses from the inner-city. Impossible.'

The clubs had yet to form a revolutionary front with Class War in a desperate attempt to blast open the perception of rugby as a cosy refuge for City toffs and Twickers twits. Instead, Keith Barwell called for an alternative *putsch*, in the form of a complete breakaway of the top twelve clubs from the jurisdiction of the RFU. But, whatever the Dirty Dozen planned, 'Freedom for the Premiership Twelve!' was not a slogan to stir hearts across Britain. Outside of rugby's narrow domain, no one cared about the Great Oval War (1996–Infinity).

Yet, onwards they marched – all the way to Brussels. The clubs presented reams of documents to the European Union, 'citing non-competitive practices and abuse of a dominant position' by the RFU. I felt for the poor Belgian who would have to spend a dreary Thursday afternoon reading through the papers. They could reduce him to madness – to a fit which left him screaming for mercy from a mindless pastime called English rugby politics.

Back in Twickenham, the RFU Council dropped Brittle's scheme to cling on to the Tetley's Cup money. They also selected a four-man RFU panel, excluding Brittle, to meet a quartet from the Premiership clubs for 'urgent negotiations' – which was a neat euphemism for 'pistols at dawn, old fruit!'. Fran Cotton, who wanted to aim a bazooka rather than a measly pistol at the head of English First Division Rugby, resigned in protest at the attempt to isolate Brittle from the duel.

Beyond the Battle of Ego, the RFU and the clubs had to scrap over four primary issues: the contracting of internationals, European competition, the size of the Premiership and negotiating rights with broadcasters and sponsors. The RFU urged that England's best players should be contracted and managed by the union or, as Cotton and Woodward tagged it, 'Club England'. They would play ten internationals a year, at least four against the southern-hemisphere giants, with a maximum of eighteen club matches a season in a streamlined league. The clubs, instead, demanded no more than seven Tests a year, with the Five Nations moved to the spring, and twenty-six league matches and accompanying cup-ties for their international stars. They also wanted to contract the players themselves, with release dates for international commitments to be agreed between the Premiership and the RFU. The clubs, finally, aimed to develop their own European competition and to control all television, radio and sponsorship deals. Rather than more jaw-jaw, they were ready for yet another war.

Vicarage Road, Watford, Sunday, 19 April 1998
They called it the most important match in the history of English club rugby. It deserved a day when the sun shone. But we were in Watford, rather than Sydney or Durban, and the low and rainy sky provided suitably English spring weather. Everything else, however, was tinged with change. Saracens, at home in a football stadium in Watford rather than a large garden shed in Enfield, had become the most glamorous club in England. Pienaar, Lynagh and Sella were the iconic names but Bracken, Constable, Diprose, Grau, Ravenscroft and Wallace had been alongside them all season as Saracens attempted a previously unthinkable league and cup double. Only Newcastle could stop them.

After sixteen matches of their twenty-two-game league programme, Rob Andrew's multi-cultural band of Geordies were closer to the title. With a two-point lead and a game in hand over Saracens, Newcastle knew that victory at Vicarage Road would assure them of their own first championship. Saracens had to win – a compulsive fact which sent the home fans spinning into a pre-match fever as hot as the day was damp. With dancing girls, a mass display of the red Saracens' fez and the 'Mars Suite' from Holst's *The Planets* blasting from the PA as the teams ran out, it was enough to make Cliff Brittle reach for the X-File marked 'New Club, New Danger' in his RFU cabinet.

On a day when the rugby was too fraught with tension, and the ground too slippery for any real fluidity, a more lasting impression resided in the ardent faces of a Watford crowd – a large percentage of whom looked as if they were fresh arrivals in the tired old world of English rugby. In one of his most inspired innovations, Peter Deakin, the Saracens marketing-whizz, had offered a 'cash-back' scheme to 150 local groups, stretching from a Watford hospice to a school PTA. Each organisation sold bundles of Saracens' tickets and, in exchange, were allowed to keep fifty per cent of the money they raised. Saracens, in expanding their 'fan-base' and increasing their profitability, also strove to become a more old-fashioned 'community' club to people who had never set foot in a Twickenham carpark.

Rob Andrew and Michael Lynagh knew their way around all the world's great Test venues – but even their expressions were taut as the significance of an already close match tightened still further. Lynagh, inexplicably, missed three penalties in the first half – and Saracens lost both Pienaar, after thirty minutes, and Bracken, at the interval, through injury.

'Those cynics,' Mick Cleary wrote later in *The Daily Telegraph*, 'who once accused Pienaar of coming here solely for his pension plan, should have seen his face as he trudged despairingly off.'

Pienaar knew that, with only a 6–3 lead at the break, Saracens were slipping away. The tension deepened in the remaining forty minutes. It became brutally nervy, almost neurotic, rugby. Lynagh landed another penalty but, with eleven minutes left, the Premiership season's best forward, the rampaging Samoan Pat Lam, found the space to crash over for the game's only try. Andrew converted. Saracens 9, Newcastle 10.

It was not Super 12 rugby – but it was almost impossible to look away. Saracens, driving and storming like the rain, kept attacking; but the Newcastle line held. Then, in the eightieth minute, and forty metres out, the drop came. Three years before, on a balmy Cape Town afternoon, Andrew had landed the last-gasp drop-goal which inched England past Australia in a World Cup quarter-final and ended Michael Lynagh's international career. But, in a suddenly barmy Watford, Lynagh achieved parity. His own drop soared sweetly and, at the whistle, it was Saracens 12, Newcastle 10.

'It's extraordinary, isn't it? Who comes up with these scripts?' Andrew asked. 'He owed me that one, I suppose . . .'

Saracens and Newcastle each had thirty points at the head of the Premiership. The Watford boys had four matches left, the adopted Geordies five – but three of those were corkers, away to the reigning champions, and relegation-haunted Wasps, and at home to the stern old guard of Leicester and Bath.

'We'll have to win all our games,' Andrew admitted, 'because I can't see Saracens losing . . .'

But, before the sleepless nights began, the Newcastle coach still had time to marvel at his opposing number 10. 'That was a world-class drop-goal from a world-class player. We didn't say much to each other at the end, but there was no reason to say anything. We looked at each other and there was respect in our eyes. It was enough. The margins at the highest levels are so narrow now, you almost can't see them. It's a privilege to be part of it. Today has been a watershed for the club game . . .'

Three days later, Lawrence Dallaglio sat in his Ladbroke Grove flat and grinned at the first sign of summer. As Dallaglio said, 'Suddenly everyone in London looks happy. Isn't it strange, but great, how London changes when the sun shines? People start smiling, they go out for a stroll, they say, "Hi ya, mate!" to everyone . . .'

'They start stripping off,' I continued.

'Absolutely! The sun's out, so they think, "Yeah, let's soak up the rays! Let's get funky!" I love it!'

But, on 22 April, another six and a half weeks of rugby were still scheduled for England's shattered players. While the Test against South Africa on 6 June in Cape Town remained in serious doubt, another five rounds of English league matches and an arduous visit to Australia and New Zealand awaited. Before we limped towards the tour debate, Dallaglio had to face the small matter of a crucial game against Newcastle that night.

'Yeah,' he sighed, 'we need the points as badly as them . . .'

The reasons, of course, were different. Wasps were third from bottom; and if they were three points ahead of the improving London Irish firebrands, they had played one more game. Defeat against Newcastle, and the play-offs loomed – perhaps. I was confused. Could the RFU scale down the First Division? If not, would the current Premiership of twelve clubs be extended to fourteen in 1998–99? If 'yes', would relegation be scrapped for one season? Or would four clubs go up while two slid down? I turned to the Wasps and England captain for clarification.

'Mate!' Dallaglio exclaimed, 'you don't know and I don't know! I don't know whether there'll be ten or twelve or fourteen clubs in the English First Division next season. Who does? And that's yet another reflection of the chaotic state of English rugby at the moment. We're working on the assumption that the bottom two will be in some sort of play-off situation. So we have to start winning games – and fast. Although we've still got much the same team as last year, we've really struggled. The difference between winning and losing in this league is very small. Last season we were organised and committed – but that's not enough this time round. Most of the teams have improved hugely while we've stood still. So it's been a rocky year . . .'

'Has your own play been affected by the struggles both on and off the field?'

'It's not been easy. I've found that, as captain, people want to hear my views on England, on Europe, on the significance of club rugby, on the future of the Five Nations – and they're all loaded questions. As players, we want to see some leadership off the field because these are not really issues which should concern us in the middle of a hard season. I want to concentrate on the rugby. But we're confronted by such massive questions that you can't just push them away. If you care about rugby, you have to care about the way these matters are being handled. At the same time, if you're going to be successful in sport, you need the right environment – and we don't have that at the moment. The chaos and discord permeates throughout the game.

'As for me, personally, I think my own level of play has dropped since we spoke at the beginning of the year. Then, I felt I was playing pretty well. But my form has tailed off. And I know that the primary reason, which comes back to the political sphere, is that I've simply played too much rugby over the last eighteen months. Each player has his optimum number of games – after you pass that mark your game suffers. You pick up knocks, you don't rest them and you never recover. Yet there's always pressure on you to play the next game and then the one after it. As a rugby player it's one of the worst things in the world being better than your opposite number and not being able to show that because you're too knackered. It's so frustrating. For the last few months I haven't been dominating games like I should. I've been getting by – and not much more. You can get away with that to a certain extent here but, in the southern hemisphere, you quickly get found out . . .'

England were in danger of abrupt exposure against Australia, New Zealand and South Africa. Although he had yet to make a public announcement, as the morning wore on it became clear that Dallaglio would not be touring in the summer. He had a badly injured shoulder, which he would attempt to play through for the remaining weeks of the domestic season; but, then, he would have to recuperate.

'As you know,' he said, 'I really love to play against the All Blacks, the Springboks and the Wallabies. That's what drives me most in rugby, to play for England at that peak of world rugby. But this tour was set up by people who had no real concept of the demands of modern rugby. There's an argument that the All Blacks and the Springboks were also tired last November but that they paid us the respect of sending out their best side – therefore we are obligated to do the same. In principle, I agree. England should always select their best players. But this is an exceptional situation. The guys who went out to South Africa with the Lions last summer have just not had any real break from rugby. We have to think long-term – it's not a matter of selfishness but of doing what's best for us. I know it's going to make it very difficult for England in the summer but it would be foolhardy to sacrifice the chance of success in the World Cup for the sake of this tour.

'You see, there is a massive difference at the moment between our levels of fitness, power and regeneration and those you see in the Super 12 and the Tri-Nations. They are way ahead of us – because they know how to prepare and they've got their structure right. In world rugby, at the very highest level, power and fitness are all-important. And they are both built on a pyramid. They grow on the foundation they've been given. If you've got three months to prepare yourself, you've got a big, wide and solid base on which to build. A couple of weeks off is ludicrous. It's not enough to create a decent enough platform. You can never regenerate yourself – either physically or mentally. And that's what we've got to do. It's no secret that the best teams in the world at the moment are in the southern hemisphere – and they are also the only three countries to have won the World Cup. Unless we start getting our act together, we've got no chance. They're going to be streets ahead.

'You only need to look at the Super 12 to see the lessons. Natal did not want to lose their identity but, in the end, they made enormous concessions – and by becoming the Coastal Sharks for the duration of the tournament they've given South African rugby an incredible boost. Now, every single one of their top players is involved in the Super 12. It's the same with Australia and New Zealand. They've got up to 150 players right up at that level. In England the situation is very different. We've got a small number of players who're playing far too much rugby and a vast number who are not playing enough high-level rugby. It's crazy . . .'

Later that night, Lawrence Dallaglio's Wasps surprised Newcastle, beating them at Loftus Road. If Wasps had crawled a little nearer to Premiership safety, Saracens and Newcastle were still locked together in a fascinating clinch at the top with four matches to play. The most thrilling English league campaign in recent memory would be decided on the very last day of the season. And, on 9 May, Dallaglio would have his own crack at picking up a piece of consoling silver, the Cup, if Wasps could beat Saracens at Twickenham. As much as I missed the Super 12, with two hours every Sunday of week-old matches being a wan imitation of the live event, there was enough good rugby in England to sustain me.

Yet it was like watching rugby in the Big Top – for the political clowns howled on. I felt real sympathy for Dallaglio. He was the lion in the middle – and wherever he turned he would have either the RFU's wooden chair or the clubs' cracking whip snapped in his face. Dallaglio was loyal to Wasps but his heart lay in international rugby. The All Blacks, Springboks and Wallabies were all contracted to their national teams for, in those countries, the black, green and gold jerseys counted above all else. And yet they also had the Super 12, for the ultimate benefit of each southern-hemisphere country. As testing as the Allied-Dunbar had become in England, it was not played at the same level. Dallaglio also knew that, whatever happened with the politicians, he would not play against the best French club sides in the 1998–99 season. English rugby was more intent on cutting off its own feet; but, stump-legged or not, Dallaglio and the rest of the England team would try to run on in pursuit of the southern-hemisphere giants.

In public, he had to be careful. He was a prized possession, for both the RFU and the clubs. On the day I left London for Auckland, it was announced that Dallaglio would become world rugby's richest player – a cool million pounds being the reputed size of a five-year contract with the RFU. The rumours swirled and then ebbed away. Dallaglio was still contracted to Wasps – and to England. Over the entire season, both the clubs and the union had made appalling and pig-headed errors. Their leading players, perhaps Dallaglio most of all, were having to endure the consequences.

But we had a memorable morning together and, turning away from rugby chaos at the end, we also had a special London handshake. 'It's really happening,' we assured each other – a league and FA Cup double for my Arsenal and a League Cup and European Cup-Winners' Cup twin-set for his Chelsea.

'London rules,' I said.

'Mate, you know it,' he laughed as we stepped out into the sunshine, 'and nothing for Man United . . .'

If only, for the sake of Lawrence Dallaglio, I thought briefly, English rugby could find a similar reason for hope.

Rob Howley and Welsh rugby, however, faced even more uncertainty. When I travelled to Cardiff, the genial but weary Welsh captain had no idea of his rugby future, either in the immediate or the long-term. 'Well, it's simple,' he explained. 'For Wales, we could be off to South Africa next month, or not. For Cardiff, next season we could be playing in the Welsh First Division or the Allied-Dunbar in England – or neither. At least I know I'm getting married on 1 August – otherwise, all is confusion . . .'

The South African tour, Howley had heard that afternoon, was likely to be cancelled. 'To be honest,' he nodded, 'it would be a little bit of a relief. I would love to go back one day – especially after I had such heart-ache in South Africa last year, having to return home early from the Lions tour. I'll never forget the tears I shed, or the touching moment when this South African fan came over to me at the airport, on the day I was flying back to Wales. He said, "Rob, you're a fantastic player and we'll really miss your great duel with Joost [van der Westhuizen] . . ." To hear that from a South African rugby supporter meant an awful lot to me. He gave me his scarf and I've kept it to this day. I would love to play in South Africa once more, especially against the Springboks, but perhaps not on this tour. I know how hard it is to play even minor provinces like Border; and we would be going out without Scott Gibbs, Allan Bateman, Neil Jenkins, David Young – and the rest. If it still happens, it will be a very long three weeks for Welsh rugby. Against the Springboks, to be honest, I fear the outcome . . .'

Rob Howley also feared for the fate of Welsh rugby. 'It's very grave,' he admitted. 'Cardiff and the Welsh union are due to go to court in June over our refusal to sign this loyalty agreement. The union originally wanted Cardiff to commit themselves to the Welsh League for the next ten years. They've now reduced that to seven years – but when we don't know where we'll be in British rugby in seven days, let alone seven years, how can Cardiff sign any document about the future? We're determined not to be excluded from the possibility of playing the best English and French teams. The lawyers, meanwhile, feel certain that they will need at least two weeks in court to reach a judgement – which means that the case will be pushed back from June until November. By then, the new season will be a couple of months old. So, at Cardiff, we're having to explore new avenues – like getting out of Welsh rugby completely and playing in England.'

Peter Thomas, Howley's chairman, was in the midst of talks with Newcastle's Sir John Hall about the possibility of Cardiff joining the Premiership. 'The Welsh Rugby Union,' Cardiff's chief executive Gareth Davies stressed, 'have not adapted well to professionalism. Things are moving forward in England in terms of the popularity of the game – and we think we might fly the flag for Wales in the Allied-Dunbar Premiership, in a more professional setting . . .'

The English Rugby Partnership's Doug Ash responded with the assertion that 'we welcome the idea of Cardiff playing in the Premiership. They have a significant amount to offer in terms of playing standards, support and commercialism . . .'

'It's a very drastic step,' Howley said, 'but, for the sake of better rugby, we might yet have to take it. But, who really knows? It's all up in the air. As players, we'll probably be the last to know . . .'

He smiled sadly. There was no need for either of us to say it – chaos, again.

'But Rob,' I suggested hopefully, 'it can only get better, surely . . .?'

'Well,' the little scrum-half said, 'we live in hope . . . but I'm not holding my breath on this one . . .'

Howley was one of the contemporary greats of world rugby – and yet his career was in limbo. I looked for a brighter ending.

'At least you've got the wedding to look forward to, Rob . . .' I said.

'Yeah,' he laughed, 'and there're no rugby committee-men involved on that day – what a relief . . .'

Chapter 20
Beyond Toulouse

The longer I travelled, the stranger the journey. And, with each passing month, the word 'home' seemed as elusive as it was beguiling. I began to say 'home' more and more, as if even its sound might unravel the knot. From Brisbane, I had flown home to London; and from London I would soon return home to Johannesburg. It had yet to merge into a perfect crack down the middle – for I had lived only a third of my life in England. My heart, more than a mathematical mastery of the fraction, told me that I would always be South African. It was a sentimental form of nationalism – but I liked it.

When I went back to South Africa, however, I often became 'that guy from England'. I also remember being quietly disconcerted when a white South African cameraman wondered if I was from New Zealand. 'I couldn't quite place you, man,' he said, 'I could just tell you were foreign.' And, of course, after fourteen years away, I was a foreigner in my own country. In Britain, meanwhile, in my adopted home, in the home of my grandfathers, my accent remained sufficiently strong for people to know that I came from elsewhere. Sometimes they picked South Africa in one; but, occasionally, it was Australia or Holland or, more oddly, Canada.

Curiously, in our own home, in our South London flat, it gave us a laugh, a right old Cockney 'larf', or, as I said when laughing in authentic Afrikaans, '*'n lag*'. Over the years, Alison's otherwise impeccable Home Counties pronunciation had been flattened and trodden a little by the South African voice rambling away in her ear. Now, whenever she meets anyone new in London, whether they're English or Iranian, they ask her a familiar question: 'So, where do you come from?'

They might have asked the same of me, if they could've heard us behind closed doors when Arsenal were on the box – and I shouted naturally at Tony Adams, 'G'arn, do 'im, Tone!' or asked, in a polite yelp, 'Bloody 'ell, look at fuckin' Parlour, ain't 'e on fire?'

Sometimes, it felt liberating to teach Alison a language as universally practical as Afrikaans; and sometimes it felt just as good to say, ironically of course, 'Wot'cher!' or 'Awright!' to our Cockney pals in the pub.

Similarly, it was great to drift between the two hemispheres, the south and the north, and to be part of both, if not belonging wholly to either. Rugby, as ever with issues of nationalism, provided an illuminating insight into the dustiest old foibles and the most sweeping generalisations.

England was the helpless constant. Everybody in rugby, it seemed, hated England. In France, Ireland, Scotland and Wales, the aversion had its roots in both ancient wounds and more recent political and cultural scrapes. The arguments were unswerving, and so England would always be the enemy in northern-hemisphere rugby. I was more surprised to rediscover how much England featured as a source of venom in rugby below the equator. It was not even the fact that they were about to send a third-string side to Australia, New Zealand and South Africa – the ridicule ran much deeper.

'Bloody Pommies,' a man growled at a television screen in Dunedin while we watched England beat Scotland in the Five Nations, 'they're so hopeless at rugby. They're bloody awful. We've got the All Blacks and they've got nothing. I really hate the Pommies!'

'Why?' I asked, suddenly bored with the usual decayed rant.

'It's the arrogance, mate. That's what gets me. They're not like us. They're bloody arrogant bastards!'

Slightly more sophisticated versions of the same polemic were trundled out during a few Australian, South African and New Zealand press conferences – and still the gist remained. 'The English are nowhere near as superbly talented or brilliantly organised as our boys – but, jeez, aren't they pompous . . .'

With a foot in both camps, an English South African *sout-piel* to the very end, I just laughed. For all the dismissive words, the southern rugby masters seemed to protest very long and very hard against the 'non-entities' they were always just about ready to ignore. They were the three rugby kings, as everyone in the northern hemisphere readily acknowledged, but they were perpetually eager to confirm that England were 'nowhere, just nowhere'.

If a fourth country had to be squeezed into rugby's oval frame of command, France would be the pick – every time. Should the Tri-Nations ever become a more balanced square of an international tournament, the mysterious French would be summoned as soon as the ritual finger had been flashed at England. It sometimes seemed as if my more cocky friends from the south took too much perverse pleasure in the contracting of world rugby. If British administrators had turned their own game into a farce, the international arena also lost a little more variety from its narrowing upper deck. But at least the French were still praised across the southern bow of the world.

'Who could win the 1999 World Cup?' I asked a couple of dozen times in Australia, New Zealand and South Africa.

The answer was unchanging. Each of the Tri-Nation countries would have a real chance.

'Anyone else?' I would persist.

'France,' was the echo. 'France . . . France . . . France . . .'

And, more often than not, the name would be uttered with the slightest of sighs. France, still, meant romance in rugby – and danger.

'Fantasy and rigour,' I thought with a typically Gallic shrug, feeling suddenly nostalgic for France, and for French rugby. There was time for one last visit.

Castres, Friday, 24 April 1998

Once I was on the train, I was fine. It was getting to the station first, buying my ticket and finding the correct platform and the right carriage which sent me into a mild spin of anxiety. If I'd been a Springbok rugby player, I would have had the multilingual Nick Mallett to look after me. But, instead, I was on my own in Toulouse, trying to remember my last sweaty coo through the most basic pidgin-pie French. I cursed those smug occasions in South Africa and New Zealand when I'd dared think of myself as cosmopolitan. Two different rugby reporters, in Johannesburg and Palmerston North, asked if I had heard of a French newspaper called 'La Quip'.

'Ah, you must mean *L'Equipe*,' I'd responded in my superior French, trying not to spoil the effect by giggling at the memory. A few years before, I had also murmured the doubtful quip.

I carried a copy of *La Quip* under my arm in Toulouse, but it didn't help. No rugby fan came to my rescue. The Toulouse railway set obviously mistook me for a sporty local on his way into the countryside to pick apples on a Friday afternoon with his rural *cherie*. Instead of *L'Equipe*, which I only bought so that I could look at the rugby photos and study the league tables, I should have flourished my Camus paperback. It would have matched the French championship's existential introspection and, possibly, prompted conversation with a helpful *mademoiselle*.

'Mmm,' she would note, clearly impressed, 'Camus?'

'*Oui*,' I would nod seriously.

I would show her the cover so that she could read the title. '*The Outsider*,' she would slowly say, her halting English made all the more charming by her French accent.

'*L'Etranger*,' I would confirm, already translating her English back into the original French.

And then, at last, she would understand. I was the outsider. I was lost and alienated – and in need of, at the very least, linguistic help.

'Let me buy your ticket, Albert,' she would say, the 't' falling away into a soft hush of nothingness, as it had done for the real Camus.

But, shit, I'd left bloody Camus at home. He had been more a football than a rugby man, after all.

Like *L'Etranger*, I was a man alone. I walked up to the ticket booth. I drew in enough of a deep breath to bark out the words 'Castres' and '*billet*', while remembering, like Albert, to lose the 't' but, confusingly, to throttle the 'l's as well. Then, I held up a finger to indicate one ticket and used my other hand to swing back and forth like a pendulum.

'Toulouse . . . Castres . . . Toulouse . . .' I said as the ticket-man watched patiently.

'Are you English?' he eventually asked, in perfect English.

I didn't even give my usual, 'South African, actually,' distinction. Instead, I just gulped thankfully.

'A return ticket to Castres, yes?' he asked. 'Platform twelve. The next train is in ten minutes . . .'

It was a doddle getting round France. I was so relaxed and happy that I sat back for an hour and watched the French landscape rush past in a pretty blur. Friday afternoon, on a train, steaming out of Toulouse, on my way to meet Thomas Castaignède – and, still, there were those fuckers who bought *The Face* and thought 'rugby' was the most unfashionable word in the English language. If only they knew that 'rugby' was also a darkly seductive French word, if only they had heard of Castaignède and *Les Bleus*.

I made it to the Castres ground bang on time, at three o'clock. It was exactly forty-eight hours before Castres's most significant match of the year, the first leg of a play-off against Perpignan. After a seemingly endless season, Castres had qualified as one of French rugby's top eight clubs. If they could beat Perpignan, at home on Sunday, and even lose by a smaller margin away the following Saturday, they would be through to the last four – a round from the decisive clash which would decide the 1997–98 *Championnat de France*. The final would be held in Paris, at the

Stade de France. Glory, for Castres and Castaignède, glinted in the gentle sunlight.

Forty old men stood around the perimeter of the ground, waiting for the last training session to begin. I couldn't understand a word they said, but they were lost in intricate discussion of Sunday's match. The names 'Perpignan' and 'Castaignède' jinked past too often for me to be mistaken. Clouds of smoke hung over each group, suggesting that, if a London ad agency were searching for a location for a new Gauloises commercial, they should puff no further than Castres before a major game of rugby.

There was a smattering of applause and a few supportive grunts when twenty-four players ran out. Castaignède was the last to emerge from the tunnel, because he preferred to walk. While the others began to stretch and yawn, he turned towards me.

'Don, 'allo, 'ow are you?' Castaignède grinned. 'I have to do this first . . .' He gestured towards the field as if he could not believe it. When had Pablo been forced to practise his art? Picasso did not need to train – he just painted and sculpted, as Castaignède did with a rugby ball.

'Professional rugby,' he shrugged, as if in explanation of his decision to humour the town of Castres, and practise for a couple of hours on an otherwise sultry Friday afternoon. 'See you later,' he said, trying to sound as stoic as he was witty.

The sombre Castres pack had jogged and shuffled to the far end of the ground. I wandered over to watch them in stark close-up. They brooded and mumbled, as if preparing to smash heads together in a friendly warm-up. The meaty hooker began to talk more loudly, while the others gathered round him in a butchers' circle. The two locks, standing closest to the sun, shielded their eyes against the glare. The chatty number 2 pointed upwards and I imagined him quoting Sartre on Camus – 'I would call his pessimism "solar" if you remember how much black there is in the sun' – as he continued his Friday-afternoon seminar. But, more likely, he was promising, in a Castres version of my Arsenal Cockney, 'Sunday, I'm tellin' ya, we're gonna do 'em, we're gonna fuckin' do 'em . . .'

Castaignède, naturally, was removed from such base motivational chatter. He was also more elegantly dressed than the rest. The others wore a motley collection of coloured and hooped rugby jerseys and shorts that were an unseemly mix of white, black and even brown. There was little thought for continuity or grace. They were just at training. Castaignède, instead, looked ready for a rugby recital. He was in the deepest blue – socks, shorts and sweater, with a distinguishing loop of red around the collar. His blond hair bobbed casually, the darker show of roots providing the kind of insouciant blend Robbie Williams would kill for on *Top of the Pops*.

The back line began to spin the ball. After a few minutes of faultless whirring, the scrum-half threw a terrible pass which Castaignède leapt high to catch. Before his feet even touched the ground again he had rectified the kink in the line and fed a smooth pearl to his inside-centre. The ball was already moving on to the next pair of hands by the time Castaignède hit earth again at a cool trot. Once, the unthinkable happened. Castaignède dropped the ball. He was in a good mood so he did not glare at his number 9. Rather, he looked down at his hands in disbelief. He shrugged and licked his fingers lightly, as if even he could bum out once and allow the ball to slip as if it were a tub of greasy KFC. The next pass came and, without even a burp, Castaignède caught it crisply and sent it fizzing away. A minute later, he slid out a delightful little reverse pop-up of a pass which made his team-mates laugh in appreciation.

Castaignède was happy. The forwards joined him and Castaignède and a big prop bounced off each other's stomachs as if they were both Michelin Men. The fun turned serious and they went through their tackling routines and defensive drills. But, eventually, Castaignède ambled away. He needed to be on his own, to prepare himself for the lonely discipline of kicking.

He took a ball with him. The noise of his team-mates hollered on but, like *L'Etranger*, Castaignède stood a little apart. He looked up at the poles and then, with a small series of steps, he moved in and kicked. Perfection. The ball not only sailed straight and true between the posts but it clattered into the advertising board behind the goal and bounced back – eventually rolling all the way to Castaignède's feet. He hadn't moved. But, then, as casually as if he were picking up his boomerang, he bent down and scooped it up. I applauded quietly, for no one else seemed to have noticed.

He moved the ball closer to the right touchline, so that the angle would make his task more difficult. Again, he studied the high H in front of him. He minced round the corner and kicked. The ball soared and then dropped, smacking against the crossbar. Castaignède shook his head slightly. It had rebounded, but he needed to walk fifteen metres to reach its final resting place. One of the assistant coaches saw the Castres star saunter past and, as Castaignède lined up his next shot, he raced behind the try-line. It was a little easier for Castaignède then – he could just land his penalties and the man behind would catch the ball and boot it back.

Still, it was work. A light sheen covered the French fly-half when, as the shadows spread across the length of the ground, he decided he had done enough for the day. 'It will be nicer to sit down and talk,' he joked as we left the field together and walked up the short flight of stairs to the club-house.

Like John Eales, he took off his boots; but he kept his blue socks on. It reminded me of a spell earlier that afternoon when, in the middle of the back-line manoeuvres, Castaignède had decided to change his boots. For ten minutes or more, while he waited for a new pair to arrive from the dressing-room, he had run around in his socks, looking even quicker on his feet.

'Yes, today,' he explained, before taking a long gulp of Coke, 'I decided I should work very hard with my team. We have a big match on Sunday. A hard match. So we must train – even when I have no shoes . . .'

'Can you beat Perpignan? I wondered.

'They are physical, they are very strong. They have also done better than us this year. But we have made it to the last eight. And now we can beat them. I think we can go on in this tournament. Y'know, my dream is to play against my old team, Toulouse, in the final, in Paris. That would be a thing of magic for me. I still live in Toulouse. It's my home but I come to Castres because they promise me I will play stand-off all season – and, of course, they pay me . . . how should I say? I think they give me very professional terms. So, for now, Castres are my team. But Toulouse is my home. When I played for Toulouse I always gave two hundred per cent. I played with my heart . . .'

'But not in Castres?'

'No, of course, it's the same. I try very hard. And I think the people here, they like me now. They know I will do some crazy things. Sometimes it's working, sometimes it's not. Last Sunday, I played a crazy move. I run with the ball and I do this . . .'

Castaignède's eyes were wide as he made the same gesture. He tilted his head to the right, staring wildly, while he flung his hands over his left shoulder as if passing the ball backwards. He laughed loudly.

'I do this without even looking but I know that someone is behind me. The defence, they are so confused. Because I look to the right they ran to the right. But the ball – it has gone to the left. It lands in the hands of the man behind me and he has no one to stop him. He scores the try! Superb! But I know that maybe I do this trick a hundred times and it will not work. But, when it does, people love it. You should hear the crowd last week – "*Ooooooooooo!*" I take life like this. I want to try – why not? Nothing is impossible in life . . .'

'But your coach at Castres will only be interested in beating Perpignan on Sunday.'

'Of course,' Thomas conceded. 'This is true. But, you see, I know I am professional. We have to win. I want to win – but I still like to be crazy. Me? I enjoy life. I like adventure. I like playing with the danger. When we have an aim I do everything to obtain it. But once we have it then I just let go – I run crazy. On Sunday I will maybe only try this pass again when we have a big lead. I won't try it when the score is 0–0. You see, I listen to the coaches. I know when to be strict. But, still, we must play for fun too. We must play for a joke, when we have the time . . .'

'I've always thought,' I said, 'how well you would have fitted in with Franck Mesnel and the "Show-Bizz" boys at Racing in Paris . . .'

'Of course!' Castaignède exclaimed with pleasure. 'It is very funny you say this – they were my example! When I was a boy I have them as heroes. They play in a new way, with a new spirit. They wear the pink bow-tie and at half-time they will drink the champagne. We love it – even in Toulouse, where rugby is serious, the people love it. It's very French . . .'

'But I bet you're glad you're too young to have played under Jacques Fouroux,' I said. 'I couldn't imagine you banging your head against the wall before a game . . .'

'No, not me,' Castaignède said in shock. 'We don't have that anymore. I'm glad because, you know, me, I hate that. If I see anyone hit his head against someone, I shout, "No! Stop! Let us not fight, boys . . ." But, really, it does not happen now at the top. We are from a new generation. Many of our players are coming from university. Maybe we have a new and young way of thinking. But, still we are very proud to play for France. Me? I will do anything on the field.'

Castaignède stood up suddenly, as if I had not seen him before. 'Look at me,' he instructed with a grin. 'I am very small. But I am afraid of nothing. Jonah Lomu can pick me up and he can throw me ten metres. I don't care. I get up and – pow – I tackle him next time . . .'

Castaignède sat down again, having just dropped Lomu in his dream. But I remembered how he had tackled relentlessly in Paris, against England.

'I love that match,' he enthused. 'I love that pressure. Everybody was waiting for me to fail. But we won. You see, how a number 10 plays, it depends on his team. But, with France, now I have good players around me like Glas, Carbonneau, Califano. Someone like Carbonneau – he is a very different man to me. I am studying at university and this year I qualify as a civil engineer. But Carbonneau, because he comes from another life, it is good. Maybe he finds in me, like I do in him, something I don't have – that's rugby. Very tall people, very small people, clever people, tough people. We have them all in our French team . . .'

The Welsh and the Scots might have been mildly comforted by the discovery that they had conceded fifty points each, just because the French team was a neat mix of 'very tall and very small people'. It felt as if something more radical was stirring in French rugby.

'I think so too,' Castaignède said. 'This team – it is maybe special. We have flair and we have the discipline. We have it more than other French teams before us, I think. Against Wales, we were on a cloud for that whole game. 51–0! The poor Welsh. Everything they were doing was returning badly. In this game we were really on the top. I think we were, you know, sublime.'

'Do you ever imagine a different Five Nations?'

'Yes,' Castaignède admitted. 'New Zealand, South Africa, Australia, France, England – for us that would be good. Me? I would really love it. If we want to progress then we must play the southern hemisphere. But, at the same time, we must not forget nations like Wales, Scotland, Ireland. They have given so much to rugby. I don't think we must just push them away and say, "No, go away!" They must keep up with us. But I don't know how we do it. Rugby is changing very fast.'

'Do you ever think it's changing too quickly?'

'No, I love it. I love the Super 12! It's fantastic! So quick! With all the skill! I love Carlos Spencer! He plays so well with Auckland. I think I take him as my best example. Whew – he's so exciting . . .'

'Would you consider leaving France for one of the southern-hemisphere countries?'

'I am going to do it! After the World Cup I will not play in France. I will not play in England. The club rugby here it's not so good. It's tough but it's also boring. Next season it is worse. There will be too many teams. I don't know why! We have too much politics in France and England. I don't like that. I like the Super 12 much more. I would love to play in New Zealand in the Super 12 – but I know it would be very hard because they only like to have New Zealand players. But they have very good teams and the way they play would suit my game. If they want me, I will play for nothing in New Zealand.

'In France, the All Blacks are our heroes – and then the Springboks.

So I get very excited when I think about the World Cup. To play those teams again will be a dream. That is even more important than the Super 12 for me – to maybe win the World Cup. I think, now, we are maybe twenty points behind the All Blacks and the Springboks. But, in one game, if we are lucky, maybe we can beat them. I am going to train very hard next year. I want to add three to five kilos in muscle. I will even push the weights to get this. And I want to play even faster. We have to do this. We will face someone like Christian Cullen – and I love him! With a full-back like him, the All Blacks will never be afraid. He's so natural, he's so strong. And maybe they play Carlos Spencer at number 10 against us. Woah! That would be my best dream – to play the All Blacks in the World Cup, to play Spencer and Cullen!'

Thomas Castaignède grinned helplessly. He held his arms up in front of him and shook them, as if he were already holding the Cup in Cardiff.

'To beat the All Blacks, next year,' he sighed, 'to beat the Springboks, to win the World Cup for France! That's why I was working so hard on the field this afternoon. You know, two times, I scored the winning points in the World Cup final today – here, in Castres, in my head . . .'

Agen, Saturday, 25 April 1998
The brutality of contemporary rugby had already begun to curtail some great careers. In France, the older men were being forced out. The bright *Tricolores* of the 1998 Five Nations had cast darkness over numerous Test lives. If the All Blacks were trying to keep their most venerable bodies together for one last crack at the World Cup, the French had already decided. Out with the old, and in with the new.

If Thomas Castaignède was nearing the peak of his talent, Abdelatif Benazzi was halfway down the long and dusky hill. But, still, he had not given up. A year before, he had been the captain of France. He still had the strength, he felt, to drag himself back up for one last tilt.

'This has been a hard season for me,' he said. 'First, we lose so bad to South Africa. Then I get injured. My knee. I am out of the Five Nations. It is a struggle, but I come back. The rugby is very hard, very physical. We have played too much rugby for too many years. And the French championship is very long. We play for eleven months a year. I think it is too much. Next season, there will be trouble with the French clubs. Aaach! Sometimes, you know, I feel old. But, no, I am not really old.'

'How old are you?' I asked the huge loose-forward, looking up at him in Agen. I was more used to seeing him and his huge white headband in the distance, or on television, when his face grimaced with determination as he began another drive.

'I am twenty-nine,' he smiled. 'It's not so bad.'

Benazzi had a seriousness about him which made Castaignède seem almost childlike in comparison. It was one of the reasons why I had wanted to see the two of them so close together. They personified different facets of French rugby. If Castaignède was the chattering superstar in the back line, Benazzi was the reflective rock in the pack. Castaignède was a peroxide charmer, Benazzi the Islamic thinker. Castaignède looked as if he had cruised through French life, Benazzi as if he had suffered.

For much of the '90s, Abdelatif Benazzi had been one of world rugby's finest forwards – as well as a more symbolic presence in French culture. As a Moroccan, he had overcome some of the worst racism in French rugby to eventually lead his adopted country. As an Arab, from North Africa, especially in France, with the rise of Le Pen and the right, he had done wonders. He was more than just an ordinary rugby player – and, in the midst of yet more South African tumult, he seemed a serene and inspirational figure.

'I know the situation in South Africa,' he said. 'I have been there and, although I like many South African people and I like the rugby, I have also seen some bad things in Pretoria and Johannesburg. But, in France, there are problems too. For me, now, because of the rugby I am okay. But for other Arab and black people in France, sometimes they have to face a very hard mentality. It is only a minority in France who are like this – because most of the French people are very tolerant. But, when the few are bad, they can be very cruel.

'I still remember coming here to Agen. It was hard. I come from Oudji in Morocco and it was there that I learned to play rugby. We play with some Frenchmen in Oudji and it is fine. It is very good. But, when you come to France, and you are an Arab – well, it is not so good.'

Benazzi was a very big man, but his voice had dropped even further. It made a low, but strangely gentle, sound as he continued, without excess emotion.

'Maybe my French, then, was not so strong. I struggle with the language. But it is not only my accent some people hate. It is the way my hair rests on my head. And, always, it is the colour of my skin. If it is not black, it is not quite white. So, they don't see me as a man. They see me only as this word – "Arab!" And, to some French people, "Arab" is a bad word. Even in rugby, I found that there were men who did not want integration with me. I hear the words on the field – "Arab, we will hurt you!" and "Arab, fuck off to your Arabic country!" I don't understand the attitude. I think, maybe, they are jealous.

'There were two internationals in Agen who were against me. The selectors see how hard I train and they promise me a chance. But my problems with these two French internationals are very bad. My priority was sport, to be part of a great rugby team like Agen, a team which has many international stars. My friends, Benetton and Sella, are from this team in Agen. It is very good. But then there are these other men – and their priority is to keep out an Arab like me. I had to wait six months in Agen before they chose me. But, in the end, the other players and the selectors, they are for me – against these two. It was very special. Before then, I would sometimes go home at night and I would cry. It was very painful. But, then, I have this team behind me – and the solidarity is very special. It is lifting my spirit. I am happy in Agen from then.'

'And when you played against other teams?' I asked.

'My own team were good, but my adversaries were bad. So I have another problem. We might play Narbonne or Toulouse and they say things against me – maybe for psychological reasons, you know, to upset my rugby. They say, "Benazzi, fuck off!" and "Dirty Arab – fuck off!" But I listened to these anti-Arabic words and they are a big motivation. I will say a strange thing now, but it is true. Racism inspired me to be a bigger player.'

'And then,' I said, 'came all the international honours with France.'

'I had to choose between Morocco and France. I am a Moroccan man – but, for rugby, I had to choose France. I had twelve caps for Morocco – but France was the big rugby challenge. There was a lot of pressure when I came in. Jacques Fouroux was near the end when I came into the side.'

'I've heard so much about Fouroux – for a little man he caused a huge stir.'

'Exactly! He has a big personality. For him every game is a war. When he picked me, he say, "Abdelatif, I need you to go to war for me!" And I did.'

'And did you like Fouroux's tactics – the way he motivated you as forwards?'

'Yes,' Benazzi said with an easy grin, 'it was very like a warrior! He liked a physical game. Smash! Smash! Smash! It was a very nice experience for me – I liked it . . .'

'But French rugby,' I said, 'has changed.'

'Yes, you are right. But I have played in many French teams. I will try to find my way back into this team too. I do not want to end here. It is too soon.'

Abdelatif Benazzi had played sixty-one times for France – and yet, far more than that, he had changed perceptions amongst French people, whether they were rugby stars in Toulouse or farmers on the fringes of Agen. We spoke for another hour; and if his simple English was not always as solid as his play in the back row, he spoke with startling lucidity, about Morocco and South Africa, as well as his ambition to return to the heart of French rugby.

Then, as the sun began to sink, he drove me through Agen, to show me the beautiful town which had once caused him such pain. And, later, when we reached the station, he turned towards me. With even more passion than before, he took off his sunglasses, wiped the sweat from his eyes, and said, 'I hope you will see me again . . .'

'I hope so too,' I said, perhaps misunderstanding him.

'I hope you will see me again in the blue shirt,' he said more clearly, 'that French shirt . . .'

Milton Keynes-Northampton, Tuesday, 12 May 1998
Within a few more weeks, the French season was over for both Castaignède and Benazzi. On an emotional Sunday in Castres, Castaignède and the home-town boys had beaten Perpignan. Once more, for me, it had been a thrill to be swept away by the noisy fervour of French club rugby. With Brive already out of the championship it was '*Allez Castres!*' all the way. But, in the end, it was only a narrow victory – and, at the far end of the cramped stadium, the Catalan support for Perpignan was almost as riotous as the local crowd. I feared for Castaignède and Castres in the return – and they were duly hammered the following Saturday. They were out – and, soon, the French Cup had also drifted away. But, still, there was the diversion of a quick summer tour to Fiji and Argentina – where Castaignède again played for a winning *Tricolores* team, while Benazzi prepared in Oudji for his dreamy return in 1999.

During my train travels between Toulouse, Castres and Agen, I kept seeing Gregor Townsend's name – either in my own copy of 'La Quip' or in the local newspapers of the passengers sitting opposite me. Townsend, it seemed, was set for either Bourgoin or Brive. We had already arranged one last interview, in May, starting in the appropriately Gallic setting of Milton Keynes railway station.

'It's Brive,' Gregor said, soon after he had met me off the train. 'I have to make a final decision this week. But it looks like I'm on my way to Brive.'

Townsend broke off with a chuckle – he could tell I was impressed. 'Ah, shit,' he said, 'it's been my hardest season ever. It's been so long. On Monday, I'm leaving for Australia with Scotland and I'm having to steel myself a little. Normally, I would be jumping for joy at the prospect of going back to Australia. I love the country but, now, it's a case of me thinking, "Will my body make it through to the end?" A couple of weeks ago, Northampton were playing London Irish and, in the middle of the game, I found myself thinking, "Only five and a half matches to go!" – and that's jus' no' me!

'But, after the Lions, the English Premiership has been very competitive. I think we've had one easy game all year. Otherwise, it's been really tough. When you're playing the likes of Newcastle and Saracens, the defences are very fierce – and I've played every game. They did a table on Sky last week about the most games played in British rugby in the last year. I was in the top three. Lawrence [Dallaglio] was on forty-three, Paul Wallace was on forty-one and I clocked in at forty. I guess I'm my own worst enemy. I just love playing.'

But, with both Cardiff and Bath attempting to lure Townsend away from Northampton, the home fans had not been as enthusiastic.

'Yeah, I've had a wee bit of barracking 'cos people know I'm probably on my way. But, still, it's not been an easy choice. I didn't go to Cardiff and I didn't go to Bath – and, as the season's worn on, the fans have been a bit more supportive. I think they know that I'm not just a typical rugby player. I want to sample other cultures and other styles of rugby. I also knew my Northampton contract was about to end. So I told Ian McGeechan, "If a Super 12 side or a French team come in for me, maybe it's time for me to make the break."'

I remembered, in Durban, with the Lions, how Gregor had stressed his desire to turn to France.

'Yeah,' he said, 'the chance to experience the French culture, and French rugby, has always been the lure. I'm getting married in a month and a bit. It's a chance for me and Claire to live in France for a while.'

'It sounds great, Gregor!' I enthused.

'Yeah, that's what I think. I was tempted by Cardiff last year, and I would love to team up with Rob Howley again, but the weakness of Welsh club rugby put me off.'

'Well,' I said, comfortingly, 'you won't have to worry about the standard or the commitment of French club rugby.'

'Aye,' Townsend agreed, 'they're pretty tough boys.'

'Especially at Brive,' I cracked. 'Laurent Seigne will have you on head-banging terms with all the team before you know it . . .'

Townsend winced. 'I used to like doing that myself, up in Scotland – but when I was much younger. I'd hate to do it now. When I went over to Brive to talk things through I told them that was my only worry about French rugby – from the outside, for all their flair, the French can look so violent and intimidating. But they said that's all changed. Since the European Cup, teams have learnt to win away. Before, in France, it was very much town against town. Away teams would be so intimidated that they would just cave in. But since they've been playing more regularly in Bath and Cardiff and Leicester, they've changed their preparation. French teams have learned that they can win away without punching each other in the face beforehand. But, still, it is a worry. I've played against teams like Toulon where they come out, at home, in tears. They're *that* emotional and *that* worked up. I'm not sure if that's my style. What do you think I should do? Should I go?'

I already knew that Gregor Townsend had made up his mind. He was too intrigued by the idea of living in Brive, of learning a new language and absorbing a different culture. He was far too intelligent not to revel in France but, still, I told him about the heady wonder of Brive against Dax and Castres against Perpignan. I told him almost everything I had heard from Benazzi and Castaignède.

'It'll be great, Gregor,' I said.

'Yeah,' he said, 'I know.'

It had been one of my more unusual interviews – for we had spoken in between moving some of Gregor's furniture from his Northampton flat into a Budget van we'd picked up on the way. He was about to drive it back to Edinburgh, in preparation for the move to Brive.

'You always knew you were going to France, didn't you,' I said, as we shifted his mattress down a tight stairway.

'Pretty much,' he agreed. 'But it's been good to hear you also like French club rugby!'

'It's fantastic,' I said. 'But Gregor . . .'

We had reached an especially cramped corner. We needed to bend the bulky mattress, just as if we were the Brive front row at work in Toulon.

'Yeah?' he panted.

'*Parlez-vous français?*'

'*Un peu. Un petit peu . . .*'

Chapter 21
A Small Ache

The old French tickler, one last time: 'There are two kinds of rugby players. Those who play pianos, and those who shift them . . .'

A year earlier, as the Lions prepared for South Africa, I might've been surprised to hear that, on 12 May 1998, on an otherwise ordinary Tuesday in England, I would shift heavy furniture in the afternoon with one member of that team and then, a few hours later, listen to a few tinkles with another while he whipped up a deliciously light pasta. At a stretch, I would probably have guessed right and come up with the names – Wood and Townsend. But, still, I would have feared for Keith Wood's rugby career. Could the captain of Ireland, and one of the English Premiership's most resilient characters, really fall so far, so fast? What desperate fate would force him into the depths of my piano-moving partnership?

In the modern game, few clichés were safe. Even the more recent, such as 'John Hart's unbeatable All Blacks', were about to be examined like never before. There was less hope for rugby's antiquated truisms – even the most romantic. New Zealand might have lost both Sean Fitzpatrick and Frank Bunce, one to retirement and the other to a lucrative pension with Castres, but they had left behind an enduring legacy for both the hulking shifters and the preening pianists. Forwards had to shove and run, skip and pass, while even the highest-stepping backs had to show the bench-pressing strength to rough it with the biggest boys.

And so, after an afternoon of lifting and packing with Gregor Townsend, I spent a more rarefied and musical evening with the man who remained British rugby's definitive piano-cruncher in the scrum. At least some things were the same – Keith Wood was still the friendly guy from Limerick who hummed Leonard Cohen ditties while crashing into his rival hooker. Yet, in keeping with rugby's more subtle variations, he was also the kind of debonair host who played Bjork while serving an exquisite pasta garnished with olives and rare sheep's cheese, a delicately tossed salad, chunks of bread and salami, with a small Italian beer each for luck.

We both had reason for optimism as an early-summer twilight fell across Twickenham. Three nights before, Louis Luyt had resigned. Even though his position had appeared untenable earlier that week, when his own Sarfu unions voted against his continued presidency, Luyt had insisted that he would not step down. He regarded the show of support against him as 'unconstitutional'. Luyt threatened to gasp on and find a legal loophole in his constricting lack of support. But, just as his white government had been forced to submit, Luyt had eventually given in. Not even a man as obstinate as him could hold on forever. 'My people folded,' he complained to *Rapport*, 'and I can't trust them anymore . . .'

Until then, I told Keith Wood, I had feared the bleak completion of a typically South African rugby circle. Despite Nelie Smith's cheery assurances from Ballymena that 'it is not too Luyt for Louis to go', there were days when I saw myself devoting the last chapters of this book to the return of boycotts and the renewal of isolation. But, as ever with South Africa, doom quickly slipped into elation. Luyt was out, Test rugby was in, the Sarfu executive would be 'democratically re-elected' and the residual problems of 'development rugby' could at least be addressed beyond the long shadow of big Louis.

The Minister of Sport, Steve Tshwete, reiterated that 'this is the best thing that has happened to South African rugby since winning the World Cup. We must applaud those rugby people who stood up to be counted in the vote against Luyt.'

Nelson Mandela, who had described Luyt as a 'pitiless dictator' in court, again sought a more reconciliatory tone – even paying tribute to Luyt's role in organising the World Cup as well as his formative meeting with the ANC near the end of apartheid. 'It is regrettable,' Mandela said, 'that people's mistakes tend to be what they will be remembered for – instead of their achievements and positive contributions. South Africans should not be blind to the fact that Dr Luyt was one of the pioneers of the movement to seek broader consensus in this country.'

Just as the Irish and Welsh tours of South Africa had been on and off and on again, so Wood's own summer plans had fluctuated. At first, he was on his way as captain but, then, as exhaustion seeped in, he decided to withdraw. The Irish management accepted his reasons. Then, with yet more injuries in the pack, there was a turnaround. Ireland needed him. Wood suggested a compromise. He would miss the first few weeks of the tour, but arrive in time for the two Tests against the Springboks – if the whole shebang was not scuppered by Luyt.

But, by that evening, all was confirmed. The tour was on, and he, like me, would fly over for the Tests. While I enjoyed the painless luxury of spectating, he faced the hurt of yet more physical clattering. By the time we'd finished our meal and moved across to his front room, the fading light had given way to darkness. Wood snapped on the small lamp above his head and sat down in his Adidas shirt and baggy shorts. In the gloom, with the glow around his bald head, he almost looked like Brando playing Kurtz – except that Woodie would always need more than a few gravelly words to explain himself and then tell a few classic stories on top. He was perhaps the easiest of anyone I knew to interview, because he always spoke with such expansive honesty. And yet, as we began by assessing the litany of terrible injuries he had suffered over the years, it was I who almost felt the need to do the Brando bit and whisper, 'The horror, the horror . . .'

Gregor Townsend had already told me that, in the dressing-room, the Lions had all seen how Wood's body was a battlefield of scars. Around the shoulders, where the surgeons had operated, the lines ran long and deep. But, more than just the familiar weals and welts, they had seen how hardly a patch of his body had avoided punishment over the last few years. He had taken some brutal batterings, both in club and Test rugby. After every game, he limped and ached – but kept talking.

'Yeah,' he admitted, 'there's been some pain. One of my shoulders was destroyed. I was out for sixteen months with that. Then it was the other one – and now I also have these knees and ankles that hurt and a whole lot else besides. It's the way I play. I'm a major runner with the ball and, as a hooker, that kills the purists – not that I care. In rugby, if you look at the runners, whatever position they play, those are the guys with the worst injuries. They're running and the hits are coming in. But that's the whole point of this game. I can play it tight, but don't tell me, "Woodie, don't put your hands on the ball!" I don't care how many times I go down, I'm still going to get up and play the same game. I love the confrontation.'

Wood rubbed, as if comforting each in turn, his left shoulder and then his right knee. 'Most mornings when I wake up, my body feels pretty stiff. At the moment it's not too bad but, in the winter, all the old joints tend to stiffen up. As Tom Billups, the American captain, says, "Woodie, all we're waiting for is a breakthrough in medicine so that they can patch us up in our old age." Tom's thirty-three, and a hooker too. I'm twenty-six, so I tell him, "Tom, they better get a move on because I'm going to have to be put back together by the time I crawl into middle-age . . ."'

'Do you ever feel,' I asked, 'that you're doing yourself permanent damage?'

'If you thought that way,' Wood said, 'you'd never play well. I don't think I'm going to be in great shape at the age of forty – but you live the life you lead. I wouldn't say, by any stretch of the imagination, that I have a devil-may-care attitude. I do think things through. I'm also conscious of what rugby can do to the body. But I can honestly say that this is one issue that I don't mull over. In certain things in life, you just need to get on and do it. This might be a strange thing to hear from the captain of Ireland, but I am not a religious person. I believe that you're only here for a while and then it's over. I don't believe in an after-life. You're just here and you do what you have to do. So, with rugby, I live it and I love it – to the full. I want to play until I'm thirty-three or thirty-four and, then, I'll deal with whatever consequences my body deals out to me . . .'

But, as for Townsend and Dallaglio, the Lions tour had exacted as much a mental as a physical toll on Wood. 'At the end of that tour,' he said, 'I was wasted. I'd hurt my back, I'd hurt my groin, I'd hurt my ankle. But there was another kind of shattering – the cracks you get from psychological fatigue. The low which followed the high of that tour was so grim it was almost hilarious. You put so much into a tour like that and, afterwards, you feel as if you've got nothing left. Two days after we got back it was my best friend's wedding – and I was the best man. I was so determined that the focus should be on him rather than me, because it was his special day. And it was great but, by midnight, I went to bed. And that's at an Irish wedding! My best mate's wedding! I should have been going until at least six in the morning. And that was the start of my difficulties this season. There were a couple of times when I just felt as if I could break out and cry.'

'And yet you had to play even more rugby just over a month later . . .'

'I think all the clubs made the mistake of not allowing us to rest. That's them still struggling to come to terms with professionalism. They brought us back immediately and, if we coped at first, the problems soon emerged. There've been plenty of times when I've been trying to build myself up for matches and then I've just said, "Jeez, I can't, there's nothing there.' I remember you coming to see me in the dressing-room after Quins had lost in Limerick to Munster. I was burnt out. In the warm-up – and this is a European Cup match in my home town – I was flat. And there was nothing I could do. And that day was a shocker for us in Limerick.

'Two weeks later, in the quarter-final in November, we went to Toulouse. I'd had some intense physio the week before and I felt okay.

Before the match, in the dressing-room, I was going through my routine, with the boys all around me. I didn't want to build it up too much – 'cos it was just about the biggest club match you could ever wish to play. There were 25,000 Frenchmen going totally crazy outside. It was a brilliant day, with a stunning atmosphere and yet, as soon as I jogged out onto the pitch, I knew I was in trouble. All week I'd been building myself up for this match. And five minutes into the game, I was thinking, "What the fuck are you doing?" I couldn't hit the line-out. We were getting screwed in the scrum – the worst it's ever happened to me. I've played in the front row against Califano and Tournaire a few times for Ireland. We've always been very comfortable. But that day it felt impossible. And I wasn't the only one. There was this lethargy running right through the team. We wanted to do well but nobody could do a thing. We got an absolute thrashing – the biggest I've ever had with Harlequins. Sure, Toulouse had psyched themselves up something massive because, in their eyes too, we're the quintessential English side and we also had a couple of Frenchmen in our team. So they were out to give us a kickin' – but the size of the defeat was down more to our being completely shattered beforehand.'

Yet the following Saturday, in Dublin, I saw Wood score two tries against the All Blacks.

'I just had to get myself up for that one – even if it fucking killed me. But that's the problem – you can go that extra game but the burn-out will hit even worse two weeks later. Against New Zealand, I tore my ankle ligaments in the first five minutes and, even now, they're still giving me trouble. But then they just numbed and I played the first half. I scored twice, made a few runs, threw well and scrummaged passably. But I was still doin' only pretty average when, suddenly, it felt like I was carrying my foot by a thread. The half-time whistle went. There were ten steps down to the changing-room and they had to help me down. They got the boot off but they couldn't put any strapping on the foot because it was too painful. Once the adrenaline stops, that's when the pain really bites. I was out.'

In the weeks preceding that game, doctors advised Wood that he needed a complete break from rugby.

'Yeah. But I played on. There was always another big game. I've had my momentary lapses of sanity and pushed myself on through the worst of it. I did it at twenty-two and I was far worse then. Fuck, at twenty-two, you're about as ridiculously stupid as it's possible to be. But, this season, I've had to cut back. I've played twenty-three games for my club

– but I've missed almost six weeks. And that's simply because of fatigue after last season and the Lions . . .'

We were back into the realm of British rugby politics. The previous season's series of forty-five or fifty-five matches still burned a hole through all the Lions. 'I said recently,' Wood sighed, 'that if the mess doesn't get sorted then I'll play fifty matches a season if they want me to. But I won't play them well. I can do it – but not at the right level of intensity. It's the same this season – I haven't played well and that's down to too much rugby.'

'Do you think the chaos can be resolved in the near future?'

'It should be! We just need these guys to show a bit of common sense. For all the egos and power-mongering, some things are definite. We have a strong club structure here. That must stay. I think the clubs should look after their own affairs. That's another definite – because it's wrong that amateur administrators dictate the clubs' professional business. A revised European competition is another definite. I say this even as an Irishman – it's completely mad that only four English clubs play in Europe while there're three teams from Ireland. But, to balance the power of the clubs, there is an even more significant definite. People should always be able to play for their country. The pinnacle of rugby is always at international level. Those are four basic definites. The problems themselves are not complicated. It's just the people – on both sides . . .'

For all the stark talk of injury, weariness and political lunacy, there were many more humorous insights into Wood's abiding passion for rugby. He spoke with particular precision about front-row play, and his own position in the middle, in those surreal moments before impact at a scrum. 'You have to be as tight as tight can be,' he said. 'It's very special. As a hooker, you have to have complete faith in your two props. You put your hands above your head and then over their shoulders. You're completely exposed. And then, together, you bend and lower. And a foot away there's these three other guys who're doing the same thing, who're revving themselves up for an almighty hit. And, you're waiting for the moment. For five seconds, you're totally uncluttered – and that's not a bad thing to be. Five seconds before the moment comes your mind is clear of everything but one pure and simple thought . . .'

Wood paused. He lowered his voice a notch, just to crank up the intensity.

'You're waiting, the three of you in a row, the three of them opposite. And I've thought about this a lot. I've really tried to break down those five seconds into a little series of distinct fragments. But it's just one pure burn where you think and feel nothing beyond one thing: "*I'm going to hit this guy as hard as I fucking can!*" Everything else is gone. That's the beauty of it – the ability to lose yourself totally in the moment . . .'

Keith Wood also found a gnarled beauty in the fleeting hurt he both caused and suffered during a game of rugby. It was as if the sport's physicality was best expressed through a camaraderie of pain. 'Well,' he said cheerfully, 'it's never a case of trying to do any real damage to each other. It's strange but this kind of thing always seems to happen most often between me and some of my best friends in rugby. When Ireland played England in the Five Nations, I was up against my old pal, Jason Leonard, the guy I pack down with for both Quins and the Lions. In the first two minutes, Jason kicked me in the head. I fell down but I didn't mind in the slightest. It meant me and Jason were going to give each other a shake all through the match. Near the end, I kicked him in the head. I had no hesitation. He was in the way. Afterwards, we were laughing and hugging each other. We found it very amusing.'

'And I guess you'll be doing that again in South Africa . . .'

'Sure. I'm feeling so much fresher now than I did earlier in the season. I'm a bit closer to my real self. Some people say I'm crazy to go out again for two Tests after the season I've had – but it's only a couple more hard games and then I go off on my holidays. I think it's going to be incredibly tough against the Springboks but, shit, you know me. That's the kind of rugby I like. I'll be happy in the thick of it . . .'

The morning after Keith Wood's illuminating soirée, a larger but more desperate gathering met down the road in Twickenham. Clive Woodward announced England's thirty-seven-man squad for their five-week, four-Test tour of Australia, New Zealand and South Africa. There were twenty uncapped players and a new captain in Matt Dawson. More significantly, fifteen names were missing, either through injury, tiredness or for personal reasons: Dallaglio, Johnson, Rodber, Leonard, Hill, Garforth, Guscott, de Glanville, Catt, Grayson, Bracken, Underwood, Rees, Greenstock and Adebayo.

Dawson claimed that 'We have every chance of winning the Tests', which qualified him for a Millennium Doom prize as Optimist of the Century. When pressed, he admitted of his young flock that 'if they cannot grow up quickly on tour they will be found out . . .'

Woodward also tried for an early smile. 'I am excited by the tour, by the squad and by the challenge. I don't feel great about leaving senior players at home, especially as all three of our opponents brought strong squads to Britain before Christmas. But I can put my hand on my heart and say that, with the possible exception of Kyran Bracken, none of those players would make the Test side on current form. If we were playing this weekend, guys like Lawrence Dallaglio and Martin Johnson wouldn't be on the field.'

While he excused Dallaglio, who had played for Wasps the previous Saturday in the Cup final, he was flatly unimpressed by Johnson being used by Leicester despite his groin injury. 'There's no criticism of Lawrence – he'll be welcome back. But I'm disappointed that Martin has been playing for Leicester in some meaningless end-of-season games. I feel for those who have to turn out for their clubs, because they could lose their jobs if they don't. Nevertheless, I wish players would give England priority, resting when necessary. But it's no good moaning – if we return home with four or five new guys having made an unanswerable case for an England place, then the exercise will have been worth while.'

Dick McGruther, the Australian Rugby Union chairman, was almost incandescent at the futility of playing what he described as 'probably the most under-equipped group of Englishmen sent to Australia since the first fleet. We are disappointed and insulted. This is the biggest sell-out by the English since Gallipoli. You have to wonder whether this mob deserves to host a World Cup pool in 1999, or why they should be rewarded with one. I think the English RFU have treated the southern hemisphere with a degree of contempt – but we invite all Australians to come out and witness a Pommie thrashing . . .'

For fourteen minutes, Australia failed to score against England in Brisbane. It took them twenty-six minutes, when they led 6–0 through two penalties from Matthew Burke, to score their first try. But then it began. A Pommie thrashing became the worst-ever defeat for one of world rugby's eight established nations. A 33–0 half-time lead was plugged in and scorched by the electrifying Wallabies. Tune, Roff, Herbert, Horan and Larkham were blistering and, when they began to really try, they caught fire. There were three five-pointer smokers each for Tune and Larkham, two for Horan and one for Kefu, Burke and Gregan. Australia 76, England 0.

As Chris Hewett reported in *The Independent*, 'There were unmistakable signs of shellshock on an awful lot of English faces yesterday and the pain was not eased by a tirade of Wallaby one-liners aimed in their direction. "The official figure, gentlemen, is 26,691," said one of the

Suncorp Stadium functionaries shortly before the final whistle. "Is that the attendance or the scoreline?" asked an Australian scribe. Under the circumstances, the Poms had no option but to sit there and take it.'

England were not alone in their torment. Scotland lost to Fiji and then, a week after England, were destroyed 45–3 by Australia – which, when set against the white shirts, must have felt like a triumph of sorts. The Scots, in Gregor Townsend's last match of a long season, improved the following Saturday too, losing a 33–11 'nailbiter' to the Wallabies. That same afternoon, on 20 June, England were blitzed 64–22 by New Zealand. Wales and Ireland, meanwhile, battled to win any kind of match in South Africa. The Welsh had already been overwhelmed by the Emerging Springboks and a second-string Natal team. In the build-up to a two-Test series, Ireland had also lost three out of four provincial games – the worst of which was a 52–13 hiding from Andre Markgraaff's Griqualand West, four days before their first Springbok encounter in Bloemfontein.

The Irish had the distinctly English figures of 76 and 0 tattooed into their brains. Nick Mallett had also not forgotten how Ireland had almost beaten France in the Five Nations. 'They made it difficult for France to launch their counter-attacks with up-and-unders into the box. They're one of the few teams that can limit a big score by the way they play the game. They keep down their attacking opportunities to the minimum so you win very little turn-over ball. Their defence is well organised, they close down space intelligently and focus on keeping the score down . . .'

They also had Keith Wood, and Paddy Johns from Saracens as captain, to show them the way. Eighteen seconds into the first Test in Bloemfontein, the Springboks' new fly-half Gaffie du Toit, a shimmering talent playing in place of the injured Honiball, was offered an instant taste of the meaty Irish stew. Teichmann and Erasmus set up a ruck from Ellwood's kick-off and van der Westhuizen fed du Toit. The twenty-two-year-old caught the ball and, coolly, found touch. With more heat under his head-gear, the blazing Johns kept running. He clattered into du Toit with a hefty shoulder. The Irish had obviously decided to get their late charges in as early as possible. Penalty to the Springboks and, already, a bruising pattern to the Irish scheme.

Although Stefan Terblanche scored his first international try two minutes later, Ireland were not about to be nailed. The key moment of the series, naturally, was hammered home in a woody slot by my bald friend, Keith. After half an hour, the Irish centre Kevin Maggs stepped out on a strong run; he was blocked by du Toit and a ruck formed.

Teichmann waited for the ball to be released, but Wood had other ideas. He came steaming in over the top and hit Teichmann high, his elbow smashing into the Springbok with a brutal smack.

South Africa were similarly disjointed and almost fractured. Although the Springboks won 37–13, with Terblanche scoring four tries on his début, they were still a shadowy print of the side they'd been in Europe six months before. Mallett promised a markedly sharper performance the following Saturday, as further preparation for the fast-approaching Tri-Nations. The Irish, too, decided to end their own season with a bang.

Loftus Versveld, Pretoria, Saturday, 20 June 1998
There was one moment of levity. It came early, soon after Franco Smith had made an astonishing break and passed to Andre Venter. The big Springbok flanker sprinted down the length of the Irish half with a speed and power which left the emerald shirts fluttering helplessly. Try to South Africa. Montgomery prepared for the conversion when, suddenly, the French referee, Joel Dumé, caught sight of Ed Morrison's waving flag. There was a brief touchline conference and then Dumé, with a shrill blast of his whistle, summoned Teichmann and Adrian Garvey.

'I think you punch,' he said to Garvey.

'No, no, no, no,' the prop answered in an accent dripping with Parisian certainty, 'no punch . . .'

Dumé hesitated, confused to find a Frenchman in a Springbok shirt. But, lest any accusations of bias could be levelled against him, he upheld Morrison's judgement. Penalty to Ireland. Garvey ran back to his forwards, no doubt muttering Gallic profanities every step of the way.

We were already on course for the dirtiest rugby international in recent memory. It was filthy stuff in Pretoria, grim bare-knuckle violence laced with boots and flying elbows. Mass brawls broke out in drunken convoy as lines of players weaved across the pitch in fist-throwing tow. It was the most dispiriting rugby match I had ever seen.

The Irish blamed Joost van der Westhuizen for starting the troubles. In the eleventh minute, the Springbok scrum-half kicked Malcolm O'Kelly – in full view of the ref. The look of alarm which spread across van der Westhuizen's face was enough to confirm his fear of a long walk to the tunnel. He escaped with a warning but, according to the Irish, every dark deed flowed from there on.

Nick Mallett was more accurate in his sombre post-match

assessment. 'What Joost did was inexcusable. He knows it too. I spoke to him at half-time and he apologised. But he was not the only one. I'll be studying the video and we'll be talking to all our players who were involved. The Springboks certainly were not guilt-free. They became frustrated and, while I'm not excusing their actions, there were some mitigating circumstances. There is a feeling that the northern-hemisphere countries are thirty or forty points weaker at the moment. And if you don't win by that amount against them then even your own public feel you haven't had a good game. Today we scored five tries and won 33–0. They didn't create one chance. But we all saw what went on out there. My impression is that the Irish decided to do everything in their power not to have a result as embarrassing as England's 76–0 loss to Australia. You can do that in rugby by not creating try-scoring opportunities and kicking the cover off the ball and slowing down the game. We were trying to score tries. We weren't trying to impede them. But they went into the game with the sole intention of keeping the score down – legally or otherwise. If teams are cheating in order to stop tries being scored against them, and they're not being penalised, then you will get this kind of reaction . . .'

Even the mild-mannered Gary Teichmann – the All Blacks' favourite 'hard but fair bastard' – resorted to a snapping jab and a mean uppercut in the face of constant Irish spoiling. Early in the second half Teichmann, chasing a bobbing ball, was pulled back again by the shirt. I blinked in surprise, if with some understanding, when he turned angrily on the Irish centre, McCall, and stunned him with an impressive series of combinations. Johns and Costello smeared into the Springbok captain furiously and, once more, cross-field mayhem ensued.

'There had been talk of aggression the whole week,' Teichmann said. 'They came out in an aggressive manner in Bloemfontein and they repeated it today. There were a few instances when the discipline got out of hand but we weren't going to back off. It was one of those games where something happened every time you went into a loose maul or ruck. Even right at the end, Naka Drotske was kicked in the back on the ground. It was hard for me to keep discipline while my guys were receiving no protection . . .'

The Irish management were no more contrite. 'Van der Westhuizen's kick set the tone of the match,' Donal Lenihan insisted, before remarking that Keith Wood was 'battered, bruised and lumped . . .' Lenihan underlined the Irish team's bitterness that the Springboks had laughed and taunted Wood when he was injured three minutes from the end. 'There was no accepted courtesy between international players,' Lenihan said, 'and we find that sad . . .'

But at least it was over. Late that Saturday evening, the headline-writers were hard at work, sharpening their Celtic clichés.

'The Fighting Irish' were leaving; 'The Singing Welsh' were coming.

Loftus Versveld, Saturday 27 June 1998

In the last few days before the carnage, the South Africans and the Welsh predicted a competitive match. 'The Welsh are attempting to play rugby,' Nick Mallett encouraged, 'and even though they have been behind from a very early stage in their games, they have come back and scored some nice tries. They are playing much more positive rugby than Ireland, which means we are going to have to improve our tackle count. This is going to be a test for our defensive lines . . .'

Despite losing all four of their provincial games, the Welsh assistant coach, Lyn Howell, remained positive. 'We have identified a few weaknesses in the Springboks,' he explained, 'and we will be targeting them . . .'

The Welsh were already missing, through a variety of reasons, Gibbs, Bateman, Jenkins, Young, the Quinnell brothers and a dozen more of the gang. Their captain, Rob Howley, was the next to fall. Howley's hamstring was torn badly enough for him to replaced by Paul John – the son of Dennis John who, only weeks before, had stepped in from Pontypridd as caretaker coach while the Welsh Union tracked Graham Henry in Auckland. There was another link with the Blues, for Wales would be captained by Kingsley Jones, the son of big Jonah's manager. Phil Kingsley Jones was still in Auckland, but I could imagine his booming pride as his boy from Ebbw Vale led the red shirts out on a warm late-afternoon. But, if it was another dry winter in Pretoria, it was still a wet summer in the Valleys. And, with the rain in Wales, came the tears of rugby men.

On hard and firm ground, the Springboks began to run. And they ran tirelessly into a blue evening tinged with gold, moving the ball across the green field with effortless pace and panache, as if sauntering through a training lark on a Tuesday morning.The Welsh never gave up. They tackled and tackled and tackled. But, even when they were not bouncing off the big South Africans, it was never enough to bring down just one Springbok – there were always five or six more green jerseys running behind at full tilt. The ball would slide out again, and the next man would take it at speed, with still four more screaming on the overlap.

At half-time, it was vaguely respectable. 31–6 to South Africa. But, then, the Springboks began to cut loose. Rossouw kept veering inside, his sudden shift of direction and lengthening of stride slashing past the Welsh as easily as an electric trimmer slicing across the red-leafed top of a small hedge. His legs were long enough for him to jump over his tacklers, but he preferred to cut through them. Snyman and Muller, in the centre, were happier punching holes in the middle while the forwards – Teichmann, Venter, Erasmus, Otto and Garvey – opted for a blend of the scalpel and the bludgeon.

It was merciless, and I felt a little ache for Wales. But as the Springboks reached for something extraordinary we, Alison and I, began to cheer more greedily. We were, after all, thrill-seekers rather than rugby traditionalists. And so we yearned for a hundred, just for the selfish pleasure of saying we had seen it. With a fresh Honiball, Skinstad, Aitken, le Roux, Swanepoel, Hendricks and Drotske unleashed against the Welsh, as Mallett took full advantage of the new replacement law which allowed seven substitutes, the score began to soar – with frightening regularity for the Welsh writers around us. We tried to be sensitive, shrugging sadly, saying, 'It's just one of those freaky days' and 'You'll be fine once you've got your full team back.' But as soon as they turned away or buried their heads in their hands, we did it. We jumped up sneakily or whispered, 'C'mon, give us another!' as the try-scoring slaughter continued.

They crossed the Welsh line seven times in the last twenty minutes and, when McNeil Hendricks burst forward again to release Rossouw, we were on our feet. The winger's legs blurred, as if Rossouw had as many speedy limbs beneath him as the number 11 on his back. He looped out a pass to Montgomery. As he arrowed down the touchline, Monty looked even quicker. He hit the target, for the Springboks' fifteenth try. It was his second and, with nine conversions and a penalty making up his personal booty of thirty-one, Montgomery had scored more points than any other Springbok in a Test. It also ensured that Wales had broken England's three-week-old record for the worst-ever defeat amongst international rugby's leading countries.

South Africa 96, Wales 13 – and time for one more attack as the Pretoria-accented cries of '*Ole, Ole-Ole-Ole-Ole* . . .' resounded around a rapturous Loftus. Venter, whom Mallett had moved from flank to lock to let in Skinstad, turned up at scrum-half and sent Aitken away. Drotske and five other Springboks were running outside him. The red line awaited a green century. Aitken passed and, shit, Drotske knocked it on. Paddy O'Brien, a kindly Kiwi, saw a chance for Welsh salvation. He lifted his arm and blew, before the big 101 could roll round in the next move. As soon as the whistle sounded, I was strangely relieved. The surrounding Welsh misery was deep; and our longing for a hundred seemed cruel. It was enough. Welsh rugby, and British rugby, had hit bottom.

Cape Town, Friday, 3 July 1998
England were in town. But the great rugby questions of the day mattered far less to me. I cared more about my friend. The gaping divide between the north and the south, the decline of some countries and the return of others, the sweeping moves and the massive scores, even the looming Tri-Nations, faded into oblivion. Alison and I were in Panini's, in James Small's coffee-shop in downtown Cape Town, and we were happy. James made us laugh. It had been great from the start. He'd hugged Alison and winked at me, and then stretched out his hand and pulled me in for a quick ruck and a squeeze to say 'howzit'.

'How are you, James?' I'd asked as we stepped back.

'Hey, bru,' he grinned. 'I'm good!'

And he was good. He was special. And that morning we again saw the reason. In Pretoria, in the press box, they had not been in mourning for James Small. Stefan Terblanche, in his first three matches for the Springboks, in Small's number 14 jersey, had scored six tries. I remembered two different local rugby writers drifting over to inquire, with their wry smiles, if I had returned to South Africa to write the biography of James Small. I knew that they really meant, in rugby terminology, to pin a Springbok obituary across his name.

'It's over,' someone said, 'he'll never play for South Africa again . . .'

At the end of May, Nick Mallett had announced a twenty-four-man squad for the Tests against Ireland, Wales and England. He chose three wings – Pieter Rossouw, Stefan Terblanche and McNeil Hendricks.We were expecting it. Small was in trouble, again. While his Super 12 had been wrecked by injury and controversy, Terblanche had been flying, ending the tournament as joint top-scorer with Joeli Vidiri and Jeff Wilson on a dozen tries.

I'd felt the first real cold threat for Small, after almost six years of Test rugby, in Palmerston North, on the day when the Sharks whipped the Hurricanes and Terblanche cruised in with a hat-trick. I'd wandered down to the dressing-room to congratulate Gary Teichmann. Afterwards, as I stepped out into the passageway again, I heard the New Zealand reporters calling for Terblanche. Small's old coach, Ian McIntosh, smiled knowingly.

'Stefan only speaks Afrikaans,' he warned the waiting Kiwis with a jokey smile.

When Terblanche emerged from the steaming room, he looked crisp and fresh. The braces on his teeth made him look very young. He spoke impeccable English and dealt modestly with the Kiwi queries.

'The guys have all made it so much easier for me,' Terblanche said, 'especially the senior players like Andre Joubert and Henry Honiball. They made me feel very welcome and I have learnt a lot already by playing alongside them.'

'What's next, Stefan?' one of the New Zealanders asked – before suggesting in the next breath: 'Have you started thinking about Springbok honours yet?'

'My aim now,' Terblanche said calmly, 'is to make the most of the opportunity I've been given. I'm going to try and prove I'm worthy of my place in the Coastal Sharks' side. That's all I'm thinking about at the moment...'

I hung back a little from the others, watching him, knowing that Nick Mallett had also seen Terblanche's trio of tries. But, then, I chose to turn away. Terblanche was affable and very talented, yet my thoughts were many thousands of miles away, with Small.

Three months later it was almost as if Small's name had been expunged from Springbok rugby. Although he still held the record for the most tries and caps, both Joost van der Westhuizen and Mark Andrews had closed in. Against Wales, van der Westhuizen had equalled Small's nineteenth try while Andrews needed only three more Tests to pass his mark for the most appearances in a South African shirt. More painfully, Small's name did not even appear in the newspapers' list of potential Tri-Nations squad replacements for the injured McNeil Hendricks. Mallett eventually recalled Chester Williams.

The week before, Mallett and I had spoken about Small. The Springbok coach was typically forthright. 'I've told James that rugby is not an individual sport – it's a team sport. I've also said to him that I will judge him first as a player because you always have to weigh up his international experience – and the experience he carries is immense. I also know that James Small always performs well in a Springbok jersey. He would never let me down on the field because, in that green-and-gold shirt, he plays with momentous pride. But you cannot have a guy who only performs well in a Springbok shirt. He's got to do well in the Super 12 first. And James only played four or five times in this year's Super 12 – and when he did play he played poorly. He wasn't committed to it a hundred per cent. Stefan Terblanche played almost all the games and he was the leading try-scorer. So we had a situation where the incumbent was clearly not motivated – and the team knew it. Some of the Western Stormers were upset with James. A lot of players are saying, "He's lost it!"

'So if you take two players of roughly equal ability then it's natural you're going to pick the team-man. I really like James – he's intelligent and interesting and talented. But he's also incredibly moody. He's prone to some dark moments. Now he has done remarkably well out of turning himself into the "James Dean of Rugby" – but you can only do that if you remain twenty per cent better than the next player. And, this year, Stefan Terblanche has performed superbly. So we have the most capped Springbok who's having a few problems on and off the field, and we have this very keen and sometimes quite brilliant youngster who deserves some credit after doing so well. If I'd ignored Stefan, I would have lost total credibility – because everyone would say, "What's the point of doing well in the Super 12?"

'I've had some very good moments with James over the last few years. So I would love to say it's not the end of the road for him but . . . well, I do think it's going to be very difficult for James. He has to have a whole sea-change of character and that's going to be very hard for him . . .'

With Small, I was moved most by his candour. We had transcended our once clear roles of rugby player and writer and yet, because my mind turned back repeatedly to this book, he allowed me to interview him. He answered questions which must have hurt him. Everything I asked was built around the theme of loss. It seemed as if a specific time in his life, perhaps the most special of all times, was about to end.

'But Don,' he said, 'it's not the world. Rugby is not life – by any stretch of the imagination. I think that's the one lesson I've absorbed most in the last six months. Once, rugby was all-consuming for me. It was everything. Nothing else mattered, as long as I played rugby for South Africa, as long as I was a Springbok. Sometimes it felt like it was the only reason I'd been put on the face of this earth. But it's not.

'Everybody's coming up to me and saying, "Shame, we're sorry to hear about your . . ." And they never finish the sentence. They're sorry that I'm not in the Springbok team any more. I'm saying, "Where's the shame in it?" I've been to countries all around the world. I've been through three passports, which is a fucking dream. I've sung my national anthem in great stadiums with my family watching me. I've won a World Cup final. I've made a great living out of rugby. I've been very lucky. I don't want to sound like I'm suddenly turning politically correct but, before isolation ended, there were some great players who were never given the chance I had . . .'

'But James, rugby's been part of you almost forever. Where else in life will you feel that intensity when you run out for the Springboks against the All Blacks?'

'That is the scariest thing. It's like I've been living in this cocoon for the last ten years and more. What will life be without it? And I'm not talking only financially – even though the end of my Springbok contract will cost me R700,000 a year and that's a fucking lot of cash for a guy who's twenty-nine years old. But the money's not so important. Y'know, not so long ago I bought this beautiful car, a little Mercedes convertible, an SLK. I loved it. It was my dream. It was fucking beautiful. I would drive it and it was like, "Burn, burn, burn!" But then the intensity fades and I thought, after a week, it's just a car. I sold it. All that kind of stuff's gone now.

'But, *ja*, I am a competitor. When you spoke earlier, about Stefan Terblanche scoring four tries on his début, I could feel it. My blood began to pump and rise to a height of pressure. It felt as if it could blow my head off. But then I just stopped myself. I thought, "Hey, c'mon, he's a good rugby player. He deserves it. He's taken his opportunities. He's the kind of player I admire. Far be it for me to begrudge a young guy like him. I was also once twenty-two and burning to be a Springbok." But, you know, to be honest, that desire of mine has been doused. You asked me how I'm going to replace that feeling I had running out against the All Blacks. Well, it's different, but when I get a deal done with my business, a deal which involves an order for 30,000 CDs, a deal that involves some creativity and imagination and an ability to put people together, I get a real rush. I feel good. I can do other things beyond playing rugby . . .'

'That's healthy,' I said.

'*Ja*,' he laughed softly, 'in terms of the big picture. But in terms of my rugby career it's not so healthy. Y'see, rugby today is fucking demanding. It requires tunnel vision. You've got to train for at least four hours a day – two hours in the gym and two hours in the field. You've got to watch what you eat and how you rest. When I started playing rugby it was just a game. Now it's a full-time occupation which you have to live twenty-four hours a days, seven days a week, eleven months a year. You've got to be like a beast to keep up with some of these guys. I know the levels you have to reach in the Tri-Nations. And, hey, maybe I'm not at that level now, maybe I'm thinking of too many other things beyond rugby . . .'

When the Super 12 season began, in February, with the Stormers playing the Hurricanes in Cape Town, I had phoned Small. He'd sounded bright, despite his run-in with the notorious Toks van der Linde.

'I started the pre-season like a cracker, bru!' he recalled in June. 'Like a fucking cracker! This was going to be my year. We went down to Hermanus for a training camp and I said, "Small, now you're going to rock and roll!" But I couldn't sustain it. And then we had our little flare-up, me and Toks. Y'know, Toks van der Linde is the kind of guy other players mock when he's not around. But I'm just straight-forward with him. I like the guy but there're times when I have to tell him, "Toks, you're a fucking idiot! You should grow-up." We were drunk and things blew up.

'And then, a few of these guys – Toks, Christian Stewart and Bobby Skinstad – went to the new Western Province coach, Alan Solomans, and told him they wanted me out the team. I never had a straight answer from Solomans. I kept calling him, to say, "What's happening? Let's meet. Let's sort this out once and for all." But I never got any clear answers. Next thing I know, after winning the Currie Cup with these guys last year, they want to terminate my contract. I have a life in Cape Town, a home in Cape Town and now I have to move back to Jo'burg to play for the Golden Lions [formerly Gauteng/Transvaal] . . . and then I'm out the Springbok team as well . . .'

I tried my best to say the right thing. I spoke of his finest days in green and gold. I still remembered how happy I had been when, at the end of '97, he had scored his record-breaking try. Did he also still derive pleasure from the memory?

Small paused, for a long time. I've since counted the seconds on my watch while I listen to our silence on tape. Ten aching seconds, heavy with thought, pass before Small emits a dry laugh.

'It might have been a good time to retire, hey?'

He paused again, more briefly. 'I dunno. That's the sad thing about it. I've been at war with myself about my form for a long time. Even on that tour, I was at war. I felt I should have reached the stage of my career where I could play in a relaxed and calm way. But I've never reached that stage. Harry Viljoen, my old coach and mentor, says that my best rugby is still ahead of me. He thinks I've matured and this wider perspective will help me . . .'

'Hey, James,' I cracked, 'you could yet become the "Frank Bunce of South African Rugby" . . .'

'Ja, that's what Harry said. Bunce played his best rugby at thirty-four. And I know that I've never really fulfilled my ultimate potential in rugby – despite the World Cup and the caps and the tries. And that's down to me. It's my own fault. And that's what keeps me signing contracts. I would love to do better than before . . .'

'But if you could go back,' I said, 'back even before the start of this season, would you change anything?'

'Not a thing!' Small said quietly. 'The lows in my life have mainly been of my own doing. If it had not been those same mistakes, I would have made them elsewhere – in other parts of my life. And, ironically, I think it's being sent off in an international, getting into a brawl at a nightclub and falling out with the odd team-mate which has created "James Small". I've sold that name for ten years now. It's been a commodity – and that commodity comprises everything I've ever done. It comprises the fuck-ups but it also comprises the good things . . .'

'And Springbok rugby,' I noted, 'has become a little cooler since "James Small" rolled in. The old days seem further away . . .'

Small laughed. 'Ja, the days of the hardcore bonehead have gone. All these advertisers now think it's pretty hip to use a rugby player. And that's great. These younger guys are coming through but, in a way, I was there first. And, one day, I'll sit on a beach and I'll write my name in the sand and I'll say, "Okay, that's mine again . . ."'

Chapter 22
Black, Green and Gold

Johannesburg had been dry for months. The days were blissfully unchanging. A wide sky of clear blue unrolled every morning, with only the position of the sun appearing to shift, climbing a little higher each hour. I was on the road at seven, winding through the waking suburban streets with a few other white cars and some more black walkers. I waved to the sleepy security guard on our corner and, a minute later, just as I neared the low dip curving towards the highway, saluted the more formal sentry standing outside his wooden box. He was another young black guy, and he answered with a grin and a big thumbs-up. He wore only a thin jersey over his purple uniform. His head was also bare and, as he shouted a few friendly words to the women on the opposite pavement, his breath did not form a misty puff as it hit the Highveld air. It was still not cold enough.

I had been home for three weeks, and every day had felt like spring. Yet, for people who lived in Johannesburg, it had been another bleak winter. The violence and the crime had escalated rather than diminished. The stories of murder and rape, of hijackings and robberies, had multiplied – and were matched only by despairing talk of the plummeting Rand as the South African economy went into free-fall. When I'd left Johannesburg in 1984, the R500 in my pocket was worth £250. In 1998, at an exchange rate of almost eleven to one, that same amount could buy £45.

There was resentment and fear, as well as resilience and compassion, wit and kindness – just like anywhere. But South Africa always felt different. It was fucked-up, but it was also special. Everything seemed especially acute in Johannesburg. Despite the encroaching gravity, people managed to live almost ordinary lives. But, for all the wealth and luxury some still enjoyed, South Africans always had to live a little closer to dread, a little further in the shadows. We had our past, both to remember and to relive.

There were strange tales from the old days, full of absurd bumbling and chilling lunacy. A few weeks before, as the Truth and Reconciliation Commission (TRC) drifted towards an end, the bizarre headlines and eerie reports returned. 'Apartheid's Lab Rats under the Microscope' focused on the news that, as David Beresford wrote in *The Mail & Guardian*, 'government scientists had investigated the possibility of developing ways of poisoning people on the basis of the pigmentation of their skin'.

Dr Schalk van Rensburg, recruited to the secret chemical and biological warfare unit at the Roodeplaat Research Laboratories in 1984, explained that 'the most frequent instruction was to create a compound which would kill, but make the cause of death appear to have been natural. That was our chief aim.'

With Roodeplaat's assistance, South African agents attempted to murder the Reverend Frank Chikane, an anti-apartheid leader, by planting lethal chemicals into five pairs of his underpants. In the mid-'80s, the military men had also considered the possibility of lacing Nelson Mandela's prison medication with a poison called thallium, which would 'progressively impair his brain over time'.

They tried further to develop a vaccine to counter fertility in black South Africans and instigated a scheme to release thirty-two bottles of cholera into the water supply of targeted areas. They also encouraged the South African Defence Force to store 'up to a billion rands' worth of the "love drug" Ecstasy'. But, without easy access to the Summer of Love, the raving men in white coats had never quite worked out how best they might use their tabs of E.

At least Louis Luyt's downfall had released almost as much exultation as the mad scientists' confessions had induced trauma. Rugby was still so central in white South African culture that Luyt had been demonised to the point where an outsider might have imagined that he personified every evil perpetrated during apartheid. The truth was less dramatic. He'd been a staunch supporter of the Nationalist government and, in a venture tainted by financial and political scandal, had set up *The Citizen* newspaper in 1977. *The Citizen* aimed to provide a daily soapbox for apartheid in English-speaking South Africa. But, ultimately, it seemed as if Luyt had two greater loves – his own personal power and, of course, rugby.

In his oval republic, Luyt had been crass and domineering. At the World Cup final post-match dinner in 1995 he'd told the All Blacks that only political sanctions had prevented his beloved Springboks from winning the two previous tournaments. The New Zealanders walked out, united by Mike Brewer's description of Luyt as a 'fat Afrikaner bastard'. It was also a popular slogan for rival South African rugby unions, like Natal, where there was virulent disdain for Luyt's arrogance.

In the same way that he'd used his position in Sarfu to boost the strength of his Gauteng province, Luyt liked to keep his rugby goodies within the family. But his son-in-law, Rian Oberholzer, as Sarfu's chief executive, had since proved himself to be a competent and enthusiastic administrator. Oberholzer also displayed a lighter and more politically sensitive touch, attributes which saved his job when Luyt was forced to resign. Luyt's son, Louis Jnr, had not carved out a comparable reputation, however. He was notorious in South Africa for the ten per cent commission he had reputedly creamed off the Springboks' tasty package with Nike. His father, naturally, had suggested that little Louis would be the ideal young man to broker that multi-million-dollar sponsorship deal.

Yet Luyt's desperation to maintain his empire seemed almost quaint when set against the wild experiments of Roodeplaat. Within the world of rugby, however, he was still a mean old mule – and his denunciation of Francois Pienaar as a 'Judas' during his last days in office was considered heretical by most South Africans. Even my mother, who had never been remotely interested in the sport, thought Pienaar represented all that was good in rugby. She also knew that Pienaar had won the Cup for Saracens and guided them to the runners-up spot in the English Premiership behind Newcastle. But my dad and I, more concerned that the Springboks' winning streak would continue in the weeks ahead against Australia and New Zealand, were heartened by her approval for our new coach and captain.

Nick Mallett and Gary Teichmann were, even to my mother, 'fantastic!'. Such was her rising rugby fervour that, for the first time in my life, I almost heard her swear when she declared: 'And at least they don't have that bloody Louis Luyt to stop them now. Thank goodness he's gone!'

Although she didn't take it a step further and yodel *'Viva, Bokke, Viva!'*, she still turfed me out of bed about an hour earlier than necessary that morning.

'You can't be late for Nick Mallett!' she warned.

And so, on a gorgeous Friday in Johannesburg, I hit the road to meet the man who had done so much to transform South African rugby in nine breathless months.

We met for breakfast. While I pulled off a passable impression of the Springboks' cheerfully hungry prop, big Ollie le Roux, his coach was more consumed by the Tri-Nations. Occasionally, Mallett speared a slice of fruit or took a sip of coffee while I spoke and opened the way for another question. But, most of the time, Mallett talked while I listened. I knew he understood the menacing black and gold threat from New Zealand and Australia. Although South Africa would play their first Tri-Nations match in Perth, we moved, inexorably, to the old masters in Black.

Mallett had visited New Zealand for the first time during the Super 12 weeks of March and April. 'I loved it,' he enthused, 'even if our results were not great. The passion for rugby in New Zealand is unbelievable. I met ordinary supporters out there who know as much about rugby as most South African coaches. And their depth of talent is remarkable. The Super 12 again highlighted some salient points for me – the most obvious of which is that, in terms of their overall structure and sense of cohesion, New Zealand are still way ahead of us.

'During the move to professionalism, they managed to ensure that every single aspect of their game would lead to a stronger All Black team. They've realised that the basis for supremacy in world rugby now begins with the Super 12 – and so, for the three years of its existence, they have dominated the tournament. This year we had an excellent team in the Coastal Sharks but, beyond that, to be brutal, it was a shambles for South African rugby . . .'

After the windy high of Palmerston North, the Sharks had lost twice in South Africa – 12–8 to a fanatically defensive Northern Bulls in Pretoria and 32–20 to the more sparkling Canterbury Crusaders in Durban. That second defeat, in the last game of the league format, was decisive. By winning at King's Park, Canterbury finished second and claimed home-ground advantage in the semi-finals. The Crusaders' Andrew Mehrtens and Norm Berryman, in particular, were scintillating, dragging the Sharks all the way back to New Zealand for the play-off seven days later.

Without the injured Henry Honiball, Teichmann's team slid to a 20–0 deficit after a quarter of an hour in Canterbury. But then, drawing on the determination they had shown against Wellington, they bit back. With fifteen minutes left, incredibly, they were ahead 32–26. But, still, the best New Zealand teams did not know when they were meant to lose. The Crusaders scored two late tries to seal their place in the final, 36–32.

The champions, meanwhile, had won nine matches out of eleven on their own track. On 26 April, in the first game since Sean Fitzpatrick's official retirement, the Auckland Blues destroyed the Western Stormers. Harry Viljoen, the South African coach, was stunned. 'That first period by the Blues was the most awesome twenty minutes of rugby I have ever seen. They were incredible.' The Blues won 74–28, to set up home-ground advantage in the knock-out stages.

They squeezed past Josh Kronfeld's Otago Highlanders in an exhilarating semi and then, the following Saturday, lost the final, 20–13, to a converted try in the last minute. The Canterbury Crusaders, repeating their 1997 NPC success over Auckland, had won the Super 12. If the Blues' two-year grip had been broken, there was meagre consolation for the South Africans and Australians. Three New Zealand teams made the final four – and if the Sharks came third, the three remaining South African sides reversed the pattern by finishing in the bottom four. With Queensland and New South Wales just missing the play-offs in fifth and sixth positions, the Australians had done better in overall terms than the Springbok combinations.

For Mallett, New Zealand's pre-eminence was notably disturbing. 'It's very worrying,' he admitted. 'The bare statistics provide a devastating insight into their superiority. The Golden Cats only won two games, while the Bulls and the Stormers scraped in with three. That's eight victories between three teams. Auckland, with nine wins in the league, won more than that on their own. There were twenty Super 12 matches between South African and New Zealand teams this year. They won seventeen of those matches – and the Sharks won the other three. The New Zealanders played ten matches in South Africa and they won eight.

'So, suddenly, after all our success in Europe, whole swathes of Springbok players were being beaten regularly. Os du Randt, Andre Venter, Joost van der Westhuizen, Andre Snyman, Pieter Rossouw and Percy Montgomery were being blitzed. Some of them looked as if they were just trying to keep the score down. There was a huge loss of confidence amongst my players. I had guys coming back into the Springbok camp who were so shell-shocked that they could not even make a simple spin-pass anymore. So, yeah, as you can tell, I was not happy.'

'Why did they fail so badly?'

'Provincial rivalry was a major reason. The composition of the teams was decided before I came on board and clearly they didn't work – the

Golden Cats being the prime example. Our rampant provincialism is a hangover from the days of isolation because, without international competition, our teams turned the Currie Cup into the be-all and end-all of rugby. It's only been in the last year or so that the Currie Cup has taken a back seat to the Super 12. So when you've got guys from Free State and Gauteng coming together, they still remember some of the old provincial wars and, unless you work hard together, the divisions can widen.

'Fortunately, in the Springbok set-up, we've been able to change the atmosphere and the players are starting to regain some of their old form. At practice over the last month I never mentioned Ireland or Wales or England – I always referred to the Tri-Nations. It was no good me saying you can't get away with that against Wales in Pretoria or England in Cape Town. So I kept dropping these allusions to Perth and to Wellington, telling them how much sharper they will have to be to prevail against Australia and New Zealand . . .'

While the All Blacks had beaten England easily in Dunedin, they had struggled for almost an hour in Auckland – before they turned a 14–10 lead into a more expected 40–10 scoreline. Alarmed by that lacklustre first hour at Eden Park, the following week's *New Zealand Rugby News* printed a cover photograph of three of the All Blacks' tight-forwards, Ian Jones, Craig Dowd and Robin Brooke, with a curt headline: 'Axe Won't Fall, But Heat Is On . . .'

The former All Black, Wayne Shelford, went further. 'Due to the high skill level and fast pace that has been exhibited by most sides in the Super 12,' he explained, 'it is not uncommon for teams to keep hold of the ball for long periods of time and attempt to run their opponents ragged. But it can't be used as an excuse for running out of puff. The reality remains that experienced "older" guys like Craig Dowd, Olo Brown, Robin Brooke and Michael Jones are taking longer to recover from the strain of their busy playing-schedule than some of their younger rivals . . . the scary thing for a couple of the senior All Blacks is that we're only a third of the way through the season and some of them are looking knackered already. The prospect of all our tight-forwards lasting through to the end of next year's World Cup must be in question . . .'

For once, John Hart was under pressure. He recalled Michael Jones and Walter Little – 'fragile buggers', as Kevin Skinner had warned me in Auckland four months before. He also retained the old grinders in the tight. Then, it had seemed the right option. Although they'd struggle to hang on for 1999, Hart needed his most experienced survivors to compensate for the loss of Fitzpatrick, Brooke and Bunce. Those three, that hard and glittering trio which had caused us so much hurt over the years, were the subject of hopeful speculation in South Africa. Could any team, we wondered, even the mighty Blacks, overcome such a loss?

I still remembered how Mallett had said, at a time when the rest of us were running around describing the All Blacks as the 'Invincibles', that 'their greatest strength, their experience, could turn into their biggest weakness. I believe we now have the team to exploit that weakness. They can't get away from it. Their leading players are ageing fast . . .'

Seven months on, I wondered if he thought New Zealand could overcome the absence of their three core players.

Mallett nodded forcefully, as if could already see a moment when the Springboks might lead the All Blacks. 'I think we'll see the real effect when they're in a situation like they were last year at Ellis Park. Then, they were 23–7 down. And, with bloody Fitzy and Zinny there, and Bunce scoring those tries, they came back and won. Even at 23–7, those guys had that inner calm and unshakeable confidence which only comes with years of winning. They work on the principle that you have to score thirty-five points to win a Test. So, if after twenty minutes they've only scored six points, they retain their composure. They've still got an hour to score another thirty. And the All Blacks won that Test – 35–32.

'Then, I was just an interested spectator. But that result really bothered me. I felt that we had played our best rugby since isolation and yet we only scored two tries. They played badly and yet still scored four tries. I felt it underlined their psychological edge. We also kicked too much. To beat the All Blacks you have to retain the ball and keep attacking them. The best form of defence against them is keeping the ball in hand. When they knock it on, you have to keep it for the next ten minutes. You can control a game of rugby once you're ten or fifteen points up. If you get a penalty you aim for the corner flag and take the lineout. And you just keep on camping there, hammering away, wearing them down. If you'd kicked for posts instead you might have picked up three more points – but they'd have the ball back. And, suddenly, they're attacking you. But if you dominate possession, that's when the doubts will creep in. If they haven't got Fitzy or Zinny calming them, driving them, it might be different. We might see some cracks then.

'But, until we get in that situation, we have to assume that they'll be much the same side. I've noticed that all their Super 12 sides have that ability – when they've been down they've just shown this serene conviction that the points will eventually come. There's no question of panicking. It's New Zealand rugby's collective psyche – keep plugging away and the try-scoring moments will come.'

As Mallett stressed, South African rugby was more fragmented. 'We have so many reasons which keep us apart in this country. It sometimes feels as if we're being pulled apart by division. The political legacy still lingers. It will take years for apartheid's effects to disappear. We're not going to suddenly have ten black or coloured stars at international level. It is going to take time because, unfortunately, people are still having to overcome some massive disadvantages. But I've got no doubt that we will eventually have a truly representative team. We've set up what we call a Talent Identification Programme which will help us target thirty or forty younger players who we can work with extensively. You can't expect them to immediately play rugby at Super 12 and Tri-Nations level. We've got to work with these guys, help them with intensive training and weights programmes and the rest of it. We have two domestic competitions – the Vodacom Cup and the Currie Cup. We're at least getting coloured and black guys who're shining at that level – but the acid test for them will be the Super 12. If you can play at that level you're ready for Springbok rugby. And so, against Ireland and Wales, McNeil Hendricks came on and did pretty well. He scored a try and showed real potential . . .'

Hendricks and Chester Williams had overtaken Small on the wing. I knew that both men would have been pleased that, in my disappoint-ment for Small, they had just become two more of his worryingly competitive Springbok rivals – rather than mere 'coloured representa-tives'. Mallett, of course, had to observe the political niceties more diligently. He had been careful to remove himself from the Luyt-fuelled crisis between Sarfu and the NSC.

'Look, I can compartmentalise the rugby politics. People were always putting me under pressure to make comments about the mood in the Springbok camp when there were threats of a boycott. But, in public, I always said, "No comment." I purposely stayed out of the in-fighting from the start. I said to all the administrators, "You stay out of my little rugby domain and I'll let you guys sort out your problems."

'I had enough on my plate improving the reputation of my Spring-boks both on and off the field – so I left the court battles to the politicians. I think, as a team, we've started to claw back some of the positive reaction we had when we won the World Cup. Certainly, in Europe, we got some terrific reviews from both the French and the

British media. We changed the perception of our players a little bit – and I've tried to do that by treating them as adults and not being dictatorial. And they've responded magnificently. But, sure, it's helped that we're making a fresh start. Under Louis Luyt there's no doubt that our reputation was badly tarnished. So it's up to us to improve on that – by winning and by being open and relaxed in public.'

Mallett, as a gregarious English-speaking coach, with his easy mastery of French and Italian, had done much to smash the traditionally dour Springbok mould. As friendly as I was with Nelie Smith, Mallett shone much more brightly in modern rugby's increasingly sophisticated world. Smith also lacked Mallett's political credibility. Earlier that week I'd visited *Oom* (Uncle) Nelie in Port Elizabeth. It was, as ever, great to see him – and we spent a few gentle hours reminiscing about Ballymena and looking forward to a season where he would rejuvenate the fortunes of Eastern Province in the Currie Cup. Yet he startled me when I asked who would succeed him in Ballymena.

'Ah, Don,' Nelie said softly and evenly, 'I asked Andre Bester to take over . . .'

I'm not sure how I did it, but I nodded impassively – despite the whirling inside. I thought of Bester and his taping of Andre Markgraaff's 'kaffir' invective, which had been at the source of the government investigation that had brought down Louis Luyt.

'*Ja*,' Nelie mused, 'Andre was my captain for Griquas against the All Blacks in 1996 . . .'

Nelie, naturally, thought in terms of rugby rather than any wider ideology. I tried to open up a small debate by suggesting that 'Markgraaff won't be too happy that Bester's working in rugby again . . .'

Nelie smiled. 'I suppose not. But I stay out of that completely. It's got nothing to do with me. I just think Andre can work well with my Ballymena pack . . .'

We returned to safer Irish ground for a while and then, as we walked towards my car, Nelie Smith recalled telling me in Ballymena 'that I have a plan to find the first black Springbok rugby player. I'm really going to try to implement that here in Port Elizabeth.'

I believed him, for I knew Nelie Smith would do almost anything to discover another Springbok, whatever his colour. I shook his hand warmly. 'I'll stay in touch, Nelie,' I promised – even though I would not be travelling to Ballymena to meet Andre Bester.

Nick Mallett shook his head in amazement. 'Bester! He's certainly not got the best reputation in South African rugby. But this whole

English-Afrikaans thing is interesting – y'know, I'm not unanimously liked here. When we played in Bloemfontein it almost felt as if we were playing overseas. There were quite a few shouts against me because, to some, I'm this wise-arse English guy. But it doesn't concern me that a few conservative Afrikaners would prefer one of the old-school coaches in my place. I'm focusing more on addressing the whole English-Afrikaans divide in Springbok rugby. It provides quite a unique mix – and it's not without its problems. It's clear to me that the guys who communicate best in my side are from an English background. Yet the Afrikaans guys are much more disciplined. They always train very well but they hate noise. If the English guys are shouting and whooping, the Afrikaans boys think it's been a bad practice. I'm having to explain to guys like Andre Snyman, who comes from the Northern Transvaal, which is quite an austere rugby province, that he must communicate and shout out moves. He's never been asked to do that before. Now, with the English boys, sometimes it gets too jokey and there's lots of noise but no inner discipline. It's anathema for most of our players to combine the two. They've been taught that if you laugh it's not serious. And then if you tell them to shut up they're too shit-scared to show any spontaneity. I'm trying to blend the best of both cultures. Slowly, it's coming.'

The Springboks had won all nine of their matches under Mallett. But with two games away in the Tri-Nations, within the space of eight days, I asked if he ever considered the first defeat. 'In any sequence of victories, one thing is guaranteed,' he said with his definitive assurance. 'You'll not remain unbeaten forever. It will come. But I'm confident I'll handle it. If you lose because of circumstances on the field, it's sad but acceptable. If you lose because of a situation off the field, that's when the players' confidence begins to erode.

'Now, to lift the Tri-Nations, we need to win three matches out of the four. We need to beat both the Wallabies and the All Blacks at home – and we've got to win either in Perth or Wellington. South Africans are very arrogant when it comes to rugby. They only really consider the All Blacks as our major rivals. They're always absolutely amazed when we lose to the Aussies – but Australia have been the only side to consistently stand up to New Zealand over the last ten years. I think it's a tremendous insult to the Australians from our public when they just dismiss them. The Wallabies have a great coach and the best back line in world rugby. They're really going to have a chance of winning this tournament – as well as the World Cup next year.

'But I firmly believe that it's harder to win the Tri-Nations than the

World Cup. To win the World Cup it's quite possible that you might only play one of the two other Tri-Nations teams. But in this tournament the three best sides in the world face each other twice, home and away, with all the travelling on top. It's incredibly taxing. So we've got to start with a win in Perth. I know Wellington is a very tall order. If there's a pissing rain and a howling wind . . . well, they're simply better than us in those conditions. But, elsewhere, I really think the Aussies and the Springboks are going to stretch the All Blacks. So far there've been two Tri-Nations tournaments and they've yet to lose a match. They won all four of their games both years. I'll be really surprised if they do that again . . .'

Durban, Wednesday, 12 August 1998
Memories of Pretoria, a year and a month before. Then, while the scrum machine was bent by the Black pack, Zinzan Brooke's voice echoed across the yellow grass. Each time, the eight would smash into the sighing cushions and, on the Zinzan cue, lower and heave. The hissing machine, carrying its young Afrikaans boys on top, would skid over shiny ground while Justin Marshall yelped, 'Keep it on, keep it on, keep it on!'

In Durban, Marshall's cry had not changed. At the back of the scrum, in Zinzan's place, Isitolo Maka bellowed and the push came, as sharp as the earlier hit had been hard. I stood a few feet away, and watched a drop of sweat fall from Josh Kronfeld's nose as they moved forward. Standing on the other side of the scrum, Ian Jones shouted, 'Good shove . . . good second shove . . .' as he clapped his hands. Craig Dowd, alongside him, was quiet, his face still reddened by their earlier exertions.

At last, they broke. Josh walked away first, adjusting his scrum-cap with a thoughtful fiddle. The others followed, four of them his team-mates from Otago – Maka, Taine Randell, Carl Hoeft and Anton Oliver, son of Hurricane Frank. Jones and Dowd looked on. They were out of the team and almost lost on the outside. Jones tried again. 'Well done!' he said simply. But he did not follow the new All Black pack as they walked another ten metres together. They stopped, drank from their bottles and gathered themselves for the next assault against the creaking contraption. There were only three days left to the next Test – and everything had changed.

The last time New Zealand had met South Africa at King's Park, the Springboks were on the brink of turmoil. It had been Gary Teichmann's first Test as captain – in place of Francois Pienaar. The All Blacks won that day, the second of their four victories over the Springboks in 1996. Teichmann, despite those Black defeats, and losing to the Lions, had led South Africa in every single international since then. He was about to equal Pienaar's record of twenty-nine Tests as Springbok captain. Teichmann's position at the head of his team was more secure than it had ever been.

New Zealand, however, were in the midst of cataclysmic upheaval. Three forwards remained from that 1996 team – Kronfeld, Robin Brooke and Olo Brown. Only Kronfeld was assured of his place in the 1998 side, for it had been a disastrous Tri-Nations tournament for New Zealand.

They had lost only one match in the previous two years – a meaningless last game out of five at Ellis Park in 1996. Yet, in the space of four Saturdays, from 11 July to 1 August 1998, the All Blacks were defeated in three consecutive matches. Australia beat them twice, first in Melbourne, when Matthew Burke scored all their points in a 24–16 win and then, far more damagingly, in Christchurch. The 27–23 margin could not obscure the harsh truth. A hapless New Zealand had been crushed by John Eales's outstanding Australia. With less than five minutes left, the Wallabies had led 27–9. Two converted tries from Cullen and Lomu restored a misleading veneer of parity. The All Blacks were humiliated in the tight and, without the concussed Kronfeld, outfought in the loose. Australia showed the kind of superior ball retention and driving play which, only months before, appeared the preserve of New Zealand. Ian Jones and Dowd were dropped – while Michael Jones, Walter Little and Mark Carter, none of whom made the squad to Durban, all seemed to have played their last Test.

In between mishap and disaster, there had been further catastrophe for John Hart in Wellington on 25 July. For the first time in seventeen years, since Nelie Smith's beleaguered Springboks in 1981, South Africa won a Test match in New Zealand. In a typically gruelling contest, South Africa's 6–3 lead was only widened ten minutes from the end. Joost van der Westhuizen darted for the line, as if anticipating a return pass. The All Blacks followed but Henry Honiball held on to the ball and then turned, to set up Pieter Rossouw on the outside. Ten metres from the line, Rossouw sailed through open space to score under the posts. New Zealand 3, South Africa 13.

The week before, Perth had been as miserable as Wellington would be oddly sunny. The rain and cold ruined the Australian spectacle – but we were transfixed by the gruesome tension as, in the last five minutes, both the Springboks and the Wallabies almost scored from a jangling chain of five-metre scrums at opposite ends of the field. Both defences held. Australia 13, South Africa 14.

In Durban, it was still hard to fathom. While the All Blacks watched enviously, Test rugby's most significant annual championship would be decided the following week at Ellis Park between the Springboks and the Wallabies. The tangled reasons were clearing. Nick Mallett and Rod Macqueen had transformed South Africa and Australia. The forlorn discord of 1997 had been replaced by methodical planning and bright conviction. If the Australians boasted the most dynamic back line in world rugby, the Springboks countered with an apparently impregnable defence. They also combined far more coherently than a New Zealand team knotted by doubt. As the season turned and the old order changed, the Springboks and the Wallabies appeared the most seamless sides in world rugby – a fact which would have been derided as fantasy exactly a year before.

Ever since Fred Allen's 1949 side lost a series in South Africa 4–0, the All Blacks had almost always followed a defeat with a furiously imposing performance. But, in the 1998 Tri-Nations, they lacked leadership both on and off the field. John Hart looked fretful and erratic while Randell, a captain at twenty-three, needed at least another year to grow into the role. It had taken Teichmann a full season to develop as a Test captain – and Randell looked as if he would have to wait a little longer for maturity. He'd also not been helped by Hart's decision to play him at eighth-man, with Michael Jones in his preferred number 6 shirt.

But, after Christchurch, Hart had been forced by an irate public to remodel his pack. The creaking Auckland foundation was ripped up – and in came Hoeft, Maka and, from Waikato, the young lock Royce Willis, who had made only nine NPC appearances, mostly as a substitute, before he'd been drafted to the Blues for the 1998 Super 12.

On their bumpy Durban training pitch, the three new boys veered in for one more tilt at the machine. Jones and Dowd again watched them walk past. As difficult as it had been for Fitzpatrick and Brooke to retire, theirs seemed a more private and less hurtful fate.

As his old partner Robin Brooke linked up with the strapping Willis, Jones chewed on the right corner of his lower lip. And, then, as the All Blacks crouched without him, he clapped his hands lightly and said, almost to himself, 'C'mon . . .'

An hour later, after the forwards had rejoined the backs and gone through the usual tackling and passing drills, looking as ardent as ever as

Hart yelled, 'Urgency . . . urgency!', Josh Kronfeld ambled over to see me with a more leisurely gait. He was still a little apart from the rest.

'This is our last one, Josh,' I consoled him as he sat down for yet another interview with me.

'Aw,' he grinned, 'it's been no drama, Donald. I've enjoyed it . . .'

'It feels a little bit different here than last year, though,' I suggested.

'Yeah,' he nodded. 'Strange how it's turned out this season . . .'

'Back in Dunedin, you said it might be interesting . . .'

'I did. But I didn't really want it to be *this* interesting! I think everybody's expectations were higher than they should have been. They weren't justified. Y'know, after Australia had put their seventy-six points on England, it gave a bit of a false picture. We were supposed to, so people thought, just go out there and post sixty points without even thinking. Without Fitzy and Zinny and Frank Bunce we were so keen to do well and carry on the good work that we didn't really concentrate on what we needed to do. The basics went awry and we tried to score points off almost everything. I think we started to try and win our matches in the first ten or twenty minutes – when they're more often won in the last twenty. And, after the loss in Melbourne, there's been more pressure.'

'How's the whole country absorbing the shock?'

'They've been pretty good, actually. They've said, "Aw, well, we had to lose some time – and better the year before the World Cup . . ." They've also been pretty fair to me. I had a great Super 12 and I've been doing okay in the Tests – apart from getting concussed against the Springboks when the big lock, Otto, barrelled into me and left a bruise the size of Africa on the side of my head. I think there's also a real understanding in New Zealand that the Aussies and the South Africans are just so much better this year. The Wallabies are really keyed-in and, in terms of skills and dynamics, they're probably just ahead. But I wouldn't back against the Springboks when they meet Australia. The South Africans really put their mark on the game – and, defensively, they're very tough. So that's a tight call.'

Knowing that, after Durban, New Zealand had one more international to play in '98, in Sydney, in the last Bledisloe Cup match, I asked Josh the seemingly impossible – was it conceivable that the All Blacks might lose five matches in a row?

'Well!' he exclaimed softly. 'That's something I haven't even contemplated. But we're already homing in on 1999 – we've got another Super 12, then two Tests against France and then five more matches against

Australia and South Africa again. Those are the four main contenders for the World Cup – so next year's going to be pretty hot. But, you know, I still think we might win on Saturday . . .'

Two days later, on the Friday morning, Gary Teichmann could not quite believe it. '*Ja*,' he said as his fingers ran doubtfully around the edge of his chin, 'I have to remind myself it's true. Two weeks ago I supported the All Blacks . . .'

Teichmann trailed away in mock despair. 'It was very hard to shout for those guys after all the pain we've had against them. But I wanted them to win. Because an All Black victory would have given us the chance to clinch the Tri-Nations by beating them tomorrow . . .'

'At your home ground . . .' I said.

'Where I've still to win a Test,' Teichmann echoed. 'I've captained South Africa twice at Kings Park – and we lost to the All Blacks and then to the Lions . . .'

But, since Nick Mallett, Teichmann had yet to explain the reasons for a defeat. He was also in the midst of his best season, as his peerless form in the Super 12 was followed by a triumphant Tri-Nations. Teichmann was also driven by the knowledge that his finest moments in a Springbok jersey had happened elsewhere in the world – in Paris, London, Edinburgh, Perth and Wellington. Only the ninety-six points in Pretoria compared, and even they were clouded by the more abject failure of Wales.

'We really need to win both of these two – the All Blacks in Durban and, next week, the Wallabies at Ellis Park. Then, I think, we can say that we're a good side.'

'Have the Australians become more difficult to play than the All Blacks?'

'I always find New Zealand very hard,' he sighed. 'Physically, they're so tough – you always know you're going to feel it the next morning after you've played them. They try to dominate you. Australia are difficult to play in other ways. They've become very organised under Rod Macqueen. They stick to their packed defence but, as soon as you go to ground, they move out in this fan. Two or three might be on the ground but the rest of them are spread in defence. So they're hard to break down. It's almost better to take a scrum because at least it will keep eight of their guys bound for a while longer. But the All Blacks have so much individual flair on top of their physical style. If you give them half a yard, Cullen, Lomu and Wilson can rip you apart. You can never ease up against New Zealand . . .'

'Although there seemed to be real cracks in Christchurch . . .'

'I was very surprised. I thought they'd win that game. I couldn't believe they'd lose three on the trot. But you saw then how much they need Kronfeld. He was missing against Australia and they were just not the same team. He makes a huge amount of difference to them because he gets through so much work. Whenever the ball's loose against New Zealand you know that you'll look up and see Kronfeld. But I noticed something the week before, when we beat them in Wellington. It was very close and they'd had a lot of the ball. And then, when we scored that try with ten minutes to go, I saw a lot of All Black heads go down. It was so unusual – because you just know that if *okes* [guys] like Fitzpatrick and Brooke had been there it would have never happened. Those guys never thought they'd lose. They'd just come back at you – especially at 13–3 with ten minutes to go. In Wellington we had absorbed so much pressure and yet they hadn't split our defence. They'd toiled away so hard but they'd got nothing. So when suddenly we scored, it was too much for them.'

We paused before I asked the one word question which mattered most to both of us: 'Tomorrow?'

'They're going to be more motivated than they've been in years. They will not want to lose all four Tri-Nations matches. It's going to be very close, and very hard – again. Beyond that, anything could happen . . .'

'But Gary . . .' I murmured, as we looked out at the grey sky which had settled over Durban's North Coast. 'I need a happy ending . . .'

King's Park, Durban, Saturday, 15 August 1998

Down to the black, and down to the green. It would always end this way.

New Zealand ran out first, their shirts billowing in the breeze. They turned away to the right, all twenty-two of them in yet one more concession to modern rugby. Even the All Blacks had become more than fifteen men. The seven substitutes, including Ian Jones and Craig Dowd, shook their legs and flexed their necks as if the call could come at any time. Josh Kronfeld sat in the middle of his half of the field, his right leg stretched out in front of him. He began to bend and twist, contorting himself into a variety of positions. He was, as usual, already dreaming of the open-side. Twenty feet away, the remaining seven members of the All Black pack had joined together in a close circle. They linked their arms just as the noise of 52,000 voices rose and reverberated against the four coloured walls of crowd.

Gary Teichmann walked to the head of the tunnel. He must have felt a sudden blast of heat as he began his run. A fattened roar sizzled and spat around the King's Park bowl. Teichmann turned to the left. I remembered him running out much harder the year before, against the Lions. But, after a dozen straight Test wins, eleven of them with Mallett, Teichmann had his composure. The All Blacks, inevitably, stood between him and lucky thirteen.

Kronfeld had joined his boys and, together, they trotted towards us in the main stand. The black rank formed and, fifteen feet along, Teichmann stood straight at the start of the green line. My eye moved slowly down the long black queue, lingering a little on Jonah Lomu and Christian Cullen as if they might suddenly wink. Mark Mayerhofler, the new All Black centre, was one of the few who did not sing. His set his face in a sombre mask, as if he were readying himself for the Springbok crushers, Muller and Snyman. Josh stood next to him. His head was covered by the black cap. He lifted it towards the blazing lights of the stadium. His eyes were closed as he sang. His mouth opened wide and the words to *God Defend New Zealand* fell from him as if, for that brief minute, he was rugby's answer to Howlin' Wolf.

I knew Gary Teichmann was less of a bluesy belter – but I would have looked down anyway. The opening came and, as much as I hid it, slipping behind my own mask, it really did mean home. I remembered a time, fourteen years before, in 1984. *Nkosi Sikelel'i Afrika* was still banned. It was then that I'd first heard it sung by thousands of voices. It was different to those earlier times, at university when, after bad protest plays or polemical diatribes, the groovy students had tried to sing it – but forty or fifty voices meant less, especially when we on the white side never really knew the words. I'd never sung with the others, mainly because I only knew the first line *'Nkosi Sikelel'i Afrika'* (God Bless Africa). But, also, I never felt I belonged – I was not black and I was also not to be about to put my white fist in the air as if I was a part of the struggle. Yet that day came in 1984 when, in Soweto, as my pal Shortie and I reeled out of a shebeen on a dusty afternoon, we saw the massed crowd and heard the singing. They made a sound which, in that moment, I thought was the most beautiful thing I had ever heard.

In a rugby stadium, it would never be the same. But it still tugged at me and I thought, in a blurring rush, of Nelie Smith and James Small, and everything that had happened between their Springbok days. And then we were into *Die Stem*. King's Park's more gracefully muted chorusing was swept away by a collective booming.

Only the *Haka* remained. The Springboks, clutching each other's shirts, faced it. Taine Randell began to cry out the ancient words. It was a fantastic *Haka*, the slaps on the thighs and shouts of death ringing out rhythmically above the noise. We watched Lomu, as his giant frame shuddered during the chanting and the gesturing. It was only near the end, as if the crowd sensed the gravity of another All Black challenge, that King's Park erupted with the '*Ole, Ole-Ole-Ole!*' stand-by. But, by then, except for Randell and Kronfeld, the black shirts were flying through their final leap.

Honiball kicked high into the swirling wind. After a minute, van der Westhuizen used his own left boot and went for his favourite dink, the ball arcing over Lomu's head, making him turn as Erasmus closed and forced him into touch, deep into the Black twenty-two. Andrews won the first line-out. After Erasmus's charge had been diverted, van der Westhuizen allowed his back line an early run. Snyman's pass was long, and it found Montgomery just as Eroni Clarke came hurtling from the dark side. He hit Monty at speed but, like a car smashing into a wall, Clarke crumpled. Montgomery stayed on his feet and managed a two-handed basketball feed. Terblanche scooped it up and flowed down the wing. He brushed aside Cullen and then Marshall. Terblanche dived in the corner for his eighth try in his seventh Test. Two minutes on the clock, 5–0 to South Africa.

New Zealand, finding the old calm inside the black shirt, came back strongly. After seven minutes, a confident delivery down a snappy black line arrived at the Lomu express. Big Jonah tore down the left touchline. He was too quick for Venter and too strong for Montgomery. As if he was back in his World Cup mood of '95, Lomu ran over the top of Percy and even held off Erasmus so that he could pop the ball up for Marshall. The scrum-half did not even bother to use his hands. He just booted it ahead and, over the touchline, fell on top of it in a delighted kill.

A quarter of an hour later, Maka again blew the locks off the previously safe Springbok defence. He exploded through the hole and waited for Randell to come through on the burst. It was a simple try under the posts for the beaming young Kiwi captain.

17–5 at half-time. The 'we always lose at King's Park' wail had already begun in the local press-room. The New Zealand writers grunted more purposefully – they were back in familiar territory.

Andrew Mehrtens was similarly at ease in the opening quarter of the second half. He landed another couple of penalties, the first of which was a wide-angled monster which he kicked from near the halfway touch-line. South Africa 5, New Zealand 23. John Hart strode up and down the touchline, a steely spring suddenly in the heel of each shoe.

The All Blacks lost the rampaging Maka. He had to be helped from the field as the blood poured from his shattered nose. Without Fitzpatrick and Brooke to guide them, New Zealand decided to defend their lead. They would stretch themselves across the eighteen-point bridge. There were, after all, only thirteen minutes left.

Penalty to South Africa and, true to Mallett, Teichmann called up Honiball. The number 10 aimed for the corner. Line-out to South Africa. James Dalton arrowed it to Teichmann at the back. As the ruck formed, Dalton came round to the front. The ball was shovelled to him and, leaning against the green wall, he offered it surreptitiously to Joost van der Westhuizen – as if it was the second-last cookie in the tin. Van der Westhuizen, ravenous as ever, devoured it. He took the sweetest little gap and raced over. Montgomery converted. 23–12.

Mallett, meanwhile, rotated his Springboks constantly. The fresh and the new men bolstered the Springboks – even in the front row where Ollie le Roux steadied the sinking pack after, all evening, Garvey had been made to crawl along a splintered plank by the mutinous Hoeft. But it was the more dashing Bobby Skinstad who scored the next try, after seventy-three minutes. The Springboks were only four points behind. King's Park palpitated, the fevered hiss of the crowd sounding like an endless gasp.

In injury-time, Terblanche chipped Lomu. It was too late. The huge number 11 could not stop his momentum. He crashed into Terblanche. Penalty to South Africa. Once more, Teichmann pointed to the corner flag and, once more, Honiball kicked. Such moments were supposed to drag but, then, it happened so quickly. Up went Otto and down into the usual ruck. Dalton came in like scrum-half and then, as if remembering that he was more of a shifter than a player, he put his bald head down and charged. A heap of bodies, some in green and more in black, crashed over the line. The arm went up immediately. Try to the Springboks, try to Dalton. South Africa 24, New Zealand 23. It was all over.

My elation faded with a delicious lag. The third beer of the night kicked in and Durban began to gently glow. I still could not quite believe it. Nineteen points in twelve minutes. 24–23 at the death. A second straight Springbok victory over the All Blacks – and *their* fourth consecutive loss. If it was a green-and-gold dream, it was also the blackest nightmare.

I'd managed to curb my leaping and whooping in time to see Taine Randell walk from the field. Even in my euphoria, a little breath caught at the back of my throat. A look of terrible blankness had spread across his face, as if he needed to block the shock and the misery.

But, a couple of hours later, Randell stood up and spoke, with some grace, at the after-match function. He even smiled and made a little joke. Sean Fitzpatrick nodded his approval. I stood at the back of the room with Josh Kronfeld and, as Randell stepped down, we clinked our tins.

'Bad luck, again,' I said.

His eye was badly bruised and cut. He'd been in the wars again. 'Thanks, mate. We thought we had you for a while there . . .'

'So did I . . .'

Josh shook his head and reached out for another small sandwich. 'It's fucking hard sometimes. Y'know, I just didn't really get going out there. Not even in the first half. I didn't have a great game – and, then, to lose it like that . . .'

'Well, at least the travelling's almost over for the year,' I said, trying for some cheer.

'Yeah, only Sydney to go now. You'll be glad to be on your way too, hey?'

'Yeah, this is the last trip . . .'

'Till you come over to New Zealand again,' he said, 'for a holiday . . .'

'That'll be good . . .'

'Next year, mate – see you in Dunedin?'

'Sure . . .'

It felt good to have moved on from the game. The following morning, as part of John Hart and Nick Mallett's plan to forge an even closer relationship between the All Blacks and the Springboks, the two teams would play a friendlier game of golf. I knew Josh Kronfeld would probably have planned something different. 'What are you doing tomorrow, Josh – not the golf, I bet?'

'Nah,' he smiled. 'I might sneak down to the beach instead – maybe have a surf, y'know . . .'

Sean Fitzpatrick, however, was all set for the golf. He and John Hart would take on the Springboks' ace pairing of Teichmann and Mallett. Fitzpatrick was as charming as ever; even when, after a few minutes, I asked him if we could do one more snippet of an interview.

'You don't still want to talk to an old boy like me, do you?' he laughed.

'Course I do,' I said as I whipped out the little recorder.

'Just like old times, this,' Sean said, even though he must have spoken to a dozen reporters in the week and slipped in a couple of television interviews. 'But, yeah,' he said as we slid back into the usual routine, 'I really felt for the All Blacks today. I thought that they played very well for sixty minutes and the new boys, Royce Willis and especially Isitola Maka, were excellent. Maka made a huge difference. I think that's why Gary [Teichmann] was quiet in some periods of the game. He had to do a lot to keep a hold on Maka.'

'Did you think the course of the game changed when Maka went off?'

'Yeah, I think it did. He made some huge drives. The momentum flagged once he went. But it's good for the All Blacks in the long-term. We might have our back row for the World Cup now. Taine, Josh and Isitola. I thought Taine Randell, at number 6, had his best game since he became captain. After this defeat, I think he and the boys have had enough character-building to last them a lifetime. He's had a pretty lousy few months – a bit like I did when I first took over. And Teichmann had it rough in his first year. Nah, Taine's the right man. I've got no doubt about that . . .'

'It must been hard for you, today, watching in the stand, especially when the lead started to dwindle . . .'

'It's strange, you know. I think I miss the playing less than I thought I would. But it's the competitive streak that you never lose. And there's nothing quite like a Test between the Springboks and the All Blacks to get the juices flowing again. Yeah, I would've loved it. But, y'know, tomorrow, I've got a little competition to fill the gap. And I reckon we might just beat the Springboks – on the golf course . . .'

From one captain to another, I completed my round with Gary Teichmann. He grinned at me and put out his hand.

'So you're also happy?' he said as, with his left arm, he pulled his wife, Nicky, towards him.

'I'm very happy,' I confirmed. 'I got my ending. A last-minute try. A one-point win against the All Blacks. It couldn't be better . . .'

September in London. Summer, which had never really begun, was over. Another British rugby season was under way. In England, the champions, Newcastle, lost on the opening day – to Richmond, who had moved from their tiny ground in south-west London to a spanking new football stadium in Reading. It was all part of the ascending whirl of Premiership rugby – tempered only by the downward spiral of political turmoil as the clubs and the English RFU raged on.

The war had crossed the border, finally, and the Welsh and English unions claimed steadfast unity against the slippery entrepreneurs. Cardiff and Swansea had broken away from the Welsh League and, although their entry into the Premiership had been blocked, they'd arranged to play friendly matches every week against the English clubs. The fourteen Premiership sides had torn up the RFU fixture list and drawn up their own, which allowed two teams a week the necessary bye to meet either Swansea or Cardiff. Yet, without English participation in the 1998–99 European Cup, there was even less to compare with the steelier Super 12.

I, meanwhile, was still lost in a greenish haze. A week after Durban, the Springboks had shimmered again in Johannesburg, on a day when South Africa overwhelmed Australia 29–15 to win the Tri-Nations. In the end, there was less tension than against the All Blacks, such was the Springboks' supremacy – exemplified by the conclusive try which saw Bobby Skinstad cross the gold line with a sumptuous feint and dive. He stood up, with the ball in one hand, and stuck out his tongue. He let it hang, in deliriously wagging delight.

'It was an emphatic win,' Nick Mallett confirmed later. 'It's the best we've played so far. And I can say now, on 22 August 1998, South Africa are the best team in the world. And, looking at the last eleven months, I would say they have to be the greatest-ever Springbok team. If you look at the record books I don't think you will find a comparable achievement. They have beaten France away twice, England both overseas and here, and New Zealand and Australia both home and away. I don't think we can give enough credit to Gary Teichmann. It's staggering what he and his team have done.'

Teichmann, as ever, was unassuming. 'We've been at the bottom – and it's far better to be at the top. But John Eales and the Wallabies should not be too down. I remember how our dressing-room felt when we lost at Ellis Park, last year, to the All Blacks. We all know – the good times come and go . . .'

It was impossible, even then, to forget the All Blacks. Nick Mallett was 'delighted with our victories in France and Britain last year – but I always felt that we needed to beat New Zealand who were clearly the best team in the world at that stage. We needed this Tri-Nations and we needed to beat Australia and New Zealand. And we've done it. It's been a fantastic year. It's almost been too good to be true . . .'

For New Zealand, who lost again narrowly to Australia the following week in Sydney, for their fifth defeat in a bleak black row, it had been a terrible year. But we all knew a clearer truth. They would be back. The All Blacks had played the Springboks fifty-one times. There had been three draws. There were twenty-four victories for New Zealand, and twenty-four for South Africa.

The story would roll on – as it would inside me. For rugby would always be more than a game. It was not just a sport, or even a symbol. It was part of me. And after everything, after the long years of apartheid and isolation, the fleeting bliss of the World Cup and the Tri-Nations, rugby always came down to the old shadowy shirts, especially those in black and those in green and gold. Already, I had begun to yearn a little for the next time, the next time I would see them together.

Afterword

Three months later, despite being at opposite ends of the earth, they were still inseparable. The All Blacks were at home in New Zealand, recovering from a calamitous year, while the unbeaten Springboks kept grinding through Britain. But they were locked together by rugby history. Beyond their extraordinary parity after fifty-one Tests, proving that not even an odd number could split them, their rivalry hit a notably higher pitch of equality.

On 28 November 1998, in Dublin, South Africa beat Ireland to rack up their seventeenth successive Test victory – and so match the world record set by New Zealand almost thirty years before. While Fred Allen's All Blacks had built their triumphant stretch over four years, from 1965 to 1969, Nick Mallett's Springboks ripped through the same number of Tests in thirteen months. The South Africans had spent 1998 on a relentless conveyor-belt, travelling and playing brutally physical rugby week after week in cities as diverse as Pretoria and Sydney, Invercargill and Edinburgh. A Grand Slam tour of Britain at the end of an especially onerous year might have appealed to TV executives, the game's administrators and the rest of us watching in the stands – but to the Springboks it felt like four more long laps of torture.

After their summer of humiliation in the southern hemisphere, the home countries had also uncovered a fresh resolve to curb the weary South Africans. They were determined to close the wide oval gap which had opened up between the Tri-Nations and European rugby, a divide whose nightmarish symbols remained England's 76–0 loss to Australia and South Africa's 96–13 devastation of Wales five months before.

With the arrival of Graham Henry as their new coach, the Welsh Rugby Union had unleashed an optimistic poster campaign. It featured the surreal sight of an inspirational Henry surrounded by the red shirts giving voice to a hopeful hymn, *Guide Me O Thy Great Redeemer*. A few churchmen across Wales were outraged by the supposed blasphemy. In the old days, the rest of the country might also have taken offence at the suggestion that their rugby salvation depended on a New Zealander.

Graham Henry, however, did not look or sound much like a messiah. He had a rough-hewn, hang-dog face and a voice flattened by laconic acerbity. He appeared to be a man who had been around too long, and seen too much, to believe in fantasy – particularly on the rugby field. It was an unlikely thought, but if Henry had turned to acting rather than rugby he would not have been interested in any of the heroic roles. Instead, he would have been a casting-director's dream to play either an 'Ordinary Bloke' or a grander 'Everyman' in a gritty drama about real people taking a gamble with life. There were even moments in Cardiff when it sounded as if Henry had ended up bang in the middle of a David Mamet play as he growled through a long series of meaningful pauses.

'Nah . . .' he finally grunted when I asked him if he missed New Zealand and the Auckland Blues. 'Been there, done that. Got the fond memories. Sometimes, y'know, you just need something different . . .'

Just when it seemed as if Henry's staccato-speech was about to burst into a hard-bitten soliloquy, he broke off with the kind of rasping laugh a New York method-actor would kill for in his next audition. 'And, yeah, I've certainly got some new challenges and new horizons here . . .'

It seemed a typically downbeat Henry irony. Two months after he'd signed his £1,250,000 five-year contract with the Welsh board, a seething Kiwi public were calling for John Hart's slick All Black head. Henry was the only viable alternative and, with the NZRFU blocking the possibility of his early return from Cardiff, Hart survived.

But who could have guessed a few months before that the All Blacks would lose five consecutive Tests?

'I was as surprised as anyone,' Henry murmured. 'No one could have predicted it. They'd only lost one match in the previous two years.'

'If you had known how the season would turn out,' I asked, 'would you ever have left New Zealand for Wales?'

Henry gave me a knowing look, and then cracked open a dry chuckle. 'Don't know,' he said. 'Didn't have a crystal ball then. But I'm not thinking about the All Blacks now. I'm totally committed to Wales. Sure, it's a different environment but I'm enjoying myself. I just want our guys to play with a huge amount of pride. If they do that then I'm sure the Welsh people will support them.'

After his opening match in charge, the Welsh were confirmed believers in their Kiwi saviour. On 14 November, two weeks before the Springboks joined the All Blacks as the most successful Test team of all time, Wales came within a minute of breaking that streak. Andre Venter's desperately late try ensured a South African getaway, but a true measure of the progress Wales had made was seen in their desolation. Far from celebrating their resurgence, they lamented the loss for, under Henry, they knew that they should have held on for the victory such bold play had deserved.

After that epic, South Africa beat Scotland and Ireland more easily. Only England remained between them and that historic eighteenth, so encouraging an even more momentous anomaly – New Zealand rugby followers yearning for a home win at Twickenham on 5 December.

In the previous fortnight England had been hapless against Italy, scraping in on their muddied knees, and disappointing against Australia – losing by a point to an exhausted but resilient Wallaby team who had shown far more sparkle and force in dismantling France the week before. England had, therefore, failed to defeat a Tri-Nations team in eight attempts under Clive Woodward.

But, after a few disasters and displays of flakiness, Woodward was learning. He still resorted to the odd vague but bubbly slogan – from 'I'm taking no backward steps in how the team is trying to play' to 'the game-plan is that the way you play, the way you coach, has always got to be evolving and moving forward'. Yet his ramblings through a rugby text apparently rewritten by Dale Carnegie were countered by as many examples of lucidity and wit. He was, as Frank Keating wrote in *The Guardian*, 'a pleasant and talkative lad'.

John Mitchell, in comparison, was a brooding man. As the forwards' coach, the New Zealander had shaped an English pack in his own image. In recognising England's dependence on that strength, Woodward cast aside his earlier claims that he would create a team as expansive as any in world rugby. As they prepared for South Africa, the onus was once more on crushing forward power and defence.

Ironically, the Springboks moved closer towards an image centred around flair on the field and amiability off it. In Dublin, Bobby Skinstad reproduced another of those tongue-lolling breaks and magical side-steps which, combined with his cheery grin and boyish appeal, had made him the Springboks' most publicised player. His legion of fans in Cape Town, especially the panting parade of 'Bobby-Girls' who screamed his name incessantly, had long believed Skinstad was the sumptuously skilled future of world rugby. The British media suddenly spoke of him in similar terms.

It all seemed a long way from the dark days of 1969, and that terrible Springbok tour of Britain. In contrast, the 1998 South Africans were admired and even liked. In our house, at least, they scored further PR points with the confirmation that their amiable press-liaison officer, Alex Broun, a former Australian stand-up comedian and playwright, had once starred in *Neighbours* – as Kylie Minogue's first boyfriend. That soapy slice of history seemed definitive proof that the smartly ironic Boks of the late-'90s inhabited the same postmodern cultural whirlpool as the rest of us.

The Springboks' press-guide contained similar nuggets. Asked to name 'The People You Would Most Like To Meet', the South Africans produced an entertaining selection. James Dalton chose Mahatma Gandhi, Genghis Khan and J.F. Kennedy; Robbie Kempson picked Madonna and Mona Lisa; Gary Teichmann opted for Mike Tyson, Lady Di and Nostradamus; Johan Erasmus for Demi Moore, Nelson Mandela and Paul Gascoigne; Percy Montgomery for Isabella Rosselini and Michael Jordan; while the burger-munching Ollie le Roux side-stepped the obvious choice of Ronald McDonald and went for a trio consisting of Albert Einstein, Jim Morrison and Jesus Christ.

Their listed ways of preparing for 'a big match' were only slightly less surreal. 'Sleep in, don't eat . . .' Skinstad suggested. 'Listen to music while eating fruit salad,' countered Andre Snyman, while Percy Montgomery produced a culinary variation by admitting that he 'listened to music while biting my fingernails'. Further advice from the new breed of Springbok rugby athlete came from Adrian Garvey, who explained that the modern front-row forward should 'think of the game while dozing'. His fellow props had similarly novel ways of steeling both mind and body before a Test. Ollie le Roux liked to 'focus from Tuesday, and watch videos featuring big tackles', while Robbie Kempson preferred to 'listen to Vivaldi, Beethoven and Verdi'.

A Wagnerian soundtrack would have been more suitable for their match against England, but the shattered South Africans looked as if they had eaten too many of their own fingernails while dozing through *The Four Seasons*, a dangerous reminder of how long they had been on the road throughout 1998. They began brightly with a Pieter Rossouw try but, slowly, the English forwards strangled them. The mistakes multiplied, the penalties to England piled up and the previously impregnable green wall cracked.

England were less than dazzling but, at last, they resembled a team strong enough to beat the best in the world. Compared to the side which had twice defeated both the All Blacks and the Australians only a few months before, South Africa were poor – but England were entitled to a form of ecstasy to match the efficiency of their 13–7 win.

Rugby was changing again, just as the seasons turned. The imbalance of power was shifting and, as the chasm between the north and the south narrowed, the old international appeal of rugby intensified. But, in that more private and unyielding battle at the bottom of the world, the score from Twickenham held a deeper significance.

South Africa had failed to win their eighteenth straight Test; and it was hard to believe that any other side would surpass that record. As always, the All Blacks and the Springboks were bracketed together – and now, perhaps forever, on that same number of seventeen.

Paris, January 1999

'In French rugby, right now, there is pessimism and dread,' murmured Richard Escot, the rugby editor of *L'Equipe*, a month before the last-ever Five Nations. Paris was covered in snow, and it was freezing on the streets outside. The city looked forlorn but beautiful; yet it sounded as if *Les Bleus* were lost in a more desolate French winter.

World rugby was still skating across the icy surface of change laid down by professionalism. For every new law or tactical approach on the field, there appeared to be an accompanying dispute over television money or the introduction of a different competition. In February 2000, with the arrival of Italy, the Six Nations would replace the world's oldest rugby tournament. But some of the game's more basic truths could not be altered. Like the ancient South African and New Zealand rivalry, French rugby's volatility represented an irreducible constancy.

'There is no unity in our game,' Escot explained. 'French rugby has been dislocated before but, in the old days, in the amateur years, it did not matter so much. But in modern rugby, especially in a World Cup year, you cannot easily accept these problems. Of course there is still a chance, a little flame of hope, that I might be wrong. But I don't think so. It feels like we are facing a helluva mess . . .'

Despite successive Grand Slams, France's failure at home against South Africa and Australia in 1997 and 1998 had induced widespread, if privately spoken, scepticism of both Pierre Villepreux's and Jean-Claude Skrela's tactical acumen and assessment of players. There were particular doubts about their pursuit of pace over power amongst the backs and their choice of Raphael Ibanez as captain. Yet, while whispers against Villepreux and Skrela were common within the clubs themselves, the French media had remained strangely silent.

'After France won the football World Cup,' Escot suggested, 'we had to cool down as journalists. You have to remember the criticism all the newspapers gave to Aimé Jacquet [France's football manager]. It was very strong. Reporters all over France wrote that he was taking the team in the wrong direction. And what happens? France become world champions. So now we are careful – because, even if journalists and coaches and players don't agree with Skrela and Villepreux, the public mood has changed.

'We are now expected to be more supportive. I have never felt this before in France. I think of Walter Spanghero and even Pierre Villepreux and Jo Maso [the French team manager] in the 1970s. If they wanted to criticise the strategy or the selection, they would do so. It was the same in the '80s with players like Pierre Berbizier and Serge Blanco – no one would try to shut them up. There was a freedom of spirit and expression then. Not now. In the professional game, no one wants to be quoted.

'So, for now, we have to keep quiet – even though many of the French players have said to me, off the record, that th0ey are astonished by the coach's selections. They're also not so happy with the style of rugby they are being asked to play for France. When they consider the year ahead, starting against Ireland in Dublin, they become very anxious.'

French paranoia had been amplified by a startling series of Gallic catastrophes in the European Cup. Without the English teams, engaged in their own sulky civil war, European club rugby had been reduced to a cross between a French romp and a Celtic farce. In the autumn of '98 I felt sympathy for Ulster, including many of my old boys from Ballymena, who had been drawn in the same group as the mighty Toulouse. The opening match of a lopsided tournament was grimly predictable – Toulouse steaming in with 108 points against doomed Ebbw Vale.

Gary Longwell, who'd been a particular favourite of Nelie Smith's at Ballymena, had locked the Ulster scrum since 1991. 'We had to play Toulouse the week after the Ebbw Vale match,' he remembered. 'It was very intimidating. The blaring horns and bands even drowned out the thunderstorm and, inside, there were French TV cameras in our changing-room. It was totally alien to us, because in Ulster we're not used to the big-time. But, after we'd lost 38–3, it felt as if we'd really let ourselves down. We were beaten even before we stepped onto the park. We didn't believe, then, that we could beat a side like Toulouse.'

But, in the most evocative story of another turbulent European season, Ulster then defeated Toulouse twice at Ravenhill in Belfast – 29–24 in the return group match and 15–13 in a fiery quarter-final. In mid-January, Ulster offered another bristling welcome to a glamour outfit from across the Channel – Stade Français.

As Longwell told me a few days before that semi-final: 'We know now that we can beat anyone at Ravenhill. We aim to get in amongst them, hit them with some really big tackles and never let them settle. If you get ahead of these French teams they can lose a wee bit of self-discipline. Ravenhill will be crammed, with 20,000 Ulster fans driving us on. Stade Français won't know what's hit them.'

In a pulsating game, Ulster fulfilled Longwell's stark prophecy and overwhelmed the starry Stade Français. A fortnight later, in the final at Lansdowne Road, they achieved an even more incredible feat – out-thinking and out-hustling a third French team, Perpignan. Ulster had won the European Cup, following Toulouse, Brive and Bath.

As Richard Escot confirmed, Ulster had also opened up the previously moderate cracks in France's professional rugby psyche. Ironically, the chasm that had existed in the 1980s between the playing styles of Villepreux's fluid Toulouse side and Jacques Fouroux's intensely physical France resembled that which separated the 1999 French team and clubs like Stade Français, Brive, Pau and Montferrand. The distinction remained that, under Villepreux and Skrela, France were asked to spread the ball wide as often as possible. The clubs, meanwhile, were committed to a far more direct approach.

From Paris I turned south, to hear Pierre Berbizier, Fouroux's successor as national coach, advocate the latter method in an increasingly bitter struggle for the soul of French rugby. Berbizier had led France to their only series win in New Zealand in 1994, and also inspired them to a World Cup semi-final the following year. His pragmatic discipline shone deep within those French milestones.

'We have good players in France,' Berbizier mused, 'but I don't know if we have a good strategy. Our backs are being told to play a game not suited to modern rugby. Power is the key today. Skrela and Villepreux know this but they want to speak about the old ideas of French flair instead. I don't think they deal with current reality.

'I had the same problem when I was coach. Wherever we played people would ask me the same questions: are France going to play with flair? But so often we make the show and the other team gets the result. They like to applaud our flair because it makes it easier for them to beat us. But the flair should only come after you have respected the basics. I believe in the spirit of winning – not the spirit of French flair.'

It said much for the affability of both Villepreux and Ibanez that they each listened patiently to my outline of the domestic criticism they could not muffle for much longer. 'But,' Villepreux argued, 'there will always be people who think we should adopt a different style. Pierre Berbizier was the coach for four years but the last World Cup was played under very different rules. We try to move into the present. We want to show a lot of fluidity. Yes, power is very important – but to play this type of southern-hemisphere game you need the right players. We believe we can beat the bigger teams if we anticipate very quickly.'

Villepreux was similarly confident about the quality of his pack, dismissing all criticism of Ibanez. 'I always had him in my mind as captain,' he revealed. 'Ibanez is a very honest player who has a great capacity to stick to our strategy. I think he will surprise his critics . . .'

Ibanez was charming enough to admit, 'We had a meeting with the whole team and the coaches after the Australia match. We talk about the mistakes – the first was that we lose our self-control. We did not find sufficient opportunities and so we forget our discipline . . .'

Ibanez laughed softly. 'It is hard for us. We are Latin people. It's always the same in France. We go up and we go down . . .'

If they had been up for most of the preceding few years, Richard Escot feared that France had once more crossed the downward path. 'Warren Gatland, Ireland's coach, gave an interview in *L'Equipe*,' Escot sighed. He said, "France can't hurt us. They won't hit us hard. It will not be the same as playing a southern-hemisphere team. If Ireland play well they can beat France." Our players read that and they felt uneasy. They also remembered the performances both Wales and England gave against South Africa. They know that they might lose to these sides.

'One of the players said to me, "It's going to be horrible if we lose in the Five Nations because then we face a terrifying tour – Samoa, New Zealand A and the All Blacks." He's right. It's not impossible for France to lose four matches before the World Cup. If that happens then, by June, we will have a big interrogation. But, now, we sit and wait – it's like a Hitchcock movie. There is a lot of suspense. Anything can happen . . .'

On 6 March 1999, the strangest and the wildest scoreline in recent Five Nations history glinted across the smoothly curving loop of the Stade de France. The blunt summary of an extraordinary game was told in French, but a clearer meaning was seen in the accompanying band of computerised digits. *France 33, Pays de Galles 34*. After an eighty-minute blur of staggering rugby, time had almost slipped away. France were on the breathless brink of losing to Wales in Paris for the first time in twenty-four years.

'We could not believe it,' Thomas Castaignède sighed. 'We never thought we might lose to Wales. Last year we played the Welsh away, at Wembley, and it was like a dream. Wales 0, France 51! Everything we did was sublime. Now, eleven months later, it is incredible. We have not lost a match in the Five Nations for so long but we are in danger. We are one point behind Wales and it is injury-time. And then, you know, we get that penalty . . .'

In the championship opener in Dublin, Castaignède had snaffled a dramatically late French lead with a serene penalty. His rival fly-half that afternoon, Ulster's David Humphreys, then had his own opportunity to win the match with a final swing of the boot. Humphreys missed. After an exhausting battle, Castaignède and France had their 10–9 victory – and Richard Escot's forecast of Hitchcock-like drama had been upheld. His more damning prediction of existential despair for *Les Bleus* was merely delayed.

As he prepared for another conclusive strike in Paris, Castaignède felt 'very calm . . . The kick should always go over. But, against Wales, and I don't know why, it went to the left. We had lost, and I had missed the last chance to save us.'

Although he'd kicked three penalties, two conversions and scored a try, his miss against Wales was the more lasting memory. 'I was so upset that for three nights after the match I could not sleep at all. I just lie there, seeing the game in my mind. Every night, we play very badly!'

The French were often typically graceful in attack against Wales. There were moments of astonishing blue guile – especially from Emile Ntamack, who scored a hat-trick of tries, and Castaignède himself, most notably when he slashed through the red line and slid out a wonderful little ruse of a reverse pass.

'We have the capacity to play this way,' Castaignède agreed, 'but we also have one main problem. It is the same struggle we always have in French rugby. Concentration! I don't know why we lose our concentration. Last year, when we won the Grand Slam again, I think that this team can bring together the fantasy and the rigour. But, this season, against Ireland, we did not show too much flair. And, against Wales, we lost the concentration. It's not good for us.'

Yet more French uncertainty, however, helped liberate the Five Nations from the moribund predictability of 1998. If that year had marked the tournament's nadir, with France and England able to register record scores against the bereft Celts, 1999's finale was as thrilling as any in history.

Gregor Townsend, who'd since moved to Brive, had promised as much even before the Welsh soared over Paris. 'The tournament is very tight,' he stressed. 'Most critics seemed to suggest early on that it would be between four countries – with Scotland nowhere. But whenever Scotland have a good year we've been written off at the start. So it suits us. I'm also sure that there won't be a Grand Slam for anyone this year. England and France are bound to lose at least a game each.'

After their narrow loss to France, Ireland were expected to be the team who would ruin England. The Irish tight five, inspired by Keith Wood, planned to break the English up front in Dublin – and yet the reverse happened.

At Lansdowne Road, we always knew it would not be pretty. We expected grinding attrition and furious defending, a match of steepling kicks and hard slabs of tackle, a boilerhouse battle of crashing front-rows and endangered full-backs. It was meant to be rugby in the raw, a real meat-on-the-bone stomach-churner – the kind of dark and low-scoring struggle which would complement the exuberant fizz seen earlier in St Denis.

While the rugby strained until the last minute, when Tim Rodber finally blasted his way clear for England's second try and a 27–15 win, the façade of tension was misleading. The compact English forwards had long before reduced the supposed green monster of a pack to a subdued shuffle. The heavy white roller pushed deep and hard across the flattened Irish field.

There were also some crunching white tackles. On three separate occasions Jonny Wilkinson cut down the bigger Irish forwards and backs with a variety of pop-eyed hits. He also kicked his every penalty and conversion with immaculate nerve.

The nineteen-year-old Wilkinson lent a youthful sheen to the brusque industry of his grizzled forwards. Yet, in attack, England only revealed flickers of creativity. Their ensuing victory over France, at Twickenham on 20 March, was hewn from a similar block of solid granite and steely kicking. There was scant sign of anything more dazzling in terms of either movement or tries scored.

England's forwards were relentlessly authoritative. The entire English defence was a similarly imposing line of organisation and bite. And Wilkinson landed every one of his seven penalties. Yet, frustratingly for England, their failure to score even a single try against the retreating French marred an otherwise comprehensive 21–10 victory.

The disconsolate French press raised a collective Gallic brow when Lawrence Dallaglio suggested that England had beaten 'a top-quality side'. 'We lost the ball too many times,' Jean-Claude Skrela countered, 'and we failed to put England under any consistent pressure. Our frustration is huge, although not quite as overwhelming as when we lost to Wales.'

Raphael Ibanez was as philosophical after an abject performance. 'We made too many mistakes and I told my team that we could not win when we gave away twenty penalties to England's nine. It was a logical result – for England competed with classic defence.'

Scotland, meanwhile, competed with classic flair. Their resurrection from Five Nations also-rans to, at least briefly, the most exciting team in Europe had its source in an enforced switch which, early in the second half against Wales, saw Townsend slip from inside-centre to stand-off to replace the injured Duncan Hodge. Within minutes, Townsend's brilliant interception and sixty-metre run, for a converted try, turned a tentative 13–8 deficit into a sudden lead. He soon caused more havoc amongst the red shirts when he cut away from a ruck and, after a ghostly feint, set up Alan Tait for a third try – which ensured a convincing 33–20 Scottish scoreline.

When I called him the following week in Brive, Townsend dryly noted 'the reappearance of so many believers. I'm pretty much used to them coming and going,' he said. 'Yeah, there were moments for me at Murrayfield, but I actually played far better the week before for Brive.

'But this is the first time in three seasons of club rugby that I've been a regular stand-off. That's helped tremendously. There were times last year at Northampton when I only played one out of every four or five matches at number 10. I feel so much happier at Brive – I've been given the chance to establish myself. I love to move the ball through my hands and out along the whole backline – y'know, the simple pleasure of just taking the ball and running and passing it. That's my kind of rugby . . .'

It matched the philosophy of Townsend's partners in central midfield – John Leslie, the newly capped New Zealander from the Otago Highlanders, and the returning Tait. I knew how inventive and dependable Leslie had been in Otago, for he was Josh Kronfeld's best friend in rugby, but his impact in Scotland was even more emphatic. He scored within the opening seconds of his début against Wales and, with Tait, was instrumental in guiding Scotland's try-scoring bravado at Twickenham. Townsend's prediction that England would lose at least one match was almost fulfilled then, during Scotland's cruel 24–21 loss.

Townsend, as against Wales and England, also scored a try when Ireland were shredded and crossed like emerald-green sprouts. He saw it as a delicious irony that, after such a difficult year in 1998, he was on the verge of becoming only the fifth player in history to score a try in every single match of a Five Nations championship – if he could also touch-down in Paris against his new Gallic colleagues.

Amid the harsh zeal of playing alongside Brive's Olivier Magne, Philippe Carbonneau, Christophe Lamaison and David Venditti, Townsend had flourished. The French championship is not a league for either the soft-hearted sentimentalist or the casual traveller. But the rigorous French terrain suited the deceptively resilient Scot.

'My game has evolved so much more in Brive,' he enthused. 'French rugby is hard and relentless, but the players' skill levels are much higher than in England. The length of passing and angles of running are superior. It's also more physical in France. There're a few more holes for you to break through but, when they come, the hits here are much bigger. So even my tackling has improved.'

But, even considering his own audacious form, a Scottish championship still appeared about as likely as the genial and thoughtful Townsend striking up an engaging friendship with his perpetually surly and aggressive half-back partner at Brive, France's incisive but occasionally vicious little scrum-half, Carbonneau.

'I know you won't believe this,' he laughed, 'but I'm a pretty good friend of Carbonneau. Most of the stuff that's written about him is true. He's tough and abrasive on the field. But, away from the rugby, he's very shy and quiet – he's a really nice guy! So, who knows? Maybe we're in for a few other shocks as well . . .'

The final weekend of the last-ever Five Nations provided the stage, with a schedule of matches shaped as much by modern television interests as old rugby traditions. While the usual early Saturday afternoon kick-off prevailed at the Stade de France, the conclusive match at Wembley was pushed back to the Sunday, on 11 April. In the end a money-driven decision escalated the rugby's more venerable drama.

Just as the All Blacks lost five matches on a gloomy roll, so *Les Bleus* suffered their own humiliation by slipping to their third straight defeat. On a glorious afternoon in Paris, Scotland were devastating – especially during a five-minute burst when they created three glittering and converted tries. Townsend's was one of them, so completing his championship quartet. Leslie and Tait also scored twice each as the Scots raced to their 36–22 victory.

A year before, Scotland had lost 52–16 at home to France – and Townsend had been ridiculed for his lack of passion. The change could not have been sweeter, and even the usually taciturn Jim Telfer agreed: 'It was unbelievable, the best I have ever seen Scotland play.'

Pierre Villepreux, instead, spoke more sorrowfully. 'In my head,' he wished aloud, 'I would like to cancel this year's Five Nations . . .'

A day later, Scotland watched with distant hope rather than tangible expectation that Wales might beat England and so help return the departing championship to Edinburgh. It seemed a routine if anxious encounter. Whenever the white lead shimmered, Neil Jenkins pulled Wales back with another of his six penalties or the conversion of Shane Howarth's lone try. After eighty minutes England led 31–25.

But, then, it all went horribly wrong for England. In the third minute of injury time, and close to the line, Scott Quinnell fed a short pass to Scott Gibbs who did not even have to reach for his typical battering charge. He was able to dance lightly through four English tackles. It happened so quickly that the white shirts slumped to the green turf in hasty disbelief.

A difficult conversion remained. But Neil Jenkins, who'd steered every one of his previous seven kicks through the middle of Wembley's towering white poles, was never going to miss. Wales 32, England 31. Scotland had won the Five Nations, and France had finished last.

Rugby was again as compelling as it was ever-changing. The Five Nations' return to equality and surprise was even more gratifying than Ulster's astonishing exploits at club level. While the French were the victims in both instances, they had suffered such agonies before and would do so again – in between bewitching us all over again.

Only a year before, in this same book, both Rob Howley and Gregor Townsend had marvelled at the French return after their 52–10 destruction by South Africa in November 1997. Neither of them believed then that either of their own teams would be able to reinvent themselves in such a way after the traumas of their 1998 tournament.

Yet the fabric of the European game had changed, especially in rugby's shifting seams of nationality. The Welsh had been saved by Graham Henry who, in turn, had introduced a former All Black, Shane Howarth, as his dashing new Welsh full-back and another New Zealander, Brett Sinkinson, as his open-side flank. Henry also picked an English-born South African, Peter Rogers, to bolster his front-row after a meek capitulation against the Scots and Irish.

Ireland and Scotland had done the same. In Dublin, Warren Gatland

and Andy Ward were former Kiwis, and Dion O'Cuinneagain an ex-South African. John and Martin Leslie, with Glenn Metcalfe and Shaun Longstaff, were the New Zealanders who had transformed the Scots. If some traditionalists lamented such mixing of patriotic identities, the rest of us welcomed the Celts' timely restoration. And, as a South African of distant Scottish descent, it was also convenient to remind my New Zealand friends that the All Blacks had been enticing players from Samoa, Tonga and Fiji for decades. More importantly, with the fourth World Cup only months away, the old game seemed more cosmopolitan and competitive than it had done for years.

London, Sunday, 23 May 1999

I read the news first in the *Sunday Times*. Stephen Jones, an equally staunch admirer of England's captain, was as shocked as I must have looked when peering blearily at the words he had written: 'Lawrence Dallaglio faces sporting ruin this morning after allegations that he has admitted to pushing drugs and also, in company with two colleagues, taken ecstasy and cocaine on the 1997 British Lions tour of South Africa. If these allegations are proven, Dallaglio will surely be dismissed from his post as England captain and from the England squad itself as it prepares for the World Cup in October.'

Reeling like a breathless centre who had just taken a huge hit from big Lol himself, I staggered out into a miserable London morning to pick up my own grubby copy of the *News of the World*. The front page was a screamer: 'England Rugby Captain Exposed As Drug Dealer'. Describing him as 'Pin-Up Dallaglio, 27, a father of two young children' and a 'six-foot four-inch sporting legend', the newspaper insisted that Dallaglio had 'confessed to astonished *News of the World* reporters that he had taken "acid", smoked marijuana and enjoyed drunken romps with vice girls', and that he 'made big, big money from dealing in drugs'.

The tabloid confessional ran on and on, wrapping round the first five pages of that saucy edition. While I recognised the damage the drug story had done to his rugby career, I was far more stunned by the fact that Dallaglio had actually made his 'confession' on tape. The man I knew was scrupulously determined to avoid controversy.

On one of these earlier pages, and with a now raw and unknowing irony, I wrote that 'Dallaglio's sole concern, that Alice [his partner] would be subjected to tabloid scrutiny because of his shock-horror status as an "unmarried father" and England rugby captain, had already disappeared. He was not about to be dictated to by anyone.'

I also noted Dallaglio's emulation of Sean Fitzpatrick: 'Even though he was nine years younger, Dallaglio had that rare presence which allowed him to match his All Black counterpart . . . I had already watched a few English press conferences where Dallaglio waxed politely, without giving away any snippet of consequence. It was another Fitzpatrick art.'

The idea, then, that Dallaglio would 'reveal all' to two strangers seemed inconceivable. The 'drunken romps' and recreational use of drugs could be held at a distance from the hysteria peddled by the tabloids. It was far more baffling that Dallaglio appeared to have lost temporary use of his considerable faculties and had blurted out reams of the quotable fodder which fed the *News of the World*'s insatiable appetite for celebrity-driven scandal.

The following day, Dallaglio was forced to announce his resignation as England captain and admit: 'This was an elaborate set-up by the *News of the World* to which I naïvely fell victim.' But he also suggested that the claims against him were 'a complete fabrication'. This enabled sympathetic newspapers to run headlines like 'Dallaglio: I Deny Everything' – yet it was already accepted by his supporters that he had contributed hugely to his own downfall.

On the Tuesday morning, at an excruciating press conference, Dallaglio explained that he had been led to believe that the two reporters, a man and a woman, were representatives of Gillette. They had requested a meeting with him to discuss a substantial promotional deal. Dallaglio never quite got round to clarifying how he thought he might secure a contract with a multinational conglomerate by stressing how cool he was when it came to discussing drugs or prostitution. But he did concede that he had boasted of past escapades in an effort to impress the pair while they drank champagne in his hotel room.

'I did lie during the course of the discussions with the reporters,' Dallaglio confirmed, 'and I can give you no sensible justification for doing it. I feel totally humiliated in having to acknowledge that now. However, I have not lied to my family, to the RFU, or Wasps, and I will not lie to you today. I have been foolish and naïve and I will always regret the effect this has had on everyone.'

Dallaglio's voice quavered as he neared the end of his statement. 'Rugby has given me everything in my life. You simply cannot operate at this level if drugs are part of your life. I will throw all my efforts at rebuilding everyone's confidence in me both as a player and as a person.'

I felt only sympathy for Dallaglio and the suffering he had caused his own family through that rare burst of immaturity. As he knew then, whatever the outcome of the RFU's inquiry into the deceit or veracity of his own claims, his life would never be the same again.

I remembered how happy he had always looked whenever I'd seen him in the months following this book's writing. He was the first player I met again to give him his own copy, on a hazy late-summer evening in September when Alison and I went to his old flat in Ladbroke Grove. Six weeks later, in a more official capacity at a Knightsbridge hotel, he was in full captaincy mode as he looked ahead to the imminent arrival of the Australians and the South Africans. I marvelled again at how much rugby meant to him. And when I next saw him, at Twickenham during the Five Nations, he forced me to relive England's defeat of my beloved Springboks. But, after that bantering torture, he made me laugh again. Lawrence Dallaglio, it seemed then, had everything.

A few hours after absorbing the impact of that *News of the World* 'investigation', James Small made his last appearance at Twickenham – for the Barbarians, who also included Andre Joubert, Walter Little, Thomas Castaignède, Os du Randt, Abdelatif Benazzi, Francois Pienaar and Zinzan Brooke in a dream-like line-up. My mood lightened as Small ran in one of the Barbarians' nine tries in a 55–33 thrashing of the new English Premiership champions, Leicester. It was one of rugby's more honeyed afternoons as old Springboks, All Blacks and *Tricolores* reminded the northern hemisphere's most powerful club there were still lessons to be learned from rugby's masters.

On the brink of retirement, Small felt relieved to have finally turned the last corner of his long and winding career. He had just become engaged to his girlfriend, Christina, and it was time to step away from the game which had defined him for so long. In the week before that Twickenham finale, both for Small and yet another English season, he'd been exuberant. 'I can't believe it,' he said when three days of rain finally ended, 'I've seen sunshine in London for the first time in my life . . .'

He had tried desperately hard to illuminate his Springbok prospects at the outset of the South African season. Small trained for the Super 12 with a purpose he had not felt in years. In the opening game, he showed much of his former drive and scored a try in a big win for the Cats over the ACT Brumbies. But, in the very next match, against New South Wales, he tore his groin. By then, he knew the truth.

After Twickenham he returned home and, on 24 June, announced his retirement in Johannesburg. As Small sighed, 'The thought of having to go through another eight weeks of rehabilitation, while putting in the same amount of hard work just to get back to where I was for the ACT game, made me look very carefully at my future. Rugby has been so good to me and there have been more ups than downs. Maybe I was too much of an individualist in a team game. But you grow and learn and I'll take those lessons into my future . . .'

Away from the Five Nations, newspaper 'honey-traps' and life-changing decisions, rugby whirred around the southern hemisphere. The Super 12 had begun with its typical law-changes, public controversy and playing confusion during an uncertain opening month. But, as in 1998, the rugby soon settled and once again offered an ardent weekly display of speed and power across the three countries.

But there were more problems for individual teams. The decline of Auckland, struggling in their first year without Graham Henry, was matched by the annual collapse of three South African sides – the perennial no-hopers, the Bulls, the Cats and, more unexpectedly, Gary Teichmann's Sharks. Teichmann and Henry Honiball struggled with injury throughout the tournament and, without the kind of compelling form or consistency of appearance they had shown in 1998, the Sharks just missed out on their usual semi-final appearance. South African hopes, instead, were carried by Bobby Skinstad's Stormers, who played some great rugby – only to lose momentum when Skinstad was injured in a car accident.

They still finished second in the league, behind the Queensland Reds, whose continuing rise was made even more impressive by the absence of another injured star, John Eales. The progress of the Reds and the New South Wales Warratahs provided sufficient evidence that Australia would have a compelling claim to the World Cup.

And then, as always in the Super 12, there were the New Zealanders. Like the Auckland Blues, the Chiefs and the Hurricanes, even the Canterbury Crusaders struggled with inconsistency – with the Crusaders needing to win matches in South Africa to ensure their fourth-place finish. Only the Otago Highlanders, especially in the form of the irrepressible Josh Kronfeld, Jeff Wilson, Taine Randell and a young scrum-half called Byron Kelleher, showed the kind of verve which suggested they had overcome those All Black blues. For the first ten weeks the Highlanders were the team of the tournament, only succumbing to fatigue and third place at the very end.

The national identity of the Super 12's four leading teams – Australia, South Africa, New Zealand, New Zealand – suggested that little still separated the Tri-Nation countries. And yet, as in the three previous years, it was left to the New Zealanders to prove that they knew how to win a tournament at the death. Although their higher league placing secured them home advantage, both the Queensland Reds and the Stormers were beaten in the semi-finals. The Canterbury Crusaders scored four tries to one as they won 28–22 in Brisbane, while the Highlanders blew the Stormers away 33–18 in Cape Town. The South Africans did not help their cause by going on strike in the days before the match. While they managed to increase their pay-packets they did nothing for their rugby – but the Highlanders were irresistible.

Once more the Wallabies and the Springboks were forced to watch a New Zealand final. On 30 May, at the Highlanders' House of Pain in Dunedin, the Crusaders displayed a fierce commitment to win 24–19 and so match Henry's back-to-back Super 12 championships with the Blues.

New Zealand's shadowy nightmare had ended. Three weeks later, against a bank of rainy cloud, the All Blacks returned on a Friday night in Albany to crush Samoa 71–13 and, as New Zealand's *Rugby News* rejoiced, 'end eleven months and seven days of mourning without a Test win'. Jeff Wilson scored four times, playing at full-back, with Christian Cullen switched to right-wing. On the left flank another Hurricane, Tana Umaga, returned to international rugby with an exhilarating brace of tries which confirmed his rise over Jonah Lomu.

South Africa were similarly ruthless against Italy – winning 74–3 in Port Elizabeth and then a week later, on 19 June, dishing out a world record 101–0 pasting in Durban. Teichmann missed his first Test in three years, but more to save himself for the following week's visit to Wales and the crucial Tri-Nations encounters in July and August. The Springboks were ravaged by injury, a direct consequence of having toured the UK at the end of the year while the All Blacks rested. But the Italian mismatch at least allowed them to cap two more coloured flyers on the wing. In Port Elizabeth, Breyton Paulse shone with four tries, while his second-half replacement in Durban, Deon Kayser, ripped through a quick hat-trick.

Yet, in Wales, Nick Mallett opted to return to his more proven wings, Stefan Terblanche and Pieter Rossouw. Terblanche had broken the

Springboks' individual record by scoring five tries in one Test against Italy, while Rossouw was the equal of any world number 11. But Mallett was accused of being 'arrogant' and 'insensitive' by leading members of the ANC government who had escalated their demand for a quota of black Springboks.

'Every player must know that he deserves his place and is there strictly on merit,' Mallett argued. 'I don't ever want Paulse or Kayser to feel they owe their position to anything other than rugby ability. The fact that they are black must have nothing to do with their chances of playing for the Boks. There is no way that I will ever take part in anything that can be construed as window-dressing.'

Kayser and Paulse echoed Mallett's stance. 'At the highest level,' Kayser agreed, 'you cannot have quotas. You have to win your place on merit.' Paulse insisted that 'I think it should remain the ultimate honour to be selected for your country – because you are good enough. You must not lower the standard of the Springboks by not selecting on merit. A quota in a Test team would be very demeaning to the players involved. It would create unnatural pressure because they would feel guilty about being in the team.'

On 26 June an all-white Springbok team lined up at Cardiff's Millennium Stadium. While the site for the 1999 World Cup was yet to be completed, 27,000 Welshmen were allowed into the ground to witness a historic day for the billowing red shirts. Across the world, in Sydney, the new Olympic Stadium held 81,000 as England, led by Martin Johnson, attempted to win their first Test in Australia. But earlier that day, in Wellington, the creaking Athletic Stadium hosted its final Test before it was torn down. The revamped All Blacks faced the disintegrating *Tricolores*, whose miserable year had continued with further defeats against Tonga and New Zealand 'A'.

As another season finally ended in the northern hemisphere and intensified in the south, the six leading powers in world rugby came together in those three very different cities. I thought of Lawrence Dallaglio, watching those matches on his own in London. He missed playing for England even more than they felt his large absence. But, at least for Dallaglio, hope had returned. The English RFU were on the verge of announcing that, in mid-July, he would return to the team's training camp. His career was about to be saved.

Without him, England's 22–15 loss over the hardened and canny Australians, exemplified by the ruthless finishing of Ben Tune and Joe Roff, was the most accurate summation of the narrow gap which still existed between Europe and the Tri-Nations.

Yet Wales's first-ever defeat of South Africa, an astonishing and almost comfortable 29–19 victory, provided the more symbolic truth that rugby had regained its status as a truly international game. Almost a year to the day after they had been crushed 96–13 in Pretoria, even the South Africans amongst us could not begrudge the boundless Welsh joy.

'This is the number-one match of my coaching career,' Graham Henry, that Welsh rugby god, muttered. 'South Africa are the best team in the world and we beat them. The guys showed courage, heart, guts, character and backbone.'

But, as a New Zealander, Henry was able to resist further Welsh delirium. The Springboks were shorn of Andre Snyman, Henry Honiball, Joost van der Westhuizen, Adrian Garvey, James Dalton, Mark Andrews and Bobby Skinstad. Henry opted for a more cautious conclusion. 'We're not contenders for the World Cup. The big four in world rugby are clearly still Australia, South Africa, New Zealand and England. I cannot see us in the final against any of them . . .'

The Welsh, however, were rising again, just as the French slipped still further. After the All Blacks' 54–7 shellacking of France, Raphael Ibanez suggested that 'we learned more in one week in New Zealand than by playing forty games in the French championship. Now we understand what the élite of rugby is all about . . .'

His beleaguered coach, Jean-Claude Skrela, could not disguise his own disbelief. 'They did not even pick Jonah Lomu,' he shuddered. 'It was incredible. Lomu was not even on the bench against us. Where else in the world would that happen?'

Two weeks later, on 10 July, in Dunedin, Lomu returned to the bench against the Springboks. He was sent out late in the second half and his first run was only halted when seven Springboks combined to pull him down. It was that sort of day: a nightmare on a winter afternoon for the team in green and gold, but a glistening dream in crisp sunshine for the black shirts.

'We won't know how far we've come until we play South Africa,' John Hart insisted before the Tri-Nations began. In the end, we knew. The revamped All Blacks had crossed a dark road. Against the depleted Springboks they roared back with luminous brutality.

For an hour, I still had vague hope that South Africa would suffer an expected loss rather than a severe beating. At half-time, New Zealand led 6–0. And, early in the second period, Gary Teichmann and Naka Drotske barged over for a legitimate try. A 7–6 Springbok lead would have tested the black nerve, at least for a while. But the score was disallowed and the terrible dance began.

Cullen, Wilson and Marshall all crossed the flat green line with either a skip or shimmer. It was a dizzying way for the All Blacks to break their parity with the Springboks. They had won their twenty-fifth Test over South Africa's twenty-four. But they'd also administered the Springboks' worst defeat. New Zealand 28, South Africa 0.

Nick Mallett, however, had not lost heart. 'I'm not shattered, surprisingly. We knew it was going to be a very difficult game. They played some great rugby prior to us coming here, and we were coming off that defeat against Wales. Today we defended well but we missed a lot of players. I think you saw our lack of experience – especially with our half-back pairing of Gaffie du Toit and Dave van Hoesslin. They made errors but they'll have learnt something from this – as we all will.'

I also felt strangely sanguine. The All Blacks were back. It was no use even saying, 'surprise, surprise!' A fortnight on, against Australia, who were then at the peak of their own ten-match winning climb, the All Blacks' rehabilitation appeared complete. The Wallabies had just pulled down the Springboks in Brisbane, a record 32–6 demolition, but New Zealand were even more magnificently belligerent.

The Australians were helpless, especially at forward, against the swarming black tide. Although the high brick wall of their defence allowed only one try, the Wallabies were forced by sheer New Zealand pressure to concede nine penalties. Andrew Mehrtens succeeded with every one – and a 34–15 win in Auckland confirmed the All Blacks as rugby's most ferocious and darkly mythic team.

Even a year before, when they were at the very lowest, we had known that they would return in vengeful mood. And if we shuddered inside at the damage the All Blacks might yet do in the months and years to come, it could only be for rugby's benefit that they were so strong again. They had suffered terribly the previous season; and, suddenly, it was the turn of others to feel similar pain.

The Springboks, like the Blacks of '98 and *Les Bleus* of '99, skidded down their own small slide. France had been defeated in six of their last ten matches. The Springboks had lost four out of six – with only an Italian holiday in the middle for respite. The depth of change in seven months was almost painful to fathom; especially when there were such sad casualties.

When Nick Mallett announced the South African squad to face New Zealand and Australia for August's concluding Tri-Nations matches,

Gary Teichmann was not even one of twenty-six players. Joost van der Westhuizen took his place as captain, while Teichmann's berth at the back of scrum was left open for the mercurial Bobby Skinstad. Teichmann was thirty-two years old. He was also still struggling with injury. So his loyalty to Mallett, and his pivotal role in leading the Springboks on their world record run, was brushed aside. It was terribly cruel.

But there had never been any room for sentiment in South African rugby – and especially not when the All Blacks were outstripping the Springboks. 'It was unavoidable,' Mallett said bluntly. 'The captain of the Springbok team has to be an automatic selection in his position and, looking at our best loose-forward combination, the selectors and I believe Gary is not assured of his place. I don't think Gary's very happy at the moment. He is pretty upset. It's been a dream of his to go to the World Cup . . .'

That dream, however, was ruined; and Teichmann, like James Small, had to recover from yet more rugby heartache. I felt desperately for him, remembering how often we had spoken of Cardiff and the World Cup. It was even more disturbing to learn that the eminently dignified Teichmann had been forced to approach Mallett himself in an attempt to discover the truth of his demotion. 'I'd had enough of reading in the papers,' he said, 'that Nick was on the verge of dropping the older players. I needed to know my position. I left a message for Nick to call me back on the Friday afternoon. He said he was going to phone me but had decided to do so after the weekend. I had an inkling of what was coming because when I spoke to Nick in Australia he told me he wanted Bobby Skinstad to be part of the World Cup and he emphasised that it would be as a number 8.'

Teichmann suggested to the South African *Sunday Times* that unreasonable expectations had been foisted on to the young and still injured Springbok by Mallett and his assistants. 'I just believe Skinstad has been managed badly by them. All you hear is that we cannot go to the World Cup without Bobby. It's Bobby this and Bobby that . . .'

While Teichmann stressed that he was still willing to play for Mallett, two weeks later he signed a £250,000 deal to play for Newport. 'My whole life had been focused on the World Cup but everything was suddenly turned on its head. When I was dropped, I pretty much knew that I would never get back. When Nick stated that I was the sixth-best number 8 in the country, I knew there was absolutely no point in hanging around. At least by joining Newport I'll get to see Wales . . .'

In August, New Zealand again crushed South Africa at Loftus

Versveld. A year before, in Durban, Teichmann had been at the pinnacle of his career while Josh Kronfeld was at the bleakest All Black ebb. Everything had changed. Kronfeld and the Kiwis were flying. But, just as I had been certain that New Zealand would rise once more, so I believed that South Africa and France would prosper again. Eventually, success would roll back, as the cycles of international rugby spun slowly round.

Like New Zealand, South Africa and France remained vibrant rugby nations. Beyond the division and controversy, the chaos and disappointment, there was still an unbreakable love for the old game. That passion had lured Gregor Townsend to Brive, and that same ardour so hurt Gary Teichmann.

It always coursed most fiercely through Springbok country. On 14 August, missing both Teichmann and the recovering Skinstad, the desperate South Africans clung on to beat Australia 10–9 in Cape Town. Their grim victory ended their five-match slump – and also handed the 1999 Tri-Nations to New Zealand.

The Springboks' ancient enmity with the All Blacks ensured that, finally, they would gather themselves and respond with the kind of rugby they had played throughout 1998's unforgettable year. For even as the seasons blurred, the still and dark core of rugby shone more brightly, remaining a world of entrenched rivalries and constantly changing fortunes.

In Paris and Cardiff, London and Sydney, Auckland and Johannesburg, as Gary Teichmann had said almost a year before, the good times come and the good times go, for all of us. There will always be another turn and another time, whether for the French or the Welsh, the All Blacks or the Springboks. The only difference is that for some, as in life, the wait will be a little shorter and just a little easier to endure.

Acknowledgements

This book began in Cardiff, with me sitting across a table from James Small. If not for James, there would be no book. Thanks go, especially, to him – both for the interviews and the good times.

Gary Teichmann, too, wherever we met, was always a friend who went out of his way to help me – and I'll particularly remember him looking out for me in New Zealand.

Josh Kronfeld was never less than engaging and interesting. He also taught me much more than I'd previously known about New Zealand . . . and surfing.

Nelie Smith helped me understand a little bit more about Springbok rugby and our shared past in South Africa. Our days together, in Ballymena, were amongst my most memorable.

All the outstanding players I interviewed were remarkably accommodating and patient with me – as well as providing entertaining and illuminating company. Thank you to Abdelatif Benazzi, Andrew Blowers, Thomas Castaignède, Christian Cullen, Lawrence Dallaglio, John Eales, Sean Fitzpatrick, Rob Howley, Michael Jones, Jonah Lomu, Francois Pienaar, Os du Randt, Gregor Townsend, Ben Tune, Chester Williams and Keith Wood.

I was also lucky enough to interview and write about Fred Allen, John Hart, Graham Henry, Phil Kingsley Jones, Nick Mallett, Macdonald Masina, Willie John McBride, Franck Mesnel, Frank Oliver, Kevin Skinner, Jeffrey Stevens, Errol Tobias, James Topping and Brian van Rooyen. I am grateful to all of them.

Alex Broun, with the Springboks, and Jane Dent, for the All Blacks, never failed to help me.

Peter Howarth, Alison Kervin, Paul Morgan and Mark Reason – and especially Ben Clissitt and Mike Averis at *The Guardian* – were good enough to publish early fragments of this book.

Richard Escot was not only my most important link to French rugby – he soon became a friend and a constant source of support in France.

Mainstream's Bill Campbell and Peter MacKenzie, as ever, showed great faith and patience as my writing rambled on past various deadlines and word-limits. Their support was unwavering – as was that of Judy Diamond, my editor, who kept me sane near the end.

Thanks also to Luke Alfred, Diane Coetzee, John da Silva, Neil Dowling, John Gaustad, Josh Georgiou, Wynn Gray, Chris Grinter, Bob Howitt, Tom Jenkins, Jason, Trent and all the Macdonalds, Jay Savage, Clinton van der Berg and Huw Williams.

John and Pat Musgrave were my essential UK press cuttings agency – a pint of Youngs Special and a schooner of sherry await at the Hand in Hand.

To Anna Fisher, my indispensable French translator, *Merci, Madame!*

Hilton Tanchum, my rugby mentor for thirty years, was invaluable during the earliest stages of the book – as well as later with his regular airport-taxi shuttle.

My sister, Heather Simpson, was again on editing duty – especially in her reading of the opening section. Thanks, as always, to her.

I owe a particularly special thank you to Tim Musgrave for all his work and encouragement. His reading was consistently clear and constructive – and, most of all, he helped make this a better book than it ever would have been without him.

My parents were great – whether they were helping me sort out my complicated plans in South Africa, setting up their 'Administrative & Travel' service – or just putting up with all the late nights out in Johannesburg. But my gratitude to them stretches way beyond the last two years.

And, again, the last words deserve to be about Alison. Apart from her stunning mastery of the *Haka*, she has lived through every page of this book. She was always the first to read, and significantly improve, each new chapter – just as she was always the one I'd turn to in every moment of doubt. And, of course, while writing these pages, it was with Alison that I had the most unforgettable times. At the end, thanks go to her, more than anyone.